IFIP Advances in Information and Communication Technology 424

IFIP – The International Federation for Information Processing

IFIP was founded in 1960 under the auspices of UNESCO, following the First World Computer Congress held in Paris the previous year. An umbrella organization for societies working in information processing, IFIP's aim is two-fold: to support information processing within its member countries and to encourage technology transfer to developing nations. As its mission statement clearly states,

> *IFIP's mission is to be the leading, truly international, apolitical organization which encourages and assists in the development, exploitation and application of information technology for the bene t of all people.*

IFIP is a non-profitmaking organization, run almost solely by 2500 volunteers. It operates through a number of technical committees, which organize events and publications. IFIP's events range from an international congress to local seminars, but the most important are:

- The IFIP World Computer Congress, held every second year;
- Open conferences;
- Working conferences.

The flagship event is the IFIP World Computer Congress, at which both invited and contributed papers are presented. Contributed papers are rigorously refereed and the rejection rate is high.

As with the Congress, participation in the open conferences is open to all and papers may be invited or submitted. Again, submitted papers are stringently refereed.

The working conferences are structured differently. They are usually run by a working group and attendance is small and by invitation only. Their purpose is to create an atmosphere conducive to innovation and development. Refereeing is also rigorous and papers are subjected to extensive group discussion.

Publications arising from IFIP events vary. The papers presented at the IFIP World Computer Congress and at open conferences are published as conference proceedings, while the results of the working conferences are often published as collections of selected and edited papers.

Any national society whose primary activity is about information processing may apply to become a full member of IFIP, although full membership is restricted to one society per country. Full members are entitled to vote at the annual General Assembly, National societies preferring a less committed involvement may apply for associate or corresponding membership. Associate members enjoy the same benefits as full members, but without voting rights. Corresponding members are not represented in IFIP bodies. Affiliated membership is open to non-national societies, and individual and honorary membership schemes are also offered.

Arthur Tatnall   Bill Davey (Eds.)

Reflections on the History of Computers in Education

Early Use of Computers and Teaching about Computing in Schools

Springer

Volume Editors

Arthur Tatnall
Victoria University
Melbourne, VIC, Australia
E-mail: arthur.tatnall@vu.edu.au

Bill Davey
RMIT University
Melbourne, VIC, Australia
E-mail: bill.davey@rmit.edu.au

ISSN 1868-4238 e-ISSN 1868-422X
ISBN 978-3-642-55118-5 e-ISBN 978-3-642-55119-2
DOI 10.1007/978-3-642-55119-2
Springer Heidelberg New York Dordrecht London

Library of Congress Control Number: 2014937322

Typesetting: Camera-ready by author, data conversion by Scientific Publishing Services, Chennai, India

Printed on acid-free paper

Springer is part of Springer Science+Business Media (www.springer.com)

Preface

Many people consider history to be about things that happened a long time ago: that it is about wars, kings, politics, nations, and such like. One could then ask why a study of the history of computers in education is important when it is a comparatively recent phenomenon beginning only in the 1970s.

This book deals with *personal reflections* on the history of computers in school education, rather than providing listings of names, dates, hardware and software details, and curriculum applications, and the authors of the chapters are not professional historians but rather people who as teachers, students, or researchers were involved in this history. They narrate their history from a personal perspective and offer fascinating stories not just of what happened, but also of how it affected them, with their chapters representing reflections on their experiences of this time.

As these stories have been told by witnesses who were involved at the time, their value lies not simply in the facts described, but rather in their mature reflections of events in this period. The book chapters are quite different to what would have been written by academic historians, and in any case few historians have exactly the same view or personal experience of past events. In many ways these chapters present a social history of the introduction and early use of computers in schools.

They cover the history of computers in education from the 1970s up to only about the mid-1990s, before the widespread use in education of the Internet, Google, Wikipedia, iPads and smart phones. Many changes have occurred since the mid-1990s, but they are a story for another time.

The chapters in this book deal with the introduction of computers in schools in many countries around the world: Norway, South Africa, UK, Canada, Australia, USA, Finland, Chile, The Netherlands, New Zealand, Spain, Ireland, Israel, and Poland. All the papers were peer reviewed before final acceptance.

Perhaps after reading all the contributions you might like to reflect on whether the introduction and use of computers in schools really resulted in significant changes to education in the way that many of us at the time thought that it would. We hope that you will enjoy reading these fascinating stories and perhaps find some commonality in how and why computers were introduced into schools around the world.

March 2014

Arthur Tatnall
Bill Davey

Table of Contents

Lessons from the Great Underground Empire: Pedagogy, Computers and False Dawn

Stewart Martin

Faculty of Education, University of Hull, UK
stewart.martin@hull.ac.uk

Abstract. The educational use of computers in the UK coincided with growing tensions between educators and government policy. This led to the imposition of a National Curriculum and policy that took scant account of research evidence or the views of professional educators. As a result of this unhappy coincidence, the UK failed to take early advantage of the educational benefits offered by this technology. The exploitation of the unique affordances of computers have seen a false dawn and dashed hopes but, slowly, a body of research has emerged that is now starting to identify where we should look and what we should do. However, the necessary changes would fundamentally alter the roles of teacher and learner within the educational system as well as government policy and this may go some way to explain government reluctance and the systemic inertia in the UK and elsewhere.

Keywords: computers, education, teaching, pedagogy, computer games, government policy, cognitive load theory, learning styles.

1 Introduction

```
West of House.
You are standing in an open field west of a white
house, with a boarded front door.
There is a small mailbox here.
```

Although many people today will never have heard of it, this is the opening text of what is arguably one of the most iconic pieces of interactive computer software ever written - and is the place where my journey into the use of computers in education began.

The software in question is the computer-based adventure-game trilogy *Zork!*, which was written in 1977 on a 'mainframe' computer by Tim Anderson, Marc Blank, Bruce Daniels and Dave Lebling, who were members of the Dynamic Modelling Group at the Massachusetts Institute of Technology [1]. Published in 1980 by the American software company Infocom, *Zork!* was part of a genre of digital interactive fiction which ran on the then emerging market of commercial computers aimed at the home. Unlike today's computer software which depends upon powerful

A. Tatnall and B. Davey (Eds.): History of Computers in Education, IFIP AICT 424, pp. 1–25, 2014.

multimedia machines to function, *Zork!* ran on much more modest technology and featured only white text on black backgrounds; it contained no colour, graphics, animation or sound effects. In the context of *Zork!*, 'interaction' therefore comprised of the user repeatedly responding to the text which appeared on the screen by typing in words at the keyboard and observing the software's response. As one commentator of the time noted:

> "Zork *is all text - that means no graphics. None are needed. The authors have not skimped on the vividly detailed descriptions of each location; descriptions to which not even Atari graphics could do complete justice." [51]*

Between 1980 and 1984 I worked as Senior Teacher at a large secondary school in Maidstone, a county town in southern England in Kent, in the UK. My main teaching role was in the English Department and as part of this I had a number of classes of low achieving students, comprised mostly of boys, who were preparing to take external public examinations. The low levels of educational attainment in that particular school during the 1980s were not uncommon, as educational achievement and aspirations in many schools around Maidstone at this time were significantly below national averages.

During this period the UK Government, under both Labour and then Conservative leadership, launched and nurtured the Microelectronics Education Programme (MEP), which ran from 1980 until 1986. The programme was managed by the newly formed Council for Educational Technology and, following the involvement of the Department of Trade and Industry in 1982, saw the introduction of a computer into every school in England. The machines provided for this purpose were Research Machines (380Z or 'Nimbus' machines), BBC 'Acorn' computers and also the Sinclair ZX Spectrum; the latter being most commonly used for control projects, such as teaching children how electronic switches in circuits or traffic lights worked.

At this time one read in much of the literature circulated to schools that the objective of the MEP was to promote the study of microelectronics and its effects, and to encourage the use of this technology as an aid to teaching and learning. When our school's computer arrived (and it was just one single computer), the Head Teacher was disposed to offer it to the Physics department for dismantling and study as part of the study of microelectronics but was persuaded by me to keep it in one piece and allow the English Department to use it as an aid to teaching and learning instead.

Initially this single Research Machines 380Z computer in my classroom was used for word processing with single students or small groups and when it was eventually supplemented by several additional 'Nimbus' machines this work was extended to larger groups, although the eight machines available still made it difficult for students to be allocated to their own computer and forced students in classes to work together in groups. It became clear later that this restricted availability proved to be an opportunity in disguise.

Whilst the curriculum work done by students with these machines was interesting and unusual, their use seemed to appeal mostly to academically able students who could take advantage of word processing software's ability to format and edit text so as to improve its clarity of expression, eloquence or persuasive power. This suggested that the educational usefulness of computers might largely be related to a student's academic ability in a given subject but it seemed equally possible that the technology simply appealed to those students who liked to learn in a particular way because the available software offered opportunities for working in a manner that somehow suited their preferences. As the technology at that time was limited in its ability to present content using different media, styles or formats, it seemed likely that if differences in these things were important for individual student engagement and learning then only those learners for whom that limited range of presentational styles and formats was valuable would be strongly attracted to its use.

The affordances offered by the word processing software we used were insufficient to encourage the majority of my weaker students who were still struggling to master basic English expression, spelling and grammar; what was unclear was whether this was more to do with the difficulties they were experiencing with the subject content itself or because their preferences for learning in certain ways were not being very well catered for by the software, or whether the ways in which content was presented to learners made a significant difference to learning for all learners, or even whether these issues were all closely related.

2 Early Exploration

I became interested in discovering whether successful learning with computers was more likely to be about providing for each individual student's approach to learning (their habitual preferences for how they liked to learn, if such a thing existed) or about being able to present subject content in particular formats that were intrinsically more likely to lead to learning because of their structure and format. Although there was no computer software available at this time that would allow me to address these issues it was whilst I was thinking of how I might make this technology useful for my students that I came across the software which introduced this chapter. This software (*Zork!*) seemed to offer ways to begin exploring the questions that concerned me about using computers, because it required highly structured learning to engage with it successfully but did not impose particular ways or styles of learning on the user, although it did use a very limited text-based format for presenting content. I therefore anticipated that, like the word processing software we had used, it was likely to appeal only to a limited number of more able students.

Zork I: The Great Underground Empire is the first part of the *Zork!* trilogy and when one lunchtime I showed it to some of the students at my computer club it provoked considerable interest, I suspected largely due to its novelty. Amongst the group that day were some of my less able students who had wandered in whilst looking for something to do to avoid the rain outside and because of their earlier poor learning experience with word processing software it was this group's fascination with this software that particularly caught my attention.

Word got around of what was happening in the computer club. In response to the pleas from my students I allowed them limited access to *The Great Underground Empire* at the end of English class sessions, as a reward for hard work and task completion. I anticipated that it would be useful in this regard only and it did seem to encourage my students, including my less able ones, to apply themselves more to class work although the latter continued to find the work itself difficult to remain engaged with, despite my best efforts to make the content more accessible and relevant.

However, over the following period of a week or so I noticed a pattern of behaviour emerging with regard to *Zork*! Whilst some students were content to use it alone, most seemed to prefer to wait until some of their classmates were also free and then explore it together. As I watched these students, it became clear that something quite interesting was going on.

Zork! has a limited vocabulary and is programmed to interact with the user in particular ways. The user assumes the role of an anonymous adventurer in this computer simulated fantasy world filled with scores of rooms, some containing traps, some containing puzzles. Hundreds of objects are scattered throughout this maze, some of which are valuable treasures, some of which are magical tools. At the heart of the program is a sophisticated piece of software (a parser) that breaks down what the user types on the keyboard into its component parts of speech, assigns each a function and establishes the syntactical relationship between each part. The software responds according to the output from the parser. Simply pressing only the 'Enter' key on the computer keyboard generates the response "I beg your pardon?", for example, so the user is required to think of what to say to the game's omniscient 'Dungeon Master' in order to access the environment in the game. When the user types words on the keyboard and then presses the 'Enter' key, the parser attempts to match the words and phrases typed (and to some extent their sequence) with its database of coded words and phrases and their relationships to known meanings. It then selects a response based on this analysis and presents this to the user on the computer screen whilst also selecting a 'move' from the software gaming engine to show the user (if relevant) the next section of, or solution to, the maze or puzzle.

Although not powerful by contemporary standards, the parser in *Zork!* is frequently able to present a reasonable if limited approximation to intelligent response that is at times quite amusing and uncannily human, thanks to the skill of the programmers. This interactive element within the software presented students with challenges and a typical encounter often went something like this (user-typed input in capitals):

```
>OPEN DOOR
The door cannot be opened.
>GO WEST
Forest
This is a forest, with trees in all directions. To
the east, there appears to be sunlight.
>CLIMB TREE
There is no tree here suitable for climbing.
>ENTER FOREST
You hit your head against the forest as you
attempt this feat.
```

```
>GO WEST
You would need a machete to go further west.
>GO NORTH
Clearing
You are in a clearing, with a forest surrounding
you on all sides. A path leads south.
On the ground is a pile of leaves.
>PICK UP LEAVES
In disturbing the pile of leaves, a grating is
revealed.
Taken.
>OPEN GRATING
The grating is locked.
>HELP
I don't know the word "help".
```

I anticipated that, faced with this kind of interaction, most students would probably give up fairly quickly, especially as the early version of *Zork!* we used had no 'save game' feature, so when students came into the classroom and began a new session, or if their adventurer character 'died' in the game, as often happened, they always started right back at the beginning again, standing in an open field west of a white house, with its boarded front door.

To my surprise many of my students did not give up, however frustrating the difficulties became. Instead they began to discuss strategies with classmates and plan sequences of instructions. They began to explore the software's vocabulary and make lists of words and phrases it 'understood' and objects and actions it 'knew' about. Inventories of objects and their locations were developed, especially when it became clear that for many situations and places further into the environment certain objects needed to have been located and 'collected' beforehand because their possession by the adventurer was required to overcome obstacles, solve puzzles, open doors or pass barriers. They made maps of the underground terrain and recorded sequences of successful instructions, often in personal diaries or notebooks. They started to look up unfamiliar words in dictionaries, particularly when exploring vocabulary and wanting correct spellings.

The level of vocabulary and the complexity of description and of sentence structure tends to increase as users progress deeper into *Zork!* and the interaction becomes semantically richer [36]. The following is from a section a little further into *Zork!* than the previous extract and is typical:

```
Living Room
You are in the Living Room. There is a door to the
east, a wooden door with strange gothic lettering
to the west, which appears to be nailed shut, and
a large oriental rug in the centre of the room.
There is a trophy case here.
```

```
A battery-powered brass lantern is on the trophy
case. On hooks above the mantelpiece hangs an
elvish sword of great antiquity.
>TAKE ALL BUT RUG
Sword:
  Taken.
Lamp:
  Taken.
>READ
Read what?
>THE DOOR
The engravings translate to ‘This space
intentionally left blank’
>LOOK UNDER RUG
Underneath the rug is a closed trap door.
>MOVE THE RUG
With a great effort, the rug is moved to one side
of the room.
With the rug moved, the dusty cover of a closed
trap-door appears.
>OPEN
Open what?
>DOOR
Which door should I open?
>THE TRAP DOOR
The door reluctantly opens to reveal a rickety
staircase descending into darkness.
>GO DOWN
It is pitch black. You are likely to be eaten by a
grue.
Your sword is glowing with a faint blue glow.
>WHAT’S A GRUE?
The grue is a sinister, lurking presence in the
dark places of the earth. Its favourite diet is
adventurers, but its insatiable appetite is
tempered by its fear of light. No grue has ever
been seen by the light of day, and few have
survived its fearsome jaws to tell the tale.
Your sword is glowing with a faint blue glow.
>TURN ON LAMP
The lamp is now on.
Cellar
You are in a dark and damp cellar with a narrow
passageway leading east, and a crawlway to the
```

```
south. On the west is the bottom of a steep metal
ramp which is unclimbable.
The trap door crashes shut, and you hear someone
barring it.
```

Faced with scenarios such as this, different groups began to collaborate to explore different regions and assign specialist roles to individuals – mapmaking, vocabulary, strategy and so on. However, not all of my students became involved in every one of these specific activities in every session and it was clear that at different times some students preferred making maps, or creating strategies, or working directly with words, or with words together with the pictures they had created. It was difficult to discern any fixed pattern in this from casual observation but suddenly these students began exhibiting higher-order thinking skills and using them confidently when previously they had exhibited no potential for such behaviour in my lessons. Above all, what was most noticeable was the degree of involvement, commitment and perseverance displayed by many students and their evident sense of achievement and enjoyment in collaborating, learning and working in highly self-directed ways to achieve objectives they had developed for themselves. What remained unclear to me was the relationship between computer use, content format, individual learning style preferences and successful learning.

I began to wonder if there were ways in which the educationally desirable behaviours of my students might be transferrable to alternative settings - such as my English Literature classes - which were not game or puzzle oriented. Could computer software produce learning benefits from content that engaged the imagination but was more demanding in scope and depth - and was not explicitly a game? My concerns were not about using computers for games or any implied trivialisation of learning in this, for it was clear that my students took *Zork!* very seriously indeed. It was the sustained attention, the seriousness of their application and the associated enjoyment they discovered from intellectual application that I sought to transfer – together with their success in learning. However, one concern was whether the computer would continue to motivate learners once the novelty had worn off. Would it encourage meaningful learning in other contexts and, if so, in what particular ways might it do this? Would different students prefer or need to use such a resource in different ways? Would any learning that took place be manifested in improved examination results or in other affective ways, or would benefits be limited to motivation and enjoyment alone? Would any benefits transpire that could not have been achieved by more traditional approaches? Would using computers produce or encourage any changes in the way I taught and in the ways my students learned? In short, would the use of this technology sufficiently repay the necessary investments of time and resources involved in using it?

Inspired by my early experiences with *Zork!*, I developed my own computer software to help students studying set texts for national English Literature examinations, drawing on my experiences in the classroom with students to refine it and take advantage of the increasingly sophisticated multimedia capabilities of home computers to introduce more ambitious programs which made use of graphics, animation and sound as these became more widely available over the next twenty years. The initial and subsequent versions of the software proved popular and eventually reached a stage of development where I published titles for eight of the most frequently set literature texts through a company I set up for that purpose. These programs, developed initially as an exploration in curriculum development, are now in use in many schools throughout the UK.

From the beginning the software seemed to be successful from my subjective point of view, but I was concerned to establish whether its apparent effects were real and measurable. Did the use of this multimedia computer software offer pupils valuable learning opportunities that were unavailable in traditional classroom environments and, if so, did these enable a useful variety of approaches to academic work for pupils which improved their learning? From my perspective as a practicing teacher I was not aware of whether there was much systematic research on these matters and I had used no published research or theoretical underpinning in the design of the software, nor had I made any systematic analysis of its effects. This would perhaps seem surprising now, but these were early days in the development of home computers, the use of computers in schools, the design of human-computer interfaces and especially the use of multimedia and because of this the training of teachers and of those in service at this time had not embraced their use.

This was brought home to me most forcefully in some of the training sessions I ran for teachers across the county of Kent at this time. During these sessions we would talk as a group about what use we were making of the school computer and any associated concerns or issues that teachers felt needed addressing. It soon became clear from these conversations that teachers tended to use their school computer mostly as a 'treat' for students who had finished their classwork early. The software available for these machines at this time was generally very limited and comprised mostly of drill and practice programs designed, for example, to help students learn basic mathematical skills or simple words in other languages. Teachers tended to let students play with these programs but did not often use them as a resource in their teaching. Usually this was because of the limited number of machines, as even those schools who had more than the original government machine tended at first not to have more than an additional four or five because of their expense. Many teachers were content to leave students playing a computerised game of 'hangman'. This struck me as a dreadful waste of the equipment and as something that sent all the wrong messages to students: hurry to get your classwork finished and you can play on the computer; computers are only useful for passing the time; teachers do not see much educational advantage in computers; computers are only for 'clever' children and so on.

To underscore my concerns I wrote a simple program in BASIC to illustrate one of the key educational and pedagogical opportunities that I thought teachers could take advantage of. The program was a version of the game 'Guess the animal". In this game, one player thinks of an animal and the other players try to work out what it is. If they do so they win the game and the player who guessed the animal correctly takes the place of the first player; otherwise the original player gets another turn and thinks of another animal. The other players are allowed to ask only one question at a time of the first player, in turn, and every question has to be answerable with the single word 'Yes' or 'No' by the first player.

The program that I wrote played the part of the other players and began by asking the pupil using the computer to think of an animal. When they had done so, they were told to press the 'Enter' key. The program always responded when the 'Enter' key was first pressed by asking 'Is it a ferret?'. The pupil would type in either 'Yes' or 'No' to every guess the computer made and then the computer would take its turn in responding with another question. The program was written in such a way that logical steps were followed through a classification structure by eliminating whole groups of animals with each question the computer asked. For example, if in answer to the ferret question the pupil typed 'No' the computer would next ask 'Does it fly?'. Depending on the pupils answer ('Yes' or 'No') to this question the program moved through to flightless animals and then might in the following turn ask if the animal lived in the sea. Similar steps were then followed to narrow down the type of animal to a single group and at that point the program would take an animal name from that group in its limited database and present it to the user in the form of 'Is it a xxxx?' where xxxx was an animal that fitted the classification tree at that point. Quite deliberately only one animal was included for each group in the database so that the computer quickly ran out of choices and ended up saying 'I give up. You win! What was the animal you were thinking of?' Students and teachers found this hugely entertaining. For the purposes of this explanation let us assume that the pupil was thinking of an elephant and the computer's last unsuccessful guess had been 'Is it a cow?'. Having conceded defeat, the computer would then ask the key question that was the whole point of the program. In this case the question would be "Please type in a single question that would allow someone to tell the difference between an elephant and a cow. The question must be one that can be answered by 'Yes' or 'No'". Once the pupil had typed in their question the computer would then ask "Please type in the correct answer to your question – is it 'Yes' or is it 'No'?

The key feature of this program was that the new animal and its question (along with the correct answer) were then added to the program's database in the correct part of the decision tree. If any future pupil reached the same point again the computer would present the key question and in light of the answer would present 'Is it an elephant?' or 'Is it a cow?'. This very simple learning algorithm underscored what I wanted to convey to teachers about the use of computers: that computers could be used to make learning engaging (there is nothing wrong with that); but they could also be used to help students to think; to re-examine what they already know; to classify and structure their knowledge, to learn how to ask the right questions; and to put more intellectual energy into the computer than came out of it. Looked at this way, the computer is indeed a 'learning machine', but not in the way most people thought about this at the time, where the consensus seemed to me to be that the computer was a machine for teaching students.

Admittedly I was a little discouraged when one teacher who had not used the program before became panicky at the machine's first response and shouted to the rest of the group "It knew I was thinking of a ferret! That's really scary - aren't computers fantastic!" It took me quite a while to reassure him that it always started by asking if the animal was a ferret and that the computer was no more able to read his mind than I was. Whilst they were still in awe of computers, some teachers could see the point I was making but were still at a loss to know how they could build upon this approach to create a very different pedagogy to the drill and practice they often used. Teachers at that time did not commonly have the training, ability or interest to start learning programming so that they could develop learning packages for pupils. Nor did that seem to me to be a sensible way forwards. I have always felt that teachers should concentrate on learning and teaching, not on such things as mastering computer programming – particularly as most software at that time that could be used for this was distinctly user-unfriendly. There was virtually nothing in the way of the high level software-building tools that are available today.

3 Teacher Training and Changing Times

So although in the early 1980s I was amongst the first small group of teachers in the UK to use computers in mainstream schools to enhance learning, my early experience had already made me aware that whilst the technology seemed to have great potential for supporting learning it also was likely to have significant limitations. In contrast, many government initiatives then and now seem to rest upon on an almost blind faith in the presence or use of computers to somehow provide solutions to many intractable, long-standing, social, educational and economic problems. My early experiences of using computers was more nuanced and had already suggested that their benefits were likely to be very dependent upon applying them in specific and particular ways, of which educators in general were only just beginning to become aware.

So the questions that first intrigued me in the 1980s remained unanswered and remained so through the 1990s and still inform much of the discussion in the academic literature I come across today. Why these same questions still remain topical and, more importantly, the answers to them still somewhat unclear after over thirty years of computer use in schools seems puzzling, but why these questions did not receive appropriate attention in the 1980s is easier to understand.

When I was preparing to become a teacher during the early 1970s, teacher training commonly included exposure to the study of the history of education, to educational philosophy and to the writings of those interested in curriculum development. Aspiring teachers at this time were also introduced to the idea that a learner-centred approach to classroom pedagogy was more desirable and effective than one centred on the teacher. As a consequence of this, teacher training in this period commonly included reference to the writings of thinkers such as Dewey and his arguments that students in schools needed to both experience and interact with the educational curriculum and should therefore become collaborators in partnership with teachers in the experience of learning. However, Dewey was also esteemed for his advocacy of the need to maintain a balance between an active child-centred approach to pedagogy that took account of the experiences and interests of the pupil as well as the need to respect the important role of the teacher in drawing meaningfully upon the pupil's prior learning and in choosing and presenting important curriculum content [16], [17].

These approaches to learning and teaching had been given impetus by publications in the UK such as the Plowden Report [23] that, although focussed largely on the primary sector, was seen to hold important lessons for education more widely, as reflected in its opening comments:

> *At the heart of the educational process lies the child. No advances in policy, no acquisitions of new equipment have their desired effect unless they are in harmony with the nature of the child, unless they are fundamentally acceptable to him. We know a little about what happens to the child who is deprived of the stimuli of pictures, books and spoken words; we know much less about what happens to a child who is exposed to stimuli which are perceptually, intellectually or emotionally inappropriate to his age, his state of development, or the sort of individual he is. We are still far from knowing how best to identify in an individual child the first flicker of a new intellectual or emotional awareness, the first readiness to embrace new sets of concepts or to enter into new relations. [23]*

Trainee teachers were encouraged to apply such ideas as well as those of Dewey and Cole et al. [7], [16], [17], and especially of Piaget [38], [39], whose thinking clearly influenced Plowden. Piaget suggested that through a process of objectification, reflection and abstraction children develop their own schemas (mental frameworks of structured groups of concepts), complex predictive models and their understanding of their physical and social environments and that they do this through exploration and the iterative use of abstract reasoning to deduce 'rules' operating in a particular environment or setting. Teacher training programmes encouraged this approach as an effective way to develop a more child-centred pedagogy and also promoted Vygotsky as an influential related thinker and in particular referred to his work on the role of play in facilitating the development of abstract ideas and meaning; the part these have in developing a child's higher mental functions were much in evidence in professional discourse at the time [7]. Vygotsky also identified the important social role of collaborative learning and related this to his concept of the 'zone of proximal development' in the advancement of individual learning through collaboration. These ideas, together with those of Piaget and Dewey, featured strongly in the newly emerging honours degree programmes of teacher training that I and my contemporaries experienced but were also subject to cautions about the use of ICT from the literature of the time which observed that children in their early school lives commonly learn to accept "delay, denial and interruption of their personal wishes and desires" [27, p.18]. Teachers in classrooms of the time were mainly concerned to "decide on a set of activities" and then "focus their energies on achieving and maintaining student involvement in those activities" [27, p.162]. Writers still felt the need to continue to make a similar point almost forty years later:

> *"New technology's potential to change the culture of the classroom and the relationship between teacher and students is important, since traditional classrooms are not ideal learning environments." [27]*

My own professional training and experiences with ICT, particularly with *Zork!*, had therefore left me sensitive to the possibilities offered by this newly available technology and its potential for promoting collaborative and individual learning, for encouraging pupils to take more control of their learning to collect and synthesise information thoughtfully, for promoting the development of critical thinking and for developing intellectual constructs and theories about scenarios and relationships. As a result of my training and early experience with computers I was persuaded of the superiority and desirability of a more student-centred and experientially-based approach to learning and teaching and excited by the possibility that ICT may be a powerful way to bring these things about. This was not a unique experience, and many of my contemporaries during the 1980s and 1990s who started incorporating ICT into the classroom practice found that its use allowed the historical continuity of teacher-centred pedagogy to be replaced by more student-centred approaches [10].

The supporters of Plowden and the advocates of collaborative and student-centred learning were, however, not without influential and powerful opponents who had been growing in prominence since the 1970s. Some commentators and politicians mounted a concerted drive against such approaches - even though their grounds for doing so often appeared to rest largely on dogma and opinion and tended to ignore evidence contrary to their agenda. They accused child-centred approaches and the dominance of what they dubbed as 'trendy educationalists' of being responsible for what they identified as a decline in educational standards [45]. Piaget's ideas of cognitive development through step-wise stages where learners developed through their own active efforts informed much of the Plowden Report and against this rising criticism the recommendations of both Plowden and therefore of Piaget fell out of favour [21]. The so-called 'Black Papers' of 1969 added fuel to the debate in blaming much of what was seen by their authors as wrong with UK education on the influence of Plowden (for example see [8]). Difficulties surrounding a small number of problematic and idiosyncratic schools, such as at the William Tyndale school in North London in 1974 [20], exacerbated matters and were seized upon by these critics of education and as a result of all this Plowden came to be increasingly marginalised.

The then Prime Minister Jim Callaghan's 'Ruskin Speech' at Ruskin College, Oxford in 1976 also marked a turning point in these debates and the emergence of more overt political control of the curriculum and teacher pedagogy. There was a prevailing view in many teacher training institutions in the late 1970s, including the one I attended, that this firmer tone signalled a clear intention to take action and was probably due to frustration at what some politicians saw as the stubborn reluctance of teachers and schools to listen and change. From 1979 onwards the Conservative government, led by Margaret Thatcher, embarked upon a process of political intervention in education that led to the imposition of a subject based National Curriculum in the 1988 Education Reform Act.

Within the National Curriculum ICT then emerged as an important area that all subject teachers were and still are required to address and the government's Office for Standards in Education (Ofsted) is required to inspect. This area was and continues to be characterised largely by 'key concepts' such as: individual capability in ICT use; communicating and collaborating; exploring ideas and manipulating information; understanding the impact of ICT; and thinking more critically about using ICT and information in general. The National Curriculum indicates that these key objectives should be achieved through the development of 'essential skills and processes'. Teachers, such as those of English Literature at Key Stage 4 (for children aged between 14 and 16) are for example required to promote the use of ICT for: 'Finding information'; 'Developing ideas'; 'Communicating information'; and 'Evaluating information' [41]. The National Curriculum emphasises the use of ICT for generic instrumental purposes and promotes its utilitarian adoption across the curriculum. In this regard the use of ICT by pupils for finding information, developing ideas, communicating information or evaluating their own work is not unlike (and arguably no better than) the way such objectives might be achieved by a teacher through the use of writing, classroom discussion, promoting the reading of books or by getting their students to use a library. This point seemed to have escaped the attention of government policy.

The introduction of ICT into schools in the 1980s therefore coincided with a more overtly interventionist stance by politicians towards mainstream public education and also with the fall-out from the continuing 'great debate' about the curriculum and the nature, purposes and responsibilities of teachers and schools. However, my own early experience, particularly with *Zork!*, had by this time led me to already conclude that the 'catch all' utilitarian approach for the use of ICT that seemed to run so strongly through government policy and the National Curriculum was unlikely to discover or exploit many important features that may be unique to this technology for enhancing learning and teaching in specific ways and in particular contexts.

4 National Policy and ICT

During the period of my early experiments with *Zork!* and my first attempts to develop my own software to support the teaching of English Literature in the 1980s, the UK government was busily promoting the wider use of computers in schools. At first this was via the Microelectronics in Education Project in 1980 but this was also supplemented by a range of other, often heavily funded, initiatives.

The transformational promise of digital and other technology for education had been an enduring feature of political rhetoric long before the member of parliament Michael Heseltine launched the 'Superhighways' initiative in the UK in 1995. Digital technology has been consistently offered to the public by politicians as an almost magical talisman for producing educational progress and excellence ever since. The sums of money committed though this field of public policy have been substantial, even when only the major events and policy initiatives during the 1980s and 1990s are taken into account (Table 1).

Table 1. Major financial initiatives for schools 1980-2002

Source	Year	£ (million)
The Microelectronics in Education Programme (MEP)	1980-1986	32
The Micros in Schools Schemes *	1981-1884	15.1
The Technical and Vocational Educational Initiative (TVEI)	1983-1987	240
Microelectronics Education Support Unit (from 1988-1998 merged with the National Council for Educational Technology)	1986-1988	13
The Education Support Grant for England **	1987-1993	90
Multi-media computers in primary schools	1992-1995	10
Education Departments' Superhighway Initiative (EDSI)	1996-1998	10
Multimedia laptops for teachers	1996-1998	27
The National Grid for Learning (NGfL)	1998-2002	700+
Training for teachers and librarians (New Opportunity Fund) ***	1999-2002	230
Total		1,367.1

* Provided by the Department of Trade and Industry (DTI) who continued to add further funding each year throughout the 1980s from surpluses at the end of their financial year.

** Supplemented since 1993 from the Grants for Educational Support and Training (GEST) scheme.

*** £1.125 billion total spend on this programme, making the overall total over £2.5 billion.

Many of the problems that dogged the ambitious policies for ICT launched in the 1980s and thereafter in the UK, especially those resulting from an over-emphasis on hardware at the expense of teacher training, should have been predictable on the basis of research and evaluation that had already been done [24]. During the 1980s the damaging effects of failing to draw upon prior research was exacerbated within the UK Department for Education and Science and the Department for Trade and Industry by a disinclination to commission any evaluation of the then current initiatives [46].

'Technology' policy initiatives at this time (and also, many would say, those launched subsequently) were also characterised by political desires for tangible success in often unrealistically short time-scales. The promotion of a 'bidding-culture' for resources also often tended to encourage inexperienced individuals and organisations to rush into offering things that turned out to be unattainable. For the ten years from 1987, when initiatives faltered or failed, the DES was under such pressure to deliver on promises made to and by government ministers that key personnel were blamed and "less experienced people were brought in because they were prepared to offer more than could actually be achieved" [46, p.23]. The situation improved in the 1990s with the formation of the National Council for Educational Technology (NCET; funded by the DES) that was required to consult the research community. However, there were still some problems and to take one prominent example the major Teaching and Learning Technology Project was in danger of never being evaluated "probably because of a fear that it might indicate a considerable waste of public money" [26, p.24].

The National Grid for Learning (NGfL) was the single largest contributor of resources for technology to education in the UK and was developed to meet two of the three recommendations of the Independent ICT in School Commission's Stevenson Report [26] - the first of which being to improve teacher training and the second being about the provision of up-to-date computers and the formation of a network to allow teachers to exchange professional information. The NGfL was focussed on promoting higher levels of practical competency in teachers' use of digital technology and on the provision of hardware and infrastructure. Notably, therefore, the NGfL was developed without an explicit overriding educational outcome in mind and in common with many of the initiatives before it, without the support of a body of research underpinning the specific outcomes for pedagogy and student learning that could reasonably be anticipated.

Like many of the initiatives from the 1980s, the NGfL seems to have been based on a belief that teachers would welcome such initiatives and changes with open arms, that these would enhance classroom practice immediately and that teachers would therefore be keen to embrace opportunities to gain expertise in the use of new technology:

> *"Teachers rapidly become enthusiastic once they have regular hands-on access to computers" [27, p.7]*

But the Commission also offered two further key observations:

> *"we do not advocate Central Government ordering large amounts of hardware for schools" [27, p.9]*
>
> *ICT "... should be used in the service of the curriculum, and made available to help teachers to manage the learning process, however that is defined by them." [27, p.15]*

The Stevenson Report was not alone in advising caution in the introduction of ICT into schools and emphasised that such change could be perceived by teachers as threatening, especially as it involved the introduction of highly technical and expensive machines which seemed set to alter the nature of teaching. Introducing effective change in education is often about changing beliefs and attitudes more than anything else and neglecting this has thwarted many interventions:

> "... if ever there is an example of the risk of "death by a thousand initiatives" it is teacher training! It is difficult to blame and easy to sympathise with the consistently critical - and exhausted! - feedback we have received about the number of knee jerk changes made to teacher training. *Changes should be made to the training of teachers to encourage the use of ICT only if Government has a genuine and clearly stated belief about the huge importance of ICT.*" [26, p.22 emphasis in original]

However, other commentators noted that the government's communication of its belief in the importance of ICT was a necessary but insufficient precondition for the successful introduction of technology into schools and that earlier lessons should not be forgotten:

"Those who introduce change treat teachers in precisely the same way as they criticise teachers for treating students. Curricula are often introduced in a way that ignores what teachers think and why." [19, p.119]

Such concerns were also echoed in the evaluation of the Teaching and Learning Technology Programme, conducted by Coopers & Lybrand, the Tavistock Institute and the London Institute of Education, who found that:

"... existing (ICT) products need to be embedded into teaching and learning structures for students. This requires the addressing of issues such as cultural change within departments, time for academics to work CBL (computer-based learning) into their teaching curricula, staff development and training and even a fundamental change in the role of teachers in some higher education institutions." [7]

In contrast to Stevenson's view that teachers generally welcome both change and the introduction of ICT [26], other writers argue that teachers are commonly perceived as opposed to change, that many of them see ICT as just another bandwagon or unwelcome experiment and that many of them feel such encroachments on their practice can safely be ignored because they have little impact on reality; in this view teachers are seen as exercising a sort of practical wisdom [14]. Given that in the event the government ordered large amounts of hardware for schools, made little attempt to involve teachers in defining how it should serve the curriculum and appeared to ignore cautions from writers such as Fullan [19], it is easy to see that an unflattering view of teachers may have gained currency in the minds of some policy makers and politicians.

The seeming preoccupation with the provision of hardware and skills training was not unique to the UK. Similar political imperatives and developments occurred elsewhere and had in common with the UK context an injunction that schools should spend more on computers, with the accompanying expectation that this would of course improve students' academic achievements. For example, in 1997 in the United States the President's Committee of Advisors on Science and Technology and Panel on Educational Technology advocated a three-fold increase for public spending on resources and services related to technology, most of which was to be for equipment and technical infrastructure [12].

In 1998 the United States spent $7.2 billion (2.7% of the total spending on education) on computers in schools, mostly on hardware (74%), although many government advisers and several major reports sought a much greater proportion on software. The five-year spend from 1994-1998 was approximately $29 billion (although by 2001 in real terms this was probably no more than $175 per pupil per year) and some observers argued strongly that this was inadequate: "Until spending levels rise substantially, the impact on students is likely to be severely constrained" [1].

Commentators have pointed out that underlying judgements were being made in decisions to spend money on computers as opposed to other resources and have, in contrast to the technology's arguably unproven worth, drawn attention to research concluding that traditional approaches, such as reduced class size and increased teacher training, confer recognised and substantial achievement benefits for pupils.

For example, the total cost of introducing computer aided instruction (CAI) in Israel between 1994-1996 has been equated to one additional teacher per school per year, and similar resource commitments in other countries have occasioned comment that "this significant and ongoing expenditure on education technology does not appear to be justified by pupil performance results to date" and that "on balance, it seems money spent on CAI ... would have been better spent on other inputs." [4, p.761].

Despite similar reservations from observers in the UK, in 1999 the New Opportunity Fund (NOF) continued the impetus of the NGfL and, using funding from the National Lottery, began training teachers in the use of information and communication technology. The express aim of the NOF was to ensure that teachers made effective use of technology and the expectation was that this would "make a significant contribution to the raising of standards of pupils' achievements" in ways "that meets their needs and is delivered in a way which fits into the culture and plans of their school" (ibid). Details of how these objectives were to be attained in practice were not provided.

Many political initiatives for greater ICT use in education, whether originating in the UK or elsewhere, seem founded more on aspiration than on research findings when politicians, government organisations and policy makers are presenting them to the public. Early failures to commission evaluation studies of the impact of ICT provision compounded the impression that political action may have been judged more important by policy makers than the cautious and more measured implementation suggested by observers such as Stevenson [26].

The introduction of ICT into UK schools may have been designed to fulfil a number of goals: manufacturers' desire profit from selling equipment to schools, whilst others may be seeking solutions to the problems perceived by them to have historically crippled education. Others may anticipate that ICT will create a revolution in classroom teaching practices; and yet others do not wish to see poor and minority children left behind in technological expertise. Such coalitions seem to be generally driven by a belief that if ICT were introduced into the classroom it would be used and if it were used it would transform education [10]. The main impetus for such development in both the USA and the UK appeared to be the interactions between a changing job market and the anticipated effects of the developing global economy, about which President Bill Clinton observed:

> *"Frankly, all the computers and software and Internet connections in the world won't do much good if young people don't understand that access to the new technology means ... access to the new economy" [44]*

In this President Clinton was echoing a similar sentiment from UK Prime Minister Tony Blair:

> *"Children cannot be effective in tomorrow's world if they are trained in yesterday's skills. Nor should teachers be denied the tools that other professionals take for granted." [15]*

However, the economic imperative for adopting new technology in education may rest upon a misreading of its probable role, an incorrect assumption about the need for workers to have ICT skills and a lack of consensus about what those skills might be and about their precise economic or educational utility. The promotion of the technology has tended to be dominated by deterministic views of education heavily characterised by simplistic 'cause and effect' assumptions about anticipated benefits [11], [46].

Even in very high-technology contexts, many skilled teachers are strongly inclined to use ICT primarily to replicate their existing teacher-centred instructional practice [11]. Dawes' early study of these phenomena classified teachers as either 'potential', 'participant', 'involved', 'adept' or 'integral' users, depending on the degree to which they integrated ICT into their practice [14]. Whilst Dawes presumed the category into which teachers fell was influenced by curriculum specialism (e.g. science teachers may find ICT more intrinsically useful than PE teachers), she also noted that even with the more specialist curriculum used with older children, where more teachers were in the higher categories, few ever reached further than 'involved' practitioner status. Follow-up studies of such work have tended to concur and have further concluded that frequent use of ICT is confined to a small minority of educators, although teachers' access, technical competence and an orientation toward a constructivist pedagogy in which depth of study is emphasised more than breadth can significantly affect whether teachers are likely to use ICT [4]. Teacher attitudes towards ICT as driven by their enthusiasms, values and existing pedagogy would therefore appear to be important for understanding how far and how successfully the technology is likely to be adopted and applied.

5 Attitudes

During the latter half of the twentieth century digital technology was frequently presented as an exciting solution to a range of educational and social concerns and also as a means by which teachers could adopt educational roles very different from their perceived traditional didactic stance as the transmitters of knowledge [33]. Such changes were thought to be desirable in part because they could enable a more student-centred approach to classroom practice which had long been seen by many as more appropriate and effective [6], [16], [17], [38], [39] and also because the ability of ICT to offer easy access to a huge range of contemporary information was seen as presenting an effective challenge to the view of knowledge as something that was static and fixed [33].

A powerful limitation on the use of computers by teachers therefore seemed to me to stem from their beliefs about the nature of student learning and, leading from these, what type of instruction is best for their pupils; beliefs that are influenced by their own theories about learning and the affordances that are offered by ICT applications [4], [42]. For example, as a result of such beliefs, some teachers then and now may feel that the internet is largely irrelevant to what they are concerned with in classrooms and, unsurprisingly therefore, may feel that its use is of little relevance to their academic values or pedagogy. Some teachers in the 1980s also argued that in any case they were too busy with many other initiatives to find time to use ICT, had no real knowledge of how best to use it and were dissuaded from considering doing so by the expense and time for training, the scarcity of ICT resources, a lack of technical support and in some cases also by the unfavourable attitude of their school's senior management [14], [53].

However, the exposure of teachers to technology can – if done carefully – encourage them to critically examine their educational philosophy and established classroom practice and can facilitate a change to even very strongly held attitudes about pedagogy, as I found during my own experiences with *Zork!* and when demonstrating its possibilities to other teachers [34].

Even today it seems clear that teachers' subscriptions to a particular pedagogy may be a necessary but insufficient condition for changing traditional teaching practices and others have observed that changes to assessment systems and a lot more professional development will also be needed [32]. In addition to this, the issue of technology adoption and its relationship to the learning outcomes desired by assessment that was highlighted by Parr and Fung when reviewing research in this area has provided conflicting guidance [37].

6 Effectiveness, Learning Outcomes and Attainment

Evidence for the effectiveness of the classroom use of ICT, in terms of impact on academic performance, has been mixed over the last 30 years. Different studies have found moderate effectiveness, minimum effectiveness and no effectiveness. Some reports and studies have focussed on the broader impact and effectiveness of ICT, others on game-based learning but relatively few on multimedia. Some observers of the field have argued that effectiveness statements are often of little use in any case because too often they are unaccompanied by details of student ages, the software used, the outcomes sought and information about how the studies were done [28]. Additionally, according to many writers, most policymakers, practitioners and parents do not appear to have examined research and seem to have taken for granted that computers are effective and have then acted to put them into schools.

From the first appearance of computers in schools, three things have made it difficult to evaluate their contribution: this lack of clarity in the research about what ICT 'effectiveness' means and how it should be measured; a lack of research that has compared computer use with other educational options not involving computers; and different assumptions that have been made in the research about the role of the teacher in technology-rich classrooms. These things have made it hard to compare different research, synthesise the results or reach conclusions, but attempts to do so, such as the 1998 study by Kikpatrick & Cuban [28] found that by the late 1990s, *single studies* made up a high percentage of the investigations. These single studies of achievement gains or improvements in student attitude reported positive, negative and mixed outcomes from ICT use in roughly equal measure. Kirkpatrick and Cuban did identify several studies that focussed on distance learning or on applications for disabled or at-risk students, all of which reported positive outcomes, but they noted that few of these studies were rigorous and ten of them that examined the use of ICT in core curriculum areas ranged from being wildly enthusiastic to cautiously pessimistic; beyond this they were unclear in their conclusions.

Following an extensive survey of the literature from this period [37] it was clear that computer assisted learning had until then been shown to be no more effective than other approaches and may in fact have been less effective than other kinds of intervention. Much that had been written about computers in education had not really been research or scholarship but comment, reporting of informal observation, opinion, or intuitive speculation. The varied and changing nature of computer assisted learning did make rigorous studies in this area difficult but the main problem for researchers was being able to deal successfully with the complex influences and interactions that arose when ICT is introduced into any learning environment.

Claims for a bivariate relationship between computer interest or availability and achievement are not uncommon in the literature although many studies tend to report only positive associations between use and benefit. Such evidence about the relationship between computer availability and the educational achievement of students is drawn upon by many commentators, not least in the political arena. However this can be highly misleading, because computer availability, for example in the home, is also correlated strongly with other characteristics of family background which, when adequately controlled for, reverses many other findings and produces a statistically significant negative correlation [18]. Some quantitative empirical studies, similar to the international 'league tables' for countries published these days, use data from the Programme for International Student Assessment (PISA) and multivariate regression within which are applied extensive controls for student, family and school background effects and a careful analysis of these shows that it is *how* and *what* computers are used for that makes an educational difference.

For example, students may use computers at home for many things (email, games, web access) but these may often distract them from learning and bivariate results for the availability of computers in schools and pupil achievement are severely biased [18], because higher levels of computer availability in schools are strongly associated with higher levels of other educational resources. The correlation between student performance and computer availability at school is "small and statistically indistinguishable from zero" when other school characteristics are controlled for [18, p.360]. As in the home environment, the amount of computer use in school does not directly correlate with achievement and there may be an optimal amount of computer and internet use significantly above zero but below the level of several times per week:

> *"Having a computer at home and using it at school will almost certainly raise some computer skills ... (but) this may come at the expense of other skills ... (which) are the ones that yield significant labour-market returns, not the computer skills" [18, p.375].*

Many of the conclusions from studies in this area have to be interpreted cautiously because they are not based on randomised controlled experimental evidence but on multivariate, descriptive and conditional correlations and may not necessarily "allow for causal inferences because they may also reflect effects of other, unobservable characteristics" [18, p.361]. Their results are, however, a substantial improvement upon the simplistic bivariate correlations found in many other studies which cannot or do not attempt to disentangle them from other factors [30].

In contrast to the emphasis found in the early policy rhetoric, there has grown more appreciation of the importance of pedagogy over and above the presence of the technology alone in achieving educational benefit from computers in classrooms. In that sense there is growing understanding that the most important questions about educational technology have never been about the technology at all but about how it is used. There appears to be a growing recognition in published research, if not yet in political policy, that the most effective educational outcomes from computer use are likely to be about identifying its unique affordances for learning and teaching, over, above and/or different from those that already exist in established (non-technology) classroom practice.

Writers have tended increasingly to echo earlier hopes that this growing appreciation will produce more one-to-one interaction (child to screen and child to teacher) that is regarded as freer and less intense, where the teacher can become more of a facilitator and co-researcher of learning and where children take more responsibility for their own learning or, as Jackson put it, can become "self-confident, independent thinkers, whether team players or entrepreneurs, capable of acquiring a range of different skills and adapting to several jobs over a life time" [27].

Although some writers conclude that there is now widespread recognition that the educative skills of teachers and not just their technical competences with technology are the determining factor in using ICT to bring about educational improvement [1], it seems clear that some teachers use ICT as part of highly traditional approaches to learning, whilst others are more adventurous and that either can be equally effective in terms of student achievement [9]. There is, however, strengthening evidence that "new technology's potential to change the culture of the classroom and the relationship between students and teacher is important, since traditional classrooms are not ideal learning environments" [49, p.98]. Despite such evidence there are important caveats, as the earlier evaluation of the Teaching and Learning Technology Programme (TLTP) conducted by Coopers & Lybrand, the Tavistock Institute and the London Institute of Education noted:

> *"...existing products need to be embedded into teaching and learning structures for students. This requires the addressing of issues such as cultural change within departments, time for academics to work CBL (computer-based learning) into their teaching curricula, staff development and training and even a fundamental change in the role of teachers in some higher education institutions." [7]*

A recurrent supposition in much of the writing about the promise of digital technology is that we are now seeing a generation of 'digitally literate' students entering education and that this has profound and inescapable implications for schools, colleges and universities. Variously labelled the 'Net generation' [52], 'Millennials' [24], [25], 'Generation Y', the 'Youtube' or 'Facebook' generation [47], the 'Backpack generation' [13], 'Digital natives' [40] or similar, these young people are presumed to represent a challenge to traditional forms of educational pedagogy and content that differentiates them markedly from earlier generations because of their sophisticated technical skills and learning preferences. Writers espousing these views presume that traditional forms of teaching and learning are therefore no longer appropriate and call for significant changes to the philosophy found within classrooms, although examination of these assumptions and assertions has led some to conclude that much of this debate lacks theoretical or empirical support [5].

One of the advantages commonly claimed for software and systems designed for these 'digital natives' is that they are learner-centred, that they apply approaches where pupils can set their own pace and control their own learning using the 'learner-as-explorer' or student as 'discoverer' model [44]. Such pedagogical approaches are concerned with learner activity and owe much to the theoretical perspectives of phenomenography and constructivism. Phenomenography [35] is derived from studies of student learning and uses the complementary concepts of 'deep' and 'surface' approaches to learning to discuss how the former involves deep immersion in a task and a focus on gaining insight into structure and intrinsic meaning whilst the latter uses rapid skimming, scanning and browsing to develop subject overview and broad meaning. Both approaches are thought to contribute essential strategies to effective learning. The origins of Constructivism have been traced back to Plato and Socrates [22] and both perspectives share the conviction that meaning is created by the learner's activities rather than being imposed or transmitted. Learning is therefore characterised as a way of interacting with and critically evaluating the world, to which the learner brings their individual intentions and motives, their existing knowledge and their established perceptions. The acquisition of information is therefore a necessary, but by itself insufficient, condition for bringing about learning, which requires the further stage of bringing about changes to the individual's established cognition. So as a result of learning an individual's conceptions and perceptions of the world become changed.

These issues, publications and theoretical models we have looked at have informed the emergence and growth of arguably the two most significant debates about how best we might understand and exploit the relationship between pedagogy, instructional design, subject content and individual learning and are especially relevant for the application of multimedia ICT in learning. These two debates are located within Learning Styles [29] and Cognitive Load Theory [51], with the latter representing the more rigorous and likely best approach.

Hopefully our current endeavours will help to focus attention on what is important about the relationship between computers and education – and what is not. The critical element will always remain the relationship between the teacher and the student, however that is mediated by communication technologies. One thing seems clear: pursuing political or educational dogma at the expense of what research evidence shows us is misguided and can often lead to the squandering of valuable resources. Worse, it can lead to us failing our children. This is a failure to capitalise on what is arguably the most powerful instrument for changing the relationship between teacher and learner that we have. Most of all we do not want the earlier mistakes to be repeated and we owe it to generations to come to ensure that when listing the evidenced and demonstrable benefits to learning, the history of the first fifty years of the use of computers does not end with an echo from the Dungeon Master in *Zork!*:

```
The engravings translate to 'This space
intentionally left blank'
```

References

1. Anderson, R.E., Becker, H.J.: School Investments in Instructional Technology, Teaching, Learning, and Computing: 1998 National Survey Report #8. Center for Research on Information Technology and Organizations (2001), http://www.crito.uci.edu/tlc/html/findings.html
2. Anderson, T.: The History of Zork, http://www.csd.uwo.ca/Infocom/Articles/NZT/zorkhist.html
3. Angrist, J., Lavy, V.: New evidence on classroom computers and pupil earning. The Economic Journal 112, 735–765 (2002)
4. Becker, H.J.: Findings from the Teaching, Learning, and Computing Survey: Is Larry Cuban Right? Education Policy Analysis Archives 8(51) (2000), http://epaa.asu.edu/epaa/v8n51/
5. Bennett, S., Maton, K., Kervin, L.: The 'digital natives' debate: A critical review of the evidence. British Journal of Educational Technology 39(5), 775–786 (2008)
6. Vygotsky, L.S.: Mind in Society: The Development of Higher Psychological Processes. Harvard University Press, Cambridge (1978) Cole, M., John-Steiner, V., Scribner, S., Souberman, E. (eds.)
7. Coopers, Lybrand: nstitute of Education, & Tavistock Institute: Evaluation of the Teaching and Learning Technology Programme (TLTP). HEFCE, Bristol (1996)
8. Cox, C.B., Dyson, R.: Black Paper 1977: Fight for Education, Critical Quarterly. John Wiley, Sussex (1969)
9. Cox, M., Webb, M. (eds.): An investigation of the research evidence relating to ICT pedagogy. Report by Becta to the DfES (2004), http://partners.becta.org.uk/
10. Cuban, L.: How Teachers Taught: Constancy and Change in American Classrooms, 1890-1990 (Research on Teaching). Teachers' College Press, New York (1993)
11. Cuban, L.: Oversold and Underused: Computers in the Classroom. Harvard University Press, London (2001)
12. Culp, K.M., Honey, M., Mandinach, E.: A Retrospective on Twenty Years of Education Technology Policy. U.S. Department of Education (2003), http://www.ed.gov/rschstat/eval/tech/20years.pdf
13. Curtis, J.M.: The Backpack Generation and Art History. Journal of Aesthetic Education 35(1), 31–44 (2001), http://www.jstor.org/stable/3333769?origin=crossref
14. Dawes, L.: First connections: teachers and the National Grid for Learning. Computers & Education 33(4), 235–252 (1999)
15. Department for Education and Employment: Connecting the Learning Society. Stationery Office, London (1997)
16. Dewey, J.: The School and Society. University of Chicago Press, Chicago (1900)
17. Dewey, J.: The Child and The Curriculum. University of Chicago Press, Chicago (1902)
18. Fuchs, T., Wössmann, L.: Computers and student learning: bivariate and multivariate evidence on the availability and use of computers at home and at school (CESifo Working Paper 1321, http://www.cesifo.de). Brussels Economic Review – Cahiers Economiques de Bruxelles 47(3-4), 359–385 (2004), https://dipot.ulb.ac.be/dspace/bitstream/2013/11947/1/ber-0300.pdf
19. Fullan, M.: The meaning of educational change. Teachers College Press, London (1982)

20. Gillard, D.: Education in England: a brief history (2011), http://www.educationengland.org.uk/history/
21. Halsey, A.H., Sylva, K.: Plowden: history and prospect. Oxford Review of Education 13(1), 3–11 (1987)
22. Hawkins, D.: Constructivism: some history. In: Fensham, P., Gunstone, R.F., White, R.T. (eds.) The Content of Science. A Constructivist Approach to its Teaching and Learning. Falmer Press, London (1994)
23. HMSO: The Plowden Report: Children and their Primary Schools. London: Her Majesty's Stationery Office: London (1967)
24. House, E.R.: The Politics of Educational Innovation. McCutchan Publishing Co., Berkley (1974)
25. Howe, N., Strauss, W.: Millennials rising: the next generation. Vintage, New York (2000)
26. Independent ICT in School Commission: Information and Communications Technology in UK Schools: An Independent Inquiry (The Stevenson Report) London: Independent ICT in School Commission (1997), http://rubble.heppell.net/stevenson/ICTUKIndex.html
27. Jackson, P.W.: Life in Classrooms. Holt, Reinhart and Winston, New York (1968)
28. Kikpatrick, H., Cuban, L.: Computers make kids smarter – Right? Technos Quarterly 7(2) (1998), http://www.ait.net/technos/tq_07/index.php
29. Kolb, D.A.: Experiential learning: experience as the source of learning and development. Prentice-Hall, Englewood Cliffs (1984)
30. Kozma, R.B.: The Influence of Media on Learning: The Debate Continues. School Library Media Quarterly 22(4), 233–240 (1994), http://www.ala.org/aasl/aaslpubsandjournals/slmrb/editorschoiceb/infopower/selctkozmahtml
31. Kozma, R.B.: Technology and Classroom Practices: An International Study. Journal of Research on Technology in Education 36(1), 1–14 (2003)
32. Lim, C.P., Chai, C.S.: Teachers' pedagogical beliefs and their planning and conduct of computer-mediated classroom lessons. British Journal of Educational Technology 39(5), 804–828 (2008)
33. Loveless, A., DeVoogd, G.L., Bohlin, R.M.: Something old, something new.. Is pedagogy effected by ICT? In: Loveless, A., Ellis, V. (eds.) ICT, Pedagogy and the Curriculum, pp. 63–83. Routledge, London (2001)
34. Martin, S., Vallance, M.: The Impact of Synchronous Inter-Networked Teacher Training in Information and Communication Technology Integration. Computers and Education 51(1), 34–53 (2008)
35. Marton, F.: Phenomenography – describing conceptions of the world around us. Instructional Science 10(1), 177–200 (1981)
36. Montfort, N.: Twisty Little Passages: An Approach to Interactive fiction. The MIT Press, Cambridge (2005)
37. Parr, J.M., Fung, I.: A Review of the Literature on Computer-Assisted Learning, particularly Integrated Learning Systems, and Outcomes with Respect to Literacy and Numeracy. New Zealand Ministry of Education (2000), http://www.educationcounts.govt.nz/publications/ict/5927
38. Piaget, J.: The Child's Conception of the World. Routledge and Keegan Paul, London (1928)
39. Piaget, J.: The equilibration of cognitive structures: The Central Problem of Intellectual Development. University of Chicago Press, Chicago (1985)
40. Prensky, M.: Digital natives, digital immigrants. On the Horizon 9(5), 1–6 (2001)

41. QCA: ICT Programme of Study for key stage 4: Qualifications and Curriculum Authority (2007),
http://www.education.gov.uk/schools/teachingandlearning/curriculum/secondary/b00199065/ict/ks4/programme
42. Ravitz, J.L., Becker, H.J., Wong, Y.-T.: Constructivist-Compatible Beliefs and Practices among U.S. Teachers. Teaching, Learning, and Computing: 1998 National Survey, Report 4. Center for Research on Information Technology and Organizations, University of California, Irvine (2000),
http://www.crito.uci.edu/TLC/FINDINGS/REPORT4/REPORT4.PDF
43. San Jose Mercury News, Silicon Valley, California (April 18, 2000),
http://www.mercurynews.com/
44. Scrimshaw, P.: Computers and the teacher's role. In: Somekh, B., Davis, N. (eds.) Using Information Technology Effectively in Teaching and Learning. Routledge, London (1997)
45. Scruton, R.: Expressionist education. Oxford Review of Education 13(1), 39–44 (1987)
46. Selwyn, N.: Guilding the Grid: the marketing of the National Grid for Learning. British Journal of Sociology of Education 20(1), 55–68 (1999)
47. Shapira, I.: What Comes Next After Generation X?, Education, The Washington Post, pp. C01 (2008),
http://www.washingtonpost.com/wpdyn/content/article/2008/07/05/AR2008070501599.html
48. Somekh, B.: New technology and learning: Policy and practice in the UK, 1980-2010. Education and Information Technologies 5(1), 19–37 (2000)
49. Somekh, B.: Pedagogy and Learning with ICT: Researching the art of innovation. Routledge, Oxon (2007)
50. Stone, D.P.: Zork!: an overview of the series. Computer Gaming World, vol. 3(2). Golden Empire Publications, Anaheim (1983),
http://cgw.vintagegaming.org/galleries/index.php?year=1983&pub=2&id=9 and
http://cgw.vintagegaming.org/galleries/issues/3.2.pdf
51. Sweller, J.: Cognitive Load Theory, learning difficulty, and instructional design. Learning and Instruction 4(4), 295–312 (1994)
52. Tapscott, D.: Growing up digital: the rise of the Net generation. McGraw-Hill, New York (1998)
53. Williams, D., Coles, L., Wilson, K., Richardson, A., Tuson, J.: Teachers and ICT: current use and future needs. British Journal of Educational Technology 31(4), 307–320 (2000)

No One Is Born a Global Citizen: Using New Technologies to Bring 'Other Stories' into the Classroom

Alnaaz Kassam

Toronto District School Board, Canada
alnkassam@yahoo.com

Abstract. In a rapidly shrinking world, a Canadian high school teacher of literature in English reflects on the increasing diversity of her students and the role of technology in bringing to them a sophisticated knowledge of the cultures of the world. In this paper, she describes her experiences from a 20 year journey with using technology in various projects that include teaching students about human agency in global politics, First Nations land issues, the portrayal of the Caribbean in the media, the impact of HIV/AIDS on Africans and the comparison of use of water resources in East Africa and Canada. Through this journey, she comes to the conclusion that technology is an important conduit but the role of the wise teacher, a high quality curriculum that fosters deep knowledge of the cultures of the world, critical literacy and an appreciation of ethics in human agency are vital in bringing about a sympathetic but deep knowledge of the "other" in our midst and increasingly in a rapidly shrinking world where we rub shoulders with all of humanity everyday.

Keywords: Classroom Teaching/Practice, Digital Divide Secondary Education, Developing countries.

1 Introduction

At a time of vast technological change, the world is undergoing a major revolution, where people the world over can communicate with each other instantaneously despite the vast distances that separate them.

We also live in a globalized world where intercultural and international understandings are absolutely essential. Nonetheless we currently have situations where both internally and externally, there is much misunderstanding and strife between peoples of different backgrounds. In a recent speech, Kofi Annan (2013), the former secretary general of the United Nations, explained that even those societies that have a long history of pluralism and policies that protect minorities such as those in Europe, face challenges in demonstrating respect and tolerance for all. This phenomenon illustrates the difficulties of governing diverse societies and fostering democracies in today's world. Annan (2013) explains:

> *Europe, for example, has well-established legal systems and arrangements to protect minorities and reach acceptable compromises. Yet even within Europe, pluralism is sometimes seen as a threat. Levels of social prejudice have been rising against religious and cultural minorities and new immigrants. Just as no country is born a democracy, no one is born a good citizen. Mutual respect and tolerance*

A. Tatnall and B. Davey (Eds.): History of Computers in Education, IFIP AICT 424, pp. 26–47, 2014.

> *have to be fostered and taught...... My experience has also taught me that strong, healthy and cohesive societies are built on three pillars: peace and security; development; and rule of law and respect for human rights. Unfortunately stability and economic growth have, for too long, been the principal responses to national and global problems. We must not fall into this trap.*

In an interview about his book, *The Global Soul*, Iyer explains how new technologies and travel affect our experience of the world, encouraging us to seek an even faster pace of change and increasingly newer technologies. He questions whether we are in charge of this fast-paced change.

According to Iyer (in Cavenett, 2007), we live in societies, where it is difficult to ask people where they come from; we all seem to have mongrel identities. However, Iyer claims that if we cannot say where we come from, we lose not only our sense of place but also our identity. In the schools I teach, in the panorama of countries of origin of my students, in the multitude of identities and loyalties that my students grapple with, I increasingly find that I must teach to these very issues.

It is increasingly obvious that students need not only to appreciate their own identities but also to live with tolerance, respect and above all knowledge of other cultures so as to create viable democracies that treat all with equity. Respect for the other is certainly a prerequisite for world peace.

Over the past 20 years, I have wondered if technology is a catalyst or an impediment in the process of having our students acquire global outlooks geared towards promoting knowledge and understanding of others around the world. Let me explain.

For Iyer, finding the global soul is about finding one's identity. The challenges of losing identity for him are in some ways a form of liberation; losing old categories of the past from which we are liberated but subsequently facing the challenge of creating something new.

However, others believe that the world can remain peaceful, economically and politically viable only if we educate our children in elementary and high schools in the knowledge of the world and its peoples. We also need to teach them the ethics of equity and a sense of responsibility to each other and the world. Citizens in democracies, who have the privilege of affecting change in governmental policies need to know not only themselves but the 'other' too. A knowledge of pluralism is a necessity in a world that is full of strife.

My question is this: in a world of breathtakingly fast communication, is technology destined to break our traditional identities and society? Or can technology allow us to communicate with each other and thereby assist us in acquiring a deep knowledge and respect of the other such that we can build peaceful societies where all can live in peace? Can schools play a role in leveraging technology for this purpose?

This is a particularly important question to pose at this point in time given that we live in a world of both local and international strife and also given that we are amidst a particularly intense era of technology, one in which computer technology is widely utilized for social networking amongst young people (Twitter, Youtube, Facebook, blogs, wikis, etc.). Will these new social networks allow different voices to enter into the classroom or are they simply mirages that will not affect what we consider to be 'important knowledge,' (of dominant societies) that which we impart in schools unchanged and untouched from generation to generation?

Over the past 20 years, I have been involved in using technology to bring diversity into the classroom. Where I have experienced success is in my ability to bring many diverse voices into the curricula. However, somehow in this journey, empathy, respect and a deep questioning and critical analysis of inequities in society and conflicting identities has eluded students. In this paper, I will illustrate why I believe this to be the case.

My journey will begin in the early days of computing in education and it ends with an action research study that ended about a year ago. I will document how despite early disappointments, I was eventually successful in getting students to incorporate knowledge of the other but also to incorporate empathy and critical analysis into the projects we studied..

My journey has taken many different paths – both in the roles I have played; doctoral candidate, educational researcher at a major university in Canada and now high school teacher. It has also taken me down the path of using ever increasing levels of computer power: from text-based simulations, networking using a single modem and print-outs and then moving to students researching using integrated technologies such as mobile phones, YouTube and wikis to link to knowledge and people across the world in order to improve inter-cultural understanding across the globe.

In this journey of my experience with new technologies and students' emerging identities, I would like to discuss several projects that I have worked on. Each of them illustrates various developments in our history of using technology in education. These developments include: the breathtakingly fast-paced development in the speed and potential of technology, its increasing ubiquity, its ability to make learning both interactive but also transparent but also an increasing awareness that educational institutions have somehow failed to use technology to its best potential.

There are 6 projects that I would like to explore: A history simulation on the *Bartlett Family,* The ICONS project on international diplomacy, The *Other Story* Phase One*:* Impact of Media on the Caribbean, The *Other Story* project, Phase One: Understanding Canadian History from a First Nations perspective, The *Other Story* project, Phase Two: Taking responsibility for the AIDS crisis in Africa and finally, Water as resource in a globalized world: blessing for few, curse for many.

For each of these I will first describe the project and what I learned about the potential of new technologies for the inclusion of diverse identities into the classroom from it. I will examine both the types of technology and my increasing personal awareness of the complexity of promoting inter-cultural understanding that I experienced through these encounters.

2 A History Simulation of the Bartlett Family

When I think about the beginning of my long journey with educational computing, I am reminded of my early days of observing the implementation of computers in the classroom. More than 20 years ago in the early 1980s, I was a researcher in an Ontario government funded research project examining the impact of computers in classrooms. My task at one point was to observe how two teachers in one school incorporated the seven computers they had each been given into their classrooms.

At one point, I sat in the back of one classroom and watched students working with what were very specific tasks assigned to them by their teacher. Soon I found myself observing a young boy named Walter. I watched him work day after day on a history simulation called the *History of the Bartlett Family*. It took a day or two for me to realize that Walter had developed an ingenious way to use the simulation to amuse himself while hoodwinking his teacher.

The *History of the Bartlett Family* simulation was an award winning, carefully researched simulation of a pioneer family in Ontario whose trials and tribulations of establishing a family farm, participating in the early political process in the still nascent society of Ontario became a fascinating way of exposing elementary students to history in an interactive and immediate fashion.

Young Walter, however, using the series of choices that allowed settlers to perish or progress through a series of simulated hardships, managed to sail through the simulation until it took him to a short program where the Bartletts had to cook a stew using ingredients available to them. Walter's sole objective and delight was to create a poisonous concoction for the stew that would render the Bartlett family too sick to survive, and would end the game. Walter enjoyed this process enormously and came up with varied concoctions of the recipe tirelessly in order to be able to 'die' in the shortest possible time. Walter was delighted at this outcome and considered this to be an achievement of success in the objectives of the program.

This observation of Walter and the Bartlett simulation has become for me a symbol of what new technologies mean for traditional classrooms and traditional modes of literacy. There were 3 lessons that we can acquire from those early observations of Walter, which I feel still apply today. They are:

a) While computer technologies have an extraordinary ability to provide interactivity and immediacy to student learning, that very feature allows students to sabotage the learning process because they are now in control of the learning outcomes. *How then do we design learning in order to avoid students hijacking our best efforts?*

b) It is clear that even from the first moments of word processing, technology changed our concept of literacy and knowledge creation. One of the ways that this change occurred was that there was interactivity in learning. For me, interactivity provided an opportunity for bringing new voices into the classroom, especially as the technology became so ubiquitous that we could communicate and interact with students even in East Africa. But I was soon to discover that the Walters of this world are very much part of the identity of our youth today. The second question to be posed is: *What are the ever increasing implications for literacy when classroom walls keep coming down? Is there going to be some impact upon the inclusion of diverse voices in the classroom?*

c) While computer technologies provide an extraordinary amount of interactivity to students they also increasingly provide *a transparency* of student work including racist remarks and shallow analysis, which will be available for perusal by all within and without our schools (even on a global basis). *Does this mean that there will be more efficient academic accountability but even more important what does this transparency bring in terms of ethical and social ramifications? What are the issues for privacy and increasingly racism across and beyond national boundaries?*

In the next sections, I will explore the ethical and social ramifications of the introduction of new technologies into our classrooms. If computers bring down classroom walls, can they bring varied perspectives and voices into the classroom? Can they assist students in learning about their own identities? Can they ultimately help build pluralistic societies through fostering inter-cultural understanding?

In the next section, I shall introduce a second project that I observed in those early days of computing where networking was limited and reserved for the privileged few.

3 The ICONS Project

In the late 80s, as an educational researcher, I was called upon to observe a Canadian classroom at SciTech school (a pseudonym) partaking in a North America wide simulation known as the ICONS simulation, which one teacher incorporated into his teaching of the geography *World Issues* course at SciTech at the senior high school level.

ICONS, which stood for International Communications and Negotiations Simulation, was as its name implied a simulation where students became negotiators representing countries of the world in the solution of a series of important issues called subgames. In the simulation that the students at SciTech took part in, these four subgames were: Arms Control, International economic problems, Nuclear Proliferation and Human Rights.

Unlike other simulations that last only a few hours, this one spanned several months - of which the first weeks were spent in preparation, the next four were the actual simulation and the last few weeks were spent in the debriefing. The actual simulation was first of a series of conferences where participants from various countries took part at the same time. However, there was also asynchronous communication in the form of messages left in the mailbox at any time during the four weeks of the simulation. All teams were linked to a central mainframe computer at an American university, where using specially designed software, the computers handled thousands of messages. The most exciting part of the simulation was the real-time conference session, where students actually 'negotiated' with students from other parts of North America. Two teams were present from Canada, with SciTech representing Canada. Similarly, one of the teams from the U.S. represented that country, while all the other schools represented other countries (e.g. Angola, Japan, etc.). This too, was part of the exercise - which students learn to place themselves in the shoes of other cultures and countries, so as to appreciate their problems and views.

This was an exciting simulation because, for the first time it allowed networking across schools. I watched students work with a primitive modem (all I witnessed was a cable emerging from the ceiling as the students shared the one modem with the rest of school. The school was also linked to NASA as part of a science project) and the modem was connected to one computer, from which everyone made printouts. This was a particularly interesting development; now the classroom walls were coming down and I believed I would witness diverse voices in the class. However, this presence of diversity of perspective and voice proved disappointing.

In the literature, the organizers of the simulation described the simulation as being created to increase inter-cultural understanding and communication, and then present one political game that could take place, which would allow participants to come to grips and deal with rather delicate international relations.

In one instance, the simulation context is that the CIA has learned that Iran has in its possession a powerful nuclear bomb - such an incident would of course upset the balance of power in the Middle East. While describing and assigning country roles to various participants (again the participants are not from the countries they represent), a statement describing Iran's position is posited by the writers of the simulation:

> *"Iran can be made to behave in more or less menacing ways, not only toward Iraq, but also toward the Gulf States, Saudi Arabia and even Israel (via Shiite proxies in Southern Lebanon). Iranian moves do not have to appear entirely rational." (Fieldnotes, Page 17)*

In an almost eerie resemblance to current global politics, we see how media stereotypes (of Iranians being irrational, menacing) are played out, even in a simulation by a major university in the U.S. This is a rather unfortunate mistake as there were many students of Iranian origin in this school.

So, yes the classroom walls came down in this project and students began to discuss other cultures, countries and civilizations, however their viewpoint of those of other cultures (here Iranians) did not change – dominant biased and racist media perspectives continued to prevail unchallenged.

What lessons can we learn from this project? New technologies can bring new subjects of study and new voices into the classroom, but this does not mean we are rid of media stereotypes in how we deal with them.

Carefully researched and carefully constructed projects should assist us in moving beyond stereotypes to a critical analysis of local and global diversities, but unless we include authentic, credible voices from the 'other' side, interactive simulations will not improve the understanding of diversity in the world.

In the next project description I will show how I created a project where I included the authentic presence of the other but I will also demonstrate how including authentic voices in the project does not always guarantee that this type of inter-cultural understanding will occur.

4 Other Story Project: Phase One: Introducing the Caribbean

It is perhaps in the next project, (which took place in the early 90s) the *Other Story* project, of which I was the Principal Investigator and creator, that the authentic inclusion of diversity (without stereotypes) had the best chance to occur. This research project entitled, '*The Other Story: Research in the Development of Telecommunications-Based Materials to Promote Anti-Racist and Critical Thinking in Ontario Schools*', was a research project funded under the Transfer Grant by the Ontario Ministry of Education from 1993 to 1995.

It is important to point out that in the first phase of the *Other Story* project I was an educational researcher at a major Canadian university. I had completed my doctoral degree in education and was thus qualified to apply for research grants and become a Principal Investigator in research work. At this stage, I was also able to visit different schools and the research funding allowed me to hire research assistants who also conducted research in schools to support my work. However, this was still the first phase of the *Other Story project* and it is also important to point out that in the 2nd phase of *the Other Story* project, I was a classroom teacher with my own students, curriculum and connections to schools around the world (see below). In a sense, I was much more in control of the learning and teaching experience when I became a classroom teacher than when I watched various classrooms implementing a project that other researchers and I had put together.

In this first implementation of the *Other Story project,* the main objective was to bring the 'Other' into the classroom through the Internet. In this first episode of the project, students in the Caribbean and Canada were linked through an online conference (mostly through a listserv). In order to deal with the primitive resources that made up the beginnings of the new communication technologies, I as researcher, carried a 1200 baud modem to each school. The modem was linked to the school phone line in the main office and then connected to one computer in the school lab using a 50 foot cable to upload the data that students had typed up on their computers. In some schools I saved the student data to a disk and then carried it to the university from which I uploaded the responses to the listserv. Students from the Caribbean school faxed their responses to me, which I then typed up and uploaded to the listserv created. These very frustrating technology experiences more than made up with the type of data that was collected through the project.

The conference participants included students from three inner city classrooms in Toronto with one school in the Caribbean. The conference participants also included one Canadian teacher and some students of Caribbean origin. There was also one professor of Caribbean origin from a local Toronto university who acted as expert and responded to students' often very racist and ignorant remarks.

The project was carried out in the form of a simulation with each classroom posing as the government of a fictitious Caribbean island. Each government was presented with the task of debating in their parliament whether they wanted to regulate TV on their island. Each classroom was divided into 4 groups representing the Ministries of Culture, Tourism, Finance and Information. The Ministers received well-researched portfolios of materials written by authors of Caribbean origin.

All Canadian schools in the project were inner-city schools. Classroom observations showed that students were for the most part apathetic, uninterested in school and classroom discussions. A discussion with one classroom teacher revealed that despite all manner of efforts in reforming the curriculum, nothing had worked in changing students' attitudes to their schooling.

Although the materials provided to the students and the experts available online were carefully chosen for authenticity, wisdom and a true reflection of the Caribbean culture, the online interaction soon disintegrated into a racist diatribe with narrow-minded views on the part of the students. Among the first comments to emerge online are students' pre-conference views of the Caribbean:

> *The Caribbean gives me a lot of different impressions. For example: Jamaica. When I think of Jamaica I think of holidays, honeymoons, sun, fun and sand. Also, I think the people would be very happy (high) because marijuana is legalized.*

In another class, students list their impressions of the Caribbean:

> *Goats and pigs running around, surfing, people living in grass huts on beaches, street markets, low paying jobs, no electricity, nude beaches, cruise ships, dreadlocks (hair style), alcohol, tropical storms, tropical fruit, people saying "Hey man", black, bare footed people, dress in grass skirts....*

The researchers, while shocked at this believe that after reading the materials provided to them and especially watching the film called *the Dish Ran Away with the Spoon,* a BBC production that explored the issue of cultural domination through TV through the perspective of the people affected: artists, writers, teachers, religious leaders, politicians, school children and other ordinary people, that Canadian students might change perspectives and become more interested in issues faced in developing countries. Yet some of the answers that emerge are patronizing and similar to the following quotation:

> *My impression of the Caribbean has not changed because I found the video to be somewhat unrealistic. I have been to the Dominican Republic and saw what it was really like. I mean I actually went out of the American resort that I was staying at and looked around, .. the video portrayed the Caribbean as this great place where everyone is happy and only worried about what the children watch on TV when they are lucky to even have a TV*

Another response refers to the local people fleecing the tourists in various ways. Through the data collected on-line and in classroom observations, a certain view of the Caribbean emerges. It is a view that reflects the North American attitudes of superiority, of ignorance of the rest of the world. At the same time, there is a flaunting of that ignorance.

While at first glance, it seems that digitized technologies only seem to exacerbate the open expression of racism and provide it an audience (a phenomenon that is increasingly seen on Twitter in response to certain news stories), closer analysis and discussion with the rest of the Caribbean experts that form part of this project, reveals other responses. The English literature teacher of Jamaican origin at one of the inner city schools in Toronto, explains that she is not surprised at the racism aimed at people of her background, but she is pleased that it is expressed publicly so that it can be dealt with publicly and *responded to* by the university professor on the project, who can then explain to the students the folly of their thoughts. Here the professor responds to students' on-line discussions:

> *Some of you have raised the issue about 'ripping-off' of tourists. Do some people in the Caribbean 'rip-off' tourists? Of course this happens! But it happens everywhere in the world as well. Does this happen more in the Caribbean than in other parts of the world? No one really knows, but probably not. Quite often, however, the Caribbean is advertised to*

> *tourists in a very unrealistic way (is it paradise?) and this creates a problem for tourists when something 'wrong' happens. Does it rain in paradise? Maybe not, but it sure does in Jamaica.*

Students from the school in the Caribbean also respond angrily to the racist remarks of the Canadian students:

> *One of the misconceptions about the Caribbean is that the people live in grass huts on beaches and that there are goats and pigs running wild. This is in no way accurate. Caribbean people live in regular wood or brick houses just like everyone else and like most people we build pens and sties for our goats and pigs, if we have any. Considering that we live in regular houses, it is safe to assume that we have electricity and running water.*

Thus this very early communication technology provided *transparency* (the racism cannot be hidden, it is overt and available for all to see), *interactivity* (such that alternate views can be expressed and shared) and finally *equity of expression* (no longer is information shared in the broadcast mode but rather even high school students from all parts of the world can express their views for all to see and tackle). These are components of social networking sites that are still very much present today and form part of their strengths and weaknesses even today.

We now turn to another experience in the *Other Story* project.

5 Other Story Phase One: A First Nations Perspective

One of the objectives of this project was that it was designed to bring the 'other' into the classroom but this was accomplished by using the 'other's own perspective'. It was hoped that through this process that we would be able to unravel history by using a critical analysis of the relationship between the dominant and other using documents that were both officially produced but also those written in the voice of the marginalized other.

The Other Story was a research project to develop curriculum for inter-cultural understanding through a critical inquiry, issues-oriented approach. The curriculum was a combination of classroom based discussion and an on-line conference linking schools throughout Canada to students and adherents of the culture being studied. The most important objective of the project was to study cultures from their own perspective. Students, teachers and adherents of the culture being studied were invited to participate in the on-line conference. It was envisaged that through this approach Canadian students would develop a deeper, more sophisticated and less media-bound understanding of different cultures of the world.

In the spring of 1995, eight Grade 8 classrooms including two from First Nations schools participated in an Internet conference that discussed issues pertinent to the portrayal of First Nations people and their relations with other peoples in Canada. The conference was entitled: 'First Nations Peoples: The Untold Story' and it took up a significant event in Canadian history and presented it to students both from the conventional text book view and from the perspective of the First Nations people.

The conference was divided into 4 sessions - in the first session, students read and responded to a story written by Susan Fletcher and Michael Dion, who were two First Nations authors. The story was about Mistahimaskwa (otherwise known as Big Bear in conventional text books) who dared to defy the encroaching Canadian government forces who wished to occupy and take over the land of his people.

In this first session, students were to read and respond to the story, after which they were to look for information on this event in other resources: textbooks, encyclopedias and/or school library books. Students were to ask themselves the question:

> *Have we been exposed to the First Nations viewpoint before? Why or why not? What does this tell us?*

The response by each classroom was uploaded to be sent to all other schools participating in the project. Schools were to be identified by the presence or absence of First Nations students and teachers in their classrooms.

In the second session, students considered responses from Session 1 from the other schools in the project and composed replies to them. The students were to discuss whether they were in agreement with views presented, if they learned anything from other perspectives and if they wanted to contribute to the overall discussion in any way. Questions directed specifically at First Nations or non-First Nations peoples were welcomed. This input was uploaded and sent to all schools in the project.

In the third session, First Nations peoples and particularly the authors of the story from the First Nations perspective were to respond to the discussion from the previous two sessions. The fourth session was to be one of reflection - have we as teachers, students and adherents of the various cultures learned anything from this exchange of experiences? How does this portrayal of Indigenous and non-Indigenous peoples affect our relationship? How can we use this learning experience to affect a change in the relationship between us?

What happened in the interaction? It is impossible in this short amount of space to outline the interaction of 8 classes over a period of 4 weeks. However, some interactions can be highlighted to show how difficult it was to get students to think in terms of complexities. The need to seek simple answers, to point to easy explanations for what happened in the encounter of First Nations peoples and the newly arrived white peoples seemed to be the order of the day.

In my analysis of what happened, I will concentrate here on the on-line interaction from 2 schools. As explained above, all schools start by reading the story of Mistahimaskwa written from a First Nations perspective and then compare it with their textbooks.

Here is the feedback from A.S. Dawson (pseudonym), a suburban school close to a large Canadian city:

> *We compared the story from the text book and the story by Dion and Fletcher and noted the differences and similarities. Some similarities mentioned in both stories was the way the native Indians were acknowledged as poor and starving from the lack of buffalo, which a main source of their survival, had been wiped out by the incoming colonizers. Surprisingly, the text books also looked at the grievances the*

> *natives had including the fact that the land given to them as part of the treaty was poor and inadequate. The location of the battles that were specified in each story was also identical. After the massacre at Frog Lake, both stories mentioned that Big Bear was tried and found guilty of the deaths caused by his warriors. The similarities that the story shared were basically the clean cut facts.*
> *Because the information in the text books was slightly more European oriented, there were a few differences in views when compared to the Natives' story. Although the text books tried to capture some of the things the Natives were experiencing, the information was still mostly factual and not as personal as the story by the Dions. The text books did a fairly good job in reporting the story of Mistahimaskwa even including the views from the Natives.*

In analyzing the data from the students, it is interesting to note that in this exercise, the most important thing in comparing the texts is to determine which one is more accurate. The students begin by identifying the similarities between the texts of the two cultural groups as being the clear-cut facts. What are facts? As Carr explains:

> *The historian is neither the humble slave, nor the tyrannical master, of his facts. The relation between the historian and his facts is one of equality, of give-and-take.*
>
> *As any working historian knows, if he stops to reflect what he is doing as he thinks and writes, the historian is engaged on a continuous process of molding his facts to his interpretation and his interpretation to his facts. It is impossible to assign primacy to one over the other.*

Thus we see that facts can never stand alone: in choosing the facts to include in their version of events, the historians from both cultural groups made choices. These choices were in some cases made to hide culpability in terms of injustice and cruelty. In other words, the facts themselves, rather than being neutral and value-free - 'what happened' in the past - become in and of themselves, an extension of the historians' perspective and interpretation. A wise and experienced teacher would and should have been able to draw these issues out.

Students from the A.S. Dawson school failed to see that what was in the history text book describes simply as the settlers taking the land of the First Nations through violent force, is actually unethical, illegal and above all cruel. It does not matter if what is reported is accurate – one must consider the legal and ethical ramifications first.

It is this exercise that Susan Fletcher (the First Nations author of the stories) was trying to get students to come through, what interpretation do we give to this event that happened to First Nations peoples, what does it tell us about ourselves as human beings, as Canadians? We cannot really complete this process until we examine the interpretation of the event from both perspectives - 'those who did it and who it was done to'.

In contrast, when the history texts and the stories written by First Nations authors are read by a First Nations school in Northern Manitoba, the students write back emotionally to the on-line conference. They say that they understand how Mistahimaskwa felt because they too had recently lost their traditional hunting grounds to the flooding from a dam built by Manitoba Hydro. Ten years later, they had yet to be compensated and they still lived in temporary housing with no access to their traditional hunting and fishing grounds. "Nothing has changed for us", they said. The story written by First Nations authors resonates strongly with them.

A.S. Dawson students, in avoiding the question of what happened in the larger context of whether it was right that it should have happened, have avoided bringing themselves and their own positions into the story. In understanding history from the perspective of history as a neutral account, with no moral accountability, students avoid the larger question of *whether the government acted fairly* in this incident. They also avoid the question of how the historian (or the textbook writer) has interpreted this event.

When A.S. Dawson receives the print-out of the other schools' responses to the story of Mistahimaskwa and their search for this event in their text books, I, as researcher was present in the class. My fieldnotes show that I am struck by the fact that these students are adversarial in their response to all the comments that they have received from other schools – constantly trying to show that their response was 'better' and that each of the schools did not respond well to the task. Some A.S. Dawson students respond to other schools' sympathy for the First Nations peoples when they lost their land, as being politically correct. Their teacher sees no wrong committed and is only interested in proving that her students are the most articulate of all the other schools. They miss altogether the suffering of the First Nations school.

While the *Other Story* project makes great efforts to bring marginalized cultures into the classroom so as to encourage students in history classes to understand history and to practice critical thinking from an ethical perspective, we find that unless the classroom teacher is engaged and knowledgeable in creating critical pedagogical environments, students descend into one up manship and petty posturing.

Instead of an ethical accountability of the government's 'stealing' of First Nations land, students are reduced to arguing which text book is most 'objective' and which class the most articulate. And later in the project, the heart-rendering accounts from a school of First Nations students living in a reserve in Northern Manitoba, where they have lost their land yet again to a hydro project is ignored, while students in cities continue to bicker on who is producing the best sound bites.

The above two simulations reveal the following:

a) Technology **does** provide unique opportunities for inclusion and interaction with diverse voices from outside the classroom.
b) Technology provides unique opportunities for the creation and introduction of non-mainstream content in the classroom
c) Technology does not guarantee a critical pedagogy in the classroom – that is contingent partly on the content of the programming but much more **importantly** on the environment created by the teacher before, during and after the introduction of any new programming.

The 5th project that I would like to report on is:

6 The Other Story Project, Phase 2: Rights and Responsibilities in a Troubled World – Students Reaching Out to Discuss Solutions for the HIV/AIDS Crisis

In this paper, I have thus far tried to demonstrate how the arrival of new technologies had allowed the introduction of knowledge of and interactivity with the 'Other' into the classroom. However, I have pointed out the importance of the presence of a wise and knowledgeable teacher to ensure that the learning exercise looks at issues of power, ethics and the complexity of diversity.

In the fall of 1999, I left my position as an educational researcher at a university and became a full-time high school teacher. Now I had the opportunity to try out the *Other Story* project in my own classroom, in cooperation with teachers in other classes in my school or indeed across the globe. Thus, in the fall of 2007, four Grade 9 English classes from my school took part in a project entitled '*Rights and Responsibilities in a Troubled World: Students reaching out to discuss solutions for the HIV/AIDS crisis*'. The project was coordinated by myself (and I brought 2 Grade 9 classes, Ms.Neuman (and her 2 Grade 9 classes) both from one Canadian school. Mr Charles Tasma (and 144 students from a Boys High School in Kenya) also participated in the project.

The basic aim of this project was to encourage students both in Kenya and in Canada, regardless of their place at the level of privilege or poverty, to consider issues of global responsibility and social justice. As part of this objective, students considered what role they could play in increasing global awareness of the issue of HIV/AIDS and how they could get involved in taking responsibility to learn about and assist others on a global level.

The second objective of the project was to expose teenagers to issues of globalization: Who is responsible for the global world order? What responsibility do Canadians have for the way poverty is distributed in the world? Why is it that some voices and perspectives are heard in the media and others are not?

Students used resources from UNICEF including a graphic text called *Asmina's Story*, movies, and they participated in other activities and in pre-arranged e-mail discussions. It was hoped that this international student exchange would foster mutual understanding and friendships. The project was for the most part, successful as seen by these comments by David, one of the Canadian students at the end of the project:

> *"From my research topic, I've learned many different consequences of our greed and demand for material goods. Knowing this point, I now understand that I'm also an indirect cause of poverty in Africa and other parts of the world. After this project, I still found it difficult to figure out a viable solution for poverty, considering the inequality most people are living in now. I also found out that only because of our aggressive ancestors that we are living in considerable wealth, while others are treated unfairly. The main message I learned from this project is that people are still living in poverty because of our unwillingness to change this fact, despite the disparity we caused."*

Why was this project successful when so many projects that link privileged and less privileged students do not achieve these ends? Warschauer (2002) believes that efforts to bridge the digital divide fail because the focus is too often solely on providing hardware and software and not on the content and social context of the interaction.

6.1 Construction of the Kenya-Canada Project: 3 Components

It is posited here that, based on Warschauer's model of effective overcoming of the digital divide, three components of projects must be taken care of. These three elements (technology, content and social inclusion) will be described as they impacted the Kenya-Canada project.

6.2 The Technology Element

In an unequal world, how do we ensure that there is at least a semblance of equity between the two schools in Kenya and Canada? At first glance, it is clear that the digital divide is vast – the school in Canada has 4 fully equipped labs, a library with 50 computers, and all rooms with Internet broadband access. Students too come from homes where broadband is normal. The school in Kenya has no electricity, a few computers that are outdated and slow, Internet connection proves impossible. As Warschauer points out, the scaffolding needed for computers – steady supply of electricity, even dial-up connection, updated software and hardware and technical support are all missing.

The only connection the school has to the Canadian students is a weekly trip that the Kenyan teacher (subsequently promoted to being Vice-Principal) makes to the Internet café, many miles away. There are gradations of access – on the one hand, the school in Canada has instantaneous access at every moment of the day, while the school in Kenya has to depend on the vice-principal driving down to a city every weekend to send messages that he must type up.

In a world of instant text-messaging, iPods, cell phone cameras and YouTube, how can Canadian students be patient with weekly e-mail that arrives in their classroom in the form of a print-out that they must share with each other? How do we stop time for the Canadian students, so that Kenyan students can catch up to participation with respect in this project? In discussion with each other, the Canadian and Kenyan teachers come up to a solution – why not have both sets of students work in groups of 5 come up with one answer per group to promote democratic discussion (and minimize typing)? Teachers would circulate to ensure that students discuss critical literacy oriented questions and acquire background information of the issues being discussed.

6.3 The Content Element

Unlike the hole in the wall project that Wershauer (2002) describes in India, in the Kenya-Canada connection, technology does not *drive* the connection, but rather technology *facilitate*s communication. The project is carefully constructed, week by week. During the first week, students introduce themselves to each other in terms of the philosophy of the project. They outline how they see themselves improving the globe.

In the first and second week, the Canadian students read about Africa. They study the HIV/AIDS crisis, the disaster approach to journalism and learn about how Africa did not need to be saved by celebrities (Adichie (2008) and Iweala (2007)). Students learn to apply critical literacy principles to reading two stories on the same subject of land and violence: one written by a colonizer and the other by the colonized whose land was taken from his ancestors. Throughout the 4 months of the projects, students in Canada conduct research projects on Africa. They learn about the unfair trade policies, the unwillingness to share anti-viral drugs with Africa, the exploitation of the mining industry, etc. But the most impact on Canadian students is a simulation called: World History of Racism in Minutes (WHORM), where they witness history from a thousand years ago to today, and they watch Africa collapsing under the European conquest and the devastation of slavery.

The focus of the project is not to use technology to share communication, but rather to share the content and context of inter-global understanding through a peer relationship across the ocean. With this preparation, when the Canadian students read *Asmina's Story*, a UNICEF text about the story of a young girl who is left to look after her young siblings upon the death of her parents to HIV/AIDS, they question why all the African people in the book are portrayed negatively while UNICEF comes across as a saviour. But when the Kenyan students (some of whom are AIDS orphans) come back with replies showing that they too have been helped by UNICEF, when no one else was there, it stops the Canadian students in their tracks and gives them a reality check.

6.4 Importance of Social Inclusion

The Kenyan-Canadian connection is a strong one in that it builds upon 3 levels of scaffolding: a strong connection between the teachers in Kenya and Canada, who communicate regularly, almost daily at times, through cell phone instant text messaging. Secondly, there is a common teaching philosophy and clear objectives. Thirdly, the project limits itself to the technology available in Kenya, and focuses instead on comprehending the social and political context of the people it studies.

To illustrate, when one of my students came up to the front of the room to present on Wangari Mathai, a Kenyan female Nobel Prize winner, she was dressed in African clothes and spoke passionately of women's rights and the importance of believing in a cause – that of protecting her country's sustainability from deforestation.

Thus, while the technology was very much present, it was not the dominant force in the project. Our weekly communication with Kenyan students brought a hush of excitement to the room. In fact, at one point, when the Kenyan teacher, Mr. Tasma, arriving at the Internet café, is faced with a black-out and has to wait outside for 10 hours for the café to open, Canadian students are fascinated by this devotion and this break-down in basic amenities. They talk of it incessantly and suddenly appreciate the ubiquitous technology that they take for granted around themselves.

The final project that I would like to report on is a geography project linking students from one Canadian school to another school in Kenya – the project looks at water as a resource comparing the Great Lakes in Canada to Lake Victoria in Kenya.

7 The Other Story Project, Phase 2: Water as Resource in a Globalized World: Blessing for Few, Curse for Many

The final project that I worked on was a project linking Canadian students, who live in the Great Lakes region of Canada with students who live in Kenya, close to Lake Victoria, the 2nd largest fresh water lake in the world. At the start of the project, Kenyan students shared their experiences of alternating floods with lack of access to even drinking water.

Canadian students talk of their water supply that is fresh, clean and filtered hourly – it arrives in their taps or in water fountains around the city. Their sole complaint is their increasing awareness of the waste created by the plastic filtered water bottles that they purchase for a dollar (the Kenyan students' family income for the day), only to be thrown away after one drink. Canadian students worry about the unnecessary landfill from these plastic water bottles.

From the girls in Kenya, we hear about how one of them, "was almost swept away in the raging floods" (her words). Others describe how they must purchase water and must conserve it carefully so that it is available for drinking. Others say that water for them brings up images of water-borne diseases that they must endure. Still others speak of Lake Victoria, which is so clogged by hyacinth flower weeds that fishermen's boats get stuck. Fish are suffocated by the clogged lake. Water cannot be drained from the lake and drinking water is unreliable.

Conservation efforts in the fresh water lakes of Canada and Kenya illustrate to the students how alternating approaches to respecting nature can lead to lives of comfort or lives full of danger. It is a sobering lesson in the importance of human agency in geography and it teaches teenagers in the North and the South, regardless of their place at the level of privilege, to comprehend other worlds: what we have been granted by nature and how important it is to use it in a sustainable manner.

8 Discussion of Findings

It can be seen from the above projects that promoting inter-cultural understanding through the use of technology can be achieved if:

a) the Curriculum drives the project, not the technology**:** complex context has to be part of the preparation for the project: both in terms of access to technology but also in terms of understanding the region one wants to work with
b) The project must have clear objectives and philosophy
c) It is important to slow one's pace to meet the needs of the region one connects to – so that social bonding, background knowledge research, acquiring of knowledge of the two cultures and technical problems can be taken care of.

d) Access to technology is not as important as critical reflective analysis and an ability to express oneself well in a common highly used language – in this case, English.

It is important to remember technology cannot drive the curriculum, nor the inter-cultural understanding – it is the slow pace of building context, social relationships, understanding of one's own global responsibility to others that must drive the building of the bridge across the cavern of the digital divide. Understanding these issues requires the presence of knowledgeable teachers and good curricula.

In his article, 'Reconceptualizing the Digital Divide', Warschauer (2002) challenges the notion of the digital divide, stating that the concept provides a poor framework for either analysis or policy, and suggests an alternate concept of technology for social inclusion.

Warschauer (2002) points out that introducing computers into an environment is a complex affair both in terms of technology but also in terms of its content that must be relevant. In terms of technology, he points out that the computer is only a conduit – it needs many other elements of technical scaffolding: electricity, access to networks, hardware, upgraded software, etc. Concomitant with each of these is an ongoing support system. In terms of dissemination in the curriculum, Warschauer explains that ICT implementation is similar to literacy. ICT has to make sense in a social context. Similarly, literacy is not just decoding – what might work for literacy in inner city North America will not work for madrasahs in Karachi. It has to work for people.

According to Warschauer (2002), access to ICT is embedded in a complex array of factors encompassing physical, digital, human, and social resources and relationships. Content and language, literacy and education, and community and institutional structures must all be taken into account if meaningful access to new technologies is to be provided.

In a similar manner, Cummins et al (2007) point out that when introducing literacy and technology into schools and environments where there are low income kids, it is important to:

> *use a pedagogical framework that identifies situated practice, overt instruction, critical framing, and transformed practice as central components. The essence of this framework is that students should be given opportunities to engage in meaningful experiences and practice within a learning community, and the development of concepts and understanding should be supported by explicit instruction as required.*

This issue becomes even more important when we consider that this divide between the privileged and less privileged has existed in terms of civic activism and expression even in the most developed democratic countries in the world. At the start of this paper, I explained that my objective was to promote inter-cultural understanding but also the building of citizenship skills for students in high schools. Ensuring that *all* students regardless of economic, cultural and racial background are knowledgeable, articulate and respectful of the rights of all is an extremely important initiative for future peace and progress. It was hoped that the new technologies would then provide that equity of access to information to all peoples but also access to interactivity for all, regardless of income, to express one's concerns in a democratic government structure.

A recent PEW research study (2013) conducted in the U.S. has some insights in this regard, It is interesting that while online political activity has grown (the number of social networking site users has grown from 33% of the online population in 2008 to 69% of the online population in 2012 and more of these users are engaging with social and political issues than in the past. While it is promising that many youth are also using social networking sites for this purpose, it is truly disappointing that those of low income are less likely to use social networking for these purposes. (Pew, 2013):

> *The well-educated and the well-off are more likely than others to participate in civic life online – just as those groups have been more likely to be active in politics and community affairs offline. Political activity in social networking spaces shows a somewhat more moderate version of the trend*

A similar study (Richtel, 2012 quoted in Kassam, 2013), shows that while *access* to technology is no longer a problem among black and Latino youth as it was perceived in the past, *appropriate* use for educational purposes continues to be a cause for concern. According to Rideout (in Richtel, 2012), author of a decade long Kaiser Foundation study:

> *Despite the educational potential of computers, the reality is their current use for education or meaningful content creation is miniscule compared to their use for pure entertainment. This means that computers, instead of closing the gap, are widening the time-wasting gap. (- quoted in Kassam et al. (2012), p. 201)*

At the beginning of the paper, I introduced the case study of Walter. I showed how technology by itself left to the resources of young people could result in a waste of expensive equipment and sophisticated digital content creation.

Thus while it is very important that we teach about tolerance and access to equal human rights through networking with others using technology, we are not going to arrive at complex but sensitive understanding of others when we leave this process to the resources of young people left to themselves in the computer lab or indeed at home, where broadband access is increasingly ubiquitous.

Teaching about civic discourse and learning about and interacting with diverse peoples of the world is an increasingly vital skill to be taught in our schools, for it is only in our public school systems that diversity of income level, aptitude, personalities, ethnicities, race and religions can be found. And it is on this foundation of diversity that we can scaffold and build an education that bridges the divide between differences but also engenders the ability to use and access new technologies to promote inter-cultural understanding, tolerance and the importance of human rights.

Moreover, it is not just the technology that creates the activism of the students – it is the content of the curriculum, the context created by the teachers and certainly the activism of the students themselves.

As Malcolm Gladwell (2010) explains in an article on the role of technology in promoting activism, not all activism in recent history has had the use of technology to spread its message and empower people. Activism does not require technology to succeed. Gladwell writes that in the 60s, as part of the civil rights movement, what started as sit-down protest by four black students in one lunch counter at Woolworths in Greensboro, North Carolina to protest the store's segregation policies against 'Negroes', spread in a month to 70,000 students who staged similar sit-ins in the South.

According to Gladwell,

> *By the end of the month, there were sit-ins throughout the South, as far west as Texas. "I asked every student I met what the first day of the sitdowns had been like on his campus," the political theorist Michael Walzer wrote in Dissent. "The answer was always the same: 'It was like a fever. Everyone wanted to go.' " Some seventy thousand students eventually took part. Thousands were arrested and untold thousands more were radicalized. These events in the early sixties became a civil-rights war that engulfed the South for the rest of the decade – and it happened without e-mail, texting, Facebook or Twitter.*

Gladwell questions the assertion that the world is in the midst of a revolution where the tools of social media have reinvented social activism, giving the powerless the opportunity to collaborate, coordinate and give voice to their concerns (Gladwell, 2013, p. 42). He states that studies by the Stanford sociologist , Doug McAdam showed that commitment to activism in the civil rights movement was determined more by personal connections to those in the movement.

Gladwell suggests that digitized social networks are much less powerful because they are networks that are not hierarchical and they are not based on institutions of peoples who know each other personally and that have established leadership structures. He also suggests that the weaker acquaintance like friendships offered by Facebook are much less powerful than the Sunday churches that black people attended each week (ibid, p. 49):

> *Enthusiasts for social media would no doubt have us believe that King's task in Birmingham would have been made infinitely easier had he been able to communicate with his followers through Facebook, and contented himself with tweets from a Birmingham jail. But networks are messy: think of the ceaseless pattern of correction and revision, amendment and debate that characterizes Wikipedia. If Martin Luther King had tried to do a wiki-boycott in Montgomery, he would have been steamrollered by the white power structure. And of what use would a digital communication tool be in a town where ninety-eight per cent of the black community could be reached every Sunday morning at church? The things that King needed in Birmingham – discipline and strategy – were things that online social media could not provide (Gladwell, 2010, p. 48-49).*

As I have tried to demonstrate in this paper, face to face interaction, teaching students in high school classrooms where teachers, students and powerful curricula can come together and build powerful relationships that can be used to teach students about activism, are much more effective than thrusting students to their own devices in front of a screen with little or no adult supervision around.

Issues of equity and power in democracies are much better explained and demonstrated in classrooms full of people from diverse backgrounds, with competing agendas but also places where young people from different backgrounds form friendships around common interests but also common feelings of powerlessness.

Teachers and students can also come together to understand history, geography and literature through learning about human problems, understanding through dialogue, respect of others and diplomacy rather than violence. These can be achieved in traditional classrooms with traditional materials and traditional teachers. The Internet has its place but as we have shown above, social media does not in and of itself bring about activism and wisdom and above all, knowledge and respect of the other. These skills and knowledge are brought about through the wise counsel of the teacher, who too must be trained in the knowledge of the world and the importance of respect and tolerance in the creation of democracies of tomorrow.

9 The End of the Teacher's Journey

As I sit back and think of the various technology projects that I have been involved in: watching Walter deal with the *Bartlett Family* reducing a complex, well-written, well-researched simulation into a mindless game of destroying the family as fast as possible in algorithmic fashion, then watching the *ICONS* project dissolving peoples of the world into the rational and the irrational (us and them), and then observing the ethical and historically accurate dimensions of the *Other Story* project being reduced to mindless politically correct posturing and provocative sound bites, I ask myself why were students and technology always sabotaging our best efforts?

After careful reflection, I do not think that the fault is that of technology, but rather that of the teacher or the curriculum writer who is unaware of this attraction of gizmo-gabble for youth. I do believe that in each of the projects discussed above, if I or the teachers involved in the project, had designed the learning environment so that it involved the principles of critical pedagogy and encouraged students to look at the significance of what they were looking at, encouraged them to look for critical analysis, marked them for critical literacy that encompassed ethical viewpoints and accountability to the marginalized, we may have seen different results.

In all the projects that I described above: the *Bartlett Family* simulation, the *ICONS* project, the *Other Story* project (phase one), students were not encouraged to question and critique reality in the tradition of Freire who considered all knowledge to be political. For Freire, education was exposing students to the relationships between the powerful and the powerless and thereby awakening the students' agency.

What then has been missing from all those projects? It is not the knowledge of the other, it is not the perspective of the diverse peoples of the world, it is not the interactive participation of students and it is certainly not the absence of the latest gizmos which students imbibe instantly; it is this critical analysis of the unequal power relationships between the Iranians and the U.S., the First Nations peoples and the government of Canada. In all the projects, the marginalized other was not a free agent to do as he or she wished. In order for a project to be successful in introducing diverse voices in a respectful manner into the classroom, one needs to focus on their relationships with those in authority in various places.

In my description of the journey that I have taken with technology in the past 20 years, I realize now that it was not the absence of a literacy approach that promoted reading and writing that was missing, nor was it literacy approach that promoted knowledge of technology that was lacking. It was **critical** literacy that had not been embedded consciously and conscientiously into the curriculum.

As the students in the Other Story project failed to realize in their work, learning about the oppressed other is not about being politically correct – it is about the relationship of the dominators and the dominated and that relationship is ultimately not about the objective reality of the relationships between people but rather the fairness and ethics of the relationships . In seeking to encourage my students to explore their identities in class I must not shrink away from those that evoke conflict.

In the final phase of the Other Story project, I succeeded because I started with that philosophy. It is a noble goal to bring the 'other' into the classroom, to deal with the story of diverse peoples not normally dealt with in the classroom. But it is simply not enough to bring them in; it is important to 'problematize' the relationship of the dominant and the less dominant – it is important to consider the conflicts and power struggles between cultures so as to engage students in more critical ways.

With the ever increasing pace of change in the development of new communication technologies, as well was with the increasing migration of peoples across the globe, new challenges in identity formation, peaceful negotiation of community, national and international co-existence, the need to learn about each other's complex identities, place greater pressures on our educational systems. This paper has tried to provide information, discussion, sample projects and above all a critical analysis on the increasingly symbiotic relationship between complex identities and new technologies.

References

1. Adichie, C.N.: Madonna's not our Saviour. The Guardian (June 8, 2007)
2. Annan, K.: Democracy a Key Challenge Against Democracy, Address at the Global Centre for Pluralism (May 13, 2013), Ottawa found at `http://kofiannanfoundation.org/newsroom/speeches/2013/05/%E2%80%9Cpluralism-key-challenge-21st-century%E2%80%9D` (November 2, 2013)
3. Au, K.: Literacy instruction in multicultural settings. Harcourt Brace, Fort Worth (1993)
4. BBC World, The World Debate - How True is Your World View is on BBC World, Sat 5 April, 0810BST, 1610 BST and 2010BST (2008), `http://www.bbcworld.com/Pages/Programme.aspx?id=156` (accessed April 8)
5. Cummins, J., Brown, K., Sayers, D.: Literacy, technology, and diversity: Teaching for success in changing times. Allyn & Bacon, Boston (2007)
6. Cavenett, W.: Global Soul: Pico Iyer, `http://citizenuniverse.blogspot.com.au/2007/08/global-soul-by-wendy-cavenett-few-years.html` (accessed November 3, 2013)

7. Freire, P.: Pedagogy of the Oppressed. Herder and Herder, New York (1970)
8. Gladwell, M.: Small Change: Why the Revolution will not be tweeted. The New Yorker (October 4, 2010)
9. Iweala, U.: Stop Trying to Save Africa. The Washington Post (July 15, 2007)
10. Kassam, A., Iding, M., Hogenbirk, P.: Unraveling the digital divide: Time well spent or "wasted". Education and Information Technologies 18(2), 215–221 (2013)
11. Kassam, A.: Changing society using new technologies: Youth participation in the social media revolution and its implications for the development of democracy in sub-Saharan Africa. Education and Information Technologies 18(2), 253–263 (2013)
12. Kassam, A.: Bridging the digital divide - Intercultural understanding and global activism across continents. In: Wheeler, S., Brown, D., Kassam, A. (eds.) Conference Proceedings, "ICT and Learning for the Net Generation". IFIP Digital Library (2008) ISBN-13: 978-3-901882-29-6
13. Kassam, A.: Critical Thinking and An Ethical Approach to Teaching History: the Case for ICT. In: Informatics and Digital Society: Social, Ethical and Cognitive Issues. Kluwer Academic Publishers, Norwell (2003)
14. Kassam, A.: Networked Technologies and Other Stories: New Paradigms for Learning. In: Hogenbirk, P., Taylor, H. (eds.) Information and Communications Technologies in Education: The School of the Future. Kluwer Academic Publishers, Norwell (2001)
15. Kassam, A.: The Other Story: a Telecommunications Journey into the World, published in Orbit 27(3), 24–25 (1996)
16. Pew Research Centre, "Civic Engagement in the Digital Age" (April 25, 2013), `http://pewinternet.org/Reports/2013/Civic-Engagement.aspx`
17. Warschauer, M.: Reconceptualizing the Digital Divide. First Monday, Peer-Reviewed Journal on the Internet 7(7) (2002), `http://firstmonday.org/ojs/index.php/fm/article/view/967/888` (accessed on November 2, 2013)

Learning Along with Your Students: Projects from the Graduate Diploma of Computer Education

John S. Murnane

Melbourne Graduate School of Education, The University of Melbourne
jmurnane@unimelb.edu.au

Abstract. This Chapter deals with the early development of Computer Education for teachers in Victoria, Australia, through a set of Research and Development (R&D) Projects that formed a large part of a Graduate Diploma in Computer Education (GDCE) at Melbourne State College, later part of The University of Melbourne. The early years of the GDCE, coincident as they were with the advent of the microprocessor and the desktop computer, reflected and indeed influenced the development of Computer Education in Victorian schools. The Projects provide an informative insight into the teachers Professional Development in Information Technology, the state of educational computing, and the uses to which computers were being put in Victorian schools in the 1980s and early 90s.

Keywords: Computer Education, Professional Development, early computing in Victorian schools, educational impact of the microprocessor.

1 Introduction

When the GDCE began in 1980 the computing tools school teachers had to work with were absolutely minimal, although many of the coming developments in IT were already clear to see, if not already in existence. The projects therefore tell a story of teachers not only struggling with the educational psychology and philosophy of using a computer in a classroom, with its consequent impact on the way they taught and their students learned, but frequently having to write the software or even build the hardware themselves. As the decade progressed and the tools because available, the projects turned to more educational and sociological matters as the teachers pioneered the IT revolution with their students.

The Research and Development Projects, being by design heavily practically-oriented, provide an informative insight into the teachers Professional Development in Information Technology and the use to which computers were being put in Victorian schools in the 1980s and early 90s.

2 Early Days

Teacher education about computers began at Melbourne Primary Teachers' College (later Melbourne State College via a series of mergers) in 1970[1]. The first students

[1] 'Primary' Teachers Colleges prepared teachers for Elementary schools covering Preparatory to Year 6, with an age-range generally from 5 to 12.

A. Tatnall and B. Davey (Eds.): History of Computers in Education, IFIP AICT 424, pp. 48–70, 2014.

were entering the final year of the then new Diploma of Teaching (Primary) and J. G. Angus, Head of Mathematics, was looking for someone 'to do something with computers' with Third Year students taking Mathematics as an option. I happened to be enrolled in the Computer Science course at the Royal Melbourne Institute of Technology (RMIT) and, having some tertiary Mathematics as part of that, was hired by Angus to teach *Mathematics Method* at First Year and 'Computers' to his group of Third Year Mathematics students. (The Dip. T. (P) prepared teachers for Elementary schools and allowed trainees to specialize in a limited number of Second and Third Year options.)

Even thinking about the role computers might play in a Primary classroom was very long-sighted for 1970. In an interview in 2003, Angus recalled some of the factors:

- Looking to the future: to have some Primary teachers who could have some input into 'what computing finally arrived at past calculating machines.'
- Transition: moving to more equality between Primary and Secondary teachers. [At the time Primary teachers were generally regarded as second-class in academic background.]
- To somehow attract College Staff who knew something about computers.
- To be prepared for the future by providing a sprinkling of teachers in Primary schools who knew about computers, rather than just having these teachers in Secondary Schools.

(J. G. Angus: telephone interview with J. Murnane, 16/9/03).

In the five years that followed, RMIT allowed the Third Year Mathematics classes to use its Elliot 803 computer for two hours once a week. The 803, a Second Generation machine, was used to run Algol 60 programs, not an activity particularly relevant to a Primary classroom but one which was in-line with Angus's desire to begin to sensitize and interest some Primary teachers in the *possibilities* they promised. (It was also about the only thing the computer could do apart from running Machine-code.) I have fond memories of standing in a classroom, most of the walls of which were taken up by the computer, with twelve rather bemused student teachers, telling them that 'One day, when you have one of these in your classroom, you won't be doing what we've just been doing, but it will be exciting and powerful, and it will change the way your students learn and the way you teach'. The students were clearly *very* skeptical, but the Intel 4004 'computer on a chip' had arrived on the market in November 1971 (Mazor, 1995) and was clearly pointing the way to the PC, if not in form, at least in promise. The potential for getting away from just writing a program towards information processing and communication were already obvious. It just took a little time[2].

---

[2]To put the birth of the educational computer in context, release dates for early Microcomputers used in Victorian schools were: Tandy TRS-80 Model 1: November 1977, Apple][: June 1977. Apple][Plus: June 1979, Apple][e: 1983. Commodore PET: 1977. VIC-20: 1981. Commodore 64: 1982. For larger machines see Tatnall and Davey (2004).

Over the next five years the College progressively acquired its own computers and at the same time more lecturers with an interest in, if not actual experience with computers were recruited, some coming with a merger with the Melbourne Secondary Teachers' College.

3 The Graduate Diploma in Computer Education

In 1978 a proposal was submitted for a Graduate Diploma in Computer Education (GDCE) (Melbourne State College, 1979). This course, the first of its kind in Australia, was designed to introduce computers in all their (current!) aspects to practicing teachers at all levels. It took in its first 30 'students,' all qualified and practicing teachers, in 1980. Given its early origins in relation to the penetration of computers into Victorian schools, the GDCE was conceived as a means to *develop* ideas about ways for using computers in Education and to implement and research some of these in practice, as well as simply teaching *about* them and their educational potential.

The course was designed to be taken part-time over two years. Generalizing somewhat, Year 1 was an introduction to all the aspects of computing relevant to education that could reasonably be crammed in. In their Second year the teachers were to consider and experiment with their own ideas for using the technology in their classrooms. A large part of this was a Research and Development (R&D) Project, conceived as a major way of progressing the use of computers in the classroom. (It is a rare moment in Education when a course involves the students in developing large sections of the discipline itself!) There was also considerable emphasis on documenting, analysing and reporting the results of trying out these new ideas: the lecturing staff, drawn from a wide variety of academic areas, were determined to explore and document ways that a student could really learn in conjunction with a computer.

To this end, fully half the Second Year of the course (one quarter of the total course points) was devoted to the R&D Project. In line with the objective of helping to develop educational computer use, copies were retained and made available for study and research[3] (Melbourne State College, 1987, p. 19). The subject ran in this form from 1981 to 1993 and the project Reports provide an interesting insight into what Victorian teachers were thinking about IT and Education, and what they were actually doing (or not doing) with it in their schools. In 1978, when the GDCE was being developed, the 'C' in ICT was largely absent. The Course Proposal refers only to 'computer technology'. The first project to even mention Communication was from 1987 and the next, 1993.

Student records show that 254 students passed the subject between 1981 and 1993 and a Report from each should have been preserved. In actuality, 147 have survived the initial collection process and several major changes in storage location. This still

---

[3] While each project was double-examined by the supervisor and another (internal) staff member, they do not have the standing of an externally-examined thesis and were not subject to external editing and peer review. Hence they are not included in the Reference list. Where a direct reference has been made to a particular Report, the name of the author, title of the project and date are given inline in the text.

represents a considerable collection of material, roughly a stack of single-sided A4 paper 2 meters high. Three years are particularly bad. Only one from each of 1984, '89 and '91 survive. A total of 39 from those three years are missing. Nevertheless, within the limitations detailed below, the surviving material gives an interesting and vibrant picture of the early development of Educational Computing in Victorian schools. They constitute a valuable background against which to study the use of ICT in education at the time.

4 The GDCE Research and Development Project

> *"The programming took up much of the time allocated to the Project." (C-A. Cartledge, The Use of Computers in Year 9 Mathematics Work on Fractions, 1983)*

The Project had two aims:

- To enable the teacher to achieve first-hand experience in the application of computer technology to a particular educational task.
- To enable the teachers to participate in the design, implementation and evaluation of a computer-supported resource for use in a school. (Melbourne State College, 1979.)

Following some face-to-face sessions dealing with research (project development, researching the literature and collecting and analysing data), a project would be agreed between each student and a supervising staff member. Assessment was on the basis of presentations at the beginning and end of the subject and a 6,000 word report. As can be seen from the Aims, the emphasis was on researching something *practical* with a computer in an educational context. The projects are notable in the large number and wide range of backgrounds in the supervising staff, an indication of the wide interest in computers in Education at the time.

In general, while the students made obvious efforts to bring academic rigor to the analysis of their data, the earliest Projects often suffer from obvious shortcomings to be expected of the period:

- The almost total absence of computers in schools. Even having one computer in the school was a challenge for many and getting time away from the Computer Science or Mathematics teachers was difficult. (GDCE students were still reporting this as a problem into the late 90s.)
- There was very little suitable software. Historical data on when applications such as word processors, spreadsheets, games and financial packages became available might suggest that this should not have been the case, but the R&D Projects make it very clear that in the early 1980s, if a teacher needed software they mostly had to write it themselves. To encourage experimentation, 'outside' help with programming was specifically allowed provided it was fully acknowledged.
- The biggest problem was lack of time.

A year might seem adequate to conceptualise, plan, execute and analyse Graduate Diploma-level research, but it was not generally adequate in the case of the R&D projects even though students were encouraged to select a topic area towards the end of their First Year. Early sessions were taken with lecturers in conducting research, then a project had to be finalised and approved. Most projects would then require the agreement of the appropriate authority: the Victorian Department of Education, Catholic Education or individual school if privately run. Approval time could be short if the teacher was a staff member in a school in control of its own administration, but for large systems this could take months. By the time the project was ready, particularly if there was programming or system development involved, there would be little time to experiment and analyse, and most early projects show signs of curtailed development. These problems notwithstanding, in the first two years eleven projects were well tested in a classroom, four of them extensively, but eleven classroom-based projects had no testing at all. It is mainly the time factor which often stunted the desire to produce solid and reliable evidence that computers could offer, and indeed demand, radical changes to education and it is not generally possible, at this remove, to assert that many do so. In the first three years, only one before-and-after study (A. Gilding *Atom Alchemy*, 1981) was performed.

In 1981 there was little if any place for computers in the organised curriculum. It is noticeable that many teachers who, for various reasons, were dependent on observing other teachers using computers or participating in their classes, reported problems in introducing them into existing subject-structures. This could have been seen as a barrier, but since this is one of the things the GDCE set out to change, it was regarded as an objective and something the lecturing staff and students were determined to break down and change.

Externally, the educational philosophy of computers *was* changing rapidly. In the 1984-6 triennium $18 million was allocated to the Commonwealth Schools' Commission Computer Education Program, a Federal Government initiative (Tatnall and Leonard, 2010, p. 103). This program recognised the need for students to have an understanding of the new technology, planned for the use of computers across the curriculum and emphasised access to the program by "girls and other disadvantaged groups" (Commonwealth Schools' Commission, 1984). The Victorian State Computer Centre was established by the Victorian State Government around the same time, offering advice and courses on educational programs, and beginning the provision of administrative software.

At this time the spread of computer types in schools was quite wide. S. J. Missen (*A Format for the Evaluation of School Administrative Software,* 1982) in a survey posted to 162 Secondary schools with 76 returns gives a typical picture. The project gives the break-down for individual schools, but collectively found: Apple][: 26, Micromation: 16, Spectrum: 12, Cromenco: 5, BBC: 5, PDP 11: 4, PDP 8: 1 and Northstar: 1. The maximum for any one school was seven. Five schools had none.

Seventy computers spread over 76 schools do not go far. Missen also provides a comprehensive report of peripheral equipment, software and computer use. Only one school had a hard disk. Not surprisingly, Secondary schools in the 80s had to expect a "very wide range of computer experience in their Year 7 intakes" (J. M. C. Disken, *Year Seven Computer Education*, 1985)[4].

The R&D Projects show the arrival of computers in Victorian schools in increasing numbers from 1981 on. At that time, Melbourne CAE possessed a Digital Equipment VAX with 20-terminals and a small Lab of six Apple][computers. Single VAX terminals were scattered around the Departments, as were a few more Apples and a Tandy TRS–80s. In the early 80s the Apple Lab was expanded to 20 and later 20 networked BBC 'Model B' added.

The remainder of this chapter is concerned with an analysis of the projects: how the teachers themselves learned about Computers and Education, what computers were used for and how they were regarded by the bulk of teachers, students and parents. There is also a pleasant story woven into many Reports telling of their author's journey into the domain of the researcher, an unfamiliar area to many teachers of the time.

Leaving aside surveys and interviews, the projects, particularly in the early years, describe what is likely to be the teachers' and students' first experience with computers, educational or otherwise. Hence, in assessing the reported results, a large Hawthorn effect must be allowed for as well as an even larger reflected 'Experimenter' effect on the teacher/researcher (See Gottfredson, 1996, Murnane, 2010b, Rosenthal, 1996). Nevertheless, when looking across all the Reports a convincing consensus can be found. Individually the results might be questionable, but collectively they spell a coherent and convincing story.

5 The 'Do It Yourself' Era

"I have found it is possible to mis-spell 'camel' in dozens of ways." (A. Biggs, *Burke & Wills*, 1982)

"These new channels will offer the possibility of a 'wired' world and will revolutionise the way we communicate with one another." (A. Hersbach, 1983)

"Accordingly I bought 100 meters of Telecom cable, unrolled it up the corridor and connected to the office system." (D. Walker, *How Useful is a Communication System at Marian College?* 1993).

In the first few years of the GDCE, unless a project involved studying an existing system, it was usually necessary for the teacher to write their own program, set up their own data system or even build their own electronics. Of 34 Reports submitted in 1981–82, 21 involved some sort of technical computing, either programming or setting up a computerised system using an existing application such as an author language. Most of these reports contained long and detailed Appendices on the program or system, often with lengthy Users' Manuals. None of this left much time for testing. Most programs were written in some form of Basic or Pascal, but one, an exploration of the historical 'Burke and Wills' expedition used 'SuperPILOT,' an

[4] Secondary Schools cater for Years 7 to 12, with students generally 11 to 18 years of age.

Author Language for the Apple][, and another 'EXAMINER,' a multiple-choice testing presentation program.

An analysis of the programs paints a quite encompassing picture of the future of educational computing, at least until the advent of the Web. The teachers were certainly aware of the *possibilities* and were determined to exploit them, even at the cost of having to write the programs themselves. The GDCE First Year did include a small introduction to programming (in VAX Basic), but all of the programs went far beyond the requirements of this subject in length, and often complexity.

Eight of the 34 used a Computer Assisted Instruction (Programmed Learning) structure. This is not surprising, given the emphasis on it in the 70s. Lecturers in the main First Year subject, *Computer Education*, used CAI to teach about computers and their educational potential. A common thread running through many of them was the realisation that it is very hard to cover all possible responses unless some type of evaluation of student's responses, as against a set comparison list, can be used (Bitzer, 1976). Interestingly, while the *Computer Education* CAI sessions were received quite well, when the teachers were required to write programmed lessons of their own as part of the subject assessment there was a general reluctance, essentially a feeling that that was not the way *they* wanted to teach.

Fourteen projects were intended to teach specific areas of various disciplines, with eight in the Mathematics/Physics areas, including a very impressive symbolic algebraic manipulation program (D. Podhorodecki, *An Experimental Symbolic Algebra Programme, POLLEX*, 1983, extra programming assistance duly acknowledged), and two to teach programming. There were three from the Humanities, including two very early social simulations, one exploring local social interactions in an Australian neighbourhood for three to fourteen students (M. Arnold, *The Great big Scoreboard of Life: An Educational Opera*, 1992), and the other International Relations (C. J. Allitt, *International Relations*, 1983).

Nine projects involved a simulation. The potential power of the computer to simulate a complex set of interacting factors under user control had been emphasised in previous GDCE subjects. Projects included teaching Gas Laws, atomic structure and the two social simulations above.

The ability of the computer to automate various administrative tasks was clearly recognised, with eight projects dealing directly with the area. Four of these involved writing a set of programs implementing some facet of school administration. Two were surveys of useful programs or packages and one was a feasibility study of computerising the Education Department's Audio-Visual resources. There is an interesting non-anticipated outcome here that demonstrates something that can be found in many of the projects from 1981 to 1993: unsuspected, positive *educational* outcomes were found only after the project was implemented in the classroom.

While the administrative packages were developed specifically to improve efficiency and cut down the time teachers had to spend on bookwork, in many cases, once the system was in place and working, improvements in *educational standards and flexibility* were discovered. A timetabling program allowed more subject choices to be made available in Year 11 and 12 than could be offered under the previous manual system. A program to automate the school swimming sports results allowed a progressive score for each House to be announced, and a program to aid the Careers Teacher provided students with "many careers that they had not previously considered because these careers related directly to information they had input personally" (R. McKenzie, *Computer Assisted Career Guide for Students*, 1981).

A 1987 survey of Principals, Computer Coordinators and 'the person considered to be responsible for computers,' sent to 100 Western Metropolitan Region State Primary Schools (with returns of 94, 91 & 79 percent respectively), gives a picture of the state of 'administrative' computing at the time (G. R. Pratt *The Application of Computers into Schools' Administrative Procedures*, 1987). The Schools Administrative Computing Unit (SACU) inside the State Computer Education Centre was in the process of implementing a computerised administration package for State Schools. The Accounting Package was in the process of progressive installation by "SACU Officers," with Student Records and Library to come. The survey showed many respondents in schools waiting for installation "showed a great deal of concern" about the Accounting Package and its implementation, which Pratt attributes largely to "a lack of information" about it. Apprehension as a result of lack of knowledge and experience was to be a constantly reoccurring theme right through to 1993.

One very notable attempt was made in analysing the 'social data' contained in the school enrolment records. The base was a 1980 student enrolment survey. Originally intended for analysis by hand, it was realised that far more could be done by computerising. Students were recruited to translate the data to mark sense cards and these were processed by a small set of analytical programs written by Buckley. In turn this lead to a revised 1982 survey with a tighter set of questions more suitable for data-processing. This required a narrowing of the type of data that could be collected: there was a limit to which open-ended questions could be replicated by selection lists, and the extent to which questions dependent on previous answers could be dealt with was also limited. One can read in this project a clear picture of things to come in the enhanced variety of information that can be economically extracted and the way computerised processing influences the array of data which can be collected and in turn imposes limits on the conclusions that can be drawn.

An obvious problem often identified in technical projects was the likely effective life of the system, given the short life of the computer or operating system it was written for. This was well demonstrated by a very ambitious computer controlled music synthesizer built and programmed by G. J. Hubbard (*Computer Controlled Music Synthesizer*, 1982). (See Mueller, 1982.) Finding existing synthesizers were well outside the school budget, (the MIDI interface did not appear until 1983), Hubbard built and programmed his own using a recently released sound generator chip. Unfortunately his choice of the COMPUCOLOR II, chosen for the ease to which it could be interfaced, doomed the project as COMPUCOLOR went out of business before the Project's due date. The synthesizer, and its programming, was not transferrable to a different machine.

Two projects from 1982 concerned Computer Managed Instruction but only one project in future years dealt with the idea. Prophetically, two dealt with Computer Crime.

A thrill of satisfaction when a program, particularly one which has proven difficult, finally works as specified will be familiar to almost any programmer. These projects, while the programming was often fairly primitive, show that teachers were well aware of the promise and potential of computers and were determined to explore and exploit them, even if it meant a considerable amount of (unfamiliar) programming. Not only that, they express palpable excitement and satisfaction when their programs were used by staff or students:

> *"[I had] no knowledge at the time of [writing the program], of the feelings of excitement and wonder that would follow in trialling and evaluating [it], in addition to the desire to experiment with it in a variety of ways, just to see the effects it had on the students learning. Watching students, who in some instances would have great difficulty in applying themselves to a Mathematical task, 'invent' Mathematics and feel a great sense of achievement in doing so without the threat of 'marks' being awarded, was extremely rewarding" (C-A. Cartledge, The Use of Computers in Year 9 Mathematics Work on Fractions, 1983)*[5].

This is an expression of perhaps the highest aim of GDCE staff: to find evidence for the belief that working with computers in a classroom could and would change the way teachers were teaching and students were learning.

6 Teachers' Attitudes in the Early '80s

"Ignorance more than fear is the major factor in this group of people confessing to being scared of computers."
D. Little, *Attitudes of Secondary Teachers to Computers and Their Use in Schools* (1982)

As might be expected, the Reports provide a uniform picture of a high level of enthusiasm for computer use in schools by those enrolled in the course. They are clearly excited at the idea of advancing the use of computers in their schools: it absolutely shines through. This might be expected of anyone prepared to enroll in a part-time course requiring two evenings a week for two years, but it is also in the interest and attitudes of their fellow teachers that future trends are evident. Not surprisingly, many of the early projects were concerned with ways to introduce computers to schools: meaning ways to interest and in-service otherwise disinterested teachers.

From the first year of the course the aim of introducing computers to schools was something that occupied the GDCE teacher's attention. Many early projects included

[5] This project utilised technology developed by A. Gilding for *Atom Alchemy* (1981) with assistance from staff member C. Bigum which allowed the students and the computer screen to be videoed as a split screen, allowing the student's operations and conversation to be analysed (Bigum and Gilding, 1983).

an early chapter headed "Why Use a Computer in a Classroom?" or "Why use a Simulation?" In 1981–2, eight projects considered needs for, and/or implementation of, teacher Professional Development (PD) in the area. This was partly from an obvious need for other teachers to learn to use the systems created as part of the projects, but also as a general means of overcoming fear of the machine. Four projects considered teacher's attitudes as their main topic. Here, a generally quite positive attitude from non-users comes through, although some of that was related to a prosaic feeling that as computers were part of society, they had better be part of education.

Some projects, without being specific, do hint at a small proportion of outright hostility to computers. Most teachers with no or little exposure to them, while generally at least open to suggestions for their use, *were* worried about their lack of experience and stressed need for in-service professional development. There is also strong support for the need for local 'experts': teachers at the school readily available for individual consultation and help. This need for PD was reflected in applications for the GDCE. In the first five or so years we regularly had some 200 applications for 30 or later 40, places. The first selection 'cut' was to discard any applicant with less than four years of teaching experience. By the early 90s the quota was 75 and we were receiving just enough applications to fill it. By 2000 applications were down to around 30 per year.

The positive effect PD could have, (perhaps also with a growing familiarity), is shown in a Project set up to provide it. S. Lyon (*Computers for Beginners*, 1995) ran a set of six Units taken by staff *and* students (Table 1). Lyon documents a progression from the Units being taught by the Computer Coordinator to staff taking over and team teaching. As staff worked through the Units, the computers were moved progressively from a Laboratory to the classrooms.

Table 1. Improvements in computer use as a result of PD

	April	October
Teachers using computers integrated with classroom activities	1	13
Classroom teachers able to 'boot up' a computer and run a program	3	15
Students capable of loading a program and following prompts	15	350
Student using word-processing without teacher supervision	4	200

Rather conversely, Lyon notes that by the end of the project "all children in the grades ... are now using Word Processing in an efficient manner, [but] only three teachers are now using the process to aid their own writing," This could be related to the Apple][‘s problem in displaying lower-case letters. This problem shows in many early projects.

Over the entire area is the requirement for suitable software. If many GDCE-enrolled teachers were prepared to write their own, their fellow teachers were, not surprisingly, uninterested, and until it was available, no amount of PD was going to attract them to computers. Further, software *had* to be accompanied by easy to understand, comprehensive documentation, preferably supplemented by relevant teaching material to help them get started in the classroom. Where programs had been written and used by other staff, mostly administrative applications, there was also a heavy emphasis on good reliability and ease of use as important factors in staff acceptance.

These attitudes echoed those in the general community. A. M. Scollary (*Willing and Able? A study of the attitudes towards and the emotions aroused in adults by computers*, 1986) found adult attitudes correlated with computer experience but had no other correlations for age or gender. A 1993 Report by J. Cullen (*Students and Teachers Attitudes to Computers*) surveyed four Secondary and twelve Primary schools with a total of 890 students. She found most staff participants had positive attitudes, though gender differences *were* evident, with female Secondary teachers the least positive. Student attitudes peaked at Year 7.

S. Keown (*The Role of the Computer Coordinator: Greythorn High School*, 1986) managed to fill 30 A3 pages with 68 tasks under thirteen main headings, many involving 'Help' and 'PD' for other staff, she considered the responsibility of the school Computer Coordinator. It would be an interesting list to compare with a current version.

7 Student Attitudes

> "... students did not want to pack up, and there is evidence of some students being annoyed because they did not have the opportunity to try out some programs that they had thought up."
>
> (C-A. Cartledge, *The Use of Computers in Year 9 Mathematics Work on Fractions*, 1983)

As noted, development of many projects, particularly those involving programming, did not leave much time for classroom testing, but of those that did, student response was strong and enthusiastic.

S. M. Shehata (*Computer Assisted Learning in Matrices*, 1981) contains a 20-question Likert Scale student questionnaire examining student response to a set of programmed lessons. Notable are very strong positive responses to "The program helps me learn quickly" and "I prefer the program to regular instruction." Interestingly, "I find myself just trying to get through the program rather than trying to learn" produced eleven "Strongly agree" with four "Disagree" or "Strongly Disagree." Other questions suggest many students felt that the program was distancing them from their teacher, but their confidence in the material they were learning was heightened by the instant feedback they were receiving. They were unanimous that they enjoyed "working at the terminal" and all agreed it was "not boring."

Most of these students were having their first computer experience and the fascination of just using a computer must be factored into the survey results. Even given the limitations of these small un-refereed studies, it would be interesting to compare these results with current student attitudes. To what extent were the positive student feelings expressed in many early Reports related simply to the novelty and excitement of using a computer? A teacher reported that a program computerising ACER Diagnostic Mathematics Tests written by me in 1980 was extremely popular with his Primary students "even though it was a test." (See Wong and Tatnall, 2009 for the "novelty effect.")

An interesting project was carried out at Odyssey House, a drug-rehabilitation facility, and Keilor Heights Secondary College (G. Pratley, *The Computer: A Motivational Aid for Teaching Mathematics to Disinterested Low Achievers*, 1987). Unusually for these Research projects, Pratley was able to use Control Groups with groups of students taught a Unit of Mathematics with and without using computers. This project showed attitudes to both computers and Mathematics in the 'computer group' showed improvement over the non-computer group. "Pride of ownership" developed. As with many studies, familiarity with the technology brought more approval. As well as being very statistical, the study contains a small mountain of related, direct observations, including the comment that the Turtle was "personalized": "What is *he* doing?" (Author's emphasis.)

8 From Writing Programs to Wider Issues

"A small number of teachers had had previous experience in word-processing or programming." (L. Bignall, *A Student Reporting System for Secondary Schools,* 1985).

From 1984 the Reports show a steady progression from writing a program or setting up an information system to more general reports of what teachers and schools were doing with computers. From 1984/5 projects begin mentioning 'closed' database packages including First Fleet (Wills, A. and Downes, 1985), Bushrangers, (House, Undated) and Gold Dust Island, (O'Carroll, 2012). Leaving aside 1984, '89 and '90 where only one Report from each year survives, the numbers of Projects involving technical computing are given in Table 2.

By 1985 most projects were concerned with broader issues and give a wide picture of what teachers and students within Primary and Secondary were doing with them. However, there is an understanding that the educational use of computers and their implications would only become clear with *universal* school use: "By 1990 we might well expect students will be all too familiar with many of the social, vocational and leisure time implications of the technology" (J. M. C. Disken, *Year Seven Computer Education*, 1985).

Table 2. Projects involving technical computing by year

1983	1985	1986	1987	1988	1990	1992	1993
6 of 12	7 of 18	10 of 26	6 of 19	1 of 6	1 of 6	5 of 12	0 of 6

There was also a gradual but significant increase in emphasis on the way computers can allow students to manage their own learning. There are many references to computers helping students to study independently, take more responsibility and make their own discoveries. This is in contrast with current trends to sheet responsibility for student learning directly home to the teacher, making teaching, in the words of Ken Robinson, "teacher-proof" (Robinson, 2009).

From 1985 the projects show progressively more classroom (or whole-school in the case of administrative programs) testing, with decreasing necessity to write programs. The Reports also contain evidence of a growing level of GDCE staff input and guidance. By 1987, First Year students were being provided with an 80-page 'Handbook,' much of which was intended as preliminary reading and help for the R&D Project. Twelve pages of the companion 41-page 'So You're Teaching in the Grad Dip Comp Ed' provided guidance for R&D Project staff.

9 Computers at Preschool and Preparatory Grade Level

There was a continuing interest in using computers at Kindergarten and Preparatory (Prep) levels with several using the same games (Kids at Work, Sticky-Bear Shapes, Juggles Rainbow and Face-Maker were particularly popular) and also 'One-Key' Logo and a Turtle. The Reports show children's interest observed to vary widely with a preference for working in a small group: "[I]t was rare to see single child at the machine" (K. N. Kean, *Computers in the Preschool; An investigative case study,* 1986).

Computing in Early Childhood Education (B. M. Todd, 1986) contains an investigation at one preschool with 24 children and a Commodore 64. To find out how intuitive the children found the computer a minimum amount of instruction was given in its use. The children were reported as finding no particular problems in its operation and to be choosing the computer as "play equipment". They preferred to participate 'hands-on' rather than watch and averaged nine minutes per turn. This type of experiment would no longer be very practical because most children will enter Pre-school with experience at using a GUI. Todd Included a comprehensive Literature Review that showed most relevant publications from the USA concentrated on teaching *about* the computer, while those from Australia largely concerned learning *with* a computer and stressed play.

Two teachers used the then-new "Tasman Turtle" [6] with One-Key Logo. H. Boyle (*Introducing Computers to a Kindergarten,* 1986) found it prompted interesting children's comments such as "Is the Turtle alive?" and reported a measure of parent interest. L. Jackson (*Young Children and Computers*, 1986) used a Tasman Turtle with 34 Preschool and Preparatory Grade children. Rather unusually for one of these projects, Jackson was able to include Pre and Post interviews to determine if there were changes in the children's understanding of what a computer was, and what it could do. Answers to 'What is a computer?' varied from "A thing that tells you things

[6] See later chapter by McDougall, Murnane and Wills.

– how to make things – how to play things" to "It's a television with buttons." A question on 'what is a Robot' was often associated with the popular Transformers toys. Answers to these questions, while not without their own difficulty in interpretation, could be usefully compared against contemporary children.

10 Programming and Robotics

"The evolving program serves to remember all of his discoveries, and continually to accumulate and synthesize them." (Dwyer, 1971).

"I still had some students within the Computer Awareness course who expressed a strong interest in programming." (G. P. Bertuna *TUTEPAK: Tutorial programming package*, 1982).

"Both boys and girls asked to use the computer with LogoWriter in their free time." (J. A. Jones, *Parent Participation, Gender Equity and Computers: One form of action*, 1993.)

A considerable proportion of the literature from the 70s and 80s deals with the perceived advantages of teaching programming. (See for instance Abelson, Barnberger, Goldstein and Papert, 1976, Dwyer, 1970, Juliff, 1982, Kurtz, 1968, Papert, 1971, Papert, 1980). Some, such as Kurtz and Dwyer document specific examples, others rely largely on Educational connections to the languages themselves, such as the need to identify structures within tasks and document their temporal execution, split tasks into procedures and allot descriptive names to these and the variables. Robotics not only involves programing but construction, in which many of the same concepts apply. Inevitably the two areas go together.

A programming language, being a precise vehicle for communication, was thought to offer a way for students to document thought processes and instructions in clear and unambiguous ways (Papert, 1980, p 32). The program, when executed, would provide feedback on the validity of the instructions. A malfunctioning program was not a target for a poor mark, it was an aid and invitation to trace the cause and rectify it (Murnane, 2010a, Papert, 1980, pps. 22, 101).

A small but continuing interest in projects involving students learning to write their own programs continued to 1992. Seven projects dealt with it, ten if One-Key Logo is included as 'programming.' The 1983 Victorian Year 12 *Computer Science* syllabus (see below) listed four approved programming languages: A structured version of Basic, Pascal, Comal and MIT Logo (Victorian Department of Education, 1983). As these examinations are used for University entrance they are an important standard. No project dealt with Comal although one school was reported as using it (below). One project reviewed the literature on PROLOG (I. M. Renwick, *Adventures in PROLOG*, 1987).

There are no particular patterns through the Reports dealing with students writing programs, other than universally reporting an enthusiasm for the activity.

S. Johnson (*A case study in Mathematical ability*, 1992) describes using LogoWriter with eight Year 8 volunteer Secondary School students. Test results in Mathematics are analysed as well as attitudes in the LogoWriter class. Weaker students showed the most Mathematical gains with improvement as high as 17%. The Report is documented with a large number of student programs. Not all Logo experiments were successful. One was declared a failure because "there was little interest [from the teachers] in the topic" (S. Lyon, *Computers for Beginners*, 1985).

Software Projects for Level 11 Computer Studies/Science Students (M. Nugent, 1986) explored the educational philosophy for teaching programming through projects rather than a 'teach the language first' approach. Once again, it would be interesting to compare the associated questionnaire with current attitudes since the Report contains good reporting and evaluation. Findings on the use of Logo and a Robotic Turtle are especially interesting. *TUTEPAK, Tutorial Programming Package Beginners Applesoft Basic* (G. P. Bertuna, 1982) was a CAI introduction to structured programming in Basic, and *Data Structures Took Kit* (J. S. Schwartz. 1985), was written for Year 11 *Computer Science. The development of a short course called An Introduction to Structured Programming in Pascal* (J. Clark, 1982) was designed as one of a set of programming units for TAFE[7]. Concise and directly to the point, it could serve as a model for contemporary manuals in structured programming.

S. J. Snipe (*Robotics in the Primary School*, 1986) used Fisher Technic, a Floor-Turtle and Lego. At the time the school had "no computers available for curriculum use" although it was developing a Computer Policy in the expectation of acquiring some. Snipe used his own Microbee computer, building and programming an interface to run Logo-programmed models. Here was another example of a teacher's work overtaken by wider events: although educational aspects met his expectations, part-way through the project Lego released its first Robotics kit containing all the elements he had been working on, albeit at a much higher cost!

F. A. Flynn used an Action Research/Participant Observation framework with eight Year 5/6 and eight Year 11 students working with Lego-Logo for the first time (*A Study of Factors Affecting the Introduction of Lego Logo to Primary and Secondary Students*, 1990). Flynn used "directed instruction" with two groups at each year-level and "open-ended tasks" with the two others. Looking for differences on the basis of gender, academic background, attitudes to school, group size and method of instruction, Flynn found inconclusive evidence for all factors and concluded that differences in achievement were due to individual students. There *were* clear differences in the 'engineering' side: students with prior experience with Lego Technic "achieved more than those students who had not used it" though students with "no previous experience with LogoWriter seemed to be at no great disadvantage. ... The students picked up the programming skills with a minimum of fuss."

[7] Technical and Further Education.

11 Year 11 and 12 Information Technology

1981 saw the introduction into the Victorian Higher School Certificate (HSC) of a *Computer Science* course at Year 12 level. The syllabus followed what could be considered as a typical computing and information technology course at the time: programming, data structures, systems analysis and information systems. In 1987 the Year 11 and 12 certificates were replaced by a two-year Victorian Certificate of Education (VCE). With the change came *Information Technology*, a two-year sequence which has undergone considerable transformations over the years. (See Tatnall and Davey, 2010.)

Even though the GDCE was deliberately set up to cater for teachers requiring PD in teaching Senior IT courses, only two projects concerned them, one each from the HSC and the VCE. Findings were very similar.

A. B. Osborne (*HSC Computer Science: A teacher's guide to some problem areas*, 1985) reviewed the HSC *Computer Science* course. Although finding that teachers and students generally liked the syllabus, he found issues such as the course being too long, inappropriate topics and especially problems arising from students having an inadequate Year 11 IT background. Osborne used a set of interviews with Computer Science teachers together with a 14-school questionnaire. The languages in use were Basic: 6, Pascal: 7 and Comal: 1.

Reviewing the later VCE IT subject, A. Moylan (*Teachers perceptions of VCE IT*, 1992) found a similar liking of the syllabus but largely the same problem areas: parts as being "open ended" and "imprecise." Much more PD was required. Student keyboard and research skills were considered to be poor. Again the research was quite wide, with Moylan surveying 40 schools with a 50% return rate, and includes responses from 100 Year 11 IT students. Most Year 11 students were planning to continue IT in Year 12. A broad range of teachers were teaching the subject with Humanities, Mathematics, Science, Computing and Commerce backgrounds. The project includes interesting data on computer ownership: 53% of students had a computer at home, 30% used it every day and 30% 3 or 4 times a week. Most use was for typing assignments or games. (Note that this was prior to the WWW).

In 2014 enthusiasm for Information Technology as part of the curriculum has waned. Programming in particular has suffered, perhaps because of the range of applications which progressively become available decreasing its impact, but it still continues in some places. Enrolment in the VCE 'Systems' stream and its successor, IT Software Development, which contains the bulk of the 'technical' computing, has decreased markedly over the years. The statistics are not totally comparable, but as an indication, in 2001, 19,413 students passed the Year 11 *IT Unit 1* and 13,356 passed Year 12 *IT Unit 4*. In 2012, 4,494 took Year 11 *Information Technology*, 2,944 took Year 12 *IT Applications* and 1,098 took Year 12 *IT Software Development* (Victorian Curriculum Assessment Authority, 2012). In my opinion, programming should be a small, but important, part of the curriculum.

12 English as a Second Language

Only three comprehensive projects concerned English as a Second Language (ESL) but they tell an interesting story spanning eight years. The overall message is, once again, potentially good results put at risk by the lack of teacher preparation and PD: teachers with little exposure were skeptical at best. Since the Reports span the years 1985 to '92, this continuing lack of teacher support is quite alarming.

Computers and English as a Second Language (M. J. Miller, 1985) contains a 'needs analysis' and a survey of 22 ESL teachers in eight schools as well as a description of a set of lessons with small groups with examples of student work. Programs used were The Bank Street Writer (found particularly effective), Logo, First Fleet, CriptoCube and Story Tree. Of the 22 teachers surveyed, only two had 'ESL in-service.' (Seventeen had no computer in-service at all.) Obtaining bookings for computer Labs was universally difficult with zero to 19 computers per school, typical numbers being nine to fifteen.

The preparatory sessions for the *R&D Project* put an emphasis on Action Research as a potentially useful methodology. Action Research is a cycle of planning, implementing and assessing a program. Because the experimenter is, of necessity, in control, it is very applicable to classroom experimentation (See Murnane, 2010a, Murnane, 2010b pp. 114–139). While many projects do show traces of this methodology, very few explicitly embed the experiment in it. One notable exception was *Using computers With English as a Second Language Classes* (A. White, 1986) which used a formal Action Research structure in a project providing in-service for seven ESL teachers at one school. White reported an initial "complete lack of confidence" in many of the staff, with the project only being kept alive by a few "committed and determined teachers." These commented on the "the effectiveness of the computers in stimulating oral language and social skills. These have been developed through the use of simulation games by all students" to Year 11 level. By the project's end, all but one were enthusiastic." The students were described as "enthusiastic and willing" though some commented computer sessions "could be boring."

D. Lazarevic (*Computers and Their Use in English as a Second Language Learning Environment*, 1992) obtained survey data from 200 students and 35 ESL teachers. A solid statistical data analysis again showed lack of appropriate software and teacher training. Over 50% of Secondary teachers gave negative answers to the question "Do you think computers useful for ESL." Attitudes to computers in ESL in schools were found to be generally poor but good in Language Centres. Some attitude and confidence differences related to gender were found with female ESL students reporting less use of computers than males.

13 Word Processing and Process Writing

An argument could be made that the Word Processor was the single most important software advance in educational computing, given its effect on written expression.

Very few Projects before 1985 mention it and none deal with it other than in passing. This is possibly a reflection of the lack of software that would run on existing school computers, although this was changing rapidly. K. Daly (*Word Processing and the Process Approach to Writing,* 1985) lists 21 available Word Processors for the Apple][, 12 for the PC, 6 for the BBC Model B and several available for other machines. At the time there were still thought to be negative aspects to Word Processors: Daly was still finding frequent references in the Literature to 'disadvantages' of Word Processors such as spelling and grammar checkers and a general fear that the Word processor would discourage students from proper essay planning.

'Process Writing' is a term applies to a cycle of development for written text. Sponsored be a variety of authors from the late '60s it is a cycle of drafting, reviewing, and rewriting, often involving other students in the review stage. (See for instance Arms, 1983, Graves, 1983, Parker, 1972.) When it came to the rewriting stage, the Word Processor was an obvious enabler.

Daly provides a very large (for a 6,000 word project) survey of computing tools useful in teaching reading and expression including the first reference to 'Choose your own adventure' games in a Project. She covers keyboard skills and touch typing, finding that 'keyboarding' can profitably commence in Prep with touch-typing classes beginning in Year 4. (Three 1990 Reports deal directly with touch-typing. It seems that in 2014 it has all but disappeared from the curriculum, perhaps because it has been largely replaced with typing with the thumbs?) Daly discusses the educational use of the Word Processor and its use in Process Writing. Daly kept an anecdotal dairy of each lesson. She timed students in physical writing at start of the project and Word Processed writing at the end, finding "substantial" improvement. She noted major problems caused by not having the computers in her own classroom, something in common with most 'classroom' projects of the time. Each student filled out an 'attitude' sheet: "All stated that the computer made writing easier but had different preferences as to how they wished to incorporate it into their work," being roughly evenly split between writing the first draft by hand and those who would type from the beginning. A notable feature of the project is the insight it provides into Daly's own learning process as a teacher.

M. Said embarked on a rare project where he was able to compare two randomly-selected groups from a Prep classroom, one using a Word Processor and the other pencil and paper (*Process Writing in the Prep Classroom using a Word Processor*, 1986) The time element here was quite extensive for a project: twenty one-hour sessions. Despite the (acknowledged) difficulty of constructing a satisfactory regime to measure differences in oral and written language at this Year level, Said was confident that Word Processing had been shown to be effective for implementing Process Writing, something echoed by H. Gofron (*Role of the Word Processor in the Process Writing Approach,* 1993). "Both Year 4 class teachers ... have been overwhelmed with the enthusiasm the children have shown for wanting to use the computer for process writing." This, using a total of three machines, which "meant three or four children to one computer for twenty minutes at a time once a week."

A very different approach to Word Processing was used by S. G. Graham (*A Unit of Work Designed to Introduce a BBC Master 128 Computer to Grade 3/4 Through an Adventure Game Leading into Word Processing Manipulation*, 1986). Graham used Adventure Games as an entry to Word Processing. He chose this as a way to promote "meaningful reading for a purpose, problem solving and group interaction specifically in the form of transactional speech and responding imaginatively in writing. … Enthusiasm was overwhelming and a pleasant change." The study was very comprehensive, using Granny's Garden leading to writing using EDWORD 2. The project included an in-service for teaching staff and two parents who helped with the Word Processing lessons, all carried out using two computers. Graham used the results of a parent questionnaire, distributed before the experiment began and obtaining 66 responses, to involve parents in their children's work and invite their participation, required because the teacher could not provide the help required while students were working at the computers. Summaries of questionnaire responses are included in the Report.

14 Gender and Social Issues

"Gender equity studies have shown that there is a need to provide programs designed to support girls' education, particularly in computing." (J. A. Jones, *Parent Participation, Gender Equity and Computers: One form of action*, 1993.)

Differences in gender related to computers occur frequently in the literature of the time, but only occasionally in early projects, becoming a focus of interest from 1987. In general, Reports do not show great differences attributed to gender. J. Morris in a study of Primary students in Years Three and Six using LogoWriter (*Gender: is it an issue in Primary computing classrooms?* 1992) did find traces of a gender gap but considered that it "may be diminishing … and may not be the issue that it once was." She concluded "the majority of children do not see computing as a male domain in the Primary school."

Similarly, M. Wilson *(An Investigation of the Factors Involved in the Differential Attitudes and Responses of Boys and Girls in Computing. 40 Year 5 & 6 Primary* 1987) in a large statistical study using questionnaires before and after a computing unit, and computer-related tasks with observation of group dynamics, found no gender differences in attitudes towards computers or "their perceived stereotyping of them. … Boys and girls displayed very favorable attitudes to computers and … perceived the computer as a neutral object." There *were* significant differences in response to 'failure' situations: girls typically faulted their own lack of ability while boys faulted the system.

One area all Reports agree on is a tendency by boys to consider that they should have priority over girls for computer access. Morris found evidence to "support the theory that boys dominate girls in computer classes." J. A. Harris (*Equity of Access and Participation in Computer Education Making a difference*, 1993) observed that following a 'girls only' computer Unit, some girls became more assertive in 'claiming' use of the computer room. Echoing Morris, she found the boys objected to this, using what Harris describes as "guerrilla warfare" to reclaim the machines for themselves.

D. Lazarevic (above), concluded, from a large survey, that female ESL students, compared to males, were less frequent computer users. S. Johnson (above) found an increase in confidence in female students during a Mathematics course using LogoWriter.

These relatively benign findings are contradicted in a 1993 study by J. A. Jones (*Parent Participation, Gender Equity and Computers: One form of action*). Jones used a multi-layered approach to assessing gender equity relating to computers, to investigate the effects of computer education on the attitudes and behaviours of female parents, and the effects on the attitudes and behaviours of her class: 21 Year 1 and 2 students. "Both boys and girls showed evidence of stereotyping. The girls were more likely to show stereotyped views, choosing one career for girls and one for boys. The boys however, were more likely to show stereotyped views when classifying work—both paid and unpaid. The boys were more likely to stereotype adult computer use. … Most of the children believed that they would use computers in their adult life for either reading or writing." Jones found there was a "definite change in the children's perceptions of gender … after their participation in [the] gender education program." Four parents took 'women only' classes. Jones found initial evidence of sex stereotyping in relation to work and play. There was also evidence of fear of computer technology. A multifaceted approach to gender issues and computer education for parents produced positive changes in attitudes and behaviour.

Two projects concerned children with Special Needs. G. E. Grigg (*An Investigation of Software Available for Special Needs Students: Intellectually and/or Physically Handicapped*, 1987) found from a survey that there was suitable software with many access devices available "which enable disabled students to interact with computers as effectively as their non-disabled peers."

M. Barcia specifically studied the Concept Keyboard and its effect on language development with 'special needs' students. He also conducted a parallel study in main-stream Prep and 5/6 grades. (*An Investigation into the Concept Keyboard and its Effect on Special Education*, 1987.) The case study confirmed positive results reported in the literature. A Logo Floor-Turtle was also used. The study also includes experiments with Special Needs students using various keyboard overlay, most of which were found to be inappropriate, though a 15-session study of one student did show progress. The overlays *were* useful in Prep but not as much in 5/6. The Report contains a very good evaluation of the stages Special Needs students were at or went through using a Floor Turtle. After some experience, and with no prompting, the students positioned themselves behind the Turtle before giving a command to move it (Papert, 1980 p. 63–4). On Methodology, Barcia notes the need to separate *observation* from being *the teacher* (See Murnane, 2010b).

15 The Last Two Years

"I hope this project will never finish." (D. Walker, *How Useful is a Communication System at Marian College?* 1993)

The twenty projects from the last two years show a progressing maturity, not only in the teachers' confidence and maturity in using the technology, but in a steady decrease in 'technical' computing and an increase in social and general educational issues. There was still considerable interest in computer use in specific subjects (Legal Studies, Information Technology, ESL, Mathematics and Process Writing). The projects also increase in size, maturity and the quality of the research.

There was still considerable interest in Administrative computing with five dealing directly with it. Staff and student attitudes to computers were prominent, being the subject of five Projects. As with earlier Projects, they conclude that considerable *Educational* benefits can flow from automating administrative systems.

A 1987 project examined Electronic Bulletin Boards (T. P. Howard, *Curriculum Dissemination via Electronic Bulletin Boards*) but 1993 brought the first project to even mention eMail and electronic student communication (D. Walker, *How Useful is a Communication System at Marian College?* 1993). The Report contains an extensive survey of the communication programs available at the time together with some heartfelt comments on the frustratingly random difficulties encountered in using some of them:

> *Noise! Success, then 'No dialtone.' Such was the pattern for the next month. Sometimes we could log in and look at the AAP files. The next time the screen would fill with garbage. Sometimes the dreaded words 'No dialtone' would appear, and I would race to the front office to check they hadn't disconnected us or that a fax hadn't steamed up the data line, causing our puny signal to drop out. Year 11 continued with their database work, happy in continued success, whilst I wrestled with technology and yearned to return to my life as a Drama teacher.*

Despite technical difficulties, Walker persevered, finally establishing a connection with a school in Vernon, Florida. This was the turning point of the project as the Year 11s were at last "beginning to believe it might be real."

As the students began to write about themselves, Walker discovered many of the problems which are discussed in relation to the Web to this day:

> *I quickly discovered that there were two groups: The Incurably Honest and the Fantasy Freaks. The Incurably Honest wrote that life was drab in Australia, Deer Park was boring and school was a drag. The Fantasy Freaks wrote about their Capri sports cars and encounters with drug runners.*

This contact showed up a difference between students in Victoria and the USA at the time in terms of sophistication and use of electronic communications. The letters from Florida turned out to be "fresh and friendly and very warm. ... Year 11 now have a splendid relationship with Vernon, Florida. ... Marian College now has two classes who can claim with quiet confidence that they exchange ideas, stories and jokes regularly with students in far-off Florida in less time than it takes to fly there."

16 Conclusion

"The intrinsic fun of real computing should be preserved at all costs. It will translate into a joy for other learning if given half a chance." (Dwyer, 1971)

The 80s and early 90s were a great time for anyone involved in the use computers in the classroom. If the Reports paint one consistent picture it is of keen and enthusiastic teachers working around the shortcomings, batting down the difficulties and frustrations, reveling in the opportunities and learning along with their students, often to even better effect, convinced that what they are doing was not only exciting and vital but was indeed changing the way their schools and classrooms functioned. Computers were indeed changing way they were teaching and their students were learning.

17 Postscript

It is often said that in the relatively near future there will be no way to access the data on the current crop of computerised media such as CDs. Many of the early reports, mostly printed on dot matrix printers are already fading and are unreadable without the aid of a magnifying glass. The bindings are also coming apart. Some things do not change.

References

1. Arms, V.M.: The computer and the process of composition. Pipeline 8(1), 16–18 (1983)
2. Bigum, C., Gilding, A.: A video monitoring technique for investigating computer based learning programs. Melbourne Advanced College of Education, Carlton (1983)
3. Bitzer, D.L.: Plato, an adventure in learning. In: Seventh Australian Computer Conference. Advanced Press, Perth (1976)
4. Commonwealth Schools Commission. Report on Computer Education. Canberra, Australia (1984)
5. Dartmouth College. Demonstration and Experimentation in Computer Training and Use in Secondary Schools, Activities and Accomplishments of the first year. Hanover, N.H. (1968)
6. Dwyer, T.A.: Some principles for the human use of computers in education. International Journal of Man-Machine Studies 3(3), 219–239 (1971)
7. Gottfredson, G.D.: The Hawthorne misunderstanding (and how to get the Hawthorne Effect in Action Research). Journal of Research in Crime and Delinquency 33(1), 28–48 (1996)
8. Graves, D.H.: Writing: teachers and children at work. Heinemann, Exeter (1983)
9. House, A. (Undated) The bushrangers database (Online). National Library of Victoria, `http://trove.nla.gov.au/work/11737119?q&sort=holdings+desc&_=1380595819424&versionId=22448430` (accessed August 2013)
10. Juliff, P.: Programming—should we enjoy it or do it properly? In: Welch, R. (ed.) Ninth Australian Computer Conference, August 26-28, pp. 38–43. Mercury-Walch, Hobart (1982)
11. Massachusetts Institute of Technology. Logo progress report 1973–1975. Cambridge, Mass (1976)

12. Mazor, S.: The history of the microcomputer—invention and evolution. Proceedings of the IEEE 83(12), 1600–1608 (1995)
13. Melbourne State College. Application for Accreditation of the Course for Graduate Diploma in Computer Education. Melbourne, Australia (1979)
14. Melbourne State College. So, you're teaching in the Grad Dip Comp Ed. Melbourne, Australia (1987)
15. Mueller, E.: New Product Review. FORUM International 2(2), 27–29 (1982)
16. Murnane, J.S.: Programming Languages for Beginners. Lambert Academic, Saarbrücken (2010a)
17. Murnane, J.S.: Researching in a Confined Environment. In: Benzie, D., Lai, K.-W., Reffay, C. (eds.) IFIP Working Conference: New Developments in ICT and Education, Université de Picardai Jules Verne, Amines, France, June 27-29. IFIP (2010b)
18. National Science Foundation, Washington, D.C. Teacher-Student Authored CAI Using the NEWBASIC/CATALYST System. Pittsburgh Univ., Pa (1970)
19. O'Carroll, R.: Gold Dust Island. Jacaranda Wiley (2012), http://www.gb64.com/game.php?id=11054&d=33 (accessed October 2013)
20. Papert, S.: Teaching Children Thinking. Massachusetts Institute of Technology, Cambridge (1971)
21. Papert, S.: Mindstorms: children, computers, and powerful ideas. Basic Books, New York (1980)
22. Parker, R.P.: Focus in the teaching of writing: on process or product? English Journal 61(9), 1328–1333 (1972)
23. Robinson, K.: We need a creative revolution. Radio. Life Matters: Australian Broadcasting Commission (January 17, 2009)
24. Rosenthal, R.: Experimenter Effects in Behavioral Research. Appleton-Century-Crofts, New York (1996)
25. Tatnall, A., Davey, B.: The life and growth of Year 12 computing in Victoria: An ecological model. In: Tatnall, A. (ed.) HC 2010. IFIP AICT, vol. 325, pp. 124–133. Springer, Heidelberg (2010)
26. Tatnall, A., Davey, B.: Streams in the history of computer education in Australia. In: Impagliazzo, J., Lee, J.A.N. (eds.) History of Computing in Education, pp. 83–90. Kluwer, Boston (2004)
27. Tatnall, A., Leonard, R.: Purpose-built educational computers in the 1980s: the Australian experience. In: Tatnall, A. (ed.) HC 2010. IFIP AICT, vol. 325, pp. 101–111. Springer, Heidelberg (2010)
28. Victorian Curriculum Assessment Authority. Satisfactory Completion of VCE Units, Information Technology (2012), http://www.vcaa.vic.edu.au/Pages/vce/statistics/2012/section2/vce_information_technology_12.pdf (accessed November, 2013)
29. Victorian Education Department. Victorian Higher School Syllabus. Australia, Melbourne (1983)
30. Wills, S., Bunnett, A., Downes, T.: Convicts and bushrangers: educational databases brought alive. In: Rasmussen, B. (ed.) The Information Edge: the Future for Educational Computing, Proceedings Australian Computers in Education Conference, Brisbane, pp. 117–126 (1985)
31. Wong, L., Tatnall, A.: The need to balance the blend: online versus face-to-face teaching in an introductory accounting subject. Issues in Informing Science and Information Technology 6, 319–322 (2009)

Introduction of Computers in Primary Schools in Norway – From Experiments to Implementation

Sindre Røsvik

6050 Valderøy, Norway
sinro@online.no

Abstract. The article presents the introduction of computers in Norway from the mid-eighties to the beginning of the nineties. In 1984 the first IT initiative on IT in education passed Parliament; White Paper no 39 (1983/84) included an action program run by a ministerial task force, an experimental activity within selected areas and schools. This White Paper was followed by a number of initiatives and more White Papers indicating a high priority and profile for IT in national policy. The experimental programs were closed according to a shift of direction presented in White Paper 24, closing down the task force and IT integrated in the ordinary administrative bodies and curricular programs. There were the years of experiments and policy developments when ICT in schools moved from the era and field of enthusiasts to implementation in regular programs and curriculum. The Norwegian Pedagogical Computer Society was founded in 1987 after a year of preparatory work.

Keywords: IT in schools, policy and history.

1 Introduction

From the 1960s till the mid-80s computers in education were the era of enthusiast teachers and single experimental schools. But around 1980 there was a shift in policy as computers became more widespread in society.

In 1985 a revised version of the curriculum guidelines for primary and lower secondary education was launched – M85. The impact of computers was one reason to present a new policy, introducing computers as part of the curriculum. The year before the government established a Ministerial Task Force (Datasekretariatet) to speed up introduction of computers in education. Substantial budget resources were allocated to the program's experimental work, including research and evaluation of the initiative. The Task Force ran a wide range of activities and sub programs till it was closed down in the early 90s when the implementation phase started. In this period several White Papers on computers in education passed the Parliament, discussing the policy and strategy of experiments and implementation. The Task Force was empowered with wide proxies both on policy strategies and resources. The initiative was followed by research programs of classroom practices, software initiatives including an evaluation of national policy in the field.

A. Tatnall and B. Davey (Eds.): History of Computers in Education, IFIP AICT 424, pp. 71–82, 2014.

This experimental phase included several elements among which some turned out to become quite controversial:

Table 1. Overview of white Papers on IT and their focal points

White Paper/Plan	Curriculum	Focus	Suggested initiatives
No. 39 (1983-84)	M74: non-obligatory subjects: Technology (Computers not mentioned) Media knowledge: TV, film, newspapers etc. (Data, computers not mentioned)	1. National programme. 2. Experiment: 'whole schools' project and limited projects 3. Software development, and import for translation. 4. Competence building on technology and methods, co-operation across the system. 5. Vocational/ special education had special attention 6. Hardware: chosen to make all software work.	1. Ministerial Task Force, evaluated by IMTEC/OECD 2. Experimental schools: 21 schools Projects: 20 schools. 3. Almost 100 educational software programmes. 4. Conferences and courses. Design and methods. Reference groups. 5. Special software, applications and hardware (switches etc.) 6. CP/M-system chosen: and within the program, brands: TIKI, Scandis
No. 37 (1987-88)	M87: Computer-/media technologies included in general part: School in Society, and Learning Environment. In subjects: *integrated* approach. IT-themes within: science and social science.	1. National developmental centre –DATOPP 2. Dissemination of results gained at experimental schools/projects. 3. Software development. 4. Competence development. 5. Vocational/special education 6. Evaluation of programme 1984-88	1. Turned down by Parliament, Task Force continued its work. 2. Regional administration, Ministry council-bodies: New Projects, conferences/courses. 3. Software programme continue. 4. Teacher Colleges critical factors. 5. Software/application projects. 6. IMTEC and OECD evaluation Presentation included.

Table 1. *(Continued)*

No. 14 and 42 (1989-90) The latter supplement ary document to the first, on organisation of the action plan)	M87	1. Permanent structure for experiment/develop ment work –and dissemination. 2. Plan of action – IT apart from traditional R&D. 3. Vocational and special education programmes. 4. Teacher competence development. 5. New electronic infrastructure	1. Task Force, Ministry bodies, intro and implementation of IT. 2. Projects, competence centres 3. Software and competence development, and projects. 4. Basic/continuing teacher education, distant education. 5. Programs to establish infrastructure. Concepts developed of Task Force.
No. 24 (1993-94)	M87	1. Ministerial strategy plan: responsibilities distributed, no dedicated task force.	1. Describes responsibilities of actors like: National bodies, universities/ colleges, regional/local authorities.

In 1984, a milestone was set when the Parliament approved White Paper no 39 (1983/84), a programme of action to introduce computer technology into schools through experimental activity in selected areas and schools. The very clear purpose was to prepare for the introduction of compulsory IT in Norwegian schools. The urge of doing this was so strong that the compulsory introduction did not wait for any results from this programme of action before information technology, in a broad sense, was made a part of every subject (integrated) in primary and lower secondary education. In 1985 a preliminary edition of a new, revised, curricular guideline was introduced. In 1987 the final version was approved by the Parliament, one year before the programme of action was fulfilled, and final evaluation results were published. The revision where IT was included in the new curriculum guidelines announced the information age and represented a broad and overall approach. The Plan of Action represented a narrow, or a project approach, to gain experience in use of computers in education. In this chapter I will concentrate upon White Paper no 39 (1983/84) and White Paper no 24 (1993/94). There are several reports to the Parliament in between which will not be dealt with here.

2 The Task Force (Data Secretarial) Period 1984 - 1988

1984 - 1988 can be named as the Data Secretarial (DS) period, but it must be underlined that there were activities throughout the school system not linked to the programme. The programme in general did not address all schools and teachers but was limited to experimental schools only. This caused some stress among teachers that were rejected assistance by the Task Force. Schools in general should be served by the National Advisory Council for Primary and lower Secondary Education, the National Advisory Council for Upper Secondary Education and the National Advisory Vocational Training in Working life. The tasks of the National Councils were to handle educational matters within their field, including professional developments and projects. They enjoyed a relatively independent role within their defined area and were considered to supply the education system with educational expertise and knowledge.

IMTEC (International Movement toward Educational Change, http://www.imtec .org/english_version/) in their evaluation of the programme found a system-conflict between the National Councils and the Task Force. It seemed clear that the project model caused some stress throughout the school system. The reason might have been unclear, or lack of, communication between central actors when it came to distribution of responsibility and tasks. This is in spite of intentions of close co-operation explicitly outspoken in White Paper 39 (1983/84). The Task Force was established in understanding with (p 49), and should co-operate closely with (p 39), the National Councils. The National Councils should by and by take care of most tasks (p 39). Access to available resource in the field is of course an important reason to conflict as well, but it is likely that the Ministry did not take enough care of its' own system understanding, and therefore was not able to sort out and distribute the tasks in a reasonable way.

Introduction of IT in general in schools lies under the Ministry with the regional School Directors and the National Advisory Councils, and was not within the mission of the Task Force. Their work could rather be defined as an innovation programme, preparing reform. Innovation in this case can be defined as renewal, or "*a considered effort to improve practice related to given goals*" (Dalin 1986: 35). Results from the programme were open to a broader educational public when it came to programming courses, development of educational software, and in providing the schools with educational software.

The main elements in the strategy outlined in White Paper 39 (1983/849) were a programme of action carried through by a task force, and evaluation of the programme by an external agency, IMTEC:

1. *A project strategy approach with experimental activity at selected areas and schools.*
2. *There were some hardware demands, specifying standards of graphics, operative system etc. To equip the project- and experimental-schools with sufficient hardware the Ministry of education, through the Task Force, paid 75% of the costs. Only two computers, TIKI and SCANDIS, were approved for use under the programme.*
3. *Access to sufficient software was defined as one of the most important tasks and software development and testing was given high priority. The software was made for the two approved models. (Schools in general which were free to buy whatever computers they wanted had to stick to TIKI or SCANDIS if they wanted this software.*

4. *Another field of high priority was teacher training or competence development. This included building of networks, mutual co-operation between schools of same and different kind, institution within and outside the school system and establishing national resource centres for the whole school system.*

It was stressed that implementation of computers had to support the major values of education in Norway by preventing emergence of new class divisions; social or gender differences, support critical thinking etc. Furthermore the programme should develop the education system's own expertise, stimulate trial teaching and debate, and stimulate collaboration across the school system, with homes and with trade and industry. The technology should be used to seek better ways of teaching and learning, and mentioned elsewhere; special education was given priority. To stimulate experiments, collect, systematise and disseminate information on the experience in this area were also to be done.

The project approach was based on schools with previous project experience. Participation in the programme was supposed to be on a voluntary basis. To be accepted as an *experimental* school the whole staff had to support the application, which the School Board then must approve, because local support and local resources were needed. *Project schools* could participate on a narrower basis, with just a few teachers. In this way accountability and ownership should be secured. The evaluating agency had several contacts with each experimental school, and to some extent had a kind of action-research element as project strategies were introduced through the first surveys. The project-leaders were made aware of important issues to discuss with their colleagues. To some extent schools may have felt the evaluation teams' survey as clarifying, and as a support to their projects. White Paper 39 (83/84) does not say that this was an intention or a purpose of the evaluation programme, a role of IMTEC. The Ministry seems to be aware of the need of guidance (CERI -report 1987: 22):

> *"A programme of action must have the character of a set of government measures which can provide guidance in the desired direction for the development in different areas of the school's activity and within all branches of the school system."*

And there was a process for the evaluation between the Ministry and IMTEC before the programme started (Report no. 15 1989: 17). IMTEC underlines as important that:

> *"The actual or perceived assumptions behind a program will often tend to restrict the possibilities of development. To conduct a genuine dialogue on the structural aspects will therefore contribute to establishing greater freedom of action, thereby increasing the possibilities for the project to provide results as originally envisaged"* (ibid.: 22 -23).

The plan of action had both an element of top-down approach and a bottom-up strategy. The programme had defined their goals and aims nationally in White Paper 39 (83/84), but the schools by invitation defined their own projects, processes and goals. The Ministry itself expresses this in this way according to the CERI -report (1987: 13):

> *"What seems to emerge is that an action programme which is either based solely on a central controlled model for development, or alternatively on a completely decentralised model, would have little chance of success."*

An action programme, however, does not have to be either completely centralised or solely decentralised. On the contrary, both elements can be represented in an action programme. The Ministry itself describes such a model (top-down combined with bottom up) in a White Paper on Research and Developmental work (No. 79 1982/83). Locally managed projects need to be more emphasised, with a growing activity as a predicted result. However, there can be two different kinds of developmental work: i) locally initiated and managed and ii) centrally initiated and guided developmental work. Information technology was defined as a national field of priority, which is centrally, initiated projects, but they were open to locally managed projects. In the CERI-report 1987, page 13 this is taken into account in this way:

> *"On the other hand, the development will demand so much concentrated effort in in-service training and at the same time extend regional and central measures which ensure quality, continuity and learning experience across the boundaries of different kinds of schools and different regions."*

Without going into it here, it does not seem that all schools were aware of their relative freedom in defining their own projects. I participated in some seminars, representing a school owner and witnessed several requests for more detailed, centrally defined instructions both on content and processes of projects. One of IMTECs' conclusions points out that maybe the most critical factors for success is the school's ability to master the trial process (IMTEC, 1987: 78). The panel at the closing session of the IFIP working conference 'Exploring a new Partnership: Children, Teachers and Technology' made about the same conclusions stating that introducing IT faces the same challenges as every other innovation project, there is nothing special about IT (Røsvik, 1994: 290). The challenge is to tackle teaching and learning strategies in an appropriate way. We will not go into the running of the programme or special details concerning courses, software developments etc. This will just be mentioned as below.

Fields of priority were special education and the development of adaptable hardware and software, special keyboards etc. Vocational training was also focused upon as the Ministerial Task Force was engaged in developing software, hardware and suitable technology to increase the level of competence in the field. The main project was MI-2000, mechanical industry towards the year 2000, developing hardware and software for the mechanical line in vocational education. Computer assisted construction and manufacture (CAD/CAM) for models and machinery was part of it. During this period the Nordic countries established a close relationship in the field, still existing, exchanging software by special arrangements and by publishing pedagogical and methodological experiences in a mutual organised educational magazine. The Task Force was very active in participating at international conferences and congresses presenting the programme, and promoting educational software for sale. Programme development was initiated through ministerial design courses (starting out as Norwegian but later became Nordic courses) and by buying and distributing other software developed by individuals or small private firms. In total the Ministry could list close to 100 programmes, mostly educational software but also some software tools.

Even though the programme period of the Task Force came to an end in 1987, its work continued till 1st August 1990. In some respect, transferring the personnel to the Ministry extended the period of the Task Force. The programme itself including the work of the project schools was ended. Final evaluations of the Task Force were conducted by IMTEC and OECD and presented to the Ministry of Education and the Parliament in 1988. Based on the evaluation reports new initiatives were suggested, referred below in the next chapter.

During these years there were a number of teachers who were eager to introduce use of computers in their own teaching. In 1986 some of these started to establish an educational computer society and in 1987 the Norwegian Pedagogical Computer Society (NPeD) was founded. The aim was both to address policy initiatives to introduce computers to schools and to run practical help and courses for teachers in the classrooms. Special education was given priority and had a focus in courses and policy initiatives. During the first years the board had members representing special needs programmes. Another purpose of the society was to inspire teachers by organising study trips to Denmark, in cooperation with their sister organisation Datalærerforeningen. The founding chairman in Norway was inspired by the Danish organisation when joining their study trip to Boston and WCCE 1985 in Norfolk (USA). During the first year NPeD organised several conferences where national policymakers and politicians were invited to present new initiatives and to be challenged on lack of initiatives and given input by classroom teachers. However, most focus was given to hands-on courses for use of computers in the classroom, raising pedagogical challenges as well as subject issues. The members of NPeD were computer pioneers and teacher enthusiasts that had high expectations for computers in education and wanted to push the development to improve and modernize education for their students, preparing them for the immediate future.

3 Intermediate Period 1988 - 1993

The second phase started when the plan of action was fulfilled. White Paper 37 suggested continuing the work of the Task Force by establishing a new administrative unit called DATOPP. The experiences of the project schools were to be disseminated by the National Councils and regional bodies. Finally it was suggested that the ministerial capacity for strategic planning should be strengthen. Special education and vocational training had been emphasised during the project period and this work should also be continued. But the Parliament did not approve the establishment of a new unit, and this led to a situation that meant that the Ministry had to continue the work within the existing organisation. The personnel of the Task Force continued working, within the Ministry.

During the period 1988 to 1993 several of the field relevant White Papers were passed to the Parliament. They will not be mentioned at all or commented upon in this paper. In the first part of this intermediate period, 1988 to 1990, there were some organisational changes within the Ministry of Education. However, the central persons of the Task Force continued working with IT programmes, supporting software development and some other limited programmes, directly or through other national educational bodies (National Councils, regional school programmes etc.). The National Councils were closed down, and personnel and tasks moved into the Ministry. There had been tensions between the different parts of the national organisation for some time.

A third phase was introduced by White Paper number 14 (1989 -90) formulating a plan for information technology for school and training for the period 1990 - 93. During these years some of the earlier initiated programmes were followed up. Some of these programmes must be mentioned especially, namely an ambitious project of distance learning through telecommunication: MI2000 and PEGASUS, giving birth to WINIX. Great expectations were put upon the WINIX concept, a sophisticated software concept handling telecommunication in an advanced way. MI2000 was developed within the vocational part of the programme and attracted attention from outside the school system. This could also be said about some other programmes that were presented internationally, and distributed within the Nordic programme of co-operation.

Without going into details, the WINIX-project turned out to be a stumbling stone for the Ministry, almost costing the Minister his seat. The media paid growing attention to critical voices attacking the concept and the Ministry's handling of it. In the end the Parliament demanded a special report on 'Certain sides of the Educational Ministry's IT-programme', also named the WINIX-case. The mixture of ministerial administration, business and policy came to an expensive end, leaving the Ministry of Education an unpleasant bill to pay. In spite of lots of good and useful work done by, or assisted by these programmes, the reputation was severely damaged by this case. Some of those involved were even reluctant to tell that they participated in the programme.

This was the background of this White Paper on information technology in education. The words of the Minister at the conference in October 1993 can be grasped in a deeper way being familiar with this political scenery. It makes it even possible to understand why this White Paper over and over again underlined that IT should be 'normalised' and that no 'special' money would be required or paid, to carry out this new programme of action. But it could not deny questions to be raised if there was a programme; with no extra money, and if the interpretation of the 'normalising' programme was that no special focus should be given to IT in education. Some of the programmes that still kept running were stopped, before, or without, any substitute programme introduced. Other programmes would no doubt have profited from some financial input to be more widespread, known and used by Norwegian schools. Once more, however, it must be underlined that the Minister heralded that a plan of action was to be worked out during the year to come. The interpretation of intentions and consequences of White Paper No. 24 (1993-94) might turn out to be different from this described scenery of withdrawal of ministerial efforts and recourses.

4 Continuing Initiatives 1993 -94

The intention of this White Paper was first of all to report from the previous programme of action (1990-93); secondly to answer questions raised by the Parliament. Finally, and what ought to be the most interesting part, was presentation of strategies for further work within the sector of education. This strategy should have been the contribution of Ministry of Education to the National Plans of Action concerning IT; completing plans of action of trade and industry, and public administration. A plan like this had been awaited, and announced, for more than a year when the Ministry of Education finally informed that there would not be a similar plan of action for information technology in education. White Paper no. 24 was launched and produced very fast, in what seemed to turn out to be the normal way for this Minister. The writing process started in October 1993. On the 24th of October the Ministry invited about 100 people from different educational and information technology milieus to a meeting where the Ministry, with the Minister in front, announced their intentions about this White Paper and the production schedule. They invited the participants to comment upon the outlines of the paper in the meeting, and eventually to contribute with proposals in writing. On the 14th of January 1994, White Paper no. 24 (93/94) was released, in print and by Internet, immediately accessible to everybody. By the 20th May the White Paper passed the Parliament, and the Ministry, co-operating with the Norwegian Computer Society, had a one-day conference presenting the White Paper and further plans to work out a plan of action. In this process the Minister invited everybody to participate in the process by giving his e-mail address. Later the Ministry confirmed that they wanted to have an open process, willing to listen to professional groups such as the Norwegian Educational Computer Society and the Norwegian Computer Society.

A main conclusion was that the work concerning IT in education was to be financed according to the ordinary administrative levels. The Royal Ministry of Church and Education prescribed that there was a normalisation of IT in education, with no extra money, no dedicated people responsible for IT at any level, if not the institutions will give priority to the field, which some will do and some will not do. The national level worked out plans and guidelines, and thereafter information and advice. Special attention might be paid to IT in education in this respect, but mainly it seemed that the Ministry would rely upon institutions, universities, and municipalities to follow up and keep in line, being responsible. But what if a municipality failed, overloaded with other local tasks, like taking care of the elderly? What if a teacher college continued to be out of line? A national plan of action ought to consider questions like these. To follow the situation in the schools the Ministry developed a system of information-collection, and also did some special investigations.

The normal management model had to be the basis in every educational matter and any plan of action. Responsibility was distributed to the different levels, where there should be a system of support and development, to spread information and link specialists, specialists and schools, and projects together, taking care of the head-milieus and facilitating international co-operation and development. With no extra money, this was to be done with 'normal money' within ordinary budgets.

Lifelong learning for individuals is based on a lifelong learning society. The Ministry of Education would execute this task through its administrative body, National Learning-aid Centre (NLS).

Throughout the chapter on practical organising (chapter 9) each section had a state of art and an initiative paragraph. The initiative paragraph should give instructions or information on actions. Mostly there was a list of aims, giving little information of actions. According to the Ministry's' presentation of the White Paper on the 24th of May this was intentional, and the Minister, therefore, heralded that a plan of action that was to be published within a year.

The White Paper also reported to the Parliament on previous ministerial work and projects on IT in education, and presented outlines of future plans. It did not intend to prescribe resources or give any details of projects or plans of action. This would be a ministerial work and responsibility. The Ministry seemed open to ideas and proposals from professionals and others who wanted to contribute to a national plan. There were many open ends and issues to be considered and decided upon.

The main keyword in the White Paper was normalisation. This meant normal distribution of responsibility and work between the different levels of educational administration, according to what was normal in other educational matters. There would be no special ministerial task force. There would not be any extra IT resources, money of personnel. There would be no special software or hardware development conducted by the Ministry of Education. The change from the Data secretarial period was clear and significant. The ministerial culture signalled to be reversed from the view of IT projects as extraordinary to the ordinary. It was back to normality. But the Ministry, underlined by the Parliament, wanted to pay attention to IT in education to make sure that education kept up to date. There was an understanding of the role and importance of IT in society, and education. The will to be active at a national level was still considerable. A plan of action was to prove that. There could then be some final questions: What a normal allocation for developmental purposes on IT in a modern society would be like? Could a growth in resources to development and innovation be expected? Was it likely that municipalities would, and were be able to finance such development and innovation programmes? Would there be new initiatives for innovation and development or to support existing milieus, network building, in this respect within and outside formal institutions?

The intentions and basic principles of this White Paper seemed in some respect to be sound and reasonable concerning what should be done. But looking into how it should be done it was not so clear, what in fact was to be done, if anything would be done. The education minister was considered to be a man of action, good at slogans. He had put forward major structural reforms changing the school system from kindergarten, primary and secondary education to higher education. When it came to ICT, however, initiatives and actions were slowed down.

The municipal economy, however, was tightening. A growing elderly population required an increased share of public care and money. The municipal financial order in Norway is mainly based on lump sum allocations from the state. However, the municipalities do not have full freedom in economic priorities. The Parliament from time to time may give attention to some special fields or tasks, offering dedicated resources to, for instance, elderly care (more and better institutions, more personnel), provided that the municipalities are spending an equal amount to the tasks. During the nineties the task programmes have been elderly care and school reforms etc. Such special reforms unbalance the municipal budgetary systems, reducing the power of local authority to set its own priorities. Still, priorities are to be done, even if it sometimes is mostly focused to get hold of state-money. The educational system might consider IT to be as important as it was in society, and act upon it, but within given economical budgets. The point here is that White Paper 24 (93/94) or state budgets didn't offer extra, dedicated resources for IT in schools which meant that this programme had to compete within ordinary municipal budgets.

A plan of action on IT in education should reflect and answer the challenge in a proper way. The Norwegian plan of action on IT in education was to be based upon White Paper 24 (93/94). If, or to what extent, it would meet future needs and challenges was to be seen. The indication, however, was that no extra money could be expected. The strategy outlined, in some respect, seemed to stress harder that this White Paper represented a different course then that from the Task Force, the one that lead to WINIX-case. In a way one could be reminded of the, at that time, on-going transition of Eastern Europe, where politicians for some time had been more clear about the *change* of policy, making it different from the previous regime, then about what to do. The ingress of the White Paper by the end stated this philosophising on IT (KUF 1995, IT in Norwegian Education. A Plan for 1996 – 1999, English version: 4):

> *"It is, therefore, becoming more and more difficult to imagine how we could manage without it, and to imagine how far it will take us. But it is because of this very development, and the speed at which it is taking place, that it is so essential both to increase the knowledge of the opportunities and our skill in availing ourselves of them. It is of paramount importance to use the learning opportunities which information technology provides, and to see that it creates a stronger sense of community not wider gaps."*

It was not possible to tell any future results for sure. The Ministry might follow up the stated intentions put forward in the White Paper, but what this was to be seemed quite open ranging from special initiatives, to nothing especially. What would count in the end were what operational steps that were taken, and the force of these actions. Some of the plans and guidelines in this White Paper seemed unclear about concrete actions as well as willingness of central authorities to invest, set resources aside to promote IT developments in education. The main impression though, was that there was both an understanding of importance, and a will to act according to the intentions of the White Paper. The intentions and will seemed present, but the ability was uncertain both concerning resources available and the concrete strategic steps to be taken. It was considered to be a challenge to make the whole school system able to deal with IT in a constructive way. It was supposed by many that this would request a proper way in allocating resources, in supporting and stimulating innovations, in disseminating experiences and knowledge to make the implementation of IT support learning. Machiavelli the famous medieval counsellor said something like: "Nothing is as dangerous as initiating change." In this respect it could be added and changed to: "Nothing is as dangerous as initiating change, except, not to do it."

References

1. Kirke- og undervisningsdepartementet: St meld. nr.79 (1982/83) Om Forsknings og utviklingsarbeid (About Research and Developmental work), Oslo (1983)
2. Kirke- og undervisningsdepartementet: St.meld. nr. 39 (1983/84) Om Datateknologi i skolen (About Computer Technology in the School), Oslo (1984)
3. Kirke- og undervisningsdepartementet (1984) St. meld. nr. 79 (1983/84) Om det pedagogiske utviklingsarbeidet i skolen og om forsøksvirksomheten i skoleverket skoleårene 1981-82 og 1982-83 (FoU-meldingen) (About the Educational Development Work in the School and about the Experiment Activity within the School System the School years 1981-82 and 1982-83, Oslo (1984)
4. Kirke- og undervisningsdepartementet: St. meld. nr. 37 (1987/88) Om datateknologi i skole og opplæring (About Computer Technology in School and Training), Oslo (1988)
5. Kirke- og undervisningsdepartementet: St. meld. nr. 14 (1989-90) Informasjonsteknologi i skole og opplæring (Information Technology in School and Training): Oslo (1989)
6. Kirke-, utdannings- og forskningsdepartementet: St. meld. nr. 24 (1993/94) Om informasjonsteknologi i utdanningen. Rapport fra handlingsprogrammet 1990-93 og strategi for videre arbeid (About Information Technology in the Education. Report on the Action Programme 1990-93 and Strategy on Further Activities), Oslo (1994)

Information Literacy in the Netherlands: Rise, Fall and Revival

Joke Voogt[1,2] and Alfons ten Brummelhuis[3]

[1] University of Amsterdam, The Netherlands
[2] Windesheim University, Zwolle, The Netherlands
[3] Kennisnet, Zoetermeer, The Netherlands
j.m.voogt@uva.nl

Abstract. This contribution describes and reflects on the development of Information Literacy in the Dutch curriculum for secondary education in the early 1980s, its place in the curriculum in the 1990s and its evaporation early 2000. After a decade without any attention for Information Literacy in the curriculum, the Royal Academy of Arts and Sciences called for a revival of Information Literacy early 2013. Based on lessons learned from the past, we will finish our contribution with some reflections on this initiative and describe emerging opportunities

Keywords: information literacy, The Netherlands, curriculum, computer science.

1 Introduction

Developments in information technology at the end of the 1970s and the early 1980s lead to policy discussions and recommendations in North America and Western Europe about implications of these developments for the education sector. In the Netherlands this resulted in a number of advisory reports [1,2] with recommendations regarding the role of information technology in education.

Although the implications of developments in information technology for education are driven by many different rationales [3], in the early 1980s the social rationale was an important argument in the debate. The social rational focuses on the need to prepare young citizens for living in a society driven by information technology. In many countries, although not without debate, discussions between different stakeholders lead to the call for a new subject in the curriculum. The new subject, often referred to as computer literacy, aimed to develop basic knowledge and skills in computing. It is distinguished from specialized computer science courses offered in vocational education programs and in higher education. Lockheed, Hunter, Anderson, Beazly and Esty [4] defined computer literacy as everything a person needs to know and to do with computers in order to function competently in an information-based society. The curriculum discussion at national or state levels did not question so much the need for paying attention to computer literacy in the curriculum, but focused on the goals and content of the new subject and the location of the new subject in the curriculum [5].

A. Tatnall and B. Davey (Eds.): History of Computers in Education, IFIP AICT 424, pp. 83–93, 2014.

From the start computer literacy did not only deal with being able to operate computers, but aimed for broad educational goals [6]. For instance programming was considered important because of the perceived link between programming skills and problem solving skills [7]. The potential of computers to store, retrieve and manipulate enormous amounts of data addressed the importance of dealing with concepts as 'information' and 'data'. In the Netherlands the call for computer literacy as a new subject in the curriculum resulted in a number of curriculum development activities in the 1980s resulting in a new compulsory subject for lower secondary education in the early 1990s.

2 Information Literacy for All: The Development of a New Subject

In 1982 the Minister of Education Culture and Sciences took the initiative to ask for advice on the place and content of new technologies in education. The Adviescommissie Onderwijs en Informatietechnologie [AOI] which was appointed published four advisory reports. Two of these reports dealt with the development and implementation of a new subject in lower secondary education [8,9].

In her first report the AOI advised to implement a new compulsory subject in lower secondary education called *burgerinformatica* ("Information technology for all"). The committee proposed four domains for the new subject: (1) experiencing computers (acquiring a functional understanding of computers); (2) computers, programming and data (acquiring an operational understanding of computers); (3) managing computer systems and (organizational, economical, societal, psychological) impact; and (4) applications of information technology [8]. Based on the comments the AOI received it was decided to add aspects of information literacy to the new subject. As a result the name for the new subject was changed into *informatiekunde* (information literacy) with the following domains: (1) information and data; (2) general applications of information systems; (3) applications of digital information systems ; (9) problem analysis and programming, and (5) design principles of hardware and software [9]. The committee advised to implement *informatiekunde* in lower secondary education as a compulsory subject taking two hours per week at the expense of mathematics and Dutch language.

In 1983 a pilot project (*100-scholen project burgerinformatica*) took off in secondary education. One hundred secondary schools were provided with eight computers (Philips 2000 and Aster CT-80) and software and curriculum materials developed by the National Institute for Curriculum Development in the Netherlands. To prepare teachers to teach *burgerinformatica* in-service education open for teachers of all subjects was provided by teacher education institutes. In the pilot project schools were asked to explore and experiment with the potential of information technology in education. A major concern at the start of *burgerinformatica* was its association with mathematics and science, and the possibility that the new subject was in the interest of boys, leaving out the girls. One reason for this concern was the emphasis on computer literacy in the initial plans of the AOI [8]. In addition in the participating schools mainly math teachers appeared to be the early adopters of the new subject, because of their knowledge, experience and interest in information technology [10]. Voogt [11] showed that this concern was indeed valid. In a survey among students in the participating secondary schools it became clear that boys had more positive attitudes towards computers than girls. To deal with this concern it was decided to broaden the scope of the subject with aspects of information literacy, as became clear in the recommendation of the AOI in 1984 [9]. In addition SLO, the National Institute for Curriculum Development, focused on curriculum materials for *burgerinformatica* that covered a broad spectrum of information technology applications, which are not only interesting for boys, but also for girls.

The preparatory work of the AOI and the experiences in the pilot project resulted in 1988 in the formal installation of a curriculum development group by the Ministry of Education, Culture and Sciences that had to develop core objectives for the subject *informatiekunde* (information literacy) in lower secondary education. The curriculum development group used much of the preparatory work done by the AOI and launched an ambitious plan for the new subject which should take 80 hours of curriculum time. The new subject had four domains: (1) data, data processing and information; (2) information processing systems; (3) applications of information technology and (4) the impact of information technology on society. Concrete core objectives were formulated for each of these four domains.

At the time an educational reform of lower secondary education took place and all subjects of the lower secondary education curriculum were reconsidered and updated. The curriculum deliberations taking place during the reform resulted in the decision for a mixed approach in the delivery of *informatiekunde* in the curriculum. A small 20-hour course called *informatiekunde* was planned as a separate subject in the curriculum. This course had to deal with concepts related to information handling and basic skills in using general computer applications. In addition to the separate course the goals of *informatiekunde* had to be addressed via other subjects in the curriculum such as Dutch language, mathematics, science and social studies. Specific subject related core objectives for *informatiekunde* were formulated such as the use of word processing in Dutch language and the use of simulations and data logging in science. It was assumed that the 20-hour course for *informatiekunde* would have a launching effect and after a couple of years all objectives of *informatiekunde* would be fully integrated within other subjects [12].

The integration of information literacy in other subjects caused new challenges for the implementation since teachers were not well prepared for the uptake of information literacy in their curriculum. To investigate the potential of the integration of information technology in other subjects several studies were conducted, amongst them three studies were conducted focusing on the integration of information technology in Dutch language [13], the integration of information technology in science education [14] and the integration of information technology in social studies [15]. In these studies exemplary curriculum materials aiming to support teachers in the implementation of *informatiekunde* objectives in their curriculum were developed and evaluated. The exemplary curriculum materials respectively focused on the use of word processing to support written communication in the Dutch language curriculum, the use of probe software to support inquiry-based learning in science education and the application of hypertext in the social studies curriculum. The three studies showed two main problems: (1) teachers not only needed a lot of help to learn how to use the technology, but also needed to change their pedagogical approach to teaching and learning in order to be able to implement the technology; and (2) the infrastructure in schools was not yet ready for the uptake of technology.

3 Implementation of Information Literacy in the Lower Secondary Education Curriculum

The new lower secondary education curriculum was implemented from 1993 onwards. *Informatiekunde* had a modest but secure place in the new curriculum both as a separate subject and integrated in other subjects, and underpinned by attainment targets schools were expected to realize in their teaching. However, due to the advisory reports by the AOI and the pilot study (*100 scholen project burgerinformatica*) *informatiekunde* had in fact already taken off much earlier in most secondary schools. Many publishers had developed textbooks for the new curriculum using the exemplary curriculum materials of the National Institute for Curriculum Development and the objectives formulated by the AOI as a starting point.

The findings of the International Computers in Education Study (CompEd), in which the Netherlands participated showed that in 1989 89% of secondary schools offered *informatiekunde* in at least one of the first three years of lower secondary education and 15% of the schools integrated the goals of *informatiekunde* in one or more other subjects [16]. However by comparing textbooks with the formal core objectives for *informatiekunde* a number of discrepancies were found [17]. In the textbooks ample attention was paid to basic computer concepts, accessory devices and software applications (word processing, databases, simulations, telecommunication and educational games). Although programming skills were not part of the goals of *informatiekunde*, about half of the textbooks paid attention to programming. The results from school practice showed that at the end of the 1980s schools in particular paid attention to basic computer concepts and word processing, implying that only a small part of the planned core objectives were realized [17].

The participation in CompEd resulted in the development of a national monitoring system to oversee the implementation of information technology in the curriculum. The results were very informative concerning the implementation of *informatiekunde* as a separate subject and the integration of *informatiekunde* in other subjects. The 1998/1999 monitor showed that only one third of the teachers in secondary education used information technology in their instructional practice but on an infrequent basis [18]. This had hardly changed since 1992. Moreover, in comparing scores of 5th (primary education) and 8th graders (lower secondary education) in 1992 and 1998 on an information literacy knowledge and skills test it could be shown that students in primary and secondary education knew more about information technology and had better skills in 1998 compared to 1992, but also that the difference between primary school students and lower secondary education students decreased significantly.

In fact there was an 70% overlap between the two groups [19, 20]. This implied that already in primary education the majority of the students mastered many of the information literacy goals when they entered secondary education. The study also found that primary and secondary school students knew more about information technology than their teachers think. Teachers tended to underestimate the knowledge and skills of their students [21]. In addition, based on an evaluation of the 1993 lower secondary education reform, it was concluded that the quality of lessons *informatiekunde* were poor and the students results insufficient [12].

Based on these findings it was decided to revise the lower secondary education. *Informatiekunde* as a separate subject was no longer compulsory. The 1998 core objectives targets were reformulated on a much more general level, implying that the specific core objectives which secured the integration of *informatiekunde* in other subjects had disappeared. By the year 2000 *informatiekunde* had a nearly invisible place in the curriculum. These developments lead to the evaporation of *informatiekunde* in the curriculum by early 2000.

4 Computer Science in Upper Secondary Education

Compared to the development of *informatiekunde*, the development of computer science for upper secondary education drew less political attention. Computer science was never considered a compulsory subject for the upper secondary science curriculum, but an optional course. The examination program for the optional computer science course was agreed upon in 1995. This course has four sub-domains: Computer science in perspective, basic concepts and skills, systems and the way they are structured and applications in conjunction. It was decided not to have a national examination for computer science at the end of secondary education, but a school-based exam instead. Through this decision the subject never is taken very serious by secondary schools. The course is offered by about 60% of the secondary schools. Computer science as a subject in upper secondary education always had its problems, which can be summarized as (1) too few students choose computer science; (2) too few qualified teachers; (3) too few means (hard- and software, including text books) to develop and teach the subject and (4) the maintenance of hard- and software is complex and expensive. An additional problem was that the subject attracted relatively few students, probably because the subject was perceived by students as too technical [22]. A recent review study of the text books for computer science in upper secondary education showed a poor quality of the curriculum materials with much attention on knowledge reproduction and hardly any practice in complex learning activities like programming. The study concluded that students in upper secondary education learn about programming without practice in programming [23].

5 A New Call for Digital Literacy in the Curriculum

At the end of the 1990s and the early 2000s the educational policy regarding the role of information technology in the curriculum had shifted. From a focus on the social rationale the policy had shifted to an emphasis on the pedagogical rationale [3]. From learning *about* information technology, as expressed in the *informatiekunde* curriculum the policy focused now on *using* information technology to learn [24,25]. For more than a decade the policy focused on the integration of information technology as a tool for learning and the uptake of information technology by teachers and not on information literacy goals.

Thirty years after the early policies on information technology in education, with its focus on understanding information technology concepts, the impact of information technology on society, and basic knowledge and skills in information technology for coping with changes in society [26] the debate on the importance of information technology for society and the need to pay attention to it not only as a means for learning but also as a curriculum goal seems to revive. Kennisnet, the public educational organization which supports and inspires Dutch primary, secondary and vocational institutions in the effective use of Information and Communication Technology, commissioned a white paper about 21st century skills. In the white paper the importance of information technology as driving force for changes in society and its implications for education was analyzed and discussed [27]. A major issue in the white paper was the need to pay attention to digital literacy[1] (knowledge and skills), not only as a tool for learning but also as a goal in itself. In particular attention was paid to the need for students to better understand technological developments in order to be able to cope with changes in society. Voogt and Pareja Roblin [27] recommended a public debate about the need for and place of 21st century skills in the curriculum.

Early 2013 the Royal Netherlands Academy of Arts and Sciences [28] published a report in which they recommended to pay more attention to digital literacy in the secondary school curriculum. The report was highly influenced by an influential report of The Royal Society [29] in the United Kingdom. The Royal Society advocated for more attention to Computer Science in the primary and secondary school curriculum and emphasized the importance of computational thinking as an important ingredient of digital literacy. Computational Thinking was defined in their report as "the process of recognizing aspects of computation in the world that surrounds us, and applying tools and techniques from Computer Science to understand and reason about both natural and artificial systems and processes" (p. 29). According to Wing [30] computational thinking is a universally applicable attitude and skill set everyone, not just computer scientists, would be eager to learn and use" (p. 33).

The report of the Royal Netherlands Academy of Arts and Sciences questioned the lack of education in digital literacy in the lower secondary education curriculum and the outdated computer science curriculum in upper secondary education. The Royal Netherlands Academy of Arts and Sciences recommended to develop and implement a compulsory subject Information and Communication for the lower secondary school curriculum and a profound renewal of the optional computer science course in upper

---

[1] The term digital literacy is used here, because it shows the development of the concept information literacy since the early 1980s.

secondary education. In both courses computational thinking was mentioned as a core skill needed in the knowledge society. Both subjects should have clear links to each other and to other school subjects. To overcome the problem of under-qualified teachers it was also recommended to redesign the preparation programs for computer science teachers.

By the end of 2013, as an answer to these developments, the National Institute for Curriculum Development was asked by the Ministry of Education, Culture and Sciences to define a conceptual framework for digital literacy in the primary and secondary school curriculum [31], which might be an indication of a revival of attention for information literacy and computer science in the primary and secondary school curriculum in The Netherlands. In addition the Dutch Government is preparing a policy document that will provide a vision on how to prepare students on the use of information technology. This policy framework will be published in 2014 and could be the formal revitalization of information literacy in Dutch education.

6 Discussion

This chapter described the rise, fall and revival of information literacy as a curriculum goal in the Dutch secondary school curriculum. Looking back at the history critical decisions were taken at specific points in time, that caused the lack of attention for digital literacy as a school subject in the current (2013) primary and secondary curriculum. Lessons learned from history may inform the current debate on the place of digital literacy in the curriculum, which we will discuss in this section.

6.1 The Gap between the Intentions and Practice

From an international perspective the debate in the late 1980s and early 1990s focused on two issues (1) a conceptual versus an instrumental approach to information technology as a school subject and (2) the place of the new subject in the curriculum [5]. In the instrumental approach computers were seen as increasingly important tool in society, and it was considered important to be able make use of them. For this reason the main focus was to become acquainted with major computer applications. A big threat to the instrumental approach is that rapid technological developments makes information literacy obsolete in a short time, as was already observed by Collis in 1988 [32]. In the conceptual approach the subject was based on a body of knowledge about information and information systems and accompanying skills. The main focus was on understanding information systems. The use of computer applications was only a minor part of the subject. In the Netherlands the latter approach was opted for, as becomes clear in the reports of the AOI. In both approaches the debate about the place of programming skills stayed unresolved, which also caused unclarity about the content of information technology. For instance, despite the fact that programming skills were not part of the core objectives of the subject, in the Netherlands many text books of the early days offered some kind of basic programming skills, leading to attention for programming skills in the curriculum in practice.

In addition to the discourse about the focus of information literacy, the place in the curriculum was also disputed. Collis [32], for instance, argued that computer literacy as a separate subject hampered the integration of information technology as a tool for learning in different subjects. She argued that teachers would not see the necessity to use computers to enhance teaching and learning if information technology applications are also offered in a separate subject. England and Wales therefore completely integrated information literacy goals in their National Curriculum. It was this approach that The Royal Society [29] in their report of 2012 qualified as unsuccessful, because of its lack in meeting information literacy goals. In the Netherlands the place of the subject in the curriculum became obscured when the domain was split: A minor part of information literacy was offered as a separate subject, and the major part was integrated in existing courses. The separate course never got beyond the instrumental approach, leading to an evaporation of the subject by the early 2000. So although the conceptual approach was aimed for by the curriculum developers it was not realized, because of poor text books and under-qualified teachers. The integration in existing subjects on the other hand was also unsuccessful, because subject teachers were not prepared to teach with technology and because there was no assessment system in place, teachers simply did not teach the core objectives which were considered relevant for their subject. Although the availability of an information literacy curriculum is a requirement, it is insufficient to warrant implementation. The start of a new subject without qualified teachers, adequate teaching resources and clear assessment procedures are a necessary condition for a successful start. But also when the goals of information literacy are integrated in existing courses these conditions are a prerequisite.

6.2 Digital Literacy to Prevent Inequity

As a result of the mixed approach to *informatiekunde* in the curriculum and the weak implementation in educational practice, the position of *informatiekunde* at the end of the 1990s was very weak. However, the position of *informatiekunde* became even worse, when research had shown that primary school students were able to perform to a large extent as well as students in lower secondary education on a test measuring information technology knowledge and skills. Instead of blaming the quality of the implementation of information literacy in the curriculum such a finding might have given rise to the misunderstanding that students automatically acquire information literacy knowledge and skills, because of the overall presence of technology in society. However, research has shown that students differ in their information technology knowledge and skills and in their use of technology [33,34]. To prevent the creation of a new digital divide between those who are digital literate and those who are not attention for digital literacy in the curriculum is needed.

6.3 A Shared Vision on Curriculum in the Knowledge Society

The international SITES[2] study [35] showed a decrease in attention for lifelong learning skills (including Information technology skills) in a number of European

[2] Second Information Technology in Education Study.

countries (Denmark, Norway, Slovenia) between 1998 and 2006, while some Asian countries (Hong Kong, Japan, Taiwan, Thailand, Singapore) showed an increase for lifelong learning competencies in the same period. A secondary analysis of the data [36] was able to show how educational policy impacted teaching and learning in schools. Findings from the recent PISA studies [37] initiated discussions about the quality of education in many countries, often resulting in calls for more attention to basic literacy and numeracy skills, stricter examination practices and schools being accountable for their results.. In the Netherlands the general educational policy became narrowly focused on basic literacy and numeracy skills as core subjects in the curriculum. This focus was accompanied by an increased emphasis on testing. This caused a decrease in attention for other subjects in the curriculum. Similar trends took place in other European countries, as became clear from the SITES data described above. For instance in Denmark an increased focus on curriculum-centred instruction, tests and individual student learning in the Danish educational policy decreased the attention on collaboration, independent learning and the use of technology in Danish schools [38], illustrating how educational policy impacts teaching and learning in schools.

Stakeholders of the education system (e.g. the corporate sector, (inter)national organizations, parents) try to influence educational policy. Some recent developments indicate that in several European countries the narrow emphasis on basic literacy and numeracy skills is changing again. In the United Kingdom The Royal Society [28] drew attention for the need of student awareness for computer science and computational thinking as a domain of study. One reason was the need for computer scientists in the workforce. Their report was highly influential as it resulted in a compulsory program of study on computing for the ages 5-14, starting in 2014. Also in the Netherlands the narrow focus on basic literacy and numeracy skills is disputed by influential bodies such as the Education Council of the Netherlands [39] which recently published a report where they questioned whether the curriculum prepares its students for the knowledge society. They advocate to put lifelong learning skills, including digital literacy, back on the education agenda. These developments show a pressing need for a shared vision on what should be learned in the knowledge society, including the place for digital literacy. Moreover it can be learned from the past that qualified teachers are a necessary condition for a successful revival of information literacy.

References

1. Rathenau, A.: Maatschappelijke gevolgen van de micro-electronica. Staatsuitgeverij, Den Haag (1979)
2. VIN: Over informatica-onderwijs, een verkenning. Rapport van de Verkenningscommissie Informatica-Opleidingen Nederland. WRRD, Den Haag, The Netherlands (1981)
3. Hawkridge, D.: Machine-mediated learning in third world schools. Machine-Mediated Learning 3, 319–328 (1990)
4. Lockheed, M.E., Hunter, B., Anderson, R.E., Beazly, R.M., Esty, E.T.: Computer literacy: Definition and survey items for assessment in schools. National Center for Educational Statistics, Washington, DC (1983)

5. Voogt, J.: Consequences of ICT for aims, contents, processes and environments of Learning. In: Van den Akker, J., Kuiper, W., Hameyer, U. (eds.) Curriculum Landscapes and Trends, pp. 217–236. Kluwer, Dordrecht (2003)
6. Plomp, T., van de Wolde, J.: New information technologies in education: Lessons learned and trends observed. European Journal on Education 20(2-3), 243–256 (1985)
7. Papert, S.: Mindstorms: Children, computers, and powerful ideas. Basic Books, New York (1980)
8. Adviescommissie Onderwijs en Informatietechnologie [AOI]: Leren over informatietechnologie: Noodzaak voor iedereen. Staatsuitgeverij, Den Haag, The Netherlands (1982)
9. Adviescommissie Onderwijs en Informatietechnologie [AOI]: Informatieleer en Computerkunde. Staatsuitgeverij, Den Haag, The Netherlands (1984)
10. Carleer, G.J., Valkenburg, H.D.: Beschrijving en analyse van uitkomsten evaluatieonderzoek 100 scholen project. Universiteit Twente, Enschede, The Netherlands (1985)
11. Voogt, J.: Computer literacy in secondary education: the performance and engagement of girls. Computers & Education 11(4), 305–312 (1987)
12. Inspectie van het Onderwijs: Informatiekunde in de basisvorming: evaluatie van de eerste vijf jaar. Utrecht: Inspectie van het Onderwijs, The Netherlands (1999)
13. Van der Geest, T.M.: Tools for teaching writing as a process: design, development, implementation and evaluation of computer-assisted writing instruction. University of Twente, Enschede, The Netherlands (1991)
14. Voogt, J.M.: Courseware for an inquiry-based science curriculum. An implementation perspective. University of Twente, Enschede, The Netherlands (1993)
15. Keursten, P.: Courseware ontwikkeling met het oog op implementatie; de docent centraal. Universiteit Twente, Enschede, The Netherlands (1994)
16. Pelgrum, W.J., Plomp, T.: The use of computers in education worldwide: Results from the IEA 'Computers in Education' survey in 19 educational systems. Pergamon Press, Oxford (1991)
17. Ten Brummelhuis, A.C.A., Rustenburg, J., Soeting, J.: Informatiekunde in theorie en praktijk: Een vergelijking tussen eindtermen, lesmethodes en onderwijspraktijk. In: Abram, I.B.H., Creemers, B.P.M., Van der Leij, A. (eds.) Onderwijsresearchdagen 1991, pp. 101–114. Amsterdam, SCO, The Netherlands (1991)
18. Ten Brummelhuis, A.C.A., Slotman, K.: ICT-monitor 1998/1999: voortgezet onderwijs, Universiteit Twente, Enschede, The Netherlands (2000)
19. Ten Brummelhuis, A.C.A.: ICT monitor 1997/1998: basisonderwijs. Universiteit Twente, Enschede, The Netherlands (1998)
20. Ten Brummelhuis, A.C.A.: ICT monitor 1997/1998: voortgezet onderwijs. Universiteit Twente, Enschede, The Netherlands (1998)
21. Ten Brummelhuis, A.C.A., Janssen Reinen, I.: Van informatiekunde naar informatievaardigheden: de transformatie van een schoolvak. In: Kuiper, W., Van den Akker, J., Voogt, J. (eds.) Portret van een onderwijskundige, pp. 31–48. Universiteit Twente, Enschede (2000)
22. SLO [National Institute for Curriculum Development]: Vakdossier Informatica. SLO, Enschede, The Netherlands (2007)
23. Koldenhof, E., Jeuring, J., Ruth, S.: Rendement van objectgeorienteerd programmeeronderwijs. Utrecht: Universiteit Utrecht, The Netherlands (2011)
24. Ministerie van Onderwijs, Cultuur en Wetenschappen: Leren met ict 2003-2005. MOCW, Den Haag, the Netherlands: MOCW (2002)

25. Ministerie van Onderwijs, Cultuur en Wetenschappen: Actieplan Verbonden met ICT. Den Haag: Netherlands: MOCW (2006)
26. Anderson, R.: Implications of the information and knowledge society for education. In: Voogt, J., Knezek, G. (eds.) International Handbook of Information Technology in Primary and Secondary Education, pp. 5–22. Springer, New York (2008)
27. Voogt, J., Pareja Roblin, N.: 21st century skills. Rapport voor Kennisnet. University of Twente, Enschede, The Netherlands (2010)
28. Koninklijke Nederlandse Academie van Wetenschappen: Digitale geletterdheid in het voortgezet onderwijs. Vaardigheden en attitudes voor de 21^{e} eeuw. Koninklijke Nederlandse Academie van Wetenschappen, Amsterdam, The Netherlands (2013), https://www.knaw.nl/nl/adviezen/adviezen-en-verkenningen/recent-afgeronde-adviezen/digitale-geletterdheid-in-het-voortgezet-onderwijs
29. The Royal Society: Shut down or restart? The way forward for computing in UK schools. The Royal Society, London (2012), http://royalsociety.org/uploadedFiles/Royal_Society_Content/education/policy/computing-in-schools/2012-01-12-Computing-in-Schools.pdf
30. Wing, J.: Computational thinking. Communications of the ACM 49(3), 33–36 (2006)
31. SLO [National Institute for Curriculum Development]: Digitale geletterdheid en 21e eeuwse vaardigheden in het funderend onderwijs: een conceptueel kader. SLO, Enschede (in preparation)
32. Collis, B.: Computers, curriculum and whole-class instruction: Issues and ideas. Wadsworth, Belmont (1988)
33. Bennett, S., Maton, K.: Beyond the digital natives debate: Towards a more nuanced understanding of students' technology experiences. Journal of Computer Assisted Learning 26, 321–331 (2010)
34. Kennedy, G., Judd, T., Dalgarno, B., Waycott, J.: Beyond natives and immigrants: exploring types of net generation students. Journal of Computer Assisted Learning 26, 332–343 (2010)
35. Law, N., Pelgrum, W.J., Plomp, T.: Pedagogical practices and ICT use around the world: findings from the IEA international comparative study SITES 2006. CERC Studies in Comparative Education. Comparative Education Research Centre, The University of Hong Kong, Hong Kong and Springer, Dordrecht, The Netherlands (2008)
36. Law, N., Lee, M.W., Chan, A.: Policy impacts on pedagogical practice and ICT use: An exploration of the results from SITES 2006. Journal of Computer Assisted Learning 26, 465–477 (2010)
37. OECD Programme for International Student Assessment, http://www.oecd.org/pisa/
38. Bryderup, I.M., Larsen, A., Trentel, M.Q.: ICT-use, educational policy and changes in pedagogical paradigms in compulsory education in Denmark: From a lifelong learning paradigm to a traditional paradigm? Education and Information Technologies 14, 365–379 (2009)
39. Onderwijsraad: Een smalle kijk op onderwijskwaliteit. De stand van educatief Nederland 2013. Onderwijsraad, Den Haag, The Netherlands (2013), http://www.onderwijsraad.nl/upload/publicaties/751/documenten/stand-van-educatief-nl-v13-def.pdf

From Student Geek to Teacher Geek Chic – Reflections on How Computers Were Used while as a Student and then as a Teacher

Therese Keane

Swinburne University, Melbourne, Australia
tkeane@swin.edu.au

Abstract. This chapter is a reflection on the use of computers in the author's time as a secondary school student, and then subsequently five years later as a qualified teacher of Information Technology. Despite the uneven teaching of computing in the 1980s low student enrolments, and the marginalization of the subject, computing flourished in the 1990s. With ever increasing enrolments for computing subjects, and a strong demand to access the computer room, resources were stretched and tensions were high. Some of the early problems that surfaced with the introduction of computing have been resolved, whilst others continue to be a challenge.

Keywords: Computers across the Curriculum, Access, Professional Development.

1 Introduction

After the introduction of computers into educational environments in the 1980s, many attempts were made to facilitate and integrate their use into the curriculum. While it was revolutionary at the time to have, at great expense, a laboratory of computers in a school, a number of issues soon became apparent. These included: access to computers, appropriate professional development and leadership to enable an integrated approach to computers across the curriculum. Some of the issues that were discovered early in the introduction of computing in schools continued to be problems for at least three decades until technology became mobile and affordable.

The use of information and communications technology is comparatively new and, more importantly, expanding rapidly, so that there is little valid past experience to draw on in constructing a map of the future. When computers were first introduced into education, they were stand-alone machines. That is, they did not network or communicate with other computers. As the computers were located in one classroom, they did not lend themselves to be used in teaching and learning by others. Apart from the highly specialist nature of operating the computer, most teachers had no concept of how to navigate their way through the operating system, unless they were trained. It was also hard to imagine other uses for computers outside the traditional uses of these machines such as programming or word processing.

The main technical decision to be made in the 1980s was whether to choose between Apple computers or IBM clones. IBM clones were known to be business

A. Tatnall and B. Davey (Eds.): History of Computers in Education, IFIP AICT 424, pp. 94–109, 2014.

machines. These computers would prepare students to enter the job market at the completion of their studies, unlike Apple, which were seen as an educational tool used in schools. Incidentally, Apple computers were considerably higher in price than the IBM clones that were flooding the market.

2 Computing in the 1980 through the Eyes of a Student

In Victorian secondary schools in Australia, computing first appeared as a subject in its own right in the classroom in the early 1980s, when Year 12 Computer Science was introduced as a Higher School Certificate (HSC) subject in the final year of secondary school. Computer Science was a formal subject that required a specialist understanding of the technology needed to teach the syllabus. Unlike other subjects, Computer Science required the use of computers, a thorough understanding of computer architecture, and the ability to navigate the operating system and use the command line interface [1, 2, 3]. Computers in the early 1980s were rather primitive and unfriendly when compared to today's machines. The teaching of Computer Science was not considered to be an easy task as there were limited classroom resources to aid in the teaching of the subject. Because there was no method study in teaching computers, teachers who taught Computer Science taught some other subject first – often Mathematics or Science. Usually teachers who taught Computer Science had either demonstrated an enthusiasm for computers or had been exposed to computers at university or work. This was because, as Jones et al. [1] pointed out:

> *Prior to 1970 very few Australian teacher education students had any contact with computers. While universities had computers and taught computer science, school computing activities were almost non-existent. Then teacher education institutions began to recruit mathematics and science staff with some computing background. [1]*

Kennedy [4] believed that "*computer teachers were seen to be 'science and maths' people capable of operating computers and were usually misunderstood*" [4]. May [5] argued that computers "*became the responsibility of people who were either interested in them or were required to use them in their teaching areas – usually the librarians and science/mathematics teachers*" [5].

In the early 1980s the Computer Science subject offered in the final year of secondary schooling in Victoria was regarded as a niche or a novelty subject as it was relatively new and attracted small numbers of students. The subject was largely technical and practical and comprised of programming, social implications of computing, hardware and electronics as an elective [6, 7]. The large capital outlay needed to purchase a classroom full of computers in a school in the early 1980s was seen to be prohibitive by some. This, combined with the high costs of insurance, and the extra effort required in security, ensured that the equipment was usually locked away [8].

Computer networking was still in its infancy, with wires and cables exposed. This was bulky and cumbersome in contrast to today's standards where they would not meet occupational health and safety standards. Apart from the highly specialist nature of operating the computer, most teachers had no concept of how to navigate their way through the operating system, unless they were trained. More importantly, it was sometimes hard to imagine other uses for computers outside the traditional uses of these machines. Moreover, Dowling [9] stated that computers used in education in the 1980s "were not developed with education in mind" [9], as they were created for and predominately used in business.

Nevertheless, shortly after the introduction of computers in schools, a great deal of thought and attention was given to using computers in educational settings and across the curriculum. Whilst the earliest approaches towards computing focused on understanding and using the computer itself, there were changes on the horizon [1].

2.1 My Student Journey

As a teenager attending secondary school in Victoria, Australia, my first interaction with a computer was in 1986. I was in Year 9 at a small, Catholic school for girls; Ave Maria College. This school was neither prestigious, nor competitive, nor affluent compared to many of the other schools in the vicinity. There were no strong female role models encouraging us that we could be anything we wanted to be, and the best we could hope for was perhaps a career in hairdressing, administration, nursing or teaching. Because the school offered domestic and commercial streams of study in addition to general academic subjects, there was a lab of electronic typewriters in place. In the 1980s, a lab of Apple IIes dedicated to learning about computing was developed in addition to the typewriting room.

Despite the school having other specialized rooms such as kitchens for home economics, textiles and science, the most expensive equipment in the school was the Apple IIe lab. Not surprisingly, these computers were heavily guarded, and locked away. As a student in Year 9 in 1986, computer classes seemed very sporadic as they were elective units and often school-planned activities seemed to interfere with them. Seemingly weeks went by without actually touching the computers.

As the prevailing idea was that we needed to learn about the computers before we could use them, very little time was spent in the computer room working on the computers. Instead, we studied theory from a textbook called *Welcome to Computers* [10] as we needed to learn about computer hardware, particularly the Central Processing Unit (CPU), the Arithmetic Logic Unit (ALU), input and outputs, memory and communication lines. Input and output were very simple in terms of keyboards, cards, magnetic ink character recognition, visual display units and printers. We spent time considering the difference between RAM and ROM and we had to recite the types of storage devices, such as magnetic tapes, magnetic disks, floppy disks and cassettes. Additionally, we studied the history of computers and the Information Revolution, Banking and Technology. We often did the theory outside of the computer lab.

Most of the theory was bland, and not very relevant to the interests of students studying computers. Much of what we were learning about computers was abstract, and irrelevant. The closest I got to a storage device was a 5¼" floppy disk, but even then, there were rules of engagement such as appropriate ways of holding the disk and replacing the cover when not used. There seemed to be a lot of rules that came with using computers, even before we were able to do anything with them.

Looking back, much of what I was taught seemed superficial. What I can't separate is whether what I studied as a student was challenging back then, or whether the standards have changed so much, that what we studied appears to be very watered down. Looking through my school reports, it was documented that the practical work we completed included using *AppleWorks – word-processing*, *Logo, Print Shop* and *BASIC*. Even programming using *BASIC* was rudimentary, as the most challenging aspect was to use variables and print output onto the screen.

My experience of using computers was limited by my teachers' own ability and confidence in using computers. Computing was only taught in the computer studies subject. However more optimistically, a report from the school Annual in 1986 mentioned the integration of computers into the curriculum particularly in Year 7 and 8, however revealing very little detail on how they were actually used [11]. As computer provision in schools was through desktops, it was difficult to provide computers for classroom use outside the computer labs, the solution was to bring the computer to the classroom as outlined in the school Annual. "*In addition, computers are trolleyed to other rooms according to teachers' needs*" [11]. The concept of bringing the computer to the classroom was way ahead of its time, but one has to question the wisdom of having a ratio of one computer to 33 students and the actual learning that took place.

Interestingly, the school maintained and ran both a computer lab and an electronic typewriter lab. The electronic typewriter lab was where we learnt touch-typing and no consideration was given that perhaps touch-typing could be taught in the computer lab. However, there was differentiation between touch-typing and word processing as the school had seven desktop PCs in the back of the Typing room segregated by glass. These PCs were dedicated to word-processing as documented in the school Annual: "The students have the opportunity to use modern equipment both for typing and word processing. All typewriters are electronic and there are seven computers available for word processing using WordStar Software" [12]. Not surprisingly, the electronic typewriters disappeared after my secondary schooling and computers prevailed!

Year 10 Computer Studies in 1987 got off to a rocky start. The first teacher who was allocated the subject resigned before the school year began so we did not have a computer teacher for the commencement of the school year; therefore we were not permitted to use the computer lab. The next teacher then only stayed for a few months and she too resigned. We were not particularly unhappy as most of our classes were dedicated to cleaning up the computer room. Upon reflection, this was a time wasting activity to avoid using computers as was replenishing the printer paper supplies by retrieving boxes of paper and bringing them up to the computer room.

For some weeks after the departure of this second teacher, we were unable to use the lab again. The school tried desperately to fill the teacher gap, and the best it could do was to find two *teachers in training* who were not fully qualified but could fill the hole. *George* and *Russell* were young, enthusiastic and brought the subject to life. Gone were the days of cleaning up the room, or learning theory. They sourced equipment that the school didn't have and demonstrated it to us, brought in guests, let us use AppleWorks and played games such as *Super-Bunny* and *Bubble Bobble*. Incidentally, that year, we were expected to purchase a textbook called *Programming Is Fun!* [13]. To this day my copy has remained unopened.

Notwithstanding the disruptions that came with learning about computing, we had to make some serious choices about our future and the subjects that would assist us to make these decisions. My father encouraged me to *like* computers not necessarily from an academic perspective, but rather because he thought it was good for me even though he wasn't sure precisely how. My father was a blue-collar migrant and he wanted a university education for me. He sacrificed a large amount of money and purchased a brand new Apple IIe with a mouse, a green monochrome screen and a LaserWriter printer. My mother disliked my Apple IIe at home as she blamed it for not having a well-deserved holiday - or money to renovate her kitchen. This expensive computer was a contentious object in the house.

Nevertheless, despite how badly computing was taught at this school, and my personal experiences, I persevered with the subject and selected it in Year 11. Gone were the days that we had to learn theory in different rooms, pick up rubbish off the floors, or do *fill in* work because we didn't have a teacher. As a result of the poor introduction to Computing in Years 9, and 10, there was a marked decline in student enrolments in this subject with fewer than 10 students studying Year 11 Computing. There was the right balance of theory and practical and the room was ours! The textbook we used was *Computer Science for Year 11* [14] focusing on word processing and databases using AppleWorks, problem solving and programming in Pascal.

At the same time, there was a big push by the Victorian Government for girls to *do* Mathematics in the late 1980s. The media campaign urged girls to realize that, *Maths Multiplies Your Choices* and encouraged parents by telling them to *Don't Pigeon-hole Your Daughters* [15]. The campaign to encourage girls to study Maths did not apply to Computing. Although the school provided computer classes, we were nevertheless conditioned that girls' didn't *do* computers and the subject was not seen as important as Mathematics. Despite these barriers in Year 11, I cemented my interest in computing. I found a geeky interest that nobody really shared, especially none of the students in my year level.

In my final year of schooling, the school did not offer Computer Science, as there was not enough interest to formulate a class. Not deterred by this, and determined to study something I was interested in, I chose to study this subject at Footscray TAFE (Technical and Further Education – an education institute for students who wanted to pursue a vocational career) on Saturdays as well as continuing to study my final year of secondary schooling at my home school. The home school did not offer Physics either – and the two students who wanted to study this subject had to also make alternative arrangements. Computer Science [3] was a real computing subject! It was rigorous, challenging and stimulating. It focused on programming and engineering and the class was predominately male, and taught by an American whose pronunciation of computer terms such as *data* and *iteration* somehow made the subject feel authentic! Computer Science challenged me, especially the programming activities, and it was the first time that I understood the importance of studying Mathematics, applying logic to solving problems and the study of Science. It was in my final year of secondary school that I found what I really enjoyed, making sense of my world and that this was the career I wanted to move into, the teaching of computers to students. After completing an Education Degree I began teaching in 1994.

3 Issues in the 1990s as Faced by Teachers

3.1 Computers across the Curriculum

Anderson [16] noted that in the early 1980s, Australia was one of the countries enthused about the use of computers in education. However, he also remarked that:

> *A majority of Australian teachers have been reluctant users of drill and practice type programs, preferring the newer possibilities offered by the use of computers in the tutee and tool modes where students direct the learning to a greater degree. [16]*

Downes and Fluck [17] noted how the "focus shifted toward emphasizing the computer as a pedagogical tool for improving learning (OECD 1987)" [17]. The term *Computers Across the Curriculum* was used to refer to the sea change that was about to occur.

The National Advisory Committee on Computers in Schools [18] released a report called *Teaching, Learning and Computers* which advocated the extended use of computers across the curriculum. The idea was to open up the computer room and invite non-specialist teachers to use the equipment in their teaching and learning. This was to be a big leap forward in integrating computers across the curriculum. However, despite the early enthusiasm and optimism by teachers, a number of factors started to emerge that hindered the progress of what appeared to be a simple enough idea. Kennedy [4] summed up these problems at the time:

> *Poor machine performance, inappropriate software, lack of organisation techniques in timetabling and time framing, difficulty in gaining computer laboratory access, inferior machine integrity and no training or awareness of proper management strategies, all compounded to cause frustration, alienation and 'fear' of the computer by the uninitiated in the schools. [4]*

3.2 Access

In the 1980s and early 1990s teachers, particularly in secondary schools experienced what was almost a universal problem of access to computer rooms. Kennedy [4] argued:

> *A laboratory is not always the ideal. Students may see the computers as a separate entity, a special area of study, a tool divorced from their learning in other curriculum areas. Music labs, art departments and trade workshops are dedicated specific areas and usually these rooms*

> *have purposeful applications and hardware/software, peculiar to a certain discipline, and are the exception to this philosophy. Computer must be accessible as possible. [4]*

Despite the large push to integrate computers into a variety of subjects, gaining access to computer laboratories was seen as a major obstacle. Teachers who were motivated to improve the teaching and learning outcomes for their students using computers found it very difficult to access the computer room as this facility was often dominated by scheduled computer studies classes.

The problem of access continued to be an issue as the popularity of Information Technology subject increased. Means, Olsen and Singh [19] put the view that:

> *Technology cannot become a useful support for students' work if they have access to it for only a few minutes a week. Technology supported, project-based instruction requires a higher degree of access to the tools of technology and to communication systems. Schools are faced with the reality of a limited budget for equipment, telecommunications, and software, and they must make hard choices about how to get the most out of what they have. [19]*

Even though Means et al. [19] were referring to student access, it was obvious that the same conditions of access in schools impacted on the teachers' ability to use computers in the classroom

3.3 Emerging Technologies

In the early years of computing in schools, the technological focus was on hardware, software and programming [20]. The major decisions that had to be made were based on which platform to implement within each school. This, in turn, also influenced the software used within the classroom. Apple computers were student friendly and were easy to use and there was considerable educational software commercially available to use in the classroom. Despite this, Dyson [21] found that software belonging to the "Apple II family and the type of software that it uses has not facilitated the integration of computers into the classroom" [21].

Some schools preferred to use IBM compatible computers, which were specifically business-oriented machines. One of the drawbacks of using an IBM compatible machine was that the need to know DOS commands made it more difficult to use than the Apple machines. Moreover, much of the software was not specifically written for educational purposes. Part of the justification for moving to the business machines was to expose students to industry used software such as word-processing, spread-sheeting and databases.

Whilst in the 1980s the issues of information technology integration into education focused on hardware and software, the 1990s saw the emergence of other technologies such as portable computing, networking of computers and then the subsequent explosion of the Internet [22].

3.4 Learning and Teaching

How students used computers in education continued to be a major issue in schools. A distinction could be made between how computers were being used in school and how they were being integrated in school. Computers being *used in education* often meant a variety of applications such as playing computer games, creating banners, word-processing and using clipart which did not have a curriculum focus. On the other hand, computers integrated into the curriculum referred to computers being used within subject content. The negative aspects of computer usage drew criticism such as that made by Dyson [21] who concluded:

> *Being used, rather than integrated, meant that the computers were used for games or activities that had nothing to do with the classroom curriculum. This information indicated that very little integration of computers into the classroom was in reality occurring. [21]*

From early on, there was a drive to introduce the use of computers into other subjects and not just in specialist computer offerings. Applications such as word processing, spreadsheets and databases were the most common types of software tools taught to students in specialist subjects such as Computer Studies or Information Technology [23]. There were several problems with this approach. It began to emerge that there was an expectation that the software application would be taught in the Information Technology subject, with the result that some teachers *opted out* of improving their own understanding of computer skills. Moreover, applications taught in the Information Technology subjects lacked a context outside that subject. Students found it difficult to make the connection of how a particular software tool solved a particular type of problem outside of the specialist computing subject. Spreadsheets, for example could be used in Mathematics and in Accounting; however, when taught in a specialist computer studies subject students, often found it difficult to apply their skills in other subjects. It was not until the use of computer based software was mandated in the final year of secondary school in Accounting that there was a formal requirement to use computers in a non-computing subject.

3.5 Professional Development

From the outset, professional development was a major issue for the integration of computers into the curriculum. The need for teachers to be confident in using and managing computer hardware in a classroom situation was important. They not only needed to be self-assured in being able to perform simple troubleshooting such as feeding paper into a printer, fixing paper jams and being able to switch on and off computers, but also competent in how to integrate computers into their subject content. However, the problem was that teachers had no formal training in how to use computers or integrate them into their specific subject area. It wasn't mandatory to learn how to integrate computers into subjects and so training was done on an ad-hoc basis.

A number of questions arose around the responsibility of who did the training. Where was training performed and who coordinated the overall way training was to occur? Leadership in this area was clearly lacking. Whilst some organizations such as the Computer Education Group of Victoria (CEGV – a subject association for the teaching of computers) were providing professional development, Keane [8] stated that attempts were made by various government agencies to in-service key staff who would act as change agents in the schools. It was evident that teachers required further, ongoing and sustained support on how to use computers in education.

Many excuses for not being able to integrate computing across the curriculum were evident, however the main problem was that the integration of computing in content-based subjects was seen as an add-on rather than a seamless integration. Little [23] believed that:

> *for computing to become integral to, not additional to, the whole curriculum, not just individual subjects or indeed a separate subject itself. Computing needs to be seen as the vital and integral part that it is of all teaching and learning. [23]*

However, in a secondary school context the integration of computers into the various subjects was problematic. It was sometimes difficult to persuade teachers of the usefulness of information technology in their specialist areas. Professional development was seen as the key to dealing with this but the way forward was not altogether clear. Professional development was seen to be system wide problem rather than being related to any one school. This point of view was expressed by Graham and Martin [24] who argued:

> *There is a need for an overall professional development strategy rather than the existing fragmentation. Professional development programs should revolve around the best practice dissemination and sharing good models, action research linked to the curriculum and collegial training in work groups. Internal training is preferable as there is often a mismatch between external professional development and an individual school's software and hardware. [24]*

Professional development, or training, remained necessary to support the innovations in teaching and learning using technology. Many educators believed that if teachers could manage computers, that is have some very basic level technical knowledge on how to maintain computers in a computer laboratory, that was sufficient. However this did not address the problem that the focus of using information and technologies should be leveled at learning and teaching. Cuttance [25] believed that:

> *This problem was exacerbated . . . by the focus of systemic training and development initiatives on technical skills, with little or no provision of programmes to support professional development in the integration of technology into the practice of teaching and learning. [25]*

To maximize the efficiency of professional development to teachers, it was important to focus on how information technology could be used in a classroom context, and the derived benefits from its use needed to be highlighted. Simply showing teachers how a software package worked was not adequate on its own, but showing how it could be used within context, and examining how it would be assessed was equally as important.

There were widespread discrepancies in information technology usage in the Independent, Government and Catholic education systems. Some Independent schools made leaps and bounds with their use of information technology through the use of Notebook computers which was pioneered at Methodist Ladies College in Melbourne (MLC – Private Independent girls school) by then Principal David Loader [26, 27]. However, there were many other schools that did not have a vision, or lacked direction in terms of infrastructure and staff professional development needs. What was apparent though, according to Roberts [28], was that:

> *Professional development is needed that is an integral part of daily practice for all teacher and schools. Such activities should respond to targeted needs and, in all facets of their planning, delivery and evaluation, model the behaviors that they advocate. [28]*

While professional development was understood to be important what form that professional development should take was by no means clear. One approach was a just-in-case mode of delivery with the danger that there was little or no consideration about the needs of the learner. Teachers may learn a skill using a particular software package, however this skill may never be applied as the teacher (learner) does not need to use it. The other, *Just In Time*, approach to professional development refers to training that is provided for a particular purpose, or as suggested by Glazer, Hannafin and Song [29], "support on demand" [29]. The advantage of just-in-time mode of delivery provides teachers with confidence to use the software just as they need to use it. Schrum [30] offered the suggestion that if information technology professional development were offered in a *just in time* model perhaps teachers would be more embracing and willing to experiment with software.

Professional development still continues to be a challenge for schools, even in the 21st century, where there are mixed abilities amongst the teaching profession to incorporate information technology into the prescribed curriculum.

3.6 My Teacher Journey

I commenced my teaching career in 1994, working at Parade College a large Catholic Boys school in the northern suburbs of Melbourne. The school had 1600 students and I was located on the Years 11 & 12 senior campus. In my first year of teaching, I taught four Year 12 (final year of secondary school) classes of Information Processing & Management (IP&M – a final year IT subject). Two of the classes had a programming focus and the other two classes were dedicated to the use of applications. For most of my early teaching career, my workload was predominantly with Year 12 and I often taught four Year 12 Information Technology classes. I also introduced Information Systems (IS – a final year IT subject focusing on programming) into the College and this subject became more popular than IP&M. Statewide, students enrolments in Information Systems were considerably lower than in IP&M, given it was a niche subject that focused on programming. However, this was not the case at Parade College, where there were, at one time nearly 60 students were studying it. Many students excelled in Information Systems and the College did well amongst the top ranked schools in the State of Victoria for a few years.

Despite only five years separating my experience as a teacher from that of a student, the educational landscape had changed. Students really enjoyed studying Information Technology at Parade College and this was evident from Years 7-12. Students flocked to the elective units in Years 9 & 10 to study Information Technology. Parade College had four large computer labs scattered across the vast campus and they were heavily used, mostly by students studying Information Technology. The labs consisted of Apple Classic Macintoshes and served their purpose well. Computing was popular at Parade College and was a subject in demand. It was not something that was only for 'geeks'; rather it was a mainstream subject.

The strength of computer studies at Parade College was a reflection of the health of the subject across the State. In 1989, there were 1627 students studying Computer Science at Year 12. Information Systems, the successor to Computer Science, attracted approximately the same number of students with an enrollment 1660 students in 1995. It was the addition of the more application focused Information Processing & Management subject which saw enrolments skyrocket to 12,109, peaking in the year 2000 with 14,004 students [31].

This dramatic increase in interest in studying Information Technology did not automatically mean that students were naturally adept at studying computers. Parents often told me that their children were amazing with computers and how much they assisted family, friends and neighbors, or how they would spend hours on their computer in their room. This conversation almost universally came up at parent–teacher interviews, when it was brought to their attention that their children were not doing as well as expected. Despite all their know how, students were often not very good with theory. They did not understand how information was managed, processed and manipulated. Some students were not very competent or proficient at creating spreadsheets with mathematical formulas, or understanding different types of systems. Some were very good at playing games, but not much else.

Whilst these numbers were remarkable statewide, at the local school level, it put a lot of pressure to accommodate the demand. As computer rooms were a finite resource, schools could not simply turn an ordinary classroom into a computer lab, due to the substantial costs involved in setting up the room such as wiring, providing adequate furniture, adjustable chairs, air-conditioning, anti-static carpets and the hardware and software licenses required. At one point when I raised the need for more computer labs with the Principal, he firmly, but politely stated that he did not have an infinite pool of funds to build another lab – and each room taken to build a new lab would be one less classroom. There were limits to how many computer labs could be utilized and we would have to make do with what we had.

To add to the complex task of balancing the number of Information Technology subjects offered within the timetabling constraints, there needed to be teachers who could teach the subject. This proved challenging, as there were many teachers who thought they could teach computing, simply because they knew how to use a computer, however without a theoretical background in Information Technology, they often preferred to teach the subject exclusively through a practical, hands-on approach. Schools struggled to employ trained Information Technology teachers who had real expertise and could teach a balanced course. These teachers were hard to find, especially ones who were also able to teach Information Systems and provide students challenges and opportunities that pseudo Information Technology teachers couldn't.

The final year of secondary school Information Technology subjects provided challenges such as the Problem Solving Project assessment task in Information Systems which made great demands on students' abilities in programming and testing. There were also groundbreaking opportunities where students could be involved in something innovative. One of the highlights in my teaching career was preparing my IT students to talk to the MIR Cosmonauts as they did a pass over Australia as part of researching telecommunications. An amateur radio station was set up at the school with the assistance of an Information Technology teacher from another school – Maggie Iaquinto (VK3CFI), to enable the communication with three space scientists – Russians Valeri Korzun and Alex Kaleri and US crew member Jerry Linenger. Whilst students in several countries had quizzed cosmonauts in the past via ham radio, this was the first time that the questioning was from Information Technology students and the questions ranged from people, procedures, hardware and software. Ten students asked questions in a space of nine minutes, and they learned that Russians used Windows 95, they used anti-virus software and they spoke about the few communication difficulties because all crewmembers spoke both Russian and English. This was the first time that students were introduced to information technology in a global context with relevance and engagement [32]

At the same time as the significant increase in enrolments in Information Technology there was a push to integrate *computers across the curriculum* whereby teachers in other areas would try to use computers in their subjects. In this era desktop computers located in computer labs was still the dominant model for computer use and, due to timetabling constraints, the rooms were often used for Information Technology classes and there were few opportunities for others to get into the computer room.

Often private arrangements were made between teachers to swap rooms – but this was not a long term, sustained proposition. There was pressure from teachers who taught other subjects to make Information Technology teachers give up their teaching space in the lab so that others could be accommodated on a long-term basis. I fought this long and hard, as I did not want the timetable dictating how to teach. Perhaps my early encounters as a student left some deep-seated scars about not spending nearly enough time in the computer room. I never divided computer classes so that X number of days were dedicated to theory and the other days were dedicated to practical classes as I often intertwined theory with practice in any given class.

In my teaching career, my office was often attached to a computer room, providing me with opportunities to observe students from other classes. On many occasions, I couldn't help but notice that some non-Information Technology classes would book the computer room for a period and play games. There was a culture that it was acceptable for teachers to use the computer room so that they could get some respite and let their students play games. On one hand, there were teachers who wanted to use the computer room to do genuine activities with their students, and on the other, there were teachers who just wanted to treat and reward their students.

Some non-Information Technology teachers believed that if they could not get access into the computer labs, then they would not have to incorporate and integrate computers across the curriculum. Often these teachers lobbied for Information Technology teachers to teach generic skills such as spread-sheeting, word-processing and databases in Information Technology classes so that the responsibility would be shifted away from them. All too often school leaders, while recognizing that this approach was far from ideal, supported the teaching of these skills in Information Technology classes on the basis that they could point to the fact that the skills were being covered somewhere.

Given that computer rooms were bookable spaces, working with students sharing common equipment in computer labs created challenges. The vandalism that occurred in computer rooms was in most cases minor, but enough of a disruption especially when the computer could not be used and students had to share. One common transgression included the removal of mouse balls so the mouse wouldn't work, or the throwing of the balls around in the room. The first line of defence to minimalize disruption was to have a large bag of spare mouse balls. However as students realized that the Information Technology technician would simply replace them, the mouse balls would be taken and not found. The technicians decided that it was best to glue the casing that held the mouse balls, however the trade-off was that when dust and dirt got into the groove, the mouse was inoperable and had to be thrown out. As technology progressed, and students had more exposure to information technology, other disruptive action was taken, such as the cutting of the cords of both the mouse and the keyboard. Other destruction included the swapping of keyboard keys so that the *qwerty* keys on a keyboard were rearranged, or that paperclips, or foreign objects were pushed into the 3½" disk drive space. Colleagues from other schools that used PCs often reported stolen RAM chips, as memory was expensive. The vandalism generally happened prior to my classes, and when I used to drill down to which class was last in the computer room, it would appear that vandalism often took place when there was an emergency teacher or when another class had done a swap with another Information Technology class.

As I was considered to be an *expert* in Information Technology simply because I taught the subject to students, I was asked to deliver professional development to my colleagues. There were two main reasons why the school believed it was important to provide professional development. The first was due to the large financial outlay in equipment and room setup the school needed to ensure that the computers were being used, and secondly because the Principal wanted to empower teachers on how to use the equipment. It was fair to say that many staff did not have any formal training on how to use computers much less how to use them in their classroom. The other reason was that the school had to be seen to be proactive in providing professional development in this area. Sending staff to one-off professional development in how to use computers was expensive, but also counterintuitive as one-off professional development sessions were often forgotten and did not add value [33]. I was asked to provide professional development workshops to teachers in the use of the common software used in the College: Hypercard, Word, Excel and Quickmail.

Parade College was exclusively an Apple school until 2001. Students and parents alike would often ask, why do we have Macs, and why don't we use business machines? This question was one of the key debates of the 1990s, along with access to computer rooms, content of Information Technology courses and appropriate professional development for teachers. Developments over the past decade and a half, including recent Australian Government policy has meant that some of these issues have been largely resolved [34].

4 Concluding Comments

Since the introduction of computers into educational environments, many attempts have been made to facilitate and integrate their use into the curriculum. Central to the problem of the integration of computers into the curriculum has been that each step along the way has been into unchartered territory. The use of information technology was comparatively new and, more importantly; expanding so rapidly that there was little valid past experience with which to construct a map of the future. Those who chose to replace their Apple computers with IBM clones in the 1980s because the clones prepared the students for business, could have hardly have imagined the current context of a world wide web, e-mail, Intranets, portals, tablets, apps, podcasts, blogs, and virtual spaces.

When computers were first introduced into education, they were considered to be stand-alone. That is, they did not network or communicate with other computers. As time has passed, and more progress has been made with technology, they have filtered down into schools where it is now the norm for computers to be networked to other computers, including the Internet. Whilst some of the early problems of computing may have been resolved, there are some that are still ongoing such as teacher confidence in using information technology tools and practices, the amount of curriculum devoted to the teaching of applications and the assessment of theory and practice.

References

1. Jones, A., McDougall, A., Murnane, J.: What did we think we were doing?: Reflections on the history of educational computing in Victoria. In: Impagliazzo, J., Lee, J.A.N. (eds.) In History of Computing in Education, pp. 63–72. Dordrecht, Kluwer (2004)
2. VISE: High School Certificate Course Description - Computer Science Victorian Institute of Secondary Education, Melbourne (1984)
3. Victorian Institute of Secondary Education: High School Certificate Course Description - Computer Science Victorian Institute of Secondary Education, Melbourne (1984)
4. Kennedy, G.: From Nowhere to Knoware. In: Computers - Contributing to Chaos or Change, pp. 135–144. Computers in Education Group of Victoria (1991)
5. May, C.: Information Technology Management in Schools. The Practicing Administrator 21, 40–41 (1999)
6. Duncan, N.: Year 12 Computer Science Exam Questions by Topics. Coghill Publishing, Melbourne (1987)

7. Holloway, K., Rae, C.: Model Practical Work For Computer Science. Computer Education Group of Victoria, Melbourne (1986)
8. Keane, W.: The Impact on Two Schools of the Victorian State Computer Education Committee "Seeding Pair" Inservice Course. Education, vol. Master of Educational Administration. Monash University, Melbourne (1988)
9. Dowling, C.: Computer - Contributing to Chaos or Change? In: Computers - Contributing to Chaos or Change, pp. 9–13. Computers in Education Group of Victoria (1991)
10. Oliver, R., Newhouse, P.: Welcome to Computers. Action Press, Morley (1982)
11. Watson, D.: Computer Studies. Vidian. Ave Maria College, Melbourne (1986)
12. Johns, C.: Business Studies Faculty. Vidian. Ave Maria College, Melbourne (1986)
13. Oliver, R., Newhouse, P.: Programming Is Fun. Napier Publications, Victoria Park (1984)
14. Tatnall, A., Davey, W.: Computer Science for Year 11. The Jacaranda Press, Queensland (1985)
15. Milburn, C.: Girls still lag boys in maths. The Age. Fairfax Media, Melbourne (2010)
16. Anderson, J.: Responses to Technological Change. In: Keeves, J.P., Marjoribanks, K. (eds.) Australian Education: Review of Research 1965-1998, pp. 327–353. ACER Press, Melbourne (1999)
17. Downes, T., Fluck, A., Gibbons, P., Leonard, R., Matthews, C., Oliver, R., Vickers, M., Williams, M.: Making Better Connections. In: Department of Education, S.T.D. (ed.) (2002)
18. National Advisory Committee on Computers in Schools: Teaching, Learning and Computers. Commonwealth Schools Commission (1984)
19. Means, B., Olsen, K., Singh, R.: Beyond The Classroom, Restructuring Schools with Technology. Phi Delta Kappan 77, 69–73 (1995)
20. Woodhouse, D., Johnstone, G., McDougall, A.: Computer Science. Jacaranda Press, Brisbane (1984)
21. Dyson, M.: Integration of Computer Software into the Primary Curriculum. In: Computers Champion Learning Tools Taking Stock, pp. 37–46. Computer Education Group in Victoria (1996)
22. Harasim, L., Hiltz, S.R., Telese, L., Turoff, M.: Learning Networks. The MIT Press, Massachusetts (1996)
23. Little, J.: Not Computers Across The Curriculum: Computing as Integral to the Curriculum - How do we Make this Change? Com 3(22), 34–45 (1997)
24. Graham, J., Martin, R.: Teachers, Schools & the New Technologies: A Discussion Paper. Australian Educational Computing 13, 6–12 (1999)
25. Cuttance, P.: School Innovation Pathway to the knowledge society. In: DEST, pp. 1–269 (2001)
26. Romeo, G.: The Impact of Computer Technology on Education. In: Townsend, T. (ed.) The Primary School in Changing Times: The Australian Experience. Routledge, London (1998)
27. Spender, D.: Nattering On the Net, Women, Power and Cyberspace. Spinifex, Australia (1995)
28. Roberts, J.: Integration of Information and Communication Technologies (ICTs) Through Teacher Professional Development: Issues and Trends in Canada. Judy Roberts & Associates (1999)
29. Glazer, E., Hannafin, M.J., Song, L.: Promoting Technology Integration Through Collaborative Apprenticeship. Educational Technology Research and Development 53, 57–67 (2006)

30. Schrum, L.: Technology Professional Development for Teachers. Educational Technology, Research and Development 47, 83–90 (1999)
31. Victorian Curriculum and Assessment Authority: VCE Unit Enrolments and Completions 1995-2012 (2013)
32. Keane, T.: Space History is Made. Tenet, vol. 6. Parade College, Melbourne (1997)
33. Fullan, M.: The Meaning of Educational Change. Teachers College Press, New York (1982)
34. Rudd, K., Smith, S., Conroy, S.: A Digital Education Revolution: Election 2007 Policy Document. Australian Labor Party, Australia (2007)

Whatever You Do . . . . Don't Put the Computer Room Near the Maths Department! or, I Was an Early Adopter, an Enthusiastic Disseminator, But Now . . .

David Demant

Museum Victoria, Melbourne, Australia
ddemant@museum.vic.gov.au

Abstract. This chapter contains accounts, descriptions and personal experiences in secondary schools in England, Canada and Australia, from the 1970s to the 1980s; a period which saw the widespread introduction of computers into schools. The chapter ends with stories from another educational institution. What I learnt:

- Think not what a computer can do for you; think what you can or cannot do with a computer
- Look for the best way to solve a problem; it might not involve a computer
- Learning always takes place in all situations, good bad and in-between [1][1], but for socially empowering outcomes:
  - there must be mutual respect between the participants, and
  - learners must have a measure of control over their learning.

Themes highlighted in this essay:

1. How computers did or did not change education
2. Teacher, parent and student expectations, concerns and visions
3. Use of computers 'across the curriculum'.

Keywords: computer, education, learning, empowerment, cut and paste, gender, professional development, cyber phobia, simulations.

1 I Fell In Love . . .

... with computing, when the first desktop machines were introduced. I played with spreadsheets, databases, controlling physics experiments, desktop publishing and word processing; I played!

[1] The 'secret' curriculum
"*The teacher who cannot speak to grief, who will not laugh and cannot weep, teaches many very deep and memorable lessons about tears, laughter, grief and shame. The secret curriculum is the teacher's own lived values and convictions written in the lineaments of his expression and in the biography of passions or self-exile written in his eyes. The teacher who appears to his children to be anaesthetized, sedated in the face of human pain may not teach them anything at all about medical racism, birth mortality, of My Lai. But he will teach them a great deal about the capability of an average adult to abdicate the consequences of his own perception and, as it were, to vacate his own soul.*"

A. Tatnall and B. Davey (Eds.): History of Computers in Education, IFIP AICT 424, pp. 110–120, 2014.

2 'Saul on the Road to Damascus'

My teaching life was a succession of infatuations – chemistry, photography, physics, science for the 'less able', school drama productions, electronics and computing.

I am a project person; I like change; routine makes me careless, there is no adrenaline to put that extra mile in. In the early 1980s, I was ready for another challenge. It came labelled with the number 64.

In 1983, I bought a Commodore 64 and spent that night programming a game of table tennis . . . but I secretly agreed with my partner's question: "why bother?"

My whole mood changed when I checked out the word processor program . . .

Liberation!

I could move text around, have headings, correct mistakes and . . . cut and paste! Word processing just automated what I had been doing – writing essays and worksheets on hundreds of separate pieces of paper, which I then cut and pasted.

Then came VisiCalc – unbelievable, mind-blowing!

But I can't remember the name of the word processing software.

3 Prologue

As a school kid, I had a major logistical problem with writing essays; I liked (still do) to produce a stream of words in no particular order, so I could get all my ideas down before I forgot them. I would then restructure the essay in a most time-consuming way by literally cutting and pasting. The tedium was increased when I was at university, having to write longer (and longer) reports and essays.

I would write paragraphs with spaces in between. Each paragraph would have a heading and, sometimes, two or three sub-titles. I would physically separate each paragraph with a pair of scissors, and arrange them in a more logical order. The process might be repeated two or three times. Finally, I wrote the essay in full.

I followed the same process when I was a teacher producing student worksheets. When I was satisfied, I would Roneo or Gestetner them or use carbon paper. My hand writing started beautifully but soon slanted, became smaller and illegible. I was rarely satisfied, often screwing up the stencils and starting again.

One day, I used my dad's typewriter. A doctor fed up with complaints about his handwriting, he had bought the machine. With it, I could produce consistently neat and legible paragraphs, and they were more interesting visually. One problem, white-out on the stencils never looked good.

Then came the photocopier; an improvement but with social problems at least in my school; only one person could operate the photocopier; he was a gatekeeper with many padlocks. You had to book weeks in advance; crawling was the only way to have your work ready on time.

On a one-year exchange in a Canadian school, I glimpsed the power of the Universal Machine. The physics teacher used four Commodore PETs and eight slide projectors to do a pictorial collage of the year at Christmas time. It was a little intimidating; he and a small group of students controlled the code and were too involved to explain it to the uninitiated.

Back home, I bought a Sinclair ZX81. It took an hour to load a game, which, at the last micro second, crashed. I never played that game. I felt left out, and not for the last time.

Then came the Commodore 64 . . .

4 Teaching the Teachers

As a teacher, I developed computer skills by myself and through various courses. I applied for a week's long professional development on setting up a computer department. I had the approval of the School Council; the Principal was very enthusiastic. There was an entry requirement: the Education Department would only allow a minimum of two teachers from a school, and one had to be female.

Only males on the staff were interested. At a staff meeting, the principal appealed for someone to join me: total silence. Then, suddenly, as if by magic, we all saw that a hand had been raised, and its owner was female: "the school needs a computer department; it's the coming thing – I'll go but it's not my thing". It never was, but I owe her.

I returned all fired up

With a good budget to support my efforts, I decided that the school needed a computer room as far away from the Mathematics and Physics departments as possible. Too many people were turned off by what they saw as unknown territory, one with fearful consequences, such as loss of control to machines.

I wanted the computer room at the very centre of the school, physically and culturally. I wanted it neutral. A sympathetic teacher gave me her room even though she did not like computers, and, previously, she had fought very hard for that room. It was perfect, opposite the main entry point for students. It had a small work room, which I used workshop cum store room. I obtained a number of Apple II Computers, disk drives, a couple of printers and a Mac. It was to be a place where the technically illiterate and fearful would feel welcome.

The school caretaker, a retired engineer, and I designed and produced mobile workstations, which could be used all over the school. They were designed to make it as easy as possible for people to use programs without any unnecessary preambles.

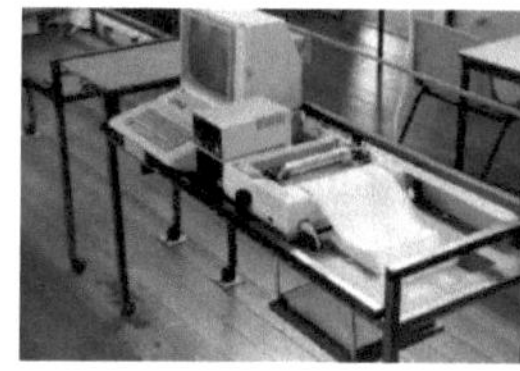
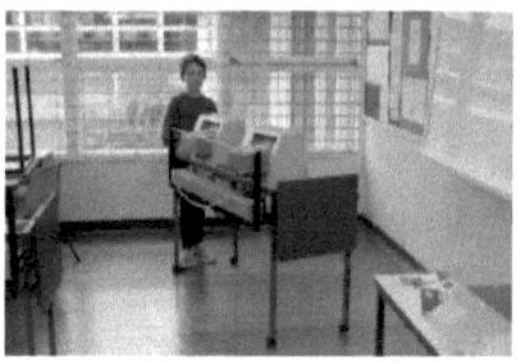

There were two spheres of activity in the computer department, training the teachers and running courses for the students. The first was much more difficult. Most teachers were very reluctant to adopt the new technology and a few could be described as 'cyber phobic'. One teacher was so fearful that he thought my choice of a different power socket, from the one used the previous week, was due to some evil desire on my part to dominate!

The teachers relied on me to assist them in the classes; the principal gave me time to do this. I ran classes in the use of applications, such as publishing, spreadsheets and word processing; the students and teachers had to collect the data themselves.

A history teacher took his class to the local cemetery and collected data from the gravestones – name, sex, date of birth and date of death. The data was entered into a spreadsheet. At first the searches were disappointing – how many were female, eighty years old and so on. The teacher felt it was not worthwhile, leading to no new historical understanding. I agreed with him secretly, but I knew this was a critical moment. If I could convince him of the value of computers for the development of historical understanding, then the other staff would be more receptive. One of the students noticed that there were a lot of deaths at an early age and at ages above 60; there were very few in the age range between. Analysis of the early deaths showed that many of them occurred in the 1920s. "The flu!" exclaimed the teacher; and the lesson developed from there. The teacher did not really take up computers independently, but others were inspired by this episode and similar ones.

Whatever a particular teacher's view, the students were mostly enthusiastic. The boys tended to want to play games while the girls were more interested generally in the word-processing and publishing software. I organised the lessons so the girls controlled access to the software and the hardware. This was accepted by most of the boys and it seemed that the girls gained much self-esteem through this. I organised a break-time club on the same basis. All went well until a group of teachers organised a girls' only computer club. One girl told me that she was sorry to leave my club but the girls felt obliged to join the other club. I soon had to pack up my club; all most boys wanted to do was to play games – the moderating influence of the girls was gone.

5 A Job at the Museum

In 1987, I joined Museum Victoria. Museums are not like schools. Museums are door openers; the best take-away message from a museum is "I must find out more . . ."

I became involved in developing exhibitions and programmes for general visitors and for teachers. In one exhibition about energy at Scienceworks, there was a section devoted to computer modelling of the climate.

Climate modelling display sponsored by the CSIRO and Bureau of Meteorology

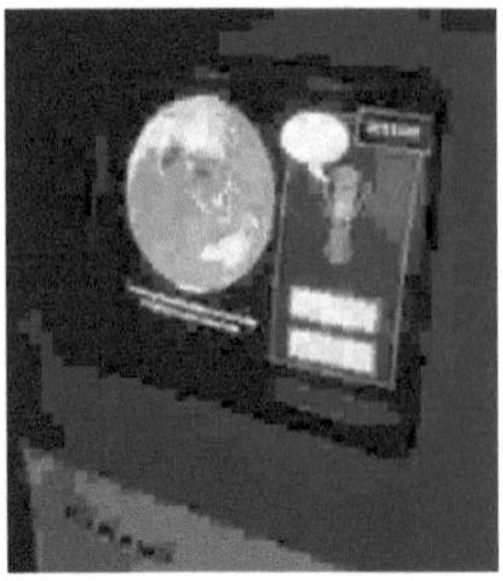

Touch screen interactive for modelling the Earth's climate

Other Scienceworks programmes included an educational package in which VCE[2] students gathered data about the old sewage pumping station. Back at school, they used appropriate software to present narratives or reports.

6 'The First Computer Mouse'

This book was part of a package of products designed to complement an exhibition on digital technology at the new Melbourne Museum, when it opened in 2000. The exhibition highlighted the history of digital technology; pride of place was given to CSIRAC – the first computer built in Australia, the fourth in the world, and the only intact first generation computer in existence. CSIRAC is an abbreviation for Commonwealth Scientific and Industrial Research Organisation Automatic Computer.

CSIRAC is currently on display in another area of Melbourne Museum

The book tells two stories in parallel: one about the humans who operate CSIRAC and one about super-technological mice [2].

'The first computer mouse' was aimed at 8 to 12 year old children and their adult carers. Illustrations and minimum text were designed to ensure that there was a clear distinction between fact and fantasy.

2 Victorian Certificate of Education.

Illustrated by Deborah Koolen

"Anna, Dan and Lucy are delighted when Grandad reminisces about the old computer he worked on when he was young. But more was happening than even Grandad realised. Under the floor was another world, whose inhabitants kept a careful watch on the humans and their computer . . . "

The take-away message of the book is that all computers, from the first to the latest, whatever their size or age, have essentially the same basic design: processor, memory, input and output. 'The first computer mouse' focuses the paper tape used as input and output, comparing it to their modern equivalents.

CSIRAC

CSIRAC, pronounced *sigh rack*, stands for Commonwealth Scientific and Industrial Research Organisation Automatic Computer. It is the only complete first-generation computer still in existence. CSIRAC was designed and built in Australia.
It was first switched on in 1949 and was switched off for the last time in 1964.
CSIRAC was one of the first digital computers the world.

Today, a simple pocket organiser has a similar power to CSIRAC.

Computer Mouse

In 1964, the first prototype computer mouse was developed. It was used with a 'windows' style screen. In 1970, the inventor, Douglas Engelbart received a patent for the wooden shell with two metal wheels. He described it as an 'X-Y position indicator for a display system.'

The 'First Computer Mouse' can be seen at the @digital.au exhibition at Melbourne Museum, Melbourne, Australia.

Note: the exhibition has been de-installed

7 You Don't Necessarily Need a Computer to Explain Digital Technology

An activity, called the Network Game, was another part of the package to support the digital technology exhibition. Simulating the net, it is best played with about hundred people. At the very beginning, the participants are told: "you are the Internet!"

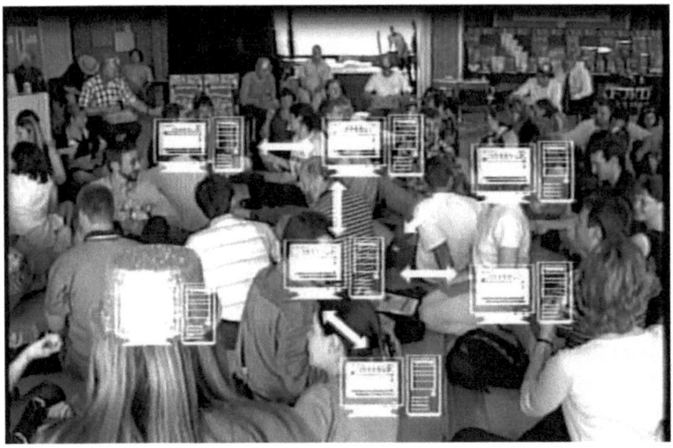

The internet consists of millions of computers connected together

Participants in the programme, which was run close to the exhibition, ranged from upper primary students to teachers.

The game is compered by a presenter and the following description is a heavily edited version of the script used by the presenter.

7.1 Introduction

The internet is basically made up of three types of computer. First is a client computer, for example your home computer. A client sends or receives messages to and from the second type - a server. Servers store the websites you want to access. Network computers (or routers) control the transport of messages between servers.

7.2 Building the 'Human' Internet

In a large space, a circle of six people (clients) sit on chairs forming a large circle. Each person wears a hat, labelled with a letter, A, B . . . or F.

Clients wear hats

Another six people (servers) sit on the floor next to each client on the inside of the circle. The rest of people are routers and sit on the floor. One router (blue circle) sits in the centre of the circle of people on chairs (clients: A, B, C, D, E, F). One server sits next to each one of the clients (A, B, C, D, E, F) inside the circle. Three routers sit around each of these servers. Four routers (black circles) sit evenly spaced at arm's length around the centre router. Three more routers (red circles) sit around each one of these four central routers.

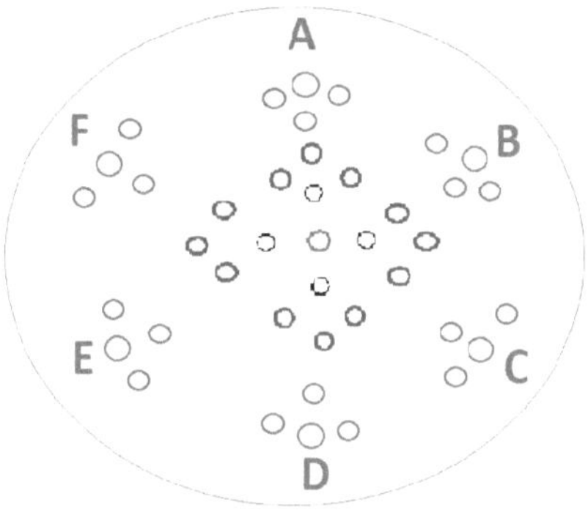

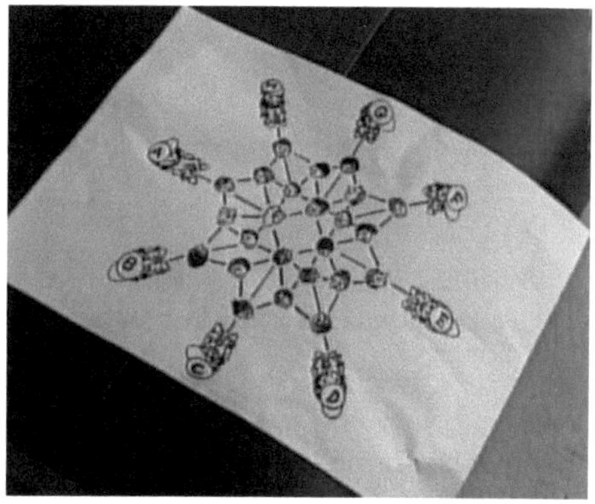

. . . each of the red routers is surrounded by three more routers . . . this goes on until there is no one left.

7.3 Background to the Game

The Internet carries an enormous volume of traffic and it is designed to deliver messages as efficiently and as fast as possible. Traffic jams are avoided by breaking messages into small packets so that each packet makes its own way to the destination server, choosing the least congested route.

7.4 Ping Pong Balls for Packets

Labelled ping pong balls can be used as packets; each labelled with a destination either A, B, C, D, E or F. Each client is given a box with lots of labelled ping pong balls (packets)[3].

7.5 The Rules

Clients give packets, one by one, to the nearest server. Servers pass packets, one at a time, to the nearest router. Routers pass one packet at a time to the closest available router. Packets can only be passed on if the other router can accept them. Routers can temporarily store packets in little baskets, but not if the basket is full. If they are full, no more packets can be accepted until one or more of the stored ones are passed on. A packet then tries another path. When the packets get to their destination, the clients store them in boxes.

[3] An extended version of the game involves the writing of messages, which are translated into digital code and labeled - see later in this chapter. Each packet is identified with symbols or numbers representing the sender, receiver, message ID, and position of packet in the message. The packets are then folded and used in the game instead of ping pong balls.

Packets stored temporarily in a router's memory

Packets can travel back as well as forwards - by any available path - it does not matter.

It does not matter which path the messages take. If you send a message to Sydney, some of the packets might go via Beijing, others via Paris, others via Buenos Aires, but they are all arrive at the same place.

7.6 The Game Is Played . . .

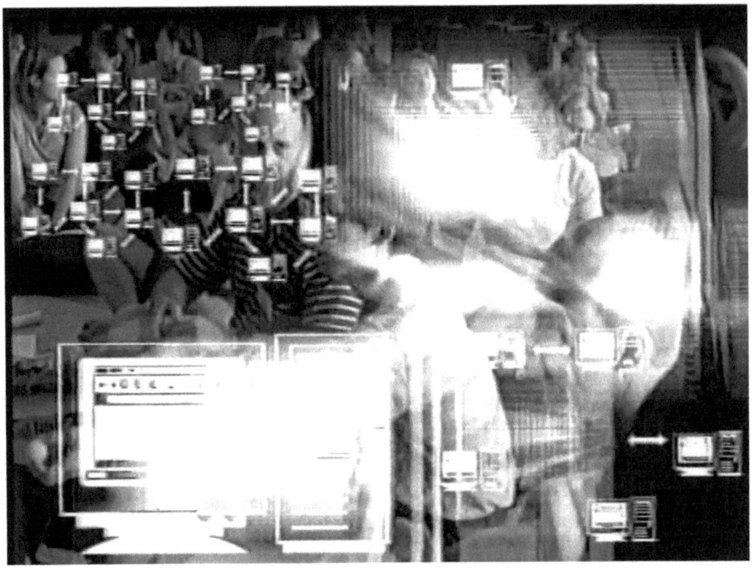

Humans simulating the net

7.7 Simulations

Once the participants have the general idea, some real life simulations can be tried.

- A cluster of 3 routers can stop passing packets to simulate sabotage or server crash. The network will still get the packets to their destinations using other routers.
- If a client fails, the packets destined for it have to be kept circulating or be stored until the client is operating again.
- If the destination mark is not clear, then the packet is condemned to circle the internet forever or until a router leaves it in its store or deletes it (i.e. chucks it on the floor).

7.8 Extension of the Game

An extended version of the game involves the writing of messages, translating into digital code on a grid drawn on a sheet of paper, cutting the paper grid into separate sections and constructing paper packets.

Coding the message on a grid

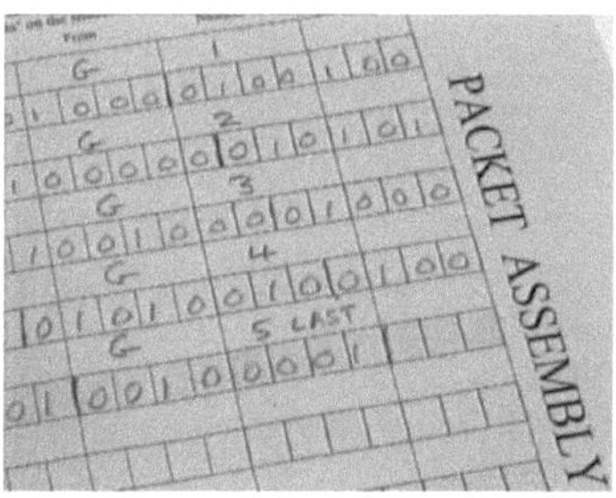

Labelling the packets

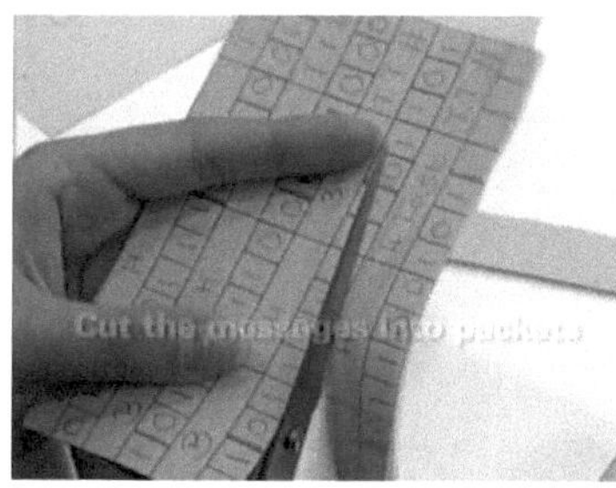

Cutting out the packets

Each packet is identified with symbols or numbers representing the sender, receiver, message ID, and position of packet in the message. The packets are then folded and used in the game instead of ping pong balls. After the game, the messages are reassembled from the pile of packets, and decoded.

8 I was an Early Adopter, an Enthusiastic Disseminator, but Now . . .

I get tired of accessing websites that are designed to trap you or are just badly designed, but I like Google and Google translation. My resistance to Facebook is still high but less to LinkedIn. One day I received 25 emails from Facebook, each informing that a friend (a real one) had added another image. On one occasion, however, Facebook gave me a pleasant surprise: a pen friend, who I last saw in 1958, contacted me. The other day, I started learning how to use Microsoft Access to document my family history and I began to reach out to others using its web facility . . . and my brother's daughter in England put a lovely picture of her daughter on Facebook . . .

References

1. Kojol, J.: The Open School Room. Quarterly Book List, 1972 (Spring 1972)
2. Demant, D.: The First Computer Mouse. Museum Victoria Publications, Melbourne (2001)

The Beginnings of Computer Use in Primary and Secondary Education in Spain

Javier Osorio and Julia Nieves

Universidad de Las Palmas de Gran Canaria, Spain
{javier.osorio,julia.nieves}@ulpgc.es

Abstract. During the late 1970s, Spain began its political transition from a dictatorial regime to a democratic one. In the 1980s, the country evolved economically and socially in a process that was speeded up by its incorporation into the European Union. The early 1990s witnessed Spain's entrance into the international arena, culminating with the successful organization of the Olympic Games in 1992. During these effervescent years, transformations in almost every facet of the country's make-up also affected the educational field. In this evolving situation, microcomputers arose and were incorporated into the educational space. At the end of the 1970s, the presence of computers at the primary and secondary education levels was practically non-existent. During the 1980s, an intense governmental effort took place to massively introduce computers in classrooms through institutional plans and policies. The results were uneven, and the greatest benefit was possibly observed in the use of the computer to manage schools, an aspect that experienced great development but was not equaled by the use of the computer to introduce new educational methodologies.

Keywords: Primary and secondary education, computers, educational history, Spain, 1980s.

1 Introduction

The second half of the 1970s was characterized by important changes in Spanish society. After the death of the dictator in November 1975, there was a progressive political transformation toward a democratic regime that culminated in 1978 with the passing of the Constitution that continues to be the basis for the Spanish legislative framework. This Constitution signified the normalization of political parties and defined a territorial model of the country based on a high level of political autonomy by its regions. These regions eventually created their own regional parliaments and governments with complete decision-making capacity in certain areas. Thus, except for defense and foreign policy, the majority of the decisions were gradually becoming decentralized, so that each region, also called autonomous communities, had the capacity to make decisions, while respecting the agreements established in the Constitution.

A. Tatnall and B. Davey (Eds.): History of Computers in Education, IFIP AICT 424, pp. 121–130, 2014.

Education participated in these political changes and was one of the decision-making areas whose management was entrusted to regional governments. The educational decentralization was carried out in a transitory way. At the beginning of the 1980s, six autonomous communities took control of their own educational management (Catalonia, Galicia, the Basque Country, Andalusia, The Canary Islands and the Valencian Community), while the other 11 postponed the transference of competences in educational matters and remained under the management of the central Spanish government through the Education Ministry. In other words, for most of this decade, the model for educational management was based on the coexistence between an institution that managed the majority of the national territory in educational matters (Education Ministry) and six other regional institutions with competences only in their own regions (Boards of Education). Throughout the 1990s, the educational administration became completely decentralized, and each region came to be responsible for managing education in their territorial setting. Figure 1 shows a map of the Spanish autonomous communities.

Fig. 1. Spanish autonomous communities as defined in the Constitution of 1978

Micro-computers and personal computers burst into this scenario, especially from 1981 on, with the appearance of the compatible IBM-PC. This device rapidly found a place in all areas of economic and professional activity. The educational field has traditionally been a step behind the economic arena in incorporating computers into its functioning. However, the wave of the PCs was so intense that the education sector rapidly became immersed in incorporating these devices in their schools. Nevertheless, the lack of computer resources and personnel trained in their use in the primary and secondary schools was a strong impediment to carrying out initiatives for the adoption of information technology by individual schools.

The exceptions consisted of initiatives by teachers who voluntarily took their own computers into the classroom, more for demonstration purposes than as a work tool.

Those responsible for the schools were increasingly aware of the importance that this type of technology could have in the learning process, but they were unable to make large scale implementation plans due to a lack of economic capacity and, above all, the scant or non-existent willingness of many teachers to change their teaching methods and receive training in the use of these devices. During the 1980s, computer science was not an obligatory subject in primary and secondary schools. This was not the case in the universities, where there was already a bachelor's degree in information technology, as well as a computer class in the majority of the scientific and technological degree programs. Young teachers who had studied computer science in their university phase were gradually incorporated into primary and secondary education, which led to the appearance of leaders and coordinators in the schools they had joined and constituted the launching pad for progressively changing the attitude of the teaching staff about the use of information technology (IT) in classrooms.

The schools' initial incapacity to carry out this process in an isolated way gave rise to policies by both the national government and the regional governments with autonomy in educational matters for the development of information technologies in primary and secondary schools. Previously, an OECD report had been published pointing out Spain's delay compared to other OECD countries, and encouraging the government to develop policies to promote the new technologies.

2 Governmental Plans to Promote Information Technologies

The new political situation in Spain influenced the way IT was incorporated into the educational system. Aware of the need to plan the transition to IT use in an orderly way, people in charge of education from the central government and from the six regions with competence in education agreed to work together on this matter, although each institution would independently manage the implantation in its own region. Thus, even though they all had similar objectives, seven parallel projects were developed with different names and plans, which were the following:

- The Atenea Project, developed by the Education Ministry and implanted in the 11 regions that did not have their own educational competences.
- Program of educational computer science Project, developed in Catalonia.
- The Abrente and Estrela Project, developed in Galicia.
- The CERED Project, developed in the Basque Country.
- The Zahara Project, developed in Andalusia.
- The Ábaco Project, developed in the Canary Islands.
- The Programa Informática a l'enseyament Project, developed in the Valencian Community.

All of these projects lasted from four to six years, up until the beginning of the 1990s. In the first half of this decade, a new educational system was implanted in Spain, which meant the attention was focused on the new model and its implications for teaching and evaluation methodologies. This change absorbed the majority of the financial and human resources. Thus, during the first half of the 1990s, once the projects for implanting IT in schools had ended, a new stage began that was characterized by the scant involvement of the educational authorities in this area. Moreover, there was a generalized feeling that IT was not a miraculous tool that would change teaching and learning methods, leading to certain pessimism about it (Area, 2008). In the second half of the 1990s, with the rise of the Internet, plans for developing IT in primary and secondary schools were revived, although this time with the objective of making the information society reach the educational setting.

The aforementioned projects shared common traits because, among other reasons, they were experimental projects with which there was no prior experience, and there was a high level of contact between the teams responsible for the different programs. One generalized characteristic of all of them was the elaboration of educational software through calls for participation directed to companies and the teachers themselves, who shared the modules they developed through calls or competitions with other colleagues. The educational software developed largely corresponded to the specific needs of each autonomous community. In some cases, it had a politically influenced bias due to an attempt to highlight historical or linguistic circumstances that differentiated some regions from others.

It can be concluded that the common denominator of all these policies was that they were projects with a Top-Down approach. In a country where the majority of the population did not have direct contact with computers, and the percentage of homes with a computer was insignificant, the priority was to make the students familiar with a new reality through the use of computers in primary and secondary schools. Then, as a result of this experience, their parents, sensitive to the importance of having tools to facilitate their children's learning, would gradually acquire these devices for domestic use.

The following paragraphs describe three of the aforementioned projects. The first project described had the greatest territorial extension, as it affected a large number of schools and teachers. The second project was developed in the Canary Islands, a group of islands that lies more than 1000 kilometers from the peninsular territory and is characterized by a broad territorial dispersion and, at that time, a lower income per capita than the national average. Finally, the initiative developed in Catalonia is described, as it is a region that has a greater income per capita than the Spanish average. Due to its proximity to other European countries, innovations are traditionally carried out sooner in Catalonia than in the rest of the Spanish regions.

2.1 The Atenea Project

Of all the projects for incorporating IT, the one that mobilized most resources and had the greatest repercussions was the Atenea Project, which, as mentioned above, was launched by the Education Ministry. It was not the first experience involving the use of computers in the primary and secondary education sector in Spain, given that Catalonia and the Basque Country, due to their autonomy in questions of education management, had already developed pioneer experiences, although with limited importance (Zufiaurre, 1994). The experimental phase of the Atenea Project began in 1985 and lasted until 1989. The budget assigned to it reached 37.5 million dollars (referenced to the year 1985). This budget was divided up, devoting 55% of the total to buying hardware, 25% to teacher training, and 20% to teaching materials (Arango, 1985). In its different stages, a total of 2,300 schools participated. The project's efforts focused on primary and secondary education, although the latter received a larger investment. Each center participating in the experience was initially given five micro-computers and a main disk unit, as well as printers.

The main objective of the project was to use the computer as a teaching tool for both the teacher and the students, in order to foster the teaching and learning efforts in both. A secondary objective was to use computers to manage the primary or secondary school. Over time this latter area was where computers' usefulness in the educational sector would be noted most, much more than in the improvements obtained in pedagogical innovation. However, the priority was always to foment the use of computers as an instrument for student learning and spread IT's utility and applications among the members of the school community (García, 2003). The plan created a teacher Responsible for the Atenea project in each center. This teacher received intensive training in the use of the computer and was responsible for training the rest of the teachers in the school in two stages. The first stage provided an initiation in the use of the computer, and another later stage focused on its educational uses.

It should be mentioned that the project was designed with the implicit objective of promoting families' demands for computer devices. Thus, the intention was to favor the national electronic components manufacturing industry, which at that time was in an embryonic stage. The technology adopted in basically all of Spain consisted of compatible IBM-PC computers with an MS-DOS operating system. The adoption of this technology was largely due to the efforts of companies like IBM and others that sell the PC compatible model to introduce it into the Spanish educational sector through donations and very competitive prices, compared to other systems such as the Apple Macintosh. In addition, the conditions for the purchase of the technology by the Education Ministry established that part of the equipment had to be manufactured in Spain, a condition that Apple could not fulfill and that definitively kept it from participating in the project. This situation was completely different from that of the United States, where Apple managed to strongly introduce itself in the educational computer market. In Spain, however, the presence of this type of computers was merely testimonial, with a very small percentage of the market compared to other countries like the United States. Only recently, with the development of the iPad e iPhone platforms, have Apple computers begun to carry some weight in the total computer park in Spain.

2.2 The Ábaco Project

The Ábaco project was developed in the Canary Islands, which form an archipelago where a stable population of 1.5 million inhabitants (INE, 1986) lived in the mid-1980s. The islands are located about 1400 kilometers from the European continent, across from the western coast of Africa. Until the 1960s, the main economic activities consisted of agriculture and commerce, gradually relinquishing the main role to tourism as the most important economic activity due to the development of commercial airlines. Therefore, the per capita income of the inhabitants of the islands has traditionally been lower than the national average. The low economic development, the distance from the continent, and the fragmentation of the territory on seven islands have been strong obstacles to the development of educational policies. With the democratic transition and a higher level of self-government, innovative educational programs that contemplated the particular socio-economic conditions of the region could be put into effect.

The Ábaco program was one of the pioneers in the Spanish ambit, beginning in 1984 and lasting until 1991. Initially, the experience was only extended to six centers in which expert personnel in IT and in psycho-education participated as the teachers. The training took place outside work hours. In each school, a computer room was created, and teachers from two other observer schools were invited to follow the project. The objective was to gradually increase the reach of the experience in an experimental phase, in order to study the effects that introducing computers in schools would have on the learning process. Once the experimental phase had ended, the project was implanted on a large scale in primary and secondary schools in the region (Fernández, 2001).

2.3 The Educational Computer Program

This project was developed in Catalonia from the year 1986. Catalonia is a region situated in the extreme northeast of the Iberian Peninsula, bordering France, and it is traditionally the Spanish region that has absorbed the most European influence and has a strong tradition of being the pioneer in adopting new socio-economic tendencies. With a thriving economy based on industry and the services sector, the income per capita is higher than the national average. Catalonia is one of the regions that have most rapidly developed their self-government, due to a historic tradition of a high level of autonomy compared to the rest of the Spanish territories. It is a geographically cohesive territory with good transportation and communications infrastructures.

The educational computer program was initially focused especially on secondary education and then generalized to primary education in 1990. As in the Atenea and Ábaco Projects, the objective was to contribute to improving the learning process and foster the use of the computer as a teaching resource and a means for renovating the educational methodology. The form of implementing the project was also similar in terms of the organization of the personnel. On the one hand, the trainers received intensive training and were freed from their teaching duties to dedicate all their time to the project. On the other hand, the teaching staff in general received courses of varying lengths depending on whether they were only to become computer literate or if there was a commitment by the teacher to use the computer as a teaching tool. The management of the project was performed through a set of specialist teachers distributed throughout territorial areas who had monthly meetings with the teachers in charge of classrooms in all the secondary schools in their territorial areas (Fernández, 2001).

3 Evaluation of the Projects

A key question in the development of these projects was the evaluation of the results in relation to the objectives proposed. As these initiatives were promoted by different autonomous communities in which the ruling governments were from different political parties, the institutional evaluation was not without a certain bias, as in many cases there was a prevailing interest in offering an image of success that did not exactly correspond to reality. The tendency to carry the political debate to all the areas, including education, meant that some of the evaluation reports elaborated were not completely believable, and in some cases showed true signs of being political propaganda. It should be noted that in Spain there has never been a state agreement that would assure the continuity of the educational model in the long term, regardless of the political party governing at any given time. However, with the perspective of time, it is possible to perform a more objective analysis of the results obtained in the period of time considered.

Thus, the Atenea Project, the largest of those undertaken in Spain during the 1980s, underwent three evaluations, the first two external and the last internal one carried out recently. The first analysis was performed by a team of evaluators from the University of Murcia in 1989. The evaluation concluded that the objective of providing the schools with information technology and increasing the teachers' acceptance of this technology had been reached. However, it showed that the improvement in the pedagogical processes was practically non-existent, and that there was no evidence that computers had the capacity to positively influence the teaching-learning process. This first report was not accepted by the national education authority, which considered that it offered a very negative image of the project. In order to have a second evaluation of the experience, a group of experts from the OECD was asked to elaborate a second report, also in 1989. This report, in contrast, praised the educational authority, highlighting the strong points of the project, so that this evaluation has been considered a political guarantee of the performance of the Education Ministry (García, 2003).

At this point, it is worthwhile to mention an event that influenced the recent history of Spain, its full incorporation into the European Union (EU). The official entry in the EU occurred in 1986. From that moment on, Spain began to carry out common actions with the rest of the countries in the Union, beginning with agricultural, industrial and, even, educational policies, whose high point was the creation of the European Framework for Higher Education in 1998. One of the most noteworthy manifestations of Spain's entrance in the EU was the influx of large amounts of communitarian capital mainly for investments in infrastructures. This influx of capital was due to the low levels of income per capita of many Spanish regions compared to the European mean. The EU, in order to promote equal conditions among all the citizens of the member countries, has a mechanism of structural funds for investment in those countries with a deficit in infrastructures. For this reason, important amounts of money could be used to buy computers, which made it possible for the chapter of purchasing computer equipment to be undertaken. Thus, one of the great problems detected in the phase prior to the development of the projects for incorporating IT in schools was solved, the scarcity of material resources (computers and rooms prepared for their use).

However, it can be stated that the greatest development was achieved in the area of educational management, as computers were incorporated in school administrations to support bureaucratic functions, such as managing students' grades, planning timetables for classes, making class lists and assigning students to groups of teachers, etc. In this context, computers at that time had more influence in the administration than in educational innovation and improving the teaching-learning process (Area, 2008).

In all of these projects, the main actors were the primary and secondary school teachers, who were given most of the responsibility for transforming the educational methods. All of the evaluations carried out on the different projects coincide in the lack of teacher training. Some reasons mentioned to explain this deficiency were (Cabero, 1989): (a) scarcity of computers in schools and for teacher training, which affected teachers' lack of familiarity with them; (b) tendency toward immobility with initial rejection of any new technology or teaching strategy; (c) lack of specialists in training trainers; (d) inexistence of training models adapted to the needs of the teacher training field; and (e) high costs of computer training, which involved not only the availability of devices and specific training for teachers, but also computers in an adequate proportion for their use by the students.

4 The Stage after the Implantation of Projects Incorporating IT in Schools

The 1990s were characterized by a certain absence of policies for incorporating IT in education. The reason may have been the concentration of efforts in adapting primary and secondary schools to the new education planning and development law (LOGSE), which meant a strong change in the teaching-learning procedures, the evaluation and management of the schools, and the schools' interrelation with the society. In addition, there was also a feeling that computers had not been the prodigious tool that would revolutionize the teaching and learning methods, so that it seemed that computers' potential had practically reached its limit.

In these circumstances, during this decade there was a boom in Internet as a global tool for dealing with large amounts of information. The impact of the Internet, not only on companies but also on citizens, gave rise to an unusual tendency toward buying computers for the home. From that moment on, there was an inversion in the process of incorporating computers into the schools, going from a Top-Down to a Bottom-Up sequence. In this process, familiarity with the use of computers created what have been called digital natives, children and young people with skills in the use of IT. They have been a great challenge to the schools, as a large part of the teaching staff does not dominate the technology with the same ability as the students they teach. This situation creates educational dysfunctions that are currently being studied.

In the second half of the 1990s, programs to incorporate information technologies proliferated again, but this time with the addition of communication, with the term information and communication technology (ICT) becoming popularized. This boom was due to the spectacular development of the Internet and the growing weight of governmental policies in favor of developing the information society. Two examples would be the National Information Infrastructure Plan, promoted by Vice-president Al

Gore in the United States in the 1990s, and the Lisbon Strategy in Europe in the year 2000. It is important to indicate that in this period the different Spanish regions developed their autonomy in matters of education under the 1978 Constitution, with the figure of the Education Ministry remaining as a merely legislative organism, leaving the development of educational innovation policies to the different regions. Therefore, numerous programs were developed of an exclusively regional ambit (Averroes in Andalusia, Medusa in the Canary Islands, Premia in the Basque Country, Ramón y Cajal in Aragón, Plumier in Murcia, Siega in Galicia, Argo in Catalonia, etc.), without any institutional coordination at the national level or among the different regions on this occasion. Nor were forums for meeting or collaboration developed that would serve to share experiences and coordinate the integration of ICT in the Spanish educational system in line with worldwide tendencies or European guidelines (Sanabria & Area, 2011).

5 Conclusions

The history of computers in education in Spain has been closely linked to the political avatars that characterized the history of Spain from the end of the 1970s to the beginning of the 1990s. During this time, the secular delay in the country's economy and education was made evident by the fact that the incorporation of computers in the educational setting was already a reality in other developed countries. The frictions between the different autonomous communities that make up the national geography gave rise to actions with a more political tone than educational. This was partly due to the fact that the autonomous communities, with their own deeply-rooted historical references, gave rise to the emergence of a territorial model that was not exempt from a certain degree of hurry. The entrance into the European Union in 1986, and with it the contribution of European funds for the cohesion among the different European regions, created the possibility of making strong investments in information technology, with which they could achieve, at the least, the objective of having computer rooms in the majority of schools at the end of the 1980s.

The initial enthusiasm and consideration that computers were going to produce a radical change in the teaching-learning process was giving way to a feeling of deception because very little had actually changed. This perception produced certain skepticism about the usefulness of computers in primary and secondary schools, so that governmental actions supporting the incorporation of IT in schools diminished significantly at the beginning of the 1990s. However, the true driving force that allowed a certain balance between the IT infrastructure in Spain and that of other OECD countries was the phenomenon of the information society, which has become deeply integrated in Spanish society and really caused the inversion in the order of the process. Today ICT can be considered an integral part of the educational process, even though the Copernican revolution that was expected with the incorporation of computers in schools never took place.

References

1. Arango, J.: El proyecto Atenea: Un plan para la introducción nacional de la informática en la escuela. Revista de Educación 276, 5–25 (1985)
2. Area, M.: Una breve historia de las políticas de incorporación de las tecnologías digitales al sistema escolar en España. Quaderns Digitals 51 (2008)
3. Cabero, J.: La formación del profesorado en medios audiovisuales. El Siglo que Viene 4(5), 14–19 (1989)
4. Fernández, M.S.: Las nuevas tecnologías en la educación: análisis de modelos de aplicación. UAM, Madrid (2001)
5. García, E.: La evaluación de programas de reforma educativa en España: tres estudios de caso desde un enfoque de metaevaluación. Doctoral Thesis. Universidad Complutense de Madrid (2003)
6. INE-Instituto Nacional de Estadística: Padrón de habitantes (1986)
7. Saez, J.M.: Apple pretende conseguir en España el éxito alcanzado en Europa y América. ABC Económico, 4 marzo, 40 (1985)
8. Sanabria, A.L., Area, M.: Las políticas educativas para incorporar las TIC al sistema escolar en Canarias. De Ábaco a ClicEscuela 2.0. In: Roig, A., Laneve, C. (eds.) La práctica educativa en la Sociedad de la Información: Innovación a través de la investigación, pp. 369–382 (2011)
9. Zufiaurre, B.: Proceso y contradicciones de la reforma educativa, pp. 1982–1994. Icaria, Barcelona (1994)

Early Uses of Computers in Schools in the United Kingdom: Shaping Factors and Influencing Directions

Don Passey

Centre for Technology Enhanced Learning, Department of Educational Research, Lancaster University, UK
d.passey@lancaster.ac.uk

Abstract. This chapter describes the early development and introduction of computers into schools in the United Kingdom from the 1970s to the evaluation of their impacts and a shift in the focus of their uses in the 1990s. The chapter explores key factors influencing the direction and deployment of uses of computers in schools. It considers influences of national initiatives and policies, the development of support, support centres and central agencies, the involvement of hardware and software manufacturers and developers, different applications of computer resources, the focus of uses in the curriculum, and impacts on education. Conclusions drawn are that original intentions for the implementation of computers in schools were re-focused in the late 1990s, particularly as pedagogies and learning effectiveness were not strong drivers during the early implementation period.

Keywords: History of computers in schools, UK, early educational technologies, computers in schools initiatives, policy and practice drivers, software development, IT industry, national curriculum, IT curriculum.

1 Introduction

Technological developments and policy actions in the 1980s can arguably be said to have had the most long-term influence on uses of computers in schools in the United Kingdom (UK). Prior to the 1980s, computers were used in very isolated instances, but policy decisions and actions in the 1980s not only set in motion a string of events that led to much wider institutional and individual access, but also led to directions focusing forms and patterns of use.

This chapter takes a part personal, and part documentary, view of the factors and influences that were involved. The author, having used computers in schools in the early 1980s, then later became involved in research into uses of computers to support teaching and learning during that same period. This chapter offers a part historical, part developmental, part policy-driven, and part pedagogically-driven perspective. Personal experiences and reflections, supplemented by documentary evidence from key individuals, from policy and from research, offered through these different lenses, provides a picture that considers key factors and features:

- National policies: how they were developed and what they achieved.

A. Tatnall and B. Davey (Eds.): History of Computers in Education, IFIP AICT 424, pp. 131–149, 2014.

- Computer education support centres, professional development and other school support activities: their presence and roles.
- The contributions of computer companies, software designers and book publishers.
- Educational application software: their development and focus.
- Use of computers 'across the curriculum' in various subjects as well as for teaching computing: practical and policy contributions.
- How computers changed education (or did not change it) and why this happened.

2 Policies and Practices

In the 1970s and early 1980s a growing concern arose in the UK for greater awareness between and potential alignment of education with industry. This alignment was driven by a concern with three main factors: that the nature and forms of industry were changing, and that these changes needed to be understood by teachers as well as by young people moving towards longer-term societal involvement in training and employment; that technologies were becoming increasingly developed and deployed in industrial and commercial practices and their uses needed to be more widely recognised by those in education; and the uses of computers in education needed to be considered from the perspectives of commercial and economic potential. These concerns for alignment and wider gaining of understanding led to practices such as teacher placements in industry for limited periods of time, and the development of courses for young people that included more commercial and industrial content (such as Business and Technology Education Council courses). Machin and Vignoles [1] discuss these changes and their implications in the context of that period, giving a view of the levels of activity arising, stating that "*Various initiatives attempted to replace the traditional apprenticeships ... These initiatives are too numerous to mention*" (p.11). These initiatives included the creation of National Vocational Qualifications and General National Vocational Qualifications. Qualifications and courses were developed regionally and nationally, so in 1987, for example, the Department of Education Northern Ireland (DENI) funded an £18m Vocational Education Programme.

In terms of technologies in education during that period of time, isolated computers in some educational institutions (generally tertiary education) could be found in the early 1970s, but these large machines had limited capabilities, and students and teachers in schools only visited such premises to 'gape in awe' at the sight of processing power handled through valve-operated systems. In 1973 the National Development Programme in Computer Assisted Learning (NDPCAL), with a £2.5m budget over 5 years, ran over 30 projects across the tertiary education sector in the UK to explore a variety of potential applications of computer assisted learning (CAL) [2]. At the same time, the Computers in the Curriculum Project, funded by the Schools Council and based in King's College London, developed a range of interactive computer programmes in a number of subject areas.

While these projects developed software or computer programs, decisions to support education through program development were also linked with decisions to support the development of a wider potential computer industry (concerned with educational computing) itself. In the late 1970s, Research Machines (RM) developed microcomputers for schools, and the Apple II and the Commodore Pet were also created in the same period [3]. Indeed, the first computers in secondary and primary schools in the UK were Commodore Pets. These were used for spelling or arithmetic practice, as well as for programming in either BASIC or LOGO [2]. As Millwood [3] says,

> *"In the entrepreneurial science parks of Oxford and Cambridge, new companies emerged to build the microcomputers demanded by society, commerce and education, leading to the establishment of Research Machines, Acorn and Sinclair. At the same time, the Continuing Education Department at the BBC noted the rise of the microcomputer as a pervasive influence on society and began to propose a national campaign, which eventually became known as the BBC Computer Literacy Project, launched in 1982" (p.10).*

RM produced a 380Z machine from 1978, but, due to the high costs of machines from early developments, schools largely had to wait to the early 1980s for their chance to acquire a computer system, from a Department of Trade and Industry (DTI) initiative at that time. The initiative was supported by the then Prime Minister, Margaret Thatcher, when she stated in a speech in 1981 [4]: "*Our future prosperity depends in large part on the quality of education today. That quality requires not only that children should learn the familiar basic subjects but that they should also be able to understand computers and how they can be used and applied.*" The initiative was called the Micros in Schools scheme, with funds of £15.1m in 1981 to 1982 to provide all secondary schools with half of the cost of a microcomputer. A follow-on DTI Micros in Primary Schools scheme similarly contributed half the cost of a cassette- or tape-driven machine (either BBC, RM480Z, or Sinclair Spectrum) for every primary school from 1982 to 1984.

Tape-driven machines were the first forms of computers accessible to schools. These gave way eventually to disk-driven machines. In 1983, the DTI provided £2.1m in funds for the Micros in Secondary Schools (Extension) initiative, so that schools could purchase printers, colour monitors, memory upgrades, disk-drives, and some other specified additional peripherals [2], and subsequently disk-drives became available for computers in primary schools in 1984. The issue for teachers at that time often was how to use such machines and their capabilities, but quickly some teachers (and some managers and administrators in schools) became interested in using these devices, exploring ways to extend not only what the technology could do, but also extending the ways certain concepts could be explored with learners (such as practising bacterial counts from example virtual microscope visualisations). In many cases initial users of these technologies had been teachers in mathematics, as there was initially less distance or distinction between software coding and application (which was perceived as a mathematical or logical problem arena). However, in some schools, teachers in other disciplines became interested in the potential for their subjects. With only one machine in a school at that time, this often led to challenges that teachers had not encountered before; a need to plan and book resources that would be school-based rather than classroom-based. Resources that would provide advice and guidance to schools on such management issues and possible approaches were to become a later major focus of research and development work, undertaken in some specific research centres [5], as well as in individual local education authority (LEA) centres [6].

Interest in the industrial and employment aspects of computers in schools led to a third government department becoming involved at an early stage. In 1983, the Technical and Vocational Educational Initiative (TVEI), was funded by the Department of Employment (DoE) at a level of £20m, rather than by the Department of Education and Science (DES) as it was at that time. These initiatives focused on curriculum development and integration of design and technology approaches, initially for upper secondary school students (14 to 18 years of age predominantly). The TVEI and TVEI Extension initiatives supported schools in the development of courses and practices that focused on industrially-linked, technologically-integrated and design-driven approaches to subjects such as engineering, and design and graphics. Through these initiatives, schools were able to gain more and wider forms of technologies, including computer-controlled manufacturing tools. As the initiatives focused often on course development and integration, technologies were often grouped and retained within specific rooms (computer rooms) or resource areas (such as a design workshop). At the same time, however, growing interest in the application of technologies to support other support areas continued to emerge strongly. Indeed, the TVEI initiatives supported wider subject interest and practices, and groups of advisers and advisory teachers to support these initiatives, outside schools and located in LEAs, often developed and promoted uses of technologies not only in subjects across secondary schools, but also in primary schools. The growing interest in alignment of industrial change and future employment to education extended to concerns that teachers and learners in primary schools should also be involved in gaining wider awareness of the changes arising and their implications for their futures. By 1984 the deployment of computers in schools had reached a level that created a demand for and led to national funding and support for in-service training in what was then called information technology (IT) for teachers.

The DTI continued throughout the 1980s in providing funds to support schools in the acquisition of newly-developing technologies. In 1985 the DTI provided £1m in funds to provide a modem for every school, and subsequently, in 1988 a grant of £140 for each secondary school to install a telephone line for data communication. This was to be a significant turning point, and heralded and ultimately led to a major focus of development on networking capability for schools, exploring networking within schools initially. In 1987, the DTI provided funding of £3.5m to support the purchase of school IT equipment, managed by LEAs, for microcomputers (but only Acorn or BBC, Apricot, IBM and RM PCs), disk-drives, printers, mice, monitors, (significantly) teletext adaptors, and turtles and some other peripheral devices. From that time, the developing of networking, in schools and then across schools, was rapid. The first networks in primary schools were installed in 1992, a UK-wide networking of schools discussed in the *Superhighways for Education* consultation was launched in April 1995 and an evaluation of the potential of the initiative was published in 1997 [7]; from the late 1990s, networking was increasingly developed to link schools and regions nationally.

Across the entire period of time that these developments had taken place, schools and teachers were in a position to make decisions about whether or not to take part, and how they would use specific resources in classrooms. In 1989 a significant policy development in the UK was the creation of a national curriculum. For the first time, subject content was specified for all sectors of compulsory education, and the specification of this content was a learner entitlement curriculum that was statutory. In the specified national curriculum, IT was not presented as a separate subject area; it was contained within design technology [8]. But, the use of computers and technologies was also spread across and indicated within every subject area of the curriculum, at every age level, although it was focused heavily, as might be expected, in design technology. A TVEI research project based at Lancaster University created maps of information technology (IT) across the curriculum, showing for each Key Stage (5 to 7, 7 to 11, 11 to 14, and 14 to 16 years of age) the statutory requirements for using IT in each subject area [9]. Within the design technology subject of the national curriculum [8], five aspects of IT capability were identified: developing ideas and communicating information; information handling; modelling; measurement and control; and applications and effects (p.73). For the end of each Key Stage, attainment targets and statement of attainment were identified at ten different levels, and an overall programme of study indicated what should be taught for learners to work at each of those ten levels. The national curriculum proposals were formalised in 1990 [10], and the programme of study within the technology in the national curriculum document rephrased what should be taught as: "*communicate and handle information; design, develop, explore and evaluate models of real or imaginary situations; measure and control physical variables and movement*" (p.45). Teachers were suddenly not able to choose whether or not to consider the uses of computers; as Griffin and Davies [11] said: "*The National Curriculum makes explicit for the first time that each pupil has an* entitlement *to a curriculum which includes information technology (IT)*" (p.255).

When the national curriculum was introduced in 1989, there was an early policy separation of the curriculum from assessment; so concerns with assessing uses of IT in subject areas (and indeed assessment concerns overall) tended in some respects to be separated from curriculum integration concerns. Some groups of LEA advisers, however, looked critically at this issue, and documentation began to emerge [12] that proposed how teachers could develop activities that would meet both curriculum and assessment requirements. The national educational technology support agency, the National Council for Educational Technology (NCET), also produced school support materials [13], and whilst assessment was covered in one of the eight booklets in that pack, this was indeed the last of the eight. It could be argued, therefore, that assessment was seen as an end product, and not as an integral element serving formative purposes.

Up to that time, strategic development of software and identification of appropriate pedagogies to deploy when using specific software had been considered to a limited extent. Prior to the national curriculum, software development tended to arise because of local interest and concerns (which had not been the case with the development of hardware and peripherals). From the time of the instigation of the national curriculum, there was a much greater focus on how the content of the curriculum could be supported by appropriate uses of software and technologies. Associated with this, a much greater consideration arose concerned with identifying appropriate pedagogies. Pedagogies applied to specific software applications at that time were being developed and were in practice, either through individual teacher endeavour, or through the practices developed and used by advisers and advisory teachers who were based in LEAs or more central national agencies. However, the centralisation of the curriculum created a more focused concern on the national identification of pedagogies and activities. The ways and reasons that support groups and agencies were developed, and their involvement in this focus, are discussed in the next section.

3 Support and Uses

In the early 1980s, when the concern and focus was on raising awareness and implications of shifts in industrial nature and practices, a part of the action taken to bring together and consider appropriate ways forward was the development of a national computer education support centre. In 1981 the DES set up the Microelectronics Education Programme (MEP), to support educational computing (initially focusing on developments in the secondary sector, but then in 1982 widened to include the primary sector). This programme was run through 14 regional consortia of LEAs, with another 4 Special Education Microelectronics Resource Centres (SEMERCs) [2].

In 1985 the DES provided £2m in funds to support LEAs through a more strategic focus, setting up the Microelectronics Education Support Unit (MESU), based in Coventry, sitting alongside Warwick University (that had already established a centre concerned with the future directions of education and work). In focusing on a more integrated strategic approach to developments of microelectronics, in 1988, MESU merged with the more higher education-focused Council for Educational Technology (CET), and NCET was formed, initially funded at a level of £20m. This agency later became the British Educational Communications and Technology Agency (Becta) in 1997, which was more strategically linked to government policy directions. These units or agencies, over time, had become linked to greater extents to LEAs as well as to the government education department.

In the 1980s, the focus of support for the national units and agencies was supplemented with support initiatives at more local levels also. In 1987 the DES provided an Educational Support Grant (ESG), with funds of £10.5m, to appoint some 650 advisory teachers in IT, to cover a range of curriculum subjects rather than the focus being on teaching IT. From 1988, MESU was provided with additional funding for induction training for these advisory teachers (including some librarians). Consequently, LEAs across England and their equivalents in the other nations (Wales, Scotland and Northern Ireland), used funds to establish their own advisory centres for computer and technology developments, headed often by an adviser of computer education, who headed up a team of advisory teachers as well as, sometimes, a technical team, either providing technical support to schools, or developing software and hardware applications for teacher use. The need for such centres to support teachers was clearly identified in the research literature of the time; needs to address management issues, skills needs, and pedagogical concerns were all highlighted. Heywood and Norman [14], for example, identified in 1988 major reasons why teachers did not use IT; these were mainly due to their lacking in confidence and competence is using IT. The authors noted at the time that,

> *"Generally the programs in use were un-demanding in pedagogical terms with much drill and practice (especially in Mathematics), little database work, and no simulation exercises. The instructional nature of this software made little extra demand upon teacher time – the machines were switched on and left to the children, therefore requiring no teacher supervision" (p.41).*

The funding for these LEA centres came through the DES, but there often were links with DTI initiatives providing funding through TVEI channels. That latter funding, however, ceased to exist to any great extent after the national curriculum was launched. IT matters beyond the launch of the national curriculum became the remit of the DES.

MESU and its successors promoted links with LEA advisers and advisory teachers. At the same time, in 1984, the advisers of computers in education established their own association, the National Association of Advisers for Computers in Education (NAACE) [15], which became a well-known body, regularly meeting with and advising government departments and agencies such as the National Curriculum Council (NCC) and the Schools Examination and Assessment Council (SEAC).

Additionally, with the launch of the national curriculum and the focus on IT in subject areas across the curriculum, subject associations also began to have increased interest in the development and uses of IT. Associations such as the Geography Association (GA) and History Association (HA), for example, set up their own internal focus groups to consider the applications of IT into subject and topic areas. In some subject areas, however, it was clear that a different focus was being suggested by the national curriculum for devices and software. Ball [16], when discussing implications of the national curriculum for mathematics teaching, said that "*Before the advent of the National Curriculum, significantly more use in mathematics classrooms was being made of smaller, more focused programs than of spreadsheets or databases*" (p.243). He highlighted the shift away from uses of calculators, adventure games, projects, games of strategy, exploratory activities and graph plotters, towards uses of content-free software.

While subject teachers in secondary schools were supported at a subject level for implementing IT needs of the national curriculum, teachers in primary schools faced very different challenges; as Govier [17] said, "*primary school teachers are teachers of English … and mathematics … and science … and technology … and history … and geography*" (p.163). She concluded that "*the demands made by the National Curriculum on the IT skills of primary teachers … are, in the short term, quite impossible to meet*" (p.162).

The development of policies and support structures over time, alongside the identification and implementation of measures to address school and teacher needs as they were arising, was coupled of course with the ways that computers and technologies were themselves being developed. In the next section, parallel technological development features and factors will be outlined and considered, before bringing this back in the subsequent sections to concerns about teaching, learning and pedagogies.

4 Computer Companies and Commercial Concerns

When computers first arrived in schools, there was little choice of machine. At that time key companies involved in developing machines were: Research Machines (RM) who had developed the 380Z; Sinclair; and the BBC who produced the BBC machine. The interest of the BBC was discussed earlier in this chapter, and from part of that interest, in 1981, the BBC awarded a contract to Acorn to produce a Personal Computer (PC), which ultimately became particularly popular in schools. Indeed, by 1986, some 650,000 BBC Model B computers (the successor of the original BBC machine) had been sold. Within a relatively short time, however, a number of other key computer companies were involved in producing machines to meet the needs of specific initiatives, that schools could acquire by choice. In reality, however, many decisions about choice were deferred to LEA advisers or advisory teams. LEAs then tended to become either: PC-based, often with RM machines; BBC-based, with Acorn machines; or Macintosh-based, with Apple machines. There was an involvement of some other computer producers, such as Apricot and IBM, but their reach into schools was much lower than the three main producers mentioned above.

From 1975, computers that educational institutions could acquire changed in terms of significant features they offered about every 5 years. These are shown in Table 1.

Table 1. Features of computers accessible to UK educational institutions since 1975 [18]

From the year	Features of accessible computers
1975	186 machines, BBC machines, standalone, using cassette and tape programmes
1980	286 machines, BBC B machines, using 5.25 inch disks
1985	386 machines, Acorn machines, with local networking
1990	Laptop machines, Compact-Disk – Read Only Memory (CD-ROM), 3.5 inch disks
1995	486 machines, 586 machines, Internet access, colour printers, shared software

Looking at this in terms of deployment and access, major technologies adopted in UK schools from 1975 not only had different features, but could also be deployed in ways that could affect both their access and the ways that teachers would use them and effect pedagogies with learners. From 1975, calculators could be used on a one-to-one basis; from 1980, standalone micro-computers could be deployed as shared items across a school or a class; from 1985, suites of micro-computers could allow half classes or groups to access them; from 1990, networked micro-computers with enhanced graphics could allow work to be retained and shared to greater extents. In 1993, there was a first trialling of portable computers in primary and secondary schools and in teacher training institutions in England, and the Acorn Pocketbook Psion Series 3 was the first small computer to be used in schools that year [2]; and from 1995, Compact-Disk – Read Only Memory (CD-ROMs) and integrated learning systems (ILSs) could enable access on a one-to-one basis for specific periods of time during a day [18].

Across this period of time schools acquired increasing numbers of computers. By 1989 the ratio of computers to learners in primary schools had reached 1:67 and in secondary schools 1:28. The focus on hardware during the 1980s was succeeded by a focus on software. The development of software to fulfil subject curriculum needs was at a height during the late 1980s, and much of the early development was undertaken by centres in universities as well as in advisory centres in LEAs. In some cases, small companies began to be established, which focused on more specialised software, perhaps to support learners with special educational needs. In some cases, these focused on hardware developments rather than, or as well as, software developments. Peripheral technology devices to support specific impairment needs, for example, were focally developed during that time period. Software designers often began their careers in professional development or advisory centres in LEAs, and the rise of small-scale companies developing software, grouped with hardware producers focusing on educational hardware developments, meant that the link between industry and education was becoming strongly established, but focused specifically on educational technologies. The industries of educational technology emerged, but these industries were much more specifically focused and at the same time more narrowly linked to wider commercial IT companies.

5 Software

It can be argued that the development of computers and technologies has followed a development path that has enabled a shift from information to communication, and from shared to individual access. The shifts in terms of software over that period are far more complex. Using a recent taxonomy of digital resources to consider forms of software accessible to schools from about 1980 [19], Table 2 summarises the ways in which specific categories of software have been accessible to and used by teachers. The software resources are roughly chronologically listed, to give an idea of the shifts in or progression of software categories over time.

Table 2. Accessibility and use of different categories of software by teachers in schools from about 1980

Category of software	Accessibility and uses by teachers
Television and video	Television and video pre-dated uses of computers and software in schools. To some extent schools replaced their uses of television and video with software (or through their access to digital resources more recently). Television and video resources have tended to focus on specific topics, but they have often provided a 'big picture' as well
Calculators	Calculators also pre-dated uses of computers and software. As they became more sophisticated, they were used for more graphical functions, but are now widely incorporated into computer resource systems

Topic-specific resources and software	Much of the early software accessible and produced by advisory and small development companies was topic based. This development approach was reinforced when the national curriculum was implemented, with many resources being developed to support specific topics within specific subject areas. However, at the same time, generic content-free software was highlighted within national curriculum documents
Word processors	Word processors have been widely used across the entire period of time that software has been used in schools in the UK
Games-based activities	Many (even early) software packages have taken a games-based approach. This was particularly the case when graphics functionalities of computers were enhanced in the mid-1980s. Games-based activities have tended to be linked to topic-specific software
Simulations and modelling	Simulations and modelling software was developed at an early stage by King's College London, and by the Computer Based Modelling Across the Curriculum Project [20], particularly focused on supporting teachers in science, mathematics, geography and business education
Project and after-school club activities involving digital technologies	Some of the early uses of software, due to there often being only one computer accessible, focused on project-based approaches, sometimes involving clubs and events after school or at break times. More recently, these forms of resources and approach have tended to become more limited
Curriculum-wide learner-centred software (ILSs)	ILSs, comprising activities to cover an entire subject curriculum, became very popular in the early 1990s. Evaluation studies of these forms of software that originated in the United States were conducted initially by NCET in 1994 [21], but after a period of some five years, their use declined dramatically
Curriculum-wide teacher-centred software	Much of the early software was developed for learner use rather than teacher use. Teachers often had to find ways to use software with learners, and to develop appropriate pedagogies. Indeed, teachers often 'left learners to use the programs' or 'allowed learners to use the programs on the computer in the corridor'. It was not until networking access became feasible that teacher-centred software tended to be developed
Projects focusing on broadcasting	Projects of this nature have been developed since networking and Internet accessibility have been possible. Increasingly, major broadcasting companies and corporations have become involved in these projects, such as the BBC News School Report projects that are run annually

Online resources supporting curriculum-wide needs	These resources were largely not developed until Internet access was feasible. Local networking did not tend to promote the development of software resources to support this form of interaction
Online resources supporting revision needs	These resources were developed more recently, since Internet access has enabled learners to use these resources in a variety of locations
Software involving and supporting parents	This was not a major thrust of the software development at early stages of implementing computers into schools. It has been a recent focus for some providers
Online learner support	This is a very recent development, and is likely to widen in scope in the future
Projects linking schools and learners internationally	Similarly, this is a very recent development, and is likely to widen in scope in the future
Projects developing video-game elements	These projects in schools have only very recently been developed, and are likely to widen in scope in the future

It is notable, perhaps, that from the early stages software development did not involve book publishers largely. The concept of resources being technologically-based or hardcopy-based remained and was retained over decades from the 1980s (and indeed in the 2010s the book publishers are still concerned with how to most effectively develop wider forms of technologically-based published resources).

Software development and availability in schools has been supported through national funded initiatives. In 1985, the DTI provided £3.5m in funds for a period of 3 years for the purchase of software, to be match-funded and managed by LEAs. In terms of the software available at that time, forms of educational application software that were developed in the 1980s tended to focus very heavily on specific subject topics, and although there was rapid development of software, limited functionality in graphics at the time limited the scope of software applications. Researchers were reporting in the late 1980s about long-term development features that they felt should be considered to ensure ease of future production and accessibility to software. Nicolson [22], for example, proposed a system of development that enabled a host machine to produce software that could be transferred to other machines, with the Acorn BBC microcomputer as the target machine identified at that time. It should be noted particularly that compatibility of developed software with a range of hardware machines was a key challenge at that time. It was not until 1990 that multimedia PCs became available to schools. CD-ROMs were developed from 1992, and the DES supported a number of specifically funded initiatives at that time, that focused on compatibility as well as on software development.

Research undertaken by Harris and Preston [23] in 1993 reported, from a survey across 196 primary and 292 secondary schools, that for both sectors the major influences affecting software purchase were levels of IT budgets, national curriculum requirements and school IT policy and development plans, and that all these factors were more prominent than LEA policies. The sources of software indicated by schools clearly did not include major book publishers notably; Sherston, Resource, SPA, AVP, Reckitts, Capedia, Longman Logotron, Macline, NCET and TAG were noted specifically as sources used by schools (p.18). However, primary schools noted that their main sources of software came through LEA computer centres, while direct commercial sources were more prevalent for secondary schools. Primary schools indicated that they mainly had computer facilities located within classroom areas; for secondary schools, teachers of mathematics, English and religious education reported most access in computer rooms, while teachers of science, design technology, music, art and special educational needs reported more access in classrooms.

The Harris and Preston report [23] indicated the prevalence of use of different forms of software in schools. These are shown in Table 3 for primary schools and in Table 4 for secondary schools.

Table 3. Types of software and their reported high levels of use in primary schools (Source: [23])

Type of software	Percentage of teachers reporting high levels of use
Word processing	67
Adventures and simulations	24
Databases	23
Computer-aided art or design	20
Programming (e.g. Logo)	6
Desk-top publishing	5
Spreadsheets	3
Computer-aided musical composition	2
Measurement and control	1

Table 4. Types of software and their reported high levels of use in secondary schools (Source based on: [23])

Type of software	Subject teachers reporting high levels of use
Word processing	Used across the curriculum, but mainly by special educational needs, English, design technology, and science teachers
Adventures and simulations	Limited use across the curriculum, with most use by special educational needs and mathematics teachers
Databases	Limited use across the curriculum, with most use by mathematics, design technology, music, geography and science teachers
Desk-top publishing	Used across the curriculum, but mainly by design technology, English, religious education and special educational needs teachers
Spreadsheets	Limited use across the curriculum, with most use by mathematics and design technology teachers

During the 1980s many questions were raised by teachers about the value of using software – including what was to become the most popularly used form of software, word processors. Researchers often undertook studies across this period that looked at uses and their outcomes in terms of teaching and learning. Pearson and Wilkinson [24] in 1986 reported a study on uses of word processors, and concluded that:

> *"The word processor was not found to be an essential prerequisite to such revision, but appeared in these cases to act as a facilitating device which increased the motivation to revise by making it so simple. The contention*

that word processors may only encourage children to tinker with surface features of their writing is not borne out by the evidence of these case studies. On the contrary, from this sample the implications are that for children who are as it were at a point of readiness to develop further in their writing, the word processor may be a most useful writing instrument which could catalyse that progress" (p.187).

Certainly in the 1980s the range of software available to schools was limited. When the national curriculum was introduced in 1989, the DES provided £750k in funds to develop new software titles to help teach national curriculum subjects. Research from the period shows how computers and software were deployed, the ways teachers across a school were able to share resources, and to develop practices that would enable individual, groups or classes of learners to gain from the software available. It can be argued that the early deployment patterns of computers supported direct and focused learner engagement and that this was a leading focus of program developers, rather than leading to an alternative focus on teacher engagement and on ways to consider appropriate pedagogies. Indeed, in a paper by Robson, Steward and Whitfield [25], the discussion about use of software is entirely around concepts of learner decisions when encountering and using a program, and how learner autonomy might be developed more in the future, rather than considering the roles of teacher support. The reasons for a learner-centred focus, however, are understandable; as Gibbons [26] concluded from her review of barriers and challenges in using BBC microcomputers in a school, once teachers had overcome the challenges of availability and accessibility of hardware, and felt confident enough to try to use a piece of software, then still the major obstacle remained, "*There is little to help the inexperienced teacher in planning and anticipating the learning situation*" (p.27). Teachers basically needed often to 'try IT out' and work out for themselves what pedagogies to use and what learning outcomes or intentions to consider for their learners.

It can be argued that how IT was used during the 1980s was developing pedagogies, and indeed the concept of IT being a 'Trojan horse' was developed from that period of time. In other words, the need for teachers to develop pedagogies that would accommodate low levels of access to IT was seen as being particularly valuable, because it meant that teachers would develop useful pedagogies around practices that would involve and lead to the benefits arising from group work, team work, shared activities, and sequential work. As Johnston reported in 1987 [27] in the context of teaching language development:

"The ways learning and teaching are altered by the introduction of software which enhances or extends the existing curriculum, offering new opportunities for classroom activities and involving a redefinition of the roles of teacher and pupil, are frequently referred to. Sometimes this is with confidence, but equally frequently the teachers express reservations concerning a perceived loss of control of pupil learning" (p.144).

Yet the author went on to say from the same research evidence that "*The most effective use of a microcomputer is found by the practising teachers to depend upon a learner-centred educational philosophy and approach*" (p.144). Indeed, the author pointed out earlier in the paper that the three most suitable areas for IT enhancement for language development were in creative writing, discussion and oral work, and vocabulary extension, where there are clearly opportunities for learner-centred approaches. The emphasis of learner-centred approaches with uses of computers is highlighted in other research findings too. Rogers [28], in the abstract of a paper exploring how IT can be used in science in the National Curriculum, certainly states how learner-centred approaches could be supported through applications of software, saying that: "*An investigative and exploratory approach to learning science is emphasised in the National Curriculum. This paper discusses the role of Information Technology in encouraging the methods of inquiry suited to this approach*" (p.246). The author discusses how data-logging, spreadsheets, databases and simulations can all support a curriculum that is learner-centred (where the learner undertakes activities and the handling of data and information).

6 Computers and the Curriculum

Undoubtedly the curriculum and its associated assessment have been major drivers in terms of how computers, technologies and digital resources have both been developed and deployed in schools, classrooms, and by teachers. The use of computers was, almost from the outset, not just concerned with use in an IT subject, but in any subject. Many secondary schools in the 1980s did start to develop IT as a subject, however, and created computer or IT rooms. In some schools, even well into the 1990s and beyond, subject teachers who were not IT teachers found they had limited access to computers and technology-based resources. Even so, from 1989, the idea of IT 'across the curriculum' was felt by many advisers and teachers to be worthwhile, but practically difficult to achieve. *HMI Curriculum Matters 15 – IT from 5-16* [29] was published that year, recommending schools to look at uses of IT across the curriculum, and to consider how to do this by developing a coherent strategy 'for making effective use of IT as an enrichment of the curriculum'.

This concept of 'across the curriculum', with use in any or all subjects, became a major focus of attention during the late 1980s, when the numbers of computers in schools had increased, but also concepts of cross-curricular value were being highlighted more generally within educational practices. Some software at that time was developed to be 'cross-curricular', that is, it did not have a specific subject focus, but covered a range of topics in a number of subjects. Software such as problem-based, simulations and modelling, developed in the late 1980s, for example, enabled teachers to undertake activities that were cross-curricular in nature rather than subject based. The national curriculum, and its subsequent assessment, both through national tests and external inspection of schools, however, tended to raise questions about the time that teachers should devote to cross-curricular activities and to devalue the cross-curricular and project-based approaches, so that schools and software developers tended to focus increasingly on producing subject and topic-based resources and software. The national curriculum in 1989 supported an 'across the curriculum' direction; as Griffin and Davies [11] said, "*The curriculum should ensure that each pupil uses IT to enhance and enrich his or her learning in every area of the curriculum*" (p.256). Schools also increasingly embraced IT teaching more; and indeed the Qualifications and Curriculum Authority (QCA), which was the merged successor of NCC and SCAA, published a scheme of work for IT. In many respects this document created a uniformity of teaching and activities for IT across schools, however, rather than generating a variety of activities and approaches.

Once a national curriculum approach had been implemented, national evaluation became much more prominent; in essence, a national curriculum appeared to support the notion that some forms of national uniformity could be identified that could be measured. In 1991 Her Majesty's Inspectorate published a report [30] on the uses of IT in teaching and learning in primary classrooms. This report highlighted how some more prevalent uses of IT had shifted over time. They stated that: "*the best practice and the most application of IT was in handling text*", but " *data-handling, control and LOGO applications produced some of the most exciting work, but only slight use was made of them*" and "*there were marked changes in the way in which many schools used IT*" (p.10). This report also indicated the fact that software use can be short-lived rather than long-standing: "*Certain programs achieved widespread, if short-lived, popularity*" (p.12).

The roles of research in driving the direction of uses of computers in schools is hard to quantify, but certainly it is clear that not only have certain research centres developed software that has had significant uses in schools, but they and other research centres have focused on the ways that software and computers have enhanced and supported learning (and indeed, many researchers have been involved in studies that have explored how IT has supported teaching and learning, such as those at King's College in the original ImpacT study [31]). Some research centres have focused on specific pedagogical concepts, while others have looked more widely across pedagogies and their uses in schools. But the distinction (and tension) between 'teaching about IT' and 'using IT to support learning' remained during this period. The Dearing review of the national curriculum in 1993 [32] certainly identified IT as a key future need, saying that "*Each National Curriculum subject should continue to be taught in the first three key stages, but the review should recognise the prime importance of mastery of the basics of learning at the primary stage, including literacy, oracy, numeracy and a basic competence in the use of information technology*" (p.8). But the statement was argued by some to be more concerned with 'the teaching of IT' than 'using IT'.

By 1997, government ministers were openly talking about the linking of uses of IT to wider concerns with learning, attainment, effectiveness and the raising of standards. A clear shift had arisen by that time; from a concern about raising awareness about the potential of computers and IT, to raising attainment in subject terms. Information and communications technologies (ICT) were then identified as a fourth basic skill. It could be said that 'a new era was emerging'. ICT was being seen as fundamental to learning, rather than it being seen as supporting raising awareness of potential for training and employment. During the 1990s the levels of computers and technologies in schools increased. By 1999, statistics from The Stationery Office [33] indicated that the ratio of a computer to learners in primary schools was 1:16, in secondary schools it was 1:8, and in special schools it was 1:4. In that same report, 62% of primary, 93% of secondary and 60% of special schools were connected to the Internet, 15% of primary, 32% of secondary and 14% of special school teachers had their own e-mail addresses, and 68% of primary, 66% of secondary and 68% of special school teachers felt confident in using ICT in the curriculum. This marked a significant shift from one teacher in some schools being aware of and interested in computers in the early 1980s.

7 Outcomes, Impacts and Directions

Computers have undoubtedly changed education in some respects, but interestingly, not in others. In terms of the original conceptions for introducing computers, no known specific evaluation of these has ever been completed. So, whilst the original intention was to develop wider awareness of industrial change and breadth of uses of computers, there is no specific evidence gathered to identify whether this actually happened. Whilst computers and technologies have become more prevalent in schools, and have been used by teachers and learners increasingly, it is not clear that this shift has enhanced awareness of industrial change, or the ways that technologies are used in industry or could be developed further. Indeed, it could be argued that whilst the development of an educational technology industry has undoubtedly happened and been successful, that this has focused the attention of teachers and learners on educational technology rather than opening up awareness to wider potential uses or enabling a focus on the development of innovation beyond education. It was the DTI that supported schools in purchasing computers, but without the DTI's continued involvement and interest in maintaining their focus, it is not clear that their long-term intentions were or could be fulfilled.

Computers have changed education in terms of resources and facilities available, in terms of a wider use of visual and auditory resources, and in terms of increasing potential uses of networking in a more modern context. But facilities have changed far more than pedagogies; but in the defence of teachers, it can also be argued that a subject content curriculum maintains a subject pedagogical focus rather than asking teachers and educators to focus on pedagogy and learning process. Johnston [34], back in 1987, highlighted this issue, stating that evaluation of microcomputer programs then lacked focus on "*the nature of the learning experiences offered*" (p.45).

Policy has driven the role of computers to a large extent. But the dramatic and frequent changes that occur with technologies themselves have not been something that has been taken up and addressed within educational policy. Policy continues to look back to a greater extent than looking forward; it is tactical rather than strategic, so whole realms of potential have been lost as a consequence.

The development of a national curriculum shifted local technology development to national technology development. Uses of computers and technologies at a local level were overshadowed by concerns with identifying national pedagogies and activities. This is not how technologies work in industry or in driving innovation; it is the specifics and the local context and detail that are important. Innovation is unlikely to arise from just a fulfilment of national activity.

Findings from a key national study published in 1993 [31] indicated that levels of computer access and use were important if learning outcomes were to be heightened. Actually evidence of the impact arising from higher levels of use and access has not definitively been identified; it still remains clear that what is done with a computer determines impact at an individual level rather than there being a formula of access and level of use that determines impact. In this respect, the development of communication facilities opens up different opportunities; levels of access are important here, but the quality of interactions and outcomes is not solely a result of that level.

The development of software across this early period of computers being used in schools shows that topic-specific and project-based activities were superseded to extents by uses of more open and content-free software. Although it can be argued that content-free software enables a wider application and opens up the possibilities for application innovation and creativity more, it can also be argued that ideas of 'a big picture' about a topic and the benefits of team working and project working have been reduced. It is clear that software developed during the early periods of computer use in schools was certainly more learner-focused than teacher-focused; unsurprisingly, it was found that pedagogies were much more difficult to develop.

Even the involvement of research has shifted across this period of time. Initially research centres were concerned with technology and software developments; these gave way to concerns with pedagogical and evaluation focuses. The national curriculum created concerns for and conceptions of national evaluation. The idea of the local innovation is not so clear within a focus that requires an identification of potential national practices.

History shows us that our intentions can be good, but if we change these intentions and do not follow them through for a reasonable period of time, then we may lose the possibility of gaining the potential we initially sought. It can be argued that the original intention of gaining wider awareness of industrial and employment change, and developing learners who could take forward interests in innovation and development, has been refocused to a much more specific use of computers within narrow areas of curriculum. Is it time to rethink the position again, and to promote the idea that education should once again partner industry in order to look to consider and address needs of the future?

References

1. Machin, S., Vignoles, A.: Education Policy in the UK. Centre for the Economics of Education, London School of Economics, London (2006)
2. Crapper, S.: Personal communication (2010)
3. Millwood, R.: A short history off-line. Becta, Coventry (2009)
4. Thatcher, M.: Speech on microcomputers in schools. Margaret Thatcher Foundation (1981), http://www.margaretthatcher.org/document/104609
5. Whole School Development in IT Project: Whole school IT development. Kent IT in Schools County Support Team, Sittingbourne (1991)
6. Birmingham City Council Education Department Curriculum Support Service: Information technology in your schools. Birmingham City Council Education Department, Birmingham (1990)
7. Scrimshaw, P.: Preparing for the Information Age: Synoptic Report of the Education Departments' Superhighways Initiative. Welsh Office, Department of Education for Northern Ireland, The Scottish Office, Department for Education and Employment, Cardiff, Belfast, Edinburgh, London (1997)

8. Department of Education and Science and the Welsh Office: National Curriculum Design and Technology for ages 5 to 16 – Proposals of the Secretary of State for Education and Science and the Secretary of State for Wales. Department of Education and Science and the Welsh Office, London (1989)
9. STAC: Mapping of IT: A View Across The Curriculum. Lancaster University, Lancaster (1990)
10. Department of Education and Science and the Welsh Office: Technology in the National Curriculum. Department of Education and Science and the Welsh Office, London (1990)
11. Griffin, J.A., Davies, S.: Information in the National Curriculum. Journal of Computer Assisted Learning 6, 255–264 (1990)
12. Advisory Centre for Computers in Education: Teacher assessment of I.T. capability at Key Stages 1, 2 and 3 – Planning for assessment. ACCE, Cardiff (1992)
13. National Council for Educational Technology: School-focused development materials for Key Stages 1, 2 and 3 – Focus on I.T. NCET, Coventry (1991)
14. Heywood, G., Norman, P.: Problems of educational innovation: the primary teacher's response to using the microcomputer. Journal of Computer Assisted Learning 4, 34–43 (1988)
15. Naace: A brief history of Naace. Naace (2013), `http://www.naace.co.uk/257`
16. Ball, D.: What is the role of IT within the National Mathematics Curriculum? Journal of Computer Assisted Learning 6, 239–245 (1990)
17. Govier, H.: IT in Primary Schools – the opportunities of the National Curriculum. Journal of Computer Assisted Learning 7, 162–169 (1991)
18. Passey, D.: Strategic evaluation of the impacts on learning of educational technologies: Exploring some of the issues for evaluators and future evaluation audiences. Education and Information Technologies 4(3), 223–250 (1999)
19. Passey, D.: Inclusive technology enhanced learning: Overcoming Cognitive, Physical, Emotional and Geographic Challenges. Routledge, New York (2013)
20. Computer Based Modelling Across the Curriculum Project: The Modelling Pack – Teacher resources for Computer Based Modelling in Science, Maths, Geography and Business Education for Key Stages 3, 4 and 16+. NORICC and The Advisory Unit Computers in Education, Newcastle-upon-Tyne and Hatfield (1992)
21. National Council for Educational Technology: Integrated Learning Systems – A Report of the Pilot Evaluation of ILS in the UK. NCET, Coventry (1994)
22. Nicolson, R.I.: A short-term plan for CAL. Journal of Computer Assisted Learning 3, 81–88 (1987)
23. Harris, S., Preston, C.: Software in schools. NFER, Slough (1993)
24. Pearson, H., Wilkinson, A.: The Use of the Word Processor in Assisting Children's Writing Development. Educational Review 38(2), 169–187 (1986)
25. Robson, E.H., Steward, A.P., Whitfield, G.E.: Pupils' choices in learning with computers. Journal of Computer Assisted Learning 4, 93–102 (1988)
26. Gibbons, L.: Escape or Run? Journal of Computer Assisted Learning 2, 22–27 (1986)
27. Johnston, V.M.: Attitudes towards microcomputers in learning: 2. Teachers and software for language development. Educational Research 29(2), 137–145 (1987)
28. Rogers, L.: IT in science in the National Curriculum. Journal of Computer Assisted Learning 6, 246–254 (1990)
29. Her Majesty's Inspectorate: Curriculum Matters 15: 1T from 5 to 16. HMSO, London (1989)
30. Her Majesty's Inspectorate: Aspects of Primary Education – The teaching and learning of information technology. Department of Education and Science, London (1991)

31. Watson, D.M. (ed.): The ImpacT Report – an evaluation of the impact of information technology on children's achievements in primary and secondary schools. Department for Education and King's College Centre for Educational Studies, London (1993)
32. Dearing, R.: The National Curriculum and its Assessment – final report. SCAA, London (1993)
33. The Stationery Office: Statistics of Education – Survey of Information and Communication Technologies in Schools 1999. The Stationery Office, London (1999)
34. Johnston, V.M.: The evaluation of microcomputer programs: an area of debate. Journal of Computer Assisted Learning 3, 40–50 (1987)

Theoretical and Epistemological Foundations of Integrating Digital Technologies in Education in the Second Half of the 20th Century

Eva Dakich

Latrobe University, Melbourne, Australia
E.Dakich@Latrobe.edu.au

Abstract. This chapter provides an overview of theoretical and pedagogical perspectives related to the integration of digital technologies in the second half of the 20th century. It evaluates dominant discourses, epistemological frameworks and theories of learning that have been influencing the deployment of new technologies into schools and their integration in learning and teaching. The four epistemological models examined in this chapter are behaviourism, cognitivism, constructivism and sociological and organisational interpretations of integrating new technologies into teaching and learning. The analysis focuses on the nature of knowledge, the nature of learning, the learning environment, the role of technology in student learning, the changing roles of teachers and learners, and the social and organisational consequences of technology integration that play a significant role in understanding the key determinants of managing pedagogical transformation and educational change.

Keywords: pedagogical perspectives, epistemological models, role of technology

1 Introduction

It has become apparent that dominant learning theories, pedagogical perspectives and epistemological models have a significant influence on the nature of integrating emerging technologies into learning and teaching. This chapter offers a historical perspective on four major schools of thought, prevalent in the second half of the 20th century, which influenced the uptake of digital technologies in education.

The impact of behaviourism, cognitivism and constructivism alongside with sociological and organisational interpretations of integrating new technologies is examined in relation to the learner, teacher and the process of learning. It is anticipated that the chapter will provide the readers of this book with an insight into some of the key thinking that provided a backdrop to a global pedagogical transformation and a cultural shift in 21st century education.

A. Tatnall and B. Davey (Eds.): History of Computers in Education, IFIP AICT 424, pp. 150–163, 2014.

2 Behaviourism and the Technology of Instruction

Behaviourism is a school of psychology that was influenced by pragmatism, functionalism and experimental animal psychology (Todd & Morris, 1995). Critics of behaviourism associated it with evolutionary epistemology that assumed that "*knowledge is entirely a product of our evolutionary history*" (Staddon, 2004, p. 234). Behaviourist approaches to student learning have dominated education in the second half of the 20th century. Their influence on teaching and learning can still be observed in educational institutions around the world. These approaches rest on the shoulders of giants such as Pavlov, Watson, Thorndike, Skinner, Keller, Binet and Terman, who made significant contributions to understanding human behaviour. The basic assumption of behaviourist approaches to learning is that learning results in a change in behaviour that can be observed and measured (Skinner, 1974; Thorndike & Hagen, 1969). Change in behaviour must be evaluated and assessed by carefully designed means of psychometrics, such as direct observation and tests. The goal of the learning process is strongly linked to learning outcomes and assessment of learning. Learning is a response to external stimuli, through classical conditioning (Pavlov, 1927) or operant conditioning (Skinner, 1984; Thorndike, 2000), and is strongly influenced by reinforcement, which comes in a form of reward/punishment or consequences (Skinner, 2005). However, behaviourist interpretations of learning and learners are often oversimplified and taken out of context in contemporary literature (Burton, Moore, & Magliaro, 2004; Catania & Harnad, 1988; Gaynor, 2004). Gaynor (2004) argued that many authors over-generalise and are making exaggerated claims. Examples of such approaches are linking radical behaviourism to logical positivism; and the myth 'tabula rasa' (blank slate) which is incompatible with Skinner's view of the learner who, in his own words, "*does not passively absorb knowledge from the world around him, but must play an active role*" (Skinner, 1968, p.5).

Behaviourist applications of instructional technology are based around basic principles related to the role of the learner, the nature of learning, and the generality of learning principles (Burton et al., 2004). According to Burton et al., learning occurs "*by doing, experiencing and engaging in trial and error*" (p. 9). The emphasis is on the active responding of the learner who "must be engaged in the behaviour in order to learn and to validate that learning has occurred" (p. 9). As discussed above the nature of learning is defined as "*a change of behaviour due to experience*" (p. 9). Central to learning is content. The learning material, based around the content, is delivered in contingencies or sequences that are broken down into small steps. The steps are taking the learner from simple to more complex tasks and reward him/her upon successful completion. Behaviourists claim that learning follows universal laws and "*the basic processes that promote or inhibit learning are universal to all organisms*" (Burton et al., 2004, p. 9).

The implications of behaviourist principles for learning environments have been summarised by Wilson (2000, p. 62) and are presented in the Table 1.

Table 1. Behaviourist insights for designing learning environments (Source: Wilson (2000, p. 62)

Learn by doing	People learn best by actively engaging in tasks. This is commonly called practice or learning by doing.
Taxonomies	Learning outcomes can be differentiated in their type and complexity – for example, simple S-R bonds, concept classification, and rule-following. Such learning outcomes are compiled into classification schemes called learning taxonomies, which in turn guide selection of learning objectives and instructional strategies.
Conditions of learning	For each type of learning, conditions can be identified that lead to effective learning. Identifying optimal conditions of learning forms the basis of prescriptive instructional theory using the formula: to accomplish X learning outcome, apply or arrange for Y conditions.
Behavioural objectives	Instruction should be based on clear, behaviourally specified learning objectives. Explicit formulation of objectives helps link instructional goals with evaluation and assessment, leading to increased accountability.
Focus on results	Teachers and schools should be accountable for their students' learning. Measurable behaviours are the best index of true learning outcomes and should be used to gauge instructional effectiveness.
Alignment	Good instruction exhibits an alignment or consistency between learning objectives, instructional strategies, and strategies used to assess student learning. Misalignment of these components results in inadequate or unfair instruction.
Task decomposition	People learn best when complex tasks are broken down into smaller, more manageable tasks and mastered separately.
Prerequisites	Subtasks often become prerequisites to larger tasks. That is, students learn the larger task more easily when they have first mastered the subtasks. This leads to parts-to- whole instructional sequence.
Small successes	Subtasks have another advantage: They allow students to succeed. Succeeding at tasks is reinforcing, resulting in greater motivation to continue.
Response-sensitive feedback	People learn best when they know the correctness of their efforts. When performance is not correct, specific information should be conveyed concerning what was wrong and how to improve the next time.
Science of instruction	Educators need to be precise and systematic in their thinking, their teaching, and their evaluation of students. Education can be treated as an applied science or technology, where through empirical inquiry, principles are discovered and applied.
Performance support	People need support as they perform their jobs, through the use of job aids, help systems, and feedback and incentive systems. On-the-job, just-in-time training and support works best. In general, the closer the training is to job conditions, the more effective learning will be.
Direct instruction	Giving clear directions, well prepared presentations, suitable examples, and opportunities for practice and transfer, are proven methods that result in substantial student learning.
Pretesting, diagnostics, and placement	Students should not all be forced to endure the same instructional program. Instead, instruction should branch into alternative treatments according to prior skills, motivation, and other critical variables.
Transfer	In order to be able to transfer a skill from one task to another, students need practice doing it. If students never have opportunities to practice transferring their skills, they should not be expected to be able to perform on demand in test situations.

According to Gillani (2003), the principles of behaviourist theories of learning have been successfully applied to instructional designs integrating technology in multimedia and e-learning environments. Such instructional designs are: Carroll's Mastery Learning; Skinner's Programmed Instruction; Personalised System of Instruction; Teaching to the Test; and the Direct Instruction Model. These applications of digital technologies utilise instructional approaches to learning such as tutorials and drill and practice tasks that are often criticised by contemporary literature on ICT. According to Yelland (2007), such applications of new technologies do not use their potential to engage students in new learning experiences, and in Bowers' (1998) opinion they result in decontextualized forms of knowledge.

3 Cognitivism and New Technologies

Cognitivism emerged in the 1950s as an alternative to behaviourist conceptions of learning. It was a response to the growing need for understanding the mental processes in human beings, such as perception, memory, attention and thinking. Cognitivism in education was influenced by new developments in cognitive sciences such as psychology, mathematics, cybernetics and linguistics (Nahalka, 1997). Theories of learning based on cognitive developmental research focused on mental processes by which knowledge was acquired and retrieved in order to solve problems (Gillani, 2003).

Departing from behaviourist explanations of learning, cognitivists brought the mind to the centre of psychology (Wilson, 2000). However, like their behaviourist counterparts, cognitivists also emphasised the importance of empirical research as a legitimate pathway in arriving at new understandings. According to Wilson, cognitive researchers used methods such as reaction-time experiments, eye-movement studies and think-aloud protocols to develop "*computational models of the human mind that filled many of the gaps left by behaviourism*" (p. 63).

The following key ideas and theoretical stances have shaped the development of cognitive theories of learning:

- Tolman's pioneering work on purposive behaviour and cognitive maps (Tolman, 1967; Tolman, 1990),
- Piaget's theory of cognitive development (Piaget, 1952),
- Vygotsky's Marxist psychology and social constructivism (Vygotsky, 1967, 1986),
- Blooms's Taxonomy of Educational Objectives (Bloom, 1956),
- Ausubel's theory of Advance Organizers (Ausubel, 1960),
- Gagne's Nine Events of Instruction (Gagné, 1985),
- Bandura's social cognitive theory (Bandura, 1989), and
- Bruner's views on education, and his theory on categorisation (Bruner, 1986; Bruner, 1990).

There are two main schools of cognitivist interpretations of learning that influenced the use of digital technologies in education. These are symbolic cognition or Information Processing Theory, and situated cognition.

Symbolic cognition or Information Processing Theory (IPT) has shaped the early cognitivist theory of learning environments and instructional design. According to Lewis' explanation in the MIT Encyclopaedia of Cognitive Sciences (Lewis, 1999), symbolic models of human cognition are perceived as computational processes. These cognitive models are made up of a set of procedures that enable the performance of specific tasks, such as memory tasks, language comprehension and problem-solving. Lewis (1999) argued that scientific explanations of these models come from cognitive psychology and artificial intelligence, which provide the theoretical foundations of symbolic cognition or IPT.

IPT had a significant influence on instructional design towards the end of the 20th century. It was anticipated that artificial intelligence and expert systems would replace the teacher. Distance learning and early online learning environments held hopes for automatising the learning process. Situated cognition viewed children's growth in knowledge "*as a series of stages from concrete to abstract forms of reasoning or as accumulation of procedural and declarative knowledge about the world*" Wilson (2000, p. 64). Wilson argued that children "*make sense of their worlds by reference to schemas, mental models, and other complex memory structures*" (p. 64). In his opinion "*differences between encountered experience and schemas can prompt further inquiry and reflection to resolve the conflict. Instruction should help learners assimilate and accommodate new information into existing schemas and cognitive structures*" (p. 64).

Situated cognition is the other cognitive theory of learning. According to Wilson (2000), situated cognition departs from rigid models of IPT and symbolic computation. It focuses on "*conscious reasoning and thought*" (p. 65) and the context of situated action. Situated cognition is often associated with social constructivism (Wilson, 2000, p. 65).

Jonassen, Davidson, Collins, Campbell, & Haag (1995) argued that while cognitivism represents a paradigm shift from behaviourism, symbolic learning and situated learning represented two distinct schools of thought. According to Jonassen at al. (1995), proponents of symbolic reasoning represented the traditional objectivist paradigm. They perceived the world as a structure that can be "*modelled and mapped onto the learner, and that the goal of the learner was to 'mirror' reality as interpreted by the instructor*" (p. 10). Because knowledge was thought to be external to the knower it was believed that it could be transmitted from one person to another (Jonassen et.al, 1995, pp. 10-11).

According to Jonassen et al. (1995), unlike symbolic reasoning, situated learning rests on different epistemological assumptions about the learner and learning. This is how they describe this new paradigm:

> *Constructivism (which provides the psychological/philosophical foundation for situated learning) begins with a different set of assumptions about learning. Constructivists believe that our personal world is constructed in our minds and that these personal constructions define our personal realities. The mind is the instrument of thinking which interprets events, objects and perspectives rather than seeking to remember and comprehend an objective knowledge. The mind filters input from the world in the process of making those interpretations. The important epistemological assumption of constructivism is that knowledge is a function of how the*

individual creates meaning from his or her experiences; it is not a function of what someone else says is true. Each of us conceives of external reality somewhat differently, based upon our unique set of experiences with the world and our beliefs about them. (Jonassen et.al, 1995, p. 11)

The authors argued that constructivist educators strive to create learning environments that require active participation of the learner with the learning environment in order to create a personal view of the world. In their opinion, the purpose of this new theory of learning is not to "*predict the outcomes of instructional interventions*" (p. 10) but as Bruner (1990) said to encourage learners to discover new meanings through their encounters with the world. Jonassen et al. (1995) maintained that this new learning theory "*transcended the behaviourism–cognitivism dialectic and entered a new era of theorizing*" (p. 9). The Jonassen et al.'s summary of the features of these two distinctive cognitive theories is presented in the Table 2.

Table 2. Contrasting assumptions of paradigms (Jonassen et al. (1995, p. 10))

Symbolic Reasoning		*Situated Learning*
	Knowledge	
Objective		Subjective
Independent		Contextualized
Stable		Relative
Applied		Situated in Action
Fixed		Fluid
	Learning	
Objectivist		Constructivist
Product-oriented		Process-Oriented
Abstract		Authentic
Symbolic		Experiential
	Memory	
Stored Representations		Connections , potentials
	Knowledge	
Functionally equivalent to	representation	Embedded in experience
the real world		Personally constructed
Replication of expert		Personalized
Symbolic, generalized		
	Instruction	
Top down		Bottom up
Deductive		Inductive
Application of Symbols		Apprenticeship
	Computational	
Symbolic reasoning	model	Connectionist
Production rule		Neural network
Symbol manipulations		Probabilistic, embedded

The above theoretical framework revealed a powerful shift in the way the knowledge-learner-teacher-technology relationships were conceptualised. Similarly to other transitions in pedagogical thought, this shift reflected the hallmarks of fresh and emerging schools of thought of the second half of the 20th century in social and natural sciences, such as postmodernism (Foucault, 2002; Giroux, 1992; Heidegger, 1977; Wittgenstein, 1953) and constructivism (Glasersfeld, 1995b; Piaget, 1970; Vygotsky, 1978, 1986); the theory of probability (Kolmogorov, 1956), neural networks and Fuzzy Logic (Kosko, 1993; Zadeh, 1973).

Cognitive theories of learning have made a significant contribution to the design and development of constructivist learning environments integrating new technologies, especially in the fields of inquiry training, hypermedia, discovery learning and simulation (Gillani, 2003). According to Gillani, cognitivists viewed technology as a tool for creating instructional materials and learning environments that allow children to "*construct, test, and refine their own cognitive representations of the world*" (p. 64).

In his book on Learning Theories and the design of E-learning environments (Gillani, 2003), Gillani emphasised the contribution of Seymour Papert, Robert Davies, Duffy and Jonassen. Papert, built on Piaget's work (with whom he worked for a number of years), and developed the LOGO project, a "*computer-based discovery learning approach*" (2003, p. 62), that enabled children to construct their own knowledge. He also created Microworlds, a learning environment which allows young children, to become designers, constructors and explorers. Robert Davies was another prominent figure in using technology to design constructivist learning environments. Davies made a significant contribution to the development of multimedia and hypermedia through his Plato project that combined text, graphics, animation and audio and the development of interactive textbooks. Gillani (2003) argued that the Plato project inspired the development of multimedia authoring software such as Hyperstudio, Director, and Flash that enable teachers to create their own interactive, multimedia teaching material. Duffy and Jonassen's (1992) application of constructivist ideas to learning with new technologies provided an alternative framework to early computational views of cognition. According to Kerr (2004), this new epistemological framework redefined the role of the learner and interpretations of how knowledge is constructed.

4 Moving Forward on the Constructivist Continuum with ICT

Constructivism has its foundations in philosophy, psychology, cybernetics (Winn, 2004), and in cultural history (Glasersfeld, 1989). The philosophical roots of constructivist thought relate back to Kant's idea of the human cognitive apparatus, Kuhn's analysis of scientific revolutions and paradigms, Dewey's conceptualisations of knowledge and knowing, Piaget's cognitive theories of personal development, and Vygotsky's interpretations of the impact of the social-cultural environment on learning.

Constructivism is an umbrella term for several schools of thought, such as social constructivism, radical constructivism and critical constructivism, that question traditional notions of knowledge, knowing and knowledge production (Glasersfeld,

1989). According to von Glasersfeld (1995a), constructivism emerged "*out of a profound dissatisfaction with theories of knowledge in the tradition of Western philosophy*" (p. 6). This Western philosophical tradition is often referred to as objectivism. Kincheloe (2005) argued that "*objectivism is grounded on the rationalist myth of cold reason*" (p. 13) and exists as a "*scientific discovery of external reality*" (p. 13).

The following constructivist ideas relevant to new learning with ICT will be reviewed in this section: Jonassen's model of constructivist learning environments, and Vygotsky's theory of Zone of Proximal Development (ZPD) in relation to learning with new technologies. These ideas provide the theoretical foundations for creating meaningful and relevant educational experiences for both students and teachers that will prepare them for the challenges and uncertainties of living, learning and working in a digital world.

Constructivist theories of learning are based on the premises that learning is both individually and socially constructed by learners through their interactions with the world (Jonassen, 1999b) Constructivist learning environments rest on these assumptions and represent an "*antidote to reproductive learning*" (Jonassen, 1999b, p. 1). Such learning environments engage learners in active, manipulative, intentional, complex, authentic, collaborative and conversational and reflective learning activities (Jonassen, 1999b, 2001) In Jonassen's opinion constructivist learning environments support the adoption of problem-based, project-based, case-based, and issue-based learning. In his opinion, new technologies, especially web-based resources provide valuable tools and resources for scaffolding such learning experiences. His model of constructivist learning environments (Jonassen, 2001) shown in Figure 1, reflect these principles.

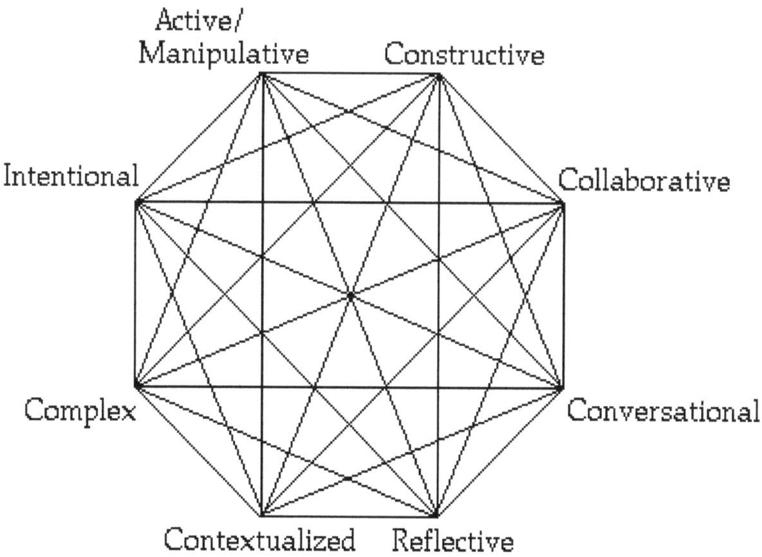

Fig. 1. Jonassen's model of constructivist learning environments (2001)

Constructivist learning is authentic, that is, it makes meaning from practice related to learners' personal contexts, and is based on scaffolding and social interaction. Yet most learning in schools occurs in learning environments that are abstract and decontextualised (Brown, Collins, & Duguid, 1989; Kolb, 2000; Polly, 2003).

One of the pioneers of recognising the implications of the social context for learning was Lev Vygotsky. He identified two levels of cognitive development: the actual developmental level, and the Zone of Proximal Development (ZPD) (Vygotsky, 1978). Learners actual developmental level reflects their cognitive maturity related to the "*development of mental functions that has been established as a result of certain already completed mental cycles*" (Vygotsky, 1978, p. 85). Through social interaction, such as scaffolding or collaboration in multi-age settings, the boundaries of the actual developmental level related to problem-solving can be extended. In such situations learners move into a new zone of cognitive maturity, the ZPD, which, according to Vygostky, is the "distance between the actual developmental level as determined by individual problem-solving and the level of potential development as determined through problem-solving through adult guidance or in collaboration with more capable peers" (p. 86). Vygotsky's theory is highly relevant for learning in the information age (Holmes et al., 2001), with research studies (Masters & Yelland, 2002; Salomon, Globerson, & Guterman, 1989; Siraj-Blatchford & Siraj-Blatchford, 2006) showing that new technologies are tools and resources that provide opportunities for higher-order thinking, inquiry and problem-solving under guidance or in collaborative settings.

5 Sociological and Organisational Interpretations of Integrating ICT in Teaching and Learning

Sociological and organisational interpretations of new technologies have been often associated with economic progress and efficiency in the knowledge society. It has been assumed, that new technologies will bring to education "*efficiency, order and productivity*" (Kerr, 2004, p. 113), and facilitate educational change, including the transformation of existing structures and organisational forms (Orlikowski & Yates, 2006) as well as social practices, which according to Giddens (1984) represent individual or collective human action, and are "*performed for social reasons*" (Tuomela, 2002, p. 78).

Kerr (2004) argued that this "*mechanistic enthusiasm*" (p. 113) expected new technologies to bring solutions to all educational problems and challenges, that would with the implementation of the 'right program' run schools and classrooms smoothly. Kerr observed a dialectic relationship between educational organisations and new technologies. He said that while the way technologies are integrated into schools depends on the "*patterns of organization*" (p. 119), at the same time new technologies affect the life of organisations and often "*translate over time into unexpected organizational and social consequences*" (p. 119).

To understand the human, social, and organisational consequences of technology integration into social practices it is important to look at the ontological and epistemological foundations of contemporary theoretical explanations in social theory and organisational science. Orlikovski and Robey (1991) interpreted technology deployment from two different perspectives: the objectivist and the subjectivist perspective. The objectivist view assigns technology the role of a "*discrete object ... capable of having an impact on social systems*" (p. 146), while the subjectivist interpretation is based on the premise of social action and human interaction. In Orlikowski and Robey's opinion objectivist interpretations seem to be mechanistic and do not allow us to foresee the real consequences of technology integration into existing social practices because they do not take into account the contextual and temporal nature of social action.

Based on the above interpretations new technologies can be viewed as 'hardware', the "*equipment, machines, and instruments humans use in productive activities*" (Orlikowski, 1992, p. 399), or social technologies that embrace "the generic tasks, techniques and knowledge utilised when humans engage in any productive activities" (p. 399). These philosophically contrasting interpretations assign different roles to technology. According to Orlikowski (1992), early organisational researchers have assumed technology to have "deterministic impacts" on organisational structures, which explains views related to the role of new technologies as 'a catalyst' or 'agent' of educational change and school structures. Other researchers have been focusing on "*the human action aspect of technology, seeing it more as a product of shared interpretations and interventions*" (pp. 399-400). Orlikowski (1992) argued that more recent studies have combined the two perspectives and drew inferences between technology as a resource and the agency of human actors in organisational contexts.

This new approach to understanding the consequences of technology integration emerged from Giddens' Structuration Theory (Giddens, 1984), where the abstract structures and human actors are in constant interaction (Giddens, 1984; Orlikowski, 1992). Giddens' Structuration Theory has been instrumental in understanding the interactions between human actors (teachers and learners), the structures and social contexts within which they operate (schools, classrooms, communities), and the structures (including rules and resources created by governments and schools) that have been influencing the social practices of teaching and learning with digital technologies.

Giddens (1984) argued that human actors and contexts of social interaction are "*positioned' relative to one another*" (p. xxv) "*along the coordinates of time and space that translate into the "character of the physical milieu of day-to-day life*" (p. xxv), embracing resources, rules and routines. Giddens maintained that routines or habitual action constitute the foundations of social life and provide its recursive nature. In his opinion routinisation is vital to human actors, granting them a sense of "trust and ontological security" (p. xxiii). In Giddens' opinion human actors try to make meaning of their social practices within a particular social context situated in time and space by "*reflexive monitoring*" (p. 5) of their activities. Through reflexive monitoring they rationalise their practices and develop theoretical understandings or personal theories of action. Reflexive monitoring and meaning-making help actors become knowledgeable agents capable of transforming their competence from 'practical consciousness' to 'discursive consciousness'. In other words, actors transition from the ability to perform the action to the ability to "*report discursively about their intentions, and reasons for, acting as they do*" (p. 6) which provides them with agency. Human agency is guided by intentions, and translates into the ability to "*intervene in the world*" (Giddens, 1984, p. 14), and/or the "ability to transform social relations to some degree" (Sewell, 1992, p. 20). The ability/power of agents to initiate change is both constrained and enabled by rules (or cultural schemas according to Sewell) and resources which constitute the structures within which they operate. Giddens' premise that resources are media through which power is exercised is particularly interesting from the perspective of this study. It helps us understand the multiple tensions between structures and individual or collective agency in teaching and learning with new technologies that can result in reproduction of existing social practices, or alternatively, through new practices it can lead to innovation, evolution and educational change.

6 Concluding remarks

This chapter offered an overview of four influential theoretical frameworks that guided the integration of digital technologies in education in the second half of the 20th century. The epistemological stances of behaviourism, cognitivism, constructivism as well as sociological and organizational interpretations of digital technologies were examined in order to understand how knowledge was contextualised, how social practices of learning and teaching were constructed and how conceptual frameworks for technology integration have evolved from teacher centred and mechanistic approaches to learner centred flexible designs.

Given the magnitude of the impact of these theoretical shifts had on learning and pedagogical design in the 20th century it is anticipated that revisiting the above epistemological frameworks will help educators critically examine and rethink current models of learning and teaching with digital technologies.

References

1. Ausubel, D.P.: The use of advance organizers in the learning and retention of meaningful verbal material. Journal of Educational Psychology (51), 267–272 (1960)
2. Bandura, A.: Social cognitive theory. In: Vasta, R. (ed.) Annals of Child Development. Six theories of child development, vol. 6, pp. 1–60. JAI Press, Greenwich (1989)
3. Bloom, B.S. (ed.): Taxonomy of educational objectives: The classification of educational goals - Handbook 1: Cognitive domain. David McKay Company, Inc., New York (1956)
4. Bowers, C.A.: Toward a balanced perspective on the educational uses of computers: Advantages, myths, and the responsibilities of educators. International Journal of Leadership in Education 1(1), 75–83 (1998)
5. Brown, J.S.: Growing up digital: How the web changes work, education, and the ways people learn. USDLA Journal (2002), `http://www.usdla.org/html/journal/FEB02_Issue/FEB02_issue.pdf` (retrieved May 21, 2004)
6. Bruner, J.: Actual minds, possible worlds. Harvard University Press, Cambridge (1986)
7. Bruner, J.: Acts of meaning: Four lectures on mind and culture. Harvard University Press, Cambridge (1990)

8. Burton, J.K., Moore, D.M., Magliaro, S.G.: Behaviorism and instructional technology. In: Jonassen, D. (ed.) Handbook of Research for Educational Communications and Technology, pp. 3–37 (2004), http://www.questia.com/read/104857577?title=Handbook%20of%20Research%20on%20Educational%20Communications%20and%20Technology
9. Catania, A.C., Harnad, S.R.: The selection of behavior: The operant behaviorism of BF Skinner: Comments and consequences. Cambridge University Press, Cambridge (1988)
10. Duffy, T.M., Jonassen, D.H.: Constructivism and the technology of instruction: A (1992)
11. Foucault, M.: The archaeology of knowledge, (reprint ed.). Routledge, London (2002)
12. Gagné, R.M.: The conditions of learning and theory of instruction, 4th edn. Holt, Rinehart and Winston, New York (1985)
13. Gaynor, S.T.: Skepticism of caricatures: BF Skinner turns 100. Skeptical Inquirer 28(1), 26–29 (2004)
14. Giddens, A.: The constitution of society: Outline of a theory of structuration. Polity Press, Cambridge (1984)
15. Gillani, B.B.: Learning theories and the design of E-learning environments. University Press of America, Lanham (2003)
16. Giroux, H.A.: Border crossings: Cultural workers and the politics of education. Routledge, New York (1992)
17. von Glasersfeld, E. (ed.): The international encyclopaedia of education, vol. 1. Pergamon Press, Oxford (1989)
18. von Glasersfeld, E.: A constructivist approach to teaching. In: Steffe, L.P., Gale, J.E. (eds.) Constructivism in Education, pp. 3–16. Lawrence Erlbaum Associates, Hillsdale (1995a)
19. von Glasersfeld, E.: Radical constructivism: A way of knowing and learning. Falmer Press, London (1995b)
20. Heidegger, M.: The question concerning technology, and other essays. In: Lovitt, W. (trans.). Garland Publishers, New York (1977)
21. Jonassen, D., Davidson, M., Collins, M., Campbell, J., Haag, B.B.: Constructivism and computer-mediated communication in distance education. The American Journal of Distance Education 9(2), 7–26 (1995)
22. Jonassen, D.H.: Constructivist learning environments on the web: Engaging students in meaningful learning. Education Technology Conference and Exhibition (1999b), http://www3.moe.edu.sg/edumall/mpite/edtech/papers/d1.pdf (retrieved August 24, 2004)
23. Jonassen, D.H.: Design of constructivist learning environments, CLEs (2001), http://www.coe.missouri.edu/~jonassen/courses/CLE/ (retrieved March 14, 2005)
24. Kerr, S.T.: Toward a sociology of educational technology. In: Jonassen, D. (ed.) Handbook of Research on Educational Communications and Technology, pp. 113–142. Lawrence Erlbaum Associates, Mahwah (2004)
25. Kincheloe, J.L.: Critical constructivism. Peter Lang Primers in Education, New York (2005)
26. Kolb, D.: The process of experiential learning. In: Cross, R.L., Israelit, S. (eds.) Strategic Learning in a Knowledge Economy: Individual, Collective, and Organizational Learning Process, pp. 313–332. Butterworth-Heinemann, Woburn (2000)
27. Kolmogorov, A.N.: Foundations of the theory of probability. In: Morrison, N. (trans.), 2nd edn., Chelsea Pub. Co, New York (1956)
28. Kosko, B.: Fuzzy thinking: The new science of fuzzy logic. Hyperion, New York (1993)

29. Lewis, R.L.: Cognitive modeling, symbolic. In: Wilson, R., Keil, F. (eds.) The MIT Encyclopedia of the Cognitive Sciences. MIT Press, Cambridge (1999)
30. Masters, J., Yelland, N.: Teacher scaffolding: An exploration of exemplary practice. Education and Information Technologies 7(4), 313–321 (2002)
31. Nahalka, I.: Kognitív pedagógia. In: Bathory, Z., Falus, I. (eds.) Pedagó giai Lexicon, vol. 2, Keraban Kiadó, Budapest (1997)
32. Orlikowski, W.J.: The duality of technology: Rethinking the concept of technology in organizations. Organization Science 3(3), 398–427 (1992)
33. Orlikowski, W.J., Robey, D.: Information technology and the structuring of organizations. Information Systems Research 2(2), 143–169 (1991)
34. Orlikowski, W.J., Yates, J.: ICT and organizational change: A commentary. Journal of Applied Behavioral Science 42(1), 127–134 (2006)
35. Pavlov, I.P.: Conditioned reflexes: An investigation of the physiological activity of the cerebral cortex. In: Anrep, G.V. (trans.). Oxford University Press, London (1927)
36. Piaget, J.: The origins of intelligence in children (1952), `http://www.questia.com/read/82225770?title=The%20Origins%20of%20Intelligence%20in%20Children`
37. Polly, D.: Anchoring student's learning in technology-rich authentic environments. Paper presented at the World Conference on Educational Multimedia, Hypermedia (2003)
38. Salomon, G., Globerson, T., Guterman, E.: The computer as a zone of proximal development: Internalizing reading-related metacognitions from a reading partner. Journal of Educational Psychology 81(4), 620–627 (1989)
39. Sewell Jr., W.H.: A theory of structure: Duality, agency, and transformation. The American Journal of Sociology 98(1), 1–29 (1992)
40. Siraj-Blatchford, I., Siraj-Blatchford, J.: A Guide to developing the ICT curriculum for early childhood education: Trentham Books Ltd. (2006)
41. Skinner, B.F.: The technology of teaching. Prentice-Hall, Englewood Cliffs (1968)
42. Skinner, B.F.: About behaviorism. Knopf, New York (1974)
43. Skinner, B.F.: An operant analysis of problem solving. Behavioral and Brain Sciences 7(4), 583–613 (1984)
44. Skinner, B.F.: Science and human behavior (2005), `http://www.bfskinner.org/f/Science_and_Human_Behavior.pdf`
45. Staddon, J.E.R.: Scientific imperialism and behaviorist epistemology. Behavior and Philosophy 32(1), 231–242 (2004)
46. Thorndike, E.L.: Animal intelligence: Experimental studies. Transaction Publishers, New Brunswick (U.S.A) (2000)
47. Thorndike, R.L., Hagen, E.P.: Measurement and evaluation in psychology and education. Wiley, New York (1969)
48. Todd, J.T., Morris, E.K.: Modern perspectives on B. F. Skinner and contemporary behaviorism. Greenwood Press Westport, Conn. (1995)
49. Tolman, E.C.: Purposive behavior in animals and men. Appleton-Century-Crofts, New York (1967)
50. Tolman, E.C.: Cognitive maps in rats and men. In: Shaw, G.L., McGough, J.L., Rose, S.P.R. (eds.) Neurobiology of Learning and Memory, (reprint ed.), pp. 67–86. World Scientific Publishing Co. Pte. Ltd., New Jersey (1990)
51. Vygotsky, L.S.: Gondolkoás és beszéd. Akadémiai Kiadó, Budapest (1967)
52. Vygotsky, L.S.: Mind in society: The development of higher psychological processes. Harvard University Press, Cambridge (1978)

53. Vygotsky, L.S.: Thought and language. In: Kozulin, A. (trans.), Newly revised ed. The MIT Press, Cambridge (1986)
54. Wilson, B.G.: Situated cognition in theoretical and practical context. In: Jonassen, D.H., Land, S.M. (eds.) Theoretical Foundations of Learning Environments (2000), http://www.questia.com/read/24455808?title=Theoretical%20Foundations%20of%20Learning%20Environments#
55. Winn, W.: Cognitive Perspectives in Psychology. In: Jonassen, D. (ed.) Handbook of Research on Educational Communications and Technology, pp. 79–112. Lawrence Erlbaum Associates (2004)
56. Wittgenstein, L.: Philosophical investigations. B. Blackwell, Oxford (1953)
57. Yelland, N.: Shift to the future: Rethinking learning with new technologies in education. Routledge, London (2007)
58. Zadeh, L.A.: Outline of a new approach to the analysis of complex systems and decision processes. IEEE Transactions on Systems, Man, and Cybernetics 3, 28–44 (1973)

The Introduction of Computers in Irish Schools

Denise Leahy[1] and Dudley Dolan[2]

[1] Trinity College Dublin, Ireland
[2] CEN Workshop on ICT Skills, Ireland
denise.leahy@scss.tcd.ie

Abstract. This chapter is a reflection on the introduction of computers and computer education in schools at primary and secondary level in Ireland. It is based on a review of the policy documents from that time and a series of interviews with teachers who were involved in the early stages of the use of computers in schools during the late 1970s, 1980s and 1990s. The use of computers in schools has developed over those last forty years, this is reflected in Irish Government policy and is discussed in the chapter.

Keywords: computers in education, ECDL.

1 Introduction

This chapter discusses the early days of the use of computers in Irish schools and contains anecdotes from people involved in computing in those early days. Teachers involved in the introduction of computing were interviewed. The interviewees were asked to describe their experiences with introducing computers into schools and in teaching using technology. The finance available for computers and the role of parents in funding the early adopters were examined.

The European Computer Driving Licence (ECDL) was created by a European Esprit project which started in 1995 and resulted in the launch of ECDL in 1997 [1]. Pilot studies were run in Ireland in 1996 and the concept was introduced to the Irish Minister for Education. Initially the ECDL was not considered suitable as a module to be presented in schools, however today ECDL is used in more than 50% of secondary schools.

The Irish Department of Education and Skills [2] is introducing a new Junior Cycle Curriculum in 2014/2015 which has been created by the National Council for Curriculum and Assessment. This defines six key skills as follows; Managing Myself, Staying Well, Communicating, Being Creative, Working with Others, and Managing Information and Thinking. It is interesting to note that working with digital technology is seen to be an integral part of each of the skills.

2 Policy

The report *Computers in Ireland* [3], which was published in 1971, proposed that a national IT strategy should be developed by a newly created Central Computing

A. Tatnall and B. Davey (Eds.): History of Computers in Education, IFIP AICT 424, pp. 164–173, 2014.

Council. The report identified 'training and education' as an area which needed attention. This training was described as being needed for management and computer specialists and would assist in understanding the potential of the computer. In 1971 computer studies had not been introduced into primary or secondary level education. Trinity College Dublin installed its first computer in 1962, an IBM 1620, and began offering computer courses in 1965. The first undergraduate degree programme in Computer Science began in Trinity College in the late 1960s [4].

The Irish Government set up the Industrial Development Authority (IDA) as an autonomous state-sponsored organization in April 1970 [5]. The brief of the IDA was the furtherance of industrial development in Ireland. This was very new for Ireland as it had always depended on agriculture and the perceived wisdom was that there were no natural resources in Ireland and that industry was very weak. The IDA carried out extensive promotional programmes worldwide and provided grants and other financial incentives to attract new and existing manufacturing and technical service industries. It provided training grants towards the costs of training workers and in general provided an environment conducive to Industrial Development and in fact attracted many industries to Ireland.

The IDA promoted the electronics industry in Ireland and by the late 1970s this industry was seen as an area of great potential growth. Initially the IDA attracted computer component manufacturers; this was followed by the mainstream computer manufacturers. Eventually these assembly type operations moved to lower cost areas of the globe and the IDA set about attracting the newly developing software industry to set up in Ireland. It was against this background of Government Policy that the initial consideration of education in computing began in Ireland in the early 1970s. At that time there were mainframe computers and mini computers in business, but access to computing was rather expensive for schools. In most cases, it was beyond the resources and finance available in schools. However, some enthusiastic teachers became interested in computer programming and borrowed time on computers belonging to local businesses, local authorities or universities. Programs were usually recorded on punched cards and compiled or assembled in batches on the available machines. It was a slow and cumbersome process as compared to the methods used today. This gave much valuable experience to the small group of enthusiasts and indeed the beginnings of a group named the Computer Education Society of Ireland (CESI) started in 1971 [6]. This was a group of teachers and academics who set the group up with an affiliation to the Irish Computer Society; the latter had been founded in 1967 [7].

Today Ireland is recognised as a major hub for ICT companies with nine of the top ten US companies having a presence in the country. Some of the largest ICT companies such as Intel, Microsoft and Google have major centres located in Dublin.

3 The Introduction of Computers in Irish Schools

The need for teacher training was recognized as being a necessary initial step towards the introduction of computing in schools. Summer courses in computing for second level teachers were introduced by the Department of Education in 1971. These were one week courses during the summer holidays. The early courses were geared towards programming in BASIC, COMAL, PASCAL and LOGO [8].

Primary school teachers started involvement in IT education in the early 1980s. The Curriculum Unit of the Department of Education established a pilot project in 1984 [9]. This project was a major curriculum development initiative which had the aim of exploring possible uses of computing as it was available at the time. Thirty four schools took part in the pilot project. One of these schools was Taney Parish Primary School where one of the authors is currently Chairman of the Board of Management.

The colleges of education and the universities also provided in-service education in computing. There were a number of diploma courses in 'Computers in Education' available as well as shorter courses. By 1992 over 1,000 teachers had completed diploma courses provided by various colleges.

3.1 The Growth of Computers in Schools

In 1982, in discussing 'Tomorrow's Classrooms' [10], the inventor of the programming language Logo, Seymour Papert, stated: "*In this written chat I use a series of encounters between children, computers and powerful ideas to build up a dream about how children might one day learn.*" Ireland has been moving along this track. In a report 'New Information Technology in the Irish School System', which was published in 1992, the growth in the use of technology in Irish schools was examined and the following results were documented [8]:

1. The children in Primary Schools gained many benefits from interacting with computers and that computers were helpful in dealing with individual educational needs.
2. It was found that children with mild mental handicap gained from their experience in using a computer.
3. Teachers working with visually impaired children found that most software packages were too highly visual.
4. Children with profound hearing impairment were found to be motivated by using a computer.

A computer studies module was introduced into the Leaving Certificate examination in 1980 as part of the mathematics syllabus. The module was optional and was monitored separately from the main mathematics course. A computer studies syllabus was introduced in 1985 into the Junior Cycle Curriculum. There was no formal examination although sample examination papers were provided to indicate the depth of knowledge expected. The technical drawing syllabus required the students should have an awareness of the developments in computer graphics. Computers were also mentioned in the Physics syllabus.

3.2 Some Experiences

Discussions were held with teachers from several schools. The experiences of three of these schools are described in three minor 'case studies' below; general comments from other teachers follow the case studies. From these discussions, it became clear that the schools that were successful in introducing computing to schools invariably had a teacher who was interested in technology. This was not always the science or the mathematics teacher, but could be anyone with this interest. The examples below are fairly typical of what happened in many schools during the 1980s:

Case Study 1: Taney Parish Primary School

Taney Parish Primary School, located in south Dublin, is one of the larger national schools in the Republic of Ireland, with 446 pupils. There are 21 class teachers and the staff includes a further 14 staff providing various extracurricular activities. In March 1984 a teacher representative to the Parent Teacher Association (PTA) proposed that should the parents be willing to assist with fund raising then the teachers (18 in all at that time) would prepare themselves to introduce the topic in the classroom.

By the end of June 1984 the school possessed 2 BBC Model B microcomputers with associated hardware and a little software. In September 1984 the school was selected to participate in the pilot project 'Microcomputers in Primary Education' set up by the Department of Education [11]. By March 1985 the school had 3 BBC computers, together with an Amstrad CPC 464 and an Atari 800.

By this time all the teachers had taken an introductory course in computers and they decided to organise an open day where parents could see what their children had been able to achieve with the computers. In addition a computer club was set up so that those enthusiastic pupils (and teachers) could pursue their interest outside school hours. The success of the introduction of computers to the school was greatly assisted by very enthusiastic and generous parents.

A report prepared in 1985, made available by one of the interviewees, outlined the results of the pilot project and contained the following comments from pupils [12]

1. *"My opinion of computers is mixed, they can be a great help and a great nuisance"*
2. *"Some boys and girls don't have computers and have never seen them. In Ireland I think there should be a course for kids and adults. My Dad only knows how to load a disc and do a few programmes for the Apple, whereas I can do graphics, sound, music and so on. If there were no computers in school I wouldn't know anything about them and I'd feel a bit old-fashioned"*
3. *"I think computers are good because you can have fun learning, not like class, which is sometimes boring"*
4. *"If computers went away there would be no fun anymore"*

In 1994, a local benefactor gave a large donation to the school which was used to set up the first dedicated computer room. This room was equipped with 10 Apple computers and all classes had an opportunity to spend time using this facility.

In the late 1990s the discussion about the relative merits of PCs versus Apples gained traction. While grants from the Department of Education were used to buy more Apples when it came to updating the facilities and moving to a bigger and better computer room the pressure from the parents, who were providing the funds, came down in favour of the PC. Today the school is fully networked and all classrooms have interactive whiteboards and all teachers have laptops. Some of the resource teachers who deal with special needs children also use iPads.

Case Study 2: Newpark Comprehensive School

Newpark Comprehensive School was established in 1972 [13]. In 1981, the Irish Department of Education decided that second level schools should have access to a computer and if there wasn't one already in the school, they would provide one. Newpark requested and were granted an Apple II. When this was delivered the box was put in a small room beside a science laboratory. While it was given to the Mathematics department in the school, only one of the teachers was interested. One of the senior mathematics pupils was aware of the computer and requested to be allowed to use it. The computer was set up and was made operational due to the knowledge and enthusiasm of the mathematics teacher and the interested pupil.

In due course, the PTA (Parent Teacher Association) became interested and bought about a dozen Apple IIs or maybe IIes. The school provided a large room at the top of a Victorian house adjacent to the mathematics teaching room. As the Apple IIs became obsolete, again the PTA became involved. This time, many of them being in business and more used to IBM PCs, they insisted on going for the PC platform. Although teachers felt the Apple system was more user-friendly but the Parents were paying. In fact, one of them later confessed that the teachers had been right. As it turned out, the PCs soon moved on from needing to know DOS to operate them. This time the school converted what had been the Language Laboratory for use as a computer room. Again this was located adjacent to the mathematics teaching room.

The Department (of Education) introduced a one-year diploma course in Computers as part of the Leaving Certificate for Fifth Year students. That was taught for many years, concentrating on programming. Later, encouraged by Trinity's Spin A Web competition, the teaching included building a website. The school also included a 10-week computer module into Transition Year. For that the focus was on using a word processing package to develop their CVs.

Case Study 3: Dundalk Grammar School

The Principal of this school has a particular interest in developing information technology in schools and prior to holding his current position he was on a number of advisory committees making recommendations to the Irish Department of Education. He did not restrict his expertise to Ireland but also contributed to Educational development in Canada, Cyprus, Estonia, Lithuania and the UK. He carries on his deep interest in ICT in Education in his current role and the computer facilities in Dundalk Grammar School are very impressive.

Although the early technology was from Apple, this changed when the parents became involved in fund raising and decision making. The Principal noted that it was not always the mathematics teacher that was involved but in some cases chemistry. The main driver was the enthusiasm of the individual teacher. The PC versus Apple debate has been solved by having two computer laboratories, one for Apple and one for PCs. In addition there is a computer graphics laboratory for woodworking design, and even a 3D printer. Dundalk Grammar School is very involved in technology and competitions involving technology; they won the F1 in schools competition in 2010 and 2011. This is a competition to design and build the fastest racing cars powered by compressed air. It is sponsored by the Irish Computer Society.

Other Anecdotes

Other teachers discussed the progress made during the 1985s and 1990s. The following list contains some of the experiences:

1985 – There was a course for primary teachers in Applesoft Basic.

1986 – School used an electronic typewriter with word processing capabilities, had an 11 character display.

1990 – School of 900 primary pupils had 4 BBC Micro Computers, 2 Acorn computers were added, using the RISC OS, eventually the BBCs were retired and school had 6 Acorns. These had no hard disk and were booted by a 3 ½" floppy disk. Major use was by the 'Remedial' teacher. The office also had a computer and an early version of Facility as a student database.

1991 – School had: Hardware – IBM compatible (an XT), amber screen, Double 5¼" floppy disk drive, Black and white printer, continuous feed paper. Software – Wordstar, Letterex (to modify fonts and styles), a label generator, Print Shop to make banners and posters.

1992 – Purchase of first PCs, Additional software: MS Works, Type to Learn, Serif PagePlus desktop publisher.

In the mid-1990s, the Irish Department of Education supplied every school with a Gateway computer - many boxes remained unopened for months, and most ended up in the office for occasional use. Schools also got a modem and one extra telephone line for a dial-up connection to the internet. The 'holy grail' was an ISDN line.

In the late 1990s, Tesco launched a 'Computers for Schools' project. A voucher was given by Tesco for every pound spent in the store. Parents collected these and the schools used them to get free computers.

4 ECDL

The use of technology was becoming more common in business and even in the home in the early 1990s. The World Wide Web was beginning to be used and the Worldwide Web Consortium (W3C) founded in 1994. At this time, there was concern in the European Union about the lack of computer skills for all European citizens, acknowledging that these skills were needed to take advantage of potential opportunities and to minimise the risks of the new technologies [14].

4.1 ECDL History

The Council of European Information Processionals (CEPIS) set up a project in 1995 to define the skills and knowledge needed to examine how to raise IT skill levels in industry in Europe. At first, the CEPIS team consisted of Norway, Finland, Sweden, Denmark, and Ireland. An extended project team, consisting of the original countries plus representatives from Austria, France, Italy, The Netherlands and United Kingdom, came together to develop the initial work and the concept. This task force looked for a skills model or syllabus definition [15].

The Finnish Computer Driving Licence had been introduced in Finland in 1988 and by the end of 1994 had been achieved by 10,000 people in Finland. The CEPIS project team examined the Finnish CDL and other skills' definitions in detail. There were similarities between the different definitions; some consisted of an outline syllabus and some consisted of tests. The Finnish model consisted of theoretical and practical tests, in seven modules. Having completed all seven modules and having passed all tests, a candidate would be given a certificate called the 'Computer Driving Licence'. The project team decided to update the Finnish CDL, develop it further and to create a syllabus.

In order to evaluate the changes made to the Finnish set of tests and to assess whether other changes were needed, pilot tests were carried out in Norway, Sweden, Denmark, France and Ireland. The project team decided to name the certification, 'the European Computer Driving Licence' or 'ECDL'. The task force created the first syllabus, re-structured and updated the questions and defined ECDL, similar to the Finnish model, as a seven-module set of skills and competencies. Module 1 was a theoretical module and modules 2 – 6 were skills based. As not every country had Internet access at the time, Module 7 was created as a theory or a practical test. Guidelines for test administration and quality assurance requirements were defined.

In order to obtain an ECDL, a candidate had to pass seven modules. As each test was passed, a 'skills card' was updated. This card could be used as proof of a specific skill and could be exchanged for a full ECDL when all seven were completed. The ECDL Syllabus version 1 was published in October 1996 and was launched in Sweden. It was planned that the Syllabus would be updated once per year.

The support of the European Commission helped the development and acceptance of ECDL. Funding was made available through the European Social Fund and Commissioner Martin Bangemann included ECDL in the Information Society Action Plan in 1994. Outside Europe, countries began to recognize the value of ECDL. In 1998, South Africa launched ECDL as the International Computer Driving License (ICDL) and presented the first ICDL to a young girl in Port Elizabeth in 1990 [16]. ECDL and ICDL are the same and adhere to the same syllabus, quality assurance standards and testing methods.

4.2 ECDL in Schools

As ECDL became more popular in Europe, many schools in Europe decided to examine ECDL, recognizing that the skills defined within ECDL were necessary for all people. In 1997, Martin Bangemann stated in 'The Information Society and the Citizen' that "greater efforts were needed in schools to prepare the next generation to participate and benefit fully from the Information Society" [17]. He said that it was vital to encourage European citizens "to create new services in education, entertainment and business in order to keep Europe at the forefront of technology" and that "greater efforts must be made in our schools, to prepare the next generation to participate and benefit fully".

Initially, ECDL was not accepted in schools in Ireland. The Minister for Education said, in 1996, that it was not appropriate at that time to be incorporated into a school syllabus. However, this has changed; in Ireland ECDL is offered in approximately 50% of the schools [18].

4.3 Issues for Teachers

Schools have progressed from the days when one computer was available in schools, to the expectations a student will have in this Information Society. As the European Commission stated in 2000, 'learning to use technology' and 'learning to learn' with technology is necessary for today's students, who need access to technology and need to know how to use technology [19].

Teachers can help if they are trained to teach the technological skills required. This has been recognized for almost twenty years. Martin Bangemann [20] stated "Preparing Europeans for the advent of the information society is a priority task. Education, training and promotion will necessarily play a central role". It could be argued that he was saying that teachers should be rewarded for obtaining technical skills and that they need to continue to develop skills with ever changing technology. Awouters et al. [21] believe "Teaching and learning with ICT requires specific competencies for teachers and lecturers" and "using a Virtual Learning Environment like Blackboard or Moodle demands more didactical than technical skills". Teachers need to understand technology, to use technology as a pedagogical tool, and perhaps, to teach programming or use of IT applications. Teachers should look at the use of technology as a teaching methodology. John & Wheeler [22] discussing the needs of learners in the classroom identify the change that technology brings - "There is a need, for example, for students to engage with digital media in a number of ways, transcending those which are required to learn from paper-based text or images".

5 Summary

The teaching profession took a leading role in the introduction of computers into schools in Ireland in the 1980s. This was supported by the parents and the Government. Government grants were often the starting point of initiatives but fund raising by parents generated the resources which allowed for widespread adoption. There were, however, a number of perceived constraints to the adoption of IT, these were;

1. The lack of a clearly stated policy by the Department of Education. There were many separate initiatives but each school was open to follow different directions.
2. The lack of funding was another constraint. When funding was available it was insufficient to provide adequate hardware and software to make a real impact. Thus, parents had to bridge the gap. This was workable in some schools but not in others.

3. The lack of standards was another constraint. Schools were faced with an ever growing number of computer manufacturers with a variety of software. There were no guidelines and this inhibited certain schools which were unwilling to invest for fear of ending up with equipment which was not approved by the Department of Education.
4. The initial concentration on programming led to disillusionment for some teachers. The lack of software in the early days made it inevitable that to use the hardware the teachers had to program. While most teachers took courses, only a proportion was suited to programming.

However, in spite of the above constraints, the use of computers in the classroom in Ireland has developed and in a report produced in 2012 by European Schoolnet and University of Liege [23] it was stated that Irish students benefit from an infrastructure and a level of connectivity which are close to the EU27 (as it was then) mean. This same report also noted that the use of ICT by teachers is considerably above other countries and that the level of confidence in using ICT is high.

References

1. User Skills Task Force, Esprit project documents and working papers, 1995 – 1997 Occhini, G, ECDL the Take-off years, Upgrade, Issue no 4 (August 2009), `http://www.cepis.org/upgrade/index.jsp?p=2132&n=2136` (accessed December 10, 2013)
2. The National Council for Curriculum and Assessment, `http://www.juniorcycle.ie` (accessed December 18, 2013)
3. Computers in Ireland, Economic and Social Research Institute (1971)
4. School of Computer Science and Statistics, Trinity College Dublin, `http://www.scss.tcd.ie`
5. Industrial Development Authority of Ireland, `http://www.idaireland.com/`
6. The Computers in Education Society of Ireland, `http://www.cesi.ie/history`
7. Irish Computer Society, the Society for Chartered IT Professionals in Ireland, `http://www.ics.ie/index.php`
8. New Information Technology in the Irish School System, Contributors: Marino Institute of Education, Commission of the European Communities. Task Force Human Resources, Education, Training and Youth, Publisher Marino Institute of Education (1992) ISBN9282647730, 9789282647738
9. Primary Science Educatio. In: Ireland Issues And Research, `http://www.into.ie/ROI/Publications/PublicationsPre2000/PrimaryScience1992.pdf` (accessed December 12, 2013)
10. Seymour, P.: Tomorrow's Classrooms? Times Educational Supplement 41, 31–32 (1982)
11. Irish National Teachers' organisation Report on Computers in Primary Education Conference (May 1985), `http://www.into.ie/ROI/Publications/PublicationsPre2000/ComputersInPrimaryEd1986.pdf`
12. Contribution from Avril Harris, sister of one of the authors, Dudley Dolan
13. School report, Taney Parish School, file documents

14. Bangemann, M.: Europe and the Global Information Society, recommendations to the European Council (1994), http://www.epractice.eu/en/library/281360 (accessed January 11, 2011)
15. Leahy, D., Dolan, D.: History of the European Computer Driving Licence, History of Computing, learning from the past. In: Tatnall, A. (ed.), Brisbane, Australia, pp. 134–145. Springer (2010) ISBN 978-3-642-15198-9
16. Dolan, D.: In Capacity building for IT in education in developing countries. In: Marshall, G., Ruohonen, M. (eds.). Chapman and Hall (1998)
17. Bangemann, M.: The Information Society and the Citizen (1997), http://www.eto.org.uk/links/infosoc.htm (accessed January 11, 2011)
18. Education Solutions for Schools and Colleges, http://www.ics-skills.ie/education/index.php (accessed December 18, 2013)
19. Communication from the Commission "Strategies for jobs in the Information Society" (February 4 , 2000)
20. Towards a European Information Society Major EU Initiatives (1996), http://eur-lex.europa.eu/LexUriServ/LexUriServ.do?uri=CELEX:52000DC0048:EN:HTML
21. Awouters, V., Jans, S., Ruben, J.: E-learning Competencies for Teachers in Secondary and Higher Education. International Journal of Emerging Technologies in Learning iJET 4(2), 57 (2009)
22. John, P., Wheeler, S.: The Digital Classroom, harnessing technology for the Future, p. 127. Routledge, UK (2008) ISBN 978 1 84312 445 0
23. Survey of Schools: ICT in Education Country Profile Ireland, https://ec.europa.eu/digital-agenda/sites/digital-agenda/files/Ireland%20country%20profile.pdf (accessed December 18, 2013)

The Rise of Information and Communication Technology Era in the Israeli Educational System

Ben-Zion Barta[1], Liora Shapiro[2], Daniel Millin[3], and Ephraim Engel[4]

[1] Retired Chief Inspector on Computers in Education, Ministry of Education, Israel
[2] Teacher and Educator, Yisgav Elementary School, Tel-Aviv, Israel
[3] Passed away, Head of the Counseling Team on ICT in Teaching / Learning
[4] Passed away, Head of the Counseling Team on ICT in High Schools
benzion@barcode.co.il

Abstract. This chapter is an overview of the development of ICT in Israeli Education, from the first pioneers in the second half of sixties to first half of the nineties, when I (first named author of this chapter) gradually passed on my responsibilities, near to my retirement. It covers policy matters, as revealed in the first published policy papers, some of the main actions and projects executed according to these policies – integrating ICT in the learning process; teaching ICT subjects; integrating use of ICT means in humanities, sciences and professional education; ICT in educational management; principals', teachers' and staff training, support and updating and some related organizational details. It ends with a glimpse to recent problems and policy decisions.

Keywords: Computers in Education, Israel, schools.

1 Introduction

I, the first author-named of this chapter, have been deeply involved with the rise of educational computing activities in Israel, as part of my responsibility as Chief Inspector on Computer in Education at the Ministry of Education of Israel, from the mid-seventies to the mid-nineties. Under my eyes, within a decade or two, computers penetrated the educational system:

- From no computers, then the first PDP8s, the first Apples Commodore, Radio Shack and IBM compatible PCs, to thousands of networked microcomputers connected to the Internet;
- Starting from a few people from academia or who industry volunteering to give a general introductory lecture about computers, ending with Computer Sciences and IT professions taught as regular subject matter similar to other sciences;
- From simple drill and practice in arithmetic to sophisticated educational applications getting into the teaching / learning of many subject matters.
- I have seen the kindergarten teachers and primary and high school teachers learning how to use computers, how to manage their computer corner.

A. Tatnall and B. Davey (Eds.): History of Computers in Education, IFIP AICT 424, pp. 174–196, 2014.

- I have seen the Chief Inspectors, the staff and the high school teachers of sciences, humanities, languages, professions, getting interest in the world of computers and finally introducing them into their regular teaching.

This chapter is an overview of the development of ICT in Israeli Education, from the first pioneers in the second half of sixties to first half of the nineties, when I gradually passed on my responsibilities, near to my retirement.

The chapter is not a precise, scholarly historical review; rather, it is based in large on personal memoirs, on some papers I published while being with the Ministry [2][3], some documents – old ones and newer ones. While I did my best to mention the main facts and events – it is obvious that many remain uncovered in this chapter and I can only apologize about this fact.

My thanks to Liora Shapiro, an appreciated ICT manager, now dedicated to ICT integrated teaching, who helped collecting the sources and preparing the text of this chapter.

I cannot write this chapter without mentioning the memory of two persons that shared the daily burden, both of whom passed away a few years ago, namely Ephraim Engel who was head of the counselling team on ICT in High Schools, and Dr. Daniel Millin, who was head of the counselling team on ICT in Teaching / Learning. Had they been alive, they would have been co-authors of this chapter. In memoria, I decided to add their names besides mine.

Tens of dedicated colleagues worked with us to accomplish the task; many are taking care of the field after us. I could not mention all these devoted colleagues.

2 Local, Institutional and National Policies

2.1 School, Municipal, Academic and Industrial Initiatives for Integrating ICT

At a time when computers were scarce and with very limited capability compared with today, promotion of computer related activities in education started by initiatives of schools, school networks, municipalities, in cooperation with academia and industry. These initiatives resulted in the first acquaintance of pupils with computer concepts and the first computer aided learning activities at the end of the sixties and start of the seventies of the last century [6].

Several schools – some supported by academia or by industry, some by their own volition - have been involved with such initiatives. Some examples: one technological high school in Jerusalem, having a computing department, used computers to teach, in addition to Computer Sciences, applications for typesetting and numerical control and developed a software package to manage students' scores and attendance; another school, in Kiryat Shmona near the Lebanese border, was among the first to get microcomputers to be used for Computer Sciences teaching and some administrative services; a third example is a school in Kiryat Ata, near Haifa that got six micros and used them for teaching computer concepts to young pupils at fifth to ninth grade. There have been several additional schools taking initiatives to teach Computer Sciences – all these initiatives received recognition by the Ministry of Education, in the form of approval to include the subject in the matriculation examinations. A few universities offered extracurricular introduction to computing to interested youngsters, and some provided regular teaching to schools.

A proposal to train computer programming professionals within the technological education schools was approved by the Ministry of Education in 1968, and several high schools offered this track – Automatic Data Processing - dedicating to it some 20 weekly hours (out of a total of 45) for 3 years.

At a larger scale, aiming at the national schooling system, the Center for Educational Technology, an institution founded by the Rothschild Foundation in 1970, set as its goal to introduce technological innovation to the Israeli educational system. Among other projects, two were directly related to Information Technology, namely: Development of curricula for teaching introductory computer science at the high school level; integrating the use of computers in the teaching process of basic subjects, in order to promote pupil's achievements, mainly for underachievers.

All these beginnings, supported but not initiated by the Ministry of Education, caused the Ministry to consider the foreseeable impacts of Information Technology on the educational system and to define its policy.

2.2 National Policies

In 1978 the Ministry of Education dedicated the first small budget to Computers in Education. Coordination of the institutional initiatives started about the same time.

In 1979 The Committee on Computers in Education headed by the Chair of the Pedagogic Secretariat of the Ministry (the highest ranking officer dealing with educational and pedagogic matters) was appointed - see # 2.2.1.

A substantial increase of funding was approved for the 1983/84 budget, following several seminars and discussions held in 1982, aiming to decide upon the policy and the main goals for using the budget.

One of the first documents dealing with the involvement of the Ministry of Education in educational computing matters was a proposal submitted to the Director General of the Ministry in 1980, dealing with the whole spectrum of issues as seen at that time. The main goals of introducing IT in the educational system, as understood at that time:

- All pupils will have a first acquaintance with computers within their compulsory education, including their operations and limitations, and will use computers and computerized systems in their daily learning activities. Understanding ways and approaches to use computers shall be emphasized, rather than programming.
- Any interested pupils will have the possibility to study Computer Sciences and professional computer applications.
- Teachers and educational employees will use computers as support for their daily activities.
- It had been envisaged that using computers within the teaching and educational activities shall start at early ages from kindergarten and up, and be effective to all levels of pupils – from special education to the most gifted ones. Computer literacy, as formal learning in schools or informal, at extracurricular activity centres, should start at fourth grade and up, while using computers for problem solving, deeper study of Computer Sciences and professional applications shall start at seventh grade and up.

Several documents written in the early eighties defined several prioritized fields of activities:

- Compulsory learning of computer concepts and educational applications of computers at all Schools and Colleges of Education to the entire student population and in-service training and updating of teachers. This learning should cover methodologies of integrating computer-based activities in teaching/learning, courseware evaluation, courseware authoring, selection and adaptation of activities to the needs of the pupils.
- Further development of Drill and Practice of basic skills, development and implementation of a variety of approaches to integrate computers into the learning process. The re-organization of the classroom has to be considered as well as individual learning and learning in small groups.
- Development and state-wide implementation of curricula for Computer Literacy, Computer Sciences and computer related vocational education and related teacher training.

There was at that time some euphoria concerning the capabilities and the expectations from computer usage in education. However, some 'cooling down' ideas have also been exposed:

- The teacher, the educator, the human being, will always be the one to take decisions, to control and guide the technological means and will be the dominant and main factor in the educational system – the technology being a tool, maybe important, to the service of men.
- Technological means have the capability to improve and modify the learning process, may help solve some difficulties and problems, but they have limited capabilities to solve the hard, real problems encountered in education. They will never be better than the men behind, that designed and developed them.

2.2.1 The Committee on Computers in Education

This committee was appointed in 1979. Its mandate was to determine policy and activities at state level. The committee members were the heads of the main educational divisions of the Ministry (e.g., primary, secondary education), representatives of administrative divisions, academics involved in computers in education, school principals and teachers.

In 1983, the committee reported on the main activities as covering [1]:

- Teachers' training and updating – pre-service and in-service;
- Curricula development – computer literacy, computer sciences, data processing professionals, professional and scientific applications;
- Computer aided learning – drill and practice, individualized learning, educational games;
- Integration of computer activities in teaching/learning, audio-visuals, data banks, use of LOGO language;
- Equipment – advice, financing;
- Support centres for schools and teachers;
- Central supervisory and advising teams.

Following several years of activity, periodical discussions about the needs and achievements, re-assessment of earlier decisions and consideration of the criticism and the variety of opinions, a two day discussion with interested and involved parties lead to a document published in November 1986, defining the policy in the field of computers in education [9]. Several tens of people from academia, industry and the educational system took part in these discussions. Suggestions and proposals from the general public were solicited and considered. When reading the following lines, one should remember the time they have been written and appreciate the vision of the participants and their deep understanding of anticipated developments. Most of the decisions and recommendations as concluded then are still accepted today some, perhaps, are still waiting for implementation.

The following is a short summary of the approaches and decisions as published in the document:

The world of computers is dynamic and rapidly changing, while the educational system has difficulty to adapt to fast changes; however decisions have to be taken even if some may be outdated and unfit for future developments.

The Information and Communication Technologies (ICT[1]) have great potential for teaching and learning and their capabilities are immense, but they carry many dangers too and have limitations.

The revolution of communications means will lead to another school, different from that of today. The ways of teaching and learning will change with penetration of ICT in each classroom and in each home. The development and the improvement of ICT will deeply influence the educational system and its operation.

ICT is not the goal; it is a means to efficiently solve some problems of the educational system but will not solve some of its hardest difficulties. In order to realize the potential of ICT many practical problems have to be solved, technical and pedagogical and while doing so, no doubt many mistakes will be made.

The big challenge is to learn and to teach using ICT wisely and soundly, for proper functioning in the ICT world.

The main areas that ICT may support:

- Planning, operating and controlling learning systems at all levels: individuals, classes, schools, regional and national (organization and management of learning);
- Collection, processing and distribution of information;
- Improvement of teaching / learning process;
- Improvement of cognitive processes: planning, systematic thinking, problem solving, abstraction.

The main fields of activity:

- Training of man-power to be intelligent users of the means of ICT:
    - All employees of the educational system, at all levels – adequate to each one's tasks;
    - All teachers and students at Schools and Colleges of education;
    - Teachers of computing at all levels and all nuances;

[1] This is the first time that the term ICT was used in relation to Computers in Education.

- Teachers of sciences, humanities, technologies, etc. – each one according to ICT uses in the relevant field;
- Specialists in ICT applications in education – students toward MA and PhD degrees;

- Infrastructure:
  - Logistics:
    - Hardware, software, courseware: specifications, evaluation, licensing, purchase, supply, maintenance;
    - Limitations as to the variety of products and the rate of their updating;
    - Guidelines concerning funding for purchase of materials;
  - Communications:
    - Set up of two logically separated regional / national networks
      - For distribution of courseware, educational information banks, learning and personal communications;
      - For educational management of the educational system;
    - Set up of two physically separated school networks:
      - For ICT based teaching /learning and management of learning at individual and school level.
      - For educational management, and downloading information from the regional / national network;
    - Defining models for integration of ICT in the operation of schools – lab, class, library, applications library, connections to homes;
  - A national network to deal with coordination of research, development and evaluation of courseware by collaboration of all institutions active in the field;
  - Planning of man-power requirements in short term and long term;
  - Planning and encouraging basic research; Evaluation of the benefits of integrating ICT in education and of its costs;
  - Defining procedures for software development, use of applications, protection of software, documentation and training; defining procedures for development of curricula; systematic check of curricula in mathematics, sciences and technologies to decide upon the need for updating them; ongoing use of computers for problem solving;
  - Creating means for distribution of information about activities in Israel and abroad in the fields of ICT in education; setting up a database about courseware and curricula in the ICT field in Israel and abroad;
  - Defining the professional-administrative structure in the Ministry for implementing and supervising operations related to ICT; guidelines for planning of buildings (new and old ones) for ICT infrastructure;
- ICT in Educational Management
  - Defining a master-plan to deal with:
    - Analysis of the data system and of the administrative structure;
    - Requirements regarding equipment for data processing and communications;
    - Evaluation of costs;
    - Long range plans of implementation;

- The first step: the school secretariat – using ICT for collection of data and decision making; usage of word processors and communications;
- Defining approaches for ICT in regional / national management;
- Building up banks of problems, questions, their selection and evaluation having in view using them for generation of examinations and their assessments – perhaps integrated with the management of the individual learning of pupils;

- Use of ICT in teaching and learning:
  - ICT as subject of learning:
    - Computer Literacy:
      - Skills shall be gained by using computer applications within the teaching of subject matters in primary schools and junior high schools – no formal teaching of ICT subjects;
      - Computer Literacy as a subject of study at junior high schools;
    - Computer Sciences and Data Processing:
      - Selective subject of learning at basic or advanced level in general high-schools;
      - Basic Computer Sciences – compulsory for all pupils of technological and agricultural high-schools;
      - Learning of specific professional applications – compulsory for pupils of almost all tracks of technological and agricultural high-schools;
      - Professional training to pupils of the Data Processing track of technological high-schools;
  - Use of ICT means and application:
    - Use of ICT means shall be intensified, as an integral part of the learning:
      - Advanced use of word processors – free writing, language learning, assignments;
      - Usage of databases; processing and display of data;
      - Access to real information banks, as part of learning any adequate subject matter and for pupils' individual assignments; creation of educational databanks as subsets of real ones; databanks specially created for pupils' use;
      - Use of software packages within learning of technologies, sciences and any other subject matter;
      - Communications – (e-mail, group and peer networks) within formal and extracurricular activities;
    - Integrating of ICT in the learning process shall be done in various ways – active and individual teaching, in laboratories, learning centres, learning corners in the class room, part of frontal teaching – but only if there is a clear advantage of ICT over conventional learning;
      - Drill and Practice shall be used to improve achievements in basic skills;

- Pupils' Assessment and Educational Feedback: this is an important field of ICT application in educational management that still needs research and development:
    - Banks of items for assessment of achievements and for diagnostic examinations;
    - Ways of integrating the assessments in the teaching / learning process;
    - Ways of providing feedback at institutional and higher levels.
- Populations: the variety of ICT related activities has impact on the different populations involved in the school system. Priorities have to be defined among the following (the list is not by priority):
    - Teachers and staff dealing with any aspect of ICT;
    - General, technological and agricultural high school pupils;
    - Primary and junior high school pupils;
    - Special education pupils –including diagnostics and parents training;
    - Kindergarten pupils;
    - Extra-curricular and informal education for youngsters and adults;
    - Any others.

2.2.2 Other Reports and Committees

The report of activities (1983) and policy document (1986) of the committee on computers in education (#2.1.1) were the first published guidelines at the level of the national educational system. Different institutions and committees have published other policy recommendations. While there have not been many new ideas, some ideas faded out; others received varying emphasis, influenced by the changes of approaches and technological means.

A report published in 1985 by the Ministry of Science and Development and of the Ministry of Communications [10] recommended initiating a national program for development of computer based teaching systems, having in view two goals: the commercial potential of export and the advancement of the national education system. A committee appointed by the Ministry of Education recommended supporting the initiative, mainly having in view that it would aim to have computers as an integral part of the educational system and the potential for far reaching changes of the whole system. Even if the program did not materialize, the related discussions in the Ministry have contributed to build up basic ideas of a national policy.

An internal document of the Primary Education Department of the Ministry, published toward the mid-eighties, was dedicated to integration of ICT into the teaching curricula. It defined as its goals:

- Improvement of the teaching / learning process:
    - Of learning achievements, of cognitive capabilities,
    - Of daily use of ICT applications;
- Strengthening of communications and cooperation among pupils, between pupils and teachers, between school and community;
- Improvement of school and class management.

These short and simple looking goals have probably been a main catalyst of the development of the vast variety of activities mentioned in #3 and of the todays' approach of 'each kid with the tablet in the bag'.

Another report, published in 1991, dealt with various subjects, some already covered by previous decisions, others rather new:

- Implementing a nationwide plan to integrate ICT in teaching / learning activities;
- Ensuring the proficiency of teachers and principals regarding selection and application of ICT based pedagogic means;
- Modification and adaptation of existing curricula to have them ICT centred;

The 'Harari Committee', headed by Professor Haim Harari of the Weitzman Institute of Science, was appointed by the Ministry of Education to assess the scientific and technological education in Israel and to recommend a plan of activities for the forthcoming years. In 1992 it published its report entitled 'Tomorrow 98' [14], fully covering aspects of education in mathematics, sciences and technologies, as basic knowledge and as advanced learning within the school system. The report dedicates a separate chapter to 'Computers as support for teaching', based and fully accepting another report, 'Proposal for a policy on Integrating Computers in Teaching and Learning in the Educational System' published in January 1992. Some of the rather new recommendations were:

- Computers in Kindergartens: improvement of learning and usage of computer environment. The activities shall cover: development of courseware and of curricula integrating computer uses. Priority shall be given to disadvantaged populations and to peripheries.
- Computers in Elementary Education: integration of computers in the learning of most subject matters with the whole range of activities enabled by ICT; equipment shall be available in the class room, the teacher's desk, laboratories, central computer room, library; a computer coordinator officer shall be appointed to take care of the whole system; pre-service and in-service training; support centres.
- Computers in Junior High Schools: Computer Literacy shall be compulsory; learning of all subject matters shall be computer embedded.
- Computers in High Schools: learning of mathematics, sciences and technology shall be computer embedded; ICT shall be used for problem solving, simulations, investigations, gathering, processing, analysis and display of data.
- Computers at Schools and Colleges of Education: computer literacy and basics of computer-based learning - compulsory subject for all students; integration of computers in teaching of all subject matters; in-service training and updating of all teachers of Schools and Colleges of Education.
- Computer communications: all aspects of ICT integration in teaching/learning shall be considered; adequate educational activities shall be developed and tried out in several pilot projects; setting up of a central information centre for the educational system shall be considered.

2.2 Organizational Details

This section describes some of the ways selected for carrying out the policy for ICT in education.

2.3.1 The Professional Committee on Teaching of Computer Sciences

The committee was responsible for creating and updating curricula, examinations, curricula for teachers training, licensing of teachers, and any other matter related to teaching of Computer Sciences at any level in the school system. Its members were computer scientists from academic institutions, people from the IT industry, teachers and supervisors of Computer Science teaching.

2.3.2 Computer Equipment for Schools

Dealing with this matter started with the appointment of 'The Committee on Computer Equipment for Schools'. Its members were administrative people and some professionals and pedagogues. Its roles: improving the terms of purchase and maintenance of equipment, promoting standardization and local development of computing equipment for schools. These activities lead to two main outcomes:

- Publishing requirements for systems to be supplied to schools and actually approving suppliers; the process of suppliers' approval was repeated every year / second year.
- Setting up of a centre for licensing courseware for use in schools.

2.3.3 Counselling and Supervising Staff

Two teams of supervisors/counsellors were set up to promote and support the ICT related activities. They had two tasks, sometimes contradictory, but mostly feasible, together: on one hand to ensure that activities in schools are carried out as expected, according to the regulations and guidelines; on the other hand, to provide guidance and counselling to teachers, principals and school staff regarding all issues related to ICT. An important role was to explain to the school principals about ICT, the related difficulties and advantages, to convince them to step into the ICT era and to introduce and support the new activities in their schools - the involvement and support of school principals was an important factor for the success.

One of the two teams dealt with the high-schools and was mainly involved with the teaching of ICT related subject matters at all levels, while the other team dealt mainly with elementary schools, being involved with the different aspects of integration of computers in the teaching / learning process. This second team was directly involved in setting up the regional support and advice centres, guiding their work, some of the supervisors becoming even part of the team of the centres.

2.3.4 Regional Support and Advice Centers for Computer Applications in Education

These centres have been created to help solve difficulties in usage of computers in schools and to promote usage of computer activities – the existing ones and those being developed. The difficulties seemed to be the outcome of the fact that many schools preferred not to use the packages distributed by organizations providing the required support. Some of these schools found that the technical problems, sometimes inadequately prepared software and pedagogical problems, caused in some cases more frustration that enjoyment.

Each centre was to provide support to schools in its region – to have enough qualified manpower to ensure personal contact with interested teachers. In the centre (available also out of teaching hours) teachers could find samples of various equipment, including networks, as used in the schools, the variety of courseware, a library of related books, full information about courses offered to teachers, and any other means considered necessary. They had to be open to interested teachers coming to the centre but had as well to go out to visit the schools and to help solving their problems on the spot. Some offered telephonic 'hot lines' to help solving operational problems that may occur in the schools.

As expected, the centre did promote the goodwill of inexperienced teachers to step into the computerized world and contributed to the progress of computer usage in the schools.

2.3.5 Budgets

The yearly budgets dedicated by the Ministry for Computers in Education were not intended to purchase equipment for schools. Purchase of equipment could be covered by this budget only as part of budgeting of a supported project. The main items covered by the budget have been:

- Development of courseware and methodology for integration of computers in the teaching / learning process;
- Teachers' training and updating;
- Supervision, guidance and on-going teachers' support;
- Development of curricula;
- General research and development;
- Educational management.

On the other hand, purchase of school equipment has been paid for from budgets of The Israeli National Lottery, local educational authorities and parents' organization. Among the criteria for allocating money for school equipment:

- Presence of a coordinator for the school computing activities and of trained teachers;
- The equipment already available – the planned usage of the equipment with the addition;
- Availability of an adequate room – size, light, ventilation, etc.;
- The distance to nearby facilities that could provide computing activities;
- At that time (mid-eighties) the concept had been that pupils get to a computer lab in groups; the recommended number of stations being not less than 25% of the class size; if the lab would be in use more than half of the available time, the number of station should be 50% of the class size or even equal to it.

- In some special cases allocation for purchase of one or two stations has been considered.
- A school could decide to divide the computers, several stations in a class room, instead of installing all stations in a lab.

3 Integration of Information Technology in the Learning Process

Computer Aided Learning, as we used to call it in the mid-seventies had some local beginnings by school initiatives, some mentioned in # 2.1. Larger scale projects, initiated by public institutions, some financially supported by the Ministry of Education started their activity at the same time (1975 – 1980) [8]:

The largest and longer lasting, the TOAM (Hebrew acronym for Drill and Practice), initiated by the Centre for Educational Technology, had as its first goal the adaptation of the arithmetic Drill and Practice developed by Suppes at Stanford University in the USA. It had to be adapted to the Israeli curricula and made available at affordable prices. A dedicated, alphanumeric multi-terminal system has been developed, capable of delivering the individualized courseware to 16 or more pupils at a time, keeping track of each pupil's achievement and adapting to it the individual teaching sequence, keeping pupils' records and generating a variety of educational reports for teachers' and principals' use.

Aiming to provide the system to tens and hundreds of schools, a logistic and administrative infrastructure has been developed to supply hardware, software, courseware and maintaining them. Another aspect of this large scale project was teachers' training about the educational uses of the system, the integration of the activity in the class room teaching, the analysis and interpretation of individual and the class reports. Ongoing educational guidance and support on the same issues, has been provided.

Further developments: courseware for a variety of subject matters (e.g. Geometry, Hebrew and English language skills, reading, basic electricity); more advanced graphic terminal; improved computing power.

The Institute for Teaching Aids, in cooperation with the Junior Technical College of the Technion - Israel Institute of Technology - developed the MACAL (Multimedia Approach to Computer Aided Learning) system. The learning materials included textbooks, computer controlled learning interaction – branched based on individual achievements of each pupil and teacher's decisions - models and simulations, short educational television shots.

The first system based on alphanumeric multi terminal mini computers was later adapted to microcomputers.

Teachers and course authors got reports of progress and achievements; template based authoring aids allowed generation of courseware without any knowledge of programming.

Teachers' training and methodological seminars helped to develop adequate pedagogical approaches.

The subject matters that have been covered aimed to high school students – introductory computer sciences, algebra, elementary English, auto-mechanics.

Although well accepted and appreciated, the use of the system faded out as team members left to other commitments and as no preparation for spreading out to large scale use were done.

Another project worth mentioning is MASHOV (Hebrew word for Feedback) initiated by the Ben Gurion University in Beer-Sheba in cooperation with two primary schools and one high school.

The basic idea was to develop learning activities with strong cooperation between the classroom teachers and the team at the University. The computer was used to provide tutorial dialogs for individual learning, drill and practice and educational games. Subject matters covered arithmetic, algebra, reading and Judaism.

At the beginning, alphanumeric terminals, connected by phone lines to the university computer had been used. Later the courseware was transferred to microcomputers with graphic and colour capabilities.

As such the MASHOV project faded out – some of the staff remaining with the university and promoting educational computing activities, in cooperation with the local schools and new projects; others left for commercial activities in the field of educational computing.

A bit later, in Kiriat Shmona, a group of teachers started the SEMEL (Hebrew acronym for Computer Assistance for Teaching) project – based on microcomputers, mainly drill and practice of basic primary school subjects, but including other learning activities, such as games and simulations with graphics as available in that times. While a full set of activities was provided by the basic system, including collection of pupils' individual data and setting each one's learning path, teachers had the liberty to add their own materials and to modify the selection of materials presented to each pupil. Thus, teaching contents and learning control have been under a mix of system decisions and teachers' control. This liberty was attractive to many teachers, even if the time and effort needed to benefit of it, were an obstacle to fully enjoy it.

Availability of SEMEL on microcomputers – rather cheap and flexible as for system size – has been another attractive property of this approach. A central institution cared for logistics and maintenance and provided teacher training and on-going support. The system was widely accepted within the schools, perhaps second in size in Israel.

One of the issues of disagreement among the different teams was the degree of freedom given to the individual teacher to manage each pupil's activity and to modify or add-on to the prebuilt teaching system.

On one hand, the prebuilt system is the result of the effort of a pedagogic team, specializing in courseware development, using feedback to improve their materials. Having this in sight, the individual teacher should just master the available system and learn to interpret the data collected about each pupil.

On the other hand, the teacher using the system and teaching his pupils, may know better what is needed for teaching the subject being dealt with, what are the needs of each one of the pupils and what would be the best way to support his/her learning.

Obviously, life is a compromise in many cases: provide self-standing systems that can operate without teacher's intervention, but provide the possibility to intervene when the teacher decides to do it.

About the mid-eighties a Department for Computer Based Curricula was set up within the Division of Curricula Development of the Ministry of Education. The role of the department was defined as help in integrating adequate usage of computers within the media available for teaching / learning. It had to be done for new curricula being under development as well as for existing curricula that was available and stable. The goals were defined as improving the teaching in general, individualization of learning, and better adaptation of the teaching process to heterogeneous classes.

Teams of teachers active in schools, dedicating some of their time to courseware development were involved in a decentralized approach promising better use of local talents, having immediate effect on the school activities and providing immediate feedback. National and regional coordinators took care of the guidelines for the regional teams and of the wide scale distribution of the finished products.

Subjects covered have been: Hebrew (as mother tongue), English (as foreign language), Arithmetic, Algebra, Geometry, Judaism, Biology – to mention just a few.

A major project, daring to computerize the educational system of a whole township – the 'Mehish' project started in 1985 by the initiative and under the management of the staff at the School of Education at the Ben-Gurion University in Beer-Sheba. It was active in two townships, mostly in Arad. It intended to reach an overall understanding of the computerization process and a comprehensive policy for the township having as its goals: to create a 'computer culture' in the schools; to create a supporting environment to the schools; to initiate changes and renewing of teaching and learning, having the computerized environment as a catalyst and provider of changes.

The project ran between 1985 and 1989 when individual personal computers were scarce. It reached some conclusions that have to be taken in account by any large scale project being execute these days. Among the conclusions of the project:

- Changes of the teaching / learning approaches in the elementary schools by the computer culture is to be expected if:
  - Pupils have at least 3-4 hours of computer activities per week (1985-89);
  - Computer based activities are integrated in most subject matters and most stages of learning;
  - Computerized activities are adjusted to the specific needs and approaches of pupils, teachers, and class;
  - Computerized activities are integrated in the normal classroom activities, by having several computers in the classroom
  - Isolated interventions cannot achieve a computer culture – everybody has to master basic computer skills: pupils, teachers, staff and management.
- Significant outcomes of computerization can be achieved after a gradual process, lasting several years, conditional upon:
  - Cooperation with the teachers and the school staff for planning and execution of activities;
  - Cooperation with and support of parents and of local authorities;
  - On-going counselling and training of teachers and staff; usage of computers in most of curricular and extracurricular activities.

The kindergartens got their first ‘computer corners’ in the early eighties by an initiative of a team at the Oranim College of Education in Tivon, near Haifa. Its basic approach was to adapt LOGO style activities aiming to develop the children’s capability to ‘define problems’, to plan solutions and test them, to be able to think about the outcomes of a sequence of actions. At the beginning, kindergartens came with groups of children to the site of development, to act under supervision, aiming mainly to study the behaviour and the acceptance by the children. Soon, it migrated to the kindergartens, each having a corner with a few microcomputers, assigned in turn to pupils. The materials were soon enriched by other sorts of educational activities, offered by the same team or by others, either from the public sector or by commercial firms.

The open minds, the enthusiasm and acceptance of the idea by the supervisors of the Ministry of Education and by the kindergarten teachers played an important role in the acceptance and success of the initiative, despite the initial doubts about its feasibility and about the capability of the teachers to overcome the technical difficulties. Large scale implementation started in 1988 and in 1991 computer based activities were included in the formal curricula of kindergartens.

In special education, the use of computers started with use of available courseware considered to be adequate to pupils with special needs. A team at the University of Tel-Aviv developed special courseware and methodologies dedicated to these pupils.

Further courseware development was carried out by teams at Universities and Colleges, by public and commercial organizations, too many to mention. These did care also for full curricula, but rather focused on specific subjects, dedicating to each subject the most adequate approach. They initiated development of courseware in a myriad of approaches – tutorials, exercises, simulations, ‘computerized’ laboratory, drill and practice, games, applications, etc. - good for execution on different computers, as stand-alone applications for use by students in their learning or by teachers in their teaching in the class room. These applications did not require dedicated computers and could co-exist on the same machine, ready for invocation by any (authorized) user. The selection of the actual means – could be managed by the computer, or the teacher, or the pupils or a mix of these options.

Once schools were ready to spend money on courseware, private, commercial firms got in the arena – some of them, set up by initiators of publicly funded projects that switched their interest to private initiatives. They dealt with production of original applications and with translation and adaptation of courseware developed in other parts of the world.

The use of commercially available word processors and spreadsheets, in some cases special educational products, started to be common in teaching humanities and sciences, in many cases by assignments specially designed having the use of these tools in sight.

Computer based activities were not restricted to the formal schooling system. Extra-curricular activities were available at various environments at youth clubs, computer clubs and even in schools out of the regular teaching frame.

The abundance of materials available and offered to the schools by many different sources soon raised the question of what materials are adequate for use. Issues of accuracy of contents, pedagogic and ethical approach, correct language, technical aspects, support of users, had to be considered when deciding about courseware offered to a school.

The need of objective (as possible!) evaluation of courseware and of providing adequate information to the interested parties brought about the decision to set up a centre for evaluation and licensing of computer baser learning materials. The Ministry of Education initiated setting up such a centre that became operative in the late eighties.

Surveys conducted in 1989/90 had as their main results, the following facts:

- There was about 1 computer per 15 pupils, most of them in computer labs, some in the classrooms;
- The variety of uses covered: teaching Mathematics, Hebrew, English, Computer Literacy, LOGO, Basic, Sciences, Geography; usage of word processors and databases; extracurricular activities.
- Daily use of computers was reported by about half of the schools. The general feeling was that the technology could be used more effectively and more sophisticatedly:
- Many teachers felt they lack knowledge and sufficient guidelines for effective use of computers;
- Printers and peripherals were insufficient;
- More courseware was needed;
- More time should be dedicated to computer activities in the school's schedule.

The operational conclusions of the surveys: more teachers' training, better planning of educational computing activities, more equipment, was needed. These conclusions may apply nowadays as well.

In the early nineties, as the Internet was growing, its potential for support of educational innovation was considered. Proposals were popping up to set up active interest groups, to improve direct and interactive contacts between colleagues and teams and inter-teams cooperation; it was considered as provider of links to global information resource, as a support of educational innovation.

First pilots were set up to provide personal mail services, bulletin boards, discussion groups, information banks, news bulletins.

All these provided a good entry point to the more developed general networking systems that became available over the years.

By the mid-nineties, as the Internet grew and became more accessible, the use of the Internet search engines became a companion of the existing learning activities.

4 Teaching of Computer Sciences – Academic and Professional

Computing appreciation courses and computer literacy courses were introduced in the late seventies in grades 7-9 (junior high school) and in grades 10-11 for pupils who did not want to go deeper into IT concepts. Computer literacy dealt with some introduction to computer structure and programming but mainly with computer applications. The appreciation courses gave more emphasis on introducing programming concepts and algorithms.

Teaching computer literacy was widely accepted and widespread in the early eighties, but faded out later, as the use of computer applications became ubiquitous at younger ages.

Teaching of Computer Sciences at high school level [5] was introduced in the late seventies, similar to teaching of sciences. It has been accorded a status similar to sciences, as part of matriculation examinations and as criteria for admission to universities.

Two policy issues had to be considered:

- Should learning of Computer Sciences be restricted to an 'elite' of pupils, high achievers in maths and sciences, or should basic principles (at least) be open to almost any pupil capable of mastering some basic knowledge. The outcome was the development of basic modules providing insight into computer operation, programming and algorithmic approach. The basic modules became an introductory course to teaching of more advanced IT concepts and of scientific or professional applications. Other modules were developed at higher level for the more interested and gifted pupils. Those willing to dedicate more time were allowed to develop individual or group projects, as part of meeting their matriculation requirements.
- The language to be used for the programming parts of the curriculum. The choice was Pascal – the structured language considered best at those times; later on, use of Visual Basic and of Object Oriented languages was introduced.

Learning Computer Sciences is strongly related to having access to programming facilities. In the seventies, when relatively low cost microcomputers were not available, programming practice was provided by central laboratories, with multi-terminal systems, card readers (cards marked with pencils) and printers. Pupils came in groups to run their programs or, much less convenient, pupils' delegates were bringing the marked cards of the class, running the batch and returning the prints to their class. These solutions, seeming ridiculous nowadays, provided the programming means to all schools that were not big enough and rich enough to provide in-school computing. Obviously, the use of central laboratories faded out at the end of seventies and beginning of eighties.

Education of IT professionals [12], as part of the technological education at high school level was introduced in the late sixties and became widespread in the seventies and eighties. It was extended to post-secondary education of one or two years, leading to education of IT technicians and practical engineers. Efforts have been made to keep the curricula updated by including new subjects of study – object oriented approach, artificial intelligence, computer communications and networks.

5 Information Technology within Learning Humanities, Sciences and Professions

Integrating IT technology within the teaching of sciences and humanities started in the eighties and has been slowly accepted and widespread. It was related to use of word processors, spreadsheets, databases, specific computational and graphic applications, use of simulators for demonstration and laboratory experiments. The effort was considerable as the whole issue was new and unfamiliar to most staff involved. The use of IT tools was accepted and integrated into most subjects of study, for several as far as becoming part of the matriculation examination requirements.

On a parallel path of activity, integrating IT technology within the professional training of pupils getting their education in the technological tracks was attempted. It involved almost any profession – electronics, instrumentation, accounting, office automation, fashions, tourism, mechanics, drawing … However, in this case the staff was more open minded – perhaps more aware that the profession is changing and the education must follow. It has been a main issue for several years, the first stage completed in the eighties. Ongoing updating will remain a necessity and never complete.

One of the difficulties related to this issue has been the complexity, size and price of real professional applications – not affordable or even justified for school uses. Using down-scaled simulators, cooperation with industry provide adequate solutions.

6 Teachers Education, Training, Updating and Support

In the early seventies, teachers had in fact no knowledge of IT or of its integration in the educational system, but the acting teachers were the ones that had to do the job. So, in-service training and updating of teachers has been a major and indispensable component of the integration of IT into any aspect of the educational activity at national scale.

On the other hand, education of new teachers, at Schools of Education and at Colleges of Education had to provide graduates competent to deal with aspects of IT in education.

6.1 Teachers of Computer Sciences and Literacy

Teaching of advanced subjects in Computer Sciences and Education of IT professionals requires teachers with adequate academic degrees and educational skills. The required number of that kind of teachers being rather limited, they were recruited among academic graduates.

Teaching of introductory Computer Sciences and Computer Literacy required a huge number of teachers. The only possible solution to this demand was to offer in-service training courses to any interested teacher. Many teachers of Mathematics, Science, Technologies and some teachers of Humanities volunteered to follow extensive training courses, about 400 hours of study, to get a license for teaching these subjects.

Teachers of technologies have been offered similar, but shorter, in-service training, covering a general introduction to computing and further specialization in the applications specific to the profession taught.

Following the basic training, updating with developments and discussing the implementation aspects and methodologies has been accomplished by teachers meetings – half day to two day seminars – and short courses, about 20 hours.

6.2 Teachers Integrating Computers in Education

The following is the opening paragraph of a paper published in 1987 [4]:

> *"With the current state of the art, and for the foreseeable future, the teacher is considered to be the principal element in any teaching/learning activity within the school system, at whatever technological level it may be found. The teacher has to master the whole range of media put at his disposal, to coordinate their correct application and to adapt them to the specific needs of his class or individual students."*

In-service teachers' training covered some basic concepts of computing, but the main topics covered methodologies of using the computers for learning and a sound knowledge of the systems used and of activities they provided. Resolving the difficulties that may occur while using computers, overcoming the fears and insecurities related to the operation of a rather sophisticated system, all these were an important aspect of the training effort.

Nevertheless, ongoing support and guidance in educational and technical matters had to be provided, in addition to the preliminary training. Involvement of teachers in the development of educational materials and in the interpretation of the records of students' activities and achievements proved to be a significant factor for acceptance by the teaching staff and for real improvement of the learning materials.

6.3 Schools and Colleges of Education

Most of the academic staff of the Schools of Education at Universities and of the Colleges of Education in the seventies had no knowledge of computers and their educational potential, some being rather skeptical about the 'new gadget'. This being the case, each year a new cohort of computer illiterate teachers joined the schools, adding to the burden of training and updating the school staff.

Two main actions aimed to change this situation [4]:

- Organizing courses, seminars to the academic staff, encouraging and providing support for research in the field improved the general approach to the subject and increased the number of interested staff members;
- A formal request by the Ministry of Education to include in the curricula computer related subjects resulted in adaptation of computer related subjects in the students' learning programs.

An introductory course on 'Computer basics and their applications in Education' became compulsory to all students of education; additional elective courses were offered – e.g., specific to integration in specific subject matters, management of school computing centres.

The academic staff was encouraged to include use of computers in their own teaching to their students.

By the mid-eighties all Schools and Colleges of Education provided these curricula.

Studies leading to a combined degree in Computer Sciences and in Education were offered in several academic institutes, providing a source of licensed teachers needed by the high-schools.

7 Computers in Educational Administration

As already mentioned, some schools started the use of computers in educational administration on their own initiative. In the mid-eighties a systems analysis and feasibility study was initiated towards a national network of computerized educational administration providing services at school level and extending to local, regional and national levels.

This project, under the management of the Division of Data Systems of the Ministry, led to the specification of school management systems, with technical requirements as well as requirements for maintenance, training and support to school staff – teaching and administrative. Commercial firms were invited to develop and offer systems based on these specifications.

The objectives were defined as improvement of the administrative and pedagogical decision-making by: compiling and analysing data; locating and displaying exceptional cases; reducing administrative burden; tools for decision making [11]. The system consisted of a standard basic software kernel to which each school could add its supplemental components interfacing with the basic software. The basic modules were: student management; teacher management; subject management; achievements record and report; statistical analysis and report. Examples of add-on modules: curriculum and teaching aids management; library management; bookkeeping.

In this case, again, adequate training and support played an important role for successful assimilation and appreciable effort was invested in it: from convincing the school principals and the main managerial staff, up to ongoing and well organized counselling and guidance.

Later on, connecting the school systems to regional and national networks was considered.

8 20 Years Later

At the beginning of 21th century wide scale networking with the WWW (World Wide Web), with all its related applications, was already a fact, and it has been expanding at a rate unknown before for any other technological means.

Several plans regarding ICT in education were published in the late nineties and first decade of 21st century.

Issues related to teaching of computer literacy, Computer Sciences, computer applications in science and technology and training of computer professionals were not mentioned anymore. This was because these matters had been already settled and accepted by the schooling system as regular subjects for teaching and examinations.

Issues related to ICT in education continue to be raised, as a main issue to be addressed. This may be explained by the fact that technology is changing, perhaps too fast for the educational system to keep track; but also it may be the outcome of a degree of dissatisfaction with the rate of integration ICT means in actual teaching: an inquiry carried out in 2010/11 revealed that many schools are lacking computers and part of the existing equipment is not advanced enough; a great part of teaching continues to be done without any involvement of ICT means. Some of the main difficulties pinpointed years ago have not been solved completely, and some reappeared, perhaps in the context of the new technologies.

A policy document published in the year 2000 [7] emphasizes the potential and expected outcomes of the information-rich new challenge. Many new issues had to be considered, while most of the existing issues and goals kept their relevance.

Some of the rather new goals mentioned:

- To provide the knowledge and proficiency needed to efficiently use the web in order to reach cultural, humanitarian and scientific sources; to provide an environment promoting self-search, collection and organization of knowledge to encourage self and autonomous learning;
- To support moral and ethical values in a society being deeply influenced by the technology;
- To give priority and to provide rich sources and encouragement for adaptation of the school staff to the new reality – remembering that youngsters are faster to grab the novelty;
- To support reliable connection of schools, kindergartens and homes to the educational network;

In January 2005, the government's Task Force for Advancement of Education in Israel published a general policy paper 'The National Policy on Education'– dealing with all aspects of the educational system, in general [13]. It was not dedicated to ICT in education but it contained several relevant recommendations. Among them some old but worth to mention, others rather new:

- In first and second grades the basic core-subjects shall be in mother tongue, mathematics and computer usage;
- The training of all educational and administrative staff shall cover integration of ICT in teaching;
- Curricula shall include integration of ICT in the contents, ways of teaching/learning and assessment. The options shall include use of computer based tools, information sources, learning materials, internet and communications;
- Education about ethical aspects of use and misuse of ICT shall be provided;

- Assessment of schools shall include, among other factors, the use of ICT in learning and in the teaching means;
- ICT shall strengthen the contact among teachers, learners and community, the contact with pupils of other schools, with experts in different fields, remote learning and coaching;

A new plan of action for integration of ICT in education started in 2011 covering 200 'basic integrator schools' and 20 'advanced integrators'. The advanced ones are schools that have proven achievements in the field and are expected to demonstrate to the basic ones and lead their activity. All schools shall get digital projection facilities, wide band wired and wireless networks, a laptop for each teacher and on-line learning contents; the 'advanced' ones will have one laptop per 5 pupils, and intelligent digital blackboards.

Schools are expected to define institutional and individual plans for accomplishing ICT integration in pedagogical, administrative and social activities; to be active in development of learning materials; to set up a school website and use it for management of learning and of assignments, for reporting attendance and discipline problem.

Teachers are expected to start posting learning materials on the school's website; pupils shall start submitting home-work through the website; pupils shall collect information from the web and be able to prepare presentations using ICT means.

Despite the problems, the criticism, the impossibility of achieving all goals and expectations, despite the feeling that more and better could have been done, even if in many schools the teaching is still very similar to what has been, far reaching changes have already been achieved and many more are under way in the future. It may take, perhaps, 20 more years till the current days' of schooling will become history.

References

[1] A report of the activities of the committee on Computers in Education, a private document (1983) (in Hebrew)

[2] Barta, B.Z.: Computers in the Israeli Educational System. Computer in Education, North Holland (1981)

[3] Barta, B.Z.: Computers in the Israeli Educational System (1980-84). Computer in Education, North Holland (1985)

[4] Barta, B.Z.: Training of Educational Staff for the Information Technology Age, Prospects, vol. XVII(3). UNESCO (1987)

[5] Engel, E., Telem, M., Barta, B.Z.: Teaching of Informatics and Information Technology at High School Level – the Israeli Experience. In: Proceedings of the World Conference on Computers in Education. IFIP. Chapman & Hall (1995)

[6] Maaseh Hoshev – Bulletin of the Information Processing Association of Israel (1976) (in Hebrew)

[7] Melamed, U.: Report of the Committee on ICT policy in the Education System. Israeli Ministry of Education (2000) (in Hebrew)

[8] Millin, D., Barta, B.Z.: Six Years of Computer Penetration into Primary Education: the Case of Israel. Education and Computing, 171–178 (1991)

[9] Policy for Activities in the Field of Computers in Education. Ministry of Education and Culture (November 1986) (in Hebrew)

[10] Proposal for a National Program for Development of Computer Aided Teaching Systems, Ministry of Science and Development and Ministry of Communications (1985) (in Hebrew)

[11] Sagi, I., Gev, Y., Feinesser, A.: School Management Information System Authority in Israel, Information Technology in Educational Management, pp. 79–92. Chapman & Hall (1995)

[12] Telem, M., Barta, B.Z.: New Trends within the Basic Training of IT Professionals in Israel. In: Proceedings of the IFIP W.G. 3.4 Working Conference. Elsevier Science Publishers (1992)

[13] The National Policy on Education, the government's Task Force for Advancement of Education in Israel (January 2005) (in Hebrew)

[14] 'Tomorrow 1998', Israeli Ministry of Education (August 1992) (in Hebrew)

The Hopes and Realities of the Computer as a School Administration and School Management Tool*

Rory Butler[1] and Adrie Visscher[2]

[1] New Zealand
[2] University of Twente, The Netherlands
randcbutler@inspire.net.nz, a.j.visscher@utwente.nl

Abstract. Software for school administration and school management started as teachers with a science background started to develop computer programs in order that school office staff did not have to repeatedly type and re-type student lists. Later, computing companies entered the market and software packages evolved. Some governments also mandated which school information systems were best suited for the schools in their country. This chapter traces the original aspirations for the school administrative use of computers (more school efficiency and school effectiveness) and compares those aspirations to eventual outcomes in schools. Some goals have been accomplished, others not yet. The reasons for the latter and the lessons that can be learned from this, are discussed.

Keywords: school administration, school management, computer use, school efficiency, school effectiveness.

1 How It All Started

In short, the following may summarize in staccato what happened. It started with a new subject in the curriculum. Software for school administration and school management was lacking and teachers with a science background started to program in order that school office staff did not have to type and re-type student lists and class lists anymore. Some teachers started programming a TRS-80, an Apple IIe, a Commodore 64, a Sinclair ZX 80 or a similar machine. Next, computing companies donated computers to schools, or provided telephone networks to connect schools using micro-computers. Programs were written in compressed Basic or machine code to deal with the limited memory of the available computers. Some governments successfully mandated which computers and software were best suited for the schools in their country. In other countries attempts to do the same were unsuccessful and schools decided for themselves what they wished to use. A range of small companies, often founded by teachers, entered the school administration market and software packages evolved including, among other things, student data, timetables, subject results, an accounting package and electronic mark book, payroll, library, resource manager, and truancy control. In the early 1990s the programs were transformed to the Windows environment, and several years later, to web-based systems.

* The authors thank Alex Fung for his feedback on the previous version of this chapter.

A. Tatnall and B. Davey (Eds.): History of Computers in Education, IFIP AICT 424, pp. 197–202, 2014.

School administration and school management software in several countries integrated with software for the storage and analysis of the results of externally developed standardized student achievement tests.

Computers were introduced into schools in the 1980s as a new subject in the school curriculum. The machines in most cases were not intended for developing and enhancing school administration and management (Bluhm, 1987; Visscher & Spuck, 1991). In fact, school administration and management only began to establish as a discipline in higher education in the early 1980s. However, the unintended effect of computer-aided school administration did happen once teachers got access to these machines in schools. In the 1980s usually mathematics or science teachers started to develop stand-alone applications within their own schools for student registration, absentee administration, test score administration and the like, These same teachers were often the ones who had to construct the school timetable, and they loved the idea that the computer would 'spit out' a completed timetable after the relevant input had been entered. Later commercial software vendors entered the stage as they saw the market evolve. They sold packages of school administration applications which, to some extent, were integrated i.e. used the same data ('Single entry - Multiple use' was the slogan). These systems were intended to be used in as many schools as possible and were therefore less tailor-made than the first applications developed by the pioneers who worked for one or a few schools.

In countries like for example New Zealand, Australia, The Netherlands and England in the nineties companies, governments, universities and others set up special projects to approach computer-assisted school administration and management in a fundamental way by analyzing schools in terms of their information household characteristics and involving school staff to become involved to some extent in the design of school information systems that could provide as many as possible valuable forms of administrative and management support to schools (Visscher, 2001). They also tried to find a balance between the need for standardization, and options for tailor-made forms of support. *Efficiency* improvement had been the primary goal during the earlier stages of school information system development but in this later stage system developers thought that the new school information systems also could promote more school *effectiveness*. In the next section we will elaborate on this concept.

2 What Was Expected/Hoped for?

Initially the idea was that the advent of the computer would make *information retrieval and document production* more *efficient* in schools (i.e. less resources in terms of time, money, and human resources would be needed for these school office activities). The computer with a central database enabled the single entry of data instead of archiving and maintaining the same data manually at various locations (e.g. school office, caretaker, counselor, deputy heads) in the school. It was expected that this would save data-entry time, and prevent errors caused by the repeated registration of data. The *computer-assisted manipulation of data* (making computations, lists, reports, sorting data, etc.) was also expected to take fewer resources and as such to improve the efficiency of schools. The idea was that, as a result, teachers, managerial staff and school counselors could dedicate more time to 'higher order' activities. Later, when web-based versions of school information systems came into existence, more efficient *data communication* between mutually connected internal and external computers (e.g. the Ministry of Education, the School Inspectorate, follow-up schools and feeder schools) was considered to be another way of improving school efficiency.

School effectiveness can be defined as the degree to which the primary goals of schools (adding as much as possible to students' entrance levels in areas considered relevant for them and for society) are met. It was expected that computerized school information systems also could contribute to improving school effectiveness by supporting more *informed decision-making* with respect to structured problems (problems with a limited number of solutions, e.g. the composition of lesson groups, the construction of timetables), and regarding more ill-structured topics/problems, with a much larger set of 'solutions'. The latter kinds of topics/problems are, for example, reflected by questions of the following kind (it was expected that questions of this kind could be answered better now by analyzing the data in the school information systems):

1. Does truancy in our school have a relationship with other school factors?
2. How do our students perform at national examinations, and which relationships exist between their performance on the one hand and student and school characteristics on the other hand?
3. To what extent do our teachers differ in terms of how much students learn in their classes, and how can we improve average teacher performance?

The fact that the computer enabled the possibility of studying these aspects of school functionality was expected to improve the quality of school decision-making and, by that, to improved school effectiveness. Moreover, school staff was expected to contribute more to school effectiveness because the computer would take over lots of the 'stupid' (routine) work they used to do. As a result teachers, school managers, and counselors were expected to be able to spend more time on trying to improve the quality of instruction and overall school functioning.

3 What Really Happened and What Can We Learn from This

Indeed, lots of routine school administrative activities are done nowadays by means of the computer. Things that were already done before we had computers can now be done more efficiently. New activities that have become possible since we have computers (e.g. web-based surveys among parents or school staff) can also be done now without requiring a large amount of resources. Although the prediction of the 'paperless office' has not become reality very few schools probably would like to go back to the days of the manual registration and manipulation of data. Exchanging data with parents, other schools, individuals and organizations, also as a result of the internet, has become much easier and efficient.

Using the computer for solving structured problems (e.g. timetable construction) will also have added to more time savings, and maybe also to more school effectiveness as the computational power of the computer enabled computing several alternatives which from an educational point of view a best alternative could now be implemented.

School staff are saving considerable time as a result of computer use. What the time that is saved is used for is uncertain. Probably part of that time is spent on computer-assisted activities that previously were not yet carried out but it does seem that more and more administrative paperwork is being demanded of teachers. Part of the time saved may be spent on other activities as well. We however have the impression that not many schools use their school information systems for making more informed decisions for ill-structured problems by answering the kinds of questions presented in the aforementioned. This may be due to various factors (Visscher, 1996):

a) The systems do not support answering these questions in a very user friendly way which means that it will be very difficult for the average school to obtain the information they would need for more informed decisions.
b) The data stored in school administrative information systems neither tell validly how much students learn in schools and to what extent that knowledge gain is satisfactory (for example, in comparison with a relative or an absolute standard) nor provide insight into the quality of the teaching processes within the classroom. As such the basis for improving the most important school process and its output is weak. There is however a trend observable that results on standardized student tests become more integrated in the systems that initially were developed purely as school information systems. That trend makes those systems more valuable for improving the primary process of schools.
c) The average school does not operate like a 'learning organization' which yearly sets very specified performance goals and evaluates their accomplishment, and as such tries to improve the quality of its functioning in a systematic way. We know from international research (e.g. Witziers, Bosker & Kruger, 2003) that few school leaders operate as instructional leaders who see improving the instructional quality of their school as the most important task. Generally, schools also are not known as very powerful policy-makers. The most important coordination mechanism in schools in terms of Mintzberg is the standardization of skills: teachers are supposed to be able to deal with the uncertainty and complexity of the teaching-learning process as a result of the profound training they have received regarding subject matter content and didactical strategies. So, teachers are relatively autonomous and most school managers do not interfere much in teacher territory by analyzing teacher work (e.g. by means of classroom observations), their results, and by looking for ways to improve these. As most schools do not have a performance-orientation that leads to the continuous analysis of the quality of the primary process (i.e. teaching in classrooms) and the related levels of student achievement, it is not surprising that providing them with an information system that could support them in important ways in analyzing the quality of school functioning, and how that quality can be improved will be a sufficient precondition for benefitting from this tool for performance improvement.

Changing schools in this respect would first of all require that managers and teachers learn to see the importance of investing in such activities. If they become motivated for improving performance they will need the knowledge and skills for doing it, like learning to ask the questions that can be answered by analyzing data from a school information system, to involve the relevant actors in decision-making processes (including the teachers who love their autonomy), to take decisions, and to implement and evaluate the decisions taken. This is all easier said than done especially if the decisions refer to the teaching process where teachers are used to much freedom. Teachers in general work hard and do their best, and many reason that, if student achievement is not as hoped for, then they should not be blamed for it as in other years they had good results with the same kinds of activities). At the same time we know from research (Hanushek, 2011; Hattie, 2009; Nye, Konstantopoulos, & Hedges, 2004) that teachers vary a lot in terms of their professional expertise, teaching skills and results, so there is good reason for utilizing the available tools for improving poor performing teachers (especially in the interest of the future of the students, and society as a whole). It will take a lot of school organizational development in order to make informed decision- making for school improvement happen. That is not so much a matter of technology (although user friendly ways for data retrieval form a necessary precondition) but especially a matter of how schools operate, and the skills school staff have for benefitting from the wealth of data in their school information systems. Schools cannot do this on their own, it will take carefully designed and tested professional development trajectories to transform schools into more learning- and improvement-oriented organizations.

In addition we would like to end with a few observations of a different nature:

a) Governmental departments proved to be the least likely to be successful in guiding the evolution of computerized administration. What seemed to happen was that a few younger people, frequently without the experience of having been teachers in schools and with little experience of the way governments interface with their communities, were given the power to make decisions which were often ill-informed. As a consequence huge wastes of energy, time and finances resulted. It seems to be far more efficient to let the market decide what works best.
b) Locally produced software is best. A package might look wonderful operating in another country but it inevitably fails to cater for the myriad of details specific to a particular country. These have evolved over time and it is not at all sensible to expect a 'foreign' package to meet the needs of a local community – even in the case of something as seemingly straightforward as school financial accounting where processes are based on international practices.
c) It is not particularly wise to build too much flexibility into your systems even if some users ask for it. For the average user lacking the skills to deal with and benefit from that flexibility, standardization is best and most attractive.

References

1. Bluhm, H.: Administrative Uses of Computers in the Schools. Prentice-Hall, New York (1987)
2. Hanushek, E.A.: How much is a good teacher worth? Education Next 11(3), 40–45 (2011)
3. Hattie, J.: Visible Learning: A synthesis of over 800 meta-analyses relating to achievement. Routledge, London (2009)
4. Nye, B., Konstantopoulos, S., Hedges, L.V.: How Large Are Teacher Effects? Educational Evaluation and Policy Analysis 26(3), 237–257 (2004)
5. Visscher, A.J., Spuck, D.: Computer Assisted School Administration and Management: The State of the Art in Seven Nations. Journal of Research on Computing in Education 24(1), 146–168 (1991)
6. Visscher, A.J.: Information technology in educational management as an emerging discipline. International Journal of Educational Research 25(4), 291–296 (1996)
7. Visscher, A.J.: Computer-Assisted School Information Systems: the concepts, intended benefits, and stages of development. In: Visscher, A., Wild, P., Fung, A. (eds.) Information Technology in Educational Management. Kluwer Academic Publishers, Dordrecht (2001)
8. Witziers, B., Bosker, R., Kruger, M.: Educational Leadership and Student Achievement: The Elusive Search for an Association. Educational Administration Quarterly 39(3), 398–425 (2003)

Computers in Schools in the USA: A Social History

Kevin R. Parker[1] and Bill Davey[2]

[1] Idaho State University, USA
[2] RMIT University, Australia
Parkerkr@isu.edu, Bill.Davey@RMIT.edu.au

Abstract. This chapter looks at the history of computers in the USA schools from a social history perspective. Instead of concentrating on innovations and leaders the story of mass adoption in schools is told. This history focuses on the 1980s when the major growth of student numbers and hours of contact with computers became a reality in American schools.

Key Words: USA, schools, computers, adoption, social history.

1 Introduction

The United States played a pivotal role in the history of computers. Everyone knows of the famous companies such as IBM and of the founders of modern computing such as Grace Hopper. A comparatively early entry to widespread commercial computing in the country should be evident in educational applications. We can be certain that large scale rollouts of educational programs had been established by 1968 as in that year, reports were being published regarding the success of the use of PLATO terminals [1-3]. Despite the certainty of facts supporting this view of history, questions remain: "How widespread were computers in education?" and "what were the real impacts on people's lives from the computer and when did they become real for the ordinary person?" For example the Plato IV terminal, an amazing educational innovation, was around in 1975, but available in 150 locations served by a donated computer. This is a significant number in normal historical terms – it could be described as a successful innovation. However, as 150 locations is a small fraction of the 109,000 schools of the time, the Plato terminal cannot be seen as a socially significant innovation. It clearly led to innovations that were significant but was not so in its own right.

History can be seen as the story of pioneers and new inventions. Another view can be obtained by following the trend of large-scale adoptions. To contrast these views of history consider two educational technologies. In the 1970s the invention of the 'Video Disc' could be seen as an important topic of conversation amongst educators. In hindsight we can see that this invention was superseded by the more flexible multimedia facilities of personal computers. Compare this with an invention that came from military training. The military historian Olsen (1982) recounts the first use of chalk to bring a multimedia experience to the classroom:

A. Tatnall and B. Davey (Eds.): History of Computers in Education, IFIP AICT 424, pp. 203–211, 2014.

> *"One of the very first uses of the chalkboard was at West Point in 1817. A Frenchman, Claude Crozet, ex-officer under Napoleon, found himself in a dilemma. He did not speak English and had no textbooks to teach his new science course – so he painted a wall of his classroom black and wrote on it with chalk" [4] p32*

We will not proffer evidence of the different impact of these two audio-visual devices, but leave it to the reader to judge the social impact of chalkboards versus Video discs. The one of greatest importance to the social historian is that which has the most impact, in this case on schools.

This chapter uses surveys of computer use to draw a picture of the social history of computers in schools in the USA.

2 An Educational Timeline

2.1 Computer Presence

The computer history museum (2014) notes that IBM had 81% of the computer market in 1961 and that Xerox PARC opened in 1970, the same year as the creation of ARPANET. A number of personal computers were released by their US manufacturers in 1977, including the famous Apple][. These momentous impacts on society created a feverish climate of innovation in many schools. To translate this story of innovation into a story of the social history of computers in schools requires some information about the spread of computing into large numbers of schools and the impact on the general population of schools. The question to be answered is: when did computers become significant in the school system?

A traditional history answer would put the beginnings somewhere in the 1950s. Commentators trace the first computers in schools to Federal funding in the 1950s.

> *"The federal government supported technology for schools as early as the late 1950s, largely through funding from the National Science Foundation and the Department of Education [5] p7.*

The social history answer to the question of beginnings is the year 1983. Detailed surveys of the number and distribution of computers showed that the widespread presence of computers was much later than the early 1950s:

> *"Between mid-1981 and the fall of 1983, the percentage of elementary schools with one or more microcomputers jumped from 10 percent to over 60 percent. During that same period, the percentage of secondary schools with five or more microcomputers grew from 10 percent to well over 50 percent" [6] p23.*

Surveys of computer penetration into schools have been continually performed in the United States. The Federal Government is concerned with equity and so considerable effort is put into measuring equity in a number of areas and computer use has been one of those areas for many years. Much of this focus is 'Title I' which provides for (amongst many other requirements):

> *"… distributing and targeting resources sufficiently to make a difference to local educational agencies and schools where needs are greatest" [7].*

The existence of Title I as a federal charter has had a significant influence on the penetration of computers into schools. The charter acts as both a basis for audits of the education system but also as a source of funding directed at those schools where resources would not normally be available for the purchase of computers and training of teachers. The 2,000 NSBA report attributes Title I funds as the basis of computer purchases in most eligible schools;

> *"Title I represents an important source of funding for this technological expansion. Indeed, Title I funds have paid for a significant portion of the computers now in use in high-poverty schools." [8] p76*

The cumulative effect of these funding programs produced a fairly uniform presence of computers across the country. A study in 1997 produced an illuminating picture of the precipitous growth of computers and sets a maturity level around the year 1990 in terms of real student access.

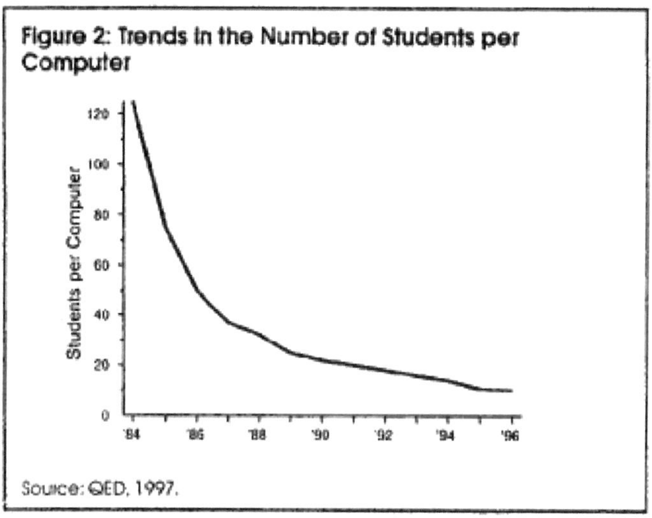

Fig. 1. Taken from [5] p13

A contemporary critic of educational computer use disputes that the presence of computers should be taken as a sign of impact. He would set 1991 as a more appropriate year of beginning on the basis of the percentage of schools with computers, student ratios and number of hours of use in a day.

> *"As an innovation, school use of computers has spread swiftly, widely, and, on occasion, deeply. But the picture is clouded. A few statistics on computer use suggest the broad outlines of the picture. In 1981, 18 percent of schools had computers; in 1991, 98 percent had them. In 1981, 16 percent of schools used computers for instructional purposes; by 1991, 98 percent did so. In 1981, there were, on average, 125 students per computer; in 1991, there were 18. In 1985, students used computers in school labs just over 3 hours a day; in 1989, that figure had risen to 4 hours a day." [9] p186*

This opinion is consistent with surveys conducted by Becker (1984) who found that the jump in computer numbers was not reflected by generous time allocations to students. He conducted surveys in 1983 and 1984 and found:

> *"... during an average week, only about one-eighth of the students in elementary schools that owned microcomputers had an opportunity to use one. More significantly, the students who did use a microcomputer spent on the average only 20 minutes at the computer during the week, some of this in a paired or group situation." [6] p27*

It seems that there might be two social beginning dates for computer presence: circa 1983 when most schools had some computers and circa 1991 when students had some level of real access to computer time.

3 Computing as an Idea

The argument that computers were not present in classrooms until 1983 or perhaps 1991 does not necessarily disprove their influence. Clearly the US Government was influenced in terms of education policy from the late 1950s. There is some evidence that this was mostly a convincing argument for the use of computers to monitor schools and make efficiency gains in administration, as had been happening with most departments since Hollerith and the census.

A telling sign that the influence of computers in education was not just a government concern was the burgeoning industry growing around educational computing. Becker [6] noted that there were at least six nationally circulated monthly publications on the subject targeted at schoolteachers and administrators. Several important thinkers were spreading the word. These included Seymour Papert [13] who saw that students could find a learning environment in the computer rather than an object of study or a vocational topic. At the same time people like Alan Kay [14] were working on educational hardware and programming systems (in this case the prescient Dynabook and Smalltalk). Each of these innovative streams in computer education was collecting adherents.

Computers had become part of the social consciousness. As industrial computer use became widespread a groundswell of interest involved parents. Becker [6] found that a principle concern of parents was the possibility of employment in their children's future being dependent upon the child's ability to work with computers. This feeling in the community is an indication of the social impact of computers in education totally independent on the existence of computers or courses in schools. Of course teachers are not immune from social trends and many were aware of the computer as an industrial fact even though their school had not yet made the move to purchase equipment. This awareness showed in people all around the system trying out the new personal computers, reading the flourishing magazines and becoming proselytizers for the value and stimulation of computers, especially in programming. Becker [6] points to this trend and the phenomenon of mathematics teachers leading the way:

> *"Many teachers and school administrators fear that they, too, need to know something about how to use computers. A number who have tried programming or using computer programs on their own find it intellectually stimulating and possibly even cost-effective. Like adventurous computerists in other professional domains, many become proselytizers for their use by others in their workplace. This happens first and most often in high schools and among mathematics teachers, for whom computers, as objects to be programmed, are most easily integrated into other instructional responsibilities" [6, p23].*

The availability of personal computers (sometimes called microcomputers because of the integrated circuit based affordable systems that came onto the market) were also a social phenomenon. A magazine of the time, Creative Computing, is available online (https://archive.org/details /creativecomputing). This magazine was published from 1974 until 1985 and is typical of magazines of the time, but with a heavy emphasis on educational and hobby computing. Skimming any set of issues shows that topics in the education section included regular articles on interesting programs to write, use of calculators in the classroom, computers to build from kits and reviews of computers. By 1980 the magazine had become mostly hobby oriented but with continued support for the programmer. (An interesting advertisement in the Winter of 1982, was for the 'new' 10 megabyte Winchester hard disc for a mere $3,095 1982 dollars!). Eventually the magazine turned to support for small business computing but could not remain viable in this market. The diffusion of educational computing through publications was mirrored by other commercial evidence. Becker [6] noted that there were more than 5,000 computer programs for classroom use in a 1983 catalogue. This tells of enormous amounts of energy being put into an education market well before the majority of schools had even one computer.

The existence of enthusiastic teachers, publications and an energetic educational software industry cannot be put into a social context as there is little evidence of the proportion of people in the relevant community. That the community was energetic is beyond doubt, that it formed a majority of people in schools is yet to be supported. The length of time in which the computer became entrenched in schools is very short. By 1998, a short 15 years after one of the 'social beginnings' of 1983 postulated above, the general public had become convinced of the value of computers in schools.

> *"An MCI nationwide poll in 1998 found that nearly 60% of the public answered 'a great amount' when asked 'How much do you think computers have helped improve student learning?'" [10, p2].*

4 The Problems of a New Technology

As argued above the existence of computer hardware in schools by 1983 was at significant levels. The rationale for computers being there was not quite so clear cut. Parents wanted employment outcomes, educational thinkers like Papert and Kay had clear ideas of what could be done in classrooms, teacher enthusiasts had become intrigued by the attraction of programming, but the existence of one computer in a school amongst many untrained teachers did not ensure a school with a clear educational imperative. Becker [6] saw this as a significant problem:

> *"With such a sudden emergence of 'computers' in the instructional repertoire of schools, it is not surprising that an intellectual and empirical rationale for their educational value has barely begun to develop" [6, p26]*

The lack of a clear direction in many schools meant that hardware purchases blossomed in the first years after 1983, but some commentators saw a lesser increase in the useful purpose for all those computers. One telling commentary on actual classroom use from as late as 1993 suggested that the computer had not achieved general acceptance as an educational tool:

> *"The overall picture, however, after the introduction of the personal computer a decade ago and persistent efforts to improve schooling, suggests at best that computers are an expanding but marginal activity in schools with wide variation in administrator, teacher, and student use. A one-line caption for all of this activity over the last decade is: Computers meet classroom; classroom wins" [9].*

The cause of this perception of failure to maximize the potential of school computers is often illustrated by a quote from Thomas Edison:

> *"The motion picture is destined to revolutionize our educational system and... in a few years it will supplant largely, if not entirely, the use of textbooks." Thomas Edison, 1922.*

The point being made is that computers are no different from other technologies that have been brought to the classroom and the inevitable outcome is that the technology will fade into the background and that this is evident by 1995.

An alternative explanation of slow uptake in the classroom is an infrastructure argument. A much later survey in 1997 shows the retrospective picture of the classrooms of the early years. The Educational Testing Service from Princeton conducted a study of schools in the country for the 1995/6 school year [5]. This can be considered to be at the very end of the widespread introduction of computers. Problems found in this study can be assumed to have existed for the previous decade and give a stark view of missing infrastructure. Relevant findings included:

- Only 15% of teachers had at least nine hours of training in educational technology
- 18 States did not require educational technology courses for a teaching license
- While 85% of schools had multimedia computers the average ratio of students was 24 students to 1 computer, nearly five times that recommended
- Only 6 to 8 percent of available courseware was judged as 'exemplary' and less than half was good enough to warrant a review.

These findings indicate that computers in schools suffered from poor teacher training, high numbers of students trying to use the equipment and poor software.

5 The Educational Computing Debates

One of the purposes of schooling is to prepare students to perform in their society. As the United States became more computerized an obvious need arose for preparation in computing. This is an obvious reason for exposing students to computers: when they leave school they need to be able to interact with the computers all around them. This made the task of those asking for funds relatively easy. Computers could be a gadget like the film projector, but they were also the stuff of commerce and students needed to use them.

> *"Because of the widespread and growing use of such technology in both the home and the workplace, computer equipment is unlikely to end up in closets or even to sit idle most of the time. Hence, for both students and teachers, there is a kind of 'authenticity' associated with using this equipment; for students, the technology represents the future" [11] p32*

One of the earliest educational computing projects to gain significant funding was the Plato system [1-3]. These systems were largely used for computer aided instruction (CAI), often in military training or in colleges. As a result of this exemplar many people justifying computers for their schools did so on the basis of teaching about computers (computer literacy) or as tools for efficient learning through CAI:

> *"There is little consensus about how computers should be integrated into school curricula in the U.S. Some argue that they should be used to teach 'computer literacy' (Winkle and Mathews, 1982), and often tacitly identify 'computer literacy' with programming skills and knowledge about the workings of computers. Others emphasize the special role that computer based systems can play as instructional aids, but people vary considerably in their views. Some valuing drill and practice in existing curricula. Others find drill and practice thoroughly pedestrian, and argue for more progressive, discovery-oriented learning in richer, student driven computerized environments" [12].*

Among those using this line of argument were those advocating computer use as a tool common in business, as a tool for learning management or as a tool for motivating students:

> *"Computer technology can be used in the classroom in three ways: 1) as tools such as word processors, spreadsheets, programming languages, and electronic network systems; 2) as integrated learning systems that present exercises for students to work on individually and that keep records of student progress for reporting to the teacher; and 3) as simulations and games that engage students in computer-based activities designed to be motivating and educational." [11, p29].*

These debates were influenced by some very strident educationalists bent on restructuring schools in a new, student centred, non-didactic model of education. Principal among these was Seymour Papert who created the Logo language and the ancillary environment to demonstrate how mathematics might be taught in a new way in which students investigated on their own.

> *"The phrase 'technology and education' usually means inventing new gadgets to teach the same old stuff in a thinly disguised version of the same old way. Moreover, if the gadgets are computers, the same old teaching becomes incredibly more expensive and biased towards its dullest parts, namely the kind of rote learning in which measurable results can be obtained by treating the children like pigeons in a Skinner box."* [13] p247.

Also in this camp was Alan Kay, of the Learning Research Group at the Xerox Palo Alto Research Center. Kay saw a chance to use computers to provide a learning environment in which students might experiment and so learn. His vision included a student using the environment in unexpected ways:

- *"to provide exceptional freedom of access so kids can spend a lot of time probing for details, searching for a personal key to understanding processes they use daily; and*
- *to study the unanticipated use of the Dynabook and Smalltalk by children in all age groups."* [14, P41].

From the viewpoint of social history these streams of educational thought are confined to the small community of educational thinkers rather than the broader school community at the times being considered. A study of the modern curriculum statements would be required to see if the ideas have spread into the general community.

6 Conclusion

Stories from the 1950s to the 1990s show that American schooling was rich in innovation from the beginnings of general purpose computing. Brilliant educational thinkers and technologists produced programming environments and hardware platforms that stand up to modern equivalents. The Plato terminal with its touch screen and well written courseware was found to be roughly equivalent to a human teacher, if a little more expensive. The Dynabook and Smalltalk system seem very similar to the modern notebook or tablet, and the Logo system is still in use today.

These amazing experiments in educational computing are historically important but are only precursors of the social history of school computing in the United States. It was not until Title I funding and the momentum of teacher enthusiasts became widespread that the social history involving all schools can be said to have started, and that can be dated to around 1983. It can be argued that the social history of educational computing not involving the actual use of computers predates 1983 as there is a broad evidence base that people around education were being influenced to a great degree prior to the widespread use of the hardware.

The social history of computers in schools is a story of faith in a new technology that came well in advance of sure knowledge of the best use. Debate raged at all levels of the education system regarding the best use. This debate asked school planners to choose between views of how a computer should be used, including using a computer in the school to:

- Teach about computers to prepare students for a technology dominated workplace
- Provide an interactive tool to provide an environment in which students can experiment and learn by doing.
- To provide a resource to increase the productivity of teaching (e.g. CAI)

An interesting recent trend in school computing has been the massive swing towards use of the Internet by schools. This may be a clue to the outcome of the debates on how computers are best used and is certainly a rich topic for further research.

References

[1] Blitzer, D.L., Skaperdas, D.: Plato IV - An economically viable large-scale computer-based education system. In: National Electronics Conference (1968)
[2] Smith, S., Sherwood, B.: Educational uses of the PLATO computer system. Science 192, 344–352 (1976)
[3] Plato Learning. History of Plato Learning (February 2004), http://www.plato.com/aboutus/company_history.asp
[4] Olsen, J.R., Bass, V.B.: The application of performance technology in the military: 1960-1980. Performance & Instruction 21, 32–36 (1982)
[5] Coley, R., Cradler, J., Engel, P.K.: Computers and Classrooms: The Status of Technology in US, Schools. Educational Testing Service, Princeton (1997)
[6] Becker, H.J.: Computers in schools today: Some basic considerations. American Journal of Education 93, 22–39 (1984)
[7] US Department of Education. Title I — Improving The Academic Achievement of The Disadvantaged (1965), http://www2.ed.gov/policy/elsec/leg/esea02/pg1.html
[8] Puma, M.J., Drury, D.W.: Exploring New Directions: Title I in the Year 2000. ERIC (2000)
[9] Cuban, L.: Computers meet classroom: Classroom wins. The Teachers College Record 95, 185–210 (1993)
[10] Anderson, R.E., Ronnkvist, A.: The presence of computers in American schools, Teaching, learning, and computing: 1998 national survey (1999)
[11] Collins, A.: The role of computer technology in restructuring schools. Phi Delta Kappan 73, 28–36 (1991)
[12] Kling, R.: Value conflicts in the deployment of computing applications. In: Proceedings of the ACM 12th Annual Computer Science Conference on SIGCSE Symposium, pp. 67–84 (1984)
[13] Papert, S.: Teaching Children Thinking. Programmed Learning and Educational Technology 9, 245–255 (1972)
[14] Kay, A., Goldberg, A.: Personal dynamic media. Computer 10, 31–41 (1977)
[15] Papert, S.: Mindstorms: Children, computers, and powerful ideas. Basic Books, Inc. (1980)
[16] Goldberg, A., Kay, A.: Teaching smalltalk, Xerox PARC SSL, p. 77 (1977)

The Dutch Situation: An Ever Continuing Story

Bert Zwaneveld[1] and Victor Schmidt[2]

[1] Open Universiteit (Open University), Heerlen, The Netherlands
[2] SLO, Nationaal Expertisecentrum voor Leerplanontwikkeling
(Netherlands Institute for Curriculum Development), Enschede, The Netherlands
g.zwaneveld@uu.nl, v.schmidt@slo.nl

Abstract. In this chapter we describe the development of teaching with and about computers, mainly in Dutch secondary education. The focus is on the years 1970 – 1995, but we also give some insight into what happens afterwards. Because there are only a few written sources available of what happened in classrooms, we give most attention to national policies during that period. With the help of some colleagues from teacher training institutions we can also present some insight in what support was offered to their students and to teachers who were already in duty. We also report about the resources for teaching: courses, the teachers' association, an advisory institution, books/periodicals and software/courseware. In our conclusions we mention, that initially there was no difference between teaching with or about computers. The most interesting point in the conclusions is that the government rather lately developed a policy and thought that that policy would be sufficient for future development of teaching with and about IT in schools. This assumption turned out to be false and each time, up to nowadays, the government had to take its responsibility on these issues.

Keywords: teaching with and about computers, Dutch national policy on the use of computers in education, teachers' resources.

1 Introduction

In general terms, the development of the use of IT in education took the following course. At the end of the 1960s and beginning of the 1970s, computers were first introduced here and there in education, especially secondary education. At that time, computers could hardly do anything compared to today. Given their limited possibilities, there was no field of IT. There was only informatics, primarily involving the teacher programming a computer in BASIC or even machine language, and then teaching the steps to his or her pupils. The computer could hardly be used for teaching purposes. During the 1980s the government started getting involved, and national projects were set up to stimulate education with and about computers. But there was still little difference between what we now call IT and informatics. Only after the first National Informatics Education Congress in 1990 in Maastricht (NIOC1990) can we finally say with some reservations that IT and informatics begin to occupy a regular

A. Tatnall and B. Davey (Eds.): History of Computers in Education, IFIP AICT 424, pp. 212–238, 2014.

place in the Dutch educational system. From that moment on the use of IT in education and teaching in the school subject of informatics started to diverge, although it would take until 1998 for the government to introduce informatics as a school subject in secondary education.

We shall employ the following terminology. Learning or teaching with the computer means education in school subjects where the computer is used in some way as a teaching tool. By learning or teaching about the computer, we mean education in what is called informatics in Dutch and computer science in English; it covers topics like programming, databases, operating systems, system development, etc. We shall use the term 'informatics' here. There are also the basic computer skills, like how to use a word-processing programme, a calculation programme, a presentation programme, use of the computer's storage options and nowadays the internet. In the Dutch educational system, the terms 'civil informatics' and later on 'IT studies of computer and information literacy' or 'information science' are used to designate those topics.

This chapter starts with a few stories in section 2 about people who came into contact with computers at school as teachers or pupils in the last century. We want to give the reader a first impression of what was going on in the classroom in those days. In section 3 we follow the developments up to the specified NIOC1990 and at the end summarise how it went on from there. In section 4, NIOC1990 is described in detail. We wrap up, in section 5, with several conclusions and suggestions for the future regarding learning with and about computers.

2 A Few Stories

During the National Informatics Education Congress of 2013 (NIOC2013), there was a session in which informatics teachers from different educational sectors talked about their experiences with computers in the teaching that they received or gave. Some of those stories are given below as a warm-up for this chapter.

The participants sharing their experiences had different backgrounds: pupil, teacher, researcher. The experiences are arranged here according to type of school. They are written from a personal perspective, referring to one of the storytellers. Although there are quotation marks, the citations are not literal.

2.1 Primary Education

> *"In the years 1994-2002 our primary school did nothing with computers until my father's company replaced its old computers and gave a large number of them to our school. The computers were primarily used to teach typing, however. The pupils prepared assignments with them. They also learned to search on the internet to research the assignment projects. I learned a bit of HTML with my father's help. The school offered these activities in group 7 and group 8"*[1]

[1] This is the end of primary school with pupils aged 10 to 12 years old.

"I think the most important explanation for why our school did this was that it could see the importance of doing so. But as a public school there was no founding available. How important this was considered is reflected in the fact that once the computers were there, they were quickly linked together in a network. Some software was available, which had been an appendix in the form of a CD enclosed with a magazine or a book, but this was not used in the class. The children could buy it for use at home.

"It was striking that many children did not start working behind the computer, but primarily sat around causing trouble. There was too little supervision, if any."

2.2 Secondary Education

"During my doctoral research into teaching modelling in physics, at the start of the 21st century, I saw the same phenomenon, pupils sat around causing trouble more than they used the computer as a learning aid.

"My research concerned the attitude of pupils to IT, more in general with regard to science and technology and the role of modelling. The software used was PowerSim, and the activities took place in the senior high school (A-level building) for havo and vwo[2]*. The idea was to expose the pupils to the procedures used in physics at the university, including the computer to simulate physical processes. From chats with the pupils (which was possible), it seemed that the learning results were definitely reasonable. This applied especially to the pupils writing short and coherent chats. It also seemed that the attitude was closely related to the course of the learning process. The better that went, the greater the motivation and the attitude. The reasoning was better and the modelling skills improved."*

"The subject informatics in secondary education at the end of the last century, at the start of the 1980s, was initially focussed on controlling the computer: working with MS-DOS. Programming has to be done at the assembler level. Assistance was provided by an IBM computer and the linked P2000-computers from Philips. Then with the development of the home computer, this training shifted to explaining about the computer and learning to programme it, especially in BASIC, sometimes even with an advanced version of it. The initial assignments were always based on mathematics. Later there were other assignments linked to other subjects, sometimes they were even subjects that were not taught at school. One example of this was the assignment to display the starry sky at night for a particular day on the screen.

[2] See appendix C.

"This informatics course was only taken by boys. It was supervised by a range of teachers, but there were actually only two who were familiar with the subject. Pupils were quickly better than most of the supervisory teachers. The school did find this subject important. Only much later was the transition made from 'how the computer works' to 'what the computer can do', as is now the case."

"In the course mathematics II, top secondary school, that existed between 1973 and 1985, there was a series of optional modules, e.g. complex numbers. At my school I studied numerical mathematics, where the pupils had to programme and solve typical mathematical problems. The programming language was called ECOL, a derivative of Algol/Pascal. Examples of such assignments were: numerical integration, the course of the path over a cloverleaf, so that it closed as smoothly as possible, estimating the number of people watching a football game on TV on the basis of the change in pressure in the water supply. At the half-time break, it dropped because of toilets being used. The pupils had to put their programme on special cards. In a specially designed box they were sent to what is now called the Freudenthal Institute, and the output sent back a few days later. Of course, there were usually some error messages."

"At my school we learned to programme in Logo rather than a language like Pascal or BASIC."

2.3 Tertiary Education

"In the 1990s Pascal was the standard language in the subject informatics. The language was the important thing, not what you could do with it."

3 A Short History of the Use of Computers in Education in the Netherlands

3.1 Global View

The use of computers in education was started by enthusiastic teachers during the period from the end of the 1960s to the beginning of the 1980s. There were hardly any female teachers involved. The starters thought, correctly in hindsight, that pupils from primary and secondary education should become familiar with computers at school, or even that working with computers could support and improve their learning. We could call these teachers 'early adopters'. The very first teachers were what we now would call 'computer nerds' or 'computer freaks'. They had access to a computer like the Tandy or the Commodore 64 that they had to programme themselves.

In the early days, the pupils in the class did not yet work with them directly but could be demonstrated certain things. The programmes often concerned the domain of mathematics, but definitely not always. From the books which appeared in this period, often with the term 'computer science' in the title – we return to these books in section 3.5, *Educational teachers' support* – it appears that hardly any distinction was made between what we now call IT and informatics. This was not surprising given the level of the architecture and the capacity of those older computers. Basically, the computers could do nothing without being directed step by step by the user, here the teacher. As a result, many books emphasised directing the computer far more than encouraging the pupils only to work with the computer. But it is clear that definitely the authors of these books, and we can assume also the early adopters, did intend for groups of pupils to start working on the computer. Several of these books contain *listings* of usually BASIC programmes that had to be entered by the teacher. Examples of such programmes are given in Table 1 in appendix A (Docters van Leeuwen 1982, p. 249):

The use of computers in schools by the pupils took off with the arrival of small, but nevertheless quite powerful computers like the Acorn from BBC and the P2000 from Philips. This latter computer was introduced in 1981. Its core was a z80-microprocessor. For both the Acorn and the P2000, the programmes and data had to be entered using a cassette tape. Wikipedia calls it a 'home computer'. The P2000 was primarily used in Dutch education because of its robust design. There was a special price for schools for this P2000 and the associated software.

Note. An outlier in the use of computers in education in this period was the possibility offered by the teaching and education computer centre of the University of Utrecht in the early 1980s. This centre was a predecessor of the current Freudenthal Institute. In the now defunct school subject of mathematics II in vwo which was intended for the better mathematics pupils who were expected to go on to study a scientific or technical programme at a university, the pupils had to choose a topic. If they chose computer mathematics, actually a form of numerical mathematics, they could put their programmes written in ECOL (a variation of Algol/Pascal) on special cards, which were sent by the teacher to the centre in Utrecht, and the result returned a few days later by post, usually with error messages. One of the stories in section 2, *A few stories*, is about this process.

In the early 1980s, the introduction of the personal computer, quickly abbreviated in the Dutch vernacular to PC, with the operating system MS-DOS provided a push from the outside. In the wake of the arrival of the PC, numerous companies and institutions introduced so-called PC-home projects. These projects were meant to encourage employees and their families to work with the PC at home; it was generally agreed in the collective labour agreements that employees would receive compensation from their employer to purchase a PC. These PC-home projects certainly helped to encourage the use of the computer in schools. Through these PC-home projects, pupils were given the opportunity to work with a computer at home. Schools had relatively limited resources to provide their pupils with computer access.

Parents who recognised the importance of computers encouraged their children's schools to employ computers in education. In addition, they could make a contribution with the PC at home. It wasn't until 1983 that 100 schools for secondary education were enabled by the government to install eight computers per school. We shall return to this topic in section 3.2, *National policy*.

With the introduction of MS-DOS and the PC, the use of computers in the classroom became much easier. Along with the development of the internet in the 1990s, we have practically arrived at the current situation. Kennisnet, a knowledge centre subsidised by the government that is meant to assist schools with implementing IT in education, to issue recommendations and to conduct research, has been saying the same thing for years about the use of computers in Dutch education (Kennisnet 2013b, p. 52):

> *"... that schools are enthusiastically embracing IT. Over several years, the use of IT has consistently grown in all sectors of education. The use of IT is important to prepare pupils for future careers and their functioning as citizens in an IT-rich and digital society.*
>
> *Scientific research supports the increasing proof that IT – with good, targeted and dosed use – contributes to the motivation, learning performance and reading speed of pupils. IT-applications support teachers with teaching and help the management to create a cost-effective school organisation. IT offers possibilities in the field of administration, organisation, coordination and personnel matters."*

But Kennisnet added as criticism (Kennisnet 2013b, p. 55):

> *"Despite the social necessity and the proven educational benefit of IT, it is still underused at many schools."*

According to Kennisnet (2013a) this lack of use is associated with the unbalance between vision of teachers, school directors, school boards and parents, expertise of the teachers primarily, availability of digital content and applications, and the infrastructure at schools.

3.2 National Policy

Following on from Ten Brummelhuis and Plomp (1993, 1994), we distinguish three phases in the government's policy regarding the use of computers in education. In the government's jargon these phases are given a label (printed in italics). We add the name of the associated project. In the detailed discussion of each phase, various matters will be clarified.

- 1982-1984: *exploration* with the 100-schools project
- 1984-1989: *basic provision and introduction* with the Informatics Stimulation Plan project
- 1989-1992: *consolidation* with the OPSTAP project.

And we add in this chapter the subsequent period, 1992 and later, to complete the picture.

3.2.1 Exploration: 1982-1984

In the 1970s there was hardly any government policy on informatics and information technology. Around 1980 the government began to realise that it could not remain sitting on its hands. The country appeared to be lagging behind its neighbours, a conclusion that was contested ten years later by the Advisory Council for Education (Advisory Council for Education 1994). Former world chess master, Prof. Max Euwe, expressed the importance of computers in education in 1980 on the occasion of the opening of an exhibition on informatics to celebrate the 100-year anniversary of the Vrije Universiteit (Euwe 1980, p. 441) as follows (see also the booklet by R.P. van de Riet in Appendix B):

> *"In secondary education as well and ultimately even in primary education, room must be made for informatics, or computer science. Schools prepare pupils for society, and computers are becoming an important component of society. Especially as far as mysterious matters like automation and computers are concerned, it is important that people are informed.*
>
> *Knowledge can allay the unfounded anxiety derived from the performance of machines that exceeds the limits of our imagination. Ignorance is a poor advisor, but is encountered everywhere, even in the highest intellectual circles. If a person becomes at least somewhat familiar with the phenomenon of computers from a young age, the anxiety will disappear and be replaced by understanding, with or without consent. It will allow any criticism to be supported by arguments, which can be discussed. People at least know what they are talking about, what they are protesting against."*

In 1983 the two-year 100-schools project was initiated, in which participating schools for secondary education were each given 8 microcomputers with the aim to acquire two years of experience with education in 'civil informatics' – nowadays we would say the 'use of information technology (or IT)' - and in informatics. In a special edition of Euclides devoted to informatics, a monthly magazine for teaching mathematics and the organ of the Dutch Association of Mathematics Teachers, which appeared in October 1983, a series of articles reported how schools were employing the computers of the 100-schools project. It revealed that along with BASIC, LOGO was also being used as a programming language. A lot of attention was paid to what was taught in the citizen informatics lessons (see the next section). As could be expected, all the contributions were positive.

3.2.2 Basic Provision and Introduction: 1984-1989

In 1984 the government took a bigger step with the Informatics Stimulation Plan, abbreviated INSP, (Ministry of Education and Science, 1984). This stimulation plan aimed to support informatics and its application in education, research, the market sector and the government. Education was expected to:

- familiarise citizens with the information technology. The term 'citizen informatics' was applied to this.
- create 'human capital' to strengthen the market sector, especially for vocational education.

To achieve these goals, a considerable sum (for its time) of NLG 267.5 million (= € 121.4 million) was reserved for the period 1984 – 1988. It was meant to pay for the development of software (educational) and for providing training (refresher courses) on a large scale. For each of the education sectors, this was elaborated in the following points of attention (see appendix C for an overview of the education system in the Netherlands):

- Vocational education: use of information technology in vocational subjects
- General secondary education: development of a citizen informatics subject in the first phase and an informatics elective in the second phase.
- Use of the computer in all subjects.
- Development of computer-assisted teaching.

The use of computers in primary education had a low priority for the government in the Informatics Stimulation Plan.

One of the components of the Informatics Stimulation Plan in the period 1985-1988 was the NIVO project, which was conducted and partly financed by the government (Casimier 1988; Ten Brummelhuis & Plomp 1993, 1994; Lepeltak 1997). NIVO stands for New Information Technology in Secondary Education. The aim of this project was to familiarise the pupils in all 2000 schools for secondary education

Table 1. Description of the software packages and courseware delivered to all secondary schools

Program	Description
Software	
PC-TYPE	Word processor for professional use
PC-FILE	Universal database management program
PC-CALC	Spreadsheet
PC-GRAPH	For creating bar graphs, pies, scatter grams, etc.
INSTRUCT	Individual training programs for the PC
TAIGA	Authoring system for development of CA1 programs
EGI	Program for free drawings
SUPERDRAFT	Simple version of CAD program
DOKA	Educational game for 'developing' an invisible text
DMS	Program for dynamic models: simulation
Courseware (lesson ideas)	
PHYSICS	Examples of PC-CALC for six topics in physics
BIOEART	Applications of PC-CALC in biology and earth science
BIODMS	DMS application in biology (blood sugar and temperature)
MATH	Examples of PC-CALC application in mathematics
TAILANG	Examples of developing drill/practice CA1 for foreign languages with TAIGA
LANGDOK	Examples of how to use DOKA for foreign language exercises

with learning with the computer from the start, by integrating the use of computers in the school subjects. The 100-schools project was incorporated in the NIVO project. The schools were given 11 computers each in a network. They were advised to set aside a classroom devoted to this. The computers were supplied by three companies: Philips, IBM and Tulip, which also provided part of the budget. The schools were also given software: word-processing programmes like PC-Type and calculation programmes like PC-Calc. Table 1 lists all the programmes the schools were given.

An equally important element was the requirement that three teachers, including at least one without computer experience and at least one woman, had to take training courses. These courses were provided by the institutes training teachers for the lower secondary school. Casimir (1988) reported that the 90-hour course developed by her institute, and intended for teachers without any computer experience, consisted of the parts:

- Data and information
- Computers and society
- Applications
- Programmable machines
- System development (automation)
- Computers and education.

A considerable proportion of the available budget was intended for what was called 'learning *with* information technology': use of information technology in all subjects with an eye on vocational preparation and increasing the attractiveness of the subjects. The focus should shift from provision of the equipment to software development.

Evaluation by external experts of the INSP and of the NIVO project. At the start of the Informatics Stimulation Plan, De Bruijn (1984), at that time professor of mathematics at the Technical University of Eindhoven, published the following analysis and criticism of the plan in a periodical on information and information policy. We reproduce here the most striking aspects of his commentary.

In general, he was satisfied with this initiative of the government. The government simply could not ignore the arrival of the computer and its use in education.

De Bruijn considered the term 'citizen informatics' for education about computers rather unfortunate. He preferred the label: training to be a consumer in the information society. For education *with* computers he used the term '*computer-aided instruction*'.

The fact that informatics was meant to be an *elective* in the second half of secondary school according to the Informatics Stimulation Plan De Bruijn considered a major error, because it would mean that no tertiary education course would require informatics as an entry requirement. It should be a mandatory subject throughout all the years of general secondary education. These two issues ensured, he felt, that the status of informatics would not be good. Not until 1998 did informatics become an elective in the last two years of academic secondary education.

The most important of De Bruijn's criticisms is that the objectives of the plans for secondary education had not been specified. Nowadays we would say that the long-term vision was lacking. The most important arguments centred around: the Netherlands is lagging behind its neighbours in this field. If computers were employed in education, this was more likely due to pressure exerted by companies and parents.

Lepeltak (1997) cited Tjeerd Plomp, advisor in the 1990s to the former Minister of Education on the subject of the use of computers in education, when he was reflecting on the NIVO project:

> *"If we look back, a few important elements are evident. To start with, we have ascertained that the idea prevalent in the early 1990s, that the Informatics Stimulation Plan activated an entire revolution, was only partly correct. Computers are now indispensable for schools. The subject of information science has a firm position in secondary education, and especially in vocational education. It has also acquired a set place in some general school subjects. For example, in physics, informatics forms part of the examination requirements. Unfortunately, there is stagnation in its use in everyday lessons; the enrichment of daily teaching by using IT. People realise now that what the ministry anticipated in the early 1990s has not come to pass."*

3.2.3 Consolidation: 1989-1992

After expiration of the subsidy period of the Informatics Stimulation Plan, schools were supposed to be able to find sufficient funding for the integration and consolidation of information technology in their education. In 1989 however a second government initiative followed instead, with the aim of expanding the attainments from the 1980s. It was given the name OPSTAP (Ministry of Education, Culture and Science 1988). This umbrella covered a wide range of projects. In secondary education an education innovation project started under the name PRINT (stands for Project Introducing New Technologies). The NaBont project was specifically oriented to vocational education. This abbreviation stands for Vocational Education Training in New Technologies. NaBont focussed on more than the use of computers, it covered all new technologies in general. And a spotlight was turned on primary education. Primary schools had obtained computers using their own funds in the second half of the 1980s (1985: 10% - 1989: 50%; 1 computer per 89 pupils) (Ten Brummelhuis & Plomp 1994). Under the umbrella of OPSTAP, the Comenius project was initiated, which made standardised equipment with software available for every primary school. In 1994 the delivery of the Comenius equipment was completed. Secondary schools were in the meantime amply supplied with an average of 21 computers per school, and most of them had one or more dedicated computer rooms (Ten Brummelhuis & Plomp 1994).

Primary schools used their Comenius equipment extensively after some initial hesitation. Half of the teachers at schools that received the equipment in 1990 were using it weekly in their lessons three years later (Ten Brummelhuis & Plomp 1994). The use of computers in secondary education was disappointing in comparison. Only in the lessons on information science - the new name for citizen informatics – were computers used because of the nature of the subject. At that time, only 3% of the teachers used the computer more than 1 hour per week (Ten Brummelhuis & Plomp 1994).

3.2.4 And Further: 1992 – …

We should now turn our attention to the first National Informatics Education Congress of 1990, abbreviated NIOC1990, which we consider a turning point in the development of education with and about computers in the Netherlands. We feel, however, that it deserves its own section in this story: section 4, NIOC1990: a turning point. We describe in this section what happened further in the 1990s.

The government's efforts seemed more or less to be finished in 1992. In the policy memorandum 'Enter, the future', it was concluded that schools were now capable of integrating and consolidating information technology in their education. In 1997 – which we realise is over the limit of the early 1990s - the government came to the conclusion that new investments must be made in the use of IT in education: the action plan 'Investing in Progress' (1997; see also Lepeltak 1997). The Advisory Council for Education, the highest advisory body of the Minister of Education, noted the following in a recommendation on this action plan (Advisory Council for Education 1998):

> *"The Council greeted with approval the ambitious action plan 'Investing in Progress'. The high priority it assigned to the use of IT in education was supported by the Council. Points of concern for the Council were the didactic foundation, the uncertainty about the next steps to take, and the financial framework. The Council felt that the action plan put too much emphasis on providing the material conditions and paid too little attention to the educational aspects of IT use. The use of IT in education should primarily be based, according to the Council, on considerations of substance: what should be done with IT, why was this necessary, and how should it be accomplished? Furthermore, the action plan stressed a mixture of objectives for all three functions of IT in education. The Council considered it unrealistic to strive for goals in the coming years that focussed on 'learning through the use of IT.*
>
> *The uncertainty about the next steps to take can slow the innovation process. Necessary expenditure to maintain the IT-infrastructure, like repairs and replacement, were not guaranteed to be covered. The financial framework of the action plan also did not take into consideration the new requirements that IT use imposed on the physical learning environment (housing, furniture, security).*
>
> *The action plan envisaged establishing vanguard schools, which are ahead of other schools in the use of IT. This implies a widening of the gap between schools. The Council feels that the differences between schools due to the policy must be completely reversed. This could mean that a larger budget would have to be reserved for non-vanguard schools than for vanguard schools."*

In the framework of this action plan 'Investing in Progress', primary and secondary schools were invited to submit project plans for the implementation of IT in education. A total of 119 vanguard schools were chosen which each produced a project plan. The plans were evaluated nationally and implemented in 1998. Again schools were supplied with PCs until there were 15 PCs per school. And teacher training was also organised. A review was published with the title 'Education Online, action in IT vanguard schools of secondary education'.

One important aspect of teaching and learning with the computer in the 21st century is the appearance of digital teaching material, often in combination with a laptop, notebook or iPad or tablet for all pupils. Often publishers of schoolbooks provided digital teaching material and tests of the methods. Teachers were not very satisfied in general with this digital teaching material and wanted to develop their own. Research by Kennisnet (2010) and Zwaneveld and Rigter (2010) revealed that there was a lot to gain here. The quality of the teaching material that the teachers produced was not often good simply because they were not developers, and the support in the form of time off from teaching duties to develop such materials was too limited. The teachers' attempts to have this done as a group effort worked to the extent that materials were exchanged, but in general they preferred using their own material than what collectively was developed. Especially older teachers were noted to prefer keeping the familiar schoolbook.

In the period 2006-2010 a number of people, including the first author of this chapter, pressed the Minister of Education, Culture and Science to bring the subject of informatics into the 21st century, especially since certain developments in that field, like the development of mobile technology – e.g. telephones and tablets, as well as social media – had no or at best a marginal place in the curriculum. This led to the Royal Netherlands Academy of Arts and Sciences setting up a commission in 2010 which produced a report in 2012 on 'digital literacy, skills and attitudes for the 21st century'. This report paid a great deal of attention to learning with the computer. The subject of informatics was another focus. We cite here the beginning of the summary (Royal Netherlands Academy of Arts and Sciences 2012) and the first four recommendations:

> *"Digital literacy refers to the ability to make prudent use of digital information and communication and to evaluate the consequences of that use critically. In the 21st century digital literacy belongs to the basic skills of every educated person. It is necessary for navigating one's way through the information society. Like language and mathematics skills, digital literacy requires instruction and education over a longer period of time. It should therefore be covered in our education system.*
>
> *Recommendation 1*
>
> *Introduce a new compulsory subject Information & communication in the lower stage of havo and vwo. This should be a broad and compact introductory subject, covering the essential facts of digital literacy.*
>
> *Recommendation 2*
>
> *Completely overhaul the optional subject Informatics in the upper years of havo and vwo. By a flexible and modular design, the subject should remain up to date and appeal to pupils regardless of their focus area.*

Recommendation 3

Encourage interaction between these subjects and other school subjects.

Recommendation 4

Make a priority to raise a new generation of teachers with new skills and attitudes. Instruct the schools for higher professional education (hbo) and the universities to collaborate in this regard."

The report seemed to confirm the proposition that not much had changed in 2013 with regard to learning with and about computers since the 1980s: a lot was happening, but not enough, and certainly considering the rapid developments in IT and informatics.

3.3 Information Science and Informatics

At the end of the 1980s, teaching with and about computers – the school subject informatics – was being separated more and more. The first sign was the school subject of information science. Learning about computers became informatics, just like the discipline in tertiary education.

3.3.1 Information Science

The subject of information science merits a separate mention in this brief history. In this subject, the pupils were taught how to deal with computers. Originally, this was only word processing, the use of calculation programmes like spreadsheets and working with presentation programmes like PowerPoint. Later, after the arrival of the internet, searching, finding and processing of information were added.

In the 1980s information science was mandatory for the first three years of secondary education. But it was left up to the schools as to how they were to meet this obligation. Two models predominated. In the first one, information science was taught as a separate subject for one year (in year 1, 2 or 3). In the other model, parts of information science were integrated in the existing school subjects. For example, word processing was associated with Dutch, working with a spreadsheet with mathematics, and working with presentation programmes and searching, finding and processing information with practically every school subject. Since 2006 information science no longer exists as a school subject, but in the subjects Dutch and English, it was still included in the main goals (Government 2010): 'The pupil learns to use strategies to collect information from verbal and written texts.' And: 'The pupil learns to search in written and digital sources of information, arrange them and evaluate their worth for himself and other people.' It is assumed that the pupils have already mastered these skills before starting secondary education, that they acquired these skills at home. In general, this assumption has proven to be correct.

3.3.2 Informatics

Although it would take until 1998 before informatics became an official school subject, part of informatics, namely automatic data processing, had already been given a place in the second half of secondary education as a result of curriculum adjustment in mathematics (havo and vwo). In 1986 the subjects mathematics I and mathematics II (vwo) were replaced by mathematics A, which paid a great deal of attention to applications in economic problem situations in particular (algebra and statistics), and mathematics B which focussed more on pure mathematics (algebra, calculus, geometry) and on their application in the natural science subjects. In mathematics A the specified section 'automatic data processing' was incorporated. Pupils learned about algorithmic situations, for example, modelling statistics (to simulate probability experiments) using programme structure diagrams (psd). See Figure 1.

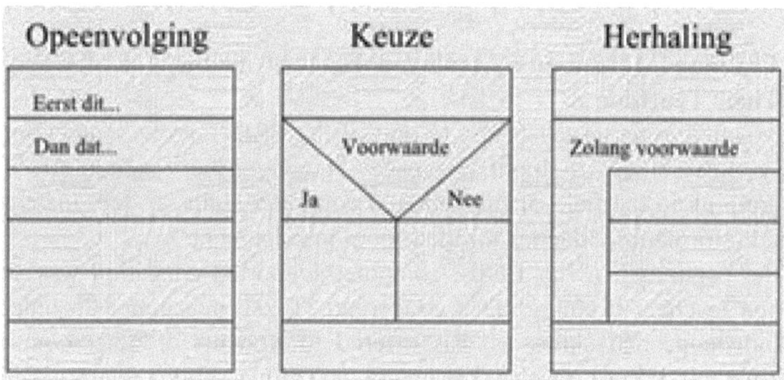

Fig. 1. The primary structures of a psd

For all vwo pupils mathematics was (and still is) a mandatory subject in the last two years. Many pupils choose mathematics A instead of mathematics B. This ensures that a relatively large number of pupils becomes acquainted with algorithms. At the next curriculum revision at the end of the 1990s, this section disappeared again.

As noted above, informatics only became a real school subject in 1998. Its aims are (Steering group Second Phase Profile for Secondary Education[3] 1995):

> *"The Informatics course at the [...] secondary education level would be focused on providing students with:*
> - *a view of Informatics and IT, and the relationship between these fields and other subject areas, as well as how they related to technology and society as a whole*
> - *a picture of the role Informatics and IT would play in their education and career*
> - *hands-on experience with Informatics and IT through:*

[3] In 1993 the Second Phase Profile Steering Committee was established. (Instelling Stuurgroep Profiel Tweede Fase) (Instellingsbeschikking), in *Uitleg Mededelingen OenW*, no.18, 30 June 1993, 55-57). The Secondary Education Profile Act dates from 2 July 1997 (Stb. 1997-322). It defines four study profiles for havo and vwo: culture and society, economy and society, nature and health, nature and technology.

- *learning the basic concepts and skills of the subject*
- *studying Informatics problems*
- *studying the structures of data processing systems*
- *working on system development in groups*

and all this within the context of how Informatics could be applied in society as a whole."

3.4 Teacher Training

Training teachers about learning with computers in the classroom deserves its own section. The following is partly borrowed from the Windesheim Magazine (1991).

3.4.1 Training Trainee and Employed Teachers in the Use of Computers in Their Teaching

As already stated, training teachers was part of the PRINT project, and courses were offered by universities of applied sciences, among other institutions. This was refresher training in the field of fundamental computer skills, system management in schools and informatics didactics for the school management.

From the beginning of the 1990s, computer-supported education was sometimes given in the teachers' training. This concerned IT use that aimed to help students acquire knowledge and skills, as was offered to students of other courses. From around 2000, all trainee teachers at many vocational colleges were offered IT-modules which aimed to prepare them for IT use in their future careers. This involved acquiring general IT skills, specific IT skills for teaching, like the use of a grading administration system and electronic learning environments, and specific IT skills for their subject. As soon as software/courseware became available, students were encouraged to use it during their practical training. Its limited availability at the training school was the most restrictive factor. The starting point of the education about the use of computers in the classroom was and is that computers are used in their own lessons and in the students' assignments with the vision: 'keep up to date and serve as an example for your students.' And 'IT-skillful teachers are found only where there are IT-skillful students'.

Since 2009 there is a knowledge basis of IT for teachers (Van der Linde 2009). This was developed at the initiative of Kennisnet for teachers in secondary education. This knowledge basis was used by the teachers' training aimed at teachers in the first half of secondary education. In 2013 a revision of this IT knowledge basis appeared (Bottema et al. 2013). In this revised version the aim of this knowledge basis was described:

> *"The IT knowledge basis describes the IT-competencies of newly qualified teachers and is thus an instrument that is used when setting end criteria in the curricula of the second-degree teachers' training (first few years of secondary education). A newly qualified teacher makes conscious and suitable use of IT in educational situations in which he makes the connection between subject-oriented learning goals, didactic forms and the employment of IT."*

3.4.2 Training Trainee and Employed Teachers for Education in Informatics

In the 1970s and 1980s there was no regular teachers' training in informatics, information science or IT. It was only from the end of the 1990s that vocational colleges offered teachers' training in IT, which led to sufficient competence for the first years of secondary education. Graduates could give lessons in the secondary (preparation) vocational education, and the training consisted of a mix of informatics subjects like programming and information analysis, and topics oriented more towards the management and maintenance of infrastructures and systems. For the prospective informatics teacher in all years of secondary education, universities have been offering since 2006 teachers' training at the level of a master of science.

The teachers' training courses have also contributed to the retraining of teachers from other subjects in IT and informatics. When a comprehensive increase of scale operation was imposed on secondary vocational education in 1991, a number of teachers was threatened with unemployment. These teachers were offered retraining in mathematics, economy and informatics. These retraining courses were also open to teachers from secondary education. The curriculum of the informatics retraining had a study load of 800 hours and consisted of subjects like information system development, programming, computer architecture, and informatics & education. To prepare for the implementation of the informatics subject in the second phase of secondary education (havo/vwo) in 1998, an extensive retraining course was offered to teachers of other subjects in all years of secondary education. This course had a study load of 1260 hours and consisted of a broad range of informatics topics and informatics didactics. Around 300 teachers attended the course in three cohorts.

3.5 Educational Teachers' Support

Teachers are generally supported in their work by:

- courses
- books or periodicals
- educational software
- advisory bodies
- associations of teachers concerned with the content of education.

We give a summary of the first three at the end of this section. Unfortunately, we are not aware of the extent to which the supportive materials are actually used.

We shall consider first the relevant advisory body Kennisnet and the relevant teachers' association i&i.

3.5.1 Kennisnet

For the support of all education in the use of IT, the expertise centre Kennisnet is the most important contributor. It was established at the end of the 1990s as part of the action plan 'Investing in Progress' (Minister of OCW 2001). On its website Kennisnet advertises itself as follows (Kennisnet 2013a):

> *"IT is interwoven in all aspects of society. IT is now commonplace in education also. The question is no longer whether IT will be employed, but in what manner. An integral approach to this is essential, and*

education recognises three domains. Along with the focus on IT in learning, the use of IT in the near future will be emphasised to increase the efficacy of the organisation and transparent justification. Kennisnet follows this development and acts as an IT-partner in these three domains.

Kennisnet facilitates the maximal use of the power of IT in all institutions in primary education, secondary education and secondary vocational education. We do this from three roles.

Kennisnet clarifies the characteristics of successful IT-applications and ensures that the knowledge, experiences and good examples are shared with education.

We create and manage the national IT-infrastructure that gives institutions freedom of choice and enables market parties to realise their own service provision.

We strive to inspire and offer a glimpse of the future by experimenting with new combinations of education and IT and sharing these insights.

By combining the available means in primary education, secondary education and secondary vocational education and coordinating and targeting their application, we can produce better and faster returns on the approximately 1 billion euros invested in IT by institutions."

3.5.2 i&i Association

The teachers' association for informatics and IT is the i&i Association. Originally, this was the abbreviation for information science and informatics, but with the establishment of the term IT and the abolition of the school subject information science, just the abbreviation i&i came to be used. Its activities contribute to the development of a vision for IT in education. Its main activity is the annual national congress for members that includes IT co-ordinates who ensure that IT is properly used by teachers in school subjects, as well as the teachers of IT and informatics:

'The i&i Association welcomes all teachers who use IT in their lessons. The association is an innovative community for teachers, education innovators, IT-coordinators and informatics teachers and wants to promote the expertise of its members and exchange knowledge in the field of didactics, teaching tools and technology. The didactics is the leading component. The association enables its members to become inspired for their daily work in education.

Vision

The i&i Association wants to promote the discussion of new educational concepts and is of the opinion that IT can act as a major stimulus and offer important facilities to realise these new concepts. The manner in which IT-resources are utilised in education is subject to change and is partly dependent on the teacher using them. In this dynamic world, i&i wants to play a prominent innovative role. Online and during the meetings organised by the association, the members encourage and inspire each other. Communal striving makes sense, responsible application of IT in education that prepares pupils for their role in a radically changing society. Through conferences, refresher training, inspiration sessions and various products, the association helps teachers to enrich their lessons with the use of IT in a responsible manner.

Target groups
The i&i Association focusses on the teachers and staff of primary/secondary education and secondary vocational education, education innovators, IT-coordinators, IT-managers, informatics teachers and anyone in whatever function who feels involved with IT in education.

Interlocutor
As an independent body, the i&i Association is an interlocutor for various organisations in the field of education and IT. In addition, i&i is the official partner of various university institutions regarding the content, status and perspective of the upper secondary school subject informatics. The association is also actively involved in setting up various new informatics courses."

3.5.3 Courses

We consider the first courses that teachers could take to be the teachers' training aimed at the early years of secondary education as part of the '100-schools project' and the NIVO project. The course books developed for these teachers' training courses are used across the coutnry. The next one to mention is the European Computer Driving Licence, ECDL. The ECDL is an international certificate, it exists in 148 countries, including the Netherlands. The ECDL covers the basic computer skills. How many teachers have already obtained this computer driving licence is unknown. We do know it is the only course with an international end exam. Furthermore, the national pedagogic centres and the teachers' training focussing on the early years of secondary education offered (and still offer) courses in the field of education using computers. This support, primarily through courses and training, is currently conducted mostly by Kennisnet. For the school subject informatics, teachers can turn to the national science support centres. These centres, which are generally collaborations between universities and polytechnics, offer support to all teachers in the science and technology fields.

3.5.4 Books/Periodicals

Regarding periodicals that supported (and still support) teachers in education using computers, the first one appeared in April 1983 and was called Computers at School. (Jan Lepeltak, mentioned earlier, was the chief editor of this periodical for a time.) It is still published ten times a year. We can confidently affirm that all aspects of education using computers have been addressed in this periodical.

At about the same time as NIOC1990, the periodical TINFON was issued which is especially oriented to informatics teachers. This timing was not a coincidence: the same people who initiated the NIOC did so on TINFON. TINFON, which stands for Periodical on Informatics Education, was the Dutch specialist periodical for education in informatics. It contributed to the professionalisation of informatics teachers and to the quality of informatics education. It contains articles about informatics education in secondary, tertiary, university, vocational education and company training. Along with articles about practical experiences with certain didactic approaches, attention was also paid to research into those approaches. In 2008 TINFON came to a premature end, unfortunately, due to too few subscriptions. Attempts to convert the periodical to a digital format have not yet succeeded.

Since1970 many books have appeared about learning with and about computers. In appendix B we provide a list that is certainly not comprehensive. We can characterise these books as follows. Most of them are meant for teachers (or other interested adults), there are just a few books for pupils, and they are mostly tied to mathematics. They almost always concern to a greater or lesser extent the architecture of computers and how they can be put to work by implementing a programme. Programming takes up a large part of the content. Applications are described, but only a few books support teachers in imagining how they are going to realise this in their classrooms, in terms of content, pedagogics or didactics. Details about books are given in appendix B.

3.5.5 Software/Courseware

The first software employed for education with computers was the packages provided as part of the NIVO project. This software was not used much because it was not standard software like Lotus 123, WordStar, WordPerfect, dBase, Office or their predecessors. Mention must be made of VU-Stat which was specially designed and developed for mathematics by someone in a teachers' training course in the 1980s to support the teaching of statistics, and that is still commonly used, in its updated form. Not only can this software deal with large data sets and carry out descriptive statistics on them, it can also do simulations and inductive statistical activities. We can also list for mathematics the computer algebra packages Derive, Maple, Matlab, and Mathematica. For the natural science subjects, we mention Coach that combines the processing of observations and scientific modelling on the computer. For informatics we cite programming languages like BASIC, Algol, Pascal.

In general, it can be ascertained that the quality of educative software/courseware was not that good, certainly in the beginning. In the special issue of Euclides, periodical for mathematics teachers, the teachers' trainer Nagtegaal (1983) covered in depth the development of educational software/courseware, and considered how that should be done professionally. He emphasised the quality of the software, referring specifically to the didactic quality. He claimed that the software supplied to schools as part of the 100-schools project left a lot to be desired. Furthermore, the teachers training institutes were involved in didactic refresher training of teachers of the subject information science from the mid-1980s.

3.6 Students' Talent Development

In this section we mention a memorable fact that is not history: the Informatics Olympiad. From 1989, following in the footsteps of subjects like mathematics and physics, the first international informatics competition was organised for talented pupils: the Informatics Olympiad. This competition consists of solving a number of rather complex programming problems in a relatively short period. The first Dutch entries date from 1990, when three pupils were sent to Minsk. A year later a national Dutch preliminary round was held, with the best participants going on to the international competition. Since then, the Netherlands has continued to send representatives each year to this international Informatics Olympiad. The Dutch participants often bring home medals and travel around half the world, except in 1995, when the international competition was held in the Netherlands itself.

4 NIOC1990: A Turning Point

As stated above, in 1984 De Bruijn remarked that – in our own words – there was little to no vision behind the government's plans with regard to the use of computers, and especially in education. The early adopters, the teachers who taught with and about computers from a very early stage, did have a vision about their use in education and in their own teaching. This vision can be formulated as follows: 'In the future it will be impossible to imagine life without computers. We have to prepare our pupils for this.' They did not know either how exactly to put this vision into practice – sometimes teachers were convinced of this vision by parents who worked in automation or computerisation, see one of the stories in section 2, *A few stories*.

In 1990 the first serious attempt was made from the bottom-up to develop a communal vision on the use of computers in education. In that year the first National Informatics Education Congress, NIOC[4], was held in Maastricht. Participants form the various relevant sectors, government-financed primary education, secondary education, vocational education and tertiary education, and the business sector with its company training, discussed for three days all aspects of education in IT and informatics in plenary lectures, parallel sessions, round tables, working groups, etc.

We consider NIOC1990 as a turning point in the education with and about computers. It is the first time that all involved educational sectors arrived at a communal vision. From the policy recommendations issued at the end of the congress, the assumption is evident that teaching with and about computers could be consolidated, as it was considered more or less self-evident. We cite here from the

[4] Since 1990 a NIOC is organised every two years.

8-page document containing the recommendations the ones for general education (NIOC1990). For the sake of completeness, we state that far more happened at NIOC1990 than what we report here. We are restricting ourselves to secondary education.

> *"Policy recommendations for General Secondary Education*
>
> 1. *The government should take decisions and provide guidance to schools and institutions on the basis of the vision produced herein about the manner in which the subject of informatics/information science should be incorporated in secondary education. If no decisions are taken, the achievements and investments made so far will be lost. For adult education modified decisions should be taken.*
> 2. *The guidance should consist of:*
>   a) *Programming the role of the institutions doing the teaching;*
>   b) *Promoting the development of educative software;*
>   c) *Providing content for the subject of informatics at the school level as in the final objectives recommendations for the basic curriculum and the PRINT-recommendation for the second phase;*
>   d) *Establishing a learning continuity pathway;*
>   e) *Earmarking resources and facilities for schools.*
> 3. *Better regulations must be created for the competence to teach informatics. The institutions must respond in turn by offering possibilities to obtain a specific, well defined level of competence.*
> 4. *Schools must develop a strategy for the creation of the subject of informatics. The school management must take responsibility for the coordination and necessary means and facilities.*
> 5. *The educational support institutions should intensify activities aimed at informatics education: curriculum and test development, research and implementation."*

There is a certain consolidation of computers in education that has become apparent since NIOC1990 as the government is increasingly reducing financial resources, and is taking a less regulatory stance in its policy.

In the meantime from the didactic viewpoint, visions are being developed for the use of computers in education. Kennisnet (2013b, p. 5) formulates this as follows:

> *"Dutch education is bursting with ambition. Excellent education, given by professional teachers in purposefully equipped schools. Education that matches the talents, skills and learning style of each pupil. Education that nurtures the best in each pupil. This is needed desperately. Society is changing at a rapid pace. The education must move with this change and the skills and talents needed in the 21st century. This ambition cannot be realised without a proper employment of IT. If IT is used in the correct manner, this will lead to greater motivation, better learning performances and a more efficient learning process for the pupil. It can also help the teacher to professionalise*

themselves. In addition, IT can lead to a better organisation in school with greater transparency and better guidance."

This statement by Kennisnet is supported by many others. The president of the Royal Netherlands Academy of Arts and Science, Hans Clevers, formulated part of the vision on learning with and about computers in the form of several questions referring to the skills and attitudes (Royal Netherlands Academy of Arts and Science 2013, p. 5) on a very tangible level.

"Is the first search result in Google the best one? How reliable is the information found? May I simply use all of the information on the internet? Who can see my profile on the internet and what are the associated risks?"

And we would like to add our vision to this: 'Citizens should be capable on the basis of their knowledge of IT and their good experiences with its use to help give direction to new developments in the field of IT.'

5 Conclusions

The history of learning with and about computers in the Netherlands in the past period of over 40 years, as described above, leads us to the following two conclusions.

At the very beginning, in the 1970s, there was no distinction between the use of the computer as a tool and informatics. The first teachers who realised the importance of computers for society and thus for education, had to program their computer using informatics. This limited the use of computers in the classroom. The advances in technology and the tendency to make computers more user-friendly allowed a growing distinction to be made between informatics on the one hand and what we now call IT on the other. Nevertheless, it took until the end of the 1990s before informatics was introduced as an independent school subject in secondary education. Furthermore, the attention paid to fundamental computer skills, was ultimately given shape in the school subject information science, but has been almost completely marginalised since then. This is also related to the increasing technological developments and greater ease of use. This progress in the possibilities of the computer, the increasing availability of educational software and the attention paid in teachers' training to teaching with the computer led to a certain consolidation of the use of computers in school subjects from the beginning of the 1990s.

Government policy also made an important contribution to this consolidation. Initially, computers were used in education only at the initiative of individual teachers, but in the 1980s and early 1990s, the government took action by stimulating computers in education with funds for equipment, software, training and other support. The government expected to achieve the desired consolidation much earlier, but again and again it proved necessary for the government to initiate new projects. Since the mid-1990s no new projects have been started by the government.

With some exaggeration, the government's policy can be characterised as lagging a bit behind the initiatives of individual teachers. The initiatives aroused the government. It then took the lead for what it hoped would be only a short time, ultimately turning it over to the educational field. This then turned out to be an underestimate, and as a result, the government had to become active again. That still applies today, as it seems that the digital world of the 21st century again has a need for a government initiative, for learning both with and about computers. We repeat here once again recommendation no. 1 of the Royal Netherlands Academy of Arts and Science (2012):

> *"Introduce a new compulsory subject Information & communication in the lower years of havo and vwo. This should be a broad and compact introductory subject, covering the essential facts of digital literacy."*

Acknowledgements. We thank Jan Timmers, Willem van der Vegt and Ton Konings for their valuable additions and improvement of earlier versions of this chapter. Further, we thank especially the teachers who participated during the NIOC2013 in the relevant session. In the person of Hans Frederik we thank the NIOC-board for the financial contribution to the production of this chapter.

References

Bottema, J., Erkelens, N., van der Hoeff, A., van der Linde-Koomen, D., Schols, M., Tollenaar-Hartogensis, A., Bos-Wierda, R., Barendsen, R.: Kennisbasis IT 2013. Algemeen Directeurenoverleg Educatieve Faculteiten (2013)

Casimir, C.: In-service Training in the NIVO-project in The Netherlands. European Journal of Education 23(4), 315–321 (1988)

De Bruijn, N.G.: Het Informatica-Stimulerings Plan. Informatie en Informatie beleid, 5 (1984)

Docters van Leeuwen, R.: Lesgeven met computers. Onderwijskundige aspecten van educatief computergebruik, vol. 2. NIB, Zeist (1982)

Euwe, M.: Deel uit de toespraak bij de opening van de V.U.-tentoonstelling over informatica bij gelegenheid van net 100 jaar bestaan van de V.U. Euclides 55(10), 441 (1980)

i&i (2013), http://ieni.org/over-ieni/ (retrieved July 2013)

Kennisnet. Vier in Balans Monitor 2009. Kennisnet, Zoetermeer (2010)

Kennisnet. Kennisnet: over ons (2013a), http://www.Kennisnet.nl/over-ons/ (retrieved October 2013)

Kennisnet. Vier in balans monitor 2013, De laatste stand van zaken van IT en onderwijs. Kennisnet, Zoetermeer (2013b)

Koninklijke Akademie van Wetenschappen. Digitale geletterdheid, vaardigheden en attitudes voor de 21ste eeuw, pp. 10–11. Koninklijke Akademie van Wetenschappen, Amsterdam (2012)

Lepeltak, J.: Nederland investeert in sprong vooruit, Educatie moet bijdragen aan de ontwikkeling van 'main port' naar 'brain port' Computable (April 4, 1997), http://www.computable.nl/artikel/achtergrond/education/1391848/1277214/nederland-investeert-in-sprong-vooruit.html (retrieved October 2013)

Van der Linde, D., Van der Hoeff, A., Pronk, H., Van Ast, M.: Kennisbasis IT. Algemeen Directeurenoverleg Educatieve Faculteiten (2009)

Ministeries van Onderwijs en wetenschappen. van Economische zaken en van Landbouw en Visserij. Informatica-Stimuleringsplan, Beleidsvoornemens tot bevordering van informatica en informatietechnologie in Nederland. Ministerie van O and W., Zoetermeer (1984)

Ministeries van Onderwijs en wetenschappen. van Economische zaken en van Landbouw en Visserij. Onderwijsappendix bij het Informatica-Stimuleringsplan, Versnelde invoering van informatietechnologie in het onderwijs. Ministerie van Onderwijs en wetenschappen, Zoetermeer (1984)

Ministerie van Onderwijs en wetenschappen. Nieuwe informatietechnologie in het voortgezet onderwijs, brief van de staatssecretaris van onderwijs en wetenschappen aan de Voorzitter van de Second Kamer der Staten-Generaal. Ministerie van Onderwijs en wetenschappen, Den Haag (1990)

Ministerie van Onderwijs en wetenschappen. Enter: de toekomst. SDU, Den Haag (1992)

Minister van Onderwijs, cultuur en wetenschappen. Onderwijs on line, actualisatie. Ministerie van Onderwijs, cultuur en wetenschappen, Den Haag (2001), `http://www.rijksgovernment.nl/bestanden/../education-on-line../actualisatie.pdf` (retrieved October 2013)

Nagtegaal, C.: De invloed van Bergen op de kwalieit van onderwijs-software. Euclides 59(2) (1983)

NIOC (1990), `http://nioc.nl/nioc/1990/docs/NIOC1990_policysrecommendations.pdf` (retrieved July 2013)

Advisory Council for Education. Advies over Informatie- and Communicatie Technologie and Onderwijs, uitgebracht aan de Minister van Onderwijs, Cultuur and Wetenschappen. Adviesraad voor Onderwijs, Den Haag (1998)

Rijksoverheid. Kerndoelen. Rijksgovernment, Den Haag (2010), `http://www.rijksgovernment.nl/documenten-en-publicaties/besluiten/2010/09/17/kerndoelen-onderbouw-secondary-education.html` (retrieved October 2013)

Stuurgroep Profiel Tweede Fase Voortgezet Onderwijs. Verschil moet er zijn. Stuurgroep Profiel Tweede Fase Voortgezet Onderwijs, Den Haag (1995)

Ten Brummelhuis, A., Plomp, T.: Lessons from Two Dutch Projects for the Introduction of Computers in Schools. Computers in Education 20(4), 333–340 (1993)

Ten Brummelhuis, A., Plomp, T.: Computers in Primary and Secondary Education: The Interest of an Individual Teacher or a School Policy? Computers in Education 22(4), 291–299 (1993)

Ten Brummelhuis, A., Plomp, T.: Informatietechnologie in het onderwijs: vijftien jaar beleid. De stand van zaken na 15 jaar overheidsstimulering op het gebied van informatietechnologie in het onderwijs: eindpunt of tussenstation? Adviesraad voor Onderwijs, Utrecht (1994)

Windesheim Magazine: Kuper, D.: Computer ondersteuning in onderwijs; van der Vegt, W.: Teachers opleiden in informatica; van der Vegt, W.: Retraining tot teacher informatica. Windesheim, Zwolle (1991)

Zwaneveld, B., Rigter, H.: Over drempels naar meer IT-gebruik in het voortgezet onderwijs, Rapport naar aanleiding van het project DigilessenVO in 2009. Open Universiteit, Heerlen (2010)

Appendix A: Examples of Early Computer Programmes about Learning *with* the Computer

Examples of courseware with which the pupils can work independently (referrals to sections of the book have been deleted):

no.	name	didactical use	specialism	computer type
1	PH-exercise	Drill & practice	chemistry	BASICODE
2	Water pollution	Simulation	biology/geography	PET/CBM
3	Verb forms1	Tutorial	Dutch	PET/CBM
4	Verb forms2	Tutorial	Dutch	BASICODE
5	Long division	Tutorial	mathematics	PET/CBM
6	Decimal division	Tutorial	Mathematics	PET/CBM
7	Fractions	Application	mathematics	BASICODE
8	Basic	Tutorial	informatics	PET/CBM
9	Alphabet	Application	informatics	BASICODE
10	Racing cars	Simulation	physics	BASICODE
11	Decision-making	Application	social sciences	BASICODE
12	Search_for the_word	Drill & practice	Dutch	BASICODE
13	Reduction	Application	mathematics	BASICODE
14	Predator/prey	Simulation	biology	BASICODE
15	Haiku	Application/AI	Foreign languages	BASICODE
16	Othello	Game	general	BASICODE
17	Titration	Simulation	chemistry	PET/CBM
18	Water management	Simulation	social sciences	PET/CBM
19	Ladder game	Game	general	PET/CBM
20	Printsit	Application	informatics	PET/CBM
21	Planetarium	Simulation/application	physics	PET/CBM
22	Chemparser	Application	Chemistry/language	BASICODE
23	Galton board	Simulation	mathematics	PET/CBM
24	Titration curves	Simulation	chemistry	PET/CBM
25	Black box	Simulation	natural sciences	PET/CBM
26	Times tables	Drill & practice	mathematics	BASICODE
27	Rectangles	Tutorial	mathematics	CBM
28	VAA-system	Real-time application	didactics	PET2001

Appendix B: A Bibliography about Learning with and about the Computer

In this appendix we present the books chronologically. Their content is described briefly in italic fond. The books aim at teachers and in some cases also at pupils. If so, it is specified.

M. Euwe (1966). Inleiding tot computer en automatisering. Alphen aan de Rijn: Samsom BV. *This book is about two aspects: computers, how they work and how one can program it and about the automation which is enabled by the computer.*

W.J. Muhring & H.A.A. van Dorenmalen (1970) Automatisering, oriëntatie op het gebied van informatieverwerking. Groningen: Wolters-Noordhoff. Met een voorwoord van Prof. Dr. M. Euwe. *After a description of a computer and how it works and can be programed, the book provides a number of applications. It offers mainly background information for teachers.*

C. Görts, S. v.d. Meulen, A. v.d. Sluis, & J. Zweerus, (1972). Computerkunde 1 en 2 voor a.v.o en v.w.o. Groningen Wolters-Noordhoff. *This book offers the students, after a short introduction to computers, an almost complete course ECOL (see the text in the frame on page x) and a very large number of examples of projects to the students.*

W. van den Camp, H. Emanuels, J. Lubke, & P. Ploeger, (1971/1972). Elementaire computerkunde, Deel 1voor mavo en havo; Deel 2voor mavo, havo en vwo. Amsterdam: Meulenhoff Educatief. *These two books aim at students. They give an impression how computers work and how they can perform tasks by use of a programming language, here a part of ALGOL.*

R.P. van de Riet (1980) Computer & Beroep. Amsterdam: Vrije University. *About an exhibition at the hundredth anniversary of the Vrije Universiteit.*

B. Camstra (1980). Leren en onderwijzen met de computer. Leiden: Stenfert Kroese. *The book offers the most important knowledge about computer assisted instruction to potential users of computers in education (and to them who are against it).*

Chr. De Boer & P. Pottjegort, (1981). Computersystemen, de computer en zijn gebruiker. Alphen aan de Rijn: Zorn Uitgeverij BV. *This book describes rather completely technical aspects of the computer. There is also a chapter about applications and about business systems. There is little attention for the role of the user of the computer.*

W.GE. Wouters (1981). De programmeertaal BASIC. Zutphen: Thieme. *This book is written in order to teach students to program in BASIC.*

W.P. Janssen (no year of publishing). Onderwijs en computer. Amphi-reeks. Den Bosch: Malmberg. *This book discuss subjects like how the computer works, how to deal with the computer, didactics of the teaching with the computer, educational software, information technology.*

D. Dijkstra & S. Metselaar (1982). Voor het eerst ... beginnen met de computer. Groningen: Wolters-Noordhoff. *This book is no more than an introduction into BASIC.*

J. Schoenmaker, W. van Zundert, & J. Engelen (1982). Informatica met de microcomputer. Den Bosch: Malmberg. *This book offers an introduction into what computers are and in programming in BASIC, but also how to apply the computer in other school subjects like mathematics, physics and economy.*

R. van Dongen en R. Docters van Leeuwen (1982). Lesgeven met computers 1, het ontwikkelen van lespakketen. Zeist: NIB. *This book offers a lot of support to the reader who wishes to design and develop educational software.*

R. Docters van Leeuwen (1982). Lesgeven met computers 2, onderwijskundige aspecten van educatief computergebruik. Zeist: NIB. *As a sequel to the fore mentioned book, this book is especially about the didactical and pedagogical aspects of the use of computers in education.*

Chr. De Boer, (1983). Computerlexicon: Educaboek. *Exactly what the title says: an elaborate lexicon of all terms used at computers.*
U. de Jong & F. van der Heijden (1983). Computerwerk. Den Bosch: Malmberg. *On the basis of about ten applications the students learn to perform tasks with BASIC.*

Appendix C: Educational System of the Netherlands

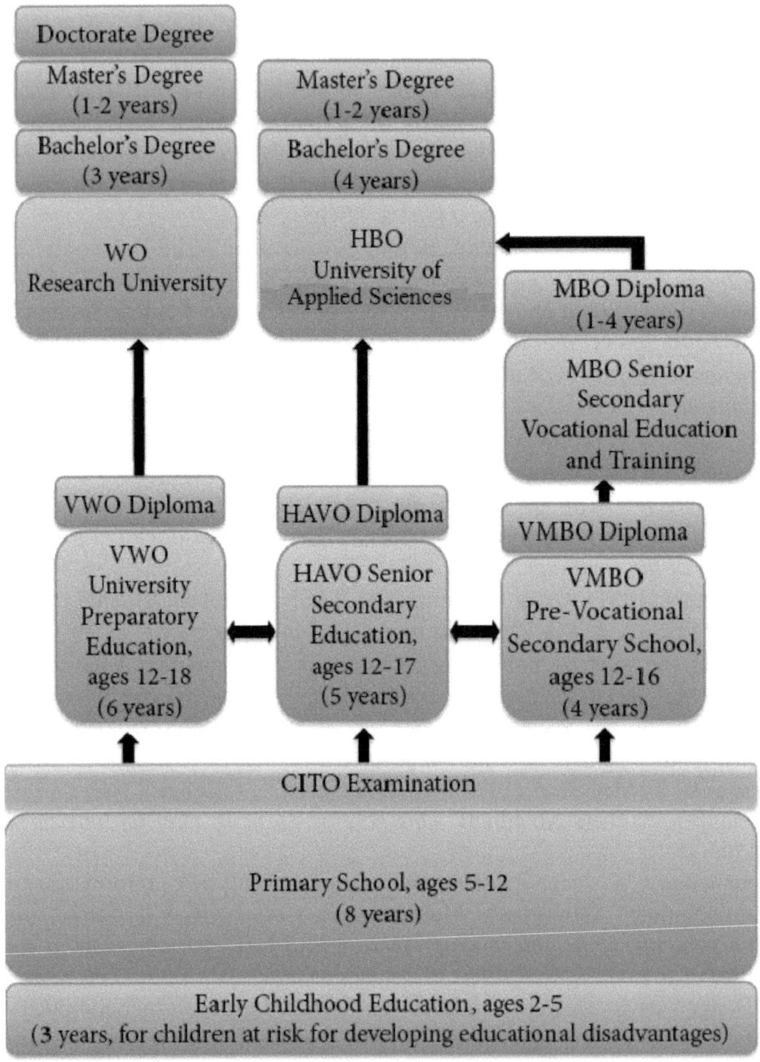

Computers in Education in Finland

Jari Koivisto

Principal, LUMO Upper Secondary School, Vantaa, Finland
jari.koivisto@vantaa.fi

Abstract. This chapter traces the history of computers in education in Finland from the early 1970s to today. It begins by noting that the history of computers in education in Finland began in the early 70s after many Finnish companies and universities acquired and made use of mainframe computers. Some of the university students who used computers in their studies afterwards became teachers and brought with them the idea of using computers in classroom education in Finnish schools. At that time, however, most teachers could not see that a computer would have any practical significance in the classroom. The chapter goes on to examine the types of computer used in schools in the 70s and 80s, the available software, networks, developments in curriculum and the future.

Keywords: Schools in Finland, ICT, programming, software, curriculum.

1 Early Technology

The history of using computers in education in Finland started in early 70s. Many Finnish companies and universities had already earlier acquired some mainframe UNIVAC and IBM computers to make their processes faster and more efficient. The students at the Technical University of Helsinki built their own ESKO computer during six years 1954 – 1960. For obvious reasons these computer services were not available for school education. Fortunately the university students could use the computers in their studies and many of those students became teachers afterwards. These people brought the idea of using computers in classroom education in Finnish schools. However at that time the general idea among the teachers was that during their active service in the school a computer will not have any practical significance in the classroom. In their mind the computers will be used in the national tax administration, insurance companies and finance.

By the end of 70s and in the beginning of 80s computer programming became increasingly popular hobby among the teachers who were allowed to use some computer-time using the university computers, and also among young people, mainly young men, who could afford to buy for themselves the first desktop computers like Commodore VIC-20, Apple II or Sinclair ZX81 machines. An important component in most of the home computers was the 8-bit Zilog 80 processor. It came into market in 1976 and it was exceptionally suitable to be used in affordable home computers.

A. Tatnall and B. Davey (Eds.): History of Computers in Education, IFIP AICT 424, pp. 239–245, 2014.

One of the curiosities in the Finnish education was the HP 65 programmable calculator which Hewlett-Packard introduced in 1974. It was a quite popular device among the technical university students, and a number of maths teachers adopted it to their daily work as well. It was very advanced at that time but using it was not so easy because its user interface was based on the reverse Polish notation (RPN) invented by Polish logician Jan Łukasiewicz. This calculation logic, and accordingly the user interface, was stack-based. This postfix notation made it complicated for the user to communicate correctly with the calculator. The same notation was also used in the FORTH programming language for its arithmetic operators. There were a number of FORTH enthusiasts among the Finnish maths teachers but the language was soon replaced by BASIC, Pascal and C languages.

The first real educational computer in Finland was the Swedish ABC-80 which came to Finland in the end of 70s. Many schools started their computer classes with ABC-80 but it was very exceptional to have a computer lab with a reasonable number of computers in the school. ABC-80 had some educational software and it was convenient for practicing BASIC-programming but otherwise it did not stand any chance against much more modern Nokia MikroMikko computers released in 1981.

The common operating system then was CP/M and the most common programming language was BASIC. In many cases young computer enthusiasts were using assembly language because the computer memory was very limited. Commodore 64 home computer became a legend almost immediately when it was launched for Christmas season in 1982. It had a MOS Technology 6510 processor with an assembly language easy enough to be used by anybody who could spare some time to learn it. Programmers exchanged their codes actively and the publicly available software library increased in a fast speed.

The pioneers of assembly programming did not bring any significant added value to education then but their experience was valuable afterwards. Home computer programming expanded quite soon to a business, and an increasing collection of educational software was soon available both in commercial and freeware form.

Nokia computers occupied the computer labs in 80s in Finland. The collection of educational software was quite extensive and the computers could be connected as an educational network inside the school. This was the first opportunity for a regular teacher to start using computers in a productive way. A certain set of language teaching software applications became especially popular because they were easy and straightforward enough for a regular teacher and student to use. The pedagogical added value of the computer lab networks was questionable. On the other hand it was convenient for a teacher to secretly monitor what the students are up to but in practice only a very few of the teachers in reality used this option. In many cases the teachers used the network only to distribute task files to the students.

Some schools bought Apple Macintosh computers but these did not become very popular because of their high price. On the other hand Mac-machines opened the eyes for many teachers to see the real possibilities of computers in education. The graphical user interface was appealing to teachers who were not interested in programming or any technical tricks. They created a certain pressure to the local administrators to buy Apple, and in many cases the administrators agreed and bought Apple computers in spite of expenses.

The Commodore 64 computer became a success in special needs education in Finland thanks to some really devoted Finnish special needs education teachers. The reason was that a significant number of those people who started with the earlier VIC-20 computer became very productive Commodore 64 programmers and they found a strong and steady demand of specialized software in the area of special needs education. Actually many of the programmers trained themselves to become special needs education teachers. By the end of 80s there was accumulated a remarkable collection of software in this area. The sound chip SID 6581 of Commodore 64 was excellent and a great amount of music has been composed using Commodore 64 computer as well.

The era of Commodore 64 in education became to a halt in practice when the PC machines with Microsoft operating system and Intel processor started to come to school computer labs at the end of 80s. They were reasonably priced and reasonably reliable. First of all an abundant collection of educational software was available and adequate for the schools to be used. It was relatively easy for technology oriented teachers to install new software, new operating system versions and new hardware to the computes. An educational network was easy to install as well. The PC labs became the standard in education and PCs have kept their leading position since then.

The common habit in Finland at the end of 80s became that one or two teachers of the school took over the responsibility to maintain the computer facilities of the schools. These pioneers became the ICT support teachers with a small financial compensation working 10 hours a week and receiving salary for one hour. They knew everything about the hardware and software and they were eager to help anybody who wanted to use computers in teaching. The computers were normally school's property and the computers were regularly updated and rebuilt when the ICT support teachers heard anything about new exciting innovations. In the 90s the municipal technology centres took over the responsibility of maintenance and the ICT support personnel devoted themselves to pedagogical support for the teachers and students.

By the 90s and thereafter all the schools have had a computer lab, and quite often some computers were installed in a public area of the school to enable the students to use the computers for educational or any other purposes. This concept has been successful because during breaks the students can find additional information about the day's topics, check their ideas, and prepare documents. The public area computers are used practically in every school and there are only a very few reports about stolen or damaged equipment.

The PC desktop computers have been the mainstream in the schools. A few schools adventured to try Sun's Java Station computers. The idea of a network computer was really ahead of time but it did not become a commercial success in USA and Sun Microsystems gave up developing Java Stations. The same lack of market enthusiasm applied to Newton by Apple or any other personal digital assistants.

The laptop computers never became important in the Finnish education mainly because of their weight, price, and vulnerability when carrying them from home to school and back. The schools do not want to purchase them because they are easy to steal and cumbersome to handle and distribute for classes. The tablet computers are much more promising for educational use.

2 Software

In the 70s there were great hopes that computers might bring a revolution to math education but the reality was that the early computers did not provide almost any tools or software for maths teaching. BASIC programming tools were only possible software for math teachers. On the contrary the language teachers got very soon used to effective ultra-behaviouristic language teaching software. The user interface in this software was simple. The students had to fill in missing words in a correct format and the software was suitably repeating the already learned concepts and producing more increasingly demanding sentences for the student to correct. It was also easy for the programmers to write software to check the answers from the student and calculate the percentage of right answers.

Some tentative maths programs had similar functionality but they were suitable only for the lower grades. However machine scored responses maintained their popularity because the feedback is immediate and clear. The learning result was to produce perfectly formulated correct sentences. Not so much attention was paid to produce meaningful communication using a foreign language. In 2010s it seems that the teachers have largely given up using educational software in language teaching in Finland and their idea is to create genuinely communicative situations in their classes using foreign languages.

VisiCalc and similar spreadsheet computer programs were popular among Apple users but the real educational use of spreadsheets started only when Microsoft Excel became available. The first popular word processor in the Finnish education was WordStar, and one generation of teachers started their computer user career by preparing their lessons and test papers using WordStar. The first massive in-service training sessions for teachers in the area of educational computing were organized in the end of 80s to prepare teachers to use WordStar. This also indicates that maths and science teachers were not especially impressed on the prospects of using computers in science and maths classes.

The Public Domain software was very popular in Finland in 80s. Many teachers had a respectable collection of PD-software and in some cases they were producing their own applications. There were quite a few programming environments suitable for serious programming work especially Borland's Turbo Pascal and Turbo-C. That software became popular in schools and toward the end of 80s Turbo-Pascal had almost a monopoly in Finland. This also meant that the teachers and more advanced students were exchanging their software and at the same time learning new programming tricks.

3 Networks

First Finnish schools were furnished in the end of 70s with Mikro-Mikko computers and computer lab pedagogical networks from Nokia. As a pedagogical tool this lab network was not very successful. The main function was to provide a possibility for a teacher to follow students' progress. Teachers did not consider this possibility very useful because the students were quite irritated about this issue. The graphics in these computers was very primitive as well, and the computers were mostly used to fill simple checkbox forms for language learning or producing short essays.

Playing computer games became popular very fast and sometimes it was possible to connect computers in the lab for playing purposes. This was great fun at that time. Many students were active readers of the computer magazines and they learned to program their own simple game software. A great amount of this kind of software was distributed among students, and this network became the first real computer based social network in Finland. An important feature of this network was that it was not in any way regulated by any official body. Software piracy was quite common, and the first computer viruses came to the Finnish schools in the end of 80s simultaneously with the PCs occupying computer labs.

Packet-switched services became popular when X25 protocol in 1976 and X400 recommendations were publisher in 1984. Since then the Finnish schools have been connected electronically to the rest of the world. It became very popular for the students to chat with students in other countries. It was really exiting both for the students and the teachers to have chatting friends all over the world. Writing messages without seeing or hearing was the only means to communicate but still people felt that the world is now open for them.

The TCP/IP protocol reached its maturity by the end of 80s and it enabled the vast expansion of electronic data exchange and especially the Internet. In 1988 Dr. Jarkko Oikarinen from Oulu, Finland created the messaging network IRC (Internet Relay Chat) which became immensely popular among young people. Practically all school students knew it and it became the first messaging system which teachers began to hate because so many students spent a substantial part of their free time in IRC in many cases at the expense of neglecting their homework.

The Internet reached the Finnish classrooms approximately in 1994. The first graphic browser ever was published in Finland in 1992 when four students at the Helsinki University of Technology wrote the Erwise browser. The students were Mr. Kim Nyberg, Mr. Teemu Rantanen, Ms. Kati Suominen and Mr. Kari Sydänmaanlakka It was designed for UNIX operating system but it did not gain any popularity afterwards. The first popular browser in Finland was Mosaic and it was widely used in the Finnish schools. For many years Mosaic and Netscape were the most popular browsers in the Finnish classrooms.

By the 2010s Internet connections are available in all the schools in Finland. This has been achieved thanks to the continuous funding from the government to build educational networks, furnish the computer labs, and most of all to train teachers to use teaching methods suitable in a computer intensive learning environment. A massive in-service training in the area of computers in education has been going for many years and it seems to bear fruits. The teachers feel themselves comfortable in social media and in electronic classroom communication. However they feel they are really uncomfortable with any special software. Even regular Microsoft Excel is difficult in spite of the fact that Microsoft Office has been the main working environment for the teachers for tens of years.

Ubuntu Linux has gained some popularity, but the percentage of Linux users is relatively low. Earlier Linux implementations gave the impression of software which is suitable only for professionals. The municipal computer centres are really reluctant to make major changes in the municipal computer setup.

4 Curricular Thinking

At the end of 80s the Finnish universities became interested in computers in education. Earlier almost the only activity in which to use a computer was programming. Gradually it became possible to communicate using the computer and at the same time an increasing amount of educational software became available for schools. This progress created interest in thinking about possibilities to implement computers in a more educational way into various subjects.

In late 80s some software developers became aware of the Market diagram model in creating educational software developed mainly in Norway. A remarkable amount of software came into Finnish educational software market at the end of 80s using the Market diagram model. In spite of active marketing and clever ideas embedded in the applications the end users of the products considered them quite clumsy and non-educative, and the numbers sold were disappointing. In practice the earlier products which were based on traditional behavioristic approach sold better.

The Finnish National Board of Education (NBE) together with researchers at the Finnish universities took an initiative to find advanced methods of integrating computers in education. Starting from 1993 the NBE have launched and partly financed hundreds of school development programmes to innovate the best way to make computers and networks part of the classroom work. The title of the national programme was 'Finland towards the Information Society'. These projects have produced a massive amount of data for educational methods developers at the universities.

Professors Carl Bereiter and Marlene Scardamalia from the University of Toronto were the main contributors in introducing the concept of 'knowledge building'. The idea was enthusiastically accepted in Finland and many researchers at the universities abandoned the traditional behaviouristic view of learning. The Finnish government supported a number of research projects and in practice Finland entered the era of constructivism and later social constructivism in the beginning of 90s. The Finnish national curriculum framework from 1994 was following the new ideas and it brought a revolution to the Finnish curriculum thinking. Finland has been evaluated highly in the OECD Programme for International Student Assessment (PISA) for many years, and the foundation for this success was laid in this particular framework curriculum and its implementation.

This idea had unfortunately a seed for disaster because programming, learning to use computer applications, and computer hardware skills were declared obsolete. It was officially declared that the students will learn the computer skills while they are using computers as tools, and no additional subject 'computer science' was needed in the schools. The immediate consequence of that policy was that the Finnish universities downgraded their teacher training master programmes in computer science, and the universities ceased to produce formally qualified computer science teachers to the Finnish comprehensive and upper secondary education. The latter part of the Finnish education system is comparable to the sixth form education in England.

The leading concept in the new thinking was that by retrieving information from the Internet and creating essays using that information will give a deep insight for the students in utilizing computers. Afterwards it became obvious that this assumption is not correct and the computer skills of the Finnish students did not develop as expected.

The Finnish National Curriculum Framework in 2004 was heavily leaning on social constructivist ideas and this significantly enforcing the role of computers in education in Finland. It became essential to use computers and computer networks as a constructivist learning tool. Unfortunately the initiative of having computer science as a subject with nationally defined learning contents was abandoned.

5 The Future

ICT has been deeply integrating into everyday work in schools. The school administration is completely dependent on extensive databases containing all necessary data on students, teachers, schedules, classrooms, school financing and document management.

The classes are becoming more active and more interesting to students. Information from many sources is always available, and the students learn to be critical when forming their attitudes and opinions. Many classical conventions like the concept of a classroom or a school will become obsolete. Everything can be made virtual.

There have been discussions about ubiquitous ICT which in practice means more digital services but also enables more possibilities to monitor and control all the persons and their activities in the school community. It is highly possible that this is not only a positive feature. A school community is exceptionally sensitive in social relations because there are a large number children or teenage students. Excessive control indicates that the students are expected to resemble more robots than human beings.

Hopefully the future school will use ICT in a way which is respecting students as valuable and individual human beings having their own aspirations and dreams worth being fulfilled.

Schools, Students, Computers and Curriculum in Victoria in the 1970s and 1980s

Arthur Tatnall

Victoria University, Melbourne, Australia
Arthur.Tatnall@vu.edu.au

Abstract. Although computers today are commonplace and are widely used at all levels of education, prior to the mid-1970s the idea of introducing school students to the use of computers, or of a school owning its own computer was difficult to imagine. This chapter tells the story of the introduction of computers into schools in Victoria, Australia in the 1970s and 1980s. It begins by looking at school computing before the PC and then goes on to describe the use of computers at Watsonia High School where I was teaching at the time. I describe my involvement and experiences with computers in schools in this exciting period, in particular looking at computing curricula: Computers in Society and Computer Science at Watsonia High. The chapter also tells of the Commonwealth Computer Education Program and the various support structures that were put in place to assist schools. It consists of a reflection on my own experiences of school computing during this period.

Keywords: Schools, Curriculum, Australia, Computers in Society, Computer Awareness, Computer Science, Apple][, Australian Educational Computer, Computer Education Support Structures.

1 Beginnings of an Interest in Computing

In this chapter I describe my involvement with computers in Victorian schools in the period of the 1970s-1980s. I provide some vivid reflections on my experiences at this time both as a teacher and as an educational consultant.

From my earliest memories at school I recall being interested in the sciences, both physical and biological. I soon also developed an interest in robotics and was fascinated by the idea of the computer or 'electronic brain' as it was then often called. I had no opportunity to do anything with a computer though until at Melbourne University in 3rd year physics we had a unit on FORTRAN IV programming. We entered our programs on punch cards at the university and then the packs of cards were sent off to an IBM mainframe in St Kilda for processing. My first FORTRAN program was to print out the first 1,000 prime numbers. My program got to 980 numbers then crashed, I don't know why. Perhaps I had dimensioned one of the variables to 1,000 when it should have been 1,001. I never found out, but I still enjoyed my first experience of programming.

After completing the Science Degree I undertook a Graduate Diploma in Education and then started work as a High School teacher. I had nothing to do with computers

A. Tatnall and B. Davey (Eds.): History of Computers in Education, IFIP AICT 424, pp. 246–265, 2014.

again for another ten years until the mid-1970s when my colleague Bill Davey arrived at Watsonia High where I was then teaching.

2 School Computing Before the PC

Australia moved into electronic digital computing quite early when the CSIR Mk1 (CSIRAC) was built by Trevor Pearcey and Maston Beard for the CSIRO[1] in the late 1940s [1], but while university computing courses began in the early 1950s, it was quite some time later that it was possible for schools to make any use of computers [2].

It was not until the early 1970s that a few computers started to appear in Australian schools, typically resulting from the exposure of certain teachers to computing during their university studies [3]. In Victoria these early instances included a PDP-8 computer loaned by Digital Equipment to Burwood High School in 1972 [4]. In 1973 an Innovations Grant enabled McKinnon High School to purchase an 8k Wang computer costing over $10,000 and because of its high annual maintenance charge (15% of the purchase price), it was shared with Box Hill High School [4]. These early computers were used almost exclusively by mathematics departments for the teaching of programming and mathematical algorithm design [4]. They had very little impact on other schools in which the idea of owning a computer was unthinkable.

A much larger impact, however, occurred in 1974 with the introduction of the Monash Educational Computer System (MONECS) developed by a group of Computer Scientists at Monash University. MONECS typically ran on a DEC PDP-11 (DEAMON) minicomputer and used mark-sense cards for program and data entry [5]. The students filled in the cards in class at their school using a pencil and then their teacher delivered the cards to a local university for execution. This allowed a class of 30 students to each get two runs in a one-hour period [5] and was designed to teach programming in FORTRAN or BASIC.

In the 1970s and 1980s Victoria had two different types of Secondary Schools – High Schools and Technical Schools, and in another development at this time some Victorian Technical Schools experimented with Control Data's PLATO System [6] of computer-assisted instruction for the training of apprentices. The system was, however, very expensive and its use did not proceed.

The arrival of the Apple][in 1977 saw the end of this period and the beginning of real advances in the use of computers in schools. At around $2,000 for a 16k Apple][that used a tape drive (not supplied – you simply used your own cassette recorder) and a television set (also not supplied) as a monitor, the Apple][was affordable for most schools.

3 Teaching at Watsonia High School

I had been teaching Physics, Science and Maths at Watsonia High School (WHS), a school of around 1,000 pupils in the northern suburbs of Melbourne, for five years

[1] Commonwealth Scientific and Industrial Research Organisation.

when Bill Davey arrived in 1974. Bill had studied some computing in his Science degree at Monash University and, before coming to Watsonia, had done some computing with one of his maths classes at Bendigo High School using mark sense cards executed at Bendigo Institute of Technology. He had also commenced some tertiary studies in computing and came to Watsonia High keen to do more work in this area.

4 WHS Student Allocation Program at La Trobe University

In the 1970s in Victoria decisions on curriculum and school organisation were school-based (within Education Department guidelines). In the early-1970s Watsonia High decided to organise its junior and middle schools students into 'vertical modular groups' depending on their choice of elective subjects. This meant that, for example, Year 9 and Year 10 students could share the same electives so providing more choice for these students and effectively giving each student an individual timetable. Organising these groups presented quite a challenge when it was done by hand. Someone at the school, however, had found a contact at nearby La Trobe University who had been developing a computer scheduling program that could assist in this task, and in 1974 (and for several years after this) we worked together using La Trobe University's program for student allocation to timetable groups on the university's DEC-10 computer. It worked this way: students filled in a form at school indicating their elective preferences (from a list of possible options) after which Bill and I went to La Trobe University and entered this data using a teletype. The university then ran the program and produced list of possible student groupings which we took back to the school for consideration. Sometimes this process had to be repeated to get useful results, but overall it made this grouping task possible. It also re-introduced me to computing.

5 Programming in Year 11 Maths at WHS

In the mid-1970s Bill and I also used the MONECS system at La Trobe University in a Year 11 maths class for teaching BASIC programming so that the students could design algorithms to solve mathematical problems. This work involved the students designing a program (in BASIC) and marking their cards in class using a pencil. Then one of us took the decks of cards to La Trobe to execute the programs. The results were frequently disappointing for the students with the only thing coming back being a print-out listing a number of syntax errors. It typically took most students several tries (with perhaps one or two runs each week) to get their program working. While students today would not persevere with frustrations like this the excitement, at that time, of using a computer and making it do something that *you* determined meant that they did keep going with it, and indicated that they enjoyed and appreciated the experience.

6 The Computer 'Travelling Road Show'

In this period the Secondary Mathematics Committee (made up of school maths teachers and personal from the Education Department) developed an interest in using computers for mathematics and other aspects of education and a Computer Education Subcommittee (including Bill Davey as one of its members) was formed. The Subcommittee then set up the 'Computer Travelling Road Show' in which groups of two or three of its members would visit schools to promote the use of computers. They normally brought with them a 16k Apple][(on loan) with cassette tape drive to demonstrate computer applications involving graphics, mathematics, commerce and word processing, rather than just programming, to teachers at curriculum days and school staff meetings [4, 7].

7 Arrival of an Apple][Computer at Watsonia High

In 1977 Bill was a member of the Secondary Mathematics Committee and teaching at Watsonia High School. With support from the Committee he put in a curriculum innovations grant submission to the Commonwealth Government to purchase an Apple][computer for the school. As a result, in 1977 Watsonia High School obtained an Apple][microcomputer with 16Kb RAM and a 110 volt power supply. The school needed to supply a television set (for use as a monitor) and a cassette tape drive as the Apple][did not come with these as part of the package. This was one of the first Apple][computers to enter Australian schools. For this year and the next the Apple][was used mainly for demonstrations and was later upgraded, at considerable expense to the school, to a 64Kb machine with a disk drive and mark-sense card reader.

On several occasions I took the computer home to do some work and to show my family. I remember how sensitive the cassette drive was to its volume setting. If this setting was not exactly right the program would not load, or save and it was very easy for our 3 year old son to accidentally knock the volume control. As the Apple][had no monitor of its own it was necessary to use our home TV set, and when there were problems with the cassette volume setting, loading and saving programs often took much longer than expected, meaning that our son was unable to watch 'Play School' – one of his favourite programs.

Bill left Watsonia High at the end of 1978 to take up a new position, leaving me with the Apple][computer and the decision of what to do with it.

8 Graduate Diploma in Computer Science

Seeing a future in educational computing, but conscious of not having a good theoretical background in this area, in 1979 I enrolled in a part-time Graduate Diploma in Computer Science at La Trobe University while still working full-time at Watsonia High. This Graduate Diploma course contained basically all the computing content, but without the other general subjects, of a Bachelor's Degree in Computer Science. Course content included the following components:

- Programming – in ALGOL (and later Pascal), 6800 assembler, PDP-11 assembler and COBOL
- Software Engineering
- Computer Organisation and Operating Systems
- Information Systems: systems analysis and design and database management,

as well as a choice of four of the five ancillary subjects: Introduction to Accounting, Management Accounting, Social Psychology, Numerical Methods and Operations Research.

9 Year 10 'Computers in Society' at Watsonia High

In 1979 at Watsonia High I introduced a new core subject: '*Computers in Society*' into the Year 10 curriculum [8]. At that time Year 10 at WHS had 150 students in five class groups. '*Computers in Society*' was a core subject taken by all 150 students for three periods per week throughout the year. The subject consisted of three parts, each of one term's duration and delivered by a teacher who understood and could relate to each particular area [9]. The teaching team consisted of one science teacher (Arthur Tatnall), a commerce teacher and a teacher of social science. Together we determined the requirements for the new subject which consisted of three parts, taught on a round-robin basis each term, with the following units:

- Preliminary Course – Introduction to the Computer (6 periods)
  - o Introduction to the course. What is a computer? What can it do? What can't it do?
  - o Demonstration with the Apple][: Apple Vision, Music, Colour Graphics, Space Invaders etc.
  - o Hands-on experience: instruction in how to operate the Apple][to run an 'Introductory Program' – printing your own name and address. While each small group of students did this the rest completed an exercise from a text book, then the groups rotated.
  - o The concept of a computer program – a computer can do only what it is told.
  - o Introduction to the social implications of computing
- Section A: Structure of the Computer – taught by the Science teacher (3 periods per week for one term)
  - o How does a computer work? Block structure of the computer: I/O, memory, CPU, integrated circuits, disk, cassette, printer, number systems and binary code etc.
  - o Programming: programming languages, flow charts and algorithm design, programming in BASIC using mark-sense cards on the Apple][
  - o Hands-on experience: graphics, games, uses for student reports, timetables etc.
  - o Excursion to La Trobe University computer centre

- Section B: Computers and Business – taught by the Commerce teacher (3 periods per week for one term)
  - Development of uses in business, impact on productivity and employment
  - Word Processing: concept, historical development from the manual typewriter, types of word processors, effect on organisation of the office
  - Stock Control: comparison of the manual, physical stock control with the latest methods of Point of Sale terminals to highlight changes required of personnel, efficiency and control
  - Accounting Systems: comparison of old and new systems to highlight job specifications, productivity, internal communications, payroll, relations with customers. Hands-on experience on the Apple][and use of mark-sense cards for a Balance Sheet exercise
  - Process Control: production-line, processing industries, effect on quality and productivity
  - Information Systems: use of a computer in collating, preparation and presentation of information for things like airline seat reservation, accommodation reservation, vehicle delivery and railway loop control
- Section C: Uses, History and Social Implications of Computer Technology – taught by the Social Science teacher (3 periods per week for one term)
  - History of the development of the computer
  - Advantages and misconceptions
  - Applications: election results, space programme and defence, crime detection, archaeology, traffic control, computer dating (using match maker on the Apple][), computers in home/leisure/entertainment, shopping, medicine, communication
  - Implications: privacy, political uses and need for protective legislation, 'Police State', harassment, economic, employment, cashless society (who benefits?) leisure, education, computer crimes, machine controlled society

The course was taken by all 150 Year 10 students using the school's *single* Apple][with a mark-sense card reader. This was to be one of the first 'Computer Awareness' courses in Victoria and was offered from 1979 to 1985. (During this period the school purchased another Apple][, making teaching this subject easier) Today it is hard to see how using a single computer and maintaining the students' interest for this course would have been possible, but such was the excitement of having access to the new world of computing, of getting some understanding and experience of using a computer, and of making the computer do something that *you* determined, that the students did put up with the limited hands-on use that was possible and continued to maintain an interest in the subject despite this. Another factor in the subject's success was the enthusiasm of the teachers involved, who worked to make the subject always interesting and exciting for the students.

10 Secondary Computer Education Committee

The Secondary Computer Education Curriculum Committee was formed in 1980 from members of the Secondary Mathematics Committee, the Board of Inspectors of Secondary Schools, three seconded Computer Education Consultants and a number of practising teachers. I was one of these practicing teachers. The main brief of the committee was the production of Computer Awareness course guidelines and investigation of Computer Science as a discipline. The committee's charter also included publication of computer education articles, collection and propagation of *public domain* software (for Apple][and CP/M computers) and provision of in-service education for teachers [2].

10.1 Computer Awareness Guidelines

In most countries around the world today secondary school students are very aware of information technology and of the many use of computers. This, however, was not the case in the late 1970s and early 1980s when the first microcomputers began to make their appearance in Australian schools [8]. It was also, significantly, the case that few teachers were then aware of how to use a computer, what computers could be used for, or what the implications of their use might be. The solution seen at the time was introduction of 'Computer Awareness' courses.

> *"Computer awareness is simply the possession of skills and knowledge which enables informed judgements to be made about what is seen or heard about computers. The emphasis in computer awareness courses is on the knowledge and skills which give an appreciation of the capabilities and limitations of computers and their applications rather than on the technical skills required to program or maintain computer systems." [10 :1]*

Later that year the Secondary Computer Education Committee produced the first edition of its Computer Awareness Guidelines [11]. The Guidelines suggested that this course be offered at Year 10 with the following objectives:

- *To reduce bewilderment and fear of the unknown in the minds of individuals and to promote a balanced view of the computer's role in society*
- *To provide students with sufficient information to enable them to use computer-based services with confidence*
- *To establish an informed basis for decisions regarding computer applications which have political implications and involve value judgements*
- *To examine the impact (actual and potential) of the computer on life styles and employment opportunities*
- *To foster familiarity with computing equipment and, by providing hands-on experience and an introduction to programming techniques, develop, through practical experience, insights into computer processes, uses and limitations*
- *To provide sufficient understanding about the way in which computers work to comprehend not only what they can do but also what they cannot do*

- *To develop an awareness of the potential abuses of computers and computer know-how*
- *To demonstrate the use of computers in solving problems and to encourage students to apply the principles of problem solving creatively.*

The document strongly stressed the interdisciplinary nature of this subject matter and that Computer Awareness should not be equated with Computer Programming [8]. Course content was:

- Section 1: (15% of available time)
  - Historical development of the computer: the abacus, Pascal's adding machine, Babbage's difference engine, generations of electronic computers, the microcomputer
  - Structure of a computer: analogue vs. digital computers, input and output, memory, central processing unit, backing store, computer electronics
- Section 2 (25%)
  - Hands-on experience – booting the system, loading programs, booting the disk operating system, obtaining a catalogue of programs, running programs, switching off the system, creation and use of files, word processing, general computer usage
  - Algorithms – the concept of an algorithm, simple flowcharting
  - Elementary programming in BASIC, marking cards, program commands, syntax, arithmetical/logical operations, debugging programs
- Section 3 (60%)
  - Misconceptions about computers – intelligence, infallibility
  - Use of computers in government, industry, commerce, science, research, the arts and at home
  - Security implications
  - Implications of computer use for society: political, economic and social implications.

11 Year 12 Computer Science

In 1981 as a result of several years of work by a group of academics, teachers and people involved in various ways with the production and use of computer technology, *Computer Science* was introduced as a Year 12 Higher School Certificate subject in Victoria [2, 12]. To many, the value of a school subject is measured in terms of its place in the Year 12 (the final year of schooling) curriculum and so as a preparation for tertiary study [3] and this was the case with Computer Science, at least to most students and parents, but not to all teachers.

The original version of course (1981) was made up of a core, optional units and school-based practical work [13]. The core (20 weeks) consisted of:

- Computer structure
- Algorithms
- Programming languages
- Data structure manipulation (in immediate access memory)
- Input/output devices
- Data processing.

There were four optional units (each of 5 weeks):

A. Social implications of computers
B. Hardware
C. Visits to installations
D. Data processing systems and case studies

of which each school needed to choose two.

Thirdly was school-based practical work.

Initially the core was weighted at 35% and examined externally, the school assessed options as 30% and the school-based practical work as 35% as the subject designers wanted to allow practical work in programming to be given considerable weight [2]. I was a member of the Computer Science Subject Committee from its inception, an Examiner for the first three years and then Chief Examiner until 1991 when the subject was replaced by the Information Technology field of study [14].

Melbourne and Monash universities initially refused to allow the inclusion of Year 12 Computer Science in admission scores for their courses, their stated reasons being that the component of assessment allotted to the formal examination was only 35% rather than the usual 50% [2, 15] and that the subject did not have sufficient academic merit. The other Victorian universities, however, had no problems with the subject and accepted it fully. When the subject came up for reaccreditation in 1984 [16] the Computer Science Subject Committee, in a compromise designed to satisfy the position taken by Melbourne and Monash universities, recommended that assessment for the subject be changed to: core external examination – 50%, consensus moderated[2] practical work – 30% [17], and school assessed, consensus moderated options – 20%. Changes were also made to the course content, principally to move Social Implications into the core and to change the options. In addition to the consensus moderated practical work, the new course structure [18] consisted of: Core (20 weeks):

[2] Consensus moderation was used by several Year 12 subjects as a technique for comparing the work of students in different schools. In Computer Science it was used for both practical work and options. The process involved holding an initial meeting of all teachers of the subject in moderation groups of about twelve at the start of the school year. This meeting would then decide on a common interpretation of the course guidelines. At a final moderation meeting at the end of the school year, a sample of the student work from each school in the group would then be re-examined by the other teachers. If the moderation group as a whole considered that a particular school's work (as judged from the sample) had been marked 5% (for example) too easily, all the students from that school had their Computer Science option work marks reduced by a commensurate amount. Similarly, the marks from a given school would be increased by the group if this was thought necessary.

- Computer structure and data representation
- The design and implementation of algorithms
- Programming languages
- Data structures
- Input/output devices
- File structures
- System software
- Social implications

There were now two optional units (each of 10 weeks) of which each school had to choose one:

A. Computers in science and engineering
B. Computers in business and government

Melbourne and Monash universities now accepted the subject. Teachers however, were not universally in favour of the new subject [15]. Some claimed that Computer Science was an elitist academic subject, too difficult for some students, and so should not be supported. (It is interesting to note that this was exactly opposite to the view earlier held by Melbourne and Monash universities.) Others noted that the ratio of girls to boys taking Computer Science was almost as low as that for physics, and expressed concern that it was becoming a *boys' subject*. Perhaps, however, the most damaging criticism came from those teachers who claimed that the presence of a specialist subject detracted from the move to encourage the use of *Computers across the Curriculum*[3]. An early move in introduction of computers to other subject areas was the use of Apple][software such as: Lemonade, Hammurabi and the First Fleet (convict) database and Acorn BBC computer software included a word processor, database manager and a role play simulation program called Suburban Fox where students took the role of a fox and learned to survive. A number of the advocates for *Computers across the Curriculum* saw Computer Science as an adversary and it took some time before these points of view were reconciled. The basis for this view was firstly the claim that the demands made on school computing facilities by Computer Science classes made it difficult for others to obtain adequate access to the machines[4], and secondly that the existence of a specialist subject would mean that teachers of other subject areas would not bother to include any mention of computing, considering it covered elsewhere. Many of us disputed these claims.

---

[3] In common with several other countries, Computers across the Curriculum was a popular, if ill-defined term in those days. It was generally taken to mean the uncritical promotion of the idea that the computer could enhance learning in all curriculum areas and should be pressed into them with all possible speed.

[4] While containing some truth, this argument misses the point that in most cases the reason that the school had purchased a number of computers at all was to support the teaching of Computer Science. Being a Year 12 subject it was easier to get funds from School Councils and the Education Ministry to buy computers for this purpose than for many other uses.

12 Year 11 Computer Science at Watsonia High

In 1981 a new 'Computer Science' subject was introduced at Year 11 at WHS. I intended this subject to follow on from Year 10 'Computers in Society', but also cover much more detail about computing, how computers work, algorithms and programming, while still containing some material on the actual and potential uses of computers and the social implications of their use [19-21]. The subject primarily made use of the school's Apple][along with use of mark-sense cards at La Trobe University. The subject's content included:

- Computer structure: basic hardware elements and computer structure, data representation, binary numbers, computer logic, coding systems
- Algorithms: concept, modelling, representation with flowcharts, Nassi-Shneiderman diagrams, pseudocode
- Programming fundamentals: top down design, structured programming, testing, errors, debugging, Pascal, BASIC, documentation
- Random numbers and simulations
- Low level programming: machine language, assembly language – Use of LOWLEV [22]
- Operating systems and system software
- Computer applications: databases and data processing, word processing, accounting and finance packages, science and engineering, leisure and education, numerical methods
- Computers and society
- Practical assignments

This subject ran from 1981 at Watsonia High for some years after I left in 1983.

13 Jacaranda Press Book: Computer Science for Year 11

In 1983 I was approached by Jacaranda Press (Wiley, Australia) to write a textbook for Year 11 Computer Science [23], and invited Bill Davey to work with me on this. We began to work on a book based on our own school subjects and teaching experiences. We tried to make the book different to the normal textbook of the time and to include student exercises that we had found worked well with our own students. The book was well accepted by schools and quickly became a best seller. It had the following chapters:

1. Introduction to programming through graphics
2. What goes on inside a computer?
3. Data and databases
4. Computers and problem solving
5. Talking to a computer in its own language
6. Computer programming languages
7. Filing, searching and sorting; database programming

8. Word-processing and communication
9. Number crunching and financial applications
10. Automation and process control – information technology and the future

The book must have made an impression, at least on some students, as even over 30 years later we still get some former students who have kept a copy of the book and would like us to sign it.

14 Commonwealth Computer Education Program

By the late 1970s the number of microcomputers in Victorian schools (and those in other Australian states) had begun to grow considerably but without any central direction from education authorities. In 1980 in Victoria to address this issue Anne McDougall was commissioned to report on how computers were then being used in schools and the possibilities for their future use [24].

Constitutionally in Australia it is the State Governments that are responsible for School Education and that determine school curriculum and how it is supported and delivered. In matters of perceived national importance, however, the Commonwealth Government adopts a policy position and supplies funding for specific education projects [25].

Following the rapidly growing interest in the use of computers in education, in February 1983 the Commonwealth Schools Commission expressed the view that:

> *"The development of a satisfactory program of computer education in Australian schools was of fundamental importance to Australia's future"* and *"... that the Commonwealth should commit itself to the development of a national computer education (or schools computing) program for all Australian schools, commencing in 1984"* [26 :1].

In April 1983 the Australian Commonwealth Government then set up the *Commonwealth Schools Commission National Advisory Committee on Computers in Schools (NACCS)*, whose purpose was to provide leadership and funding for Computer Education across all Australian states and territories [25, 26]. NACCS included representatives from the Education Departments of each Australian State and Territory (Queensland, New South Wales, Victoria, Tasmania, South Australia, Western Australia, Australian Capital Territory and Northern Territory), parent organisations, teacher unions, equal opportunity organisations, Catholic Schools, Independent Schools, State School organisations, Universities, the Commonwealth Schools Commission and the Commonwealth Department of Science and Technology [27].

In its report *Teaching Learning and Computers in Schools* [26] the Committee made comprehensive recommendations covering curriculum development, professional development, support services, software/courseware, hardware and organisation. The report indicated that priorities for curriculum development should be:

- provision of Computer Awareness activities for all students in the early years of secondary schooling
- integration of computing into the school curriculum

- in-depth (optional) Computer Studies courses at the senior secondary level
- curricula which meet the special needs of relevant disadvantaged groups.

For the period from 1984 to 1986, the Commonwealth Government provided $19 million in support of the program [3].

NACCS regarded Education Support Services as essential and suggested that appropriate use of funds could include the appointment of education consultants, the further development of comprehensive computer education centres and the provision of grants to support innovative practices in schools [26].

15 Computer Education Support Structures

15.1 Computer Education Consultancy

In 1981 I was appointed as a Computer Education Consultant. These Consultants were practicing school teachers who were seconded from their schools, usually on a part-time basis, to work from their Regional Education Office. Consultants were subject specialists, chosen for their subject expertise, teaching ability, willingness to adapt to and lead educational change and their ability to get on with and work with other teachers [25]. They were appointed only for a period of twelve months at a time so that they would not lose contact with the school classroom. Unlike most other subject consultants, however, Computer Education Consultants were pioneering a new area of education and had little in the way of established precedent, techniques or materials to assist them. As the use of computers in education was an entirely new area and few teachers had any experience with it the Consultant's task was to introduce and offer suggestions on the use of computers in schools of all types: Primary, Secondary and Technical. Despite working only part-time on this job I typically visited two or three schools each day to discuss matters with individual teachers from a variety of subject areas [28-30], demonstrate software, assist with the configuration of hardware and to conduct whole-school professional development activities.

I remember that after I gave a whole-school demonstration of the use of computers, as part of a professional development activity in a metropolitan primary school, one of the teachers came up to me and said: "*But won't some of the kids know more about computers than me*". Although we don't always like to admit it, many teachers feel that they must know more than the students about something before they can make use of it or teach it. I suggested an alternative approach of getting one of the more computer-literate students to demonstrate using the computer to the class. This would both be empowering for the student and overcome the teacher's lack of knowledge of computers. I don't know whether she took this advice.

At this time those of us involved in computer education consultancy really attacked the task with 'missionary zeal' believing, rightly or wrongly, that the use of computers in schools could fundamentally change education for the better. I continued in this position in 1982.

In 1983 I became a full-time (seconded) General Curriculum Consultant and in 1984 a full-time Computer Education Consultant. This was hard work but very rewarding as our services were highly appreciated by teachers and by schools. We rarely, however, had any interaction with school students, working instead with teachers and school principals.

During this period I also developed several computer programs for Apple][and MS-DOS, the main ones being LOWLEV (a pseudo assembly language / machine code system), Seasen-PILOT (programming language) and Match-Maker (a student dating program to teach about databases). I also wrote training manuals for Microsoft Works for Windows and for Macintosh.

15.2 The State Computer Education Centre (SCEC)

In Victoria, the early development of Computer Education in schools was certainly 'bottom up', beginning with the efforts of a small number of teachers. When the Computer Education 'explosion' began in 1983 the Victorian Education Department saw the need for some form of 'top down' planning and control, and formation of the State Computer Education Centre (SCEC) was the result. After an initial trial in 1984, in 1985 the centre was formalised with a Senior Computer Education Officer, Software Co-ordinator, Professional Development Co-ordinator, Curriculum Co-ordinator, Educational Computer Systems Analyst, and Equal Opportunity Officer all holding deputy-principal positions. seventeen senior-teacher positions (five at SCEC and twelve in the regions), and four assistant teacher positions making up a total staff of twenty-seven professional officers [2]. I was appointed to the position of Educational Computer Systems Analyst and continued in this role for the next three years.

SCEC played a significant part in setting the direction of educational computing in Victoria for the next three years by developing policy, producing curriculum documents, evaluating and distributing educational software, evaluating computer systems and producing the 'recommended list' of computer systems for use in schools.

15.2.1 List of Recommended Computers for Victorian Schools

The Schools Commission had recommended that computer hardware purchased with program funds "*should … be used to purchase computer hardware which is on the appropriate State Education Department approved list*" [31]. As Educational Computer Systems Analyst it was my job to draw up specifications, collect and evaluate submissions and produce this recommended list, which was for computer *systems* and not just hardware, for all Victorian Government Schools. Apart from providing advice to schools, this recommendation process was necessary to fulfil certain Government contractual and offset[5] requirements.

---

[5] Victorian Government offsets policy required an investment in Victoria by suppliers, proportional to sales, and noted preference for Victorian manufactured goods, approved decentralised secondary industries, anti-dumping policy and apartheid sanctions against South Africa.

The 1986 Educational Computing System Specifications [32] document noted that recommended computing systems in schools should offer software, running on the recommended computer hardware, for a substantial number of the following applications:

- Useful tools for teachers and students: word processing, database management systems, spreadsheets, graphic design, expert systems, telecommunications and control technology.
- Problem solving: adventure games, logic games, Logo and Prolog.
- Courseware: simulations, information retrieval systems, data collection and analysis packages, computer controlled experiments, drill and practice and computer aided instruction.
- Programming.
- Vocationally oriented studies.
- Special education.

The document said that these systems should be easy to use, serviceable and ergonomic. They should also be as small be provided at the lowest cost possible. Also, system suppliers should offer upgrades, provide training materials and offer company support to schools and to SCEC. I performed this task for three years before moving to higher education in 1988.

15.2.2 Designing the Australian Educational Computer

Such support for the purchase of microcomputers from a State's recommended list was considered to be only an interim measure, necessary only until an *Australian Educational Computer* could be developed and built. In 1985 two Schools Commission Working Parties were set up to determine 'Educational User Requirements' and 'Educational Technical Requirements'. The idea was then that a 'System Concept Study' and 'Development Proposal' for construction of the computer would follow [15]. The intention was both to develop a high quality computer appropriate for school use but also to provide an opportunity for Australian industry to build the machine. I was appointed as an 'expert' member of the 'Educational Technical Requirements' working party.

In its report [33] the Educational User Requirements working party considered developmental characteristics of school children and learning situations in which computer use was considered appropriate, then attempted to draw up user requirements from each of these. The report gave examples of the learning activities in schools as including: use of computers as a tool in existing subject areas and in Special Education, studying Computer Science, co-operative large group and project group use [27].

Our Educational Technical Requirements working party produced a report [34] containing two main sections:

- The Technical Requirement which gave detailed coverage to: user interface, input/output devices, processing resources, networks, telecommunications and system requirements.
- A section dealing with possible implementations of these requirements to satisfy at least three types of use:

- Personal
- Classroom
- School-Wide.

The idea was that these uses could be catered for by a family of compatible systems having a common user interface, and that at some stage in the future the way should be left open to connect these systems to computing facilities at the district, regional, state or national levels [27].

This, however, was all before the days of the ascendancy of the IBM-PC, MS-MOS and the Apple Macintosh and schools made use of a large variety of computers including the Apple][, BBC (Acorn), Tandy TRS-80, Commodore Vic20, Commodore 64, Microbee, (an Australian designed computer) and the CP/M machines: Cromenco and Micromation. When the Computer Education Program funding ended in 1987 the idea of the *Australian Educational Computer* was not taken up by the Department of Science and Technology and so was dropped. In retrospect this was probably a good thing as it was not long before the PC and Macintosh had, between them, captured almost all the school market and our new computer would have stood a good chance of becoming an expensive white elephant [27].

15.3 The Australian Computer Society (ACS)

The ACS was always supportive of school computing, especially Computer Science and other aspects of this area that is saw as potentially leading to careers in computing, but also use of the computer in other subject areas. In 1985, as part of the ACS hosted 'First Pan-Pacific Computer Conference (PPCC-1)', we ran a Schools' Congress [35] that attracted several hundred senior secondary students to listen to a series of speakers discussing issues including: movie making with computers, computing careers, computers in business, videotext in education, robots, communications, artificial intelligence and logic programming, computer science, magnetic storage media and computers in the sciences. Two years later, as part of The Australian Computer Conference (ACC-87) we again ran a Schools' Congress [36]. Topics this time included: expert systems, desktop publishing, computers and music, systems life cycle, computer animation, banking, business, manufacturing, the future of technology in Australia, Electronic Funds Transfer, educational computing, careers and robotics.

Following these Congresses, in a 1988 position paper on education [37] the Australian Computer Society stated its view that:

> *"The ACS sees the need to widen the facilities made available to academic and secondary teaching staff to develop a closer understanding of the changing business and industry sectors."*

In addition to these initiatives, for many years the ACS provided speakers at school careers evenings (including people like Peter Juliff) and to discuss computing careers with students and teachers.

15.4 Teacher Subject Associations

The Victorian Curriculum Assessment Board (VCAB) which controlled Year 12 subjects in Victorian schools was never in a position to assist teachers, spending all their available resources in designing and modifying courses and administering examinations. The VCAB Computer Science Course Management Committee likewise did not itself have the resources to assist teachers, except with advice [38]. Clearly, other forms of support were required.

The Computer Education Group of Victoria (CEGV) was originally formed in the late 1970s as an association of teachers, teacher educators and others interested in the use of computers in education. It came into prominence in 1979 when it launched the first national computer education conference in Australia. The CEGV, and its counterparts in other states, have exerted a considerable influence on computer education through professional development activities, annual conferences, journals and the provision of other publications and resources [2]. Another type of group to emerge in the early 1980s was the *user group*. Victorian Apple Computers in Education (VACE)[6] was such a group, formed at the grass roots by teachers in 1982 to share knowledge between those using Apple][computers. At this stage, computer education had not progressed to the stage of being, to any degree, hardware independent. Schools using Apples had little to discuss with those using TRS-80, Acorn BBC, Cromenco or Commodore computers as the software and applications had little in common [2].

In mid-1988, the Year 12 Computer Science Course Management Committee (of which I was a member) met with the Executive of the CEGV to put the view that the CEGV should be more involved in the provision of assistance to teachers of Computer Science, and of the new Information Technology Field of Study. The result was the establishment of the Victorian Information Technology Teachers Association (VITTA), largely through the efforts of Arthur Tatnall and Bill Davey [38]. Many IT teachers appreciated that much 'real computing' was done in a business setting, and that they themselves did not have sufficient knowledge of the way that business operated or what it did. The answer was to arrange a series of monthly evening meetings of VITTA, many of which would involve site visits. The program for the first half of 1989 was as follows:

- **February:** Kambrook factory – process-control technology and computer-assisted management.
- **March:** Discussion session of the new VCE Information Technology Field of Study.
- **April:** Hewlett Packard: 'Micros and Mainframes'. Tour of HP's Australian Headquarters and a series of talks on HP's 'New Wave' software, RISC technology and computer peripherals.
- **May:** Ford Motor Company's Broadmeadows production line: 'Robots and Production'. Tour of the Ford plant with special attention to the use of robots for welding and sub-assembly. Comparison with the other 'human operated' parts of

[6] VACE was the successor of Melbourne Apple Computers in Education (MACS), formed in 1981 by Denis Kennedy, Bill Davey and Arthur Tatnall.

the production line. Discussion of the social issues of robots replacing workers, quality control with human workers vs. robots, boredom on a production line and training of workers.

- **June:** Space Time Research's Supermap CD – use of compact disk optical storage technology.

Later activities included visits to: Australian Airlines avionics centre, Fallshaw Casters – a manufacturing company making considerable use of robotics and Information Technology and Carlton United Breweries to see the use of mainframe computers to run a large business.

In the early 1990s a Year 12 '*IT Field of Study*' involving three new subjects was introduced to replace Computer Science. Teachers for this field typically came from two quite different backgrounds: former Computer Science teachers, and former commerce / secretarial studies teachers. Finding commonality between these groups was not easy [38].

16 Conclusion

This is where these reflections end. After the conclusion of the Commonwealth Computer Education program in 1987 I left the Education Department to take up an Information Systems position in the Faculty of Business at Footscray Institute of Technology, later to become Victoria University. 1991 was the last year of Year 12 Computer Science and the point at which I bowed out of this area. This then was the end of my direct involvement with the school system (but not my interest) except for some work with Lego on evaluation of their Lego Technics kits, two years as President of the CEGV in 1990-1991 and Chairing of the Australian Computers in Education Conference in 1992.

This chapter could have discussed many other computer education innovations and activities in Victoria at this time, but I have restricted it to my own personal experiences. These other activities would have included software issues such as the development of Apple][software by a couple of teachers at Myrtleford High School and the subsequent establishment of Seasen Software Pty Ltd, educational software created in conjunction with SCEC and developed by Prologic, development of software for school management, use of other software from MECCS[7], use of software in science [39], computer games and their use in education, and more. Professional development issues that could have been discussed included SCEC's 'Seeding Pair' in-service education program, the 'lighthouse schools' and the contribution to teacher education of the Graduate Diploma in Computer Education at Melbourne University. Other possible issue for discussion could have been the role of computer hardware and software suppliers, the falling costs and increasing power of microcomputers, the contribution of the ACS, the attempts to involve girls in the use of computers, to assist students with learning disabilities and the development and use of Lego robotics. Much more still needs to be written.

---

[7] Minnesota Educational Computing Consortium.

References

1. Pearcey, T.: A History of Australian Computing. Chisholm Institute of Technology, Melbourne (1988)
2. Tatnall, A.: The Growth of Educational Computing in Australia. In: Goodson, I.F., Mangan, J.M. (eds.) History, Context, and Qualitative Methods in the Study of Education, pp. 207–248. University of Western Ontario, Canada (1992)
3. Tatnall, A., Davey, W.: Streams in the History of Computer Education in Australia. In: Impagliazzo, J., Lee, J.A.N. (eds.) History of Computing in Education, pp. 83–90. Kluwer Academic Publishers / IFIP, Assinippi Park, Massachusetts (2004)
4. Salvas, A.D.: Personal communication, Melbourne (1985)
5. Monash Computing Museum. MONECS Deamon Educational Computer system (2003), `http://www.csse.monash.edu.au/museum/` (February 2004)
6. Plato Learning. History of Plato Learning (February 2004), `http://www.plato.com/aboutus/company_history.asp`
7. Davey, W.: Personal communication (1985)
8. Tatnall, A., Davey, W.: Early Computer Awareness Courses in Australian Secondary Schools: Curricula from the late 1970s and early 1980s. In: Impagliazzo, J. (ed.) History of Computing and Education 2. IFIP, vol. 215, pp. 107–116. Springer, Boston (2006)
9. Tatnall, A., Davey, W.: Improving the Chances of Getting your IT Curriculum Innovation Successfully Adopted by the Application of an Ecological Approach to Innovation. Informing Science 7(1), 87–103 (2004)
10. Montgomery, A.Y.: Computers and Society: Teaching Computer Awareness. In: Computer Awareness Conference Papers 1980 Secondary Computer Education Committee. Victorian Commercial Teachers' Association Melbourne (1980)
11. Secondary Computer Education Committee, Year 10 Computer Education: Guidelines for Secondary Schools. Education Department of Victoria, Melbourne (1980)
12. Victorian Institute of Secondary Education, New Computer Science Course. VISE, Melbourne (1980)
13. Victorian Institute of Secondary Education, Computer Science (Group 1), in Higher School Certificate Course Description. VISE, Melbourne (1980)
14. Tatnall, A.: A Logic Error is a Misunderstanding Between the Programmer and the Computer. COM3 Journal 16(1), 15–17 (1990)
15. Tatnall, A., Davey, B.: The Life and Growth of Year 12 Computing in Victoria: An Ecological Model. In: Tatnall, A. (ed.) HC 2010. IFIP AICT, vol. 325, pp. 124–133. Springer, Heidelberg (2010)
16. Victorian Institute of Secondary Education, Computer Science, a Course for the Eighties, in VISE News. VISE, Melbourne (1984)
17. Davey, W.: 1991 VCE (HSC) Computer Science Information and Examples, Melbourne (1991)
18. Victorian Curriculum Assessment Board, Computer Science (Group 1). VACB, Melbourne (1990)
19. Tatnall, A.: Computer Science: New Curricula at the Senior Secondary Level. In: CEGV 1985. Computer Education Group of Victoria, Melbourne (1985)
20. Davey, W., Tatnall, A.: Computer Science; Year 11. In: Salvas, A.D. (ed.) Computing and Education - 1984 and Beyond. CEGV, Melbourne (1984)
21. Tatnall, A.: Watsonia High School: Computer Studies, Year 11. Watsonia High School (1981)

22. Tatnall, A.: Lowlev for Windows - an Introduction to Low Level Programming. Data Publishing, Melbourne (1995)
23. Tatnall, A., Davey, W.: Computer Science for Year 11. Jacaranda Press, Brisbane (1985)
24. McDougall, A.: Computers and Post-Primary Education in Victoria: a Study of Needs. Education Department of Victoria, Computer Policy Committee, Melbourne (1980)
25. Tatnall, A., Davey, W.: Computer Education Support Structures in Victorian Schools in the 1980s. In: Impagliazzo, J. (ed.) History of Computing and Education 3. IFIP, vol. 269, pp. 1–22. Springer, Boston (2008)
26. Commonwealth Schools Commission, Teaching, Learning and Computers. Report of the National Advisory Committee on Computers in Schools. Commonwealth Schools Commission, Canberra (1983)
27. Tatnall, A.: The Australian Educational Computer That Never Was. IEEE Annals of the History of Computing 35(1), 35–47 (2013)
28. Tatnall, A.: Computers and Science Teaching. Lab Talk 24(4), 5–6 (1980)
29. Tatnall, A., Neville, L.: Artificial Education and Education: a new direction or more of the same tired old thing. In: Australian Computer Education Conference - Tomorrow's Technology Today. CEGV, Adelaide (1987)
30. Tatnall, A., Tatnall, B.: Logo in Control: Control Technology in Education. In: Australian Computer Education Conference - Tomorrow's Technology Today. CEGV, Adelaide (1987)
31. Commonwealth Schools Commission, Teaching, Learning and Computers. 1984 Information Kit. Commonwealth Schools Commission, Canberra (1984)
32. Ministry of Education Victoria, Educational Computing System Specifications 1986. State Computer Education Centre, Melbourne (1986)
33. Commonwealth Schools Commission, Australian School Computer Systems: Educational User Requirements. Commonwealth Schools Commission, Canberra (1986)
34. Commonwealth Schools Commission, Australian School Computer Systems: Technical Requirements. Commonwealth Schools Commission, Canberra (1986)
35. Tatnall, A. (ed.): The First Pan Pacific Computer Conference - Schools' Congress, PPCC-1. Australian Computer Society, Melbourne (1985)
36. Tatnall, A. (ed.): The Australian Computer Conference - Schools' Congress, ACC 1987. Australian Computer Society, Melbourne (1987)
37. Australian Computer Society, Position Paper Number 6, 'Education'. Australian Computer Society, Sydney (1998)
38. Tatnall, A., Davey, W.: Making Information Technology Real. In: ACEC 1989 - Backup the Future. CEGACT, Canberra (1989)
39. Tatnall, A.: Fibre Optics, Breakfast Cereal and Computer Science. COM3 Journal 18(1), 6–8 (1991)

The First 25 Years of Computers in Education in Poland: 1965 – 1990

Maciej M. Sysło

Institute of Computer Science, University of Wrocław, Poland
syslo@ii.uni.wroc.pl
http://mmsyslo.pl/

Abstract. The first regular informatics lessons in schools were organised in Poland in the second half of the 1960s. Some of the lessons in Wrocław were devoted to programming a mainframe computer located at the university, and school students in Warsaw had a chance to learn theoretical models of computers and foundations of computations.

In the mid-1970s, the government of Poland recognised the importance of computers in the state economy and also in preparing the society for new challenges in the job market and social life. Several national programs and projects were initiated and funded by public money which brought to schools the key components of computer education technology, such as: microcomputers (Elwro 800 Junior), curriculum and syllabuses, educational software, textbooks and materials for teachers, journals. In this paper we shortly characterise all these components and describe their role in informatics education in Polish schools.

The 'investments' in the area of new educational technology, hard and soft, technical and intellectual, made in the 1960-1980s to the education system in Poland, have paid off in the next years and until today, when technology, such as the Internet and mobile tools, are rapidly changing our lives and education.

Keywords: Education, Poland, schools, types of computer, teacher training.

1 Introduction and Preliminaries

The development of educational technology based on computers closely follows the development of computer technology. First regular lessons on informatics were organised in Poland in the second half of the 1960s – see Section 2. At that time there were only a few computers (mainframes) in Poland and none of them was installed in a school. Pioneers of informatics education in Wrocław decided to allow school students to spend some time programming a real computer in the university computing centre, whereas in Warsaw the first informatics lessons in a school were on theoretical models of computers and computations. In both cases leading mathematicians and computer scientists played the main role in introducing informatics ideas to schools and running the first lessons in classrooms.

A. Tatnall and B. Davey (Eds.): History of Computers in Education, IFIP AICT 424, pp. 266–290, 2014.

Shortly after the first informatics lessons in schools it became obvious that a proper preparation of school teachers would be crucial for the success of computerisation of learning and teaching. The first in-service course for future teachers of informatics was organised in the mid-1970s in Warsaw.

In the mid-1970s, a first sign about the importance of the electronic revolution to the most crucial branches of economy, industry, education, and social life came from the government (as a resolution). In the highly centralised political system in Poland of the 1960-1980s, such resolutions opened many doors and were followed by specific programs and projects, and, the most important – by the state funding. New resolutions, government programs and projects had been announced in the 1980s.

The official history of computers in Polish schools started in 1985, in the beginning of the personal computer era, with the first official informatics curriculum proposed by the Polish Information Processing Society (PTI) and approved by The Ministry of National Education (MEN).

In the second half of the 1980s one could observe very intensive activities of various state, public and private institutions which resulted in many ideas and products delivered to 'the education market', in particular to students, teachers, and to schools. Among them were: curricula and syllabuses, textbooks, educational software, journals and magazines, conferences.

We are proud in Poland that informatics, introduced to the curriculum in 1985, has reminded in the core curriculum for all these years till today.

The chapter is organised as follows. In this Section we shortly present the education system in Poland in the last 50 years and explain some terms used here. In Section 2 we characterise the first informatics classes which were organised in the second half of the 1960s in schools in two cities in Poland, and Section 3 is devoted to the first in-service training of informatics teachers which was ran in the mid-1970s in Warsaw. Government resolutions, programs and projects are presented in Section 4 and Section 5 is on the Polish school microcomputer Elwro 800 Junior and its software. In Section 6 we describe the situation in schools in the second half of the 1980s with regard to the main components of informatics education: curriculum, textbook, educational software, journals, conference for teachers, partners. At the end we list some of the sources, in majority in Polish.

1.1 The Education System in Poland in the Second Half of the 20th Century

In the period from 1948/1949 to 1998/1999 the formal school system at primary and secondary levels in Poland consisted of two stages; from 1948/1949 to 1965/1966:

- primary school – 1-7 grades (age 7 to 14);
- high school – 8-11 grades (to 12 in certain vocational schools) – (age 14 to 18);

and from 1966/1967 to 1998/1999, to better prepare young students for their further education and personal vocational career in the future, primary school was extended by one year:

- primary school – 1-8 grades (age 7 to 15);
- high school – 9-12 grades (to 13 in certain vocational schools) – (age 15 to 19);

Since 1999/2000, the formal school system consists of three stages:

- primary school – 1-6 grades (age 7 to 13);
- middle school (in Polish: gimnazjum) – 7-9 grades (age 13 to 16);
- high school – 10-12 grades (to 13 in certain vocational schools) – (age 16 to 19).

Formal education started in Poland at the age of 7 and now it moves down to 6 (in 2014 all children will go to school when they are 6). The school grades in Poland in the period 1965-1990 were in the range [2-5], with 2 as fail.

1.2 Terminology

In this paper we use today's terminology: computer, informatics, informatics education, Ministry of National Education (MEN). In Poland, a computer was called 'a mathematical machine' in the 1960s, although the term 'computer' was used for the first time in 1963, and the term 'informatics' for computer science was introduced in the late 1960s. The ministry responsible for education in K-12 has changed its name several times.

In the education system in Poland, **informatics education** consists of two types of classes or/and activities:

- separate computer (in elementary school) and informatics (in middle and in high) classes;
- across-curriculum integration of computers, information and communication technology, and Internet with learning and teaching of all subjects.

In this article, in which we describe early activities in Poland in the area of computers in education, our focus is mainly on learning and teaching about computers. In the beginning, with a few exceptions, informatics (understood as computer science) dominated as a subject, since there was no subject-oriented software and first computers coming to schools were used to build computer labs then used mainly by teachers of informatics. This fits into the model for technology development in education [UNESCO, 2002], which consists of four stages. In the first stage – *Emerging* – schools begin to get equipment and software (technology in general) and teachers are learning new educational technology and exploring the possibility and consequences of adding technology to the curriculum. Integration of technology with other subjects is the goal of the next stages – *Applying* and *Infusing* – which follow the first stage.

2 First Informatics Classes in Schools

In this Section we describe two initiatives which in the 1960-1970s appeared in two academic centres in Poland, in Wrocław and in Warsaw. They were different in nature, since they were born in different circumstances. At the University of Wrocław in 1962, the Numerical Methods Division (KMN) was established within the Mathematical Institute and the mainframe computer (Elliott 803, made in the UK) was installed as the first commercially made computer in universities in Poland. In 1964/1965, academic teachers from KMN offered some school students informatics classes with a possibility to write programs and to run them on a real computer.

On the other hand in Warsaw, although there were several institutions which hosted mainframe computers (also University of Warsaw), the informatics lessons, which started in 1970, were run in two university mathematics classes and were devoted mainly to some theoretical foundations of informatics. Other initiatives born in Warsaw in the 1970s were: informatics syllabus for schools and in-service courses for mathematics teachers on teaching informatics in high schools, both supervised by the Institute of Teacher Education (IKN) – see Section 3. According to Andrzej Walat, in the second half of the 1970s, informatics was taught in about 1000 high schools in Poland, mainly by teachers who were prepared during the IKN courses.

There were several other institutions and companies all over Poland which in the 1960-1970s offered lessons, courses and regular classes to students from primary and high schools. They were ran by the personnel of those institutions/companies graduated in informatics related fields and using their computer equipment.

It is worth mentioning that the first classes of informatics in schools in Poland were initiated by leading mathematicians and computer scientists of their time working in academic institutions in Wrocław and in Warsaw. Informatics lessons, addressed to students in mathematics classes extended their knowledge and skills by including computer (numerical) methods and programming of a real computer in Wrocław, and theoretical foundations of computers' design and calculations in various models of computations. Teachers and instructors in schools and also students involved in the first informatics classes in Poland admit today a great concern, engagement and activity of the initiators of those first classes – professors Stefan Paszkowski in Wrocław and Hanna Szmuszkowicz and Zdzisław Pawlak[1] in Warsaw – their enthusiasm was shared by all participants in these activities, students and teachers, in schools and in academic institutions.

2.1 Numerical Methods and Programming in Wrocław

The first informatics class in Poland was established in the Adam Mickiewicz High School III (grade X) in Wrocław in the 1964/1965 school year[2]. It was partly initiated by The Science and Technology Council of the Regional Party Committee (PZPR)[3] and approved by MEN (the Ministry of Education). The decision was influenced by the University of Wrocław initiative (in 1962) to buy a commercial computer Elliott 803, to open a numerical track (specialisation) and offer it to mathematics students. The school subject was called 'Programming and using a computer' and its syllabus was proposed by KMN, University of Wrocław (see [Witek, 1966], [Zuber, 1966]). Since those days a computer was mainly used for numerical calculations, students in this first informatics class learnt some basic numerical methods for solving mathematical problems and some programming languages for Elliott 803 (assembler, autocode Mark III, and Algol) and finally ran their programs on the real computer.

---

[1] See short bio of Zdzisław Pawlak:
`http://chc60.fgcu.edu/EN/HistoryDetail.aspx?c=12`

[2] Another such class in Wrocław was open in the High School I in the next school year.

[3] PZPR – the Polish United Workers' Party.

The students enrolled for informatics classes (also from other high schools in Wrocław) were supposed to have grade 4 or above in mathematics in the previous year. Out of 36 school hours a week, students in the informatics class had 8 hours of mathematics, 4 hours of informatics and 1 extra hour for elements of electronics (as a part of physics). The syllabus of mathematics (proposed by S. Paszkowski [Witek, 1966], [Zuber, 1966]) was extended and augmented by adding some sections and topics related to numerical methods and computer calculations such as: error analysis, mathematical tables and interpolations, polynomials, solving algebraic equations and systems of linear equations, numerical integration.

Informatics, taught by Roman Zuber, Jerzy Kucharczyk, Henryk Bogdanów and some other members of the University Computing Centre, covered: programming (first in autocode Mark III, then in assembler, and finally in Algol 60) binary representations, computer organisation, and computer implementations of numerical algorithms. For a particular problem to be solved or a topic to be discussed, time of teaching and learning was split into 4 parts: designing a solution as a computer program (50% of the time assigned), making a program ready (punching) for running (12,5%), running a program (12,5%), discussions in groups (25%). Parts 1 and 4 took place in the school classroom, and Parts 2 and 3 were held in the Computing Centre. Today, it is interesting to notice that during part 4, a teacher was helping and advising students how to cope with problems which may occur in the process of algorithm implementation and when verifying correctness of a solution, also in the case of home assignments. It reminds what today is called **a flipped learning**, a learning and teaching method in which a teacher spends most of his time on advising students on the problems they meet in their personal learning.

While solving a problem, students proceeded through all stages of solving a problem with a computer, what today is called **algorithmic thinking** (or **computational thinking**): describe a specification of a problem, choose an algorithm and data structure, implement an algorithm as a computer program, run a computer program, analyse outputs obtained and verify the correctness of your solution, discuss possible applications of your solution. In his evaluation of programming lessons, R. Zuber [Zuber, 1966] considered the stage of computer implementation of an algorithm as a specific communication dialog man-machine in which, contrary to a teacher, a machine is a formal and objective partner (tool), what Donald E. Knuth described precisely:

> *It has often been said that a person does not really understand something until he teaches it to someone else. Actually a person does not really understand something until he can teach it to a computer.*
>
> [Donald E. Knuth, *AMM* **81**(1974)]

In the first years of informatics classes there were no textbooks for the school lessons. Teachers had to use hand-outs. In the next years, some texts were published on: Algol [Paszkowski, 1965], programming Elliott 803 [Łukaszewicz, 1966] and numerical methods and programming [Zuber, 1972].

The first class was attended by 19 students, and only 2 of them quit due to some health problems. In the beginning, there was a problem with different levels of students' competencies in mathematics brought from various schools they came, however after 2-3 months this problem disappeared. Close to 90% of students completed the first year of informatics lessons with the grade 4 or higher, [Witek, 1966], [Zuber, 1966].

Most of the students who graduated from informatics classes in high schools III and I in Wrocław continued their study in informatics related disciplines and found jobs related to computers, some of them in University of Wrocław, where a few of them are still employed.

2.2 Theoretical Foundations of Computer Science in Warszawa

In contrast to the Wrocław initiative, in which the specialisation of S. Paszkowski group in KMN and the access to a computer decided that informatics lessons were devoted to numerical methods implemented on the real computer, a Warsaw initiative of introducing informatics to schools, undertaken in the beginning of the 1970s, was not tied up with computer programming. It was not a result of lack of computer access – computers were in operation in many places in Warsaw – it was the result of the idea of those who carried the initiative that teaching informatics to school students should focus mainly on the foundations of informatics to build a solid base for the future needs and interests in informatics related topics when students find jobs in different areas.

Informatics lessons in Warsaw were initiated in 1970 by mathematicians Hanna Szmuszkowicz, Stanisław Mazur, and Zdzisław Pawlak, in two university mathematics classes in the Klement Gottwald (today Stanisław Staszic) High School XIV (LO XIV). In the beginning, Andrzej Skowron, Andrzej Walat and Piotr Dembiński taught the theory of mathematical machines (Pawlak's machines, [Pawlak, Skowron, 1970], [Pawlak, 1971]) and the foundations of the finite automata theory. The focus was on understanding the meaning of algorithm and algorithmic problem solving using: a notion of the program for a von Neumann machine (in connection to universal Turing machine), algorithms coded in assembler, and algorithms represented by flow charts. In general, an algorithm was determined as a constructive method defining its transition function and the function calculated by the algorithm. In the next years, A. Walat taught some elements of programming – students wrote programs in Pascal in the classroom and then they could run their programs in one of the computing centres in Warsaw.

In the fall of 1970, H. Szmuszkowicz established in the Institute of Pedagogy a weekly seminar for teachers from Warsaw high schools interested in informatics and its teaching. The seminar was supervised by Z. Pawlak, who shaped its program and suggested topics and materials for discussion, and ran by A. Skowron and A. Walat. Topics of the first meetings of the seminar covered the theory of Pawlak's machines and analysis of the syllabus of informatics and educational materials used in High School XIV. Z. Pawlak, A. Skowron, and A. Walat wrote a textbook and classroom materials for students in LO XIV, [Pawlak, 1971], [Skowron, 1970, 1976], [Walat, 78].

In the beginning of the 1970s in IKN, a group of academic and school teachers started to work on a syllabus for informatics lessons in mathematics classes in high schools in Poland and on another syllabus for in-service training of mathematics teachers to prepare them for teaching in informatics classes. The first in-service course for 300 teachers, coming from different high schools in Poland, was organised in 1974 (see Section 3). A group of 20 teachers was selected who were asked to teach informatics for 2 hours a week in their schools according to the syllabus completed in IKN. Feedback from those teachers, from their schools, and from their students were used to modify the syllabus. The same group of teachers prepared materials for teaching informatics in schools and to run a course on didactics of informatics for participants of the IKN in-service course.

Informatics for High Schools – Syllabus [Hallay, 1981]

I. Introduction of basic concepts (4 hours)
II. Algorithms (16)
III. Algorithmic languages (14)
IV. Digital machine, machine and symbolic languages (14)
V. Technical realization of basic blocks of the machine (6)
VI. Informatics systems and their software (6)
VII. Methods of applying informatics 6)

A visit to a computing centre.

In contrast to the Wrocław syllabus for informatics, it was assumed in the IKN syllabus that informatics may be taught with no access to computers. It was only advised to visit a computing centre equipped with a computer.

Jerzy Hallay, one of the authors of the first Warsaw informatics syllabus and an instructor at the IKN in-service courses for teachers commented on the syllabus [Hallay, 1981]:

> *The ability to use a computer … is not any more a competence of a small group of experts. We may assume that informatics systems will significantly influence everyday life of a whole society, as well as our personal life. … additionally, there is no doubt that the way of thinking supported by informatics … contributes to better organisation of a man in every domain of her/his activity. Knowledge and skills acquired when constructing algorithms perfectly form attitudes of honest and consequent behavior. In particular, the syllabus puts the main stress on elements of general education which develops critical and effective thinking. The syllabus does not impose teaching of effective programming, however it is assumed that students will understand the main ideas behind programming and know basic programming constructions from various programming languages. Moreover, no particular computer should be the object of instruction, however students should learn general ideas and laws of how computers work and their importance in the contemporary world.*

Note, that these words, written a long time before the microcomputer and mobile technology era, almost exactly describe what today is known as **computational thinking** – the mental competence, based on the power and limits of computers and computations, useful when solving problems in various domains with the help of computers, and augmenting traditional 3R literacies.

Syllabuses for informatics classes, informatics lessons in selected schools, and teacher training, initiated and conducted in the 1960-1970s in several regions in Poland, especially in Wrocław and in Warsaw, stimulated awareness of teachers in schools, decision makers in the area of education, and politicians and then activities and decisions, which in the mid-1980s, when computers became easily available for schools, universities, and private homes, formed a solid base for computerization of all schools and universities – see Section 4.

3 First Initiatives in Teacher Preparation

Teachers and their preparation are the most important factors when introducing any change to an education system, especially when introducing a new education technology. The first informatics classes described above were taught by academic teachers with the background mostly in mathematics, according to syllabuses written by teams which were also rooted at academic institutions. There are two types of preparations expected from teachers in the area of computers in education:

- to teach informatics as a separate subject;
- to incorporate and integrate computers, technology and informatics with other subjects.

It is also expected that informatics teachers can help teachers of other subjects in their schools to use computers and technology in various disciplines. Graduates from informatics-oriented faculties are not really interested in teaching in schools since they are convinced that all other informatics jobs are much better paid. On the other hand, new teachers of other subjects are prepared in a very traditional way with the main emphasis put on psychology and pedagogy and with only general ideas about the use of technology in teaching and learning and the impact technology can make on students learning and on teaching methods. Most of the teachers get their preparation to teach informatics or to use technology as a learning and teaching tool during in-service training.

As mentioned above, the first in-service course for 300 mathematics teachers to learn what and how to teach informatics in high schools, supervised by H. Szmuszkowicz (in the beginning) and then by J. Hallay, was organised in the summer of 1974 by IKN. This course was preceded by a seminar on teaching informatics which ran for more than 2 years by IKN in cooperation with Universities in Warsaw and in Wrocław, and attended by academic and school teachers not only from these academic centres. In the first years, the course consisted of two parts, theoretical (held in Nowy Sącz, Pułtusk, Kalisz, Piotrków Trybunalski) – with no access to computers, and practical in computing centres equipped with mainframes (in Gdynia and Warsaw).

In the beginning, the course for teachers was dominated by two topics (subjects): organisation of mathematical machines (a textbook was written by M. Stolarski) and foundations of informatics (a textbook was written by J. Hallay). Moreover, A. Walat published two collections of exercises on foundations of informatics [Walat, 1978], and A. Skowron wrote a text on foundations of the theory of mathematical machines [Skowron, 1974].

Teachers who attended in-service courses ran by the IKN, used in their schools the syllabus for informatics classes prepared also in IKN (see Section 2). The feedbacks from schools were then used to modify the informatics syllabus for schools and, after some years, were collected in the form of didactic materials for the next groups of teachers attending the in-service training courses.

The first in-service course for teachers of informatics was highly evaluated by MEN and all instructors received medals from the minister of education, Jerzy Kuberski.

It was estimated by A. Walat that by 1980, more than 1,000 teachers attended in-service courses for teachers of informatics, and informatics was taught in more than 1,000 high schools in Poland, however most of the classes had no access to any computer.

The in-service course for teachers ran by IKN has changed its syllabus in the mid-1980s when microcomputers (ZX Spectrum and compatibles) became popular in Poland and also arrived in schools, see [Wasiak, 2014]. A team arranged by PTI and supervised by S. Waligórskiego (University of Warsaw) published a new syllabus for informatics in high schools, approved by MEN to be used in schools, see Section 6.1. Another team, also supervised by S. Waligórski, prepared a Polish-language version of Logo for ZX Spectrum. S. Waligórski modified also the syllabus for the in-service teacher training course – the teachers were supposed to use computers during all lessons of the course – in the beginning it was ZX Spectrum, then Elwro 800 Junior, and finally IBM PC. Theoretical lessons (lectures) almost disappeared replaced by practical lessons with microcomputers. The subject on organisation of mathematical machines was gradually replaced by exercises with application software which was just in the beginning of its route to today's popularity. Programming started with Logo, and then continued with Pascal. In the second half of the 1980s, teachers attending the preparation course could use textbooks published for students in schools or for other users of microcomputers, which became popular also at homes.

In the 1980s, many universities and computer training centres started to offer teachers in-service courses on different aspects of microcomputers and their use in schools for separate informatics classes and for supporting learning and teaching other subjects.

Learning programming in general and programming in Pascal in particular were among the most popular courses offered for teachers as well as for students, in schools and also as off-school activities. Jan Madey from Warsaw University was a leading teacher in these courses; he also co-authored a textbook on Pascal ([Iglewski et al., 1979]) and wrote many educational materials on programming.

4 Government Documents, Decisions and Actions

In the mid-1970s the government of Poland adopted the Resolution No. 175/75 'The Program of Electronisation of the National Economy to 1990'. The main goal of this program (called **Program I** hereafter) in the area of education was: *to popularise and modernise the education system, and as a result, to upgrade the education of the society by implementing and using in instruction modern electronic tools, such as: TV, language labs, didactic machines, electronic calculators, computer terminals.* It was the first sign that the government had recognised the importance of the electronic revolution to the most important branches of economy, industry, education, and social life.

In 1983 Program I was evaluated as not meeting the original goals and expectations. It was due to the increase of its public funding and, more important, due to rapid changes in computer technology after the world premiere of a personal computer IBM PC in 1981. In 1983, Program I was replaced by **Program II** established by the Resolution No. 77/83 'The Program of Electronization of the National Economy and the Directions of the Development of the Electronic Industry to 1990'.

4.1 Government Programs

As a follow up of the Resolution 77/83, two programs addressed education were established by the government based on the proposals submitted by the committees of specialists in informatics and education:

1. **Program III:** 'Program for Public Education in the Area of Informatics and for Computer Techniques Applications in General and Vocational Schools in 1986-1990', Warsaw, March 1986.
2. **Program IV:** 'Program for Development of Computer Techniques Applications in Higher (University) Education in 1986-90', Warsaw, December 1985.

4.1.1 Program III

The main goal of Program III was: *to make it possible for school and university students to learn informatics methods and tools to be able to use technical tools based on computer techniques as ordinary tools in their jobs and in daily life.* Moreover, it was assumed that *computers will be used as educational tools and this will lead to better and new achievements in education …One of the goals of our education system is to create and develop in students informatics culture understood as ability of applying computers as modern job tools, used also in exploring various application areas … Informatics content should not be designed only according to informatics and computer techniques standards but also taking into account general education goals, corresponding to levels of education and types of schools.* Four areas of the Program activities were distinguished:

- teacher preparation;
- hardware and software (application and educational);
- publications (journals and textbooks);
- research and development.

Program III was signed by the vice-ministers of education and of higher education, and also by a government member Aleksander Kwaśniewski, a future President of Poland, who was in charge of youth affairs in the government.

4.1.2 Program IV

Program IV was devoted to computerisation of higher education institutions (universities) in the area of education and research. It was assumed that *informatics education of all students in higher education institutions is the most important way for the effective development of informatics and its applications in the national economy.* Program IV consisted of two main components:

- education of future specialists in informatics, responsible for the development of informatics methods and tools, and also for training of other informatics specialist and educators;
- informatics education addressed to all students, to prepare them for using informatics methods and tools in their future jobs regardless of the area of interests.

4.1.3 Ministry of National Education (MEN)

In the mid-1980s, a special department was established in the Ministry of National Education which was (and still exists) to manage and monitor activities ran by government agencies and other institutions in the area of computerisation of schools. In the 1960-1980s the education system in Poland was highly centralised. In the 1980s the department was chaired by Zbigniew Rogowski with the help of Krzysztof Święcicki.

4.2 Government Projects

In the second half of the 1980s, several projects were established to accomplish the goals of Programs III and IV. Two of them, RRI.16 and RRI.14, were the most important with regard to their achievements for general informatics education.

Project RRI.16

The goal of Project RRI.16: 'Informatics for Schools – Development of Informatics Education in High School and Preparation of Education Software and its Implementation in Schools' was to:

- prepare educational materials for the subject Elements of informatics (EI) in high schools;
- provide methods for teaching and learning with computers;
- produce sample packages of educational software.

Twenty seven teams from universities, technical universities (polytechnics), schools for teachers, and independent institutions took part in Project RRI.16. The most important results obtained in this Project were: the first textbook for informatics in Poland (see Section 6.2) and several systems and packages of educational software (see Section 6.3). All these products were made available for students and for schools – they were either bought by MEN and then sent to schools (software) or they were made available for purchase (textbooks).

Project RRI.14

The goal of Project RRI.14: 'Informatics and Computer support of Education and Research in Higher Education Institutions' was to:

- equip higher education institutions with modern computers and informatics tools;
- produce sample software packages for supporting education processes;
- prepare and train academic teachers and school staff for incorporating modern computer technology with their teaching and research.

Project RRI.14 was coordinated by Wrocław Polytechnic – coordinator Professor Wacław Kasprzak. Almost all higher education institutions in Poland participated in this Project, mainly as recipients of some modern computer labs to be used for introductory informatics courses. A curriculum for these courses was proposed by a team from the University of Wrocław, supervised by the author. Hundreds of software systems and packages were designed and produced by the participating schools then made available for all other schools participated in the Project, see the catalogue [Katalog_1].

It is worth to mention that one of the software packages designed by another team supervised by the author was later produced in 1300 copies and sent to high schools as supporting software for learning and teaching elements of informatics (see Section 6.3 for more details).

Today one should acknowledge that the two Projects from the second half of the 1980s laid a solid ground for the future decisions and activities in the area of informatics education in all types of schools on all levels of education. Schools had got modern computer systems equipped with application and educational software to support education and research (in universities). The software was listed in a uniform way in three volumes, two produced in Project RRI.14 [Katalog_1] and one in Project RRI.16 [Katalog_2]. Although the production and distribution of the Projects' results (books and software) were not the Projects' responsibilities, the participating institutions could freely copy and use the results for non-commercial purpose in education and research.

5 A School Computer – Elwro 800 Junior

In the mid-1980s Polish customers were able to buy 8-bit microcomputers abroad and bring them to Poland officially (there was no COCOM restriction on 8-bit microcomputers), they could also purchase imported microcomputers at computer bazaars (with local currency) or in Pewex or Baltona retail stores. Schools and universities were buying microcomputers in some quantities to form their first computer labs and to offer students the first regular classes on informatics or on using them in other subjects. Quickly, ZX Spectrum became the most popular 8-bit microcomputer in Poland. Taking this into account, MEN organised a competition for a Polish school microcomputer – the winning computer was to satisfy the following conditions:

- to work in one of its mode as ZX Spectrum, so that rich software for ZX Spectrum available in Poland could be used;
- to work under control of a disc operating system, so that the software working under CP/M could be used;
- to communicate with a user in Polish when editing texts or programming in Logo.

Four constructions competed and the competition jury, launched by OFEK, on the basis of the findings and the results of the surveys selected microcomputer Elwro 800 **Junior** (called Junior hereafter) as the winner, see Figure 1. It was designed by a team from the Institute of Automation, Poznań Polytechnic, supervised by Wojciech Cellary and Paweł Krysztofiak [Cellary, Krysztofiak, 1988].

Fig. 1. Elwro 800 Junior: microcomputer, screen, tape recorder

The most important feature of Junior, in particular for schools, was its operating system CP/J compatible with CP/M and moreover it could control the local network Junet consisting of up to 15 microcomputers Junior. ZX Spectrum could be also connected to the Junet network. A class configuration of Juniors consisted of a local network of students' Juniors with no disc drives, a teacher's Junior with an external disc drive which was a server of files and printers, and a printer. It was very economic and effective design – all students had access to discs and to printers.

Microcomputer Elwro 800 Junior was produced in 4 versions: version 1 – a student's Junior with no disc drive, version 2 – a teacher's Junior with an external disc drive, version 3 – with an external disc drive, available for private users, and version 4 – a Junior equipped with an internal disc drive.

5.1 Software for Juniors

A microcomputer Elwro 800 Junior, operated under the OS CP/J, was equipped with basic software tools to control a disc drive, a magnetic tape memory, a local computer network Junet, and a graphic printer. The Basic interpreter and the program for magnetic tape control were compatible with those in ZX Spectrum, hence the programs for ZX Spectrum could be run on Junior. Moreover, the extended Basic interpreter for Junior controlled external devices, communication in the network, and could be used to save files on discs read from the magnetic tape memory. One could also use application software, such as: text editors ED/J (designed in Elwro) and WordStar and the database system dBase under the control of CP/J, and also spreadsheet SuperCalc in the ZX Spectrum mode.

The team which designed Junior produced also an interpreter for Logo and an environment for programming in this language [AC-LOGO]. MEN bought the rights to this software and disseminated it among school in Poland which had got Juniors. Moreover, Sinclair Logo and Polish Logo, implemented by a team supervised by S. Waligórski, and also other programming languages, such as C, Prolog and Pascal (Borland Turbo Pascal) could be also used on Junior.

After several years of presence of Juniors in education institutions (schools and universities), software companies and in private hands, a large number of computer programs and written materials were available. A largest collection of educational software was presented during the conference 'Informatics in Schools, IV' in Błażejewko (17-20 September 1990). There were presented: 51 programs for Junior, 32 – for the IBM PC, and 7 – for both computers. The programs were designed to support a variety of school subjects: technique – 5 programs, chemistry – 16, physics – 30, geodesy – 2, geography – 3, history – 1, informatics – 26, mathematics 7, English – 1, natural environment protection – 2, pedagogy – 1, and statistics – 3. Software designed for Juniors, due to its compatibility with ZX Spectrum, ran also on other 8-bit microcomputers used in schools and at homes.

We would like to comment here on some software packages presented in Błażejewko which made Junior a real school computer:

- A package of 11 programs to support experiments in chemistry, designed by a team from Adam Mickiewicz University in Poznań;
- Authoring tool JU-LEK, designed and implemented by Witold Rudolf in his master thesis, supervised by Ewa Gurbiel (Institute of Computer Science, University of Wrocław, 1989). JU-LEK was used to prepare and execute lessons of presentation type (PT CAI – Presentation Type Computer Assisted Instruction) – lessons in JU-LEK reminded of today presentations prepared in PowerPoint. It was used to prepare lessons in various subjects – see a frame on physics in Figure 2.

  Lessons made in JU-LEK consisted of at most 99 frames (or screens) connected (ordered) according to a lesson plan (graph). Each frame could contain at most 150 objects such as: texts (of at most 62 characters), graphics (a piecewise linear curve with at most 10 vertices, circle, disc, rectangle, vector), commands (delete, break, repeat, pointer, answer, run an external program in Turbo Pascal). Graphical objects could have attributes: type of a line, colour, intensity of a colour.

  JU-LEK consisted of two sets of modules – for an author (a teacher) and for a student. The author's set contained two main modules, GEN – for building a lesson, EXE – for executing (trying) a lesson created by GEN. The purpose of the student's set was to execute a lesson built in JU-LEK. JU-LEK was implemented in Turbo Pascal 3.02A and additionally a graphics library GSJ 0.0 was used (author: K. Pielesiak, Poznań Polytechnic). JU-LEK and its author were awarded the III Prize in the 1990 National Competition for Master Degree Thesis in Informatics. The system was purchased by OFEK Jelenia Góra, which published its guide book and then disseminated to schools equipped with Juniors.

- 'Elements of Informatics' – a package of systems on various topics in informatics and in its applications, designed by a team of almost 50 authors and programmers, supervised by the author [Sysło, 1993]. The package was created in Project RRI.14 then MEN ordered 1 300 its copies and sent to high schools in Poland (for more details about these programs see Section 6.3).
- a package of application software offered by VULCAN, see Section 6.6. The package consisted of: a file management system (VCOMMANDER), a text editor (VEDIT), a graphics editor (VGRAPH), spreadsheet (VCALC), database (VBASE), and a program for data visualisation (VCHART).

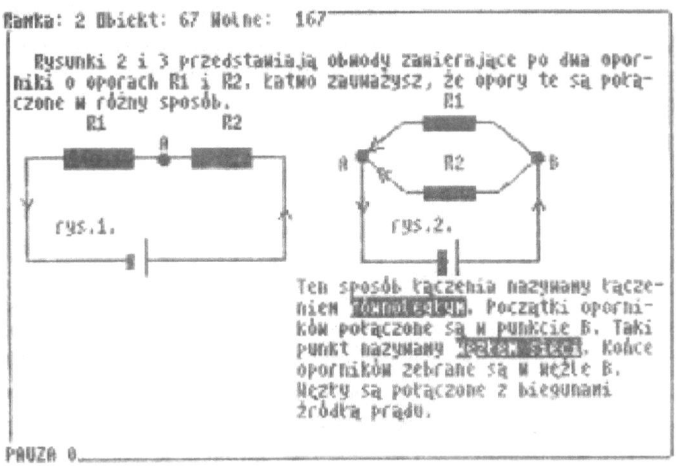

Fig. 2. A sample frame from the authoring system JU-LEK

The Software for Junior (SO CP/J, Logo, Turbo Pascal) comprised the basic computer environment for informatics lessons conducted according to the first textbook in Polish *Elements of Informatics* written by a team from the Institute of Computer Science University of Wrocław, supervised by the author.

5.2 Elwro 800 Junior: Epilogue

Elwro 800 Junior was produced by Elwro Computer Company (ZE Elwro) in Wrocław, which specialised in producing mainframe computers. Elwro was founded in February 1959 and in the beginning produced computers designed in Poland, then switchcd to a series of computers based on ICT/ICL license, and in the 1970s produced computers of the unified system based on IBM Series 360 in cooperation with other countries in the Eastern Block.

Production of Juniors was a big challenge for ZE Elwro. The company had no experience in production of personal computers in large quantities and, on the other hand, there was no supply of good quality elements for microcomputers in Poland. In fact, some elements for Juniors were imported from East Germany (processor), Soviet Union (memory), Bulgaria (disc drives), and from other countries (integrated circuits). The elements were rather of low quality and this effected the quality of the final products, microcomputers Junior.

As a producer of mainframe computers, ZE Elwro did not have a qualified service to deliver and to install personal microcomputers Junior to schools and to provide maintenance and repair service in schools. Moreover in schools, teachers were not prepared to manage with new equipment, how to: install new software, set and maintain a local network for different groups of students, or react in the case of small breakdowns, failures or malfunctions of Juniors.

In the beginning of the 1990s, with all these problems faced by the producer and the users of Juniors when the era of 8-bit microcomputers was coming to its end, MEN decided not to buy Juniors anymore and stop sending them to schools. Almost 10,000 Juniors were installed in almost 1,000 schools. In 1993, due to MEN's report, 60% of computers in schools were still 8-bit computers and more than half of them were Juniors. (Meritum, also Polish made, was another microcomputer popular in schools.

When the IBM PC begun to replace Juniors in schools, ZE Elwro designed a special drive JunServ to use IBM PC as a file and printer server for the network of Juniors. Moreover, VULCAN designed an emulator of Junior on IBM PC.

In conclusion we admit that in the second half of the 1980s, introducing microcomputers Elwro 800 Junior to schools created opportunity for thousands of students to make the first steps in learning how computers work and how to use them in a number of intellectual activities. The lesson learnt was a big step towards the future in the environment of new and rapidly changing technology. On the other hand, a number of government, public, and private initiatives made their first investments in the movement which in the years to come would cover all levels of education and far beyond any formal and non-formal education system, especially when the Internet entered the stage.

6 The Mid-1980s – Curricula, Textbooks, Educational Software, Conference and Journals

In this Section we shortly review the situation in educational use of computers in the second half of the 1980s, when 8-bit microcomputers dominated, just before the Internet era. Today one can observe that the activities and their results in many areas related to computers in education obtained in the late 1980s laid down a solid ground under their successful continuation in the 1990s. We focus on curricula, textbooks, educational software, annual conferences for teachers, and magazines and journals. Finally, educational activities of three entrepreneurs are shortly described.

6.1 Curricula

First curricula for teaching informatics in schools were designed in the 1960s and 1970s, for local initiatives in schools in Wrocław and in Warsaw (see Section 2). Then in the mid-1970s, another curriculum was proposed for teachers who attended in-service training in IKN and were to return to their schools to teach informatics (see Sections 2 and 3).

The first curriculum for the subject called *Elements of informatics* (EI), addressed to all high schools, was proposed by a team of PTI supervised by S. Waligórski and then approved by MEN in 1985. The curriculum was designed for 75 lessons (each 45 min. long) and covered the following topics (numbers in parenthesis denote the number of lessons) [Program_1]:

1. The Use of a microcomputer (2) – first steps in using a computer and its software.
2. Practical applications of a microcomputer (6) – learning how to use various computer applications for text editing, creating graphics and sounds, building tables and simple databases, making simulations.
3. Drawing pictures on the screen (4) – individual creation on the screen of simple elements of drawings, such as: points, lines, curves, and use them to obtain a more complex drawings; use of colors and background.
4. Procedures (12) – elements of programming using procedures, Logo environment, recursion.
5. Elements of programming style (12) – elements of structural programming, procedures and structural relations between them; top-down programming.
6. Non-elementary methods in creating graphics (12) – the use of graphics procedures with parameters.
7. Operations on texts (12) – operations on texts as lists of characters (in Logo).
8. Individual problem solving (15) – the use of acquired knowledge and skills in solving more advanced problems.

In 1990, MEN also approved another curriculum for EI in elementary schools (in fact, for the last year in elementary schools). The curriculum was designed for 60 lessons (each 45 min. long) and covered the following topics (numbers in parenthesis denote the number of lessons) [Program_2]:

1. The use of a microcomputer (6) – preparation for using a computer and its software.
2. Practical applications of informatics (12-36) – learning in action various computer applications for text editing, creating graphics and sounds, building tables in a spreadsheet, creating a simple database of information.
3. A student as a teacher of a computer – first steps in programming (12-6) – elements of programming, mainly to draw pictures (in a Logo environment).

4. Programming more complex actions – elements of programming style (24-6) – elements of structural programming: writing procedures and planning cooperation between them.
5. Recreation with computers (6) – educational computer games.

In both curricula there was a restriction that informatics classes can be organised only in those schools which had got a computer lab for running such classes. In 2013, MEN has introduced the regulation that during informatics lessons each student should have a computer for her/his personal use (1:1 strategy).

In the mid-1990s there were three EI curricula for schools which were approved by the Ministry of Education in 1994-1995. Two of them were designed mainly for those schools in which EI classes were run for one or at most two years. One of these two curricula is focused on problem solving and algorithmics and the other – on the use of application software. The third curriculum which was proposed by the team from the Institute of Computer Science, University of Wrocław, supervised by the author, had a very general structure and consists of a number of modules which can be used to design a plan for teaching EI from one to four years with the emphasis on different aspects of informatics, e.g. problem solving, algorithmics, application software.

It is worth mentioning that *Informatics* (in the beginning, as *Elements of Informatics*) has, in Poland, been a part of the national curriculum since 1985.

6.2 The First Textbook

The first textbook for *Elements of Informatics* (under such title) was written by a team supervised by the author [Textbook_1]. It was one of the products of Project RRI.16 (see Section 4.2). It appeared in 1988 (first edition) and then, it is perhaps interesting to mention that, this textbook had a new, unchanged edition (printing) every year (two in 1995) till 1990 and more than 100,000 copies have been sold out. It is unusual for a book on informatics to remain unchanged on the market for so long. It was mainly due to the approach adopted in the book – computers and software tools were not described in full details but only with respect to the main theme (problem) of the presentation and discussion. The content of the textbook was universal although there were some key components of the contemporary informatics and technology missed, especially related to computer networks and computer supported communication, which entered schools later in the 1990s. The content of the book was (and still is) universal and we are not surprised today to see our book in hands of students and teachers:

1. What is informatics. Elements of history of computers and informatics.
2. How computers are designed and how they work (operating systems).
3. Playing and learning (turtle graphics – Logo).
4. From problems to programs (elements of programming in Turbo Pascal).
5. Designing one's own directory (database in Turbo Pascal).
6. Calculations in mathematics (elements of numerical methods).
7. Computing faster – efficiency of algorithms (elements of algorithmics and algorithms complexity).
8. Writing with no paper and pencil – text editing.
9. Easy and effective managing of a small business (spreadsheet).

The textbook was accompanied by a book with some solutions of all problems from the textbook [Texbook_2] and by a guide book for teachers [Texbook_3] which was the first text in Polish on the methodology of using computers in schools – it can be considered as a textbook on the didactics of informatics. Package EI (see Section 6.3) was used in all three volumes as supporting software for students and teachers.

6.3 Educational Software

In Section 5.1 we have described in details educational software designed and produced for Juniors. These software packages were sent (from ZE Elwro or from MEN) to schools equipped with Juniors and then were available for all Junior users in schools.

6.3.1 Educational Software for Chemistry

A team from Adam Mickiewicz University in Poznań, supervised by Andrzej Burewicz and Hanna Gulińska, designed a package of 11 programs for Juniors to support experiments in chemistry (see Section 5.1). This team has been (and remains today) very active in providing students and schools with tools for computer assisted learning and instruction in chemistry [Burewicz at al.].

6.3.2 Educational Software for Elements of Informatics

A software package – EI (*Elements of Informatics*) – was designed for IBM PC by a team supervised by the author in Project RRI.14 (see Section 4.2) to support teachers of informatics and of related subjects [Sysło, 1993]. The software was comprehensively tested and accompanied by its documentation and educational materials (more than 1,000 pages). Then Foundation OFEK produced 1,300 of its copies and delivered them to high schools.

Package EI consisted of 10 educational systems:

1. SB – a system for constructing and executing flow-charts of algorithms.
2. DYSKIETKA – a system for presenting basic operations on a computer file system and demonstrating their effects.
3. TP-TOOL – a set of tools for supporting learning of programming in Turbo Pascal.
4. ESO – a system for demonstrating operating system commands and learning elements of concurrent programming.
5. DISC-MATH – a system consisting of 6 programs for supporting learning algorithms and data structures: operations on list and tree data structures, sorting algorithms, operations and algorithms on graphs, backtracking algorithms, a model of a universal computer.
6. EKO-SYM – a system for simulation of eco-processes.
7. MAT-STAT – a system for supporting lessons on probability and statistics and also for estimating parameters based on experimental data.

8. PS-STAT – a system for analysing experimental data addressed to non-specialists in other areas.
9. ASD – a system for demonstrating and analysing algorithms and data structures.
10. MET-NUM – a system for supporting learning numerical methods (computer realisation of mathematical calculations) and for performing some numerical calculations.

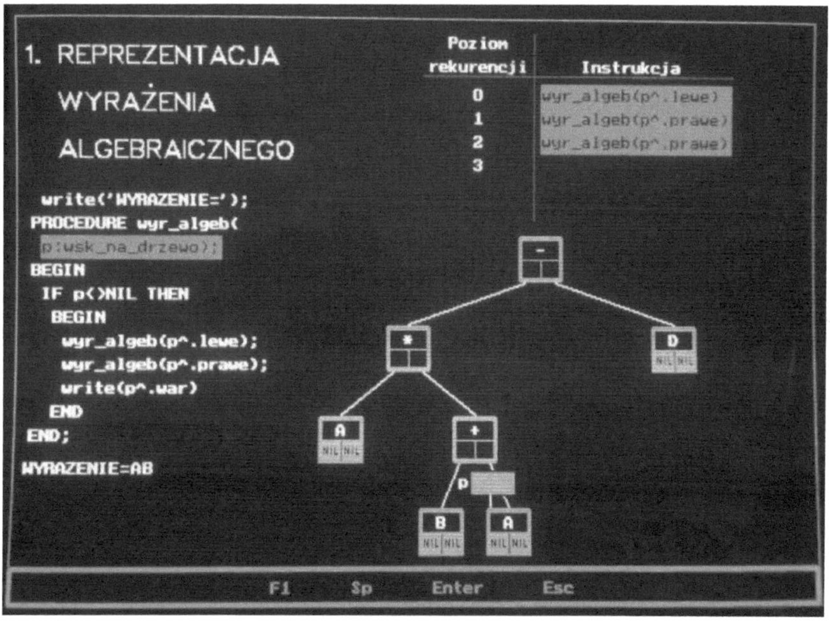

Fig. 3. A screen with Package EI – demonstration of a tree data structure

The package was used to support learning and teaching of informatics (systems: SB, DYSKIETKA, TP-TOOL, ESO, DISC-MATH, ASD, EKO-SYM, MAT-STAT, PS-STAT, MET-NUM), mathematics (systems: DISC-MATH and ASD, MAT-STAT, MET-NUM), statistics (systems: EKO-SYM, PS-STAT, MAT-STAT), and biology (system EKO-SYM).

Package EI, supported by very rich written educational materials, could be used in a number of ways: by a teacher, during a lecture or exercises – to illustrate concepts and their properties, and to demonstrate methods and algorithms; by students – during a teacher's demonstration, when working in groups and individually. Depending on the preparation and expertise level of students, package EI could be gradually used:

- as a tool for demonstrating concepts, their properties, methods and algorithms;
- as a demonstration tool in which the user can make experiments with different values of parameters of her/his own choice;
- to plan and design exercises supported by the package;
- to write their own programs utilising some software modules available in the package.

In our vision, when we were designing and implementing Package EI, similarly to Seymour Papert [1980]: *the student programs the computer* instead of *the computer is being used to program the student.*

From today's point of view, package EI appeared ahead of time – teachers were not prepared and trained to use it. Some of the systems from EI have been redesigned and implemented for the Windows environment, and now are available as open educational resources, see `http://mmsyslo.pl/Materialy/Oprogramowanie`.

6.3.3 Educational Software for Mathematics

As indicated many times in this paper, mathematicians were very active in introducing computers to classrooms to support instruction. Several packages of software for mathematics were designed and produced for Junior (see Section 5.1), e.g., by VULCAN. Some packages for mathematics were also designed in Projects RRI.14 and RRI.16, e.g. a package Kartezjusz. Package EI described above, contained some systems for augmenting and supporting mathematical topics, mainly from an informatics point of view, e.g., for numerical calculations.

Very active was a group of mathematicians from a seminar of Wacław Zawadowski at Warsaw University – A. Walat, M. Dąbrowski, K. Dałek, E. Sepko-Guzicka, W. Guzicki, W. Jędrychowski and others – who designed and produced many software packages (for Junior and Windows environments) for mathematics education, in particular in the form of textbook extensions (see [Walat, Zawadowski, 1988]) – computer programs were used to better explain and visualise mathematical concepts and to perform some sample calculations to demonstrate behaviour of mathematical formulas and problem solutions.

6.4 Conference 'Informatics in Schools'

In 1985, MEN and two local computer institutions in Wałbrzych (ZETO Świdnica and NOT Wałbrzych) initiated an annual conference 'Informatics in Schools' which has been organised for the next 20 years (the author was the program chairman of the last 15 conferences). Now these annual meetings are continued as 'Informatics in Education'.

The conference was organised in cooperation with local higher education institutions in different cities of Poland and gathered each year 400-600 participants coming from schools and universities, software and hardware companies and also decision makers from the institutions which ran schools. The conference was an opportunity to exchange ideas, solutions, and school experience. School and academic teachers had a chance to present research and practice papers, and companies arranged exhibitions of new software and hardware products. It was the main place in Poland where the school (education practice) was meeting the market (companies) proposals.

6.5 Magazines and Journals

The most influential computer magazine in Poland in the second half of the1980s was Bajtek. It was established in 1985; Władylsaw Majewski was his first editor in chief. *Bajtek was popular among the Polish youth and played an important role in disseminating computer knowledge. … Its goal was described as follows: Bajtek is a popular magazine dedicated to all issues linked with information processing.* [Wasiak, 2014]. The second Polish magazine, Komputer, established in 1986, addressed readers interested in using computers in their professional careers.

In 1990, a monthly journal Komputer w Szkole (eng. Computer in School) was funded by OFEK, fully dedicated to the use of computers in formal and in-formal education. The journal published: curricula and syllabuses, official documents and reports from MEN, reports on school initiatives and experiences, research papers by school and academic teachers, conference reports, and translations of articles written by international experts (e.g., by A.P Ershov, Eric de Corte). The journal was a very important source of information and materials for school teachers.

Computer magazines and journals were very popular among members of computer clubs which provided young people access to computers and programming courses. Such clubs were established under the auspices of local and central youth associations, companies, and schools. In 1993, at a total of 3,792 state-sponsored cultural centres, 842 had computer clubs and 422 with computer rooms. The clubs totaled 15,283 members, including 11,499 children under 15 (see [Wasiak, 2014]). In many cases computer clubs were children's first contact with computers.

6.6 Institutions Supporting Computers in Education

As indicated above, in the 1980s, before the democratic break-down in Poland in1989, several associations, private or non-public institutions, and companies were funded in Poland, which were involved in computerisation of schools by: sharing their knowledge and experience with MEN and with schools (PTI), providing schools with software and hardware solutions, training teachers and decision makers. Below, we shortly describe the role and achievements of three such institutions.

6.6.1 PTI – Polskie Towarzystwo Informatyczne

The Polish Information Processing Society (PTI) was established in May 1981 in Warsaw. One of its goals was (and still is) to support education (informatics education and computer use in other disciplines) on all levels and in all types of schools. PTI was very active in education when the first personal microcomputers arrived in Poland, in particular – in schools. The Society donated microcomputers to teachers' training courses, and funded and established computer clubs in public places and in schools. Very active was the Society's Branch in Wrocław led by Zygmunt Mazur, which initiated a movement 'Komputer w tornistrze' (eng. Computer in a School Backpack) and in 1985 organised 'Wakacje z komputerem' (eng. Vacations with a computer).

As mentioned above, the PTI team led by S. Waligórski, in 1985 proposed a curriculum for the subject *Elements of informatics*, which then was approved by MEN for the use in schools. PTI was also very active in the process of choosing Elwro 800 Junior as a Polish school computer.

6.6.2 VULCAN

The VULCAN company, founded in Wrocław in 1988, was involved in designing and producing software for education and for school administration. First programs ran on ZX Spectrum and Elwro 800 Junior, and then the company switched to Windows software. In 1989 VULCAN sold to MEN 40 education programs for ZX Spectrum and Elwro 800 Junior (see Section 5.1) and invested the profit into its development.

In the second half of the 1980s, Vulcan participated in the government Project RRI-16 (see Section 4.2), as a software designer and producer. In the beginning of the 1990s, VULCAN represented Poland in the Program EPES (European Pool of Educational Software), and its duty was to adopt foreign programs to the requirements of Polish schools. (System DISC-MATH from Package EI, see Section 6.3, represented Poland in the Pool).

6.6.3 OFEK – Ogólnopolska Fundacja Edukacji Komputerowej

National Foundation for Computer Education was founded in Wrocław in 1986, as an initiative of Wrocław companies and academic institutions. The Foundation specialises in teacher training and in delivery of computer equipment to schools. It operates through branches. In the 1990s, the OFEK branch in Jelenia Góra was responsible for publications – it published the second edition of the first textbook for informatics in Poland (see Section 6.2) and it was a publisher of the journal *Komputer w Szkole*.

The most active branch of OFEK is now in Poznań. It was involved in editing, publishing and delivering to high school the Package EI (see Section 6.3). Now this branch of OFEK is mainly involved in teacher training – in the project *Intel – Teach to the Future* almost 80 000 teachers were trained.

7 The Years That Have Followed

In the 1990s, the history of computers in schools and in education was greatly influenced by a new communication medium – the Internet. IBM PC standard (in hardware and in system and application software) dominated the school equipment, which recently is moving towards mobile solutions. Now our students are always connected to the world by devices they carry in their pockets. Recently a new challenge has emerged – can they learn while they are connected?

In the mid-1990s in Poland, the term 'information and communication technology – ICT' was accepted by the education policy makers and a new subject *Information Technology* was introduced to the curriculum by the Education Reform of 1997 and then to high schools in 2002. Informatics as a separate subject for all students returned to high schools in 2012 as a result of the next reform of 2008, for more details see [Sysło, Kwiatkowska, 2008; Sysło, 2011].

Acknowledgements. The author wishes to thank many colleagues who provided him with many historical materials and memories. Special thanks go to: A. Skowron, A. Walat, J. Nowak, W. Rudolf, W. Cellary, P. Krysztofiak, G. Hardt-Olejniczak, Z. Rogowski, and K. Święcicki.

References

AC-LOGO: Podręcznik użytkownika AC-LOGO. Wersja 1.2 dla IBM PC, OFEK, Jelenia Góra (1993)

Bielecki, J.: Turbo Pascal. Oprogramowanie Elwro 800 Junior. WN-T, Warszawa (1988)

Burewicz, A., Gulińska, H., Miranowicz, N., Szmidt, H.: Edukacyjne programy komputerowe w nauczaniu chemii. OFEK Jelenia Góra 1992. Biblioteka metodyczna 'Komputera w Szkole' (5) (1992) Burewicz, A. (red.)

Cellary, W., Rykowski, J.: System Operacyjny CP/J dla mikrokomputera Elwro 800 Junior. WN-T, Warszawa (1988)

Cellary, W., Krysztofiak, P.: Elwro 800 Junior. WN-T, Warszawa (1988)

CP/J, Basic – Opis języka, Oprogramowanie Elwro 800 Junior, Wrocław (1987)

Czyżo, E., Zawadowski, W.: Pierwsze kontakty z mikrokomputerem ZX Spectrum. WSiP, Warszawa (1987)

Gurbiel, E., Krupicka, H., Płoski, Z.: Programowanie i Logo. Wydawnictwo Uniwersytetu Wrocławskiego, Wrocław (1987) Płoski, Z. (red.)

Hallay, J.: Algorytmy. In: Matematyka, Część 2. Informatyka, Zeszyty Naukowe IKN, pp. 6–46. WSiP, Warszawa (1981)

Iglewski, M., Madey, J., Matwin, S.: Pascal. Język wzorcowy. Pascal 6000. WN-T, Warszawa (1979)

Kania, J.: Pierwsze kroki w Logo. WSiP, Warszawa (1987)

Katalog_1: Katalog oprogramowania użytkowego opracowanego przez szkoły wyższe w ramach programu RRI.14 (1988-1990), Część I i II. Wydawnictwo Politechniki Wrocławskiej, Wrocław (1990)

Katalog_2: Katalog oprogramowania dydaktycznego, M.M. Sysło (red.), Materiały Konferencji 'Informatyka w szkole, VI', Błażejewko, Wrzesień 1990, IIUWr-MEN-OFEK (1990)

Łukaszewicz, J.: Programowanie dla maszyny Elliott 803. PWN, Warszawa (1966)

Papert, S.: Mindstorms. Children, Computers, and Powerful Ideas. Basic Book, New York (1980)

Paszkowski, S.: Algol 60, Wydanie I. PWN, Warszawa (1965)

Pawlak Z., Skowron A., Elementy teorii maszyn matematycznych dla IV klasy, Skrypt dla uniwersyteckich klas matematycznych w XIV Liceum Ogólnokształcącym im. K. Gottwalda w Warszawie, Instytut Pedagogiki, Warszawa (1970)

Pawlak, Z.: Maszyny matematyczne. PZWS, Warszawa (1971)

Program_1: Program Liceum Ogólnokształcącego. Elementy informatyki, MOiW, WSiP, Warszawa (1985)

Program_2: Program Szkoły Podstawowej. Elementy informatyki, Klasa VIII, MOiW, WSiP, Warszawa (1990)

Rudolf, W.: JU-LEK wersja 1. System autorski dla mikrokomputera Elwro 800 Junior, OFEK, Jelenia Góra (1990)

Rudolf, W.: System autorski JU-LEK. Informatyka 8, 18–21 (1990)

Sepko-Guzicka, E., Guzicki, W.: Zastosowanie komputerów w nauczaniu matematyki. IKN, Warszawa (1987)

Skowron, A.: Zbiór zadań z teorii maszyn matematycznych dla uniwersyteckich klas matematycznych w XIV Liceum Ogólnokształcącym im. Gottwalda w Warszawie, Instytut Pedagogiczny, Warszawa (1970)
Skowron, A.: Podstawy teorii maszyn matematycznych, Materiały pomocnicze dla nauczycieli. Tom 6. IKN, Warszawa (1974)
Skowron, A.: Konspekty lekcyjne eksperymentalnego nauczania informatyki w III klasach szkół średnich, Część V. Algorytm Uniwersalny, IKN, Warszawa (1976)
Sysło, M.M.: Pakiet 'Elementy Informatyki'. Komputer w Edukacji 1, 15–25 (1994)
Sysło, M.M.: From elements of informatics to information technology across curriculum: the Polish approach. Int. J. Cont. Engineering and Lifelong Learning 11, 526–533 (2001)
Sysło, M.M., Kwiatkowska, A.B.: The challenging face of informatics education in Poland. In: Mittermeir, R.T., Sysło, M.M. (eds.) ISSEP 2008. LNCS, vol. 5090, pp. 1–18. Springer, Heidelberg (2008)
Sysło, M.M.: Outreach to prospective informatics students. In: Kalaš, I., Mittermeir, R.T. (eds.) ISSEP 2011. LNCS, vol. 7013, pp. 56–70. Springer, Heidelberg (2011)
Textbook_1: Dańko W., Gurbiel E., Jarzębowski Z., Kołczyk E., Krupicka H., Łukojć K., Płoski Z., Sysło M.M., Witkowski J., Zuber R.: Elementy informatyki, M.M. Sysło (red.). Wydawnictwo Uniwersytetu Wrocławskiego, Wrocław (1989); WN PWN, Warszawa (1991)
Textbook_2: Gurbiel E., Jarzębowski Z., Kołczyk E., Krupicka H., Łukojć K., Płoski Z., Sysło M.M., Zuber R.: Elementy informatyki. Rozwiązania zadań, M.M. Sysło (red.). OFEK Jelenia Góra (1990); Biblioteka metodyczna 'Komputera w Szkole' (4). WN PWN, Warszawa (1995)
Textbook_3: Gurbiel E., Hardt-Olejniczak G., Kołczyk E., Krupicka H., Łukojć K., Płoski Z., Sysło M.M., Witkowski J., Zuber R.: Elementy informatyki. Poradnik metodyczny dla nauczycieli, M.M. Sysło (red.). WN PWN, Warszawa (1997)
UNESCO: Information and Communication Technology in Education. A curriculum for schools and programme of teacher development, UNESCO, Paris (2002)
Walat, A.: Ćwiczenia z podstaw informatyki. Zbiór zadań z rozwiązaniami przykładowymi i uwagami metodycznymi, Część I i II. IKN, Warszawa (1978)
Walat, A., Zawadowski, W.: Instrukcja do kasety 'Matematyka 6'. WSiP, Warszawa (1988)
Walat, A., Zawadowski, W.: Matematyka III. Podręcznik dla liceum ogólnokształcącego i liceum zawodowego. WSiP (1988)
Walat, A.: Wybrane problemy dydaktyki informatyki, OFEK Jelenia Góra. Biblioteka metodyczna 'Komputera w Szkole' (6) (1990)
Waligórski, S.: Programowanie w języku Logo. Oprogramowanie Elwro 800 Junior. WN-T, Warszawa (1990)
Wasiak, P.: Playing and Copying: Social Practices of Home Computer Users in Poland During the 1980s. In: Alberts, G., Oldenziel, R. (eds.) Hacking Europe: From Computer Cultures to Demoscenes, History of Computing. Springer, London (2014)
Witek, S.: Próba kształcenia programistów w liceum ogólnokształcącym. Matematyka XIX 1, 24–30 (1966)
Zuber, R.: O realizacji przedmiotu 'Programowanie i obsługa maszyn cyfrowych'. Matematyka XIX 2, 76–83 (1966)
Zuber, R.: Metody numeryczne i programowanie. PZWS, Warszawa (1972)

Catching the Bug: Pupils and Punched Cards in South Africa in the Late 1970s

Martin S. Olivier

Department of Computer Science, University of Pretoria, Pretoria, South Africa
ms.olivier@olivier.ms

Abstract. This paper describes my memories as one of the pupils taking computer studies in South Africa in the late 1970s, when such programs were still uncommon. The differences between how the subject was approached back then and current approaches are not only due to technological developments; the 1970s curriculum reflects a fundamentally different approach.

Keywords: Computer studies, high school/secondary school, education.

1 Introduction

This paper is an account of my personal experience of studying computing at school level in the late 1970s. Where possible I verified my recollections, but this was not possible in all instances. The ENIAC was arguably the first 'real' computer built and switched on in 1947 [1]. The UNIVAC I followed as the first commercial computer. In 1951 one was installed, in 1952 two, in 1953 three and then, in 1954, twelve [2]. These installations were, however, mostly for government (and, in particular, military) use. The late 1950s saw the introduction of Fortran — a high-level programming language for engineering (and scientific) use [3]. Cobol — ostensibly for business use — was the next landmark event. Its design was completed in 1959 and the first compiler was available in 1960 [4]. But the academic differences — about software rather than hardware — reached boiling point in the 1960s. Algol-68 lead to significant unhappiness and the design of Pascal, not only as a programming language, but as an alternative philosophy to programming language design. IBM's OS/360 operating system was late and over budget [5]. The complexity of Honeywell's Multics operating system inspired Ken Thompson and Dennis Ritchie to design the much simpler Unix. As the issues emerged it became obvious that the problems were hard and required thorough academic inquiry. Often studied in other departments (such as mathematics or engineering) it became clear that computing had its specific problem characteristics that could not be addressed by these other disciplines. The first computer science departments in the world were established in the late 1960s. In addition, the use of the computer spread, providing those who wished to learn more about computing with opportunities — if they were lucky enough. And so it came that the study of computing started finding its tentative roots in schools in many countries around the world. This is my account of being one of the early pupils who enrolled for such a course in 1978 in South Africa.

A. Tatnall and B. Davey (Eds.): History of Computers in Education, IFIP AICT 424, pp. 291–301, 2014.

2 The Beginnings

My father bought his first calculator in about 1972. It could add, subtract, multiply and divide. But, perhaps more importantly, it had a bright eight digit 7-segment LED display. And there were riddles that, when one performed the calculation, yielded answers like 71077345. Turning it upside-down revealed the real answer. This was clearly an amazing machine — and we were into the computer age.

I am not sure when the various education departments in the country introduced Computer Studies as a school subject. It arrived at the neighbouring school in 1977. Back then our schooling started with a grade 1 and grade 2 (or sub A and sub B in some provinces). This was followed by another ten years referred to as standard 1 to standard 10 (with standard 10 also known as matric). In standard 8 one had to select the six subjects that one would take until matric. Computer studies was introduced as a seventh subject for standards 8, 9 and 10 offered at only a few schools. The following year I was in standard 8 and enrolled for computer studies, along with three or four classmates. The subject was to be offered at the neighbouring school, which made it particularly easy for us to attend. A large proportion of the class came from schools as far as 35km away. Classes were scheduled for one afternoon per week from 15:00 to 17:00. (The normal school day ran from 7:45 until 13:45.) Unfortunately for many these classes clashed with sport and cultural activities scheduled for the afternoon. Hence all my classmates except one dropped the subject pretty soon after it started. The two of us who persevered through the first year did continue until the end of matric, but in different schools. However, that is a story for somewhat later in this tale.

When I think back to computer studies 30 odd years ago, the main memories are about programming and programming languages. However, after digging up my old course material I was reminded that the course was about much more than just programming. Let us rather continue with these primary memories.

3 Programming and Programming Languages

Our introduction to programming (and, in fact, most other topics) followed a clear bottom-up approach — something that would probably be frowned upon today, but an approach that did have its benefits. Our language for standard 8 was Samos — an interpreted language based on assembly language. To design a program the logical starting point was a flowchart, which was, of course, hand-drawn using a stencil with all the necessary shapes (including some shapes that I to this day do not know what their purpose was). The primary shapes were the processing rectangles, the decision diamonds, the input/output parallelograms and the beginning and end ovals. The major concession in Samos was the ability to input and output variables with one simple instruction — compared to the usual effort required in a real assembly language.

In fact, Samos was more than a language: Samos was a hypothetical computer, with architecture and programming intermingled. The discussion of Samos begins with a discussion of ferrite cores and how they could be magnetised in one or the other direction to represent a 0 or a 1. Words on this computer consisted of 61 bits — that is, ten bytes and one bit (at a time when many real computers used 6-bit bytes). The memory consisted out of 500 such words (numbered from 000 to 499).

The memory formed the basis of the comprehensive architecture that followed: The CPU, an arithmetic unit and input and output units were added to complete the picture. A handful of registers in the CPU (and arithmetic unit) were described, and it was said that the input unit is a card reader and the output unit a printer. Encoding data in the 6-bit bytes formed part of this exposition.

At this point we were almost ready to begin to discuss programming, but there was one other obstacle that remained before programming was possible. How would instructions be encoded on this computer?

The lone leftmost bit of the 61-bit word would normally be used to indicate the sign of the number stored in that word; for instructions this was not used. The next three (6-bit) bytes would be used for an opcode. This was followed by a 3-byte indexing value (which is not important for our immediate purposes). The remaining four bytes were the operand address.

The opcode was not the binary value we would (now) expect on a real computer; the three bytes were rather used to encode three characters, which was the mnemonic representation of some instruction. The very first program instruction we encountered was:

```
RWD 50
```

which meant 'read a word and store it in address (or memory word) 50. More specifically, it meant *read the first 11 characters from the next punched card and store it in word 50.*' The first character on that punched card would normally be the sign of a number, but is could also be blank for non-numeric input. The spacing of this RWD instruction was also important. To illustrate consider

```
s  012  34567  89 (Not part of the program)
   RWD         50
```

where s indicates the sign, bytes 0, 1 and 2 the opcode and bytes 6, 7, 8 and 9 the address to be used. Hence, no true assembly was required; this computer was literally programmed in machine code.

The next instruction introduced was `WWD` — write a word. And suddenly we were ready for our first program:

```
RWD 50
WWD 50
```

which would of course read a value from the punched card and print it on the printer.

The remaining instructions included some arithmetic instructions.

- `LDA` — Load accumulator
- `STO` — Store accumulator
- `ADD` — Add to accumulator
- `SUB` — Subtract from accumulator

In each case the operand indicated which value (which memory word) should be loaded, used for storage, added or subtracted. The list continues with MPY (multiply), DIV (divide) and even POW to raise the value in the accumulator to the indicated power. Later in the course SHL and SHR were added, that would shift the accumulator the indicated number of *bytes* left or right. This was often useful to isolate, say, the month, day and year of a date read in as a single line.

Note again that addressing was direct (rather than immediate). To square a number one would put the value 2 into one of the words and use that word. The program was always read into memory starting at word 0. Hence a program could have looked as follows (with lines consisting out of dots unimportant at this stage).

```
000...........
001+         2
002...........
003...........
004...........
005 POW      1
006...........
```

On the coding sheet the first three columns were used to number statements. The actual content of each word therefore was represented from column 4 onwards. Since word 001 starts with a + that word contains the constant 2. When, at `005` we say `POW 1`, we therefore square the number in the accumulator.

The next set of instructions dealt with flow control, and the names are self-explanatory.

- `HLT` — Halt
- `BRU` — Branch unconditionally
- `BMI` — Branch if minus (that is, if the value in the accumulator is negative)
- `BPL` — Branch if plus
- `BRZ` — Branch if zero

In each case the operand was the destination address to jump to if the condition was true. These instructions were complemented by `CMP` (compare), `BRL` (branch if low), `BRE` (branch if equal) and `BRH` (branch if high) instructions.

At this point it was possible to write basic programs. However one still desperately needed some way of dealing with array-like structures. This was provided by three index registers, which could be loaded, incremented, tested, stored and manipulated in a number of ways. The purpose of the index registers was to modify the operand address to support loops that could indeed process an array of numbers. Recall that bytes 4, 5 and 6 in the instruction word were reserved for indexing. They indicate whether the contents of index register 1, 2 and/or 3 should be added to the operand address. Therefore

```
S 012  3456  789 (Not part of the program)
  STO  010   100
```

would add the contents of index register 2 to 100 and use this sum as the effective address where the contents of the accumulator would be stored. If indexing was not used these three columns were left blank. As an aside, in the case of instructions that do not use an operand (such as `HLT`) the operand field was also left blank.

Note that the convention was to start every program with a `BRU`, followed by words occupied by constants or reserved for variables. The actual program started after this 'data part' and was the target of the `BRU` instruction in word 0. This is still standard practice in those rare situations where programmers work at such a low level. However, in courses I currently teach about malware analysis I note that 'modern' students find this concept (or even the concept of programs just being data that happens to be executed) rather foreign.

As noted, programming consisted of designing a flowchart that represented the solution; the flowchart had to be at a level low enough to easily translate into the (mnemonic) machine code described above. The flowcharts were then duly translated to Samos, where, just like in any other assembly language, every decision diamond was translated into code that contained a conditional jump (to a numeric destination!). This was a decade after Dijkstra's famous letter about the inherent harms of the goto statement [6]. And while Dijkstra was obviously correct in his assessment, I often did wonder if we did not gain some insight into the operation of computers that was missing for those who started by learning structured programming (or any of the subsequent or alternative paradigms). Yes, goto is harmful when developing code — especially if that code needs to be maintained. However, I doubt that the expected outcome of computer studies was that we would be trained programmers — just like the expected outcome of mathematics was not that we would be mathematicians. And those who went on to study computer science after school seemed to make the switch quite easily.

Once the program was flowcharted it was converted to code and this code was copied to coding sheets — in pencil so that writing errors could easily be corrected. And then those coding sheets were sent to the education department's regional headquarters, which had a computer (or remote access to one). There our coding sheets were punched onto punched cards and the programs were run. A few weeks later one would receive the stack of cards back, as well as the printout of this initial run. If the program (based on the test data) was correct, one was awarded full marks — ten out of ten — for that assignment. Else one was allowed to correct the program by (if I recall correctly) inserting notes into the stack of cards. These stacks were returned to the regional centre, where the "punch ladies" made the necessary corrections by punching new cards to reflect the changes we requested and inserting them at the appropriates places in the card stack. The program was run once more using this amended stack, and the cards and printouts arrived back at the school two or three weeks later. If the program worked this time one earned eight out of ten marks for the assignment. If it failed yet again, the teacher had to mark it and assign a mark between 0 and 7 to one's attempt. The process was sometimes slowed down a bit when punching errors occurred and one, in principle, deserved another chance.

One of the elements that would later become part and parcel of programming — test runs and debugging — did not exist for us. Careful coding and checking algorithms using trace tables were implicit in our curriculum. Even in later years — at university — when we could fit in a couple of test runs to debug our programs before submission — each run was time consuming, initially requiring hours per attempt, but later still with a single digit number of attempts that could be tried in a day, careful coding and clear thinking was still the norm. My observation was that this really changed when Borland's Turbo Pascal was introduced at universities, where press of the F9 button yielded results within seconds, and students could afford to move from a thinking strategy to a trial and error strategy.

In the following year — 1979, standard 9 — we were ready to face a high-level language, and the (obvious?) choice was Fortran. What made it 'obvious' was the fact that not that many compilers were available for the mainframe computer(s) the department of education was operating. Perhaps some perspective is required in this regard. The first microprocessor, the 4-bit Intel 4004 was released at the end of 1971. The Intel 8080, an 8-bit processor that could form the basis of a microcomputer was released in 1974. The first real microcomputer, the famous Altair 8800, was designed in 1975, based on this chip. Various kit-based computers followed. The first complete personal computers followed in 1977 and later (Commodore PET, Tandy Corporation's TRS-80 and Apple Computer's Apple II — all in 1977; the Atari 400/800 in 1978/1979; the Sinclair ZX80 in 1980; the Texas Instruments TI-99 in 1979; the Commodore VIC-20 and Commodore 64 in 1982 and 1980; the Acorn Atom in 1980; the BBC Micro in 1981; and, of course the IBM PC in 1981). The only high-level language available on these microcomputers was Basic, with Microsoft's implementations very common (and, the language that was the reason Microsoft was formed at all). However, for us those microcomputers remained a dream — often costing upwards of 1980 USD 500 it was not even a thinkable option to bring computers into schools. Many universities had access to minicomputers and the esoteric languages, such as Pascal and Algol were running on them. But neither the department of education, nor the schools had access to them. It is also worth noting that the University of Pretoria — my current employer — established its computer science department in 1976. So, in 1979, Fortran was indeed the obvious choice to introduce us to high-level languages.

However, the modern reader will probably not even know about the various flavours of Fortran that existed. In 1979 the FORTRAN-77 standard was already published, but the language in common use was Fortran IV. FORTRAN 77 would introduce some major improvements, of which the block IF-statements would arguably have been the most important for pupils learning to program. However, FORTRAN IV it was, which by implication meant an IF-statement was to be followed by a single statement that would be executed if the tested condition was true. There wasn't really any ELSE part associated with an IF-statement, unless one interprets the *arithmetic* IF-statement in this manner. The arithmetic IF-statement looked something like this:

```
IF (N*K+5) 100,200,300
```

The `N*K+5` could be any arithmetic statement. If this statement evaluated to a negative value, the program would jump to the statement next to the first label following the IF; in this example, a negative results would cause execution to be continued at the statement labelled 100. Similarly, a zero result would transfer control to the statement associated with the second label in the list (which would be 200 in the current example). Finally, a positive result would cause it to jump to the final label.

A 'normal' IF-statement would look something like the following

```
IF (N.GT.2) K=5
```

The `.GT.` in this example is the logical condition and is an abbreviation for *greater than*. One typical way to code a modern `if n>2 then k=5 else k=6;` back then was

```
K=6
IF (N.GT.2) K=5
```

However, in most cases one simply resorted to a `GOTO`-statement after an `IF`-statement, so our experience from the assembly-like Samos did come in very handy. As an aside, another 'strange' feature of Fortran was the fact that spaces were immaterial almost anywhere. Therefore writing `GO TO` was equivalent to writing `GOTO` or, for that matter, `G OT O`.

Our programs were developed in the same manner as Samos programs were — by flowcharting them. The remainder of the process was also similar. Programs were written (in pencil) on coding sheets and would be sent away for punching and *the* run. If errors were found, a second attempt was again allowed, after which a failed attempt meant that the teacher had to assign an appropriate mark.

In matric the language changed again, but in more ways than one. Our standard 8 and 9 teacher was not yet qualified to teach computer studies on matric level. We had two options: either go to the regional centre in Boksburg for matric or attend the English classes which were offered at Springs Boys High — about 10km from my own school. Boksburg was way too far for me, so once a week I cycled the 7km to my school in the mornings, the 10km to Springs Boys' High after school and the 8km back home in the evening — dressed in the fashion we inherited from the British: Trousers, long-sleeved shirt, tie and blazer.

The previous paragraph adds a number of elements to the story that has little to do with computer studies, but does add some historical context. Back then South Africa was a bilingual country with Afrikaans and English as the official languages. My home language was (and is) Afrikaans, which evolved from Dutch which my ancestors spoke when they came to South Africa twelve generations earlier (at various points in the 1600s). When I started my school career in 1969 it quickly became obvious that there was a huge divide between the Afrikaans and English communities with insults (and sometimes other objects) being flung between the two groups of pupils at bus stops and the few other points of contact. It was something I never quite understood. When I started cycling to school in the mid-1970s the problem disappeared from my view since shared bus stops were no longer an issue. But it was with some trepidation that I awaited my final year of education.

My classmates who came from afar could go to Boksburg at little additional cost. The only classmate from my own school could also make a plan to attend the Boksburg classes. About five of us joined the English group in Springs. However, the strife was something of the past and no language-related incidents occurred.

It should perhaps be pointed out that not too far from us incidents that were ostensibly language-related did occur. Just a short while before this — in 1976 — the Soweto uprisings occurred; the stated reason was the fact that some of the courses for black pupils were presented in Afrikaans. Whether that was the true reason for the riots may possibly be answered in due course. While the school children from the townships would probably never have phrased it like this, a better justification for the riots was arguably the fact that the future for which they were being prepared differed markedly from the future for which I was being prepared. I had the opportunity — with some effort — to study computing. I never asked, but I knew there was no such option in the townships.

In 1980 the *other* must-do computer language was Cobol, which was our programming language to study in matric. The process we followed when programming remained unchanged, apart from the new opportunities introduced by the new language.

However, 1980 was special because I got three opportunities to actually interact with computers. My matric teacher, Martin de Klerk, was a wonderful man who went out of his way to create opportunities for those of us who were clearly interested in the subject. There were a couple of factories in town and I have no idea how many of them had computers. However, one — Ultra High Pressure Units which manufactured diamonds — had a computer and Mr De Klerk arranged a visit for me. At long last I could punch some cards, put them on the hopper, read them in and see my program produce results. This introduced a few challenges because I never before had to deal with JCL (Job Control Language) or whatever the control language was for that particular computer. So, I only managed a few runs during the day, but I was inside a computer room and, for the first time in my life, saw a real computer.

The second event was not related to computer studies as a subject. During the latter part of the year some of us (pupils in general, rather than those taking computer studies) were invited to a weeklong visit to the nearest university — the then Rand Afrikaans University in Johannesburg. During the week we had lectures from the computer science, mathematics and mathematical statistics departments. The computer science department used an internally developed language that they called *Staal* (*Studente taal*, Which translates to *students' language)* to teach us the basics of programming. Staal was a rather simple language based on PL/I (and translated by a preprocessor into PL/I before it was compiled by the PL/I compiler). Given our earlier languages, this language was wonderful: It supported while loops, if-then-else structures that could include arbitrary content in the then and else clauses and this was supported without the 'bloat' of Cobol. We again coded our programs on coding sheets, but stepwise refinement replaced the initial flowcharting. The coding sheets were punched, but we had access to punches and could correct our own programs. We still had to submit them to an operator to get run (but this happened within an hour or so). While the course was aimed at those without programming experience, the few of us who had some experience were given the freedom to explore — an opportunity which I grabbed. The next year I enrolled for my first degree (in computer science and mathematics) at the Rand Afrikaans University. An interesting fact is that the department of computer science there was established in 1970 — quite early in global terms.

The third event was also not related to computer studies per se. I managed to save enough money to buy an HP 33E programmable calculator. The calculator was programmed in RPN (Reverse Polish Notation) and had 49 memory 'steps' to store one's program. This taught me another skill: how to optimise one's programs to fit into that tiny space. I never succeeded to properly program it to play tic tac toe despite several attempts…

4 The Rest of the Curriculum

As noted earlier, the memories that remain of computer studies mostly relate to programming. I have, however, kept a file of the material we received as handouts. (Obviously suitable school-level textbooks were not available at the time.) Unfortunately I have not kept a record of what non-programming material was covered in which year. I therefore list them in the order in which they are in my file. Note that my handouts were in Afrikaans and the translated titles I provide below may not be the title that was in fact used on the English version of the handout. The ideas would be identical.

Not surprisingly, the first handout is entitled *Algorithms and flowcharts.* This consists of 27 A4 pages explaining what an algorithm is and how one represents it using a flowchart. It ends with a document reference IDR/DVN/76.01.13, which suggests that it had been created for a course starting in January 1976; it is very likely that 1976 would have been the first year the subject was offered in the province, meaning I was part of the third cohort.

The second document is the Samos 'manual', explaining how one programs in Samos. It consists of 41 A4 sheets and ends with the reference SJPK/REKENAARWETENSKAP/DVN/75.09.08.

The third document (undated) is about the *social implications and future development of computers*. Such historical documents about the future often make for interesting reading. Unfortunately this brief (three page) document says more about the history of computing than its future. It does note that the use of electronic data banks (as they were called then) was gaining popularity. It notes that one of the concerns is the storage of confidential data, but expresses the optimistic assumption that we may assume that (freely translated) "suitable protection measures will be introduced." It also notes that the replacement of cash by cards is promising, and notes the "immense value of a permanent record" of an individual's transaction history. Finally, it notes how beneficial an appropriate combination of computing and television may be for education.

A recurring theme is the representation of data in the computer. Almost all handouts start with the reminder that data is stored in binary and then say something about the operation of ferrite core memory (which can be magnetised in one of two directions). However, from that point of departure a rather diverse set of notions is covered. *Numbers in the computer* is a 44 page handout dealing with binary representation, binary operations and conversions to and from binary. This is followed by a brief discussion of the use of any base. Then the bases 2, 4, 8 and 16 get special attention — in particular conversions between numbers represented in these bases. Next (binary) code decimal systems are introduced. The attention then returns to binary for a discussion of fixed and floating point numbers, and a discussion of complementary arithmetic in binary.

Another 19 page handout deals with logical variables. Logical operations, gates and truth tables form the essence of this document (which is also undated).

A thorough 38 page treatise on arithmetic in any base for integers, fixed point and floating point numbers carries the reference IDR:HS:JF:1979-03-01.

A handout about data structures and data storage continues the theme of data representation. Viewed from today's perspective it addresses an almost incoherent range of topics. The first item on the agenda is (logical) files mentioning that they consist of records, fields and characters. Then "expression trees" (in essence, parse trees for arithmetic expressions) are discussed. This is followed by a discussion of physical media such as disc packs (as typically used on mainframes) and floppy discs (which, it is stated, contain 77 tracks divided into 26 sectors. The discussion of tapes that follows continues the theme of physical media, but the emphasis is on how logical data blocks are recorded on tape. Some remarks about tape cartridges follow. Then the logical concepts of sequential and random access are introduced. Finally a few brief remarks about data banks follow. The final paragraph seems to predict the Web. Freely translated it reads as follows:

It is envisaged that telephone will in future serve as terminals and everyday television sets as video screens. Home occupants, students and pupils will then be able to telephonically connect to these databases and extract data from these data banks such that the results will be displayed on the television sets. They will, for example, be able to obtain information about aspects of the weather, information about plants, chemistry, astronomy, etc. by connecting to a specific data bank.

The final document in my file covers Cobol in (only) 24 pages, with three additional pages of handwritten notes (probably written by our teacher) completing our introduction to Cobol.

The fact that my file contains nothing about Fortran implies that my set of handouts is incomplete; however, I think it is complete enough to provide a fairly complete overview of the computer studies curriculum.

5 Conclusion

These were my experiences in the late 1970s in computer studies at school. My future was determined. I enrolled for a degree in computer science, eventually obtained a PhD in computer science and am currently a professor of computer science. I am still fascinated by these wonderful machines and the line between work and fun is often blurred.

In the 1990s, as a lecturer, I experienced classes full of students who grew up with (personal) computers and shared the love of the technology. For me work was fun and (hopefully) for many of them studying was fun. We were a community of people with a shared love who were given the opportunity to discuss it (and call it 'work' or 'studying'). I was just in the fortunate position to get to know something about these machines long before most had the opportunity.

There is also a counterpoint. I am appalled by the extent to which computers are often misused. Perhaps the new apparent simplicity to use them is incommensurate with the impact they yield over people's lives. However, that is a point for another essay.

As far as I know very few of those of us who took computer studies became computer scientists. What value it added to others' lives I don't know. On me the impact was profound.

References

1. McCartney, S.: ENIAC: The Triumphs and Tragedies of the World's First Computer. Walker & Co (1999)
2. Ceruzzi, P.E.: A history of modern computing. MIT (1998)
3. Backus, J.W., Beeber, R.J., Best, S., Goldberg, R., Haibt, L.M., Herrick, H.L., Nelson, R.A., Sayre, D., Sheridan, P.B., Stern, H., Ziller, I., Hughes, R.A., Nutt, R.: The Fortran automatic coding system. Papers presented at the Western Joint Computer Conference: Techniques for Reliability, IRE-AIEE-ACM 1957 (Western), February 26-28, pp. 188–198. ACM, New York (1957)
4. Sammet, J.: The early history of Cobol. ACM SIGPLAN Notices 13(8), 121–161 (1978)
5. Brooks, F.P.: The Mythical Man-Month: Essays on Software Engineering. Addison Wesley (1975)
6. Dijkstra, E.: Go to statement considered harmful. Communications of the ACM **11**(3) (1968) 147–148

From Mathematics Teacher to Computer Assisted Learning Researcher

Richard Millwood

University of Dublin, Trinity College,
School of Computer Science and Statistics, Dublin, Ireland
richard.millwood@tcd.ie

Abstract. In this article, I discuss a journey from Mathematics and Computer Studies teacher in secondary school to an educational researcher in computer assisted learning. Along the way, in collaboration with other early pioneer teachers and encouraged by visionary education advisors a personal kit computer was constructed in 1978, an educational simulation created in 1979, before employment as an educational simulation developer as part of the UK Computers in the Curriculum project from 1980 to 1990. Although a specific case, issues of general interest about major upheavals in the educational and technology worlds and personal issues in an unusual and ground-breaking career are discussed.

Keywords: mathematics education, computer assisted learning, computing, computer studies, curriculum development, educational research.

1 Introduction

1.1 University

I graduated from university in 1976 with a degree in Mathematics and Physics. I had undertaken two computing courses in my studies, one to develop programming skills in Fortran and the second, described as Advanced Computing, was simply to develop a more ambitious project, which I failed! These early days at university involved the punching holes in 80-column cards and constructing a stack of such cards, each of which represented one line of program code. The cycle of trial and error to improve programs took a day, leaving the cards at the computing centre reception on one day and collecting them and a printout on the next.

1.2 Teaching

When I left university, it was to work at an inner London school to teach mathematics – there were no facilities to pursue computing in this job, but the next year in 1977 I left and took up a post at another London school where programming was taught and thus begun my educational computing career.

A. Tatnall and B. Davey (Eds.): History of Computers in Education, IFIP AICT 424, pp. 302–309, 2014.

2 The Early Days of Educational Computing in UK Schools

2.1 The State of the Art

This early career coincided with the development of microcomputers which became increasingly affordable for any school to explore as a focus for teaching computer studies or a tool for engaging children in thinking about other subjects. Until this moment, very few schools in the UK had any direct contact with computers except through local authority and higher education services to take mark-sense 80-column cards, carefully coded in BASIC with pencil marks before being whisked away on a motorbike to the local centre only to return a week later with a print-out saying 'Syntax error at line 10' and ready for corrections to be made by the learner – such was the experience in 1977 at the second school I joined.

2.2 Mathematics

My main activity was to teach mathematics and it was notable then that the Schools Mathematics Project (SMP), first developed in 1961 and taught to me in school, was coming to the end of its popularity. SMP was a mathematics curriculum designed partly in response to the Sputnik launch by the Soviet Union, which also led to the 'New Maths'. Much was done in SMP mathematics to provide an intellectual foundation for computer science, and just as real computers began to be available to children to explore, its modernism began a decline in popularity! In this school, the mathematics department and indeed the whole school was beginning a reappraisal of all curricula to focus on the challenge of mixed-ability teaching and seeking curriculum developments which could tackle this. One such development was the Secondary Mathematics Individual Learning Experiment (SMILE), which invited teachers to collaborate to design a resource-base scheme for students to follow individual pathways through an agreed mapping of tasks to key curriculum areas and levels. Although this school did not adopt the scheme, SMILE became hugely influential in my development and understanding of design for learning.

2.3 Computer Studies

Computers Studies in the school was taught to Certificate of Secondary Education (CSE) level, an examination through which students could attain an award at school leaving age (16) which was equivalent to a pass at the then predominant O-level qualification. The curriculum focused on a theoretical and historical account of the development of computers, an analysis of their component parts, a sense of the wider societal use of computers and their applications, some skills in flowcharting and a small amount of programming. In my first year, this programming was undertaken, as described earlier, through mark-sense cards on a weekly turnaround, but each year I taught brought change and new opportunity. The development of this subject was supported by an advisory service led by inspector Derek Esterson and advisor Bryan Weaver who organized courses and meetings for teachers. In addition the school was part of a consortium of schools developing the CSE examination in what was called 'Mode 3' form – both the questions and syllabus were developed by teachers with both examination and coursework marked by teachers checked by the examination boards' moderation processes to assure quality. This creative and participative design opportunity was very influential for me and my future career.

2.4 Teletype Interactivity

A telephone line and teletype was installed in the mathematics staff preparation room. The teletype was an electronic typewriter that could print onto a roll of paper at the mercurial pace of 11 characters per second (a page of 60 lines and 80 characters per line might thus take around a minute to print). This equipment allowed interactive programming through the telephone handset placed in an acoustic coupler and modem connected to the City of London Polytechnic's minicomputer.

Fig. 1. An acoustic coupler and modem – the telephone handset rested on the two cups to transmit and receive digital data encoded as sound frequencies

Although slow by modern standards, this facility permitted a quicker turnaround to develop a program, but was not located in the classroom and thus hard to integrate into lessons. On the other hand, it became a route to connect with other professionals, the local authority advisory staff and indeed other computer services in other higher education institutions through email. The only drawback was that the head of department ran an after school meat butchery business using the telephone for customers to place orders, and was not best pleased if I used it after lessons!

2.5 Kit Computers

In 1978, many kit computers began to be available to the general public to purchase and build. In my case, I saved up the £230 (about £1,100 in 2013 terms) for a NASCOM II single board computer. This computer used the then powerful Z-80 central processing unit, boasted 2 kilobytes of memory, three quarters of which was available to me to use in my programs, came with a keyboard and connected to a domestic television. I could (just about) save programs to audiotape, but had to write programs by directly entering hexadecimal codes into the memory, so spent time poring over the Z-80 instruction set to discover what was possible, and acting as my own assembler – writing mnemonics for instructions and translating into the hexadecimal alongside. A great deal of learning went on after assembling the kit with a soldering iron and I developed a profound understanding of the fetch-execute cycle and the underlying operation of a computer.

2.6 A Microcomputer for Education

In 1979 the school set aside budget for the purchase of a microcomputer which was designed and marketed to education. The Research Machines 380Z had been adopted as the standard for use in the Inner London Education Authority and some money offered to schools to help with purchase. This computer, although still storing programs onto audio cassette, was considerably more powerful, including the opportunity to use computer graphics on an 80 by 60 grid and a BASIC interpreter so that programming could be more readily related to real world problems. This computer displayed its output on a small black and white television monitor and was also capable of being connected through the telephone/acoustic coupler to interactive services and, more powerfully, to resources so that computer programs could be downloaded and used after saving to audio cassette. This connection could be made to both the City of London Polytechnic service and to other local authorities – I remember downloading new software from the then Hatfield Polytechnic in Hertfordshire. Unlike the modern internet, these were point-to-point connections made through individual telephone numbers, but despite this, there was a powerful sense of connectivity and opportunity that was remarkable for the time in such a humble setting.

3 Designing for Learning

3.1 Creating a Simulation

The new school computer became a regular visitor to my home, despite weighing several kilograms and being a two handed, two journey job to carry to my car. Ever since as a child seeing a computer simulate a frictionless ball, bouncing around a perfectly elastic snooker table on the television programme 'Tomorrow's World', I had craved the chance to make a program like it. I now set about writing a BASIC program to do just this, purely for my own gratification, and thus the program

SNOOKER was born. I added pockets, friction, restitution (energy lost on bouncing) and an interactive opportunity to set the direction and pace of the ball. If it landed on a pocket a success message was displayed, varied to reflect the number of attempts it had taken. I had conceived it as a test of my capability and as a game, so proudly showed it to my students in the school. I was surprised to find they liked it, wanted to play with it together and argue with each other about the angles. One even went to the cupboard to find a protractor to hold up against the screen in order to estimate the angle to pocket the ball. It was my first experience of the power of the computer to support learning of another subject, and launched a career in computer assisted learning. The motivation, persistence and delight in the students' eyes had made a huge impact on my educational thinking.

3.2 Consolidating the Design Thinking

As a consequence of this success, I signed up to a course titled 'BASIC Programs for Teaching – a course on program writing' on the design of educational software which was being offered by the Polytechnic of the South Bank in London. This course was led by Morfydd Edwards and Susan Eisenbach and introduced me to the evaluation outcomes of the National Development Programme in Computer Assisted Learning (NDPCAL). Although that project had been at higher education level, the evaluation findings proposed four categories of computer use which might support learning: instructional, revelatory, conjectural and emancipatory. This offered me an early practical analysis to inform my own designs.

3.3 Professional Development

Through all of these activities I met with other teachers in London who were developing educational software and joined the group 'Microcomputers in Computer Education' (MICE) led by Bryan Weaver, the advisory teacher for computer studies in the ILEA. Our goal was to collaborate to create interactive programs for learning concepts in computer studies itself – a typical example was to visually portray sorting algorithms.

My own proposed program was intended to visually simulate the layout and operations of the central processing unit of a computer and would respond to a simplified assembly language program. My intention was to bring these to life in a 'revelatory' mode (Millwood 1987) and relate them visually to the computer hardware.

Although there had been a growing interest in teaching programming concepts through animations in the context of higher education, it was new to be focussing such innovation on secondary school. Our work made impact on the practice of colleagues in the Inner London Education Authority and at the time was considered a vital part of the development of teaching computer studies there, with its work reported regularly in the newsletter distributed to computer studies teachers in London by the advisory service.

4 Research, Design and Development as a Career

4.1 Programming Full Time

By 1980, I realised that I wanted to spend all of my time developing educational programs and I set about looking for posts that might permit it. There was little or no commercial market at the time for such materials and the only place where I could see opportunity was in university education departments where curriculum development projects had been undertaken to research this new area. There were two key projects at the time. The first was titled 'Investigations into Teaching with Microcomputers as an Aid' (ITMA), a collaboration between The College of St Mark and St John and Nottingham University – it focussed at first on Mathematics education, but broadened into Geography and other subjects. The other was the 'Computers in the Curriculum Project' (CIC) based at the Centre for Science and Mathematics Education at Chelsea College London University. This project focussed at the time on science simulations for sixth form students and had been distributing software to schools globally on punched paper tape to be loaded onto central computers and operated by the kind of teletype that I had been using in school. Posts were advertised in both projects and I was offered the job with the CIC project, in the beginning to redesign the paper-type / print-out simulations for the new screen-based microcomputers.

4.2 Interoperability and Standards

A major concern for the CIC project was to ensure that owners of the varied kinds of microcomputer then available could access the software we developed. This meant either re-writing each program to suit the specific variant of BASIC and computer graphics / keyboard that each computer had to or find a way to write once using standards that would enable easy implementation in each platform. The latter course was developed by creating a library of subroutines in BASIC which attempted to provide a layer to separate machine specific issues from the educational and logical design of the program. I eventually became the leader on this task and created and maintained the guidance for a growing team of programmers in the project.

4.3 Development Methodology

The project also deployed and developed a methodology for the design and development of the educational experience. This involved groups of subject teachers working together with a programmer – ideas would be generated based on challenges faced in teaching together with perceptions of what a computer could do to tackle the challenges. Simulations of expensive equipment, complex or time consuming experiments or indeed dangerous manufacturing processes were often at the heart of the work, only lightly touching on the use of the computer to encourage debate, collaboration or make choices within difficult issues, although this became more prevalent as the project matured.

To develop a unit, the teachers would complete a form which outlined the design, share these with the project's leadership and once agreement found, the programmer would begin to work with one or two of the teachers on each idea. Key concepts included the program's navigational structure, the underlying scientific model and the development of a teachers' and students' guide.

The result of the team's work would be trialled in all the schools of the wider disciplinary group and observations brought back to an evaluative discussion which may have led to change, improvement or rejection.

Finally the guides would be typeset for publication, edited by a member of the CIC project, and the computer program would be checked on the platforms for publication before being duplicated on floppy disk.

Materials were then distributed through publishers Edward Arnold or Longman Group and promoted at conferences, professional development events and subject discipline meetings.

For me as a programmer, exposure to the educational and pedagogical debates as each program was designed led to an increasing mastery of these as key issues to the success of our work and thus programming alone did not satisfy!

4.4 Lecturing in Education and National Leadership

Towards the end of the decade I began to be more and more involved in the core business of the teacher education department within which I was employed. My new-found understanding of educational issues allowed me to lecture and supervise student's work. My role became part time as a mathematics education lecturer, visiting students in practice in schools and as a lecturer on a Masters level course relating particularly to computers in education.

At the same time, I took the post, based in the Computers in the Curriculum Project sponsored by the then national organisation Microelectonics in Education Support Unit (MESU) as a research fellow in software interoperability. I helped found the Educational Developers Software Forum, where I could exercise national leadership on the way in which we could tackle the burgeoning range of hardware and systems becoming available in the late eighties. I published studies which clarified the role of new software environments and their potential in educational computing.

4.5 Mental Models and Doctoral Research

As I was based in a highly respected educational research unit, attending seminars and taking part in meetings related to education more widely, I was invited to join the London Mental Models group led by the late Joan Bliss. This multidisciplinary research group involved staff in science, mathematics and history education, but also in language, cognitive psychology, educational computing, expert systems and artificial intelligence. The group provided me with a regular and powerful discourse to engage with in relation to the role of computers in learning and in particular, analysing the nature of modelling and simulation software and its potential for learning. I participated in the meetings and contributed ideas to seminars considering models of learning with technology.

This engagement led to a proposal to undertake PhD research with Prof Paul Black. I was invited to undertake two tasks to enter the course – an essay on technology and learning and to follow the Masters level course in Research Methods. I completed both and was about to set out on this course until swept up in the technological wave of interest in multimedia, which led me to work with Prof Stephen Heppell in 1990 to build the Ultralab research team. The PhD has recently (2013) been re-engaged with, but now reported as a retrospective reflection on my practice!

5 Conclusions

This article describes the first half of a career which has always been inter-disciplinary and constantly compromised by the emergence of technologies inviting re-appraisal of the direction taken. As Alison Hudson points out, there are many professionals now operating as learning technologists or educational developers, with much confusion about their academic and professional status as the disruption made by new technologies continues to be felt in both schools and higher education.

Hudson's study suggests that:

> *"…both groups occupy a highly politicised position, are affected by the shifting value of social, cultural and economic capital in the constantly changing higher education, are subject to struggle regarding 'position' and agency and are susceptible to the demands of new power regimes and technological solutions."* Hudson, 2009, Abstract

This struggle with 'position' has made identity difficult, since the combination of disciplines necessary to carry out my work has shifted from instructional design, to multimedia creativity, and although not reported here, to course design and ultimately the design of school and higher education itself. Thus I have never 'settled down' in any subject disciplinary sense, instead obtaining coherence from the focus on design, development, marketing, teaching and leadership in the creation of innovative 'products' at many levels.

References

1. Millwood, R.: Strategies for Computer Assisted Learning Masters Thesis, King's College London (1987), `http://phd.richardmillwood.net/en/bibliography/mastersthesisreference.2013-08-08.2648031096`
2. Hudson, A.: New Professionals and New Technologies in New Higher Education? Thesis, Nationella Forskarskolan i Pedagogiskt Arbete, Umeå University, Umeå University, Department of Interactive Media and Learning (IML), SE-901 87 Umeå, Sweden (2009) (ISBN: 978-91-7264-824-1)
3. Millwood, R.: The design of learner-centred, technology enhanced education, PhD Thesis (2013), `http://phd.richardmillwood.net`

The Victorian State Computer Education Committee's *Seeding Pair* In-Service Program: Two Case Studies

William F. Keane

Emmaus College, Vermont South, Melbourne, Victoria, Australia
William.Keane@emmaus.vic.edu.au

Abstract. Following the introduction of microcomputers into schools in the late 1970s, National Policy was developed which focused on the use of computers in non-computing subjects. The Victorian strategy for the implementation of the National Computers in Education Program was the development of a week-long in-service course which aimed to develop *seeding pairs* of teachers who would act as change agents when they returned to school. This chapter looks back at the case studies of two schools which sent teachers to the in-service. The case studies were initially presented in a Master of Educational Studies degree at Monash University. This chapter looks back at the way that professional development was designed to bring about change in schools with respect to computer use, how two schools made use of the *seeding pair* teachers and what issues emerged as a result.

Keywords: change agents, professional development, in-service programs.

1 Introduction

In 1970, as third form student at Xavier College, I was privileged to be able to do computer programming one period a week as part of the Mathematics curriculum. Under the guidance of our teacher 'Basher' we straightened paper clips to make holes in punch cards and place the cards carefully in stacks to send to a computer at Monash University. At one stage it was mooted that we might go on an excursion to see the machine but our hopes of doing that were dashed when we were told that the pristine environment which housed the computer would be compromised by a visit of thirty 14 year olds. It seemed that the closest any of us would get to a computer was the imagined ones in the pages of the *Fantastic Four* comic book.

However, within a few short years the development of the so-called microcomputers meant that computers could begin to come into schools [1]. From a comparatively modest, hobbyist beginning there was rapid change; so much so that by 1982 in Victoria a subject association, the Computer Education Group Victoria (CEGV) had been formed, a journal (COM 3) had begun and Computer Science had been accredited as a Year 12 subject [2].

Interest in the provision of computers in schools developed rapidly to the point where it became a focus of government priority. Following the election of the Federal Labor Government in 1983 the Commonwealth Schools Commission established the

A. Tatnall and B. Davey (Eds.): History of Computers in Education, IFIP AICT 424, pp. 310–323, 2014.

National Advisory Committee on Computers in Schools (NACCS) which, among other things, set aside money for the development of in-service courses [2]. School education is largely a State Government responsibility which meant that "*while the Schools Commission's Computers in Education Program was a Commonwealth initiative its delivery was via state instrumentalities*" [2]. As the program was to be administered in each state, there would be differences between the states and evaluation of the programs and their impact would be at the state level.

At the time I was looking around for the topic for my Master of Educational Studies project at Monash University. My supervisor, who was involved in the evaluations, suggested that I take part in the case study evaluations. The resulting project was a study of two schools which sent teachers to an in-service course which was part of the Victorian response to the National Computer Education Program. With each state given considerable latitude, the Victorian response, which began in 1984, was designed by officers at the State Computer Education Centre. The result was the deployment, in Stage 1 of a number of week-long courses [3]. Later, in 1985, a Stage 2 course was developed so that, between 1984 and 1986 over 2000 teachers attended courses on the applications of what were called, at the time, microcomputers. It is interesting and instructive to look back at what was a major professional development and change initiative at a turning point in education.

2 The *Seeding Pair* In-Service Courses

As indicated above, the in-service courses in Victoria were designed through the State Computer Education Centre (SCEC) to operate in two stages. Initially, schools were invited to send two teachers, one of whom had to be from a non-Maths or Science background and one of whom had to be female. The week-long in-service program was designed with the non-user in mind. It was hoped that the in-service would make these users proficient in computer use, break down barriers in the use of computers and provide an introduction to the range of software available. In terms of computer use the main aim for the non-user could be simply described as familiarisation [3].

In addition to having the teachers who attended the course become familiar with computers, the course planners had a second agenda. It was intended that the teachers who attended the in-service courses would act as change agents when they returned to their schools. This second agenda was a key driver about the selection of the teachers who attended from the school. The seeding pair teachers, as they were called, were expected to carry the seeds of what they learned on the in-service back with them to their school. It was intended that they would provide training at the school level on what could be done with the computers in the classroom. The idea was that the seeding pair teachers would use computers in their own teaching and preparation, contribute to future discussions and inspire and be of assistance to their colleagues in the use of computers. They would be expected to take part in policy development and make a contribution towards future directions in the use of computers in their school [3].

2.1 The Use of Computers in Schools

It was clear that there was a vision of what a good school would look like as a result of the *seeding pair* in-service. This vision was a reflection of the literature of the time. Whereas there was, by 1984, an established Year 12 Computer Science course in Victoria there was a concern that the use of computers was being held captive by specialist computer interests. Part of the concern at the time was that "*it appears that computers are increasingly becoming a sign of a 'good school' and that the acquisition by the school of computers has an important 'symbolic role'*" [4]. The consequence of this was the seemingly unbreakable link between the maths/ science area and computers, the crowding of the timetable and the problem of adequate access for students and teachers. One of the battles of this time was between the dominant model of computers being housed in rooms or laboratories and the fear that this model was a barrier to others making use of the computers. This might not have been such a problem if the computer rooms in schools had remained empty of formal classes but, in fact, the opposite tended to be the case. It seemed that it was important to principals that such an expensive facility be fully utilised.

The link between computers and the maths and science areas led to fears that girls would be either excluded or less inclined to pursue computers. Typical of the concerns expressed at the time was the argument that, with respect to computing, "*teaching methods, content, classroom dynamics and lack of female role models all work to discourage girls from participating in this area*" [5]. It was not just the use of computers but how they were being used which was vitally important. There was a belief that computer use in education needed to move beyond the specialist study of the computer itself. This led to the debate about whether computers were better understood as tools or topics [1].

It was soon understood that any attempt at making educational use of computers across the curriculum was predicated on teacher development [4]. While one way to make use of computers in different subjects was to use packaged programs, some critics thought that this had significant limitations on the kind of learning that was likely to take place and that it would be better and more effective if teachers designed the programs themselves [6]. At the same time there was much concern that there were insufficient software resources for teachers to use. Some writers thought that a program such as LOGO would have a major impact in a number of classrooms across a range of disciplines [7].

The emphasis on teacher development led to the second agenda of the in-service program: the role of the *seeding pair* teachers as change agents.

2.2 Change Agents

Arguably the most significant aspect of the *seeding pair* in-service program was their role as change agents in schools. It is sobering to look back to the early 1980s and see how much was already known about the effectiveness of professional development and how much was already understood about the difficulty of creating change in schools. It is fair to ask what lessons have been drawn from this work and how much has changed in practice over the last 30 years or so.

It was already well understood that one- off in-service workshops were ineffective, largely because, "*the absence of follow-up after workshops is without doubt the greatest single problem in contemporary professional development*" [8]. This was a crucial issue for the designers of the *seeding pair* in-service as the purpose of the course was to develop and change the way that computers were used in schools. A centrally designed course would be unlikely to have the desired effect of changing practice within the schools themselves.

What was understood to be more effective in terms of implementing programs in schools was peer interaction [8]. We would be likely today to describe this peer interaction in terms of mentoring or coaching and there was an emphasis in the literature of the day on developing in-services courses which were more in tune with what participants needed [9-11]. This meant that the in-service course needed to provide sufficient time to develop confidence in new practices.

For change to be effective, then, it is important to have people operating at the school who can foster and initiate change by facilitating the new practices. One obvious candidate for fostering change was the principal. However, educational research at the time demonstrated that the principal was not always best placed to either initiate or foster change as they spent a large part of their time maintaining stability rather than initiating change [8]. In any event, the principal hardly had time – then or now – to sit with and assist staff members in the development of new skills. Despite this important limitation of the principal's time it was equally clear from the research that "Whether it is direct or indirect, the principal plays a fateful role in implementation and continuance of any change proposal" [8]. However, it is not possible for a principal to drive change without help:

> *Principals need to be knowledgeable about the goals and expected uses of an innovation in order to understand the needs, progress, and problems teachers experience during implementation. They may choose to undergo training and become users themselves and to provide teacher assistance directly. Their participation at that level is not essential however, so long as they provide access to resources, training, and assistance from others. Research indicates that principals often depend on assistance from a "second change agent" in the school—for example a vice-principal, a key teacher, or a central office consultant—especially in secondary schools. [8]*

A key goal of the *seeding pair* program was having people in the school who could assist in leading change. The fear was that computer use could be held hostage by the few teachers who had expert computer knowledge. Writing about the *seeding pair* in-service program Ingvarson and McKenzie [3] described in vivid detail the fears that some held about the role of the computer coordinator in schools:

> *Forebodings were expressed before our study began about the possibly negative role such people might play in the outcome of the courses, given that their background was usually a specialized one in Mathematics, Science, or Computer Science; and given that they were sometimes caricatured as introverted, anally retentive males with a strong sense of territory in relation to 'their' computers [3].*

The *seeding pair* structure was intended to guard against the 'gatekeepers' by developing skills in those who attended the course. It was intended that the seeding pair teachers would acquire skills, become involved in the development of school computer policy and work together to empower others.

3 Case Study of Vista College

The case study investigation of the impact of the *seeding pair* program at Vista College was undertaken in the second half of 1986.

3.1 Context

At the time of investigation Vista College was a Catholic boys' school in a south-eastern suburb close to Melbourne with an enrolment of approximately 770 students, a quarter of whom were from non-English speaking backgrounds. The school was not resource rich by any means and there were class sizes nearing 40 in many year levels.

Given the lack of resources, the decision to obtain the original computer system in 1981 showed great daring and foresight. The Headmaster of the time was known for pursuing modern approaches to curriculum provision. One notable example at about the same period in the school's history, was the building of an Arts and Technology wing – despite great opposition from some of the staff - to offer these subjects for the first time.

Along with the Headmaster's determination to provide a modern education at Vista College, his decision to purchase the Northstar computer was a reflection of the confidence he had in the Maths Coordinator and the friendship and trust he had developed with her husband who had left the academic world to get into the fledging computer business. He sourced the computer and wrote much of the software the school relied on in the early days of computer use.

The Headmaster had faced opposition from conservative staff members in building the Arts and Technology wing based on their objection that he was introducing 'Mickey Mouse' subjects into the curriculum. In contrast, there was little opposition to the introduction of a computer. The idea that computers were needed in schools had achieved rapid acceptance. In describing the developments at the College during the course of 1981 the Headmaster had this to say about the latest school developments:

> *Among these should be noted the setting up of a computer within the school. We are grateful for the advice of the Head of our Mathematics Department and her husband who have, this year, established this computer, which is better and more advanced than those usually found in Secondary Schools.*

In 1982 a room next to the library was set aside to house the Northstar computer and a teacher was appointed to teach the Introduction to Data Processing (IDP) course as part of the Certificate of Business Studies course offered to Year 12 students as an alternative to the Higher School Certificate. The decision to offer the IDP subject rather than the newly accredited Computer Science course was a reflection of the view that it was becoming imperative to provide access to computers for a generation of students who would need computer skills when they entered the workforce. The IDP subject was designed to be relevant to the general business student and this was seen to be more important than catering to the specialist computer studies student. To some extent this choice represented the nearest thing to a computer policy in the early years.

Other year levels were also given exposure to the computers. The large class sizes (35-40) meant that students went to the computer room in half class groups linked to the Mathematics classes. The Maths teacher remained behind to teach the rest of the class while the computer teacher taught the half class.

Because of the circumstances which led to the original purchase the computer area remained under the wing of the Mathematics Faculty. Rapid staff change led to instability in the computer area. There were six different teachers in the first five years of computer use and changes of Headmaster in both 1984 and 1987.

The Northstar computer did not prove very resilient and frequently broke down to the point that it was reserved for administrative purposes rather than student use. Students then used newly purchased Apple IIe computers. Up until late 1986 there were only 8 of these Apples which often meant that there were three students for each computer. In term 4 of 1986 an additional six Apple IIe computers were purchased with three added at the beginning of 1987. This allowed full classes to use the computers so long as there were two students for each machine.

In 1987 the curriculum included Computer Studies for Years 7-10 as well as the Data Processing subject. This meant that the room was timetabled with formal computer classes for 25 out of a possible 31 periods, thus greatly reducing the possibility of other subjects using the room. Year 12 Accounting and Year 11 Practical Maths classes managed to squeeze into the timetable.

3.2 The Decision to Send Teachers to the *Seeding Pair* Course

The decision to send two teachers to the Stage 1 *seeding pair* course in 1985 and another teacher to the Stage 2 course in 1986 was driven by the Curriculum Coordinator in conjunction with the Computer Coordinator. It was clear to the Curriculum Coordinator that more teachers in the school needed to know about computers, about what they could do and how they might impact on the students. The availability of funding was an important factor as Vista College did not routinely employ replacement teachers and the commitment to having two staff members at a week-long course was significant.

The two staff members who attended the Stage 1 course in 1985 were quite senior in the College. This was deliberate as it was thought that their seniority would mean that they would be more likely to be respected by their colleagues and less likely to be intimidated by negative members of staff. Susan, in her thirteenth year of teaching when she went on the course, taught English, History and Religious Education, had been English Coordinator and would later take up the role of Year 10 Coordinator. Patrick, having taught for 12 years, had a primary teaching background which enabled him to teach Religion, English, Social Studies and Mathematics. He was the Year 7 Coordinator.

The following year Steve, a first year Maths and Science teacher, attended the stage 2 course. While the Stage 2 course was supposed to be for senior staff or computer coordinators, Steve was proficient with computers and would be the main teacher of computer subjects the next year. In a reflection of how these kinds of extended release courses were regarded at Vista College the second teacher who was to attend the Stage 2 course with Steve was not allowed to go as no suitable emergency teacher could be found to replace him.

The views of the participants about the courses varied widely. While Patrick and Steve were enthusiastic about what they had learned, Susan felt that the course did not meet her needs. In summary, her complaints were that there was too much 'preaching' about what constituted good computer use in a school, the course was not really for the uninitiated and that the course did not really help her to understand how computers could be used in her teaching. Susan expressed a lack of confidence in what she had learned and this had an impact on the extent to which she felt she could help others subsequently. Susan felt that she lacked sufficient skills to make effective use of a computer and, like Patrick and Steve, was disappointed that there was no follow-up from the original course.

3.3 Acting as Change Agents: Professional Development of Staff

The teachers who attended the *seeding pair* in-service course were full of good intentions but very little happened in terms of staff development. While Susan felt that she lacked the necessary skills to assist other staff members, Patrick and Steve were more than willing to provide professional development. The initial plan was to have them deliver professional development on one of the staff curriculum days. There were problems with this proposal, though, as time was limited. There were, on average, six such days in a year and they were taken up with the usual administrative matters and meetings which were considered essential to the good running of the school. The other complication was that the College had to complete a mandated School Development Project which took up much of the available time and was seen to be more urgent as there were timelines to follow. After-school sessions for professional development were considered but dismissed as an option because there were a great many extra-curricular activities which took place.

The lack of formal opportunities to deliver professional development meant that the seeding pair teachers had to resort to informal opportunities such as talking to colleagues, leaving work lying about and offering help. Steve even offered to put the timetable for the following year into a spreadsheet so that it could be saved and printed and could be edited at a later date if necessary.

The *seeding pair* teachers, the Curriculum Coordinator and the Headmaster were all conscious of the resistance of many staff members to the use of computers. Some staff members could not see the relevance of computers to their teaching and there were many complaints at the time that there was a lack of suitable software for educational purposes. This perspective then became entwined with the belief that trying to come to grips with computer use was likely to time consuming. The lack of access to the computer room was seen to be a real disadvantage. Before 1987, bringing a whole class to the computer room meant having four students sharing a terminal. At this time there was simply no possibility that a teacher might have a computer on their desk at school or at home as part of their day to day work practice.

All of the participants of the study believed that there was an urgent need for further professional development as this was seen to be the key to improvements in the use of computers in schools. Despite this strong belief, there was no plan of action. It was almost as if the act of sending teachers to the course was enough in itself. There were no support structures in place to facilitate the work of the *seeding pair* teachers or were any seen as necessary.

3.4 Acting as Change Agents: Policy Development

Emily, the new Computer Coordinator in 1986, believed that she could easily develop the computers in education policy for Vista College but such a document would not be inclusive of the views of others and would, therefore, have limited usefulness in the College. The then Headmaster had a sense of the need for direction in the areas of computer literacy, understanding the impact of computers on society and determining a direction in computer education for the future. Nevertheless, despite agreement that a policy was desirable, six years after the introduction of computers in the school, no policy had been developed.

The *seeding pair* teachers all expressed a willingness to be involved in policy development as they believed the course had given them insight and skills in the area and that they could not have made a worthwhile contribution to policy development with their experience at the course.

As with professional development, there was no structure in place which would have facilitated the development of policy. Certainly there were competing priorities for attention and resources but, perhaps, the lack of support by the Headmaster was the crucial factor. The Headmaster had not actually used a computer and, while he might have been supportive of the establishment of general directions, he had neither the expertise nor the sense of urgency to develop policy in this area and, by the end of 1986, he had moved on to another position.

Towards the end of 1987 the Year Coordinators discussed whether the College was making the best use of the computers in the lab at one of their weekly meetings. Some believed that, while students needed exposure to the fundamentals of computer use at some stage, there should be less formal teaching of computers and more access to the computers for other subjects.

The opposing view was that the computers were too expensive a resource to run the risk of not being used except when someone decided to make use of them. Moreover, it was argued, access to computers was a matter of fairness. What if a Maths teacher in Year 10 wanted to use the computers while another did not; would it not be unfair to the students who missed out? It was this view which prevailed which meant that computer subjects remained in place and dominated the timetabled space in the computer laboratory. Without being able to access the computers there was little incentive to encourage teachers to try to make use of computers in their teaching.

To make matters worse, there were no computers available for staff use. Even the Timetabler had to use a computer in the back of the computer room to do his work.

3.5 Summary

Without regular access to a computer to further develop their skills and without structures in place to enable them to carry out their role, the *seeding pair* teachers were ineffective as change agents. There was an urgent need for on-going professional development but, again, without a structure to facilitate this there was no progress made with improving the skills of the *seeding pair* teachers or the teachers in general.

4 St Christopher's Grammar School

4.1 Context

At the time of the study St. Christopher's Grammar school was a co-educational grammar school with an enrolment of over 1000 students from primary school through to Year 12. By comparison with Vista College, St. Christopher's was a resource rich and competitive school in the independent school tradition.

In keeping with the beginnings of computer provision in Victorian schools, St. Christopher's began by setting up a separate computer laboratory and teaching classes in computer awareness to middle schools students. By 1986 there had been a move away from what was described as computers as topics and towards using computers within other areas. The computer awareness course at Year 10 continued as a more or less permanent feature of the curriculum. There was a well-resourced computer laboratory of Apple IIe computers in the secondary schools with more to come (as we shall see).

The Computer Department began, as was typical of the era, as part of the Mathematics Department and the Head of Computers was also the Sub-Head of Mathematics. The Computer Awareness course at Year 10 was delivered to students via their Maths class groups. The issue which arose from this organisational arrangement was the extent to which other staff felt that the computers in some sense, belonged to the Mathematics Department. Balanced against this was the obvious encouragement which the Head of Computers, Frank, gave to anyone wanting to use the computer facilities.

4.2 The Decision to Send Teachers on the Course

Frank, with the support of the Headmaster, chose the first of St. Christopher's Seeding Pair teachers to attend a Stage 1 course in 1984. This was understood to be a major commitment as the school was always reluctant to send teachers away on in-services at all, let alone ones which ran for an extended period. Despite his enthusiasm for sending teachers to the course, Frank admitted that he did not immediately grasp the importance or the potential benefits of the in-service. The two teachers were chosen with a view that the course would help them to introduce and use computers in their teaching rather than how their attendance might benefit the whole school.

In fact the two teachers did not have a significant impact on computer use at St. Christopher's. Sylvia, a middle school English and History teacher had to go to hospital during the course and was off work for some weeks afterward. The other teacher chosen to go left the school at the end of the year.

Despite these setbacks, a second pair was sent to another Stage 1 course in 1985. Thomas, the Senior Master and Head of English and Jane, the Head of Geography, had significant positions in the school and it was felt that they would be better able to influence policy and help set directions for the future, especially in terms of computer use in their subject areas. Frank and a colleague applied to attend a Stage 2 course in 1986 but they were not selected because four teachers from the school had already attended a Stage 1 course.

There were divergent views about the appropriateness of the course strategies from the three participants. Sylvia was complimentary about the course and felt that is was pitched at the right level for her but it is worth remembering that she did not complete it due to ill health. Perhaps not surprisingly she made less use of computers after the course than either of the other two participants did. Her particular contribution was running a lunch time girls only computer group. Her experience on the course had led her to set up the girls' only group as she had formed the view that it was necessary to ensure that girls had exposure to computers.

Jane was positive about the course despite feeling that there should have been more hands-on activities. While she made great use of computers in teaching Geography, Jane felt that computers were another teaching tool and that they should not be seen as the answer.

Thomas felt that the conveners of the course spent too much time trying to push particular policy perspectives rather than providing the kinds of hands-on experience that he believed he needed. He had written to the organisers to express his views and vowed that computer in-services at St. Christopher's would be very much a hands-on experience.

4.3 Acting as Change Agents: Professional Development of Staff

The *seeding pair* teachers at St. Christopher's felt that they had little impact on staff members directly, despite their best intentions. They saw a divide already emerging between those who were willing to embrace the use of computers and those who were strongly resisting them. All three *seeding pair* Teachers could point to teachers they felt were doing "wonderful things" with computers in their classrooms.

St. Christopher's routinely set aside one of its staff development days to meeting staff requests for professional development and there was a sense of pride on the part of the *seeding pair* teachers that the staff voted to devote their curriculum day to the use of computers. Frank was pleased that ten teachers, including the *seeding pair* teachers, had volunteered to help put the day together. It was felt that much staff resistance would be broken down when the resisters could see what their colleagues were accomplishing.

The contrast with Vista College was obvious. Whereas any thought of offering professional development at Vista College had been somehow lost or simply never become a priority, there was clear action at St. Christopher's. Devoting a day to learning about computers sent the message that learning about them was important. While one day was of only limited value in the long run it did represent a base on which to build.

4.4 Acting as Change Agents: Policy and Strategic Development

The St. Christopher's Headmaster established a Computer Policy Review Committee in February, 1986. While he set the terms of reference the Headmaster chose not to be on the Committee. Because of their involvement in the course the Seeding Pair Teachers were invited to join the Committee. Jane was the only woman on the Committee.

The brief provided to the Committee was extensive, covering all aspects of computer use in the school. It met once a fortnight for three months and the methods of investigation included a questionnaire and school visits. In addition to the needs of administration, the library, the finance department and careers, the Committee considered a number of areas of concern including access to computers, the future of a computer subject, computer literacy and professional development for staff.

Access to computers was considered to be the most important question in 1986. As well as the Year 10 Computer Awareness course taking up space on the timetable, the demand for spaces by other teachers for the senior school computer laboratory exceeded the availability. The Committee considered deploying computers to classrooms but rejected it because the demand did not justify the cost. It was understood that, in general, teachers at the school preferred that students all work on the same task together and so the preference was for additional laboratory space which would serve this purpose. Only Jane objected to this recommendation, arguing that other ways of working might be better.

Instead of deploying computers in other spaces, the recommendation of the Committee was to provide for another laboratory. This second laboratory would have IBM compatible computers in a deliberate move to provide for business level machines. The direction was set that computers would provide an important point of contact with the business world. This meant that computers were being seen as, in the parlance of the day, topics rather than tools.

The computer curriculum was also considered. Computer Awareness at Year 10 was seen to be an important subject but the Committee also came to the conclusion that it was important to build computer literacy into the curriculum. The Committee believed that Computer Awareness could be phased out as other subjects moved to increase their use of computers. The plan for Years 7-10 was for the following:

- Mathematics to undertake programming
- English to cover word processing
- Geography to deal with the social implications of computing

It was thought that Computer Awareness should continue as an option for those who wanted to study computers and that Computer Science should be introduced for Years 11 and 12 for those who wanted to peruse a serious study of computers.

The original brief from the Headmaster did not provide for a consideration of the need for professional development of staff members. This was added by the Committee who surveyed all staff:

- 75% of staff members wanted to learn how to use computers in their teaching
- There was a strong demand for 5 week courses
- There was strong demand for 1:1 tuition by teachers
- There was strong demand for an external ISE course on computers
- Instructional posters were needed in laboratories
- Strong demand for access to a laboratory
- The feasibility of selling old computers to staff members should be investigated

The Committee identified a clear need for access to computers and for targeted professional development.

Most of the recommendations of the Committee were adopted, with the creation of the second laboratory seen as being being crucial. Professional development was provided which helped break down resistance to the use of computers. Frank was delighted to discover that there were fewer hard core resisters than he feared but some remained and would not prove easy to shift.

4.5 Summary

In the area of policy the contrast with Vista College was striking. At St. Christopher's the formation of the Committee was a vital step in establishing a direction for the use of computers in the school. Including the *seeding pair* teachers ensured that their professional development was not wasted and that decisions about computers were being made by a group which included members of staff who were up to date with the latest thinking. Because the Committee was representative it sought to include the views and needs of other members of staff in a systematic way that tried to take account of their learning needs.

5 The Changing Times

The problems associated with facilitating change in schools are no less pressing today than they were in the mid-1980s. In fact the *seeding pair* in-service was quite sophisticated in the way that it made use of the research of the times to design an approach to change that was different to a centralised, top-down model. It is sobering to look back over thirty years to realise that there have not been any real advances in the way that professional development is used to create change in schools. Moreover, much of the recent emphasis on professional development for registration purposes has produced providers who have designed programs to cater for the individual teacher with little thought or interest in how the whole school might benefit.

One of the glaringly obvious issues to emerge from the case studies was the very different ways that the schools made provision for change. Vista College floundered about without direction and the expertise of the *seeding pair* teachers was never put to good use either in policy terms or to provide professional development. St. Christopher's, on the other hand, provided a structure through which the seeding pair teachers could make a real contribution, especially in terms of providing a direction for the school to take in the short to medium term.

The role of the principal in creating that strategic direction remains important. In terms of technology strategy this is problematic. As a number of writers have pointed out the principal does not always have expertise in technology and yet is often the one who insists on a particular direction [12, 13]. One principal I know declared that he and the computer coordinator determined computer strategy over a cup of tea before school on a Friday morning. The question of who makes the decisions remains a vital one [12]. In the case of Vista College, the change in headmasters in 1984 and again in 1987 resulted in a computer policy vacuum. The emphasis became one of providing resources rather than providing direction for teaching and learning. The contrast with St. Christopher's could not have been more striking. There the Headmaster set a policy committee in place and they were able to add professional development to their brief. The result certainly provided the school with a sense of direction and a plan of action for the future.

Along with leadership, perhaps the major question of the 1980s was access to computers. At the time the thinking was very much concentrated on providing access to students and this was reflected strongly in the expansion of the numbers of computers at Vista College and the provision of a second computer laboratory at St. Christopher's. At Vista College little thought was given to providing access to teachers while at St. Christopher's computers were stationed in staff rooms. Providing notebook computers to teachers was some way off yet. Thanks to government policy [14] the problem of access to computers is no longer the pressing issue it once was. The Digital Education Revolution might well prove to be the beginning of a new chapter in the history of computers in education.

References

1. Walker, R.: The development of educational computing policy in the Victorian school system, 1976-1985. Australian Journal of Education 35, 292–313 (1991)
2. Bigum, C., Bonser, S., Evans, P., Groundwater-Smith, S., Grundy, S., Kemmis, S., McKenzie, D., McKinnon, D., O'Connor, M., Straton, R., Willis, S.: Coming to terms with computers in schools. Report to the Commonwealth Schools Commission. Deakin Institute for Studies in Education, Deakin University (1987)
3. Ingvarson, L., MacKenzie, D.: Factors affecting the impact of in-service courses for teachers: implications for policy. Teaching and Teacher Education 4, 139–155 (1988)
4. Firkin, J., Davidson, M., Johnson, L.: Computer Culture in the Classroom. VISE, Melbourne (1985)
5. Davidson, M., Hartley, R.: Women and Computers Workshop. VISE, Melbourne (1984)

6. Kelly, A.V.: Microcomputers and the curriculum: uses and abuses. In: Kelly, A.V. (ed.) Microcomputers Across the Curriculum. Harper and Row, London (1984)
7. Papert, S.: Mindstorms: children, com puters and powerful ideas. Harvester, London (1980)
8. Fullan, M.: The Meaning of Educational Change. Teachers College Press, Columbia University (1982)
9. Joyce, B., Showers, B.: Improving inservice training: the message of research. Educational Leadership 37, 379–385 (1980)
10. Showers, B.: Teachers coaching teachers. Educational Leadership 42, 43–49 (1985)
11. Wood, F.H., Thompson, S.R.: Guidelines for better staff development. Educational Leadership 37, 374–378 (1980)
12. Keane, T.: An investigation of the role of the information and communication technologies leader in secondary schools. Leading and Managing 18, 50–64 (2012)
13. Lee, M., Gaffney, M.: Leading Schools in a digital era. In: Lee, M., Gaffney, M. (eds.) Leading a Digital School. ACER, Camberwell (2008)
14. `http://www.alp.org.au/download/labors_digital_revolution_campaign_launch.pdf`

The Historical Relationship between Affective Variables and ICT Based Learning and Instruction and Achievement in the Israeli School System

Yaacov J. Katz

School of Education, Bar-Ilan University, Israel
yaacov.katz@biu.ac.il

Abstract. ICT methodologies have been part and parcel of learning and instruction in the Israeli educational system since the mid-1970s when the behavioral theory based TOAM closed minicomputer based drill and practice learning methodology was introduced into Israeli schools. Later in the late 1970s the first PCs adapted for educational use were introduced into Israeli schools and continued in the drill and practice tradition. Thereafter, in the mid-1980s with the introduction of more advanced PCs into Israeli classrooms, open courseware coupled with electronic spreadsheets and databases came to the fore in ICT based learning and instruction. In the early 1990s when constructivist learning theory became accepted in the Israeli educational system, simulations and computer-learner interaction became popular ICT based learning methodologies used in Israeli schools. In the late 1990s reality technology was introduced as an ICT based learning methodology and in the mid-2000s ICT based distance learning became a permanent feature of learning and instruction in the Israeli educational system. Alongside the process of ICT introduction into the Israeli educational system, affective aspects of ICT utilization in schools was closely monitored. Much effort was expended in research designed to examine the relationship between ICT use in learning and instruction and scholastic achievement of students at all levels in the school system. Research evidence accumulated over the years indicates that teacher and student autonomy, computer self-confidence, computer efficacy, locus of control, need for innovation, extraversion, and control of the learning process are just a few of the affective variables found to significantly enhance ICT use in Israeli schools. Bearing in mind the progress made in the assimilation of ICT based learning and instruction in Israeli schools, it appears justified for educational policy makers and administrators to consider the importance of affective variables of both teachers and students when assessing their capability to best utilize ICT in school.

Keywords: ICT based learning and instruction, behavioral theory, constructivist theory, scholastic achievement, affective variables.

1 Introduction

Information and Communication Technology (ICT) as an educational medium has not made the impression on educational outcomes as expected. Since the 1960s when the

A. Tatnall and B. Davey (Eds.): History of Computers in Education, IFIP AICT 424, pp. 324–338, 2014.

first attempts were made to implement ICT based learning and instruction in the school classroom, much experience has been gained and much frustration that has been generated. The idea of using ICT based learning and instruction as a foolproof educational methodology is far from being fulfilled. Achievement levels attained by students in different subjects in which ICT has been used for learning and instruction have not improved dramatically, neither has affective education progressed significantly resulting from the use of ICT. Research studies have indicated that only under certain circumstances are educational outcomes improved by the use of ICT in the learning and instructional processes. This chapter will address the Israeli context of the direct relationship between ICT based learning and instruction and enhanced educational achievement as well as the mediating contribution of affective variables to the relationship.

2 ICT Based Approaches to Learning and Instruction: Past and Present

In order to understand the complex issues and problems associated with the utilization of ICT based approaches to learning and instruction in the Israeli school system, the development and progressive implementation and utilization of different ICT learning and instructional methodologies will be examined. Naim (2010) described the significant reasons for the implementation of ICT based learning and instruction in the educational system in Israel. The first reason was the rapid development of technology that put computers within reach of Israeli schools. The second reason resulted from the belief that computerized learning programs would significantly improve the learning process and suit it to the needs of the individual learner. A third reason proposed by Naim was the fact that Israeli public opinion positively adopted the belief that computers were vitally necessary all walks of daily life including the educational arena. Therefore the educational system could not possibly halt progress and began using computers in the school system just as computers became popular in commerce, industry, medicine, transportation and other fields in daily life.

Offir, Katz and Passig (1994) historically described the development of ICT use in the educational process and indicated that the "closed - open" courseware continuum succinctly and accurately depicts the progress made in the use of technology for learning and instruction. The "closed - open" continuum provides an insight as how ICT methodologies evolved and developed in the Israeli educational system since the early 1960s up till the present time.

The theoretical basis of the early ICT learning approaches used in Israel drew from the behavioral school of thought. Skinner (1954, 1958) published a series of papers predicting that "teaching machines" would make learning dramatically more efficient and emphasized the "the constant interchange between program and student". Thus the first computer introduced into the Israeli educational system in the mid 1970s was a Digital "Toam" minicomputer to which individual terminals were connected. These terminals were used by individual elementary school students for diagnostics, drill and practice and evaluation of their work in English and mathematics. The system was totally "traditional", i.e. closed, with teachers unable to effect any changes in the computer software and served as a complementary learning system to the traditional classroom lesson. The general atmosphere that pervaded the use of the "Toam" system was one of precision regarding the diagnosis and evaluation of students' ability in English and mathematics. Teachers religiously followed students' progress as mapped out by the Toam computer and planned their English and mathematics lessons accordingly. The Toam system was widely used and popularized the initial use of ICT in the Israeli classroom.

In the late 1970s when first generation of personal computers became commercially available in Israel, Apple IIs, Ataris, and Commodore CBMs personal computers connected in rudimentary networks, began replacing the Toam system in the Israeli school system. Offir, Golub and Friedel (1993) reported that the first PCs were used for traditional computer assisted learning and computer assisted instruction, based on drill and practice. Teachers closely followed inflexible computerized syllabi in a number of subjects, among them languages, mathematics and science. All students in elementary and junior high schools studied the same content and learning materials and progressed according to a rigid timetable. This generation of PCs also drew on behavioral theory and the software offered to the educational system was used to complement traditional teaching and was considered to be especially advantageous in providing students with a sound revision platform.

In the mid-1980s Israeli educators began asking pointed questions regarding the validity of behavioral learning as a valid theoretical source and inspiration for ICT use in the educational system. Addition questions raised addressed the relative advantages, effectiveness, and cost-efficiency of ICT based drill and practice as well as the advantages to be gained from the study of basic programming. Heated debates characterized the Israeli educational establishment regarding the direction to be taken in the use of ICT in the educational system (Mevarech and Hativa, 1996) and as a result of these debates other theoretical approaches were suggested. The constructivist theory of learning came to the fore in Israel, albeit alongside the behaviorist approach (Salomon, 1996), and led to the development and adoption of more flexible learning and instruction programs that were introduced into the Israeli educational system. These included the development of the use of electronic spreadsheets (Dreyfus, Feinstein and Talmon, 1997; Givon, 1996) that enhance learner independence and creativity and provide students with sophisticated graphic assistance that enhances the understanding and dissemination of complicated subject matter. Databases, which were also developed and incorporated in this stage of ICT development (Appelberg, 1997), provided students with the opportunity of enriching their knowledge and comprehension of subject matter by facilitating the search for sources hitherto available only in libraries and museums. Ernst (1991) noted that the introduction of the use of spreadsheets and databases in the educational process contributed to the promotion of improved learning and instruction and superior ICT applications in education. He added that the use of electronic spreadsheets accounted for almost 90% of computer assisted instruction and computer assisted learning in the late 1980s.

In the next stage of development in the 1990s, the constructivist learning model almost totally replaced the behaviorist approach and motivated the introduction of simulation software into the Israeli educational system (Hativa, 1996). Simulation, as described by Offir and Katz (1994), is a sophisticated, progressive and improved ICT methodology designed to electronically generate situations that exist in reality and to introduce these situations into learning and instruction. Baranauskas and De Oliveira

(1995) noted that educational computer simulations are based on dynamic interaction between the learner and the computer program and may be defined as part of a modeling process that involves the execution of the model by the learner. Through the methodology of simulation, teachers are able to provide their students with realistic models of subject matter as experienced in real life situations thereby facilitating students' understanding and mastery of the learning situation. Givon (1996) cited simulation as especially effective for the science and technology subjects where experiments can be conducted using ICT instead of having to prepare and use materials in the traditional science or technology laboratory. Leary (1995) confirmed that the achievement of learners using ICT simulation are on a par with and even outstrip achievement in non-simulation learning situations.

The next stage of ICT development in the Israeli educational system took place in the late 1990s and early 2000s and focused on virtual reality software. Turman and Matton (1994) defined virtual reality as a highly interactive ICT based environment in which the user becomes a fully-fledged partner in a virtual world. When experiencing virtual reality the user becomes an immersed participant in the computer generated virtual reality program. Bricken and Byrne (1992) stated that in order to enter the world of virtual reality the learner wears a computerized helmet and gloves which allow him or her to see, hear and touch objects in the virtual world. Henry (1992) stated that on entry into the virtual world the learner feels physically immersed in that world. Regain and Shebliske (1992) reported that learners who enter a virtual world undergo physical and emotional experiences very similar to those that exist in the real world in which they really live. Thus virtual reality provides an all-encompassing learning opportunity that promotes constructivist learning and understanding that surpass other ICT approaches (Katz, 1999). Passig and Sharbat (2001) as well Passig, Klein and Newman (2001) confirmed that the use of virtual reality technology in learning and instruction positively contributes to enhanced performance of both teachers and learners.

In order to take advantage of all the ICT developments in the Israeli educational system that took place from the mid-1970s until the present time, much educational thought and effort has been put into developing the various stages of software development into an integrated multimedia system. Multimedia methodology, which includes closed and open software as well as simulation and virtual reality packages, has become an important component of the ICT based educational process. Passig and Levin (2000) provided an in-depth analysis of multimedia packages suitable for the educational process and stated that when utilizing multimedia methodologies in learning the student does not only study the subject matter, but also learns how to deal with the synthetically programmed environment. The relatively easy use of technology and the uniformity of the multimedia interface have significant implications for both teacher and student, since they may provide a platform for a higher level of motivation, concentration, and understanding of the content being studied. The design of multimedia educational packages provides a clear, consistent and attractive ICT platform, which contributes towards the ability of teachers and students to reach excellence through user-friendly learning and instruction methodologies.

3 Distance Learning Approaches: Past and Present

Since its inception as a mass delivery system in the early part of the twentieth century, distance learning has been utilized in order to provide students in the educational system the opportunity to study in locations separated by large distances from centers of learning. Chu (1999) intimated that the first generation of distance learning approaches, which utilized traditional printed material and communication by mail and telephone, served essentially as a one-way communication technology that, while providing students with content matter, inhibited interaction between teachers and learners. In the late 1960s and the early 1970s first generation distance learning technology was superseded by second generation audio recordings, radio and television broadcasts (Southworth, Flanigan and Knezek, 1981) which provided students with an improved delivery platform. Both first and second generation distance learning delivery systems were designed primarily to produce and distribute learning materials as efficiently as the technology of the day permitted. Both generations of distance learning lacked the key element of real-time interactive communication between students and teachers.

The 1980s and 1990s saw the development of sophisticated third generation distance learning systems which include interactive video, email, internet, and intranet technologies. Learning and instruction activity through the medium of these distance learning systems was redefined to include and focus on teacher-student interaction (Trentin, 1997). Interactive videoconferencing, and interaction through the medium of internet or intranet offer one-to-many or one-to-one tuition in which teachers and students are able to communicate on-line thereby solving key instructional and learning problems in real time (Katz, 1998). Third generation distance learning systems are flexible and present teachers with the opportunity of continuously monitoring overall progress of their students. These systems also allow tutors to modify, reinforce and even model educational processes, thereby fulfilling the cognitive as well as affective needs and requirements of students. Interactivity, which characterizes third generation distance learning, has also been shown to meet student needs more fittingly and comprehensively than the older distance learning modes. Interaction provides the student with a new cognitive environment that both activates and motivates learning and contributes to student satisfaction as well as to a feeling of control of the learning process (Finnie, 1989). Trentin (1997) confirmed that interactivity available in third generation distance learning methodologies promotes active engagement of students in the learning process and leads to improved academic achievement.

Katz (1998) described how the three generations of distance learning technology sophisticated were utilized in the Israeli educational system beginning with first generation technology in the 1960s, continuing with second generation technology in the 1970s and 1980s, and with the implementation of third generation technology in the 1990s. Third generation distance learning systems that include synchronous interactive video, asynchronous learning and instruction, email, internet and intranet technologies are still popular in the Israeli educational system mainly at the elementary, secondary and tertiary levels. According to Katz learning and instruction through the medium of synchronous distance learning methodologies has been redefined to include and focus on teacher-student interaction. Interactive video-conferencing, and interaction through the medium of internet or intranet and email, offer one-to-many or one-to-one tuition in which teachers and students are able to communicate on-line thereby solving cardinal instructional and learning problems in real time. Third generation distance learning methodologies are characterized by their flexibility and allow teachers to continuously monitor overall progress of students. These methodologies also permit tutors to modify, reinforce and model educational processes, thereby fulfilling the cognitive needs and requirements of students. Interactivity available in third generation distance learning methodologies enhances active engagement of students in the learning process and leads to improved academic achievement. The implementation of distance learning technologies at different educational levels (elementary, secondary, tertiary) has been found to promote efficient and effective learning and instruction (Katz, 1998; Katz, 1999).

As a result of the increasingly successful adoption of distance learning methodologies in the Israeli educational system, fourth generation distance learning is gradually being introduced at the secondary and tertiary levels. Ismail et al (2010) confronted the implications of learning and instruction using fourth generation technology based distance learning courses. Learning has become significantly more flexible and content sources more accessible. Creating, sharing and knowledge capitalization are all facilitated by fourth generation distance learning. Wider sources of learning are provided in ICT based distance learning courses and worldwide expertise can systematically be brought to the student's desktop.

With the rapid development of fourth generation distance learning delivery, increasingly more research studies have been conducted in an attempt to evaluate the major issues related to ICT based distance learning. For example Chandra and Watters (2012) indicated that learning physics through the medium of fourth generation technology not only enhanced students' learning outcomes, but also had a positive impact on their attitudes toward the study of physics. Valaitis et al (2005) found that students who experienced up to date technology based distance learning courses perceived that the methodology increased their learning flexibility and enhanced their ability to process content, and provided access to valuable learning resources. Abdallah (2009) found that latest technology based distance learning methodologies contributed to improved quality of students' learning experiences.

One of the emerging learning strategies that has developed in technology based distance learning in recent years and is receiving growing attention from both students and teachers is in the domain of mobile learning (Prensky, 2005). It should be noted that the use of mobile learning is multi-dimensional and mobile technology now provides technological possibilities including voice, text, still-camera, video, paging and geo-positioning capabilities. These tools provide a rich variety of platforms that enhance the learning process. Moreover, mobile learning is not bound by space or time and students can choose to engage in learning without almost any limitations (Dieterle & Dede, 2006). Thus fourth generation distance learning technologies and methodologies are perceived to make a positive contribution to education and the Israeli educational authorities are increasingly insistent on the adoption of such technologies for teaching and learning (Naim, 2010).

4 Affective Variables and ICT

The research to date conducted to determine the relationship between ICT based learning and instruction and achievement is inconclusive. On the one hand, Hunley et al (2005), Gonzalez (2011), Alsafran and Brown (2012), Townsend (2012), Fairlie and Robinson (2013) in the United States and Mevarech (1988), Katz (1993) as well as Katz and Yablon (2009; 2011a; 2012) in Israel found no significant relationship between the use of ICT technologies in learning and instruction and academic and scholastic achievement. On the other hand Huffman, Goldberg and Michlin (2003), Lowther, Ross, and Morrison, (2003), Judge (2005) in the United States, Cheema and Zhang (2013) in the 2003 Program for International Student Assessment (PISA) study, and Liao (2007) in Taiwan found that ICT based learning and instruction are positively related to academic and scholastic achievement.

The evidence regarding the relationship between ICT based learning and instruction on the one hand and achievement on the other is inconclusive, Mevarech and Hativa (1996) and Katz and Yablon (2011a) suggested that the findings and results of research projects that examined the mediating effect of affective variables on the relationship between ICT based learning and instruction be studied. Mevarech (1988), Katz (1993), Ellington (2003), and Liu et al (2006) indicated that the relationship between ICT utilization in the educational system and academic and scholastic achievement is largely dependent on affective variables that seemingly mediate ICT based learning and instruction on the one hand and achievement on the other. Thus it was postulated that affective variables that act as mediators may hold the key to understanding the relationship between ICT based learning and instruction and academic and scholastic achievement.

Mevarech (1988) emphasized the fact that affective variables are of major importance when assessing the effectiveness and efficiency of ICT based learning and instruction approaches. According to Mevarech attitudinal research can shed light on how effectiveness and efficiency may be enhanced in the course of the educational process. One of the major issues apparently related to positive ICT attitudes as well as to efficient ICT in the classroom, is that pertaining to teachers' as well as students' attitudinal profiles (Kulik, Bangert-Drowns and Williams, 1983). Chandra, Bliss & Cox (1988) stated that the attitudinal sets that teachers bring with them to the instructional situation seem to be important factors in their decisions to utilize ICT in the instructional process or to disregard them as instructional aids.

Research studies carried out in a number of countries have indicated the relationship between affective variables characterizing teachers and ICT based learning and instruction. Stibble (1984), Smylie (1988) and van Deusen and Donham (1986) suggested that self-need for innovation among teachers contributes significantly toward their utilization of ICT based learning and instruction processes. Yaqhi (1996) indicated that teachers felt that the use of computers in the school classroom made a positive contribution to students' achievement. They emphasized the motivational advantages of computer use in the instructional process. Bradley and Russell (1997) indicated that Australian teachers perceived that attitudes such as anxiety and social embarrassment were negatively correlated with a feeling of computer competence and inversely related to a feeling of control when using ICT based learning and instruction in elementary schools. Harris (1999) postulated that teacher autonomy and product involvement are two major attitudinal factors that positively correlate with enhanced computer use by teachers at the tertiary educational level. van Braak, Tondeur, and Valcke (2004) found that technological innovativeness and positive feelings towards the efficacy of ICT based instruction as well as gender (male) were related to effective computer use in the school classroom. Sadik (2006) confirmed that Egyptian teachers, characterized by computer confidence, computer liking and computer usefulness (factors developed by Loyd and Gressard, 1984), were able to more efficiently utilize ICT to enhance the instructional process in their classrooms. Karim (2012) found that head teachers as well as deputy head teachers in Pakistan who held positive attitudes toward the use of computers in learning and instruction were confident that the use of ICT enhanced the quality of the educational process.

Research studies were conducted in a the United States as well as in a number of European and Asian countries in order to examine the relationship between students' attitudes to ICT based learning and instruction and scholastic achievement. Griswold (1984) found that positive attitudes such as self-recognition and self-confidence in computer assisted learning are related to higher levels of achievement attained by elementary school students. Munger and Loyd (1989) found that both male and female high school students who held more positive attitudes toward computers were found to attain a higher level of achievement in than students of both sexes with more negative attitudes. Woodrow (1991) described the existence of a significant relationship between locus of control and students' attitudes toward the use of computers in the classroom. Kirkman (1993) indicated that 12 year-old students who held more enthusiastic attitudes toward computers, were more confident using computers and spent more time using them, attained a higher level of scholastic achievement that students whose attitudes and experiences with computers were less positive. Anderson and Hornby (1996) pointed out that participation of students in ICT based learning at the tertiary level leads to more positive computer attitudes than those held by students who did not experience ICT based learning. Tsai and Tsai (2003), in their research study of elementary school students, indicated the existence of a positive relationship between higher computer mastery, more positive computer attitudes, and lower computer anxiety on the one hand and higher-order metacognitive skills in selecting main ideas and using resources helpful for learning language comprehension on the other. The results of a study conducted by Pilli and Aksu (2013) confirmed the existence of a positive relationship between fourth grade students' attitudes toward computer-assisted learning of mathematics, their attitudes towards mathematics and their scholastic achievement in mathematics.

Studies have been conducted over the years in the Israeli educational system with regard to the relationship of affective variables towards ICT based learning and instruction. These studies have yielded empirical evidence similar to that found in other countries as described in the above paragraphs. Following are studies that examined affective attitudes of Israeli teachers to ICT based learning and instruction. Offir and Katz (1990) indicated that risk-taking was an important variable related to teachers' positive perceptions of computers as making a significant contribution to the learning and instructional processes. Teachers were took risks in their daily lives were more positive about ICT based learning and instruction than teachers who were more cautious and avoided risk-taking behavior. Katz and Offir (1991) reported that teachers, whose attitudinal profiles included a clear tendency toward extraversion, personal stability, and tough mindedness, were more positive about using computers in learning and instruction and were more successful in their educational roles than teaches who were introverted, less stable and sensitive.

Katz (1999) studied a group of kindergarten teachers who underwent 10 hours of ICT based virtual reality simulation as opposed to 10 hours of workshop activity experienced by a comparison group of their counterparts. Both ICT and workshop methodologies were designed to promote improved understanding of kindergarten children's needs. Results of the study indicate that the kindergarten teachers who were trained through the ICT virtual reality technology developed a better understanding of children's needs and perceptions than those trained through the workshop method. Passig and Levin (2000) indicated that in schools where sophisticated multimedia learning and instructional packages were introduced into the school curriculum, teacher motivation and interest in the instructional process was increased and contributed to the enhancement of student achievement. Katz (2005) studied two groups of final year teacher trainees who were exposed to instruction presented in two different distance learning delivery systems. The first group of teacher trainees experienced instruction via a sophisticated flexible ICT based platform and the second group was exposed to an advanced but rigid video-conferencing instructional delivery system. Results of the study indicate that the students exposed to the flexible ICT based instructional approach indicated significantly higher levels of student satisfaction and control over the learning process than their counterparts who were instructed via video-conferencing methodology. Katz (2002) noted that affective attitudes such as independence, creativity, tough-mindedness, sociability, risk-taking, and stimulus-seeking have been shown to make a positive impact on teachers in their willingness to use ICT based learning and instruction in their classrooms. It is evident from the empirical evidence quoted above that these affective attitudes of teachers are vital to positively enhanced ICT utilization that conceivably leads to an improvement in the educational process.

Studies were conducted in Israel in which the relationship between students' affective attitudes and ICT based learning and instruction was examined. Katz and Offir (1990) found that positive attitudes toward ICT based learning and instruction were related to self-esteem, school motivation and satisfaction. Elementary school students with positive self-esteem preferred ICT based learning as did students who expressed dissatisfaction with teachers who used traditional and conservative teaching methods. Katz (1994) investigated attitudes of Israeli junior high school students who excelled in their ICT based learning. Results of the study indicate that pupils with higher learning self-image, higher social self-image, and internal locus of control tend to hold more positive computer related attitudes than pupils not characterized by these personality traits. Barak, Waks and Doppelt (2000) described how Israeli high school students, characterized as having high scholastic potential but functioning as underachievers, were taught higher order thinking skills and strategies via ICT based learning and instruction. As a result of the utilization of computers in the learning process these students' scholastic achievement, self-efficacy and study motivation were significantly enhanced. Katz (2002) demonstrated how affective attitudes held by students, such as self-image, social-image, self-confidence, internal locus of control, satisfaction, and study motivation are related to students' willingness to participate in ICT based learning and instruction. Katz and Yablon (2011b) showed in their study that students who received ICT based learning and instruction were significantly more positive on three affective variables, namely learner motivation, learner autonomy and learner control of the learning process than students who received traditional class-based instruction.

5 Conclusions

Empirical evidence has clearly indicated the existence of a relationship between affective variables and teachers' as well as students' perceptions of ICT based learning and instruction. Need for innovation, risk-taking, stimulus seeking, tough mindedness, extraversion, personal stability, sociability, self-image, social image, self-confidence, study motivation, learner autonomy, control of the learning and instructional process are just some of the affective attitudinal variables related to enhanced ICT based learning and instruction as well as to enhanced scholastic achievement. There is growing empirical evidence that the abovementioned affective variables serve as mediators between ICT based learning and instruction and achievement. Because of the affective nature of the mediating variables and the vast intricacies of the psychological basis of these variables, it is impossible to suggest a unitary model that can adequately describe the relationship between ICT learning and instruction and achievement under all circumstances. Therefore the model, being dependent on the affective make up of teachers as well as students, is one that can only address the principles of the relationship between ICT based learning and instruction and educational achievement.

Furthermore it would be a serious misjudgement to assume that all teachers and learners perceive ICT in the educational framework from the same point of view. Just as in traditional learning and instruction teachers usually prefer instructional approaches that impress them as suitable for their own particular instructional needs and students usually prefer learning methods that correlate with their own particular learning needs, the same is correct vis-à-vis the use of ICT based learning and instruction. Not all teachers perceive ICT based teaching as suitable for their needs and not all students feel that ICT based learning is suited to them. Thus differential ICT based learning and instruction is necessary in the educational process, a situation not yet recognized as valid or necessary by educators and educational policy planners.

It should be noted that although ICT based learning and instruction is now part and parcel of daily educational routine and one could intuitively conclude that attitudinal structures or constraints are relatively unimportant when considering the motivation to use ICT based methodologies in education in general and in the learning situation in particular, the evidence presented in this chapter confirms the chain of findings reviewed above that indicate that affective variables and attitudes of teachers and students are primary differential factors to be taken into consideration when assessing their capacity to best utilize ICT in learning and instruction.

References

Abdallah, S.: Learning with online activities: What do students think about their experience? International Journal of Web- Based Learning and Teaching Technologies 4(2), 1–25 (2009)

Alsafran, E., Brown, D.S.: The relationship between classroom computer technology and students' academic achievement. Research in Higher Education Journal 15, 1–19 (2012)

Anderson, M.D., Hornby, P.A.: Computer attitudes and the use of computers in psychology courses. Behavior Research Methods, Instruments & Computers 28(2), 341–346 (1996)

Appelberg, L.: Communication-learning-information technology applied examples. In: Passey, D., Samways, B. (eds.) Information Technology: Supporting Change Through Teacher Education, pp. 216–221. Chapman and Hall, London (1997)

Barak, M., Waks, S., Doppelt, Y.: Majoring in technology studies at high school and fostering learning. Learning Environments Research 3(2), 135–158 (2000)

Baranauskas, M.C., De Oliveira, O.L.: Domain oriented modelling: A balance between simulation and programming. In: Tinsley, J.D., De Weert, T.J. (eds.) WCCE 1995: Liberating the Learner, pp. 119–126. Chapman and Hall, London (1995)

Bradley, G., Russell, G.: Computer experience, school support and computer anxieties. Educational Psychology 17(3), 267–284 (1997)

Bricken, M., Byrne, C.M.: Summer students in virtual reality: a pilot study on educational applications of virtual reality technology, University of Washington (1992), `http://www.hitl.Washington.edu/projects/education/` (retrieved)

Chandra, P., Bliss, J., Cox, M.: Introducing computers into school management issues. Computers and Education 12(1), 57–61 (1988)

Chandra, V., Watters, J.J.: Re-thinking physics teaching with web-based learning. Computers & Education 58(1), 631–640 (2012)

Cheema, J.R., Zhang, B.: Quantity and quality of computer use and academic achievement: Evidence from a large-scale international test program. International Journal of Education and Development using Information and Communication Technology 9(2), 95–106 (2013)

Chu, C.: The development of interactive distance learning in Taiwan: Challenges and prospects. Educational Media International 36(2), 110–114 (1999)

Dieterle, E., Dede, C.: Building university faculty and student capacity to use wireless handheld devices for learning. In: van 't Hooft, M., Swan, K. (eds.) Ubiquitous Computing in Education: Invisible Technology, Visible Impact, pp. 303–328. Lawrence Erlbaum Associates, Mahwah (2006)

Dreyfus, A., Feinstein, B., Talmon, J.: The electronic spreadsheet and cognitive skills in inquiry oriented biology. In: Passey, D., Samways, B. (eds.) Information Technology: Supporting Change Through Teacher Education, pp. 278–284. Chapman and Hall, London (1997)

Ellington, A.J.: A meta-analysis of the effects of calculators on students' achievement and attitude levels in precollege mathematics classes. Journal for Research in Mathematics Education 34(5), 433–463 (2003)

Ernst, M.L.: The personal computer: growth patterns, limits and new frontiers. Center for Information Policy Research, Harvard University, Cambridge, Mass (1991)

Fairlie, R., Robinson, J.: Experimental evidence on the effects of home computers on academic achievement among schoolchildren. American Economic Journal, Applied Economics 5(3), 211–240 (2013)

Finnie, G.: Switching the U.S. on to ISDN. Telecommunications 23(7), 66–69 (1989)

Givon, Y.: The characteristics of open-ended software. In: Mevarech, Z., Hativa, N. (eds.) The Computer in School, pp. 39–59. Schocken Publishing House (Hebrew), Tel-Aviv (1996)
Gonzalez, R.: A comparison of online with onsite learning of undergraduate students in behavioral science and criminal justice as related to their attitudes toward computers and academic achievement. Unpublished doctoral dissertation, School of Education and Human Services, St John's University, New York (2011)
Griswold, P.A.: Elementary students' attitudes during two years of computer-assisted instruction. American Educational Research Journal 21, 737–754 (1984)
Harris, R.W.: Attitudes towards end-user computing: A structural equation model. Behaviour and Information Technology 18(2), 109–125 (1999)
Hativa, N.: Integrated learning systems. In: Mevarech, Z., Hativa, N. (eds.) The Computer in School, pp. 96–115. Schocken Publishing House (Hebrew), Tel-Aviv (1996)
Henry, D.: Spatial perception in virtual environments: evaluating an architectural application, University of Washington (1992), http://www.hitl.Washington.edu/projects/education/ (retrieved)
Huffman, D., Goldberg, F., Michlin, M.: Using computers to create constructivist learning environments: Impact on pedagogy and achievement. Journal of Computers in Mathematics and Science Teaching 22(2), 151–168 (2003)
Hunley, S.A., Evans, J.H., Delgado-Hachey, M., Krise, J., Rich, T., Schell, C.: Adolescent computer use and academic achievement. Adolescence 40(158), 307–318 (2005)
Ismail, I., Idrus, R.M., Johari, S.S.M.: Acceptance on mobile learning via SMS: a Rasch model analysis. International Journal of Interactive Mobile 4(2), 10–16 (2010)
Judge, S.: The impact of computer technology on academic achievement of young African American children. Journal of Research in Childhood Education 20(2), 91–101 (2005)
Karim, D.: Exploring head and deputy headteachers' attitude towards using computers in education. International Journal of Information and Communication Technology Education 8(2), 20–32 (2012)
Katz, Y.J., Offir, B.: Computer assisted instruction and students' social orientations. In: Proceedings of 5th Jerusalem Conference on Information Technology, pp. 660–664. IEEE: Computer Society Press, Los Alamitos (1990)
Katz, Y.J.: Achievement level, affective attributes and computer oriented attitudes: a profile of a successful end-user. In: Knierzinger, A., Moser, M. (eds.) Informatics and Changes in Learning. SectionVII, pp. 13–15. IST Press, Linz (1993)
Katz, Y.J.: Self-image, locus of control and computer related attitudes. In: Lewis, R., Mendelsohn, P. (eds.) Lessons from Learning, pp. 105–109. Elsevier Science Publishers, Amsterdam (1994)
Katz, Y.J.: The relationship between distance learning methods and satisfaction and achievement of college students. In: Davies, G. (ed.) Teleteaching 1998: Distance Learning, Training and Education, pp. 569–578. Austrian Computer Society (OCG) and IFIP, Vienna (1998)
Katz, Y.J.: Kindergarten teacher training through virtual reality three-dimensional simulation methodology. Education Media International 36(2), 151–156 (1999)
Katz, Y.J.: A model of the psycho-pedagogical and ICT interface. In: Watson, D., Andersen, J. (eds.) Networking the Learner, pp. 311–318. Kluwer Academic Publishers, Boston (2002)
Katz, Y.J.: Distance learning approaches in teacher training. In: Nicholson, P., Thompson, J.B., Ruohonen, M., Multisilta, J. (eds.) E-training Practices for Professional Organizations, pp. 255–262. Kluwer Academic Publishers, Boston (2005)

Katz, Y.J., Offir, B.: The relationship between personality and computer related attitudes of Israeli teachers. Education and Computing 7, 249–252 (1991)

Katz, Y.J., Yablon, Y.B.: Mobile learning: a major e-learning platform. In: Szucs, A. (ed.) New Technology Platforms for Learning Revisited, pp. 121–126. European Distance Education Network, Budapest (2009)

Katz, Y.J., Yablon, Y.B.: Affect and digital learning at the university level. Campus Wide Information Systems 28(2), 114–123 (2011a)

Katz, Y.J., Yablon, Y.B.: Student assessment of affective variables in an internet-based 'Introduction to quantitative research methods' course. In: EURODL, Special Issue on the Best Research Papers Presented at EDEN Conferences 2010, pp. 70–83 (2011b)

Katz, Y.J., Yablon, Y.B.: Acquiring vocabulary at the university level: a comparison of three learning strategies. In: Doyran, F. (ed.) Research on Teacher Education and Training, pp. 267–276. Athens Institute for Education and Research, Athens (2012)

Kirkman, C.: Computer experience and attitudes of 12-year-old students: Implications for the UK National Curriculum. Journal of Computer Assisted Learning 9(1), 51–62 (1993)

Kulik, J.A., Bangert-Drowns, R.L., Williams, G.W.: Effects of computer-based teaching on secondary school students. Journal of Educational Psychology 75, 19–26 (1983)

Leary, J.J.: Computer simulated laboratory experiments and computer games: A designer's analysis. In: Tinsley, J.D., De Weert, T.J. (eds.) WCCE 1995: Liberating the Learner, pp. 963–973. Chapman and Hall, London (1995)

Liao, Y.C.: Effects of computer-assisted instruction on students' achievement in Taiwan: A meta-analysis. Computers & Education 48(2), 216–233 (2007)

Liu, M., Hsieh, P., Cho, Y., Schallert, D.L.: Middle school students' self-efficacy, attitudes, and achievement in a computer-enhanced problem-based learning environment. Journal of Interactive Learning Research 17(3), 225–242 (2006)

Loyd, B.H., Gressard, C.: Reliability and factorial validity of Computer Attitude Scales. Educational and Psychological Measurement 44, 501–505 (1984)

Lowther, D.L., Ross, S.M., Morrison, G.M.: When each one has one: The influences on teaching strategies and student achievement of using laptops in the classroom. Educational Technology Research and Development 51(3), 23–44 (2003)

Mevarech, Z.R.: Intrinsic orientation profiles and learning mathematics in CAI settings. Journal of Educational Research 81, 228–233 (1988)

Mevarech, Z.R., Hativa, N.: Computerized learning environments: For whom and why? In: Mevarech, Z., Hativa, N. (eds.) The Computer in School, pp. 9–15. Schocken Publishing House (Hebrew), Tel-Aviv (1996)

Munger, G.E., Loyd, B.H.: Gender and attitudes toward computers and calculators: Their relationship to math performance. Journal of Educational Computing Research 5(2), 167–177 (1989)

Naim, Y.: Attitudes of elementary school pupils and teachers towards a technology-based learning environment, Ramat-Gan, Israel: Unpublished M.A. Dissertation, School of Education, Bar-Ilan University (2010)

Offir, B., Golub, M., Friedel, S.: Attitudes toward courseware as a function of high school students' creativity level. In: Knierzinger, A., Moser, M. (eds.) Informatics and Changes in Learning. Section VII, pp. 17–19. IST Press, Linz (1993)

Offir, B., Katz, Y.J.: Computer oriented attitudes as a function of risk-taking among Israeli elementary school teachers. Journal of Computer Assisted Learning 6, 168–173 (1990)

Offir, B., Katz, Y.J.: The computer as an instructional aid for studying the humanities. In: Brunnstein, K., Raubold, E. (eds.) Applications and Impacts: Information Processing 1994, vol. 2, pp. 660–665. Elsevier Science Publishers, Amsterdam (1994)
Offir, B., Katz, Y.J., Passig, D.: The utilization of "open" courseware for developing an inquiry approach in the study of non-scientific subjects. In: Benzie, D., Wright, J. (eds.) Exploring a new Partnership: Children, Teachers and Technology, pp. 97–101. Elsevier Science Publishers, Amsterdam (1994)
Passig, D., Levin, H.: Gender differences of favored multimedia learning interfaces. Journal of Computer Assisted Learning 16, 64–71 (2000)
Passig, D., Sharbat, A.: The why and how VR in schools: A preferred future pedagogic mission by a group of worldwide experts in VR and education. The International Journal of Virtual Reality 5(1), 1–11 (2001)
Passig, D., Klein, P., Neuman, T.: Awareness to toddlers' initial cognitive experiences with virtual reality. Journal of Computer Assisted Learning 17(4), 332–344 (2001)
Pilli, O., Aksu, M.: The effects of computer-assisted instruction on the achievement, attitudes and retention of fourth grade mathematics students in North Cyprus. Computers & Education 62, 62–71 (2013)
Prensky, M.: Listen to the natives. Educational Leadership 63(4), 8–13 (2005)
Regain, J.W., Shebliske, W.L.: Virtual reality: an instructional medium for visual and spatial terms. Journal of Communication 42(4), 136–149 (1992)
Sadik, A.: Factors influencing teachers' attitudes toward personal use and school use of computers: New evidence from a developing nation. Evaluation Review 30(1), 86–113 (2006)
Salomon, G.: Technology based learning environments: a conceptual framework. In: In, Z. (ed.) The Computer in School, pp. 17–38. Schocken Publishing House (Hebrew), Tel-Aviv (1996)
Skinner, B.F.: The science of learning and the art of teaching. Harvard Educational Review 24, 86–97 (1954)
Skinner, B.F.: Teaching machines. Science 128, 969–977 (1958)
Smylie, M.A.: The enhancement function of staff development: Organizational and psychological antecedents to individual teacher change. American Educational Research Journal 25, 1–30 (1988)
Southworth, J.H., Flanigan, J.M., Knezek, G.: Computers in education: International multi-node electronic conferencing. The Printout, 8–13 (1981)
Stibble, J.L.: Managing the curriculum. School Organisation 4, 27–33 (1984)
Townsend, M.C.: Computer technology, student achievement, and equity: A multilevel analysis of the relationship between high school students' use of computers, Gender, and mathematics achievement. Unpublished doctoral dissertation, Graduate School, North Carolina State University, Raleigh, NC (2012)
Trentin, G.: Telematics and on-line teacher training: the POLARIS project. Journal of Computer Assisted Learning 13, 261–270 (1997)
Tsai, M.J., Tsai, C.C.: Student computer achievement, attitude, and anxiety: The role of learning strategies. Journal of Educational Computing Research 28(1), 47–61 (2003)
Turman, R.A., Matton, J.S.: Virtual reality: towards improvement in simulation based training. Educational Technology 34(8), 56–64 (1994)

Valaitis, R.K., Sword, W.A., Jones, B., Hodges, A.: Problem- based learning online: perceptions of health science students. Advances in Health Sciences Education 10(3), 231–252 (2005)
van Braak, J., Tondeur, J., Valcke, M.: Explaining different types of computer use among primary school teachers. European Journal of Psychology of Education 19(4), 407–422 (2004)
van Deusen, M.R., Donham, J.: The teacher's role in using the computer to teach thinking skills. The Computing Teacher 14, 32–34 (1986)
Woodrow, J.E.J.: Locus of control and computer attitudes as determinants of the computer literacy of student teachers. Computers and Education 16, 237–245 (1991)
Yaqhi, H.: The role of the computer in the school as perceived by computer using teachers and school administrators. Journal of Educational Computing Research 15(2), 137–155 (1996)

Predicting the Future of Computers in Schools – A Reflection Paper?

Richard Taylor

International Baccalaureate Organisation, Cardiff, UK
richard.taylor@ibo.org

Abstract. Over the last 25 years advances in Information and Communication Technologies (ICTs) have led to significant changes in the way that computers[1] are used within an educational context. As schools in many ways reflect a microcosm of society, one consequence for the school community is that the relationship between the computers and the computer users has become increasingly complex. There has been a blurring of the traditional clearly defined boundaries, not only between home and school computer use, but also within schools in the way that teaching and learning are carried out. This blurring may be attributed to many factors, but the continuing miniaturisation, portability and ubiquity of the computer itself is probably the most important. For many students the computer, as well as being an obligatory fashion accessory, is seen as indispensable. The thought of having to function without a computer is something for many students is hard to envisage. The only certainty for students, teachers and school managers is the continuous evolution of computers will lead to a constantly changing digital landscape.

Keywords: Computer, convergence, ubiquitous, ethical norms, behavioural norms.

1 Computers in Schools – Case Studies

In such an ever-changing landscape, school managers[2] will need to be aware of both the physical environment related to the computer and network infrastructure as well as the wider ranging social and ethical impacts related to computer use. They will need coherent strategies to harness the benefits that computers bring and to minimise any potential problems that may result. This is something that has not always been done successfully in the past.

---

[1] Computers are used as a generic term to include any digital device such as a desktop personal computer, laptop, tablet or mobile device. The software and platforms that are used alongside computers are included within this generic term.

[2] The term manager is used to refer to senior managers (school administrator in the United States of America (USA)). Within a school managers can exist at a range of levels from the classroom teacher who will manage the use of computers within the classroom, to departmental or faculty heads who will manage the teachers and computer use at a departmental level and senior managers.

A. Tatnall and B. Davey (Eds.): History of Computers in Education, IFIP AICT 424, pp. 339–346, 2014.

The advances in computers have impacted on schools in a number of ways. These increasing capabilities that result from upgrading the computers every few years have led to the expansion and further development of the network infrastructure, the introduction of new software as well as changes in curriculum development and pedagogy to utilise these new opportunities. However, this increasing usage of computers can be a 'double-edged sword'. While computers can provide opportunities, each of these changes usually requires professional development for staff and may inadvertently shape behavioural and ethical norms. One example in the United Kingdom (UK) is the use of statistical packages such as a School Information Management System (SIMS), introduced during the 1990s, to track the progress of students. While in some ways SIMS can provide significantly more information about student performance, it may have unintentional longer term effects; the over-reliance of a data driven approach in the performance management of teachers, and a modification of pedagogy leading to the compartmentalisation of learning to ensure the meeting of short term targets at the expense of allowing the students to develop a holistic subject knowledge.

The mid 1970s saw a drastic change in the use of computers in schools. As the cost of personal computers (PCs) became increasingly affordable, increasing numbers were purchased. By the early 1980s many managers could see the potential benefits that computers could bring, for example purchasing the BBC Micro for tasks such as data logging in subjects like Science and Geography or to enable the introduction of Computer Science. Throughout the 1980s computers became widespread across schools as their capabilities continued to increase and their relative cost continued to decrease. One result was the development of a small number of classrooms that provided each student with sole access to a networked computer for duration of the lesson; a dedicated computer room.

By the mid-1990s there was a realisation by managers that computers could be included in whole school strategies that extended beyond a few dedicated computer rooms supported by small clusters[3] or individual computers scattered across the school. These strategies included becoming a laptop school, or implementing 1:1 (one computer per child) schemes or Bring Your Own Device (BYOD) / Bring Your Own Technology (BYOT). The aim of these strategies was to increase the availability of computers for students, with the ultimate goal of providing every student with continuous access to a computer such as an iPad™, tablet or laptop.

Carey Baptist School (Melbourne, Australia)[4] was a pioneer among laptop schools. In the mid-1990s a decision to introduce one laptop per student was based on the potential educational benefits from allowing each student continuous access to a laptop computer. There were also other factors that lay behind this decision such as recognising the marketing potential of introducing the laptop initiative in a highly competitive marketplace with many fee paying schools within a few kilometres of each other, as well as a relatively affluent parent community that would enable, if necessary, the costs of implementation being shared between the school and the

---

[3] Clusters refers to a small numbers of computers, usually about 5, that were located in a classroom to assist with the teaching and learning that students could use as and when required.

[4] Information provided by Mike Fitzpatrick, Carey Baptist School, Melbourne, Australia.

parents to ensure each student had access to a laptop. However, this scheme was not straightforward as it required an intensive and protracted staff training programme (estimated to be at least 8 years before the laptops became fully integrated into daily teaching across the whole school) and the purchasing of a sizable number of computers to effectively create the critical mass for the scheme to succeed. In addition to the purchase of computers, other hardware was purchased such as data projectors to supplement the use of laptops, the school IT network infrastructure was upgraded providing access to the Internet from every classroom through Wi-Fi. A significant proportion of resources were also allocated to create a dedicated IT Support Team whose sole role was to the support all members of the school community without any responsibility for the teaching of the students.

As computers have become increasingly less expensive and portable, other schools have introduced 1:1 policies. Some 1:1 policies have been made possible by collaboration between the school, such as Nan Chau Primary School (Singapore) which has teamed up in 2012 with Microsoft and Qualcomm Incorporated to create a 21st century classroom using smartphones (Tech&Learning International 2012). It provides a learning environment accessible to its 350 third grade students as well as staff and parents. Staff training has been provided through the National Institute of Education of Singapore to ensure a successful implementation of the policy. Other schools such as Essa Academy in the UK market themselves as iPad schools where every teacher and student uses an iPad rather than traditional pen and paper (Muffett 2013). Like Carey Baptist School, these schemes rely on significant investments in infrastructure, staff training and parental "buy-in" and the benefits of this intensive use of computers may take a number of years to reach fruition.

Other schools, such as Westwood High School (South Carolina, USA) have taken a different approach. Since 2012 Westwood has mixed 1:1 and BYOD policies. "We have a system that is 1:1 take-home. That requires parents to pay a self-insurance fee each year to cover the cost of repairs for damages. For parents who don't want to pay the fee, we offer a daily checkout option. We also allow students to bring their own devices, provided they run Google Chrome. We use Google Apps for Education and help students set up their Google Drive Offline so they can work on projects at home without internet access" (Coulter 2013).

Unlike laptop and 1:1 initiatives, the decision to use BYOD to ensure the intensive use of computers is one that may reflect the ability of schools to raise the necessary capital; the average cost of a tablet in 2012 was about $US200. In the UK, in a survey carried out by the British Educational Suppliers Association (BESO) between 50% - 80% of schools indicated they would be prepared to implement some form of BYOD policy (Ghosh 2013). Although this approach would enable students to have constant access to computers and not overstretch school budgets, it does raise significant questions about management of the school network and the computers themselves. With a more decentralised BYOD approach come potentially significant compatibility, appropriate use, ownership and ultimately trust issues which may not have been fully investigated in the initial implementation of the BYOD scheme.

2 Computers in Schools – A Blurring of the Boundaries

The delineation of the computer-based environment within and beyond schools is becoming more and more blurred. In the early 1990s, many homes in the UK had access to a computer but not to the Internet. It would not be until 2000 that 25% of the population has Internet access. Throughout the 1990s computers were used in designated spaces such as in the home or at school to provide additional skills, for example being able to proficiently use word processing, spreadsheet, presentation, data logging and database software to complement learning activities. Any transfer of information between the home and school computers would have been on a floppy disk. Today, the school student exists in a networked world, (Wenmoth 2013): the "cloud" acts as the mechanism to ensure the continuity of access to resources and ubiquitous use of computers. Some schools such as United World College (Singapore) have since 2011 implemented cloud storage strategies, such as Google Drive. This cloud-based approach could be used to support laptop, 1:1 or BYOD strategies.

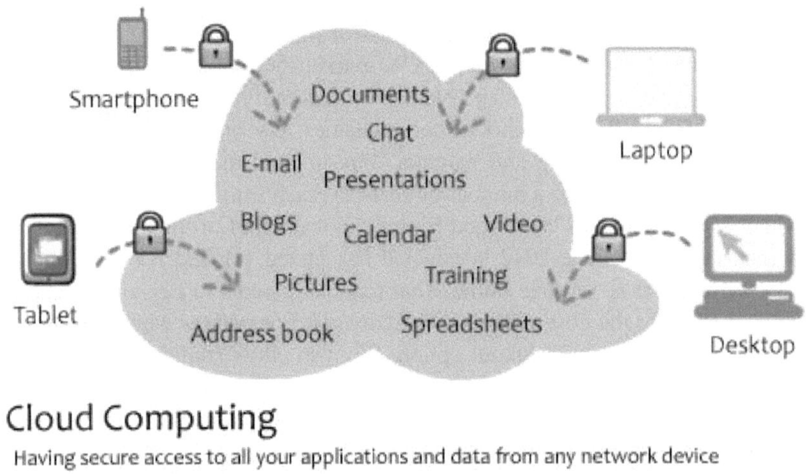

Fig. 1. A representation of cloud computing environment that many school students use (Wikipedia 2011)

This ubiquitous use of computers in a networked world is also represented in the Bradley Convergence Model, in particular in the life role of the individual. The model focuses on the convergence and integration for people through the technology which is becoming increasingly ubiquitous, the different roles of people such as their private or public role, their life environment which may be home or at work and the effects of increasing globalisation which may shape their work patterns, values and norms (Bradley 2010). This merging of roles, as illustrated in Figure 1 above and the image below, encapsulates the problems that may arise when developing school policies linked to contemporary computer use. In many cases it is almost impossible to distinguish whether the computer is being used for school work, for gathering images for the writing up of field work outside the classroom on return to the classroom, for example, from a museum, or for social purposes.

Fig. 2. A museum visit: educational or social use of computers?[5]

3 The School as a Digital Society – Developing New Strategies

While many schools have seen the use of computers as a mechanism to support the digital citizenship (people who use IT systems extensively) of the students and teachers, BYOD schools may extend digital citizenship into the development of a digital society. Kwon et al (2013) define this as being when the "social and cultural impact of digitalization has increased to a point where it cannot be separated from

[5] Photo used courtesy of Gunilla Bradley.

daily lives of citizens". A digital society, or digital school, is characterised by three cultures: the digital tools which allow humans to maintain his/her social life in the digital society and considered as the ground for other elements of the digital culture, the digital values which form a belief system that provides meanings or goals for human behaviours or social activities in the digital society and the digital norms which represents normative procedures and rules that are socially acknowledged in carrying out digital activities. (Kwon et al 2013). The culture of tools, which equates to the acquisition of computers, may be easier and quicker to achieve than the other two elements, those of the values and norms.

With such profound changes to computers and the digital landscape occurring so rapidly, many managers have struggled to adapt their strategies accordingly. A prerequisite for the successful implementation of BYOD policies is manager readiness: "in many cases managers in schools will to ensure they remain up to date with their understanding of role of technology and how this will be reflected through school policies, pedagogical practices and change management as their ICT resources will be undergoing an almost constant evolution" (Kelly 2013). However, these disparities between the manager's understanding of the role of technology and the nature of the digital landscape they exist within are not a recent concern. Many "managers do not include staff development in the equation, instead they provide programs that do little more than ensure that teachers are able to unjam the printer or use one piece of canned instructional software" (Stager 1995). Therefore in the intervening 18 years, rather than reducing these disparities, they appear to be increasing.

If managers are not able to understand the implications of the changing digital landscape, the rapid evolution and proliferation of computers may outstrip the capabilities of the school's infrastructure. This may result in technical problems for both teachers and students. The managers also face a range of technical, social and ethical issues when the same computer is used by the student or teacher in schools, at home and socially. This constant use of computers is also leading to intended or unintended changes in the behavioural norms of the computer user. Managers need to decide to what extent they accept that the ubiquitous nature of computers is leading to ethical and behavioural changes, for example the perception of privacy being less important for students, 'the Facebook generation', and how the school will need to adapt their acceptable computer use policies accordingly.

Many schools are already struggling to formulate appropriate computer use policies as almost all students carry cell (mobile) phones and many use them during lessons. One teacher in the United States (US) noted that its managers have already adapted their cell phone policy to address this issue: "School cell phone (electronic device) policy changed this year. They can only be used before school, during lunch, and after school. It seems too many students were busy texting and were tardy to class. I do like the fact that students are not tempted to pull phones out of their pockets/purses/backpacks during class anymore[6]." However, if the school decides to implement a BYOD policy, this will require a significant re-evaluation of this type of policy and a re-education of students about the appropriate use of cell phones. It is possible that this dash towards technology may have unexpected results and not lead to the desired outcomes.

[6] Information provided by Carol Mathis, St Petersburg High School, Florida, US.

There is also the risk of managers being "seduced" by technology as they attempt to enable the school to keep pace with the advances in computers. An alternative approach, the slow tech approach, is based on the premise that "society has been seduced by a rapid pace of development of ICT, progressively celebrated year on year for its growing speed and power". For society in general, and in this case for school managers, they may need to reflect on "a new way of thinking about ICT in the future: a slower, more careful, more considered, and more ethical manner; a slow tech approach" (Whitehouse and Patrignani 2013).

A key role of schools is to prepare their students to act as informed citizens in a digital world so managers must decide to what extent they wish to reflect the changing nature of computer use in society. These changing patterns of use are leading to an evolution of new behavioural norms. These include the need for immediate gratification (an almost instantaneous response to a call, text or tweet), the development of a new lexicon that include terms such as 'Big Data', lol, folksonomies, and verbs such as 'to Google'. Managers must determine the extent to which these changes should be incorporated into the formal and informal curriculum.

Furthermore, all societies experience inequalities. They face difficult decisions in determining what can be considered as an acceptable level of inequality between citizens. For schools the poorly managed implementation of strategies such as becoming a laptop, iPad, 1:1 or BYOD School may unknowingly exacerbate these inequalities. For the school to ensure its transition to an effective digital society, it is not enough to simply increase the provision of computers. Digital values and digital norms must also be addressed.

4 Towards the Future: The Difficult Decisions Ahead

If the boundaries between students' homes, schools and leisure lives become so indistinct, the traditional home / school model, and the policies and procedures associated with computer use will need to be constantly updated. In 10 years time, the role of the computer will most probably be as the facilitating device that enables students and teachers to remain constantly part of a networked world. In such a rapidly evolving digital landscape it is almost impossible to envisage what computers will be like in 2024, perhaps all students will be wearing Google Goggles™. It is almost inevitable that if the continued rate of the evolution of computers remains unchecked, schools will always be playing catch-up with any policies linked to computer procurement and usage. Alternatively, after so much change, perhaps a period of reflection will take place with managers adopting the slow tech approach.

Acknowledgements. Mike Fitzpatrick and Carol Mathis for sharing their thoughts and experiences from their respective schools.

Gunilla Bradley for the image from the museum.

Sandra Stark and Diane Whitehouse for their feedback during the authoring of this text.

References

1. BBC News Channel. Superpower: Visualising the Internet (2013), `http://news.bbc.co.uk/1/hi/technology/8552410.stm` (last accessed December 23, 2013)

2. Bradley, G.: The Convergence Theory on ICT, Society and Human Beings – towards the Good ICT society (2010), http://www.triple-c.at/index.php/tripleC/article/download/170/186 (last accessed October 7, 2013)
3. Bradley, G.: The Convergence Theory on ICT, Society and Human Beings – towards the Good ICT society. In: Kommers, P. (ed.) Proceedings of IADIS multi-Conference on ICT Society and Human Being, Prague, Keynote address (2013)
4. Coulter, L., et al.: Have any of you had a BYOD or 1 to 1 initiative in your districts whereby parents wanted to opt out? If so, were teachers at your school willing to provide alternative assignments? (2013), http://www.linkedin.com/groupItem?view=&gid=2811&type=member&item=270733219&commentID=162270305&report.success=8ULbKyXO6NDvmoK7o030UNOYGZKrvdhBhypZ_w8EpQrrQI-BBjkmxwkEOwBjLE28YyDIxcyEO7_TA_giuRN#comme (last accessed September 26, 2013)
5. Ghosh, S.: Schools warm up to BYOD for tablets (2013), http://www.pcpro.co.uk/news/education/382006/schools-warm-up-to-byod-for-tablets (last accessed October 7, 2013)
6. Kelly, A.: What are the biggest challenges facing BYOD and BYOT in education? (2013), http://www.naace.co.uk/byoddiscussion (last accessed October 7, 2013)
7. Kwon, M., et al.: Index development and application for measuring the level of digital culture. In: Kommers, P. (ed.) Proceedings of IADIS Multi-Conference on ICT Society and Human Beings, Prague, pp. 88–95 (2013)
8. Murdock, E.: History, the History of Computers, and the History of Computers in Education (2007), http://www.csulb.edu/~murdock/histofcs.html (last accessed November 25, 2013)
9. Muffett, T.: Essa Academy: Bookless school where everyone has iPad (2013), http://www.bbc.co.uk/news/education-20930195 (last accessed October 7, 2013)
10. Patrignani, N., Whitehouse, D.: From slow food to slow tech, a reflection paper. In: Kommers, P. (ed.) Proceedings of IADIS multi-Conference on ICT Society and Human Beings, Prague, pp. 160–164 (2013)
11. Stager, G.: Laptop schools lead the way in professional development. Educational Leadership 53(2), 78–81 (1995), http://www.ascd.org/publications/educational-leadership/oct95/vol53/num02 (last accessed November 25, 2013)
12. Tech&Learning International. Singapore primary school launches 3G smartphone initiative (2012), http://www.techlearning.com/Default.aspx?tabid=67&EntryId=4094#disqus_thread (last accessed October 7, 2013)
13. The Journal. Computers in Education (1997), http://thejournal.com/Articles/1997/06/01/Computers-in-Education-A-Brief-History.aspx?Page=4 (last accessed December 23, 2013)
14. Wenmoth, D.: The emerging paradigm (2013), http://blog.core-ed.org/derek/2013/09/learning-in-a-networked-world.html (last accessed October 7, 2013)
15. Wikipedia. Cloud Computing (July 4, 2011), http://en.wikipedia.org/wiki/File:Cloud_applications.jpg (last accessed October 7, 2011)

Experiences as a Student in Chile with only Pre-computer Technologies

Fernando Toro

Victoria University, Melbourne, Australia
c-fernandot@hotmail.com

Abstract. This chapter takes the form of a narrative and describes a mix of experiences dealing with exclusion, poverty, teaching methods, and reforms in the school system in Chile, which not only included monetary injections but also the consideration and research into the use of ICTs in its early manifestations, such as TV as a teaching tool. The chapter also describes some of the experiences during the early days of the Pinochet Dictatorship as a student. The events experienced by the writer, as described in this chapter, took place between 1966 and 1975.

Teaching methods in the 1960s in Chile, as experienced as a primary school student in Arica, were repetitive and required a good memory rather than striving to engage the young eager student. Despite the increased emphasis on improving education during the 1960s in Chile, whilst attending a rural school, a new reality was presented which in retrospect, seemed to reveal that there was still much more to be done and/or that the measures were missing the intended mark. However, as a child, the realities faced by the rural students were evident, even to a young student who had never attended a school outside Arica before. Computers were unknown to us at the time and I could not have imagined those students from a low socio-economic background having easy access one, had they been around back then. I can state though, that the earliest mathematical tool, I used as a student, was an abacus that we made as part of a project.

By the 1970s education and the socio-economics aspects of it took centre stage and new reforms and an increased budget was allocated to it. Yet, there was no silver bullet to solve those socio-economic deformities that existed at the time. Thus, the lack of Social Inclusion and Social Capital remained an issue and which was bound to marginalise students from a low socio-economical group, especially those in rural school. Later on, the Pinochet coup was to change the whole of the education landscape.

Keywords: social inclusion and education, education in Chile, ICT, education, teaching method, learning; rural education, actor-network theory, innovation translation.

1 Arica – A Very Brief History

I was born in Arica, Chile. Arica is a port city with a current population of just over 196,000. The city is the northernmost city in Chile, sharing a border with Peru and Bolivia Arica is also the capital of the Arica Province and the Arica and Parinacota

A. Tatnall and B. Davey (Eds.): History of Computers in Education, IFIP AICT 424, pp. 347–364, 2014.

Region (Wikipedia Contributors; 2013a). In 1970, Arica had a population of 92,500 (Instituto Nacional De Estadisticas - Direccion Regional Arica y Parinacota 2003). In Arica, it is common to see Chileans, Peruvians and Bolivians co-existing. Apart from those that consider themselves as 'Chileans', the region of Arica-Parinacota has a significant number of Aymara people, who have inhabited the region since pre-Columbian times and their descendants have continued to live in the region (Wikipedia Contributors; 2013b). According to the 2002 census, 4.6% of the total population was considered to belong to an indigenous ethnic group. Out of those that belonged to an indigenous ethnic group, the Mapuche encompass just over 87%, being the biggest ethnicity of the eight recognised original indigenous inhabitants. The next group is the Aymara, with 7% (Instituto Nacional De Estadisticas 2008).

Arica has a long history, in fact, the people of the Chinchorro culture are the first known inhabitants of the region who made Arica their centre and who are well known for the mummification of their dead. Their mummies date from around 7020 BC to 1050 BC (Colaboradores de Wikipedia; 2013) and preceded the Egyptian mummies. However, the Chinchorro people are sometimes considered an oddity, given that their society was mainly hunter-gatherer and did not appear to have an advanced society, such as the Egyptians' during the peak of their culture.

The Arica Culture followed the Chinchorro and dated from 1050 to 1350 DC. The Arica culture was tied to the Tiwanaku Culture, mainly centred in what is now Bolivia. The Arica people developed irrigation techniques, relied on agriculture and trade. The Arica culture is also known for their textiles and ceramics (Colaboradores de Wikipedia; 2003).

Arica was later occupied by the Spanish in 1536 (known as the Viceroyalty of Peru) and after the rich silver mines of Potosi were discovered it became an important port and in 1570 Arica was given the title of city by the Spaniards and was named 'La Muy Ilustre y Real Ciudad San Marcos de Arica' (Colaboradores de Wikipedia; 2003) . Due to the amount of riches being shipped from Arica, it was not uncommon that it soon attracted a myriad of pirates. Amongst those that 'visited' Arica, we come across such names as, Drake, Cavendish, Hawkins, van Spilbergen, Watling, Sharp, Cordes, Dampier and Clipperton, to name a few (Colaboradores de Wikipedia; 2003). To this day, the cemetery in Arica has a tombstone bearing the name of Sir Francis Drake. I do not know who put it there or why but I remember my Father taking us to see the burial place of the famous Pirate Drake. I doubt that Drake is buried in Arica but for some obscure reason, a tombstone bears his name and remains in place in Arica's Cemetery.

Eventually, Peru was liberated from Spanish rule and became a republic (Colaboradores de Wikipedia; 2003) and thus, it was the end of the Viceroyalty of Peru (Harvey 2002). Arica was then designated as a Province of the Department of Arequipa, which is in Peru (Colaboradores de Wikipedia; 2003).

Later when the Industrial revolution was in full swing, the nitrate rich lands of Bolivia and to some extent Peru, attracted many Chilean workers to work in the 'Salitreras'. However, due to foreign interests, Chile declared war against Peru and Bolivia (Galeano 2004). The conflict lasted from 1879 to 1883 (Punto Final 2003) and eventually annexed Arica to its territory. The reasons behind the conflict, to this day, remain hotly contested and Peru together with Bolivia still disputes the outcome.

Bolivia is now landlocked and wants access to the sea. Peru has never given hope on reclaiming Arica. The fact remains though that Bolivia lost their access to the sea and one of the most mineral rich areas on the planet.

2 My Early School Years in Arica

I attended school in Arica during the late 60s until early 1975. During that time, I attended three different schools, namely, Escuela No.18 – Escuela Republica de Israel (Escuela Republica de Israel, 2013), Colegio No. 1 or otherwise known as Colegio Modelo and now named 'Colegio Integrado Eduardo Frei Montalva' and a rural school in San Miguel de Azapa, which is 13 kilometres from Arica and which has now has been classed as an agricultural school and named 'Liceo Agricola Jose Abelardo Nuñez M.' (Departamento de Administraci6n de Educación Municipal de Arica, 2013) catering from pre-school to high school level education.

I first attended Escuela No. 18. This was a mixed primary school close to home and originally built to cater for the children of teachers who lived in this area of Arica. The school was located in the Magisterio suburb and was two short blocks from our home.

I remember that my first teacher was a former classroom friend of my mother when she was at high school. We called him Señor (Mr.) Fonseca. His full name was Leonardo Fonseca Alday. Some years ago I wanted to find the whereabouts of past students from Escuela 18 only to find out that Señor Fonseca had passed away. I learned that most of his students referred to him, as the 'memorable Profe Fonseca'. The term 'Profe' being short for 'Profesor', which translated to English means 'Professor', which is how teachers are usually referred as in Chile. Just to clarify, Profesor is used to address male teachers and Profesora is used for females. The Castellan language has gender-differentiated words, but I will not delve into the language semantics to confuse the reader.

3 The Learning Process

As I remember, my first year was spent learning to write and read. For the lessons we used a text titled the 'Silabario HispanoAmericano'. This textbook, which had been used for many years before, was the preferred textbook for teaching students to read and write. At this point, I must make a small deviation and dedicate a few lines to the Silabario HispanoAmericano. This text was first published in 1945 by Adrian Dufflocq Galdames (Wikipedia Contributors; 2012) and was based on an earlier text first published by Claudio Matte in 1884 (Millas 2010). Needless to say, the textbook had been around for a while and it still appears on the list of recommended textbook by the Ministry of Education and which, to this day, has not been surpassed in its effectiveness in the use of the Phonetic-Sensorial-Objective-Synthetic-Deductive method of teaching students to read and write (Ministerio de Educaci6n 2013). I personally found it easy to associate the pictures with the sounds and words that the book was trying to teach the avid learner. Nowadays, in keeping up with the changes, the textbook has mainly been updated in the pictorial sense to include pictures which would be easily identified by the young learner (Ministerio de Educación 2013).

The lessons in the classroom were mainly based on memorising letters, sounds and short words. The process was repetitive and we had to repeat the sounds of vowels, consonants and basic words. The same process was replicated when learning basic numbers. The teacher would then test the class by writing a letter or number and we had to put our hands up if we knew the answer. As the months progressed we could read short phrases and started to write. However, most of the first years were spent learning the intricacies of the Castellan language. In addition to our learning in the classroom, it was not uncommon to be tested on our progress. This involved being asked question during class or made to stand in front of the class and then answer a variety of questions related to previous lessons. This meant that we had to devote some time after school doing homework.

In later years, the testing during classes translated to a mere exercise in remembering key dates of events that took place in Chile's history or other events related to the Greeks, Romans and Carthaginians, to name a few. It must be noted that while lessons were being imparted there was minimum or no interaction with other students; teachers demanded absolute attention and the students listened. It was not uncommon for some teachers to physically punish students and some had a reputation of being strict teachers. Fortunately for me, Profe Fonseca was not one of those. I cannot imagine how much of an effort it must have been for those students, who found it hard to remember or had learning difficulties not yet identified. In retrospect and even when my education was in need of change and as argued by Hopenhayn (2003) that education requires a:

> *"Paradigm shift in the style of education: from memorizing to understanding, from absorbing information to discriminating between messages, from the encyclopaedic acquisition of knowledge to a selective approach, from mechanical discipline to responsible autonomy, from learning to learning to learn." Hopenhayn (2003, p. 171)*

In hindsight, I can infer that my earlier years in school had been spent doing a lot of memorising, absorbing and learning. Dewey (1958) argued that as societies become more complex, there is an increased need for formal and intentional teaching and learning. He also argued that students tend to perform better in an environment where they can interact with their curriculum and be active in their own learning (Wikipedia contributors; 2013c) and which Hopenhayn (2003) also reiterates. However, it seems that these arguments may to have been missed during my early schooling years (Cazanga Moncada, 1999).

At his point, I must add that in Chile, during my school years, you needed to satisfy a minimum standard, which was measured by regular testing, homework, as well as semester and a final year exam. If students did not satisfy the minimum standard and passed the required tests and completed the required work during the year, they would repeat the year. And so, it was not uncommon for students to repeat even at grade 1 level. I do remember in later years that some students who were frequent repeaters, stood out from the rest of the grade, as they were usually older and taller than the rest of younger students in their grade. Somehow, the lessons and testing and was not having an impact on these students, rather, it appeared to be accentuating other issues which were not being adequately addressed by the educational system at the time (Cazanga Moncada, 1999).

4 Not Always Relying on Memory Alone

Another aspect of my education was the fact that at Escuela 18 and like most schools still do around the world; it taught arts and craft lessons, where you would be shown how to paint and make a variety of objects from bits of wood, cardboard and paper. Unfortunately, you also got graded on some of the work done in these classes. I must admit that I was really bad at drawing, painting and crafts in general. And finally, after many years of silence, I must come clean and admit to the fact that my mother helped me with many of the drawings and other objects that I had to do for arts and crafts. Perhaps, I was not the only one being ‘helped’ with my work artwork. In any case, I still cannot draw better that a ten year old. I must clarify that have nothing against art. In fact, I do love the arts in all forms and expressions but I’m just awful at expressing myself through art. I have no aptitude for painting and as I would not enjoy doing something I do not like. I found it hard all those years ago doing something I had no aptitude for or interest in doing.

5 The Interesting Maths Class

I do remember with interest is one particular maths lessons, we were told to bring a piece of board (wood) with some long nails through it. Careful instructions were given, so that our parents could make this for us. Well, at least for me, I could actually say that my dad had helped me out with my work and not be penalised for it. All we had to do was to get some small pasta tubes of about a 1 cm each (almost found in every kitchen in the country) and paint a number of them in the colours that were we told. In fact, what we were making was an abacus. This was so interesting because the teacher seemed to have deviated from the usual format of imparting lessons. Using the abacus, we were taught to count and perform various exercises using this simple yet very capable instrument used by Sumerians, Egyptians, Romans and the Chinese, to name a few, a few thousand years early. I was in awe, at how easy it was to perform many mathematical exercises using this simple, early day’s calculator.

I cannot imagine how much more we could have learned, had we been allowed to continue using abaci for learning math. We learned to use the abacus and its history but as education was very rigid, we had to accomplish our mathematical exercises using our heads and not much room was allowed for making mistakes or using a calculator, in our case the abacus. Electronic calculators were not around then in their smaller versions we know nowadays. Thus, the closest we could get to technology was an instrument created a few thousand years before our time. A case in point was the fact that as students, we were also required to hand in, from time to time, our exercise books and marked for tidiness. We were not allowed to have many eraser marks on our books. However, as a gesture of flexibility, were allowed to only use pencils and a rubber. Ink pens were not part of the school utensils until much later into the life of the Chilean students. In fact, I was only asked to use ink pens sometime in 1970 or 1971, if my memory does not fail me.

6 Studying at a Rural School

In 1970, my grandfather, decided to buy a property in San Miguel de Azapa. Azapa is a small valley that has been carved out by the perennial San Jose River and is home to small farmers, who tend to olive groves as well as a variety of other vegetables, poultry and small animals, destined for the local market.

During the late sixties and early seventies, San Miguel seemed a far away place. So much that we considered it and referred to it as being located in the country. Even though, it was a mere 13 kilometres from the centre of Arica.

As soon as our grandfather had renovated the property, my brother and I decided to spend our summer vacations in San Miguel. During which, we made many new friends. Our new friends were in their majority poor and the majority from the Aymara ethnicity. As children I remember that we could identify their status by their torn clothes, some did not wear shoes or runners and their houses resembled old and worn out houses. Towards the end of our holidays, we had become really close to our new friends and so we asked our parents to enrol us at the 'country' school (San Miguel), which close to our grandparents' house. Fortunately, one of our aunties was also a teacher at the school and so we had no problem in enrolling. Usually, the student has to leave within a certain distance from the school to be able to enrol, but exceptions are always possible. For the next two years we would spend six month at the country school and the next semester at our original school back in Arica. We were happy at the school and we were willing to commute the distance from Arica every morning to arrive at the school by 8.30 am. On other occasions we would stay for a few days at my grandparents' place.

I do not have figures dating back from the early seventies that would give us the ratio of Aymara students at the school. But I can only infer that it may have been a greater proportion of what it is now. San Miguel had an influx of new inhabitants during the eighties under the Pinochet years in which people from other cities moved to usually country locations with the promise of jobs and a better life. During a visit to San Miguel in 1994 and speaking to a few of the new residents, most indicated that the jobs never materialised. On the other hand, the original inhabitants resented the new arrival and indicated that there were sometimes antagonistic attitudes amongst the different inhabitants. Getting back to the San Miguel School, figures from 2009 indicated that from a total of 420 students, 210 were Aymara and 4 Mapuche. Therefore, the school had 51% of students classified as indigenous (MINEDUC 2009).

What was interesting about the school in San Miguel, was the fact that although the students in my grade were mostly of the same age group, that is, very few repeaters, there were differences in the learning capacity by some of the students. I remember my aunty (I was not allowed to call her Aunty) spending extra time with some students in particular, so that they would catch up to the rest of the students, whereas, in my school in Arica, most students were at the same level. What was also striking, was the fact that some students, did not have proper exercise books, rather, they used books that were made by their parents from paper that had been recycled from cement bags. In my school in Arica, I wore a navy blue blazer, white shirt, tie and grey pants. In San Miguel's school we could wear a navy blue knitted cardigan, grey pants or jeans, but this was not overly enforced. Some students had very old shoes and old cardigans. It was easy to see that their parents were not, in my understanding at the time 'well-off'.

7 Social Capital and Exclusion as a Result of Belonging to an Ethnic Minority

Of the new friends that I made, I remember one of them in particular. He did not live in San Miguel, he came from further up in the valley (eastward). We became friends at school and he was undoubtedly the smartest student in the class. He was clearly of Aymara descent but unusually tall for his age, if not the tallest in the classroom. When I arrived at the school, he always sat towards the back of the class and was a quiet student but often smiling. I sat towards the front of the class and through competing for the best marks, we became really good friends. I must admit that most often than not, he would get better grades than me. Needless to say, but my aunty never showed any favouritism. I have often wondered whatever happened to my friend. Did he go onto study further or was he did he end up as many had before him? Work in the fields in the valley? I cannot answer that question but I hope that Doroteo has had a good life.

In retrospective, I believe that the time spent at San Miguel's school was to enabled me to see a bit more than the usual circle I was used to. It also showed me the unfair situation these students were forced to exist in. I started to question, compare and talk about my experience in the 'country' school with my friends and schoolmates in Arica. I then started bringing some of my friends from Arica to San Miguel, so that they could meet my other friends.

It can be disconcerting, looking back on those years, that a mere 13 kilometres from the centre of Arica made so much difference in perception, inclusion and mobility. By perception, I refer to the learned idea that San Miguel was far and isolated and we called it as being in the 'country'. Yet in a city like Melbourne (Australia), that same distance can be negligible. In addition, this distance from Arica appeared to hinder the students' ability to be included as part of the greater society. For me it was odd that very few of them would make trips to the beach, yet I failed to realise that this would be an extra cost for them. Also, most of their lives revolved around the valley and a trip to Arica was not the norm. Having said that, clearly the better schools were in Arica. Therefore, the students in San Miguel were not able, due to financial and or distance reasons, to access the schools that may have given them an opportunity to progress further with their studies. Openhayn (2003) argues that education is regarded as a crucial link in the chain of cultural integration, social mobility and productive development (Hopenhayn 2003). In addition, Warschauer (2003) indicates that social capital can be derived from the interpersonal relations that people have in their families and communities. For example, as explained by Lin (2001 as cited in Warschauer, 2003), these relations can provide social credentials, influence, information and reinforcement. An example of social credentials can be interpreted in the point of view that an elder holds a position of respect within a particular community. The same can be said for influence that can be excerpted by certain members of a tribe or commune. With reference to reinforcements, including group, personal or emotional support in times of crisis or need, Warschauer (2003) mentions an important factor to social capital, referred to as 'Norms' which relate to the general expectations of the groups around the individual and provides an important example, whereby, 'a child benefits greatly if he or she attends a school where everybody is expected to attend college'. With these arguments in mind, I find that the students in San Miguel lacked the basics of social capital from a very early age.

Following the abovc quote, two types of social capital are explained, one of these is, bonding social capital and the other is bridging social capital (Warschauer, 2003). The former relates to the ties that are shared by close-knit, inward-looking social networks, such as, among family members, a church group or an ethnic fraternal organisation. The latter, refers to the ties that are formed with those from other social circles. According to, Warschauer (2003), bridging social capital is an important factor for social and economic development, since it provides links to other sources of information and support, yet, this was absent from very early days within the San Miguel kids. For example, Glaeser, *et al*, (2006), Sen (1999) and Kurey (2006) (as quoted in United Nations Educational Scientific and Cultural Organization 2009) argue that education is conductive to democracy, enabling people with skill, being a crucial determinant by which the marginalised can participate in society.

8 On the Road to Inclusion

The rest of my school years were at Escuela Numero 1 or otherwise known as Colegio Modelo (Model School). The 'model' term was based on the premise that it produced good students and had very good teachers for a public school. During the 70s the school had an influx of young teachers who I felt were better than the older, stricter and rigid teachers who in their majority were conservative and opposed the Popular Unity government of Dr Salvador Allende. Their opposition to the government was made clear at every opportunity. I remember one teacher in particular who would frequently go into a diatribe of the government and liken it to crooks and criminals. I'm not sure how that fitted our curriculum but we would make jokes about the teacher, who to his detriment had a keen interest in shoving pens into his ears to scratch them, this was a constant routine, which we would mimic the moment he stepped out of the classroom.

As indicated above, the new teachers brought with them more dynamic teaching and I welcomed this approach and in turn, it awakened a new willingness to learn. For example, I struggled with math classes. Not that I struggled with the content but with the boring uninterested teacher and the repetitive lessons. Whereas, the new teachers were more engaging, did not pressure those students that struggled with math, rather, they would engage with them and show them various manners by which to solve mathematical problems. On the other hand, it was not uncommon for some of the older teachers to single out students who struggled with a particular subject and then test their knowledge in front of the class. This practice often ended in ridiculing the student and putting more pressure, rather than motivating the student. I'm not sure how Dewey would have interpreted these sessions, had he been a fly on the wall.

9 Education in a Time of Change and the Reality Faced by Governments

Cazanga Moncada (1999) writes that the Chilean education system of the late 1960s was, despite being on the margin of a scientific and technological world revolution, still almost invariable since the 19th century. In addition, the mechanisms for qualifications were based on a regime of exams, requiring the memorising of the subjects being imparted in the classroom (Cazanga Moncada, 1999). Which in turn, were highly frustrating to the students. Furthermore, the participation in the school system did not guarantee the progression nor the permanency in the system to lead to higher education (Moncada Cazanga, 1999). Freeburger (1964) provides some figures, which are indicative of the percentage of the national budget being spent on education by the governments of the time:

Year	Percent
1955	10.95
1956	17.52
1957	18.38
1958	17.59
1959	19.76
1960	14.34
1961	21.09

Adapted from (Freeburger 1964, p. 8)

The amount spent on education in 1961 was the highest ever spent on education in the nation's history. However, it is important to note that that the previous year, 1960, this figure had fallen to 14.34% (Freeburger 1964)

10 Government Initiatives to Improve Education at the Time I Attended School

10.1 President Eduardo Frei Montalva

In October 1964, a new Chilean president assumed power, Mr Eduardo Frei Montalva (from 1964 to 1970) and immediately, a commission is established to assess the state of the education system and its outcomes at the time (Cazanga Moncada 1999). The new government found itself with a high number of children marginalised from the school system. Figures estimated the number to in excess of 180,000. About 32% of those that entered primary school completed only six years of schooling. The number of illiterate over the age of 15 was almost 1.5 million. The siblings of blue-collar workers and rural workers who entered university did not reach 3% of the total number of students who entered tertiary education. These are only some of the figures and the reality that faced the new government and the environment in which I started school in 1966.

To tackle the problem, as mentioned by Cazanga Moncada (1999) the government embarked on a number of reforms to make education accessible to all the social sectors and in 1968 reforms were implemented to the existing educational laws and new grants and scholarships were now available, as well as an increase to the education budget. And so, it meant an increase in the food programs, clothing and utensils which were given freely to students and medical and dental programs which were to cater for students, to name a few. Apart from the changes that involved capital expenditure, other structural changes were made to the schooling system, namely the primary school years were extended from 6 to 8 years. Thus, these years could be from 6 or 7 years of age to 14 or 15 years of age.

President Frei did recognise the need to reduce illiteracy, improve the quality of education and expand the educational facilities in the country. Whilst, at the same time, the demand for these services increased, especially at the primary school level, it was necessary to implement a fast track course for primary school teachers that resulted in an additional 2,668 teachers by the end of 1966 (Cazanga Moncada 1999). This influx in the primary school level created also demands on the secondary level and thus it was necessary to create 511 new classes to cater for 20, 440 students. In addition, Cazanga Moncada (1999) explains that it was also necessary to create 265 first year (secondary level) classes to absorb 10,000 students that were once again reincorporated into the education system. Furthermore, Cazanga Moncada (1999) describes how the government also implemented important measures to educate the adult population by which new audio visual methods were used to teach. As a result, Cazanga Moncada (1999) explains that by 1965, basic education of adults increased by 56.5%, high school level for the same population increased by 228.5% in the sciences and humanities subjects. Perhaps, one of the more important contributions of President Frei's government to education was that by the end of his term, funding to universities had increased by 143% being 29% of the education budget, whereby the university population for this period was of 3.5% of the total school population (Cazanga Moncada, 1999). The increases in the funding to did not however, materialise entirely from a government initiative. Rather, during the tumultuous 1960s, university students exerted tremendous pressure, seeking modernization and democratisation (Austin 1997). In general, most student representative bodies concurred that universities should be open, democratic, universal and autonomous (Austin 1997). A series of strikes took place, with one lasting 50 days in 1967 by the university students in Valparaiso (Austin 1997). The students, as a result, became an organised force and were able to converge different populist ideals in their ranks giving rise to unprecedented elections at the Valparaiso University of all the administrative authorities of that establishment, but on a bigger scale, they made possible through the instigated changes, that the access to university was now possible to a wider range of students, as opposed to being the realm of the elites (Austin 1997).

10.2 President Salvador Allende Gossens

President Salvador Allende (1970 - 1973) was elected with a populist agenda and was the first elected Marxist government in Latin America (Fundación Salvador Allende 2013), at a time when revolutions were common in the American zone (Galeano, 1976). President Allende, who was also a Medical Doctor, gave great emphasis to education and health. And so, he designated a teacher as the new Minister of Education, Mr. Mario Astorga Gutierrez (Cazanga Moncada, 1999). Cazanga Moncada (1999) describes how President Allende criticised previous governments' measures in education, which placed too much importance on the expansion of school places whilst ignoring the socio-economic realities that existed within the classes that translated into inequalities in the educational system.

To combat these gaps that existed within the country, the government allocated 20% of the national budget towards education, the highest amount as compared to that of the other Ministries (Cazanga Moncada, 1999). Per capita spending on education, as compared to 1970s figures, showed an increase of 65% by 1973 (Cazanga Moncada, 1999). It is also described by Cazanga Moncada (1999) that by 1973, 37% of the Chilean population was studying. In addition, university places were doubled from 18,827 in 1970 to 40,000 in 1973 (Cazanga Moncada, 1999). Furthermore, Cazanga Moncada (1999) explains that by 1971, the government had fully funded the construction of 2,000 new classrooms.

Not only was the government concerned with improving the education, but also the dietary deficiencies that were present in the country's school population. Thus, from 1971, the breakfasts provided at school surpassed 64% student population (Cazanga Moncada, 1999), as well as, over 700,000 lunch rations being provided (Cazanga Moncada, 1999). Dr Allende also ensured that every student had half a litre of milk per day. For this measure, the government provided powdered milk to every student to take home on a regular basis (Cazanga Moncada, 1999). Amongst the many changes and improvement to education during President Allende's government and the continued preoccupation with improving education and the quality of teachers; the government pursued new technologies in order to impart better education (Cazanga Moncada, 1999). As Cazanga Moncada (1999) describes, how the government envisaged using television as an educational tool. As a result, a project with convened agreements with the United Nations Educational, Scientific, and Cultural Organization (UNESCO) and the Organizacion de Estados Americanos (OEA and in English, Organisation of American States) was developed and via the Centro de Perfeccionamiento, Investigaciones y Experimentaciones Pedagogicas where expert personnel were also trained in the use of television as an educational tool. Other measures also included the availability of books. The Allende government concentrated on intellectual production and more importantly in reclaiming the cultural aspect being influenced from the North (Austin 1997). As a result, Quimantú, the state publishing house (Quimantú is a Mapuche words which means 'sunshine of knowledge') published 5 million books in two and half years (Austin 1997). This record figure, as Austin (1997) states, doubled what had been published in Chile over the previous 70 years.

Evidently, the efforts to combine expenditure on infrastructure, human resources and new methodologies, was aimed at improving education and making it relevant to the times. Yet at the same time, some analysts argued that radio and television as educational tools were destined to wither away (Carnoy, Martin 2004). An early form of information and communication technology (ICT), television was considered as an educational tool that could provide content rich lessons. Livingstone (2011) argues that ICT can expand the quality of teaching and learning, thus, leading to raising standards. We must bear in mind that nowadays, ICT is misunderstood to only include digital technologies, mostly centred on the Internet and includes, computers, tablets, whiteboards and so forth. However, during the 70s in Chile, computers were far from the horizon of every student. Unfortunately, the government of Dr Salvador Allende was short lived. A violent military *coup d'état* overthrew the government on the 11th of September 1973. Therefore, there are no known records of any results or outcomes or if Television was ever used in any school during the short three years of the government. It may have been interesting to juxtapose the results in Chile to results of more integrative and interactive ICTs. If we refer to Livingstone (2011), who indicated that ICTs can have positive outcomes, whilst at the same time, offers examples of negative outcomes where computers are involved. Thus, arguing that a simple introduction of and or investment on ICTs do not necessarily mean an increase in educational performance (Livingstone, 2011). At this point, the reader notes that we have jumped across decades to make comparisons. In the same vein, let us proceed to more recent years and consider what Tatnall (2011) describes with reference to investigating the adoption of technological innovation. Tatnall (2011) indicates that not all innovations are adopted in their originally intended manner and that not all are without change (Tatnall 2011). Interestingly, Cullingford and Gunn (2005) offer a similar premise in their discussion concerning the implications of Globalisation and change by arguing that change can either be assimilated, modified or rejected by those groups or individuals faced by these changes. Thus, to summarise, the idea to use television as an educational tool may have been innovative, however, it would have been interesting to see how it was adopted, had the technology been implemented as a teaching tool.

11 The School Experiences under a Dictatorship

As indicated earlier, a violent military coup overthrew the Government of Dr Salvador Allende. Initially, a Military Junta took charge of the country and in later years, General Pinochet took control.

On the day of the *coup*, school was suspended for a few days. When we went back to school, our mother walked us to school that first day. By that time she had was not walking us to school anymore. However, for some reason, she thought it safe that she did on that day. Anyway, when we arrived at the school, at the entrance, there were two army soldiers on each side of the school gates, armed with a rifle held across their chests. As usual, just before the lessons were about to start, we lined up in the playground. This time a military officer, not our school principal, addressed us. We were told that *things* would change, that we needed to cut our hair short, that our task to help the motherland was to study. Then we proceeded to our classrooms.

Later, we found that the school Principal and some of the new teachers were no longer at the school. In fact, very few of the new teachers were at the school. The only ones that remained were those had opposed to the Allende Government. I cannot elaborate on what happened to the teachers and Principal but I imagine that they were expelled. In later years, the reality of the Military Junta and the Pinochet dictatorship became known and has been well documented. I can only hope that no worse fate than being expelled from the school befell on those teachers.

During one of our lessons, on the first day at school after the *coup*, the same officer who addressed us earlier came into the classroom with two armed soldiers and he interrupted the lesson. He addressed us using the same phrases he had used earlier. However, this time he singled out students, who in his opinion had long hair. They were instructed to cut their hair and that only women used the hair long. Whilst he was addressing us, suddenly the classroom above us, started shouting "Allende, Allende, long live Allende" and banging on their desks. The officer instructed one of his armed soldiers to see what was going on upstairs. Shortly after, the shouting stopped.

When the officer finished, he left the classroom and proceeded to visit the rest of the school to most likely repeat the process. More than addressing us, he scared us. He came in the room, armed and with two armed soldiers and he sounded very serious.

Later on the day, when I was coming back to my classroom after lunch break. I saw that on the ground level, the students from the classroom above ours, where lined up facing the wall, with their arms against the wall and legs wide apart. The officer was overseeing how the soldiers were punishing them for what they had done earlier. The students were being slapped and kicked from behind between their legs. Once they realised that some of us had seen what was going on, we were told to leave and come back later.

Despite of what was going on in Chile, school life went on, we got used to the same tired lessons with the only difference that this time, there was much more content based on the history of Chile and its military conquests. There were contests on Chilean history where students had to answer correctly, dates, names, battle locations, et cetera. In short, memorise a lot of military history.

My time as a student in Chile was being decided by other events and so it was coming to an end. Later on, one of the most significant changes took place in education. This was the introduction of the voucher system in 1981 that had been conceptualised by economist Milton Friedman (Carnoy, M. 1998). These reforms were the initial base for subsequent reforms that were to follow in the 1990s. The basis for the adoption of this voucher system, as argued by Friedman in Carnoy, M. (1998) was to improve school quality, control spending on education and privatise education delivery. However, in the case of Chile, the aim was to, put a price in education, eliminate or reduce the teachers' union bargaining power and to free school from following the national school curriculum and standards, create incentives for parents to choose schools for their children and to further deregulate the market (Carnoy, M. 1998).

12 Education Changes During Pinochet

During the Pinochet dictatorship, one of the most significant changes that took place in education during this time was the introduction of the voucher system in 1981. This model had been conceptualised by economist Milton Friedman (Carnoy, M. 1998).

Chile's educational system began a process of decentralisation (Hinostroza, JE, Guzmán & Isaacs 2002) and these reforms were the initial base for subsequent reforms that were to follow in the 1990s. The basis for the adoption of this voucher system, as argued by Friedman and explained in Carnoy, M. (1998) was to improve school quality, control spending on education and privatise education delivery. However, in the case of Chile, the aim was to eliminate or reduce the teachers' union bargaining power and to free school from following the national school curriculum and standards, create incentives for parents to choose schools for their children and to further deregulate the market (Carnoy, M. 1998; Schiefelbein (2000). As described by Carnoy, M. (1998) under this proposal, students would receive an entitlement (a voucher) from the government and which could be used in any school, either private or public. In order to implement the decentralisation measures, Schiefelbein (2000) explain that 150 'Chicago Boys' were employed by the Pinochet regime to lead the government elite staff to carry this vision forward. According to Carnoy, M. (1998) to evaluate these reforms, 4th and 8th grade students were tested in 1982. These tests would be conducted annually on the same grades in order to compare the figures (Carnoy, M. 1998).

According to Carnoy, M. (1998) and Schiefelbein (2000) the results and analysis of these tests for the period from 1982 to 1988 showed that average overall scores in Spanish and Mathematics declined for 4th graders. Carnoy, M. (1998) also describes that an increased in the scores was recorded in the 1990s. However, this was after a new democratically elected government had decided to spend substantially more on education and in particular to low-income schools (Carnoy, M. 1998). And despite the alleged and expected outcomes, Chile's education has featured as an important political agenda for the subsequent governments that have followed the dictatorship of General Pinochet. But despite these efforts, as reported in the El Mercurio (2004) and by Zuniga (2004) Chile's education continues to demonstrate the fallacies of the system when a comparison in university entrance scores are compared between students from private and public schools and also between school in the capital to school in the outer regions of the country. For example, Alvarez (2005) argues that despite increases in educational expenditure, the country still lacks the schools which can counter these differences, which are based on family and social background.

13 ICTs in Chilean Schools

Chile's education system has been going through reforms since the 1980s with the introduction of the voucher system previously mentioned (Carnoy, M, 1998; Schiefelbein, 2000). The second wave of reforms originates from the transition to a democratic government and focused on improving teachers' working conditions (Schiefelbein, 2000) and most importantly, the recognition by the new democratic governments that ICTs could bring prosperity, as well as create a digital divide (Alvarez 2005). Therefore, as indicated by Alvarez (2005) the government implemented, as part of the educational policies, the Enlaces Program to be an essential component to improve the quality of education. This program (Enlaces

Program) was created to introduce ICTs in both public and subsidised schools and by 2002 more than 70% of schools (primary and secondary) participated in the program and also received hardware and software, unlimited internet access and specially created content (Hinostroza, EH, Pedro; Cox, Christian 2009; Hinostroza, JE, Guzmán & Isaacs 2002). The third reform was implemented in 1994 and as argued by Schiefelbein (2000) was focused on the effectiveness of the classroom, better teaching material and improved learning/teaching process.

Since my time at school in Chile, it is evident that massive changes have taken place. Notwithstanding the changes made during the dictatorship years, the introduction of ICTs has been a major change compared to using blackboard and chalk, an abacus and repetitious methods. Most Chilean students can access a computer at school, although, some schools may have limited ICT resources. However, the impetus has been driven by government policy that recognises the benefits of ICTs. Albeit, the issue of social inclusion and the gaps within the education system remain present. For example, during a visit to two rural school in Chile in 2010. I was able to see not much difference in the situation that I saw at San Miguel School all those years ago Arica. I learned that the majority of the students were considered at 'risk' in terms of poverty line, came from very poor families, in most cases, their parents had not completed secondary school and some, not even primary level. Their level of performance, as compared to urban schools was lower and according to the teachers at the school, they predicted that finishing secondary school for these students would be great feat. On the other hand, the classrooms had from one to two working computers to share between 16 and 34 students. To date, the expected improvements had not materialised in the form of better grades on these students.

14 Conclusion

About a year and half after the *coup*, my family left Chile and I did not go back to visit until almost twenty years had passed. In meantime, I completed my education in Melbourne having survived high school. Later on I completed my University Degree, then a Master and currently I'm progressing with a PhD. The doctorial work investigates the impacts and challenges as a result of introducing and using ICT in schools for Mapuche students. I'm also using Actor Network Theory (ANT) to identify the human and non-humans actors, as well as, an innovation translation approach to understand how ICTs are being adopted, as Tatnall (2011) argues that not always, innovations are adopted as originally intended.

In hindsight, the years that I lived in Chile and spent at the different schools, in particular, the rural school at San Miguel, made me ask a lot of questions and sparked an inquisitorial longing for finding out what are the realities being faced by students in Chile and in particular, those starting their education in rural schools. Having visited a rural school in the south of Chile in 1994 and two other rural schools in 2010, I observed the state of the classrooms, the teaching methods, the lack of resources, as compared to urban schools, the level of poverty of the students, the poor nutrition of the students and their performance, as compared to those in urban schools. Those images from the 1960s and 1970s came back. These students were now part of the voucher system implemented by the Pinochet Dictatorship and were now having some access to ICTs in their classroom. Yet, the realities remain the same as I had experiences all those years ago. Evidently, much needs to be done and not necessarily the cash injection that manages to be accentuated by the government of the time. Rather, the problem requires a more holistic view and further research is required to understand the underlying issues, which continue to accentuate exclusion, the actors involved and the possible solutions that may be found. On the other hand, young students require to be motivated and integrated. Today's students need new a teaching and learning approach, one that engages them and teaches them to learn. As opposed to dictate and instruct as a one-way communication model and which would appear to prepare students for a time that is no longer in existence, that is, yesterday.

References

1. Alvarez, C.: ICT as a Part of the Chilean Strategy for Development: Present and Challenges. In: Castells, M., Cardoso, G. (eds.) The Network Society: From Knowledge to Policy, Center for Transatlantic Relations, The Paul H. Nitze School of Advanced International Studies The Johns Hopkins University, Washington DC, USA, p. 434 (2005), http://www.umass.edu/digitalcenter/research/pdfs/JF_NetworkSociety.pdf#page=28 (viewed May 5, 2011)
2. Austin, R.: Armed Forces, Market Forces: Intellectuals and Higher Education in Chile, 1973-1993. Latin American Perspectives 24(5), 26–58 (1997)
3. Carnoy, M.: National voucher plans in Chile and Sweden: did privatization reforms make for better education? Comparative Education Review 42(3), 309(29) (1998) via Academic Search Elite, http://0web36.epnet.com.library.vu.edu.au:80/citation.asp (viewed June 9, 2004)
4. Carnoy, M.: ICT in Education: Possibilities and Challenges. In: Inaugural Lecture of the UOC 2004-2005 Academic Year, Barcelona (2004), http://www.uoc.edu/inaugural04/dt/eng/carnoy1004.pdf (viewed March 7, 2008)
5. Cazanga Moncada, O.: Notas Para Un Curso De Historia De La Educacion Publica Chilena, Ediciones Logos, Santiago - Chile (1999)
6. Colaboradores de Wikipedia. Historia de Arica, Wikipedia, La enciclopedia libre (2003), http://es.wikipedia.org/w/index.php?title=Historia_de_Arica&oldid=69517941 (viewed December 1, 2013)
7. Colaboradores de Wikipedia: Cultura Chinchorro, Wikipedia, La enciclopedia libre (2013), http://es.wikipedia.org/w/index.php?title=Cultura_Chinchorro&oldid=68373690 (viewed December 1, 2013)
8. Cullingford, C., Gunn, S.: Globalisation, education and culture shock, Monitoring change in education. Ashgate Pub., Aldershot (2005)
9. Departamento de Administración de Educación Municipal de Arica, Liceo Agricola Jose Abelardo Nuñez, (2013), http://www.daem-arica.cl/site/web.php?page=22&establecimiento=Jose%20Abelardo%20Nuñez

10. El Mercurio: Prueba de Selección Universitaria: Se mantienen las diferencias educacionales, El Mercurio (2004), http://diario.elmercurio.com/2004/12/22/_portada/_portada/noticias/A6FC8E29-62BD-47CE-9BEB-230-2B93F59CE.htm?id={A6FC8E29-62BD-47CE-9BEB-2302B93F59CE} (viewed December 23, 2004)
11. Escuela Republica de Israel. Escuela Republica de Israel (2013), http://www.serme.cl/sitios/d4/nuestraescuela.html (viewed December 1, 2013)
12. Freeburger, A.R., Haugh, C.C.: U.S. Department of Health Education and Welfare 1964, Educatiion in Chile - Studies in Comparative Education. U.S. Government Printing Office, http://files.eric.ed.gov/fulltext/ED046812.pdf (viewed March 29, 2013)
13. Fundación Salvador Allende 2013, Línea de Tiempo, http://www.fundacionsalvadorallende.cl/salvador-allende/linea-del-tiempo/# (viewed November 14, 2013)
14. Galeano, E.H.: Las venas abiertas de América Latina, 21a edn., Siglo Veintiuno, Mexico, Buenos Aires (2004)
15. Harvey, R.: Liberators - Latin America's Struggle for Independence. The Overlook Press, Peter Meyer Publishers Inc, Woodstock, New York, USA (2002)
16. Hinostroza, E.H.P., Cox, C.: National Policies and Practices on ICT in Education - Chile (Enlaces). In: TA Plomp, R., Law, N., Quale, A. (eds.) Cross-National Information and Communication Technology: Policies and Practices in Education, 2nd (revised) edn., pp. 157–170. IAP-Information Age Pub. (2009), http://books.google.com.au/books?id=blJW2IfgVN8C
17. Hinostroza, J.E., Guzmán, A., Isaacs, S.: Innovative uses of ICT in Chilean schools. Journal of Computer Assisted Learning (18), 459–460 (2002)
18. Hopenhayn, M.: Education, communication and culture in the information society: a Latin American perspective, CEPAL (Comision Economica para America Latina y el Caribe) (2003)
19. Instituto Nacional De Estadisticas, POBLACIÓN Y SOCIEDAD · ASPECTOS DEMOGRÁFICOS, Instituto Nacional De Estadisticas (2008), http://www.ine.cl/canales/chile_estadistico/demografia_y_vitales/demografia/pdf/poblacion_sociedad_enero09.pdf (viewed February 2, 2013)
20. Instituto Nacional De Estadisticas - Direccion Regional Arica y Parinacota, Base Datos Regional INE - Arica y Parinacota (2003), http://www.inearicayparinacota.cl/archivos/files/xls/bancodedatos/base_datos_XV_region.xls (viewed December 1, 2013)
21. Livingstone, S.: Critical reflections on the benefits of ICT in education. Oxford Review of Education 38(1), 9–24 (2011)
22. Millas, H.: La Sagrada Familia, 4th edn., Editorial Planeta Chilena S.A. Avda. 11 Septiembre 2353, piso 16, Santiago, Chile Santiago, Chile (September 2010)
23. Programa de Educación Intercultural Bilingüe, BD_Escuelas_Matricula_Indigena2009.xls, by MINEDUC, Ministerio de Educación (2010) (viewed Received via email from Mr. Rodrigo Alejandro Carvajal Aceituno on the April 29, 2010)
24. Ministerio de Educación, Catalogo de Textos, Textos Escolares - Unidad de Currículum y Evaluación - Ministerio de Educación (2013), http://w4app.mineduc.cl/catalogo2013/catalogo_2013/catalogo_pub.php#app=aefd&1aa8-selectedIndex=0&4eb3-selectedIndex=0&f5ca-selectedIndex=1 (viewed August 2, 2013)

25. Punto Final, Chile y Bolivia - La Guerra del Salitre, vol. (555) (2003), http://www.puntofinal.cl/555/chileybolivia.htm (viewed December 2, 2013)
26. Schiefelbein, E., Schiefelbein, P.: Three decentralization strategies in two decades: Chile 1981-2000, 5. Emerald Group Publishing Limited (2000) (March 22, 2010), http://www.emeraldinsight.com/journals.htm?issn=0957-8234&volume=38&issue=5&articleid=839183&show=abstract
27. Tatnall, A.: Information Systems Research, Technological Innovation and Actor-Network Theory. Heidelberg Press (2011)
28. The EFA Global Monitoring Report Team, Overcoming inequality: why governance matters, by United Nations Educational Scientific and Cultural Organization. Oxford Univerisity Press jointly with UNESCO Publishing (2009)
29. Warschauer, M.: Technology and social inclusion: rethinking the digital divide. MIT Press, Cambridge (2003)
30. Wikipedia Contributors, El silabario hispanoamericano, Wikipedia, The Free Encyclopedia (2012), http://es.wikipedia.org/wiki/El_silabario_hispanoamericano (viewed September 30, 2013)
31. Wikipedia Contributors, Arica, Wikipedia, The Free Encyclopedia (2013a), http://en.wikipedia.org/w/index.php?title=Arica&oldid=582950722 (viewed December 1, 2013)
32. Wikipedia Contributors, Aymara People, Wikipedia, The Free Encyclopedia (2013b), http://en.wikipedia.org/w/index.php?title=Aymara_people&oldid=578039034 (viewed December 7, 2013)
33. Wikipedia Contributors, John Dewey, Wikipedia, The Free Encyclopedia (2013c), http://en.wikipedia.org/w/index.php?title=John_Dewey&oldid=584781263 (viewed December 2, 2013)
34. Zuniga, V., Cerda, R., Reed, P., Correa, T.: Calidad de la enseñanza: Se mantiene inequidad entre colegios públicos y privados. El Mercurio (2004), http://diario.elmercurio.com/2004/12/22/nacional/nacional/noticias/526B39B8-57E6-4077-8344-FE22F5E407B5.htm?id=526B39B8-57E6-4077-8344-FE22F5E407B5 (viewed December 23, 2004)

Reflections on Computers in Education 1984 – 2001: The Logo Continuum

Martin Chambers

The Hutchins School, Tasmania
mch@hutchins.tas.edu.au

Abstract. These reflections describe Martin Chambers time in the mid-1980s as a computing student; the early 1990s at University and from the early 1990s to the early 2000s as a computing educator.

Keywords: Computing student, university student, computing education.

1 1984 – 1987: First Experience with Computers in Education

My enjoyment of computer programming began in 1984 as a high school student in Northern Tasmania where I was introduced to Logo on an Apple IIe. I had previously spent some time gaming on consoles such as the Hanimex and Atari 2600 and later on personal computers such as the Vic 20 and the Commodore 64 but I had never used a computer to actually write programs. Logo, complete with its sixteen colours and pixelated turtle, intrigued me and the wonderment of 'creating cool images' with simple computer instructions filled my young, impressionable mind.

With this new found passion, I convinced my father that computing was an area of great importance to me and after much persuasion he purchased a Dick Smith branded 'Cat' computer. This was a clone machine that emulated the Apple IIe via a plug-in cartridge on the side. Apple IIes were virtually impossible to purchase for the home as the price was prohibitive and they weren't being sold in mainstream electrical stores.

Memories come back to me of the salesman (a Greg Evans look-a-like from Perfect Match fame) being so enthusiastic about this Cat computer that 'could do everything'. This machine was going to change the world! I was thoroughly convinced and being an over excited 14 year-old, I pushed the case to my father to purchase one very hard. My father, a bank manager at the time, who relied heavily on his own computational thinking ability instead of that offered by any computer, was less convinced about this deal but never-the-less he cautiously purchased the computer as perhaps he saw there was a flicker of hope it may indeed help in my education. Maybe, on reflection, he did see that one day I may end up working in the computing field and was happy to support me in this way.

The Cat lasted a couple of years, but before long the lack of hardware expansion became extremely limiting and now that I was working part-time I was able to upgrade to another Apple IIe clone. With this brand less new computer you could use

A. Tatnall and B. Davey (Eds.): History of Computers in Education, IFIP AICT 424, pp. 365–372, 2014.

third party peripheral cards in the expansion slots, just like the original Apple IIes. I remember vividly the various video enhancement cards, copy cards, network cards and the like that I purchased over time to improve the capability of my clone. Thinking back, this opened my mind to the importance of having truly expansive systems, a tenant still valid today.

I purchased this new computer from a partially blind, fanatical backyard supplier who had quite a band of followers in my region. Not only did he build and sell clone machines, he imported many and varied expansion cards from the United States of America. I remember one card in particular was used to bypass software protection and enable most software titles available on the market to be backed up. I was on the waiting list for a long time for this card – the demand obviously out stripped the supply!

Soon after I purchased the clone, the Apple IIc appeared on the scene and one of my close friends purchased one. Whilst being faster, having a built in disk drive and generally looking a better machine, it did not excite me as much as my expandable Apple IIe clone. We both joined the 'Australian Software Library' based in Renmark, South Australia, where Apple titles could be rented for a short period of time. Newsletters were posted out with a listing of titles included in the library, much like a catalogue of video rentals. You would simply select which items you wanted, return the slip with a cheque and your software would arrive in the mail a week or so later. You used the software for seven days and then returned it when finished. This scheme was a major coop for users (particularly down in Tasmania) because there was now access to a whole range of software not ever heard or seen of before.

2 1988 – 1991: The University Experience

In 1988 and after completing my Higher Schools Certificates' computing subjects, Computer Science and Information Systems, I arrived at the Tasmania State Institute of Technology (the next year it was to merge with the University of Tasmania) looking for an appropriate course, however, there was not a full-time computing course on offer. As a result, I majored in computing and physics within an Applied Science Bachelor degree.

My computing experience at University was mainly based around using MS-DOS driven machines. I remember in the third year of my degree (1990) Windows 3.0 was released and installed on the 286/386 IBM machines in the physics laboratories. The excitement of this moment was memorable as it appeared that finally the clunky computers we were using now somewhat resembled the slick Apple Macintosh computers that were being used in the design areas of the University. Our physics lecturers did remind us, however, to make sure we didn't get carried away with this superficial new interface.

The student computing learning areas in the late 1980s and early 1990s at my University were basically confined to laboratories. In time this started to change, however, and I recall what an astounding moment it was when a number of 'mobile computing stations' appeared in the physics laboratories.

These stations comprised of a large 386 IBM computer, set up with its own printer, keyboard, mouse and large display monitor all mounted on a portable desk with wheels. The mobile stations could wheel back and forth from one laboratory to another, giving us an unrivalled sense of computing freedom. Looking back now it must have been absolute chaos trying to organise ten or so mobile workstations into a physics laboratory where the stereotypical benches and stools took pride of place. At the time though, we thought this new mobile computing solution was an absolute revelation.

With the Applied Science Bachelor degree all but finished, I turned my attention to studying education, as I had now decided to become a high school computing teacher. During my Diploma of Teaching in 1991, I had my first exposure of how using computers could be useful in an educational setting. Theoretical study centered around some of the early constructivist approaches to learning and I now understood why programming in Logo was so exciting for me as a teenager back in 1984.

As well as the theory, there were a number of practical tutorials we attended on teaching with computers. One such class, as I recall, was structured around reviewing educational software and reporting back to the other students the purpose and effectiveness of what was reviewed. This process was quite enjoyable but at the same time, very dysfunctional!

Classmates would attempt to load their software into a computer (usually a BBC Micro or Apple Macintosh) in front of 25 odd eager fellow students, but inevitably the software wouldn't load or would crash at some point during the explanation. The presenter, more times than not, simply had to reflect on 'how it worked at home.' Looking back now, this experience was indicative of the pitfalls I would face later on in my teaching career running stand-alone software with groups of teenage students.

All of the educational computing at that point in time relied on the hardware and software to work flawlessly. Of course there was no Internet available at that stage.

3 1992 – 2002: Teaching Computing in Catholic and Government Schools

Graduating from University in 1992, I was ready for the workforce and was granted a secondary teaching position in a K-12 catholic school in Hobart, an institution I would teach for the next ten years. Along the journey I also become Technology Co-ordinator and Manger of Information Systems.

Nervously starting out, I remember the Principal at the time not being concerned with my mathematical or science teaching skills (although I was employed to teach those subjects as well), but more interested if I was 'The computer man who could fix everything'. He chaperoned me down to the main corridor of the school where on the floor lay a pile of BBC Micro, Archimedes and Apple IIe computers as well as metres of old networking cable. I did have a slight nauseous feeling of 'what have I got myself into here!'

As the year progressed, we (including a technician from the Catholic Education Office) managed to set up the computer laboratory which included a network hard drive where students could save files. This drive (which resembled the size of a large shoe box) was unfortunately unreliable and students, in the main, used 3.5 inch disks to save their work.

Loading up programs was conducted in a controlled manner by handing out disks to students, passing them on, loading the software up on the next computer, and then finally being ready to teach twenty minutes later. Class sizes were generally of thirty students and programs consisted of Logo programming, basic office (word processing, database and spreadsheet) programs as well as some other general educational titles which the Archimedes and BBC Micros were renowned for. At this time in Tasmania there was a healthy debate on the most suitable platform for education; the traditional UK based computers (BBC Micro / Archimedes) or the increasingly popular IBM or Macintosh machines.

In this my first year of teaching, computing was very much seen as an elective but much of the content was heading for the mainstream curriculum. The illusion was that all students needed to experience time on a computer to receive a 'modern education'. As a teacher in this learning area my popularity was unsurpassed, and other colleagues in some of the more traditional subjects were experiencing fluctuating student interest. It was a good feeling indeed to be so popular. I had landed the right job at the right time! We were now ready for the next big thing.

My earliest memory of being connected to the Internet was in 1993. By this stage the school had increased the number of computer laboratories and computing teachers, reduced student numbers down to twenty per class and even employed a full time technician to look after our systems. Running parallel to the computing needs of students was the push to fully computerise the administration. The demands on the ICT staff seemed many!

By connecting to the Internet via a sufficient 2400 baud modem, our class was able to participate in text based online bulletin board discussions. I remember there was a large community of Bulletin Board System (BBS) users in Austin, Texas who we would chat with now and again, but the time differences made this exercise somewhat problematic. Students, however, seemed less impressed than I was with these sessions and at times I felt they didn't actually believe we were chatting with people on the other side of the world.

My first experience of the power of the Internet as a genuine learning tool came when we performed 'ping and trace route' tests in class. The entire class would be looking at a largish monitor in the computer laboratory and then we connected to a computer on the other side of the world via the ping or trace-route communication tools.

As the Internet traffic jumped from one server to the next in various places, students would record these locations and plot them later on a world map or whiteboard in the classroom. This notion of plotting Internet traffic versus location engaged the students for many lessons. I doubt whether this would have the same impact today.

As experiences like this were happening in our classroom, there were many new developments building in the wider Internet community. In the latter half of 1993 I recall attending a particular ICT based, professional development meeting at our school, which at the time, I thought gave us an insight into the way teaching would be crafted in the future. Others were not so convinced.

A guest speaker from the University of Tasmania was invited to run this session and demonstrated to approximately sixty staff a new software program called 'Mosaic'. As we found out on that day, Mosaic was a 'web browser' which could not only download text information form the Internet, but also download and display images on the same 'web page'. We did not fully appreciate it at the time, but this was our first introduction to Hyper Text Markup Language (HTML) and the new way of finding, sorting and displaying information.

I sat in complete awe when I viewed an image being rendered from the other side of the world. I couldn't stop thinking about the implications that this would have on my future classes. After all, I had been exposed to the sending of plain text across the world – this new 'web browser' would open up new learning opportunities. The image did take approximately thirty minutes to download and render and was quite low in resolution but that did not deter my enthusiasm at all.

Contrary to my own personal excitement and to my complete amazement, I recall many colleagues were not impressed at all with this demonstration. 'I just don't see the use of it', 'It is just too slow', 'Books are much better' were just some of the comments that resonated on that day. I don't believe the classroom teachers attending that meeting were being negative towards this new teaching tool, it was more they couldn't see a legitimate use for anything like 'the Internet'.

On reflection, it would still be a few years before mainstream Internet usage was accepted as a legitimate teaching tool in the classroom.

In the years 1993 through 1995 there seemed to be a reorganisation of ICT in the curriculum. Should typing or secretarial studies still be taught? Were teachers of those subjects now expected to teach computing? Which faculty did this new subject computing belong to? Did it follow a design, science or mathematics based pedagogy? Steering committees had to be established to manage computers not only from a technical viewpoint but also to answer these burning issues.

With the rapid change of technology at this time, there was an increase in CD-ROM based educational materials, particularly the multimedia encyclopaedias. When not too long ago, shelves were filled with volumes of encyclopaedias, now students could sit at a work station and be provided with endless facts and imagery found on the CD-ROM. Students enjoyed this immensely.

Little did we know the open-source movement and the prolific rise of information available on the Internet would overtake in popularity that of the CD-ROM materials, which in turn overtook the popularity of printed encyclopaedias.

Libraries were definitely moving with the times. New searching and booking systems seemed to appear regularly and the push for web-based integration was paramount. There was nothing better than being a student at the time and able to search the library catalogue internally via a computer and web browser from the other side of the school. Previously, sending a student on a journey to the library to quiz one of the text based OPAC's or even ask the librarian for help, seemed in many cases an exercise fraught with danger.

Back in the computer laboratory, I recall teaching robotics for the first time during the years 1993 – 1995. The availability of any ready to go 'Lego' style robots was scarce so instead unassembled robotic kits were purchased and soldered together before becoming operational. Each robot had only one sensor or function. This was fine in a classroom situation as groups of four or five students could examine the 'light sensor robot' and the following week swap it with another group's robot. By the end of a four week block all the students had experienced (to a degree) a range of operations which these robots could perform. The students did enjoy the robotics unit giving them a healthy break away from the computers.

Secretarial studies were still quite popular in the early 1990s, and the challenge of integrating new computing hardware into the course was obvious. Typing laboratories had undergone a transformation whereby the legacy mechanical typewriters were upgraded to electronic typewriters but computers were considered, for some time at least, to be unsuitable for this type of course. Opinions soon changed as more sophisticated integrated software packages were developed and introduced. Eventually all the electronic typewriters were replaced.

With the creation of new laboratories for the technology subjects, printing was becoming more and more of an issue. Each laboratory contained dot-matric style printers, the bigger and louder the better. After a while, however, a revolution took place when the stand-alone 'printing station' and computer were replaced by computers that could share their printer over a network. This was great as students could now print from their own machines without having to save their work on a disk and walk over to the dedicated printing station to print it out. As time progressed shared printing machines were replaced by shared network printing devices, which removed the need for a computer to be involved in the printing production altogether. The advent of laser printers in later years changed the ambiance in the computer laboratories, with the slicker looking, better print quality and quieter machines being very popular. Soon printing quotas and ink management policies had to be introduced to keep costs under control.

Community support for all the new technology was also on the increase. As I recall in the early 1990s numerous educational technology user groups appeared which half rivalled the popularity of Apple User Groups of the late 1980s. Computing in education was becoming a legitimate player in the ICT Industry and suppliers were ready to support community initiatives that were being developed.

As the awareness of computers in education changed in the community so did the role of the computing teacher. By the middle of the 1990s the role was very demanding and I recall one of my extra responsibilities was to create and maintain the school website. For me, new scripting technologies were being developed which built on my prior HTML knowledge and I was able to integrate this dynamism into our school website.

As there were no human resources allocated for the creation of the website student help was crucial. I talked with the senior computing classes (Year 10) about ways we could make the website more interactive and what we could do to offer something back to the community. We didn't want to just display our school's contact information and some nice pictures. We wanted to make it of some use to others. At the time students were now creating word-searches and crosswords with automated software, so we decided to have them available for download. Some of the more able students attempted to create interactive quizzes using online forms and database queries. These were also integrated into the website.

A further idea was to create the 'Australian Schools Directory', since as far as we could tell there was no publically listed database where we could find all the Australian schools contact information. Taking this challenge on, we attempted to collect all the printed directories that we could find (from Catholic, Independent and Government Schools) and enter them into a database which we eventually published online in 1996. This was an extremely arduous task and many students soon understood the tediousness of data entry and the extremely important notion of data validation.

By now, the idea of creating their own personal websites was quite within the realms of many students and 'The Australian Schools Web Challenge (1997 - 2000)' provided a perfect opportunity for students to work in a team, learn HTML and showcase their work against others on a national level. Students competed annually in this event. The notion of learning through a challenge continues today through such competitions as the highly successful Grok Learning Python Challenge.

By the end of the 1900s the transformation from schools with stand-alone computers and printers, connected to unreliable networks and poor Internet connections to schools with fully networked computers and printers, support provided by dedicated technicians and relatively fast internet speeds had been completed. As I moved into my next computing teaching position at a government high school (years 7-10) in Hobart, this transformation was quite evident and attention now was starting to focus on providing students with a useful learning interface and the ability to access their work remotely.

It was at this time, I had my first experience at using a Virtual Learning Environment (VLE) and the school Intranet provided students with the ability to manage their learning assets easily. Laptops and more mobile solutions were becoming popular and affordable as was specialised printers and scanners. In the computing curriculum around 2001, there was still a need to teach business type applications and the sophistication of some of these, such as Office XP, were making an impact on the general curriculum as well. Soon the notion of 'every subject teaches computing' was becoming popular and some of the more traditional computing topics such as programming seemed to diminish in focus.

4 2002 – 2013: Internet Safety and Teaching Computing at Independent Schools

In 2002, I moved out of the classroom and worked on the Australian Governments first national Internet Safety program. From there, I returned to teaching in 2007 at an Independent k-12 in Tasmania, where I am presently still employed.

My journey has seen the popularity of computers in education rise and fall and rise again. A learning area where there is always a new challenge or new technologies to become excited about. Where students can find a passion and engage in higher order thinking. I have enjoyed every minute of this journey.

Ironically, with the pending release of the Digital Technologies Australian Curriculum in 2014 and due to their ability to stimulate computational thinking in students, programming languages such as Logo are regaining popularity once again – a language that started my thirty year computing in education journey back in 1984. The Logo Continuum!

From Learning to Use Towards Learning to Code: Twenty-Five Years of Computing in Dutch Schools

Jan Lepeltak

The Netherlands
j.lepeltak@learningfocus.nl

Abstract. In the mid-nineteen eighties of last century computers in the Netherlands were broadly introduced in secondary education, and a few years later also in elementary schools. As described in Lepeltak (2006) [1] there has been for the past 25 years a development from learning to use ICT towards using ICT to learn. Learning to use is in terms of being able to operate the machine and its basic applications. Using to learn was focused on using ICT in learning processes for various subject areas. Since 2010 the focus has been slowly moving to the creative, explorative use of ICT. This goes along with the current concept of coding. In the Netherlands coding has not a formal status in education only in the optional subject of information science ('informatica') in upper secondary school. When coding, nowadays mainly practiced by young people outside school, will become a permanent activity is hard to say. There is a strong lobby by the Dutch Royal Academy of Science (KNAW) and industry. Coding in relation to robotics has a lot of potential. It is active, exploring pedagogy and its relations with technology, biology, science. Coding provides schools with a lot of opportunities within the curriculum.

Keywords: Netherlands, using computers, coding.

1 A Short History of Educational Computing

A survey in the Netherlands in 2005 [2] showed that in secondary education (from 12-18 years), 47% of the Dutch teachers use ICT in their lessons. What we see is a very slow growth in the use of computers in the learning process within the schools. In 2002 66% of the interviewed teachers expected that they would use ICT within three years. From a 2013 survey we learned that in fact 50% of the teachers actually used digital content in their lessons [3]. It seems almost as if the use of ICT is slowing down in secondary education in the Netherlands.

It is not the availability of hardware or the access to the internet which is holding them back. Is it the software? Or has it to do with the training and the professional development of teachers? Nevertheless about 64% of the Dutch teachers feel self-confident enough to use computers in their classroom [4]. In 2012 the use of ICT in schools shows an increase.

In primary and secondary education about 78% of the primary school teachers' use on a daily or weekly basis learning supported software, very often combined with a

A. Tatnall and B. Davey (Eds.): History of Computers in Education, IFIP AICT 424, pp. 373–383, 2014.

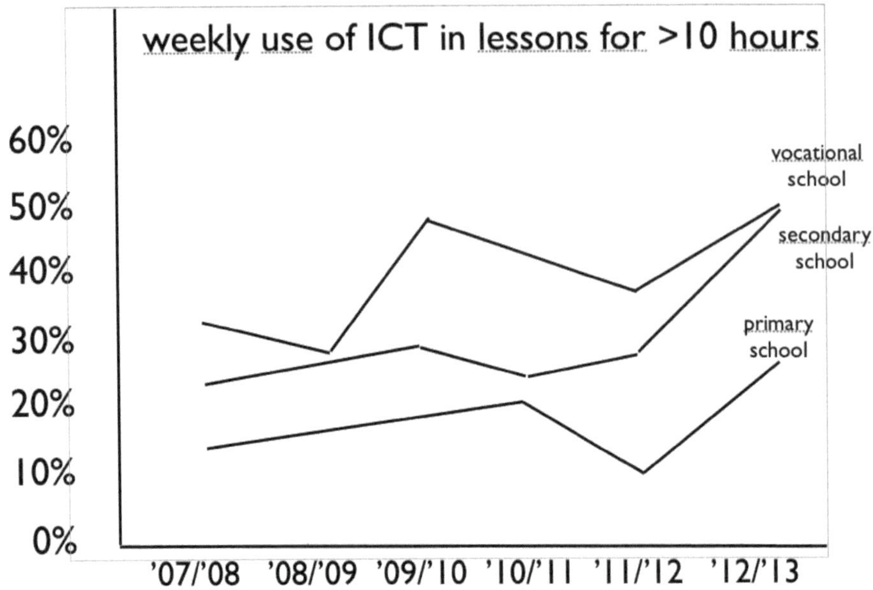

traditional method/schoolbook. In the graph below we see the percentage of teachers in the various school types that use ICT content in their lessons.

The lowest line represents the use of ICT by teachers in primary education (4-12 years), the middle one represent secondary education (12-18 years) and the above line represents vocational education (14-18 years). After a downfall in 2011 the use of ICT shows an increase. The use of internet is not taken account of in this graph. 80% of the teachers use internet on a daily basis.

Schools for secondary education started in 1984 with a new experimental subject area called 'civil information science' (burgerinformatica) a project for students from 12 – 16 years. The National Institute for Curriculum Development coordinated the project. The curriculum combined computer awareness and computer literacy. Its main purpose was: "*The development of knowledge and skills that makes it possible for students to react adequately in situations where the use of data-processing systems is possible or necessary. Students should also be able to make critical evaluations of the social implications and impact of the use of such systems.*" [5] On the basis of rather generic goals four areas for learning were identified.

1. Use of applications
2. The social implications
3. Problem analysis and programming
4. Building principles ('architecture') of hard- and software

After a large school reform in the Netherlands in 1993 Informatiekunde (the new name for an introduction in computing and informatics) became a school subject with a curriculum of 80 hours. However it was practiced for only 20 and 40 hours on the school timetable. The Dutch school inspectors also claim in a report [6] that this is not enough to make this a serious subject within the curriculum. The National institute for Curriculum Development developed the core objectives for this subject area with the long term objective of integrating these 'learning to use skills' in the regular subject areas (maths, language and sciences).

A strong lobby for the Apple approach started, without success. In 1990 Bill Gates signed in the Amsterdam Hilton a Windows contract with the Dutch government to supply elementary schools with a special MS-DOS computer named the Comenius-computer, after the famous 17th century Tsjechian philosopher and pedagogue Jan Amos Comenius. It was installed with the new Windows interface.

In 1985 the MS-DOS personal computer (PC) was introduced in secondary education in the Netherlands. With its command driven interface the PC was not an easy tool to handle.

In 1984 Apple introduced the first PC with a graphic interface for the consumer and small business market. It formed the basis of modern personal computing. "*The Mac's elegant system software was its great accomplishment. It displayed a combination of aesthetic beauty and practical engineering that is extremely rare*" [7] wrote Paul Ceruzzi in his history of modern computing.

The choice was made on the basis of a report from the Centre for Education and Information at Twente University. Although the cost aspect played a role as well, the main argument for not choosing the Apple Macintosh line was the fact that only one company manufactured them. [8]

Ironically we see in 2013 a strong but controversial movement about building elementary school education around the use of an iPad. The first so called Steve Jobs school opened in august 2013 with a lot of (inter)national publicity. Apart from this we notice a lobby for the introduction of coding and programming in elementary schools.

2 Hard and Software in the 21st Century

The schools in the Netherlands, like most northern European schools, are nowadays well equipped with hard and software. In 2012 the ratio pupil: device (desktop, tablet, laptop) in Dutch elementary schools is 1:5. In secondary education it is 1:4.9 and in vocational schools 1:5.7 [9].

In recent years educational publishers in the Netherlands produced almost no schoolbooks without any software. The part of printed content is diminishing. For the past five years several large and well known publishing houses merged and were sometimes taken over by hedge funds.

What is left is a small number of well-known educational publishing companies in the Netherlands. In 2013 these firms developed together with other players (e.g. school material distributors), a single login portal named basispoort (http://info.basispoort.nl/) which gives access to their digital content.

Because of the monopoly of the educational publishers, school managers complain that they are obliged to buy a school license. This combined with a lot of technical problems during the start in September 2013 made things worse.

Since 2005 schoolbooks in secondary education are free. Schools get a special budget for every student. This makes it very interesting for schools to develop their own content. There is a strong open source and open content movement in the

Netherlands. They promote the use of free content on the basis of a wiki-concept called Wikiwijs (say 'Wikewise'). But the complete free exchange of content seemed too idealistic. Nowadays schools can subscribe to meta-tagged content and arrange their own curriculum content.

The budget for free schoolbooks is part of the lump sum (€7500) that secondary schools receive for every student. This enables school administrators to develop their own policy for using, buying or developing learning material. According to the national council for secondary schools (VO-raad) this will make it easier for schools to change from analogue, printed content towards digital content and lesson material. It could make it also easier to make more personalized learning possible. For free schoolbooks the secondary schools receive €321.50 a pupil. For most schools this is not sufficient. Parents have to pay an extra contribution for digital material or licenses that give access to educational databases of publishing companies or Wikiwijs.

In the Netherlands there is not a national curriculum as for example in England. But pupils (also very young ones) are more and more tested. In primary education there are several tests obliged. The primary school ends with a national school test at the age of 12. At the end of secondary education there is a final national examination. Although there is no national curriculum for primary education and general secondary education, certain objectives are formulated. The situation in vocational education is more complex. Although there is not a national curriculum it doesn't mean that schools develop their own curricula. The authors of schoolbooks develop on the basis of curriculum examples most of the curricula. The majority of the schoolbooks are more or less traditional in their pedagogy. This implies that they are course driven. They have an instructional character. ICT comes with it as an asset. Educational publishers are willing to develop more innovative material which differs from the so called book plus production (traditional course with some software). They claim that the majority (70%) of the market asks for 'traditional' material in 2005. Recent surveys show that the majority of the teachers still use traditional schoolbooks although they all have strong digital component. [10]

3 Informatics, Computing, Critical Skills and Coding

Despite the fact that every school in the Netherlands has a free broadband connection with the internet, the existence of a national educational network (kennisnet) and an average pupil-computer ratio of 9:1 in elementary and secondary education, [11] educational use in secondary education is below expectation.

We consider learning to be more effective if it is perceived to be meaningful and embedded in authentic situations. [12] It is in what we now call the social constructivist approach of Lev Vygotsky where we find a great emphasis on the importance of interaction between people (children, teachers, parents) in cognitive development. Situated learning - anchoring instruction in real life problems that have to be solved and creating rich environments that stimulate learners to interact about real life problems is becoming more and more mainstream in the use of ICT for learning. [13] By situated learning we mean the physical and social context within which learning takes place. This remains an integral part of that which is being learned [14]. This is hardly the case in the traditional technology-driven courses where one is supposed to learn to work with software applications in an isolated way. Children learn to use word processers by learning to express themselves by writing, learning to use spreadsheets by e.g. during statistic research in their environment and by learning to use creative tools and mind maps by exploring their creativity.

What we learn from the Dutch situation is that it is difficult to change patterns that have been followed for years. In countries where ICT has been recently introduced we could learn from new approaches by action research methods and the exchange of free open source material. Education should primarily be a matter of students, pupils, teachers and parents. The involvement of large soft- and hardware companies is not automatically a benefit for the development of school systems with ICT. Teachers in secondary schools are subject oriented i.e. they are teaching maths, language, physics, history etc. It is for this reason that success lies only in the development of concrete plans and projects for the use of ICT that is integrated in their subject areas and in all their teaching. This is why in physics teaching in the Netherlands, where there is a longstanding tradition in the use of science labs, ICT is well integrated in the curriculum. From the beginning in the 1980s tools like IP-Coach and coachlab, were introduced to support the modern teaching of physics. But a new generation of tools is developed e.g. VinciLab an advanced educational data logger for measuring and simulation, available since autumn 2013 [15].

The arrival of a new generation of young teachers is giving a boost to the use of ICT and the development of the so called 21st century skills. They use social media and they organize successful informal meetings like Edcamps.

4 New Technologies in the Classrooms: The Digital Whiteboard

The first digital whiteboards (DWB) were introduced in Dutch schools in 2002. In 2006 one could find a digital whiteboard in 10% of the elementary schools. [16]. Most of the time the DWB was used for instruction and presentation by teachers. But we see nowadays a growing amount of use by pupils.

The introduction of DWB was criticized. Many educational innovators feared that the DWB would support the traditional instructional approach in the classroom. The Institute for Education and Communication of the NHL-University for Applied Science in Leeuwarden organized in 2006 a seminar about the educational use of digital whiteboards in elementary schools. The emphasis during the seminar was on the use of the digital whiteboards by pupils. Dughall McCormick, a British educational expert, showed examples of the creative use of digital whiteboards by pupils at this seminar.

At this moment about 40% of the classrooms in The Netherlands are equipped with digital whiteboards. In the US this is around 15%, Germany 5% and France 2%. Only the UK is far ahead with a penetration of about 70%.

The presence of a DWB doesn't mean that it is used differently from the traditional blackboard in using it only as a beamer showing/exploring the internet. In a report from a Dutch television youth panel in 2013 58% of the pupils say that their teachers don't use their DWB appropriately [17].

Worldwide or even national statistics on whiteboard penetration in classrooms are difficult to gather, but one survey of about 1,400 full-time teachers in the United States found that 59% of respondents said whiteboards were available in their schools, with 36% saying they had access in their own classrooms. Penetration in the United Kingdom is as we saw far higher, with the government having directed funding for whiteboard purchases at virtually every public school and in most classrooms during the past decade. A recent OECD report shows comparable figures about the penetration. [18] Remarkable are the differences within the EU. The total number of classrooms (teaching spaces) in each country is given in parentheses.

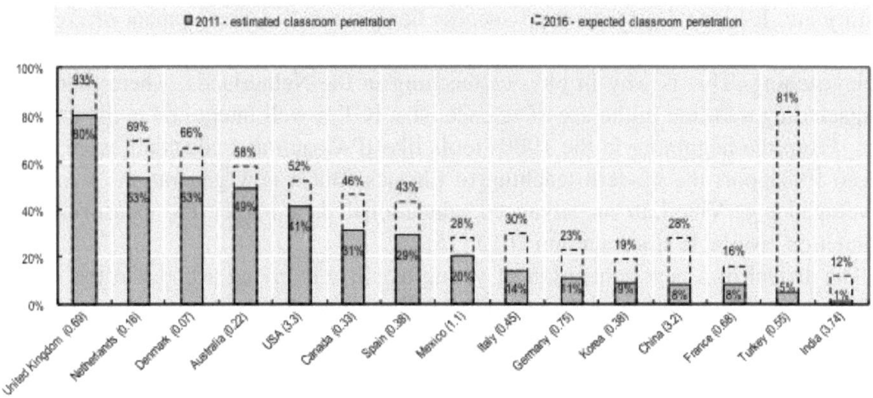

Source: Futuresource Consulting (2012) cited in the OECD report.

The OECD in their report concluded as follows. They use the term Interactive Digital White Board (IWB) instead of DWB:

1. First, IWBs as such have no transformative power on pedagogy. Teachers' diverse beliefs about pedagogy and student learning, their preferred uses of conventional boards, their goals and their prior experiences, shape the way in which they use all educational tools, including the IWB. New approaches can be developed if supported by adequate investments in professional development, but not imposed.
2. Second, professional learning about IWBs and their effective use takes time. Pedagogical change only comes with significant investment in professional development and is generally only observed after at least one year of full-time use by teachers.
3. Third, because their impact on pupils is mediated by their use by teachers, there are no robust, clear-cut positive effects on pupil learning associated with IWBs as such: the context and the nature of use of IWBs are all-important. Nevertheless, effects on learner achievement attributed to IWBs are generally more positive than for all other forms of technology.

5 New Trends: Social Media and Coding

In spring 2013 the second conference on social media in education took place in the just opened Eye-film Institute at the Amsterdam harbor front. The use of social media as an educational tool is rather new and its use is not very widespread. Social media in the schools is a big issue in terms of safety, privacy and protection. Serious incidents concerning cyber bullying, harassment, threats and grooming also took place in the Netherlands.

The use of smart phones by pupils is widespread. 60% of the children from 8 to 12 years have a mobile phone [19]. In schools, teachers and various organizations are trying to make their pupils and their parents more aware of the potential dangers that exist when one is using social media such as Facebook, Skype, Twitter etc. A growing number of schools is now using a protocol for the use of mobile phones of their pupils. Schools forbid the use of mobiles during school time or on the school premises.

About the educational use of social media within Dutch schools not much research is yet available. One could say that the use of social media is widespread within the group teachers that are early adopters of technology. More than 200 active educational bloggers ('edubloggers') are active in The Netherland. They form a community of teachers, researchers, parents, journalists, developers, publishers etc. This community is one of the leading informal groups in ICT innovation and education in the Netherlands.

A very interesting eScience [20] project at Radboud University (Nijmegen) and the Netherlands eScience Centre (Amsterdam) in Twitter is TwiNL. It provides a large database with all the daily tweets in the Netherlands, with anonymous time and location information. The database is freely accessible. Physicist as well linguist, sociologist, epidemiologists already use this D-base for research. [21]

6 Revival of Coding?

European business and industry are promoting coding in education, since ICT-experts are shortcoming now and in the near future. For The Netherlands the shortage for the forthcoming years is estimated between the 6.000 and 40.000 professionals. Depending on how the economy develops. [22]

In the Netherlands there is traditionally a large emphasis on digital literacy. It was the Dutch Royal Academy of Science (KNAW) which wrote a report for the Dutch government about ICT, programming and digital literacy. Digital literacy refers to the ability to make prudent use of digital information and communication, and to evaluate the consequences of that use critically. In the 21st century digital literacy belongs to the basic skills of every educated person in the KNAW states. It is necessary for navigating through the information society. Like language and mathematics skills, digital literacy requires instruction and education over a longer period of time. It should therefore be covered in our education system.

The KNAW reports that the relevant school subjects are below standard and do not prepare pupils for the information society. It is urgent for the government to revise current teaching of digital information and communication in secondary schools. If not the Netherlands will be behind similar countries. Our leading position as a knowledge and innovation economy will be at risk. At general secondary (havo) and pre-university (vwo) levels the subjects information science and informatics had in 2013 a marginal status. Their quality is insufficient and their content is outdated. Urgent action is needed, the KNAW claims.

In developing its views the Netherlands is neither in the vanguard nor in the rear guard. The challenge is to move beyond discussion and take action, as similar countries are doing. The Academy recommends that the relevant part of secondary education is redesigned from the ground up. We must give digital literacy our ongoing attention, first offering pupils a sound common basis and then allowing for an individual and in-depth study.

The Academy made five recommendations to the Minister of Education, Culture and Science:

1. Introduce a new compulsory subject Information & Communication in the lower years of havo and vwo. This should be a broad and compact introductory subject, covering the essential facets of digital literacy.
2. Completely overhaul the optional subject Informatics in the upper years of havo and vwo. By a flexible and modular design, the subject should remain up to date and appeal to pupils regardless of their focus area.
3. Encourage interaction between these subjects and other school subjects.
4. Make it a priority to raise a new generation of teachers with new skills and attitudes. Instruct the schools for higher professional education (hbo) and the universities to collaborate in this regard.
5. Promote instruction in digital literacy, in coordination with the initiatives taken by the Minister of Education, Culture and Science. This will help in achieving the aims of your ICT policy (Digitale Agenda.nl). The Academy's report focuses on havo and vwo, the sectors of secondary education with which it is most concerned. It is beyond question, however, that digital literacy is equally important in pre-vocational (vmbo) and primary education. Each of these needs a separate set of recommendations, to be formulated by organizations that are involved.

Because of the involved political and legislative discussions the adoption of these recommendations the implementation will take at least several years.

In the meantime, in 2013 international initiatives are under way. So we see that The Council of European Professional Informatics Societies (CEPIS), a non-profit organization seeking to improve and promote a high standard among informatics professionals in recognition of the impact that Informatics has on employment, business and society. CEPIS represents 35 Member Societies in 32 countries across greater Europe. The decline of computing/coding in education seems a western problem. US students already significantly lag their global counterparts where maths and science skills are concerned. But computer science is in even worse shape: Of 12 technical subjects examined in a recent study by the National Centre for Education Statistics, computer science was the only one that declined in student popularity from 1990 to 2009 [23].

CEPIS started in 2013 a lobby with the EU-commission to stimulate coding in elementary and secondary schools in Europe. Meanwhile in England we see since 2012 a strong pressure from the government. Lessons about ICT should be replaced by lessons about coding. This is a policy that seems to be controversial because of the increasing influence of industry on the national curriculum.

7 New Trends and Initiatives

In the Netherlands all kind of non-formal initiatives are manifest. In 2013 the World Robocup Junior was organized in the city of Eindhoven. This very successful competition got a lot of (international) media coverage. More than a 1000 youngsters from 8-18 originating from more than 30 counties were in competition for about a week in Eindhoven.

In the Netherlands one also notices various local initiatives. For example workshops are provided in elementary schools in making your own app or game. Because of the lack of knowledge and experience at elementary schools these workshops are organized at an ad hoc level.

In the Netherlands about 14% of the teachers in elementary schools are men. Other European countries show a similar development. [24] Male instructors resign after a few years of teaching [25]. 25% of men leave the teaching profession in elementary school after four years.

Because of the criticism of the quality of teacher training in 2010 some universities established so called renewed training institutions called the Academic Pabos. They maintain specific admission standards and a more academic curriculum inspired by the way teachers are trained in Finland.

Since 2011 the policy of the Dutch Ministry of Education is focused on promoting technology in the elementary schools. The participation of women in beta-studies is significantly less than that of men. The ambition is that in 2020 science and technology will be part of the elementary school curriculum – a challenge for the existing teacher training centres.

Several initiatives are often from women who worked in the IT-industry and are now giving workshops in elementary schools.

There is a group called Codekinderen (Codekids) that gives pupils in groups 3 to 8 of primary school the chance to discover their digital talents. In workshops the children are introduced to the media they use every day.

There is also an international network of 27 countries of clubs that focus on coding called CoderDoyo. In the Netherlands there are three clubs (Amsterdam, Rotterdam and The Hague) in which children e.g. develop games. These activities take place outside the school.

Strong open source programming languages like Scratch, developed by MIT-media lab, are available for free.

The new Mindstorms EV3 robotic platform makes it possible for children to build very powerful robots. Scratch can be used as a programming language for the first and second generation of Mindstorm Robotics platforms but not for the EV3 in due time, because of its different architecture.

In general one can say that we see several initiatives most of them that take place outside the school and school hours. In the elementary school the focus is on technology and science and not as much on ICT and coding.

In secondary education we see that the position of informatics is rather difficult because of the following reasons:

1. Shortage of qualified teachers
2. Low status. It's a subject that can be offered on a voluntary basis but is not mandatory
3. It is not part of the central examinations
4. There is no overview of the number of pupils and schools that offer information science

In the UK the government made coding a mandatory subject of the curriculum. The plans are controversial. The criticism in the educational social media like the Mirandenet is that these days industry (Microsoft and Cisco) seem to determine part of the computing curriculum.

In October 2013 a new BBC Director General announced an ambitious nationwide technology initiative to encourage the public to take up computer programming. The education secretary Michael Gove's ambition is to revolutionize learning in England's schools. One will see five-year-olds studying fractions and writing computer programs in their first year of school, according to final versions of the new national curriculum. [26] From age seven, the new curriculum says, children should be taught computer-aided design, and from 11 they will learn 3D and mathematical modelling, as well as using computer-aided manufacturing tools and including programmable components in design. UK government wants to implement the new curriculum in September 2014. It is not clear if there are enough qualified teachers.

The Dutch government hardly supports coding unless it is part of science and technology in the elementary school or as part of information science (an optional subject). It's a course that a lot of secondary schools don't offer. The Dutch school system does not have a national curriculum, as mentioned earlier. There are only core objectives stated. By testing and central examinations the school inspection is monitoring schools for their results. The challenge for 2014 and further will be 1) to introduce coding in schools and 2) to get coding on the political agenda. Serious experiments with coding in elementary and secondary education should be explored.

References

[1] Lepeltak, J.: From learning to Use Towards using to Learn. About lessons to be learned from ICT-education in the Netherlands. In: History of Computing and Education 2. Springer, New York (2006)

[2] TNS NIPO onderzoek ['research'] in opdracht van St.Ict op school (Januari 2006)

[3] Vier in balans monitor 2013. De laatste stand van zaken van ict en onderwijs. Kennisnet, Zoetermeer (2013)

[4] Vier in balans monitor 2013. De laatste stand van zaken van ict en onderwijs, p. 37. Kennisnet, Zoetermeer (2013)

[5] Raamwerk ['framework'] Burgerinformatica. Stichting voor leerplanontwikkeling. Enschede (1983)
[6] See also note 3
[7] Ceruzzi, P.E.: A history of modern computing, pp. 273–276. MIT Press, Cambridge (1998)
[8] Schoenmaker, J.: Apparatuur en besturingssystemen voor het basisonderwijs. COI, Enschede (1987)
[9] Vier in balans monitor 2013. De laatste stand van zaken van ict en onderwijs, p. 42. Kennisnet, Zoetermeer (2013)
[10] See ICT in the Netherlands. Fact and figures 2003-2004. IVA/ITS Ni-jmegen/Tilburg (2004), `http://www.ict-onderwijsmonitor.nl/`
[11] See note v
[12] Bereiter, C.: Education and mind in the knowledge age. New Jersey LEA Publishers, Mahwah (2002)
[13] Maddux, C.D., Lamont Johnson, D., Willis, J.W.: Educational Computing. Learning with Tomorrow's Technologies, 2nd edn., Boston (1997)
[14] Wood, D.: How children think and learn. The social contexts of cognitive development, 2nd edn., London (2005)
[15] See also `http://cma-science.nl/support/vincilab/index.html`
[16] ten Brummelhuis, A.: Digitale schoolborden in het PO. Onderzoek naar implementatie, gebruik en meerwaarde van digiborden in het primair onderwijs, Zoetermeer (2008)
[17] See, `http://1vjongerenpanel.eenvandaag.nl/`
[18] Hennessy, S., London, L.: Learning from international experiences with interactive whiteboards: The role of professional development in integrating the technology. OECD – Working Paper 89 (2013)
[19] see, `http://www.gsminfo.nl/blog/nieuws/4282/zestig-procent-basischoolkinderen-heeft-gsm-wat-zijn-kindvriendelijke-smartphones`
[20] eScience combines big data analysis and modelling with the use of supercomputers for research in various disciplines
[21] the website is, `http://twiqs.nl/`; a short video (English) about this project is available, `http://www.youtube.com/watch?v=ZRUpdUiOGVE`
[22] The prognostic figures differ but lie between the 6000 end 40.000 depending on the job level and the economic development
[23] Report USA Ministerie of education (2011), `http://nces.ed.gov/nationsreportcard/pdf/studies/2011462.pdf`
[24] Feminisering van het primair onderwijs (the feminization of elementary education) CAOP-report (January 2013)
[25] Vakkundig meesterschap en meesterlijk vakmanschap Wim van de Grift, Michelle Helms-Lorenz, Dik Maandag & Siebrich de Vries Groningen (2012)
[26] See the Guardian (July 8, 2013)

Pioneering the Internet in the Nineties – An Innovative Project Involving UK and Australian Schools

Angela Lecomber

Victoria University and See Differently
angela@seedifferently.com.au

Abstract. The author discusses the challenges and shifts of pedagogy in incorporating an innovative Project to link UK and Australian schools between 1996 and 1998. Despite the UK government's *National Grid for Learning* policy in 1997, only four schools (out of the total of 125 schools) in Sunderland, UK had a computer connected to the Internet. Schools still functioned as classrooms of the Industrial age.

Keywords: Science teaching, laboratory, Sunderland, Internet.

1 Background

In the nineties, I was a Secondary School Science teacher in a Girls Catholic School in Sunderland, in the North-East of England. This was a career change for me having previously been a COBOL programmer and systems analyst in a London Bank. Consequently I had a personal interest in the use of computers.

My experience was typical for teachers in the early nineties in Sunderland. There was no such thing as an ICT teacher nor was there a subject called ICT. Subjects were taught strictly within the discipline with little if any cross-over with other subjects. For example, year 7 students covered Water and Energy in Science but the overlap into the separate subject of Geography was frowned upon.

There was one computer per science laboratory and this was used by the Head of Science to write reports and for the laboratory technician to record orders on supplies. It was only very occasionally used for students. If at all, it was used for the very brightest who had finished all the assigned work to access a CD-ROM disc which had some material on the subject being studied. In essence, the CD-ROM was a glorified Encyclopaedia with photos. Invariably a crowd would gather around the computer. There was no local area network (LAN) and computers were not connected to the Internet.

1.1 Little Incentive to Explore the Use of the Computer in the Classroom

Disappointingly, there was little incentive to alter curriculum planning and delivery to explore the use of computers to assist with delivering subjects. Although teachers were allowed the freedom of how material was delivered (exercises, homework and class activities that would suit the interest and aptitude of pupils), we had to cover the

A. Tatnall and B. Davey (Eds.): History of Computers in Education, IFIP AICT 424, pp. 384–393, 2014.

curriculum. There was nothing in the biology and chemistry curriculums that had any reference to the use of computers (or technology). It was puzzling to me that there was software (such as data logging tools, assorted CD-ROMs and floppy disks) in the laboratory cupboard, most still unopened in their packaging.

When I attempted to explore this, I was often reminded by the Head of Biology that it was a waste of time to bother with the computer or experiment with software. The Head of Science was a little ambivalent and did not mind if I dabbled with the software. My superiors considered computers to take time away from the valuable task of teaching. In any event, I would get no support from the laboratory technician.

Assignments were handwritten and desk-top publishing with word processing programs was not available to students to use.

2 Sunderland – Backwater or Typical of Cities in the UK?

According to the Science Advisor who oversaw science throughout Sunderland from nursery to high school at the time, "the development of computer usage was behind that I had known in Leeds, probably because Leeds University, the Leeds Local Education Authority and the Yorkshire Region had been at the forefront of many developments in the UK."(Valerie Wood-Robinson, Jan 2014).

2.1 Personal Reflections of a Science Advisor

Valerie Wood-Robinson was Sunderland's Science Advisor from late 1993 to early 1997. She oversaw my teaching in Science and had previously been involved in seminal initiatives to use computers in education in the UK. Although 'seminal', many of the seeds fell on stony ground and others took a very long time to germinate, as the following observations indicate.

In the early 1980s, Valerie was asked to join a working group of teachers at Leeds University to devise or adapt school experiments to make use of a data logging tool called VELA (Versatile Laboratory Aid). VELA was a stand-alone data logger or could be connected to a BBC Microcomputer or other suitable computer to allow the downloading of data for analysis. She was on the group as a biology specialist to design sensing and data capture uses in biological experiments. In 1986 VELA was dispatched to four thousand teachers across the UK. However, there was a suspicion that the uptake by teachers was low. This was confirmed later when as Sunderland science advisor, and subsequently as an Inspector in other parts of England, she found VELAs in cupboards still in their packaging, never used.

In 1984, Valerie was invited, as Head of Science of one of the biggest schools in Leeds, to be the Leeds representative on a Regional Project involving eight Local Authorities in Yorkshire and supported by the large-scale national Microelectronics Project (MEP). Each representative was given a kit of about twenty different pieces of software for their school and after being shown how to use this was expected to cascade professional development (known as INSET sessions) to staff out of school hours.

This Project started well until it was scuppered by a Teachers' Unions "work-to-rule" which forbade its members doing any in-service training or curriculum development at lunch times or after school. Responding to this directive, the teachers in schools in the Project refused to cooperate with the training and reporting. It is not known to what extent other Projects within the national MEP initiative suffered the same fate. Valerie has recently contacted the co-ordinator of the Project who recalled that it was also hampered by difficult relations between the MEP "people in London" and the organisers in Yorkshire. The coordinator wrote a report to MEP but it was never published. Consequently, in most of the Regional Project schools, the software was stored away in cupboards un-used.

Her first recollection of training in using computers in teaching were sessions provided, in the early eighties, by the ASE (Association for Science Education) in conjunction with Leeds Education Authority Teachers' Centre. Teachers attended in their own time after school or at weekends, so only enthusiasts would be there. Training was also provided by LEAs (Local Education Authorities) in school time but usually only the Head of Science would be allowed to attend, and only if the Head teacher thought the topic was worthwhile and many did not. Courses were also run by some Universities. Again, a limited number of teachers would attend, and schools often thought it was just for Physics teachers.

Valerie relates being on a Project supported by a UK government national initiative TVEI (Technical and Vocational Education Initiative announced in 1982) focussed on the use of technology, with an emphasis on computers across the curriculum. There were cultural barriers as many secondary school teachers were entrenched in their subject allegiances and were reluctant to concede any territory to cross curricular interventions. Despite the intentions of TVEI to implement technology across the curriculum, this was derailed by heads of departments who viewed those with funding as empire builders.

She relates how in writing newsletters on behalf of the St William's Foundation Technology Education Project, she had only the simplest computer facilities provided to her even though the Project was funded from the TVEI. She used a minimal word processing programme and literally cut-and-pasted (scissors and glue), then photocopied. She appealed to teacher readers to ask if any who had desk-top publishing facilities would guest-edit issues of the newsletter, but none were forthcoming.

The cultural hurdles encountered by these Projects in which Valerie was involved elsewhere provide a context for the Sunderland Project described in the case study in this chapter.

3 1991 and ICT

In 1991, the first World Wide Web page was created in the world and in that same year Margaret Thatcher had just stepped down as Prime Minister. Sunderland had the highest unemployment rate in the United Kingdom.

I was eager to exploit the potential for the Internet in revolutionising the way subjects were taught and to provide interest in finding new ways to use Information and

Communications Technology (ICT) in the classroom. ICT refers to technological tools such as CD-ROM technology, interactive video technology and the Internet.

4 1996 - UK Government Urged to Make 'an Act of Faith'

In 1996, the Stevenson Report *'ICT in UK Schools'* produced by the independent ICT in School Commission for the UK Government justified why funding of ICT for education was necessary. The report stated that the claims made about the value of ICT for student learning outcomes were laudable and although these were not entirely proven, "... it is important that Government makes this act of faith and that we use technology rather than study it over the next decade" (Stevenson, 1996). The report suggested a framework for both primary and secondary schools: The Role of Government, Teacher Training, Software, External Networks, Hardware and Funding.

The report pointed to the commitment that the Australian Government was making by the year 2001: targeting a ratio of one computer for every 7.5 students and ICT used for all eight key learning areas at all year levels from pre-school to year 12 and for students of special needs.

5 Sunderland – Teleport of the World

Also in 1996, the local Sunderland council launched its City's Telematics Strategy. The strategy was to develop the City of Sunderland as a Teleport, the only one outside of London in the United Kingdom. A teleport is a port of electronic information that would link the community together: business, education providers, health authorities among sectors of the community.

With the potential for funding from the Sunderland Telematics Strategy, I responded with a compelling Business case. I proposed an innovative Project to pioneer the use of the Internet in schools with a view to engendering environmental citizenship. I had based this on suggestions made by Vockell and Brown (1992) that the computer was a technological tool that was able to support the education of schoolchildren to become citizens who are able to participate in social, civic and political processes and in some meaningful way further the values and beliefs that characterise active and involved citizens in a democratic society.

The Business case was approved with 36,000 Pounds provided from the Telematics Strategy and Local Agenda 21 Environmental Action Plan. Furthermore the University of Sunderland offered me the opportunity to undertake a PhD study on the use of Internet in Schools with a focus on environmental citizenship.

There were ninety-seven state primary and seventeen state secondary schools in Sunderland but only four of them had a computer connected to the Internet. Consequently these four schools were selected to be part of the pilot. These were Hillview Junior, Springwell Dene, St Robert of Newminster Catholic and Washington School. A fifth school, Southmoor was selected based on their commitment to get computer connectivity by the end of 1997. The University of Sunderland offered me the support of a part time technician to work with five schools consisting of 40 teachers.

It was disappointing that my own school (St Anthony's Catholic Girls school) were reluctant to be involved. There was no commitment to get connected to the Internet. There did not want to change tried and tested formulas for achieving academic results which at the time were the best in Sunderland. Perhaps and more likely the reason was the lack of confidence that the teachers had in their skills with ICT. Nevertheless I was compelled to resign from teaching to manage this innovative Project.

In 1997, Sunderland was heralded the 'Teleport of the World'. Tony Blair became Prime Minister that year and spearheaded the UK Government's Consultation Paper 'Connecting the Learning Society'. This paper explained the Government's proposals for securing the benefits of advanced network technologies for education and lifelong learning.

By the publication of this Consultation Paper, there were 32,000 state and independent schools with over 450,000 teachers and over 9 million pupils in the United Kingdom. Of these 6,000 had connected to the Internet and some 4,000 had installed local area networks of varying extents. The Times Newspaper reported that UK schools had the biggest 'take-up' rate in Europe on the Internet (17 Nov 1997).

Pilots were being pioneered and assessed throughout the country and my Project known as 'ICT for Environmental Citizenship' was one of them.

6 The Project

The promotional literature for the Project described the objective as:

> *'To use computers in schools to communicate with each other, across the country and the rest of the world, to learn more about the environment and the ways in which they can work with one another to preserve it.'*

I was keen to find partner schools in another part of the English speaking world. This would promote novelty for the schoolchildren and promote cross-country partnerships in exploring the new Internet capability. The Association of Science Education provided funding to link schools in Australia with the existing group of five selected schools. Australia was a focus because it was English speaking and had similarities in the Year 7 and 8 Environmental Curriculum. Australia's distance from the UK would be of interest in exploring collaborative learning across the globe.

I piloted a twinned collaborative curriculum between Hillview Junior School, Sunderland, UK and Greensborough Primary School, Melbourne, Australia. Both schools had a committed Head Teacher, a network of ten computers with a ratio of one computer to three schoolchildren available at one site or classroom and at least one Internet address specific to the Project. They both had a supportive co-ordinating teacher, technical support, a commitment to the Project throughout the year and an interdisciplinary approach to the Project.

In fact Greensborough Primary was more equipped than Hillview Junior with sixteen networked computers in their computer labs, largely through raising their own funding and getting parents to install the necessary wiring.

7 The Journey

7.1 Internet - A Galaxy of Trashcans

The Project targeted Year 7 and Year 8 students and had a ten stage plan. The first three stages of the Project involved engaging the head teachers and environmental subject specialists of the schools to ensure that they were fully on board and that they were interested in exploring a new way of incorporating the Internet into the environmental curriculum. At the time, there was a great deal of scepticism of the authenticity of material on websites and validity for education since anyone could create material. One head-teacher described the Internet as 'a galaxy of trashcans'. This was the very narrow view of its capability other than the capacity for electronic mail. One of my challenges was to find sites that were authentic, accurate and attractive for teachers and students to use.

Environmental subject specialists were not entirely convinced of the Internet's value and would have preferred the same allocated time to taking their pupils to look at the local pond-life, for example. Other teachers who were supportive were interested in the ICT technology but not interested in using it for environmental curriculum. They were the school's first appointed ICT teachers who invariably had a technical bias.

The website for the Project (http://cei/sunderland.ac.uk/schools) was developed largely using 'HotDog' one of very few HTML editors on the market at the time. It was easy to use and the teachers and students learned to use this too.

This central website would provide ideas for teachers about what they could do with the Internet within the curriculum and provide sample ways in which schoolchildren could use it. I had to also provide them with accredited websites and to network with others. The website was to be a co-ordinating platform and 'window' to an observer of the Project. The idea was to get each participant teacher to create a web page reflecting their work around a particular part of the curriculum.

7.2 Overcoming Blandness and Waiting Periods

The cost of using on-line services (not the fixed subscription fee) had not been established. High speed transmission was not available which affected waiting periods for a webpage to download. ISDN2 lines were used. However if a total page size of a home page was up to 30k, then it would take 30 seconds to download.

The challenge to be overcome was the perception that children had of websites. In 1996, the World Wide Web pages did not have the sophistication and interactivity as they do today. Web pages were uninteresting and bland. They were not designed to be read or used by children. The pages were unappealing and were not designed for children with an accessible, lively and informal format to encourage them to send emails and to discuss their work. Web pages did not offer the differentiation for the different audiences and interests as they do today. The design of websites was at its infancy and good design principles were not used to make presentation of material appealing to young people.

7.3 Technologically Barren

By January 1997, the schools in the Project had a dedicated computer room with access to the Internet. However it was disruptive if children were allowed out of the classroom to use the computer room. This could have been solved with extra telephone lines made available and connected to classrooms with extensions. However, schools were 'technologically barren' with any extra telephone lines going into the head teacher's or senior member of staff's office.

Most teachers in the five schools had to share electronic mail. There was no individual electronic mail. In two schools, there was only one address for the whole school. Problems existed on the Project because only one email address was used by all teachers and pupils. Hence in these cases, the co-ordinator of the Project would divert incoming messages to virtual files belonging to each of the participating teachers and their classrooms.

Teachers on the Project had to be taught the necessity of emptying their mailbox regularly, organising access to the electronic mail messages as soon as they came in. The importance of replying to messages within two days was a useful recommendation raised by the ICT teacher of one of the schools. Otherwise the momentum and the interest in the exchange is lost and subsequently the value in the collaborative partnership. For example, webpages were created about a particular environmental interest like reduction in the use of energy. Then this was shared by sending electronic mail in a purposeful way. Receiving feedback through electronic mail was valuable as it encouraged students to recall their work in a way different from the usual context. However if electronic mail took more than two days to get a response, then often interest waned in the collaboration.

7.4 Politics of the Computer Room

A curious problem was that of the 'blocker'. This was the teacher with ICT skills who would deliberately make access to the computer room difficult for other teachers e.g. keys were not available, passwords not made known, changes to software not explained. There was an underlying political agenda in a number of schools where those who were seen to be in charge of the new technology were not prepared to share knowledge readily and openly with their non-ICT literate colleagues. Typical complaints from non-ICT teachers would be "*Cannot understand why the IT department have locked up the computer room. I am very keen on using computers and want pupils to have easy access. It is very frustrating as computers are rarely available to teachers, let alone pupils*".

7.5 Pedagogy

With the fourth stage of the Project, I was challenged into fitting the use of the Internet into existing schemes of work used by the teachers. Even when the Internet was used in the pilot schools, the use of the Internet was 'tacked on' at the end of a unit of work rather than linking it within the schemes of work and what the teachers were already doing. The way in which the computer was used with schoolchildren was simply the mastery of basic skills of using the Internet. Pedagogy was still teacher-centred and not student-centred.

Regrettably, there was little shift in pedagogy in those early days with the introduction of the Internet into the classroom. The computer was seen as a supplement to teacher-controlled activities rather than intrinsically part of it. Even though I had produced new material in order to refine and expand instructional strategies knowing that students would be on their own with the computer, technology had not yet influenced teaching styles.

There was the need to shift perceptions: from being 'fount of knowledge' to being a facilitator of student learning.

7.6 Taking the Terror Out of ICT

The fifth stage of the Project was to 'take the terror out of ICT' i.e. the challenge of developing the expertise and confidence of teachers in the use of the Internet.

With regard to the production of webpages, down-to-earth, user-friendly advice was provided including template webpages to assist and show how teachers could produce these offline. Classes were provided and support was available.

Teachers were shown how to bookmark sites before a lesson so as to direct pupils to a site quickly and allow them to navigate their way to the necessary pages. In addition, teachers were instructed on the mechanisms to avoid unsuitable websites. They were concerned about what personal information they could allow pupils to divulge over the Internet without putting themselves or others in 'danger'. Concerns about reports of children being abducted over the Internet had pre-occupied them. They sought guidelines and standards from the local education authority as to the standards of use of the World Wide Web and the Internet as a learning medium for schoolchildren.

Another consideration was that of online resources that were largely inaccessible to schoolchildren because of their reading ability. Teachers where guided to create simpler versions of the online resources and store these offline for access by their pupils as these were simpler to read.

Individual classes were encouraged to produce webpages and teachers were provided with ecological packages on disk and CD-ROM as springboards for new ideas and approaches. Teachers were also encouraged to develop their own material.

7.7 Findings

Although forty teachers undertook the personal training on the use of the Internet, few actually succeeded in accommodating the Project in their schemes of work. Most devoted only three lessons to the Project citing reasons such as lack of time and need to cover more pressing curriculum commitments. According to Valerie-Wood Robinson (2014), as an adviser she met resistance to using computers in schools on the justification that there was so much curriculum material and administrative procedures to cover, that there was no time for this innovation.

In fact, many teachers were reluctant to accept the changes required, mainly due to fear of the unknown, and the fact that they (teachers) were less competent with computers than their pupils who were beginning to develop computer skills by playing games on home computers. This latter problem was not prevalent in Primary schools, and, although terrified of the new technology, most primary teachers were willing to give it a try in a whole school enterprise.

Towards the end of the Project in September 1998, some teachers were moving towards a more individualised model where the teacher assumed the role of facilitator and students made their own enquiries and engaged in collaborative activities. These teachers were invariably the experienced teachers in their field e.g. head of departments in geography, science and ICT. Perhaps heads of departments have more time to devote to innovative Projects. Perhaps they have nothing to prove in terms of their knowledge and more open to a shift in pedagogical approach: from 'founts of knowledge' to facilitators of learning. Whatever the reason, it was significant that those who were very familiar with the knowledge content of their specialisms were noticeably embracing ICT.

It was difficult enough to get teachers to use ICT, let alone for non-ICT subjects like environmental citizenship. The Project required a shift in teaching methods and styles to a student-centred approach. There was a lack of support for how to do this. Furthermore, teachers up until 1998, were not formally taught pedagogy (Times Education Supplement, 12th June 1998).

This Project made the following recommendations for both primary and secondary schools:

- Professional development of teachers in the use of ICT and student-centred pedagogy
- The need for regular support of teachers in the use of ICT in the classroom
- More work with Heads of Departments to ascertain where ICT fits into schemes of work
- The need to convince and support Head teachers and Heads of ICT to involve ICT in non-ICT subjects like environmental education.

8 Conclusion

Despite the rhetoric and objective of the UK Government in preparing schools for the twenty first century, in practice, they were still functioning as classrooms of the Industrial age. There were technological limitations and the lack of affordability in terms of connectivity to the Internet. However, probably the key factor in its lack of adoption in schools was the fear of using computers due to the lack of skills. Issues of shared ownership of computers and its place in the curriculum may have been underlying factors. In any event, there would need to be a shift in pedagogical approach from teachers as 'founts of knowledge' to 'teachers as facilitators of learning'. Nevertheless, computing in schools took off not because of educational initiatives but because teachers, as well as pupils, developed their skills in home computing.

It was indeed a time of great promise for citizenship and hope for young people who felt that something different was happening in education to make the world a better place.

Acknowledgements. The author gratefully acknowledges the rich contribution of Valerie Wood-Robinson, Science Advisor (Inspector) for the City of Sunderland during the period 1993 to 1997.

The author also wishes to thank the opportunities afforded by those who supported this cutting-edge Internet Project. In particular the University of Sunderland (Dr Tony Alabaster), Sunderland Telematics Strategy, Local Agenda 21, the Association for Science Education and the teachers involved in the pilot schools both in the UK and Australia.

References

DfEE, Connecting the Learning Society. National Grid for Learning. Government's Consultation Paper (1997)

Stevenson, D.: Information and Communication Technology in UK Schools. Report by the Independent ICT in School Commission 1996/97 (1996)

Vockell, E., Brown, W.: The Computer in the Social Studies Curriculum. McGraw-Hill, California (1992)

Wood-Robinson, V.: Email communication to Angela Lecomber (2014)

The Educational Programming Language Logo: Its Nature and Its Use in Australia

Anne McDougall[1], John S. Murnane[1], and Sandra Wills[2]

[1] Melbourne Graduate School of Education, The University of Melbourne, Australia
[2] Australian Graduate School of Education, Charles Sturt University, Australia
{jmurnane,a.mcdougall}@unimelb.edu.au, swills@csu.edu.au

Abstract. Although Logo was expressly designed as a Mathematical language for use in Education its early versions were very logic-orientated. With the addition of Seymour Papert's 'turtle' the system became far more accessible to students and teachers. This paper explores some of the educational ideas behind its development and describes its first use in schools in Australia through reminiscences by two of the co-authors, Sandra Wills and Anne McDougall. The paper concludes with a reflection that educational research has not been able to *prove* the educational benefits of a ground-breaking approach that empowered students with computers. However, many rich case studies of successful implementation by passionate teachers abound in the literature to provide inspiration to teachers working with the new digital natives.

Keywords: Logo, turtles, Logo in Australia, Lego Logo, constructivism.

1 Introduction

Early in 1973 one of the co-authors, Anne McDougall, commencing a newly created position as Research Fellow in Computer Assisted Instruction at the University of Melbourne, set out to read every research paper then published concerning the use of computers in educational contexts. She found accounts of innovative work with drill and practice programs for learning, computer managed instruction, and some preliminary computer simulation and modelling programs. She also found a set of papers from a group working at MIT in the USA (Papert, 1971a; Papert, 1971b; Papert & Solomon, 1971). These argued that most current work in educational computing involved the computers 'programming the children,' and by contrast suggested that students should themselves learn to program the computers to enable powerful learning through exploration of novel ideas, situations, concepts and problems. These papers described a programming language called Logo, developed specifically for this purpose. Reading them, and being delighted by their approach but reflecting on the current state of computer hardware and software, she wondered whether such an opportunity might be provided for students during her lifetime. Just three years later, thanks to some extraordinary initiatives by two teachers in Tasmania, her own students were using Logo.

This paper is concerned with the development and nature of Logo, and describes some innovative and influential Logo work done in Australia. We begin by examining

A. Tatnall and B. Davey (Eds.): History of Computers in Education, IFIP AICT 424, pp. 394–407, 2014.

the educational concepts behind Logo—and its subsequent versions such as LogoWriter and MicroWorlds.

2 A Language for Learning

The creation of a programming language of any sort is a complex business and the province of a special elite in the world of programming. Yet the difficulty of the creation of a language for fields such as business or mathematics, for which there is an existing set of well-tried models, pales into insignificance compared to the task of creating one for educational purposes: a space where a choice must first be made between various pedagogies, all with their own built-in advantages and disadvantages, advocates and detractors, before even the form of the language is decided on. Nor will the educational aim be simple. Is it to be a language to introduce the forms and disciplines of programming itself, or is it to facilitate a more general development in problem solving and analytical and logical thinking? Are we teaching computing and its applications, or are we using programming for some wider educational purpose?

Looking back at the a-priori positions on the benefits that writing programs could bring to students, we find a remarkable unity of spirit among the pioneers of educational computing languages. Cynically, it could be argued that in the 1960s, apart from some rather inflexible Computer Assisted Instruction (CAI), and some (mostly non-interactive) simulations, writing a program was about the only educational thing students could do with a computer. But the pioneers, and particularly those with a hand in writing specialised educational languages, such as Kemeny and Kurtz who developed Basic, and Feurzeig and Papert, the developers of Logo, were all convinced that great educational advantages would come from programming a digital computer, although often for different educational and cognitive reasons. Weyer and Cannara (1975, p.3) put it this way: "If … any ideas which can be formalised may be studied concretely via a computer program, then, by learning programming in full generality, students can learn to construct laboratories to study any ideas they wish to think about."

The decade that produced the first educational computer languages is now 50 years in the past. With the singular exception of anything written by Seymour Papert, looking back through the papers and reports leaves a distinct impression of teachers striving towards goals imperfectly grasped, using computing equipment barely up to the task, and hampered by primitive translators, operating systems and input/output devices. Yet the *overall* feeling is of high optimism, more positive than one finds across the more recent literature. (Papert who had worked with Jean Piaget for many years, knew what he was doing from the outset, and Wally Feurzeig and Papert, working with Lisp at the Artificial Intelligence Laboratory at MIT in the USA, not only had an example of a language congruent with their educational ideas, but one in which their new language could be written.) The pioneers, from their own experiences, *knew* that programming a computer had educational benefits, and were going to set about proving it to the world.

3 A Language for Learning Mathematics

Feurzeig's Logo group began with *education* and worked *back* to the form of their language. Early Logo was very simple. Like Basic, it came with built-in editing and file manipulation commands. If these are ignored, the 1971 version consisted of just 26 'operations,' five of which accessed the calendar and clock, and 15 'commands.' Most operations were concerned with program logic or list manipulation. An essential part of the design was to produce a language of such simplicity that it forced users to write their own library of commonly used routines, such as multiplication and division. From such a library, complex programs could be built. "Ideally, by the end of the course, each student would have created his own extended version of Logo" (Brown & Rubinstein, 1974, p.10).

There is no mention of the degree of difficulty inherent in learning to program generally, and certainly not in learning Logo, in Feurzeig's papers. The entire emphasis in *The Final Report* (Feurzeig et al., 1969) is on the difficulty of learning Mathematics, and how Logo was developed to make that easier. The programming language followed as a result of a specific educational need. The designers of Logo intended it not only as a vehicle to express Mathematical ideas and make Mathematical concepts concrete, they saw it also as a meta-language in which to express Mathematical thought (Feurzeig et al., 1969, p.5). Here is the origin of Papert's often expressed need to teach 'thinking about thinking' (Papert, 1971a, p.2) and the decision to write a computer language whose primitives and predicates inherently contained and *expressed* the mechanisms of logic and Mathematics. "Do we give children the instruction 'think!' without even telling them how to think?" (Papert, 1971a, p.4). The mathematical purpose expressed by Feurzeig is actually at odds with Papert who is at pains to stress the general problem solving capability of the language (Papert, 1971a; Papert & Solomon, 1971). Lisp's origins in Artificial Intelligence were supposed to support this (Evans, 1992, p.14; Abelson et al., 1976, p.16), but no author we have read ever explained how it was to happen.

The 'Lo' in Logo suggested 'Logic,' and the earliest versions of the Logo system were written in Lisp, a list processing language. It is curious then that early papers (Feurzeig et al., 1969, p.1; Feurzeig et al., 1971, p.1) make it clear that Logo was "expressly designed" for the teaching of Mathematics. At that time there was no Turtle Geometry, and indeed no arithmetic functionality beyond addition and subtraction. Brown and Rubinstein (1974, p.3) flatly describe it as 'non-numeric'.

Many of the programs in the *Final Report on the Logo Project* (Feurzeig et al., 1969) seem forced, elementary and repetitive. Many from the primary level, ages 7 to 9, are examples of programs to reverse the letters in a word, print a set of consecutive numbers or simply print strings. The first lessons did not involve writing code at all. This did not happen until Lesson Seven (p. 67). In the secondary curriculum, many essential elementary functions such as divide and multiply were written by the teachers and given to the students to try to understand (p. 215), the inference being that students could not be expected to write these routines themselves. Johnson (2000, p.201) found "The position that the programming environments themselves, e.g., Logo microworlds, would become the school mathematics curriculum has clearly failed to gain the support of the educational system."

None of this suggests a language easily taken up by beginners and used for their own purposes. Part of the reason has to be the use, initially, of recursion for all loops, definite or indefinite. Recursion is, as Papert has said repeatedly, a powerful problem solving tool (Papert, 1980; Papert, 1971a; Papert & Solomon, 1971; Papert, 2002) and indeed it is. But then, so is calculus!

Papert's work with Jean Piaget resulted in a passionate belief in the idea of 'learning by doing,' something he later extended to what might be termed 'learning by *making things*.' Papert in particular has always insisted that Logo is designed to encourage experimentation, with students writing and testing their own creations. Given this emphasis, it is difficult to understand the reliance on recursion at the expense of a general iterative statement. We can find nothing in the early literature that asserts that students can be expected to discover a recursive solution to a problem on their own. All we can find are examples provided *to* students to explain, understand, and adapt. In his seminal book, *Mindstorms*, published in 1980, Papert states that "recursion stands out as the one idea that is particularly able to evoke an excited response." That might be so, but he devotes less than two pages to it, mentioning it once more in the Appendix in the context of 'circular logic' (p109). Brown and Rubinstein suggest that with suitable prior experience, students can write their own recursive routine to traverse a tree, but these writers give no clue to their success rate. They did find that "if a student couldn't figure out how to write a function, we could not slowly lead him down the path to discovery" (Brown & Rubinstein, 1974, p.43). Once acquainted with WHILE—DO in Basic or Pascal, or even the primitive Dartmouth-Basic GOTO, students have no trouble in writing their own indefinite loops (Murnane, 1991; Murnane, 1992). (See also McDougall, 1985.)

4 Enter the Turtle

Even allowing for difficulty in conceptualising recursion, Logo is not English, and in its early versions Logo struggled to make progress. The cure for many of these problems was provided by Seymour Papert. Logo is often associated specifically with Papert, and particularly with his Turtle Graphics. He joined the project in January 1969 as a consultant (Feurzeig et al., 1969, p.1) and his invention of the Turtle and its commands transformed the language.

A Turtle is a small robot which, when connected to a computer, can move and turn on the floor. At a stroke this eliminated the gap between entering a program and observing its outcome, since the Turtle could execute a command as soon as it was entered. It also solved the problem of students understanding what the command did. While they might need to be taught the meaning of "TEST IS COUNT /SENTENCE/ 1 (Feurzeig et al., 1971, p.45) they could easily appreciate what FORWARD 100 meant because it accorded with their own body actions and their natural language. Turtle Geometry provides an immediate and meaningful environment for the beginner.

Along with Turtle commands came definite iteration: REPEAT :N, relieving the programmer of the need to write all loops recursively. A recursive loop can only be executed by writing a procedure and then executing it. In keeping with the idea of observing actions as the commands were entered, you could now type REPEAT 4

[FORWARD 100 RIGHT 90] and *watch* a square being drawn. Note also the close correspondence to English syntax. Once the Turtle migrated from the floor to the screen, Logo became accessible and viable in any classroom.

5 Logo Comes to Australia

In 1975 Scott Brownell, a teacher in Australia's island state of Tasmania, saw Logo at MIT on a study tour and in a visionary move brought a magnetic tape copy of Logo from Boston to Hobart to run on a PDP-11 mini-computer at the Tasmanian Education Department's Computer Centre (Richardson 1997). With a Commonwealth Schools Commission Innovation Grant, he was able to recruit a Tasmanian teacher, Sandra Wills, to extend into primary schools the work on computer awareness and computer science already underway in secondary schools in the state, using Logo as the vehicle. He secured a rare and expensive robot Turtle from the General Turtle Co. in the USA. This was at a time when the telephone system was used to connect every senior high school in Tasmania with a terminal to the PDP-11. Over the next few years, Sandra would load the turtle into her car and travel all over the island visiting the Education Department's 300 schools. At each school the children would connect the Turtle and a Tektronix graphics terminal to a home-made modem to dial up the PDP-11 in Hobart.

Fig. 1. General Turtle Inc. robot (interface box in background) with Sandra Wills at the controls of the PDP-11 terminal, 1976

The Logo project was instrumental in spreading computing, not only into primary schools, but also middle high schools because it changed people's perceptions of computing. At a time when the general population had never seen a computer nor knew what it might do for them, the Turtle and the English–like Logo language, particularly Papert's geometric Turtle commands, dispelled perceptions that computing was only for the Mathematical geniuses.

John Gilbert, originally from Hatfield in the UK but then working at the Centre in Hobart, wrote a version of Logo in which a virtual turtle left lines of asterisks on the screen to approximate the path the floor turtle was taking. (Wills, 1980; Wills, 1981). In 1976 the Tasmanian group sent Anne McDougall this version of the language to introduce Logo to her students in the Faculty of Education at the University of Melbourne.

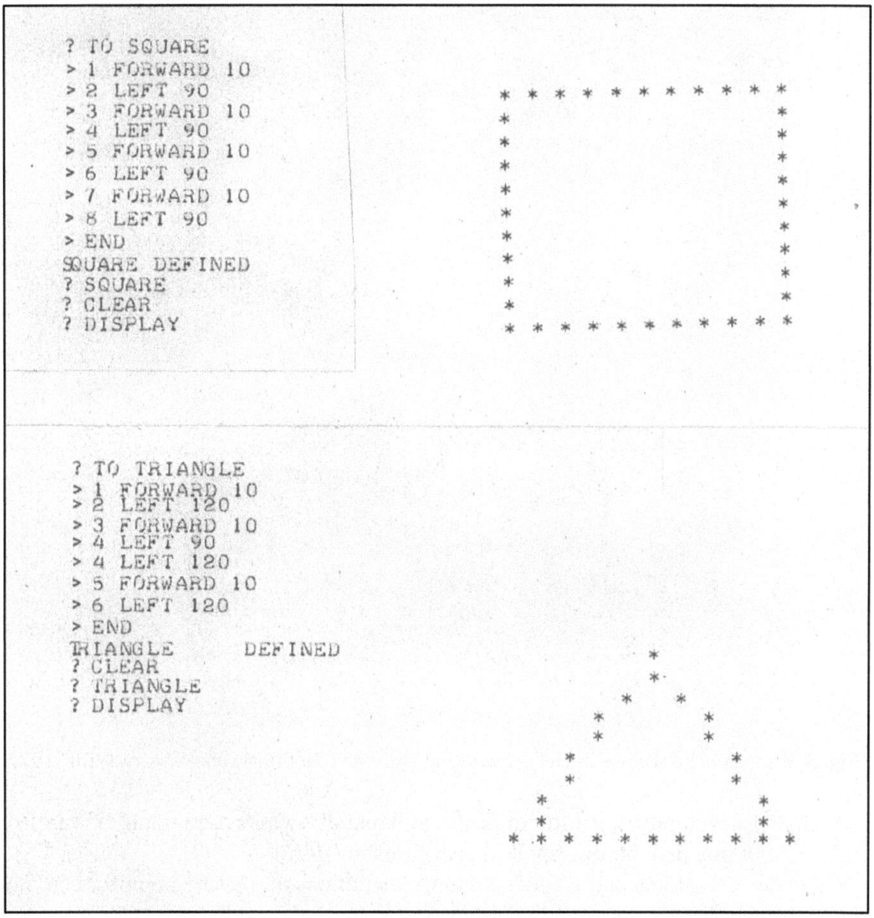

Fig. 2. Virtual turtle tracks

Once personal computers were invented in the late 70s early 80s, Richard Miller of the University of Wollongong in New South Wales wrote the first version of Logo to run on the Apple][, specifically to drive the Turtles in the Tasmanian project. Wills, in collaboration with Miller and Allan Branch, a Tasmanian engineer, oversaw the design and manufacture of a smaller and relatively inexpensive floor turtle, the Tassie Turtle, which achieved a degree of accuracy and precision that had eluded similar

Fig. 3. Primary school class in Hobart working with the robot turtle and Sandra Wills, 1977

research and development efforts in Edinburgh and elsewhere, and could be run from a 5.25 inch floppy disk on the Apple][(Richardson, 1997).

A number of schools and teacher training institutions across the country were now using Richard Miller Logo and the Tassie Turtle to explore what might be done with Logo. In 1981 Seymour Papert visited Australia. Arriving in Melbourne to speak at a conference, he was moved to tears when he found himself in a room surrounded by a swarm of buzzing, beeping robot Turtles (Richardson 1997).

Papert's visit built on the pioneering work of the Tasmanians to inspire a generation of Australian Logo workers. The next few years saw the publication by Australian authors of several widely used Logo books (McDougall et al., 1982; Nevile & Dowling, 1983; Carter, 1987; Newell, 1988a; Newell, 1988b). *Learning Logo on the*

Apple II, by Anne McDougall and Tony and Pauline Adams, was translated into German, French and Chinese. In Victoria, Logo was included as one of the recommended programming languages for senior secondary school Computer Science courses. A Special Interest Group of the Computer Education Group of Victoria, OzLogo, was established, and a quarterly newsletter, POALL, was produced and edited by Peter Carter at the University of Adelaide in South Australia.

Contingents of Australians attended, and some presented at three Logo conferences, Logo84, Logo85 and Logo86, held at MIT. In the ensuing years Logo leaders from the USA, including Hal Abelson, Andy diSessa and Brian Harvey, also visited Australia, to speak at conferences and to work with locals in several of the states. Gary Stager from the USA did extensive work in teacher professional development in Australia and Seymour Papert presented a memorable closing keynote address at the 1990 World Conference on Computers in Education in Sydney.

A conference, *Logo in Australia: Ten Years On*, was held in Melbourne in 1985 to mark ten years of Logo work in Australia. By then Logo use was being investigated in many parts of the country, at all levels of education from kindergarten, where a single-key version of the language developed by Pauline Adams was used (Adams, P. 1985) through primary (Wills 1985) and secondary (Squires & Sellman 1985; Clarke 1985) schools, to teacher pre-service and in-service education (Jones 1985; Nevile 1985). Selected papers from this conference were subsequently published (McDougall 1996).

Fig. 4. Seymour Papert and Sandra Wills with Tassie Turtle robot at Computer Education Group of Victoria Conference, 1981

Consistent with developments in computer hardware, new and enhanced versions of Logo appeared from development centres in the USA. These included LogoWriter, TurtleMath, GeoLogo, StarLogo, Lego TC Logo, Object Logo and MicroWorlds, and investigation and adoption of these continued in a variety of school settings across this country. Associated with the adoption of laptop computers in some schools, in 1989 the Australian Council for Educational Research and Liddy Nevile set up the Sunrise Project—laptop computers in two pilot schools, Coombabah Primary School on the Gold Coast in Queensland and Methodist Ladies' College in Melbourne (Richardson 1997). Children in Years 5–7 were each given a laptop computer with LogoWriter. The entire curriculum was conducted and expressed by the children as LogoWriter projects. Many schools emulated this approach, and LogoWriter and then MicroWorlds were used in laptop initiatives all over the country.

A second conference, *Learning in Logo Microworlds* was held in Melbourne in 1996, marking twenty-one years, the 'coming of age' of Logo in Australia. The Proceedings were published (McDougall & Dowling 1997) along with another book of Logo-related research papers, *Logo in Australia: Selected Readings* (Oakley 1996). The across-curriculum use of LogoWriter or MicroWorlds was associated with increasing use of thematic and project work approaches to curriculum planning, more collaborative, group and discussion work, and greater flexibility of timetabling (Chapman 1997; Best 1997; Betts 1997; McDougall & Betts 1997; Costa 1997; Kerwin 1997). As well as these cross-curricular applications, Logo use for enhancement of understanding of concepts in specific subject areas continued, for example in Science (Duncan 1997; Hopkins 1997), Mathematics (Yelland & Masters 1997), and as a stimulus for reflection about natural language (Dowling 1985). Student competence in programming (Oakley and McDougall 1997) and issues in the teaching of programming (Betts 1997) remained matters for discussion.

6 Research

In Australia, as in other countries, many research studies were undertaken investigating aspects of the use of Logo by students of all ages (see for example Gibbons 1997, p.10) and in a wide range of settings (for example Hopkins & McDougall, 2003). We will outline here several more distinctive topics studied in this country.

Almost from the first, Logo has gone hand-in hand with Robotics, a natural extension of Papert's invention of the Turtle. Early experimenters often built their own interfaces to run computer-controlled models constructed from Fisher Technic and similar kits. One of the authors, John Murnane, built on ten years experience with Lego TC Logo and internally constructed interfaces for the Macintosh Classic by Jon Pierce at Melbourne State College. He was particularly interested in investigating recursion, as programming a robot in Logo not only requires it but provides a concrete model for students to explore directly (Murnane & McDougall, 2006). He also used Lego kits to investigate linguistic differences between using a written programming environment and a graphical one (Murnane 2010). Debora Lipson built on this work, concentrating on the mechanical design and construction of the robots, and providing new insights into teaching the Mathematics of gearing (Lipson, 2008). Interestingly, Lipson found confusing differences in the notation used by Mathematicians and Engineers to describe gearing ratios. Meanwhile, Peter Carter, working at Plympton High School in South Australia, was developing models in Lego/Logo to enable students to explore some of the issues in robotic locomotion (Carter, 1990).

The use of recursion in Logo has been the focus of a number of projects. Murnane and Warner (2001) illustrated examples where children with prior experience in LogoWriter but without specific teaching about recursion, could have, but failed to use recursion in programming. In fact, there was almost no trace in their algorithms of them having encountered Logo at all.

The nature of some of the difficulties students have with using recursion in programming were analysed by McDougall in her Doctoral thesis (McDougall 1985). Anne was as able to show that young children can recognise, devise and interpret recursive structures and processes presented independently of the computer, in pictures, stories and everyday situations in their experience. She used techniques based on this finding to facilitate effective use of recursion in programming by children of upper primary school age (McDougall, 1985; McDougall, 1990b). Pamela Gibbons (1995a; 1995b) extended this work in a study of individual differences among adult students learning to program with recursion.

Gibbons (1997, p.7) discusses the value for a researcher of listening to students talking about their learning with Logo, and comments on students' remarkable ability to analyse and articulate their own thinking when they talk about their Logo experiences. John Vincent, working with upper primary school children and MicroWorlds found similar articulateness. He also studied individual differences, but focused on the visually rich aspects of the technology and interaction of these with children's writing. He found strong interactions, with excellent support for writing development in some students previously considered weak in language skills but with preference for visual communication (Vincent, 2001; 2002; Vincent *et al.*, 2010).

The weight of international research suggests that programming in Logo, by itself, does not teach Mathematics. Ross and Howe (1981, p.147) found that "the research of the last decade into 'mathematics through programming' has been more encouraging than discouraging, but only mildly so." Students, unless specifically taught about these points, keep Logo and Mathematics entirely separate in their minds, and few teachers seem to work to overcome this, or do so with much success. Even Abelson, Bamberger, Goldstein and Papert (Abelson et al., 1976, p.10) rather sadly remark that "Logo did not succeed in displacing Basic as the almost universal computer language for schools."

Despite encouraging results such as those with robotics, recursion and visualisation, Australian research on wider use of Logo and its subsequent versions has been consistent with the above. Tony Adams wrote "The Logo community has never come to terms with lists, they are just too hard to manipulate. Unlike turtle graphics they do not have a low entry threshold and for most applications a good working knowledge of recursion is required." (Adams, 1985, p.22). Pam Gibbons adds, "Despite what I have seen in the classroom, I know that Logo struggles into adulthood. ...[I]t fights the perception that 'real programmers don't program in Logo, that is, it's just for kids; in a discipline where obtuseness and mystique command respect, Logo is its own worst enemy." (Gibbons, 1997, p.17)

This problem has been exacerbated by a turn-around in one of Logo's original, fundamental, principles: keep the language small and have the student develop their own set of useful procedures. This forces them to write most of their own material and, the theory says, thereby understanding it.

Logo has been extended far beyond the limits any of its creators could have imagined: the Computer Science of the 60s gave no inkling of the possibilities the personal computer and object-oriented programming would bring. Logo, in the form of MicroWorlds, is part of a full-blown multi-media/robotics environment and in 2014 is probably the only language that makes Cobol look small, or offers the same invitation to write the same thing in so many different ways. Feurzeig's successors seem to invent a new command every time they have a new idea, even when existing commands would seem to be perfectly suitable to the purpose. For instance, the MicroWorlds Robotics version adds a completely new, quite separate set of commands to talk to the Logo RCX 'brick.' This leaves the existing, and quite adequate, 'Talkto' protocol in the main body of the language and separates Lego Robotics from the use of its rich array of logic. Redundancy in the language is therefore rife, while it is axiomatic in computer language design that there should only be one way to do something. On the other hand, the MicroWorlds Backpack is a brilliant model of an object, though the language itself cannot really be said to be object-oriented

Gibbons is correct: commercial programs are not written in Logo, and it was never intended that they should be. Instead, it was developed as a vehicle for learning to work with and physically model otherwise complex and difficult situations and problems, making their nature visible, documented and testable. Automating the glittering array of operations offered by later versions does not materially add to the educational possibilities, it just changes their nature. It may well prove even more difficult to show the new multi-environments enhance learning and the general curriculum than did the simple original.

7 Conclusion

Sadly, the weight of research concludes that Logo's advocates have not demonstrated the gains that exposure to its ideas are supposed to bring. That said, given the enormous number of contributing factors, research demonstrating that experience with programming carries over into written expression, problem-solving and clear-thinking is inherently extremely difficult. Essentially the teacher of today is in no better position than the pioneers, and is really just dependent *on their own belief in the promise that having students write programs will bring educational and other advantages*, a belief shared by the authors of this paper. The pioneers of educational computing *knew* that programming a computer had educational benefits and set out to prove it, but at the moment, when programming has all but disappeared from the curriculum, it seems that the world was not listening.

References

Abelson, H., Bamberger, J., Goldstein, I., Papert, S.: Logo progress report 1973–1975. Cambridge, Mass., Massachusetts Institute of Technology. AI Memo 356, p. 22. ERIC ED 128 181 (1976)

Adams, P.: Various Computers in the Kindergarten. In: McDougall, A. (ed.) Logo in Australia: Ten Years on, Computing in Education Group of Victoria, pp. 81–87 (1985,1996)
Adams, T.: Towards a Theory of Microworlds. Logo in Australia: Ten Years on, Computing in Education Group of Victoria, 13–24 (1985,1996)
Best, N.: MicroWorlds in a Year Seven Class. In: McDougall, A., Dowling, C. (eds.) Learning in Logo Microworlds, Computing in Education Group of Victoria, pp. 70–77 (1997)
Betts, J.: Teaching Programming Without Teaching Programming. In: McDougall, A., Dowling, C. (eds.) Learning in Logo Microworlds (1997)
Brown, J.S., Rubinstein, R.: Recursive functional programming for the student in the humanities and social sciences, Irvine, California, University of California, UCI–ICS–TR–27a. ERIC ED 108 664, p. 53 (1974)
Carter, P.: Thinking Logo: An Introduction to (the Universe through) Programming. Loxleys, South Australia (1987)
Carter, P.: Step by Step: Logo Legged Locomotion. In: McDougall, A., Dowling, C. (eds.) Computers in Education Amsterdam, North-Holland, pp. 743–746 (1990)
Chapman, T.: Logo and MicroWorlds at Westall Primary School: A 4 Year Tale. In: McDougall, A., Dowling, C. (eds.) Learning in Logo Microworlds, Computing in Education Group of Victoria, pp. 101–108 (1997)
Clarke, V.: Logo Tool Kits. In: McDougall, A. (ed.) Logo in Australia: Ten Years on, Computing in Education Group of Victoria, pp. 38–45 (1985)
Dowling, C.: Logo and Language Development. In: McDougall, A. (ed.) Logo in Australia: Ten Years on, Computing in Education Group of Victoria, pp. 31–37 (1985)
Duncan, C.: Microworlds: Making the Connections between the Abstract Concepts in Elementary Science. In: McDougall, A., Dowling, C. (eds.) Learning in Logo Microworlds, Computing in Education Group of Victoria, pp. 109–121 (1997)
Evans, P.: What is Logo? Deakin University Press, Geelong (1992)
Feurzeig, W., Kukas, G., Faflick, P., Grant, R., Lukas, J.D., Morgan, C.R., Weiner, W.B., Wexelblat, P.M.: An Introductory LOGO Teaching Sequence: LOGO Teaching Sequence on Logic, ERIC ED 057 579, p. 329. Beranek and Newman, Cambridge (1971)
Feurzeig, W., Papert, S., Bollm, M., Grant, R., Solomon, C.: Programming-Languages as a Conceptual Framework for Teaching Mathematics. Final report of the first fifteen months of the Logo project, p. 329. Beranek and Newman. R–1889, Washington, D.C (1969)
Gibbons, P.: A Cognitive Processing Account of Individual Differences in Novice Logo Programmers' Conceptualisation and Use of Recursion. Journal of Educational Computing Research 13(3), 211–226 (1995a)
Gibbons, P.: Recursion: An Analysis of Individual Differences in Logo Programming. Ph.D. thesis, University of Sydney (1995b)
Gibbons, P.: Logo Learning: What the Learners Say. In: McDougall, A., Dowling, C. (eds.) Learning in Logo Microworlds, pp. 7–19. Computing in Education Group of Victoria, Melbourne (1997)
Hopkins, J.: Stars and Sprites. In: McDougall, A., Dowling, C. (eds.) Learning in Logo Microworlds, pp. 133–141. Computing in Education Group of Victoria (1997)
Hopkins, J., McDougall, A.: Constructionist Learning and Teaching in a Computer Clubhouse Environment. In: McDougall, A., Murnane, J., Stacey, C., Dowling, C. (eds.) ICT and the Teacher of the Future, pp. 65–66. Australian Computer Society, Sydney (2003)
Johnson, D.C.: Algorithmics and programming in the school mathematics curriculum: support is waning—is there still a case to be made? Education and Information Technologies 5, 201–214 (2000)

Jones, A.: Logo in Preservice Teacher Training: An Australian Experiment. In: McDougall, A. (ed.) Logo in Australia: Ten Years On, pp. 54–61. Computing in Education Group of Victoria (1985)

Kemeny, J., Kurtz, T.: The Dartmouth Time-Sharing System. National Science Foundation, Washington, D.C. (1967)

Lipson, D.E.: Gearing Up for Robotics: An Investigation into the acquisition of the concepts associated with gears by teachers in a constructionist robotics environment. In: Proceedings of the International Federation for Information Processing TC3 Conference, Milan (September 2008)

McDougall, A.: Teaching and Learning about Recursion. In: McDougall, A. (ed.) Logo in Australia: Ten Years On, pp. 46–53. Computing in Education Group of Victoria (1985)

McDougall, A.: Student Difficulties in Programming with Recursion in Logo. In: McDougall, A. (ed.) Back to the Future, Forward to the Past, pp. 108–115. Computer Education Group of Victoria, Melbourne (1990a)

McDougall, A.: Children, Recursion and Logo Programming: An Investigation of Papert's Conjecture about the Variability of Piagetian Stages in Computer-Rich Cultures. In: McDougall, A., Dowling, C. (eds.) Computers in Education, pp. 415–418. North-Holland, Amsterdam (1990b)

McDougall, A. (ed.): Logo in Australia: Ten Years On, Computing in Education Group of Victoria (1996)

McDougall, A., Adams, T., Adams, P.: Learning Logo on the Apple II. Prentice-Hall, Melbourne (1982)

McDougall, A., Betts, J.: Logo Supporting the P – 12 Curriculum in a Technology Immersion School. In: McDougall, A., Dowling, C. (eds.) Learning in Logo Microworlds, pp. 92–100. Computing in Education Group of Victoria (1997)

McDougall, A., Dowling, C. (eds.): Learning in Logo Microworlds, Computing in Education Group of Victoria (1997)

Murnane, J.S.: Models of recursion. Computers & Education 16, 197–201 (1991)

Murnane, J.S.: To iterate or to recurse? Computers & Education 19, 387–394 (1992)

Murnane, J.S.: Programming Languages for Beginners. Lambert, Saarbrucken (2010) ISBN: 978–383836987–7

Murnane, J.S., McDougall, A.: Bad Computer Science in Beginners Programming Courses: "Considered Harmful"? A case study of the Tufts graphical programming language. In: Watson, D., Benzie, D., D. (eds.) Imagining the future for ICT and Education. IFIP WG 3.1, 3.3, & 3.5 Joint Conference, Ålesund, Norway: 329-340, June 26-30, pp. 13978–13982 (2006); ISBN: 1082-92186-33-6 FISBN: 13978-82-92186-33-6, Published online by Springer and in CD-ROM format

Murnane, J.S., Warner, J.W.: An empirical study of secondary students' expression of algorithms in natural language. In: McDougall, A., Murnane, J.S., Chambers, D. (eds.) 7th IFIP World Conference on Computers in Education. Computers in Education 2001: Australian Topics, vol. 8, pp. 81–86. Australian Computer Society, Bedford Park (2001)

Nevile, L.: Some Comments on Logo after Ten Years. In: McDougall, A. (ed.) Logo in Australia: Ten Years On, pp. 101–108. Computing in Education Group of Victoria (1985)

Nevile, L., Dowling, C.: Let's Talk Apple Turtle. Prentice-Hall, Sydney (1983)

Newell, B.: Turtles Speak Mathematics. Curriculum Development Centre, Canberra (1988a)

Newell, B.: Turtle Confusion. Curriculum Development Centre, Australia (1988b)

Oakley, J. (ed.): Logo in Australia: Selected Readings, Computing in Education Group of Victoria (1996)

Oakley, J., McDougall, A.: Young Children as Programmers: Fantasy or Flight? In: McDougall, A., Dowling, C. (eds.) Learning in Logo Microworlds, pp. 32–51. Computing in Education Group of Victoria (1997)

Papert, S.: Teaching Children Thinking. Cambridge, Massachusetts, Massachusetts Institute of Technology. p. 241, ERIC ED 077 241 (1971a)

Papert, S.: Teaching children to be mathematicians vs teaching about mathematics. Cambridge, Massachusetts, Massachusetts Institute of Technology Artificial Intelligence Laboratory. p. 26, ERIC ED 077 243 (1971b)

Papert, S., Solomon, C.: Twenty things to do with a computer. Cambridge, Massachusetts, Massachusetts Institute of Technology, p. 240, ERIC ED 077 240 (1971)

Papert, S.: Mindstorms: Children, Computers and Powerful Ideas. Basic Books, New York (1980)

Richardson, J.: Logo in Australia: 21 Years On. In: McDougall, A., Dowling, C. (eds.) Learning in Logo Microworlds, pp. 3–6. Computing in Education Group of Victoria (1997)

Ross, P., Howe, J.: Teaching mathematics through programming: ten years on. In: Lewis, R., Tagg, D. (eds.) Computers in Education, vol. 1, pp. 143–148. North-Holland (1981)

Squires, D., Sellman, R.: Designing Computer Based Microworlds. In: McDougall, A. (ed.) Logo in Australia: Ten Years On, pp. 25–30. Computing in Education Group of Victoria (1985)

Vincent, J.: The role of visually rich technology in facilitating children's writing. Journal of Computer Assisted Learning 17(3), 242–250 (2001)

Vincent, J.: MicroWorlds and the Integrated Brain. In: McDougall, A., Murnane, J., Chambers, D. (eds.) Computers in Education 2001: Australian Topics, pp. 131–137. Australian Computer Society, Sydney (2002)

Vincent, J., McDougall, A., Azinian, H.: Visualisation, multimodality and learning with information technolgy. In: McDougall, A., Murnane, J., Jones, A., Reynolds, N. (eds.) Researching IT in Education, pp. 192–199. Oxford, Routledge (2010)

Weyer, S.A., Cannara, A.B.: Children learning computer programming: experiences with languages, curricula and programming devices. Stanford, Calf., Stanford University. p. 228, Technical Report No. 250. ERIC ED 111 347 (1975)

Wills, S.: Computer Education in Tasmanian Schools: ACS Lecture of the Year. Australian Computer Bulletin 4(7), 22–28 (1980)

Wills, S.: Computer Education in Australian Schools. Australian Computer Bulletin 5(4), 4–5 (1981)

Wills, S.: Doodle Design Debug: Process vs Content Issues in Classroom Computing. In: McDougall, A. (ed.) Logo in Australia: Ten Years On, pp. 1–12. Computing in Education Group of Victoria (1985)

Yelland, N., Masters, J.: 21 Years of Logo: Logo for the 21st Century. In: McDougall, A., Dowling, C. (eds.) Learning in Logo Microworlds, Computing in Education Group of Victoria, pp. 122–132 (1997)

My Work among the Keyboards: Remembering the Early Use of Computers in the Classroom

Michael Hammond

University of Warwick, UK
m.hammond@warwick.ac.uk

Abstract. This paper reflects on the early use of computers in school. It begins with an account of the author's own introduction to computing, while a school student himself, and his first attempts to teach computing and information technology courses. The next section of the paper describes his enthusiasm for teaching in another school and the challenge of engaging students' interest. The teaching of Logo is then described in a third section and a following section discusses a project to promote the use of data handling with computers. The paper concludes by reflecting on: the role of computer studies in the curriculum; the romantic versus rationalist view of technology; the purpose of schools and schooling; and the unpredictability of the take-up of computing. It makes an appeal for schools to provide children with an opportunity to reflect on their own use of technology.

Keywords: computing, small programmes, early career teaching.

1 First Experiences of Computing

I first became aware of computers and computing when at secondary school. This would have been in the early 1970s. Those of us who were considered mathematically minded were invited to attend a short course, which drew on materials designed by ICL[1], to learn the rudiments of programming and get an idea about the impact of computers on society. I was a little reluctant as these classes were offered instead of sports and I was a sports enthusiast. The point I am making is that I began an engagement with computers through the study of computing. I was taught to write simple programmes using, as I recall, an early version of COBOL. Our lines of code were punched on cards; the cards were sent to terminals and returned with printouts. Very often the programmes did not work - two cards stuck together or the holes were not punched cleanly enough. I am not sure that really mattered, the construction of the algorithm was interesting enough in itself. As for the impact of computers on society, the set of video recordings we saw implied that there were going to be big changes in every sphere of life. You can argue that this has turned out to be the case, but on nothing like the timescale suggested to us. One scenario I remember showed patients

[1] International Computers Limited, or ICL, was an early British company engaged in the manufacture of computer hardware, computer software and computer services. It operated from 1968 until 2002.

A. Tatnall and B. Davey (Eds.): History of Computers in Education, IFIP AICT 424, pp. 408–416, 2014.

turning to a computer to diagnose their ailments through an early kind of Artificial Intelligence software. Patients would find the process quicker and easier and they would not have to leave their house or interact with an overstretched medic. The scenario might be seen as prescient given that most of us today self-diagnose through any number of medical web sites but it had got something significantly wrong. Interaction at the computer was presented as an individualised process and the scenario had not built in our need to discuss our symptoms with each other or indeed our need to invest trust in someone, in this case a medical practitioner, who had a 'warrant' of professional expertise. I do not recall the course making a deep impression on us. However it did invite a way of thinking about computing and the power of computing and, at the very least, it created an awareness that tasks which were being carried out 'manually' would be automatically processed in the future. This was not, however, enough for me to follow up an interest in computing and I went off in other directions.

2 Becoming a Teacher

After various career and determinedly non-career excursions I qualified to teach and I found myself working in three different secondary schools in the periods covering 1984 – 1989. In the first I was filling in short term for an absent teacher. I was to teach mathematics and this 'of course' involved computing. I was asked to illustrate examples of programming and, if possible, get the pupils to write a few lines of code themselves. This was not going to be easy. There were only a couple of computers (BBC[2] ones) in the whole school – one had to be rescued from a broom cupboard - not enough for any meaningful 'hands on' programming in the classroom. Rather than punching cards programmes could now be recorded on cassette tapes. This was famously unreliable. As a teacher you could spend a break time loading a programme for your next lesson only for it to crash at the last minute. Thankfully the computer studies course was a short one, only a lesson a week over six weeks with one group and then repeated with the next.

Within this short introductory course I was asked to involve youngsters in debates about the impact of computers on society and I had access to recordings of two or three short films produced for schools. These films had the potential to be interesting but I failed to engage the youngsters' imagination. We were back to considering future scenarios. I recall one film showed a handheld machine which enabled text to be displayed digitally and which would alter the notion of a 'book'. Using this device you could change font and font size and you could store a whole book on it, even a mini library, which you could, with difficultly, take around with you. Again prescient but it had missed out something quite essential. Digital books did not take off until devices were affordable and truly portable and until it was possible to comfortably read from the screen in natural conditions.

---

[2] As is well known the BBC 'badge' was given to a series of microcomputers and built by the Acorn Computer company to tie in with the BBC Computer Literacy Project during the 1980's. BBC computers were very popular in schools due perhaps to their reliability. They were seen as more robust too. Eventually of course schools moved over to PC and some to Apple Macintosh machines.

After this first brief introduction to school teaching I took on my first 'proper' teaching appointment. I was again teaching some computing and I was now able to access a whole room of computers in a small local area network. I had by now a little more experience of the computing curriculum but no formal training in the subject. My subject knowledge was shaky and I tried to keep one step ahead of the syllabus. When it came to practical 'know-how' I would circulate the class, pick up a skill by observing or troubleshooting a problem with one pair of students. I could then confidently demonstrate the skill I had only just picked up to the next pair of students. I gained what I needed 'just in time'. However I do recall one lad – Andy – asking me week after week 'when were we going to do assembly languages?'. I had little idea as to what he was talking about and had to 'gen up' furiously to prepare a lesson that bore some relation to the description of assembly languages in the text book. The great day finally arrived when I could confidently present assembly languages as a topic and impress Andy with my knowledge. However he was not there. I learnt that he had a troubled background and had moved home and school a lot, his family had now moved on. Someone thanked me for taking an interest in him but that was that. My view at the time was that he was a programmer with potential but let down by a stodgy curriculum and my lack of knowledge. He certainly had copied many programmes from books and magazines and was an enthusiast for coding. However, looking back, I do not think he had understood the logical structure of programming and he had no more idea of an assembly language than I had or he would have seen through me straight away.

During this period I was learning my trade as a school teacher. The classes were challenging - to be fair more at the level of tiresome low level disruption rather than any outright hostility. It was an uphill struggle to engage students in computer studies classes, particularly in issues of computer architecture. The impact on society should have been more interesting for them but it took me time to realise that what was happening in the world outside often had limited appeal. One of the scenarios we looked at in depth was at how computer algorithms were able to control and coordinate traffic light signals to speed up traffic flow. However my students did not drive, and their parents tended not to have cars and, for that matter, neither did I. The scenario washed over them. I have nothing against traffic lights and I have seen and worked with youngsters really who enjoyed working with programs such as Flowol[3] to set up and control simple traffic light systems. The problem lay in the lazy assumption on my part that computer control was necessarily interesting *because* it was about real life – there was nothing necessary about this.

After some reflection on my lessons I decided that I could better engage my students by turning to more immediate examples to illustrate how computers were affecting their lives. I created a module on educational technology in which they could review whatever titles I could get hold of (this was largely software developed within the Microelectronics Education Programme (MEP) programme[4]). I recorded a couple

---

[3] Flowol is described by its designers as an easy to use drag and drop approach to flow chart programming and has been widely used in UK schools.

[4] The Microelectronics Education Programme ran from 1980 to 1986 in UK. Its brief was to explore and promote the use of computers in schools. MEP could be seen as a forerunner of NCET, and then Becta.

of BBC television programmes about information technology in schools for them. A key idea in these programmes was that computers needed to be in subject classrooms rather than in specialist computer rooms alowing technology needed to become a normal part of teaching and learning. The films also took a critical look at 'instructional technology' something later made more familiar in England and Wales in the form of Integrated Learning Systems (Wood, 1998). My module on educational software went much better, particularly the software evaluation, though it did not generate any outright enthusiasm for, or critique of, computer supported learning. Interspersed with this module I carried on with computer coding and programming. Students were able to produce simple programmes in BASIC. Key for assessment was the writing up of the design, implementation, testing and evaluation process and by and large this was something students did not take easily to. However a fair number enjoyed the work at the computer and I felt I had developed a comfortable way of working with the class which allowed me to troubleshoot and support pupils at machines and to present tips and guidance to the whole class at odd points during the lesson.

I found little use of computers around the school and perhaps this was due to lack of interest on the part of colleagues or simple lack of access. I did, however, notice that teachers of English were using word processing in some classes and the language support teachers were experimenting and enjoying working with *Developing Tray*– a text revelation package. In mathematics, which was my main subject, we used a lot of equipment: number blocks, dice and of course calculators but nothing in the way of desk top computing. I had not seen or used *Logo*. Later I got hold of a *MicroSmile*[5], a suite of programmes for learning and teaching mathematics containing games, puzzles, and simple 'revelatory' scenarios. As a new teacher I was ambitious and I wanted to challenge students to investigate mathematics not just carry out the controlled practice that the textbooks provided. My efforts met with a mixed reception. I particularly remember one child I taught, let us call him Roy. We were doing an investigation of some kind and he was having none of it: 'Why are we doing all this investigative stuff, can't we do something useful like square roots like we did with our previous teacher?'. Roy had, what I would describe without irony as, 'natural wit and intelligence' but he was a challenging boy, and had made very little progress in any of his subject work. Why on earth would he find square roots useful? He would never do anything with square roots after he left school. Only now can I now see he was not asking for square roots, he wanted familiarity and order. I think if I met him today I would not be so dismissive and I hope I would understand him a lot better.

It was logical that I would turn to computers in my maths lessons. After a great deal of asking I was able to book a networked room and I set Roy's class to work on various *MicroSmile* scenarios. The students worked in pairs or threes. I tried to prompt them as I went round the room. Of course I wanted them to focus in on the maths, but, to be honest, I was looking more than anything to change their attitudes to their learning. The use of the software kept them busy and made me feel much more comfortable in my role of teacher. In fact I had been worried that Roy might mishandle the keyboard or disks but to my surprise he became an enthusiast for the use of

---

5 For more on *MicroSmile* go to the national Archive of Educational Computing `http://www.naec.org.uk/artefacts/software/micro-smile`

computers and for me as a teacher. It was a breakthrough that meant a lot to me. On the flip side I was aware that a lot of what the students were doing was playing at the machine. In particular they were attempting to solve puzzles and problems by trial and error rather than generalising from their attempts, which was the underlying rationale for the programmes[6]. When commentators say too much software is only used for motivational purposes they are right but it is the word *only* I object to. I needed to see pupil motivation at that point in my career though the problem of motivating students does not ever go away.

In reminiscing on the use of technology I have described some of my feelings about the software and the teaching of computer studies but I have not really communicated the intensity of being a new teacher. If I looked around my school I could see mixed teaching and mixed outcomes but this did not matter. I was engrossed in my enthusiasm for the job and in awe of many of my colleagues. What struck me was the deep moral compass of the school. It had, at the time, a remarkable mix of students from different ethnic backgrounds and it sought very much to create a sense of belonging for all students and for the wider community. For example music teachers promoted a strongly inclusive steel band, 'community' languages were taught, some post 16 teaching was open to the community and at Christmas lunches were put on for local pensioners. Many teachers spent a lot of time mentoring youngsters both informally and formally. I saw impressive 'active' tutorial work and a constant appeal to students to behave responsibly and be reasonable when considering other people. Those struggling for language or other reasons were given whatever boost to self-esteem and self-confidence was possible. I remember one girl, let us call her Shahira, an eleven year old who had been working with a teaching assistant in one of my mathematics classes. The assistant sent her to me to show off some work she had done. I said 'thanks that was good, well done'. Perhaps it was a little perfunctory and Shahira looked a little disappointed. The teaching assistant picked up on this and said: "well done Shahira, this is very good, you are pleased with it? Mr Hammond is very pleased with it, shall we now show the head of the department and see if he is pleased with it? Shahira duly went out to show her work to the head of department and was told, with more enthusiasm than I had mustered, how well she had done. The point is that the teaching assistant understood Shahira's fragility as a learner in a way that I did not. She would not let Shahira go until she had been convinced about the value of her work and was willing to accept that she had the capacity to learn. I know this kind of reinforcement is maddening for conservative commentators who see explicit ranking of performance as core to the work of a school and ultimately in the best interests of students themselves. However the liberal ethos in my school was very inspiring for me and very different from my own schooling. I had never properly understood what it might be like to struggle academically or lack belief in my potential for learning and the teaching assistant had, whether intentionally or not, pointed this out to me. I thank her to this day for doing so.

---

6 These observations led me later to consider the importance of intervention when pupils work on classroom mathematical puzzles: Hammond, M. (1995) Exploring a World of Number, Journal of Information Technology for Teacher Education, 4, 3, 363 - 376. [A version of this paper can be accessed on line at: [http://wrap.warwick.ac.uk/]

The school in which I worked played an important role in the lives of all the young people, not just those that were struggling. This was demonstrated to me in the weeks leading up to the Christmas holidays. Students' excitement mounted and with even three weeks to go I was asked 'we are not doing a proper lesson today are we sir, it is nearly Christmas?'. This went on and on until the end of term finally came, the students went home and I imagined how pleased they would be. Leaving the school later that day I was astonished to see the same children who had been desperate for the holidays congregating around the playground. They told me they were bored at home and looking forward to coming back to school.

3 Working with Logo

After two or three years I moved to another school and the story moves on apace. What is worth mentioning was that this new school gave me my first experience of using *Logo*. All students were taught to create simple programmes and those that took to it were able to go on and write their own procedures and super procedures. Some students really enjoyed *Logo*, some did not, some went along with it in the same way that they went along with most things that school offered. It made no great impression on me and I was astonished later, as I became interested in educational technology as a field of study, to see how *Logo* played such a central part in the story of computing. *Logo* was about handing control to children over computing and over their learning and so many hopes for curriculum change seemed to have coalesced around its use. Papert [2], at least it seemed to me, saw children as having an intrinsic interest in problem solving and almost saw 'debugging' of programmes as a transferable and lifelong skill. Through *Logo* the invitation was laid out for us to think differently about schooling. I can see Papert's point, in fact I can see the point better now than before. Later I was more than happy to promote the use of *Logo* amongst student teachers I trained and I would explain the principles on which Logo was designed. I know colleagues who have found the teaching of *Logo* creative and life changing[7] and I have no reason or wish to argue with them on this. However *Logo* was very much a footnote in my story of using computers.

4 Software for Handling Data

At the beginning of the 1990s I was unexpectedly able to work full time on a project, led by Peter Holmes, to promote the use of databases and spreadsheets for data handling. I had the best of times. I visited teachers, went on courses, collated exemplar materials and made up activities for classroom use[8]. Some, at least, of the ideas worked

[7] I learnt this in greater depth when researching colleagues' careers in educational technology – see Hammond, M. et al (2010): *What does our Past Involvement with Computers in Education tell us?* Coventry, University of Warwick: The Association for Technology in Teacher Education. [On line at: http://www2.warwick.ac.uk/fac/soc/wie/research/centre /centre_projects/current_projects/voices/book/

[8] For example: Hammond, M. (1993) *Handling Data with Databases and Spreadsheets*, London, Hodder and Stoughton.

well in the classroom. Overall I could see the project as part of a push for using general purpose programmes in school and, in doing so, creating a 'tie in' with software, such as *Word, Excel* and *Publisher*, used in industry. One argument for general purpose programmes was that students could use the same software right across the curriculum: in an ideal scenario subject teachers would be able to take students' IT skills for granted and students could reinforce and extend their knowledge of IT. As I visited schools I found computers in teaching rooms not just computing / IT rooms. I saw examples of desk top publishing and word processed text displayed on classroom walls, it looked a bright new world. I also saw some strikingly original approaches to data handling. For example a history advisor showed me a data file of miners who had died in an accident that had taken place in a nearby coal colliery in the nineteenth century. She described setting up teams of student journalists tasked with writing up a story of the mining disaster. These teams had to interrogate the data files in order to find out who had died, how old the causalities were and how many of the dead were related to each other. They wrote up their stories on a front page simulation package – this package could be pre-set to deliver news flashes to students and provide reminders of deadlines. I was intrigued and it seemed to me that this kind of 'real life' problem solving approach, backed up by technology, was becoming mainstream.

I could see and had always seen the motivational value of technology but as my data handling project progressed I wanted to go further and understand how the software could be used to enable students to do things that would not be otherwise possible. For example the use of software for data handling enabled children to work with authentic data - large sets of data could be searched quickly and easily and these data could be easily manipulated and visualised. Data loggers allowed data to be collected over very short or very long time periods. Word processing allowed easy amendment of text. However my enthusiasm for general purpose programmes meant that I had not noticed the passing of small programmes and had missed the close link that had existed between programme designers and teachers. A host of programmes, including *Microsmile* or *Developing Tray*, were on the wane. And in terms of software for data handling I was aware that relational office data bases were becoming widely used in school even if they were largely unsuitable for the simple searches and graphical representation pupils needed for classroom data handling. Of course teachers could get around the use of, say, *Access* by creating templates in spreadsheets, but as soon as you start talking about getting round things with technology you are in trouble. Small database programmes (I was, for example, familiar with *Key* and *Grass* as school programmes) were quite suitable but largely disappeared in the following years. In a similar way the programme *Model Builder*, which had been developed through classroom research into school based modelling, lost out to *Excel*.

5 Reflections

The period covered in this book was a significant one for me as I was able to develop a stance on computing and the use of computers in the curriculum. I had experiences of teaching, I visited many schools early on in my career and I had acquired subject knowledge alongside a level of pedagogical expertise. I was innovative and enthusiastic about teaching even if I felt at times ineffectual and weighed down. This was an intense period for me personally coinciding with an important time in the history of computing in schools. What then had I learnt from my experiences and to what should I draw the reader's attention? Four things stand out.

Firstly, I came away feeling that the teaching of 'computer studies' was problematic - perhaps not less or more so than any other subject but claims that it held a special interest for all children at school were wrong. The teaching of programming was interesting for some, the impact of computing on society could be made interesting, but the teaching of computer architecture would always be a challenge. This left me a sceptic in regards to the teaching of computing as a specialist subject for *all* pupils. My experience of using general purpose packages would have led me to argue for a cross curricular approach to information technology and for computing to stay as a minority subject. Yet ironically I later became a tutor for training pre-service teachers with a specialism in ICT, as it became called, as a subject and this became one of the highlights of my professional career. I changed my mind on the value of ICT as a subject and valued the approach to problem solving it implied[9].

Secondly, I can see that I was, and indeed I have remained, a 'rationalist' rather than a romantic in regard to the use of technology. I was aware, and I was keen to show, that the use of technology enabled students to work in ways that would not otherwise be possible, but I did not see the use of technology as turning the curriculum upside down or doing anything particularly revolutionary in how I thought about teaching and learning. Others have argued that if you put computers into school nothing would or should remain the same, but this is not how I felt. Of course there must have been something that drew me into technology. I liked to be identified as one of the technology enthusiasts and I was one of a minority of teachers who wanted to give computers a go. I overcame difficulties such as room bookings and a lack of subject knowledge in order to do this. In my early career it never occurred to me to say 'I can't teach computing I have not been trained for that'. However I was as likely to be inspired by colleagues who did not use technology as much as those that did. The first book I read at length about using technology in school was Olson [1]. Olson explained the importance of routines in teaching, for better or worse these were needed for the teacher to manage his or her classroom and as a new teacher I could see how important it was for me to establish routines with my students. In my view Olson had got it right, computers would be very disruptive for teachers who had already settled into routines with which they were comfortable. As it happened in my own case I could establish routines with technology and the use of computers could make the classroom a more comfortable place for me to be in. However I was new to teaching and the use of computers was core to my role. I was not a typical case.

Thirdly, if I was a rationalist about technology I was a romantic about school. I was very influenced in how I thought about schools by my first permanent teaching

---

9 In brief Information Technology became a subject in itself to address the limitations of the cross curricular approach and to provide progression in terms of data handling, modelling, communication and control. The more problem based approach set out in the IT and the later ICT curriculum was hampered by the promotion of a rather narrow, vocational assessment framework 14 -19. However I could see via my visits and the work of my student teachers that it was possible to teach an IT curriculum that had appeal to all children at least some of the time. I discuss this in more detail in: Hammond M. (2004) The peculiarities of teaching ICT as a subject: a study of trainee and new ICT teachers in secondary schools, *Technology, Pedagogy and Education*, 13,1, 29 - 42.

appointment. This enabled me to see how schools could draw on the local community and support that community, but also transcend limitations within the community. I came to believe that schools were custodians of moral principles and had a special role in developing a sense of self efficacy for all, including the least able and most vulnerable. Even when I felt overwhelmed and ineffective a sense of optimism about schools as institutions never left me. Sometime after reading Olson I read Papert [2] in which it was argued that schools had not changed, indeed had barely changed over the centuries, and perhaps were impervious to change as could be seen by their failure to embrace technology. This had no resonance for me. Schools had changed appreciably from what I could remember of my schooldays. Schools were offering students greater opportunities to exercise creativity and teachers were learning to be authoritative without being authoritarian, no matter how often they might fall short. I know many people will, with good reason, disagree with me here and I know much better today how schools are compromised by the wider social structures in which they operate. I know how the work of schools in most educational systems has been distorted by top down change and rapid shifts of policy. However, when I think of schools I still feel optimistic and I have felt it a privilege to spend most of professional career working with teachers and student teachers.

Finally, from my work with computers I learnt that the take-up of technology is, to some extent at least, unpredictable. I had presented scenarios based on the use of technology but I could see that those who predict the future often get it wrong. If it is assumed that something will happen just because it has now become technically possible some quite basic economic, psychological or sociological dimensions, let alone financial and production issues, will be left out. Computers, it was predicted, would offer us less intensive working lives when the opposite seems to have happened, computers would offer a more individualised and differentiated society but new media seems to have strengthened not weakened social bonds. I think it is important for us to present the future as uncertain and to show we can have a say in how the future pans out. Schools can help here. It is not the job of schools to mimic the use of technology in the home or indeed in the world outside or be cheerleaders for the use of technology. Rather the job of the school is to notice changes and to provide a window for reflection on those changes.

References

1. Olson, J.: Schoolworlds/Microworlds: Computers and the Culture of the school. Pergamon, Oxford (1988)
2. Papert, S.: Mindstorms: Children, Computers and Powerful Ideas. Basic Books, New York (1980)
3. Papert, S.: Children's Machine: Rethinking School in the Age of the Computer. Basic Books, New York (1993)
4. Wood, D.: The UK ILS Evaluations: Final report, Coventry: Becta (1998)

Reflections on the Beginnings of an Educational Revolution (?)

Arthur Tatnall[1] and Bill Davey[2]

[1] Victoria University, Australia
[2] RMIT University, Australia
Arthur.Tatnall@vu.edu.au, Bill.Davey@RMIT.edu.au

Abstract. If you have read through all the chapters in this book you will have encountered reflections and stories from around the world from the 1970s up to the mid-1990s. An analysis of all of these stories, set in very different countries and systems, shows that the revolution can be said to have begun in the late-1970s and early-1980s. The book also describes some significant events into the 1990s and beyond, but does not go much further into this area: that will have to be for another book! Chapters relate to the introduction of computers into schools in Canada, Norway, The Netherlands, Australia, Spain, Ireland, Israel, New Zealand, USA, Finland, UK, Chile, Poland and South Africa.

In this chapter we will attempt to draw together themes common to the stories from the previous chapters. Many chapters have dealt with more than one of these themes even though many countries and systems are covered. We will also consider the aspirations and motivations of these pioneering efforts to introduce computers into the classroom and contemplate outcomes at the end of this period.

Keywords: National policies, personal reflections, teachers, students, teacher education, curriculum.

1 National Policies, Issues and Developments

Many chapters of this book have dealt primarily with how the introduction of computers in education happened in the country of the author, and described national policies and issues that arose in this early period. Some chapters were written from a very personal perspective, others just described what happened. The contributions related to: Norway (Sindre Røsvik), The Netherlands (Joke Voogt and Alfons ten Brummelhuis, Bert Zwaneveld and Victor Schmidt, Jan Lepeltak), Spain (Javier Osorio and Julia Nieves,), UK (Don Passey), Ireland (Denise Leahy and Dudley Dolan,), Israel (Ben-Zion Barta and Liora Shapiro, Yaacov Katz), USA (Kevin Parker and Bill Davey), Finland (Jari Koivisto), Australia (Arthur Tatnall, William Keane) and Poland (Maciej Sysło). It is interesting to note similarities between the countries, both in what they did and when they did it. We can consider this time in terms of four periods.

A. Tatnall and B. Davey (Eds.): History of Computers in Education, IFIP AICT 424, pp. 417–422, 2014.

1.1 The Punch Card Period

In the first half of the 1970s students in many countries were writing programs using punch (or mark sense) cards run on a mini or mainframe at a local university. Their programs mostly related to mathematics, and their teachers were typically mathematics or science teachers who had done some computer programming in their university degree courses. The punch card era could be seen to have evolved from the efforts of these teachers.

This could really be seen as a 'pre-computers in schools' period. In this era the ability to make a computer do *anything* seemed a huge accomplishment. Those who tell of this era speak of the unbelievable patience of students waiting days to be told something like: 'syntax error in line 2'. The existence of punch card based computing did, however, provide a vehicle for convinving parents and administrators that computers were in some way relevant to schools. One should not discount the importance of public opinion on the later massive governmental and local efforts to find the resources to get computing going in schools.

1.2 Experimentation with the Microcomputer

By the late 1970s and early 1980s most countries were experimenting and coming to grips with what to do about the microcomputer and how it could best be used in their schools. Hardware was pre-eminent during this period, as there were few standards in common between manufacturers in hardware or application software. There was much discussion on whether it would be best to use Apple, Commodore, BBC, IBM PC or CP/M computers. Seymour Papert's book Mindstorms [1] was published in this periods and experimentation began in many schools with the use of Logo. (Logo was, of course, developed in the early 1970s but was then running on minicomputers not easily accessible to schools.) The statistics in the Parker and Davey chapter show that it was the accessibility of microprocessor based systems that provided the impetus to make computing a viable classroom alternative. The first classroom computers were little more use than a card punch machine as student/computer ratios were initially very poor. The champions in each school could, however, leverage their experiments to justify further purchase and that was the principal channel for widespread computing in the countries we have presented.

1.3 Development of National Policies

The first half of the 1980s was the time when most countries started to take computers in schools seriously: to develop national policies and curriculum guidelines and to provide support and funding to schools. This was an important time and has been discussed in detail in many chapters. It is clear that many countries had significant vision when it came to both curriculum and policy. Many countries had policy in place well in advance of the widespread use of computers and those policies seem to be broad in their vision of computer use.

1.4 Consolidation

By the second half of the 1980s things had begun to settle down and there was more constructive discussion of curriculum and the most productive ways of using the computers. The number of computers in schools continued to increase rapidly.

2 A Student View

Several chapters described what it was like to be a school student in this period. These included: Australia (Therese Keane, Martin Chambers), South Africa (Martin Olivier), Chile (Fernando Toro) and the UK (Michael Hammond), and a number of these former students are now themselves teachers. These chapters provide a quite different perspective on this history. As many of us were past school age by this time it is good to see the other side of the story from a student perspective.

3 Teachers' Personal Reflections

Many of the chapters describe their author's personal teaching experiences with computers. These include a chapter by David Demant who describes his personal experiences in secondary schools in England, Canada and Australia as well as working in the Melbourne Museum. Another by Arthur Tatnall relates his personal experiences as a teacher, as an educational consultant and when working in an educational support unit in Melbourne. Alnaaz Kassam from Canada relates her journey as a teacher and her efforts to use new technologies to create inclusive curricula that were reflective of diverse societies. Other personal reflection chapters include those by: Stewart Martin, Therese Keane, Jari Koivisto, Richard Millwood, William Keane, Martin Chambers, Angela Lecomber and Michael Hammond.

4 Teacher Education

Most teachers both now and in the 1970s and 1980s came to their schools with a good background from 'teaching method subjects' in their own university teacher education. These teaching method subjects were designed to acquaint the potential teachers with standard approaches to teaching material relevant to their speciality. In the 1970s and 1980s this was, however, rarely the case for teachers working with computers. These teachers typically had no pre-service teacher education relating to educational uses of computers as there was none available at the time. One of the chapters in this book (by John Murnane) describes a Graduate Diploma in Computer Education course in Melbourne, Australia. Other similar courses existed elsewhere, but these were a new development. Another way that new teachers have an understanding of how to teach their material is by remembering how they were themselves taught, and their own experiences as a school student. Sometimes these experiences were positive, sometimes not but they had at least seen how someone else taught the subject material. This also was not the case for teachers involved with computers in the 1970s and 1980s. Most teachers at this time had to work out for themselves what best to do with computers in the classroom. Some help was provided in many cases through day or half day long professional development activities, typically provided by education department support groups, but more assistance would have been desirable.

The important issue of teacher education was mentioned in many papers from around the world. These included: UK (Stewart Martin, Don Passey, Angela Lecomber, Richard Millwood), Australia (John Murnane, Therese Keane, William Keane, Anne McDougall et al.), Norway (Sindre Røsvik), USA (Kevin Parker and Bill Davey), Spain (Javier Osorio and Julia Nieves), Poland (Maciej Sysło), The Netherlands (Joke Voogt and Alfons ten Brummelhuis, Bert Zwaneveld and Victor Schmidt, Jan Lepeltak), Israel (Ben-Zion Barta and Liora Shapiro), Ireland (Denise Leahy and Dudley Dolan) and Finland (Jari Koivisto).

5 Curriculum Issues

The introduction and use of Logo [1] in schools is discussed in several chapters. The chapter by Anne McDougall, John Murnane and Sandra Wills describes the development and use of Logo in Australia. They note that Logo was expressly designed as a mathematical language for use in education and was very logic-orientated. Their chapter particularly mentions how the addition of Seymour Papert's 'Turtle' made Logo far more accessible to students and teachers. Logo is also discussed in chapters by Martin Chambers and Michael Hammond.

Another major curriculum issue at the time was whether the main emphasis should be to 'teach about computing', to use computers in many subject areas 'across the curriculum', or both. This issue arose in a number of chapters. In many countries teaching about computing – often called computer studies or computer science, was very popular during the first half of the 1980s, but after this time began to lose its place as teachers were keener to make use of the computer just as a tool in other subject areas. Schools in many countries spent much of their time in activities like teaching word processing or the use of a spreadsheet. Of course this need not have been an either/or situation, but in a number of countries it was with the result that computer studies lost out. It is interesting to note recent developments in which a number of countries are again stressing the importance of computer studies (or computer science or whatever name it is given).

6 Other Issues

A number of chapters also deal with other important issues related to computers in education. Developments in the use of computers in school management are described by Rory Butler and Adrie Visscher, and also by Richard Taylor. Pedagogy, in relation to the use of computers in schools, is discussed by Stewart Martin, Don Passey, Eva Dakich and Angela Lecomber. Richard Taylor writes on a blurring of boundaries between home and school computer use, and also within schools in the way that teaching and learning are carried out. Eva Dakich describes the dominant discourses, epistemological frameworks and theories of learning that have influenced the deployment of new technologies and their integration into learning and teaching.

7 But Has Education Really Changed for the Better as a Result?

In the 1970s and 1980s many of us who were involved in the introduction and use of computers in schools believed that we could fundamentally change education for the better. We believed that in using computers, students could achieve many new things such as making use of science simulations, creating their own applications in different subject areas, developing thinking through the design of algorithms and writing of computer programs, expressing ideas and experimenting through play with things like Logo and through learning how to use sophisticated graphics and audio applications. Senior secondary school students could also learn about and use computers as preparation for jobs in science, business and industry. In many cases our own motivations to get into this area related to our excitement and sense of achievement in making a computer do something that *we* had determined: in programming.

In an article in The Australian newspaper in 1990, however, Peter Juliff [2] argued that in using the computer only as a tool, "*We have succumbed to the terminal atrophy of imagination*". He goes on to say that: "*In the process of moving the mystique of the '60s to the blasé reality of the '90s, we have lost sight of the magic and the wonder.*" Juliff suggests that schools need to be more adventurous and creative in their use of computers. He notes that: "*Often they are only used as labour-saving devices in the same way as dishwashers and microwave ovens.*"

This sentiment seems not to have been restricted just to Australia, as many authors from around the world have expressed similar sentiments. It could be said that in the early 21st century computers in schools are used largely for typing (word processing), access to an encyclopaedia (the Internet) and communication (email). Is this what we envisaged at the beginning?

In the 1960s in the USA and in Australia (and in many other countries around the world) the physics syllabus in the last two years of secondary schools was given a significant boost by the introduction of PSSC Physics [3]. The Physical Science Study Committee (PSSC) in the USA set out to integrate experiment and theory and to introduce principles through the use of lost cost, but interesting and accessible equipment. The idea was that the students could get a good understanding of what was going on, rather than just getting lost in the use of complex equipment or being taught pure theory.

If we compare this with approaches to the use of computers in education, many current computer applications just teach the student how to use tools; how to use 'complex pieces of equipment' such as Microsoft Word, Microsoft Excel, Google, Wikipedia, Facebook etc. rather than to integrate practice with theory. By contrast, approaches involving algorithmic design and programming, as well as the use of tools, could bear some relationship to the PSSC approach. Papert also had some ideas on this [4]. A commentary from 1993 foretells of a fundamental difficulty in attaining the ideals of Papert:

> *"the seemingly marginal use of computers and telecommunications in schools and classrooms is due less to inadequate funds, unprepared teachers, and indifferent administrators than to dominant cultural beliefs about what teaching, learning, and proper knowledge are and how schools are organized for instruction."* [5 :15]

Has the use of computers in education changed education in the way we thought it might in the 1980s? Has it resulted in a significant difference and an improvement, or just a different way of doing the same old things? Have we lost sight of the magic and the wonder?

References

1. Papert, S.: Mindstorms - Children, Computers and Powerful Ideas. Harvester Press, Sussex (1980)
2. McIntosh, T.: Schools are Trapped in 'Typewriter' Mentality, in The Australian, Melbourne, p. 35 (1990)
3. Chiaverina, C.: Teaching PSSC Physics: A Remembrance of Things Past, in PSSC 50 Years Later. American Association of Physics Teachers (2006)
4. Papert, S.: The Connected Family: Bridging the Digital Generation Gap. Longstreet Press, Atlanta (1996)
5. Cuban, L.: Computers Meet Classroom: Classroom Wins. The Teachers College Record 95, 185–210

Author Index

MIX
Papier aus verantwortungsvollen Quellen
Paper from responsible sources
FSC® C105338

If you have any concerns about our products,
you can contact us on
ProductSafety@springernature.com

In case Publisher is established outside the EU,
the EU authorized representative is:
Springer Nature Customer Service Center GmbH
Europaplatz 3, 69115 Heidelberg, Germany

Printed by Libri Plureos GmbH
in Hamburg, Germany